The Go Workshop

Learn to write clean, efficient code and build high-performance applications with Go

Delio D'Anna, Andrew Hayes, Sam Hennessy, Jeremy Leasor, Gobin Sougrakpam, and Dániel Szabó

The Go Workshop

Authors: Delio D'Anna, Andrew Hayes, Sam Hennessy, Jeremy Leasor, Gobin Sougrakpam, and Dániel Szabó

Technical Reviewers: Arpit Aggarwal, Philipp Meiden, and David Parker

Managing Editor: Pournami Jois

Acquisitions Editor: Sarah Lawton

Production Editor: Shantanu Zagade

Editorial Board: Shubhopriya Banerjee, Bharat Botle, Ewan Buckingham, Megan Carlisle, Mahesh Dhyani, Manasa Kumar, Alex Mazonowicz, Bridget Neale, Dominic Pereira, Shiny Poojary, Abhishek Rane, Brendan Rodrigues, Mugdha Sawarkar, Erol Staveley, Ankita Thakur, Nitesh Thakur, and Jonathan Wray

First Published: December 2019

Production Reference: 3220221

ISBN: 978-1-83864-794-0

Published by Packt Publishing Ltd.

Livery Place, 35 Livery Street

Birmingham B3 2PB, UK

Why Learn with a Packt Workshop?

Learn by Doing

Packt Workshops are built around the idea that the best way to learn something new is by getting hands-on experience. We know that learning a language or technology isn't just an academic pursuit. It's a journey towards the effective use of a new tool—whether that's to kickstart your career, automate repetitive tasks, or just build some cool stuff.

That's why Workshops are designed to get you writing code from the very beginning. You'll start fairly small—learning how to implement some basic functionality—but once you've completed that, you'll have the confidence and understanding to move onto something slightly more advanced.

As you work through each chapter, you'll build your understanding in a coherent, logical way, adding new skills to your toolkit and working on increasingly complex and challenging problems.

Context is Key

All new concepts are introduced in the context of realistic use-cases, and then demonstrated practically with guided exercises. At the end of each chapter, you'll find an activity that challenges you to draw together what you've learned and apply your new skills to solve a problem or build something new.

We believe this is the most effective way of building your understanding and confidence. Experiencing real applications of the code will help you get used to the syntax and see how the tools and techniques are applied in real projects.

Build Real-World Understanding

Of course, you do need some theory. But unlike many tutorials, which force you to wade through pages and pages of dry technical explanations and assume too much prior knowledge, Workshops only tell you what you actually need to know to be able to get started making things. Explanations are clear, simple, and to-the-point. So you don't need to worry about how everything works under the hood; you can just get on and use it.

Written by industry professionals, you'll see how concepts are relevant to real-world work, helping to get you beyond "Hello, world!" and build relevant, productive skills. Whether you're studying web development, data science, or a core programming language, you'll start to think like a problem solver and build your understanding and confidence through contextual, targeted practice.

Enjoy the Journey

Learning something new is a journey from where you are now to where you want to be, and this Workshop is just a vehicle to get you there. We hope that you find it to be a productive and enjoyable learning experience.

Packt has a wide range of different Workshops available, covering the following topic areas:

- Programming languages
- Web development
- Data science, machine learning, and artificial intelligence
- Containers

Once you've worked your way through this Workshop, why not continue your journey with another? You can find the full range online at http://packt.live/2MNkuyl.

If you could leave us a review while you're there, that would be great. We value all feedback. It helps us to continually improve and make better books for our readers, and also helps prospective customers make an informed decision about their purchase.

Thank you,
The Packt Workshop Team

Table of Contents

Chapter 2: Logic and Loops   55

Chapter 3 Core Types 83

Chapter 4: Complex Types — 109

Chapter 5: Functions   169

Chapter 6: Errors   217

Chapter 10: About Time   353

Chapter 15: HTTP Servers   515

Chapter 16: Concurrent Work — 559

Chapter 17: Using Go Tools   605

Preface

| About

This section briefly introduces the coverage of this book, the technical skills you'll need to get started, and the software requirements required to complete all of the included activities and exercises.

About the Book

The Go Workshop will take the pain out of learning the Go programming language (also known as Golang). It is designed to teach you to be productive in building real-world software. Presented in an engaging, hands-on way, this book focuses on the features of Go that are used by professionals in their everyday work.

Each concept is broken down, clearly explained, and followed up with activities to test your knowledge and build your practical skills.

Your first steps will involve mastering Go syntax, working with variables and operators, and using core and complex types to hold data. Moving ahead, you will build your understanding of programming logic and implement Go algorithms to construct useful functions.

As you progress, you'll discover how to handle errors, debug code to troubleshoot your applications, and implement polymorphism using interfaces. The later chapters will then teach you how to manage files, connect to a database, work with HTTP servers and REST APIs, and make use of concurrent programming.

Throughout this Workshop, you'll work on a series of mini projects, including a shopping cart, a loan calculator, a working hours tracker, a web page counter, a code checker, and a user authentication system.

By the end of this book, you'll have the knowledge and confidence to tackle your own ambitious projects with Go.

About the Chapters

Chapter 1, Variables and Operators, explains how variables hold data for you temporarily. It also shows how you can use operators to make changes or make comparisons to that data.

Chapter 2, Logic and Loops, teaches you how to make your code dynamic and responsive by creating rules that must be followed based on data in variables. Loops let you repeat logic over and over again.

Chapter 3, Core Types, introduces you to the building blocks of data. You'll learn what a type is and how the core types are defined.

Chapter 4, Complex Types, explains that complex types build on core types to allow you to model real-world data using data grouping and by composing new types from the core types. You'll also look at overcoming Go's type system when needed.

Chapter 5, Functions, teaches you the basics of constructing a function. Then, we will dive into more advanced features of using functions, such as passing a function as an argument, returning a function, assigning a function to a variable, and many more interesting things you can do with functions.

Chapter 6, Errors, teaches you how to work with errors, covering topics such as declaring your own error and handling errors the Go way. You will learn what a panic is and how to recover from one.

Chapter 7, Interfaces, starts by teaching the mechanics of interfaces and then demonstrates that interfaces in Go offer polymorphism, duck typing, the ability to have empty interfaces, and the implicit implementation of an interface.

Chapter 8, Packages, demonstrates how the Go standard library organizes its code and how you can do the same for your code.

Chapter 9, Basic Debugging, teaches the fundamentals of finding bugs in our application. You will use various techniques of printing out markers in code, using values and types, and performing logging.

Chapter 10, About Time, gets you a head start in the concept of how Go manages time variables, and what features are provided for you to improve your applications, such as measuring execution time and navigating between time zones.

Chapter 11, Encoding and Decoding (JSON), teaches you the fundamentals of a JSON document, which is heavily used throughout various parts of software today, along with the great support that Go has for reading and creating JSON documents.

Chapter 12, Files and Systems, shows how Go has great support for working with files and the underlying OS. You will be working with the filesystem, learning how to create, read, and modify files on the OS. You will also see how Go can read a CSV file, a common file format used by administrators.

Chapter 13, SQL and Databases, covers the most important aspects of connecting to databases and manipulating tables, which are very common tasks nowadays, and you'll learn how to work efficiently with databases.

Chapter 14, Using the Go HTTP Client, instructs you how to use the Go standard packages to create an HTTP client and interact with REST APIs. You'll learn how to send GET requests to a server and process the response, as well as how to POST form data to a server and how to upload a file to a server.

Chapter 15, HTTP Servers, teaches you how to use the Go standard packages to create an HTTP server and build websites and REST APIs on top of it. You'll learn how to accept requests from a web form or from another program and respond in a human- or machine-readable format.

Chapter 16, Concurrent Work, demonstrates how to make use of Go's concurrency features to enable your software to perform several tasks at the same time, splitting the work across independent routines and reducing the processing time.

Chapter 17, Using Go Tools, familiarizes you with the tools that come with Go and explains how you can use them to improve your code. You'll learn how to automatically format your code with gofmt and goimports. You'll also learn how to do static analysis with go vet and how to detect race conditions using the Go race detector.

Chapter 18, Security, builds your understanding of how to identify and fix security attacks such as SQL injection and cross-site scripting. You'll learn how to use the Go standard package to implement symmetric and asymmetric encryption, and how to secure data at rest and data in transit using hashing libraries and the TLS package in Go.

Chapter 19, Special Features, lets you explore some hidden gems in Go that will make development easier. You will learn how to use build constraints to control application build behavior. You will also learn how to use the wildcard pattern with Go and how to use reflection in Go using the reflect package. This chapter will also build your understanding of how to access the runtime memory of your application using the unsafe package.

Conventions

Code words in text, database table names, folder names, filenames, file extensions, path names, dummy URLs, user input, and Twitter handles are shown as follows:

"A panic() function accepts an empty interface."

Words that you see on the screen, for example, in menus or dialog boxes, also appear in the same format.

A block of code is set as follows:

```
type error interface {
  Error()string
}
```

New terms and important words are shown like this: "These behaviors are collectively called method sets."

Long code snippets are truncated and the corresponding names of the code files on GitHub are placed at the top of the truncated code. The permalinks to the entire code are placed below the code snippet. It should look as follows:

main.go

```
 6  func main() {
 7    a()
 8    fmt.Println("This line will now get printed from main() function")
 9  }
10  func a() {
11    b("good-bye")
12    fmt.Println("Back in function a()")
13  }
```

The full code for this step is available at https://packt.live/2E6j6ig

Before You Begin

Each great journey begins with a humble step. Our upcoming adventure with Go programming is no exception. Before we can do awesome things using Go, we need to be prepared with a productive environment. In this small note, we shall see how to do that.

Hardware and Software Recommendations for Windows with Docker

To be able to run all the recommended tools used in the course, it's recommended that you have:

- 1.6 GHz or faster desktop (amd64, 386) processor.

- 4 GB of RAM.

- Windows 10 64-bit: Pro, Enterprise, or Education (1607 Anniversary Update, Build 14393 or later).

- You must have virtualization enabled in BIOS, which is usually enabled by default. Virtualization is different from having Hyper-V enabled.

- CPU SLAT-capable feature.

Hardware and Software Recommendations for Windows without Docker

If the system you are using is below the recommended requirements to use with Docker, you can still do the course. You have to complete an extra step to do so.

To be able to run all the tools (excluding Docker), you'll need:

- 1.6 GHz or faster desktop (amd64, 386) processor

- 1 GB of RAM

- Windows 7 (with .NET Framework 4.5.2), 8.0, 8.1, or 10 (32-bit and 64-bit)

Skip the steps, which explain how to install Docker. You'll need to install the MySQL server instead. You can download an installer from https://packt.live/2EQkiHe. The default options are safe to use if you are not sure which to pick. MySQL is free to install and use.

Once the course is complete, you can safely uninstall MySQL.

Hardware and Software Recommendations for macOS with Docker

To be able to run all the recommended tools used in the course, it's recommended that you have:

- 1.6 GHz or faster desktop (amd64, 386) processor

- 4 GB of RAM

- macOS X or newer, with Intel's hardware **Memory Management Unit** (**MMU**)

- macOS Sierra 10.12 or newer

Hardware and Software Recommendations for macOS without Docker

- If the system you are using is below the recommended requirements to use with Docker, you can still do the course. You need to complete an extra step to do so.

- To be able to run all the tools (excluding Docker), you'll need:

- 1.6 GHz or faster desktop (amd64, 386) processor

- 1 GB of RAM

- macOS Yosemite 10.10 or newer

Skip the steps, which explain how to install Docker. You'll need to install the MySQL server instead. You can download an installer from https://packt.live/2EQkiHe. The default options are safe to use if you are not sure which to pick. MySQL is free to install and use.

Once the course is complete, you can safely uninstall MySQL.

Hardware and Software Recommendations for Linux

To be able to run all the recommended tools used in the course, it's recommended that you have:

- 1.6 GHz or faster desktop (amd64, 386) processor

- 1 GB of RAM

- Linux (Debian): Ubuntu Desktop 14.04, Debian 7

- Linux (Red Hat): Red Hat Enterprise Linux 7, CentOS 7, Fedora 23

Install the Go Compiler

To turn your Go source code into something you can run, you'll need the Go compiler. For Windows and macOS, we recommend using the installer. Alternatively, to get more control you can download precompiled binaries. You can find both at https://packt.live/2PRUGjp. The install instructions for both methods on Windows, macOS, and Linux are at https://packt.live/375DQDA. The Go compiler is free to download and use.

Install Git

Go uses the version control tool Git to install extra tools and code. You can find the instructions for Windows, macOS, and Linux at https://packt.live/35ByRug. Git is free to install and use.

Install Visual Studio Code (Editor/IDE)

You need something to write your Go source code. This tool is called an editor or an **Integrated Development Environment (IDE)**. If you already have an editor you like, you can use it with this course if you'd like to.

If you don't already have an editor, we recommend you use the free editor Visual Studio Code. You can download the installer from https://packt.live/35KD2Ek:

1. Once it's installed, open Visual Studio Code.

2. From the top menu bar, select **View**.

3. From the list of options, select **Extensions**.

4. A panel should appear on the left side. At the top is a search input box.

5. Type **Go**.

6. The first option should be an extension called *Go* by *Microsoft*.

7. Click the *Install* button on that option.

8. Wait for a message that says it's successfully installed.

If you have Git installed, follow these steps:

1. Press *Ctrl/Cmd + Shift + P* all at the same time.A text input should appear at the top of the window.

2. Type **go tools**.

3. Select the option labeled something like **Go: Install/Update Tools**.

4. You'll see a list of options and checkboxes.

5. The very first checkbox next to the search input checks all the checkboxes. Select this checkbox, then select the **Go** button to the right of it.

6. A panel from the bottom should appear with some activity in it. Once this stops (and it may take a few minutes), you're all done.

Once done, select **View** from the top menu bar, then select **Explorer**.

You'll now need somewhere to put your Go projects. I recommend somewhere in your home directory. Avoid putting it in the Go path, which is the folder the Go compiler is installed in. If you are having problems with the **modules** later in the class, it may be due to this. Once you know where you want to store the projects, create a folder for them. It's essential that you can find your way back to this folder.

In Visual Studio Code, select the *Open Folder* button. From the dialog that opens, select the folder you just created.

Create a Test Application

1. In your editor, create a new folder called **test**.

2. In the folder, create a file called **main.go**.

3. Copy and paste the following code into the file you just created:

```
package main
import (
    "fmt"
)
func main() {
    fmt.Println("This is a test")
}
```

4. Save the file.

5. Open a terminal and go into the **test** folder.

6. If you are using Visual Studio Code:

- Select **Terminal** from the top menu bar.

- From the options, select **New Terminal**.

- Type **cd test**.

7. In the terminal, type **go build**.

8. This should run quickly and finish without displaying any messages.

9. You should now see a new file in that same folder. On Linux and macOS, you'll have a file named **test**. On Windows, you'll have one called **test.exe**. This file is your binary.

10. Now let's run our application by executing our binary. Type **./test**.

11. You should see the message **This is a test**. If you see the message, you have successfully set up your Go development environment.

Install Docker

If your computer can run it (see the *Hardware and Software Requirements* section), you should install Docker. Docker allows us to run things such as database servers without having to install them. Docker is free to install and use.

We only use Docker to run MySQL for the database part of the course. If you already have MySQL installed, then you can skip this part.

For macOS users, follow the instructions at https://packt.live/34VJLJD.

For Windows users, follow the instructions at https://packt.live/2EKGDG6.

Linux users, you should be able to use your built-in package manager to install Docker. Instructions for common distributions are at https://packt.live/2Mn8Cjc.

You are safe to uninstall Docker, if you wish, once the course is complete.

Installing the Code Bundle

Download the code files from GitHub at and place them in a new folder called `C:\Code`. Refer to these code files for the complete code bundle at https://packt.live/2ZmmZJL.

Variables and Operators

Overview

In this chapter, you will be introduced to features of Go and will gain a basic understanding of what Go code looks like. You will also be provided with a deep understanding of how variables work and will perform exercises and activities to get hands-on and get going.

By the end of this chapter, you will be able to use variables, packages, and functions in Go. You will learn to change variable values in Go. Later in the chapter you will use operators with numbers and design functions using pointers.

Introduction

Go (or golang as it's often called) is a programming language popular with developers because of how rewarding it is to use to develop software. It's also popular with companies because teams of all sizes can be productive with it. Go has also earned a reputation for consistently delivering software with exceptionally high performance.

Go has an impressive pedigree since it was created by a team from Google with a long history of building great programming languages and operating systems. They created a language that has the feel of a dynamic language such as JavaScript or PHP but with the performance and efficiency of strongly typed languages such as C++ and Java. They wanted a language that was engaging for the programmer but practical in projects with hundreds of developers.

Go is packed with interesting and unique features, such as being complied with memory safety and channel-based concurrency. We'll explore these features in this chapter. By doing so, you'll see that their unique implementation within Go is what makes Go truly special.

Go is written in text files that are then compiled down to machine code and packaged into a single, standalone executable file. The executable is self-contained, with nothing needed to be installed first to allow it to run. Having a single file makes deploying and distributing Go software hassle-free. When compiling, you can pick one of several target operating systems, including but not limited to Windows, Linux, macOS, and Android. With Go, you write your code once and run it anywhere. Complied languages fell out of favor because programmers hated long waits for their code to compile. The Go team knew this and built a lightning-fast compiler that remains fast as projects grow.

Go has a statically typed and type-safe memory model with a garbage collector. This combination protects developers from creating many of the most common bugs and security flaws found in software while still providing excellent performance and efficiency. Dynamically typed languages such as Ruby and Python have become popular in part because programmers felt they could be more productive if they didn't have to worry about types and memory. The downside of these languages is that they gave up performance and memory efficiency and can be more prone to type-mismatch bugs. Go has the same levels of productivity as dynamically typed languages while not giving up performance and efficiency.

A massive shift in computer performance has taken place. Going fast now means you need to be able to do as much work parallel or concurrently as possible. This change is due to the design of modern CPUs, which emphasize more cores over high clock speed. None of the currently popular programming languages have been designed to take advantage of this fact, which makes writing parallel and concurrent code in them error-prone. Go is designed to take advantage of multiple CPU cores, and it removes all the frustration and bug-filled code. Go is designed to allow any developer to easily and safely write parallel and concurrent code that enables them to take advantage of modern multicore CPUs and cloud computing - unlocking high-performance processing and massive scalability without the drama.

What Does Go Look Like?

Let's take our first look at some Go code. This code randomly prints a message to the console from a pre-defined list of messages:

```
package main
// Import extra functionality from packages
import (
    "errors"
    "fmt"
    "log"
    "math/rand"
    "strconv"
    "time"
)// Taken from: https://en.wiktionary.org/wiki/Hello_World#Translations
var helloList = []string{
    "Hello, world",
    "Καλημέρα κόσμε",
    "こんにちは世界",
    "السلام عليكم",
    "Привет, мир",
}
```

The **main()** function is defined as:

```
func main() {
    // Seed random number generator using the current time
    rand.Seed(time.Now().UnixNano())
    // Generate a random number in the range of out list
    index := rand.Intn(len(helloList))
    // Call a function and receive multiple return values
    msg, err := hello(index)
    // Handle any errors
```

```
    if err != nil {
    log.Fatal(err)
    }
    // Print our message to the console
    fmt.Println(msg)
}
```

Let's consider the **hello()** function:

```
func hello(index int) (string, error) {
    if index < 0 || index > len(helloList)-1 {
    // Create an error, convert the int type to a string
    return "", errors.New("out of range: " + strconv.Itoa(index))
    }
    return helloList[index], nil
}
```

Now, let's step through this code piece by piece.

At the top of our script is the following:

```
package main
```

This code is our package declaration. All Go files must start with one of these. If you want to run the code directly, you'll need to name it **main**. If you don't name it **main**, then you can use it as a library and import it into other Go code. When creating an importable package, you can give it any name. All Go files in the same directory are considered part of the same package, which means all the files must have the same package name.

In the following code, we're importing code from packages:

```
// Import extra functionality from packages
import (
    "errors"
    "fmt"
    "log"
    "math/rand"
    "strconv"
    "time"
)
```

In this example, the packages are all from Go's standard library. Go's standard library is very high-quality and comprehensive. You are strongly recommended to maximize your use of it. You can tell if a package isn't from the standard library because it'll look like a URL, for example, **github.com/fatih/color**.

Go has a module system that makes using external packages easy. To use a new module, add it to your import path. Go will automatically download it for you the next time you build code.

Imports only apply to the file they're declared in, which means you must declare the same imports over and over in the same package and project. Fear not, though you don't need to do this by hand. There are many tools and Go editors that automatically add and remove the imports for you:

```go
// Taken from: https://en.wiktionary.org/wiki/Hello_World#Translations
var helloList = []string{
  "Hello, world",
  "Καλημέρα κόσμε",
  "こんにちは世界",
  "السلام عليكم",
  "Привет, мир",
}
```

Here, we're declaring a global variable, which is a list of strings, and initializing it with data. The text or strings in Go support multi-byte UFT-8 encoding, making them safe for any language. The type of list we're using here is called a slice. There are three types of lists in Go: slices, arrays, and maps. All three are collections of keys and values, where you use the key to get a value from the collection. Slice and array collections use a number as the key. The first key is always 0 in slices and arrays. Also, in slices and arrays, the numbers are contiguous, which means there is never a break in the sequence of numbers. With the **map** type, you get to choose the **key** type. You use this when you want to use some other data to look up the value in the map. For example, you could use a book's ISBN to look up its title and author:

```go
func main() {
...
}
```

Here, we're declaring a function. A function is some code that runs when called. You can pass data in the form of one or more variables to a function and optionally receive one or more variables back from it. The **main()** function in Go is special. The **main()** function is the entry point of your Go code. When your code runs, Go automatically calls **main** to get things started:

```go
// Seed random number generator using the current time
rand.Seed(time.Now().UnixNano())
// Generate a random number in the range of out list
index := rand.Intn(len(helloList))
```

In the preceding code, we are generating a random number. The first thing we need to do is ensure it's a good random number, so to do that, we must "seed" the random number generator. We seed it using the current time formatted to a Unix timestamp with nanoseconds. To get the time, we call the **Now** function in the **time** package. The **Now** function returns a struct type variable. Structs are a collection of properties and functions, a little like objects in other languages. In this case, we are calling the **UnixNano** function on that struct straight away. The **UnixNano** function returns a variable of the **int64** type, which is a 64-bit integer or, more simply, a number. This number is passed into **rand.Seed**. The **rand.Seed** function accepts an **int64** variable as its input. Note that the type of the variable from **time.UnixNano** and **rand.Seed** must be the same. Now, we've successfully seeded the random number generator.

What we want is a number we can use to get a random message. We'll use **rand.Intn** for this job. This function gives us a random number between 0 and 1, minus the number you pass in. This may sound a bit strange, but it works out perfectly for what we're trying to do. This is because our list is a slice where the keys start from 0 and increment by 1 for each value. This means the last index is 1 less than the length of the slice.

To show you what this means, here is some simple code:

```
package main
import (
  "fmt"
)
func main() {
  helloList := []string{
  "Hello, world",
  "Καλημέρα κόσμε",
  "こんにちは世界",
  "السلام عليكم",
  "Привет, мир",
  }
  fmt.Println(len(helloList))
  fmt.Println(helloList[len(helloList)-1])
  fmt.Println(helloList[len(helloList)])
}
```

This code prints the length of the list and then uses that length to print the last element. To do that, we must subtract 1, otherwise, we'd get an error, which is what the last line causes:

```
  ~/src/Th…op/Ch…01/Example01.01    go run .
5
Привет, мир
panic: runtime error: index out of range

goroutine 1 [running]:
main.main()
        /home/sam/src/The-Go-Workshop/Chapter01/Example01.01/main.go:17 +0x12c
exit status 2
```

Figure 1.01: Output displaying an error

Once we've generated our random number, we assign it to a variable. We do this with the := notation, which is a very popular shortcut in Go. It tells the compiler to go ahead and assign that value to my variable and select the appropriate type for that value. This shortcut is one of the many things that makes Go feel like a dynamically typed language:

```
// Call a function and receive multiple return values
msg, err := hello(index)
```

We then use that variable to call a function named **hello**. We'll look at **hello** in just a moment. The important thing to note is that we're receiving two values back from the function and we're able to assign them to two new variables, **msg** and **err**, using the := notation:

```
func hello(index int) (string, error) {
…
}
```

This code is the definition of the **hello** function; we're not showing the body for now. A function acts as a unit of logic that's called when and as often as is needed. When calling a function, the code that calls it stops running and waits for the function to finish running. Functions are a great tool for keeping your code organized and understandable. In the signature of **hello**, we've defined that it accepts a single **int** value and that it returns a **string** and an **error** value. Having an **error** as your last return value is a very common thing to have in Go. The code between the {} is the body of the function. The following code is what's run when the function's called:

```
if index < 0 || index > len(helloList)-1 {
// Create an error, convert the int type to a string
return "", errors.New("out of range: " + strconv.Itoa(index))
}
return helloList[index], nil
```

Here, we are inside the function; the first line of the body is an **if** statement. An **if** statement runs the code inside its **{}** if its Boolean expression is true. The Boolean expression is the logic between the **if** and the **{**. In this case, we're testing to see if the passed **index** variable is greater than 0 or less than the largest possible slice index key.

If the Boolean expression were to be true, then our code would return an empty **string** and an **error**. At this point, the function would stop running, and the code that called the function would continue to run. If the Boolean expression were not true, its code would be skipped over, and our function would return a value from **helloList** and **nil**. In Go, **nil** represents something with no value and no type:

```
// Handle any errors
if err != nil {
log.Fatal(err)
}
```

After we've run **hello**, the first thing we need to do is check to see if it ran successfully. We do this by checking the **error** value stored in **err**. If **err** is not equal to **nil**, then we know we have an error. Then, we call **log.Fatal,** which writes out a logging message and kills our app. Once the app's been killed, no more code runs:

```
// Print our message to the console
fmt.Println(msg)
```

If there is no error, then we know that **hello** ran successfully and that the value of **msg** can be trusted to hold a valid value. The final thing we need to do is print the message to the screen via the Terminal.

Here's how that looks:

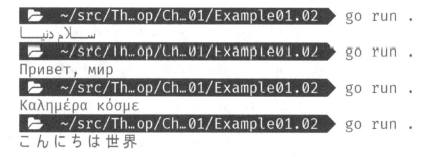

Figure 1.02: Output displaying valid values

In this simple Go program, we've been able to cover a lot of key concepts that we'll explore in full in the coming chapters.

Exercise 1.01: Using Variables, Packages, and Functions to Print Stars

In this exercise, we'll use some of what we learned about in the preceding example to print a random number, between 1 and 5, of stars (*) to the console. This exercise will give you a feel of what working with Go is like and some practice with using the features of Go we'll need going forward. Let's get started:

1. Create a new folder and add a `main.go` file to it.

2. In `main.go`, add the `main` package name to the top of the file:

```
package main
```

3. Now, add the imports we'll use in this file:

```
import (
    "fmt"
    "math/rand"
    "strings"
    "time"
)
```

4. Create a `main()` function:

```
func main() {
```

5. Seed the random number generator:

```
rand.Seed(time.Now().UnixNano())
```

6. Generate a random number between 0 and then add 1 to get a number between 1 and 5:

```
r := rand.Intn(5) + 1
```

7. Use the string repeater to create a string with the number of stars we need:

```
stars := strings.Repeat("*", r)
```

8. Print the string with the stars to the console with a new line character at the end and close the `main()` function:

```
fmt.Println(stars)
}
```

9. Save the file. Then, in the new folder, run the following:

```
go run .
```

The following is the output:

```
~/src/Th…op/Ch…01/Exercise1.01   go run .
*****
~/src/Th…op/Ch…01/Exercise1.01   go run .
****
~/src/Th…op/Ch…01/Exercise1.01   go run .
***
```

Figure 1.03: Output displaying stars

In this exercise, we created a runnable Go program by defining the **main** package with a **main()** function in it. We used the standard library by adding imports to packages. Those packages helped us generate a random number, repeat strings, and write to the console.

Activity 1.01 Defining and Printing

In this activity, we are going to create a medical form for a doctor's office to capture a patient's name, age, and whether they have a peanut allergy:

1. Create a variable for the following:

- First name as a string

- Family name as a string

- Age as an **int**

- Peanut allergy as a **bool**

2. Ensure they have an initial value.

3. Print the values to the console.

The following is the expected output:

```
~/src/Th…op/Ch…01/Activity01.01   go run .
Bob
Smith
34
false
```

Figure 1.04: Expected output after assigning the variables

> **Note**
>
> The solution for this activity can be found on page 684

Next, we'll start going into detail about what we've covered so far, so don't worry if you are confused or have a question about what you've seen so far.

Declaring Variables

Now that you've had an overview of Go and completed your first exercise, we're going to dive deep. Our first stop on the journey is variables.

A variable holds data for you temporarily so you can work with it. When you declare a variable, it needs four things: a statement that you are declaring a variable, a name for the variable, the type of data it can hold, and an initial value for it. Fortunately, some of the parts are optional, but that also means there's more than one way of defining a variable.

We'll now cover all the ways you can declare a variable.

Declaring a Variable Using var

Using **var** is the foundational way to declare a variable. Every other way we'll cover is a variation of this approach, typically by omitting parts of this definition. A full **var** definition with everything in place looks like this:

```
var foo string = "bar"
```

The key parts are **var**, **foo**, **string**, and **= "bar"**:

- **var** is our declaration that we are defining a variable.

- **foo** is the name of the variable.

- **string** is the type of the variable.

- **= "bar"** is its initial value.

Exercise 1.02: Declaring a Variable Using var

In this exercise, we'll declare two variables using the full **var** notation. Then, we'll print them to the console. You'll see that you can use the var notation anywhere in your code, which isn't true for all variable declaration notations. Let's get started:

1. Create a new folder and add a **main.go** file to it:

2. In **main.go**, add the main package name to the top of the file:

```
package main
```

3. Add the imports:

```
import (
    "fmt"
)
```

4. Declare a variable at the package-level scope. We'll cover what scopes are in detail later:

```
var foo string = "bar"
```

5. Create the **main()** function:

```
func main() {
```

6. Declare another variable using **var** in our function:

```
var baz string = "qux"
```

7. Print both variables to the console:

```
fmt.Println(foo, baz)
```

8. Close the **main()** function:

```
}
```

9. Save the file. Then, in the new folder, run the following:

```
go run .
```

The following is the output:

```
bar qux
```

In this example, **foo** is declared at the package level while **baz** is declared at the function level. Where a variable is declared is important because where you declare a variable also limits what notation you can use to declare it.

Next, we'll look at another way to use the **var** notation.

Declaring Multiple Variables at Once with var

We can use a single **var** declaration to define more than one variable. Using this method is common when declaring package-level variables. The variables don't need to be of the same type, and they can all have their own initial values. The notation looks like this:

```
Var (
    <name1> <type1> = <value1>
    <name2> <type2> = <value2>
    ...
```

```
    <nameN> <typeN> = <valueN>
)
```

You can have multiple of these types of declaration, which is a nice way to group related variables, thereby making your code more readable. You can use this notation in functions, but it's rare to see it used there.

Exercise 1.03: Declaring Multiple Variables at Once with var

In this exercise, we'll declare multiple variables using one var statement, each with a different type and initial value. Then, we'll print the value of each variable to the console. Let's get started:

1. Create a new folder and add a **main.go** file to it.

2. In **main.go**, add the **main** package name to the top of the file:

    ```
    package main
    ```

3. Add the imports:

    ```
    import (
        "fmt"
        "time"
    )
    ```

4. Start the **var** declaration:

    ```
    var (
    ```

5. Define three variables:

    ```
    Debug       bool    = false
    LogLevel    string  = "info"
    startUpTime time.Time = time.Now()
    ```

6. Close the **var** declaration:

    ```
    )
    ```

7. In the **main()** function, print each variable to the console:

    ```
    func main() {
        fmt.Println(Debug, LogLevel, startUpTime)
    }
    ```

8. Save the file. Then, in the new folder, run the following:

    ```
    go run .
    ```

The following is the output:

```
📁   ~/src/Th…op/Ch…01/Exercise1.03    go run .
false info 2019-11-16 14:08:51.1632775 +0000 GMT m=+0.000162601
```

Figure 1.05: Output displaying three variable values

In this exercise, we declared three variables using a single var statement. Your output looks different for the `time.Time` variable, but that's correct. The format is the same, but the time itself is different.

Using the var notation like this is a good way to keep your code well organized and to save you some typing.

Next, we'll start removing some of the optional parts of the var notation.

Skipping the Type or Value When Declaring Variables

In real-world code, it's not common to use the full var notation. There are a few cases where you need to define a package-level variable with an initial value and tightly control its type. In those cases, you need the full notation. It'll be obvious when this is needed as you'll have a type mismatch of some kind, so don't worry too much about this for now. The rest of the time, you'll remove an optional part or use the short variable declaration.

You don't need to include both the type and the initial value when declaring a variable. You can use just one or the other; Go works out the rest. If you have a type in the declaration but no initial value, Go uses the zero value for the type you picked. We'll talk more about what a zero value is in a later chapter. On the other hand, if you have an initial value and no type, Go has a ruleset for how to infer the types that are needed from the literal value you use.

Exercise 1.04: Skipping the Type or Value When Declaring Variables

In this exercise, we'll update our previous exercise to skip the optional initial values or type declarations from our variable declaration. Then, we'll print the values to the console, as we did previously, to show that the result is the same. Let's get started:

1. Create a new folder and add a `main.go` file to it.

2. In `main.go`, add the `main` package name to the top of the file:

```
package main
```

3. Import the packages we'll need:

```
import (
    "fmt"
    "time"
)
```

4. Start the multi-variable declaration:

```
var (
```

5. The **bool** in the first exercise has an initial value of false. That's a **bool**'s zero value, so we'll drop the initial value from its declaration:

```
Debug    bool
```

6. The next two variables both have a non-zero value for their type, so we'll drop their type declaration:

```
LogLevel  = "info"
startUpTime = time.Now()
```

7. Close the var declaration:

```
)
```

8. In the **main()** function, print out each variable:

```
func main() {
    fmt.Println(Debug, LogLevel, startUpTime)
}
```

9. Save the file. Then, in the new folder, run the following:

```
go run .
```

The following is the output:

```
      ~/src/Th…op/Ch…01/Exercise1.04    go run .
false info 2019-11-16 14:51:16.3478841 +0000 GMT m=+0.000197801
```

Figure 1.06: Output displaying variable values despite not mentioning
the type while declaring the variables

In this exercise, we were able to update the previous code to use a much more compact variable declaration. Declaring variables is something you'll have to do a lot, and not having to use the notation makes for a better experience when writing code.

Next, we'll look at a situation where you can't skip any of the parts.

Type Inference Gone Wrong

There are times when you'll need to use all the parts of the declaration, for example, when Go isn't able to guess the correct type you need. Let's take a look at an example of this:

```
package main
import "math/rand"
func main() {
    var seed = 1234456789
    rand.Seed(seed)
}
```

The following is the output:

```
  ~/src/Th…op/Ch…01/Example01.03  go run .
# github.com/PacktWorkshops/The-Go-Workshop/Chapter01/Example01.03
./main.go:7:11: cannot use seed (type int) as type int64 in argument to rand.Seed
```

Figure 1.07: Output showing an error

The issue here is that **rand.Seed** requires a variable of the **int64** type. Go's type inference rules interoperate a whole number, such as the one we used as an **int**. We'll look at the difference between them in more detail in a later chapter. To resolve this, we will add **int64** to the declaration. Here's how that looks:

```
package main
import "math/rand"
func main() {
    var seed int64 = 1234456789
    rand.Seed(seed)
}
```

Next, we'll look at an even quicker way to declare variables.

Short Variable Declaration

When declaring variables in functions and functions only, we can use the := shorthand. This shorthand allows us to make our declarations even shorter. It does this by allowing us to not have to use the **var** keyword and by always inferring the type from a required initial value.

Exercise 1.05: Implementing Short Variable Declaration

In this exercise, we'll update our previous exercise to use a short variable declaration. Since you can only use a short variable declaration in a function, we'll move our variable out of the package scope. Where before **Debug** had a type but no initial value, we'll switch it back so that it has an initial value since that's required when using a short variable declaration. Finally, we'll print it to the console. Let's get started:

1. Create a new folder and add a **main.go** file to it.

2. In **main.go**, add the **main** package name to the top of the file:

```
package main
```

3. Import the packages we'll need:

```
import (
    "fmt"
    "time"
)
```

4. Create the **main()** function:

```
func main() {
```

5. Declare each variable using the short variable declaration notation:

```
Debug := false
LogLevel := "info"
startUpTime := time.Now()
```

6. Print the variables to the console:

```
fmt.Println(Debug, LogLevel, startUpTime)
}
```

7. Save the file. Then, in the new folder, run the following:

```
go run .
```

The following is the output:

```
 ~/src/Th…op/Ch…01/Exercise1.05  go run .
false info 2019-11-16 15:35:17.2406485 +0000 GMT m=+0.000170701
```

Figure 1.08: Output displaying the variable values that were printed after using short variable declaration notation

In this exercise, we updated our previous code to use a very compact way to declare variables when we have an initial value to use.

The := shorthand is very popular with Go developers and the most common way in which variables get defined in real-world Go code. Developers like how it makes their code concise and compact while still being clear as to what's happening.

Another shortcut is declaring multiple variables on the same line.

Declaring Multiple Variables with a Short Variable Declaration

It's possible to declare multiple variables at the same time using a short variable declaration. They must all be on the same line, and each variable must have a corresponding initial value. The notation looks like **<var1>, <var2>, …, <varN> := <val1>, <val2>, …, <valN>**. The variable names are on the left-hand side of the :=, separated by a ,. The initial values are on the right-hand side of the := again, each separated by a ,. The leftmost variable name gets the leftmost value. There must be an equal number of names and values.

Here is an example that uses our previous exercise's code:

```go
package main
import (
  "fmt"
  "time"
)
func main() {
  Debug, LogLevel, startUpTime := false, "info", time.Now()
  fmt.Println(Debug, LogLevel, startUpTime)
}
```

The following is the output:

```
  ~/src/Th…op/Ch…01/Example01.04   go run .
false info 2019-11-16 15:56:47.1617309 +0000 GMT m=+0.000098301
```

Figure 1.09: Example output displaying the variable values for the program
with a variable declaring function

Sometimes, you do see real-word code like this. It's a little hard to read, so it's not common to see it in terms of literal values. This doesn't mean this isn't common since it's very common when calling functions that return multiple values. We'll cover this in detail when we look at functions in a later chapter.

Exercise 1.06: Declaring Multiple Variables from a Function

In this exercise, we'll call a function that returns multiple values, and we'll assign each value to a new variable. Then, we'll print the values to the console. Let's get started:

1. Create a new folder and add a **main.go** file to it.

2. In **main.go**, add the **main** package name to the top of the file:

```
package main
```

3. Import the packages we'll need:

```
import (
    "fmt"
    "time"
)
```

4. Create a function that returns three values:

```
func getConfig() (bool, string, time.Time) {
```

5. In the function, return three lital values, each separated by a ,:

```
return false, "info", time.Now()
```

6. Close the function:

```
}
```

7. Create the **main()** function:

```
func main() {
```

8. Using a short variable declaration, capture the values returned from the function's three new variables:

```
Debug, LogLevel, startUpTime := getConfig()
```

9. Print the three variables to the console:

```
fmt.Println(Debug, LogLevel, startUpTime)
```

10. Close the **main()** function:

```
}
```

11. Save the file. Then, in the new folder, run the following:

```
go run .
```

The following is the output:

```
    ~/src/Th…op/Ch…01/Exercise01.06    go run .
 false info 2019-11-16 16:38:29.2623608 +0000 GMT m=+0.000117201
```

Figure 1.10: Output displaying the variable values for the program with the variable declaring function

In this exercise, we were able to call a function that returned multiple values and capture them using a short variable declaration in one line. If we used the **var** notation, it would look like this:

```
var (
    Debug bool
    LogLevel string
    startUpTime time.Time
)
Debug, LogLevel, startUpTime = getConfig()
```

Short variable notation is a big part of how Go has the feel of a dynamic language.

We're not quite done with **var** yet, though. It still has a useful trick up its sleeve.

Using var to Declare Multiple Variables in One Line

While it's more common to use a short variable declaration, you can use var to define multiple variables on a single line. One limitation of this is that, when declaring the type, all the values must have the same type. If you use an initial value, then each value infers its type from the literal value so that they can differ. Here's an example:

```
package main
import (
    "fmt"
    "time"
)
func getConfig() (bool, string, time.Time) {
    return false, "info", time.Now()
}
func main() {
    // Type only
    var start, middle, end float32
    fmt.Println(start, middle, end)
    // Initial value mixed type
    var name, left, right, top, bottom = "one", 1, 1.5, 2, 2.5
    fmt.Println(name, left, right, top, bottom)
```

```
    // works with functions also
    var Debug, LogLevel, startUpTime = getConfig()
    fmt.Println(Debug, LogLevel, startUpTime)
}
```

The following is the output:

```
📁  ~/src/Th…op/Ch…01/Example01.05    go run .
0 0 0
one 1 1.5 2 2.5
false info 2019-11-16 17:00:22.3841258 +0000 GMT m=+0.000290701
```

Figure 1.11: Output displaying variable values

Most of these are more compact when using a short variable declaration. This fact means they don't come up in real-world code much. The exception is the type-only example. This notation can be useful when you need many variables of the same type, and you need to control that type carefully.

Non-English Variable Names

Go is a UTF-8 compliant language, which means you can define variables' names using alphabets other than the Latin alphabet that, for example, English uses. There are some limitations regarding what the name of a variable can be. The first character of the name must be a letter or _. The rest can be a mixture of letters, numbers, and _. Let's have a look at what this looks like:

```
package main
import (
    "fmt"
    "time"
)
func main() {
    デバッグ := false
    日志级别 := "info"
    ረጋሟት := time.Now()
    _A1_Μεíγμα := "
"
    fmt.Println(デバッグ, 日志级别, ረጋሟት, _A1_Μεíγμα)
}
```

The following is the output:

```
  ~/src/Th…op/Ch…01/Example01.06  go run .
false info 2019-11-16 17:17:19.963412 +0000 GMT m=+0.000095801 ✔
```

Figure 1.12: Output showing variable values

> **Note**
>
> **Languages and Language**: Not all programming languages allow you to use UTF-8 characters as variables and function names. This feature could be one of the reasons why Go has become so popular in Asian countries, particularly in China.

Changing the Value of a Variable

Now that we've defined our variables, let's see what we can do with them. First, let's change the value from its initial value. To do that, we use similar notation to when we set an initial value. This looks like **<variable> = <value>**.

Exercise 1.07: Changing the Value of a Variable

1. Create a new folder and add a **main.go** file to it.

2. In **main.go**, add the **main** package name to the top of the file:

   ```
   package main
   ```

3. Import the packages we'll need:

   ```
   import "fmt"
   ```

4. Create the **main()** function:

   ```
   func main() {
   ```

5. Declare a variable:

   ```
   offset := 5
   ```

6. Print the variable to the console:

   ```
   fmt.Println(offset)
   ```

7. Change the value of the variable:

```
offset = 10
```

8. Print it to the console again and close the **main()** function:

```
    fmt.Println(offset)
}
```

9. Save the file. Then, in the new folder, run the following:

```
go run .
```

The following is the output before changing the variable's value:

```
5
10
```

In this example, we've changed the value of offset from its initial value of **5** to **10**. Anywhere you use a raw value, such as **5** and **10** in our example, you can use a variable. Here's how that looks:

```
package main
import "fmt"
var defaultOffset = 10
func main() {
   offset := defaultOffset
   fmt.Println(offset)
   offset = offset + defaultOffset
   fmt.Println(offset)
}
```

The following is the output after changing the variable's value:

```
10
20
```

Next, we'll look at how we can change multiple variables in a one-line statement.

Changing Multiple Values at Once

In the same way that you can declare multiple variables in one line, you can also change the value of more than one variable at a time. The syntax is similar, too; it looks like <var1>, <var2>, …, <varN> = <val1>, <val2>, …, <valN>.

Exercise 1.08: Changing Multiple Values at Once

In this exercise, we'll define some variables and use a one-line statement to change their values. Then, we'll print their new values to the console. Let's get started:

1. Create a new folder and add a `main.go` file to it.

2. In `main.go`, add the `main` package name to the top of the file:

```
package main
```

3. Import the packages we'll need:

```
import "fmt"
```

4. Create the `main()` function:

```
func main() {
```

5. Declare our variables with an initial value:

```
query, limit, offset := "bat", 10, 0
```

6. Change each variable's values using a one-line statement:

```
query, limit, offset = "ball", offset, 20
```

7. Print the values to the console and close the `main()` function:

```
fmt.Println(query, limit, offset)
}
```

8. Save the file. Then, in the new folder, run the following:

```
go run .
```

The following is the output showing the changed variable values using a single statement:

```
ball 0 20
```

In this exercise, we were able to change multiple variables in a single line. This approach would also work when calling functions, just as it does with a variable declaration. You need to be careful with a feature like this to ensure that, first and foremost, your code is easy to read and understand. If using a one-line statement like this makes it hard to know what the code is doing, then it's better to take up more lines to write the code.

Next, we'll look at what operators are and how they can be used to change your variables in interesting ways.

Operators

While variables hold the data for your application, they become truly useful when you start using them to build the logic of your software. Operators are the tools you use to work with your software's data. With operators, you can compare data to other data. For example, you can check whether a price is too low or too high in a trading application. You can also use operators to manipulate data. For example, you can use operators to add the costs of all the items in a shopping cart to get the total price.

The following list mentions groups of operators:

- Arithmetic operators

  Used for math-related tasks such as addition, subtraction, and multiplication.

- Comparison operators

  Used to compare two values; for example, are they are equal, not equal, less than, or greater than each other.

- Logical operators

  Used with Boolean values to see whether they are both true, only one is true, or whether a **bool** is false.

- Address operators

  We'll cover these in detail soon when we look at pointers. These are used to work with them.

- Receive operators

  Used when working with Go channels, which we'll cover in a later chapter.

Exercise 1.09 Using Operators with Numbers

In this exercise, we are going to simulate a restaurant bill. To build our simulation, we'll need to use mathematic and comparison operators. We'll start by exploring all the major uses for operators.

In our simulation, we'll sum everything together and work out the tip based on a percentage. Then, we'll use a comparison operator to see whether the customer gets a reward. Let's get started:

> **Note**
>
> We have considered US Dollar as the currency for this exercise. You may consider any currency of your choice; the main focus here is the operations.

1. Create a new folder and add a **main.go** file to it:

2. In **main.go**, add the **main** package name to the top of the file:

```
package main
```

3. Import the packages you'll need:

```
import "fmt"
```

4. Create the **main()** function:

```
func main() {
```

5. Create a variable to hold the total. For this item on the bill, the customer purchased 2 items that cost 13 USD. We use * to do the multiplication. Then, we print a subtotal:

```
// Main course
var total float64 = 2 * 13
fmt.Println("Sub  :", total)
```

6. Here, they purchased 4 items that cost 2.25 USD. We use multiplication to get the total of these items and then use + to add it to the previous total value and then assign that back to the total:

```
// Drinks
total = total + (4 * 2.25)
fmt.Println("Sub  :", total)
```

7. This customer is getting a discount of 5 USD. Here, we use the - to subtract 5 USD from the total:

```
// Discount
total = total - 5
fmt.Println("Sub  :", total)
```

8. Then, we use multiplication to calculate a 10% tip:

```
// 10% Tip
tip := total * 0.1
fmt.Println("Tip  :", tip)
```

9. Finally, we add the tip to the total:

```
total = total + tip
fmt.Println("Total:", total)
```

10. The bill will be split between two people. Use **/** to divide the total into two parts:

```
// Split bill
split := total / 2
fmt.Println("Split:", split)
```

11. Here, we'll calculate whether the customer gets a reward. First, we'll set the **visitCount** and then add 1 USD to this visit:

```
// Reward every 5th visit
visitCount := 24
visitCount = visitCount + 1
```

12. Then, we'll use **%** to give us any remainder after dividing the **visitCount** by 5 USD:

```
remainder := visitCount % 5
```

13. The customer gets a reward on every fifth visit. If the remainder is 0, then this is one of those visits. Use the **==** operator to check whether the remainder is 0:

```
if remainder == 0 {
```

14. If it is, print a message that they get a reward:

```
        fmt.Println("With this visit, you've earned a reward.")
    }
}
```

15. Save the file. Then, in the new folder, run the following:

```
go run .
```

The following is the output:

```
~/src/Th…op/Ch…01/Exercise01.09    go run .
Sub   : 26
Sub   : 35
Sub   : 30
Tip   : 3
Total: 33
Split: 16.5
With this visit, you've earned a reward.
```

Figure 1.13: Output of operators used with numbers

In this exercise, we used the math and comparison operators with numbers. They allowed us to model a complex situation – calculating a restaurant bill. There are lots of operators and which ones you can use vary with the different types of values. For example, as well as there being an addition operator for numbers, you can use the + symbol to join strings together. Here's this in action:

```go
package main
import "fmt"
func main() {
   givenName := "John"
   familyName := "Smith"
   fullName := givenName + " " + familyName
   fmt.Println("Hello,", fullName)
}
```

The following is the output:

```
Hello, John Smith
```

For some situations, there are some shortcuts we can make with operators. We'll go over this in the next section.

> **Note**
>
> **Bitwise Operators:** Go has all the familiar bitwise operators you'd find in programming languages. If you know what bitwise operators are, then there will be no surprises here for you. If you don't know what bitwise operators are, don't worry – they aren't common in real-world code.

Shorthand Operator

There are a few shorthand assignment operators when you want to perform operations to an existing value with its own value. For example:

- --: Reduce a number by 1
- ++: Increase a number by 1
- +=: Add and assign
- -=: Subtract and assign

Exercise 1.10: Implementing Shorthand Operators

In this exercise, we'll use some examples of operator shorthand to show how they can make your code more compact and easier to write. We'll create some variables then use shorthand to change them, printing them out as we go. Let's get started:

1. Create a new folder and add a **main.go** file to it.

2. In **main.go**, add the **main** package name to the top of the file:

```
package main
```

3. Import the packages we'll need:

```
import "fmt"
```

4. Create the **main()** function:

```
func main() {
```

5. Create a variable with an initial value:

```
count := 5
```

6. We'll add to it and then assign the result back to itself. Then, we'll print it out:

```
count += 5
fmt.Println(count)
```

7. Increment the value by 1 and then print it out:

```
count++
fmt.Println(count)
```

8. Decrement it by 1 and then print it out:

```
count--
fmt.Println(count)
```

9. Subtract and assign the result back to itself. Print out the new value:

```
count -= 5
fmt.Println(count)
```

10. There is also a shorthand that works with strings. Define a string:

```
name := "John"
```

11. Next, we'll append another string to the end of it and then print it out:

```
name += " Smith"
fmt.Println("Hello,", name)
```

12. Close the **main()** function:

```
}
```

13. Save the file. Then, in the new folder, run the following:

```
go run .
```

The following is the output:

```
~/src/Th…op/Ch…01/Exercise01.10   go run .
10
11
10
5
Hello, John Smith
```

Figure 1.14: Output using shorthand operators

In this exercise, we used some shorthand operators. One set focused on modification and then assignment. This type of operation is common, and having these shortcuts makes coding more engaging. The other operators are increment and decrement. These are useful in loops when you need to step over data one at a time. These shortcuts make it clear what you're doing to anyone who reads your code.

Next, we'll look at comparing values to each other in detail.

Comparing Values

Logic in applications is a matter of having your code make a decision. These decisions get made by comparing the values of variables to the rules you define. These rules come in the form of comparisons. We use another set of operators to make these comparisons. The result of these comparisons is always true or false. You'll also often need to make multiples of these comparisons to make a single decision. To help with that, we have logical operators.

These operators, for the most part, work with two values and always result in a Boolean value. You can only use logical operators with Boolean values. Let's take a look at comparison operators and logical operators in more detail:

Comparison Operators

- == True if two values are the same

- != True if two values are not the same

- < True if the left value is less than the right value

- <= True if the left value is less or equal to the right value
- > True if the left value is greater than the right value
- >= True if the left value is greater than or equal to the right value

Logical Operators

- && True if the left and right values are both true
- || True if one or both the left and right values are true
- ! This operator only works with a single value and results in true if the value is false

Exercise 1.11: Comparing Values

In this exercise, we'll use comparison and logical operators to see what Boolean results we get when testing different conditions. We are testing to see what level of membership a user has based on the number of visits they've had.

Our membership levels are as follows:

- Sliver: Between 10 and 20 visits inclusively
- Gold: Between 21 and 30 visits inclusively
- Platinum: Over 30 visits

Let's get started:

1. Create a new folder and add a **main.go** file to it.

2. In **main.go**, add the **main** package name to the top of the file:

   ```
   package main
   ```

3. Import the packages we'll need:

   ```
   import "fmt"
   ```

4. Create the **main()** function:

   ```
   func main() {
   ```

5. Define our **visits** variable and initialize it with a value:

   ```
   visits := 15
   ```

6. Use the equals operator to see if this is their first visit. Then, print the result to the console:

   ```
   fmt.Println("First visit    :", visits == 1)
   ```

7. Use the not equal operator to see if they are a returning visitor:

```
fmt.Println("Return visit   :", visits != 1)
```

8. Let's check whether they are a Silver member using the following code:

```
fmt.Println("Silver member    :", visits >= 10 && visits < 21)
```

9. Let's check whether they are a Gold member using the following code:

```
fmt.Println("Gold member    :", visits > 20 && visits <= 30)
```

10. Let's check whether they are a Platinum member using the following code:

```
fmt.Println("Platinum member :", visits > 30)
```

11. Close the **main()** function:

```
}
```

12. Save the file. Then, in the new folder, run the following:

```
go run .
```

The following is the output:

```
~/src/Th...op/Ch...01/Exercise01.11    go run .
First visit      : false
Return visit     : true
Silver member    : true
Gold member      : false
Platinum member  : false
```

Figure 1.15: Output displaying the comparison result

In this exercise, we used comparison and logical operators to make decisions about data. You can combine these operators in an unlimited number of ways to express almost any type of logic your software needs to make.

Next, we'll look at what happens when you don't give a variable an initial value.

Zero Values

The zero value of a variable is the empty or default value for that variable's type. Go has a set of rules stating that the zero values are for all the core types. Let's take a look:

Type	Zero Value
`bool`	false
`Numbers (integers and floats)`	0
`String`	"" (empty string)
`pointers, functions, interfaces, slices, channels, and maps`	nil (covered in detail in later chapters)

Figure 1.16: Variable types and their zero values

There are other types, but they are all derived from these core types, so the same rules still apply.

We'll look at the zero values of some types in the upcoming exercise.

Exercise 1.12 Zero Values

In this example, we'll define some variables without an initial value. Then, we'll print out their values. We're using **fmt.Printf** to help us in this exercise as we can get more detail about a value's type. **fmt.Printf** uses a template language that allows us to transform passed values. The substitution we're using is **%#v**. This transformation is a useful tool for showing a variable's value and type. Some other common substitutions you can try are as follows:

Substitution	Formatting
%v	Any value. Use this if you don't care about the type you're printing.
%+v	Values with extra information, such as struct field names.
%#v	Go syntax, such as %+v with the addition of the name of the type of the variable.
%T	Print the variable's type.
%d	Decimal (base 10).
%s	String.

Figure 1.17: Table on substitutions

When using **fmt.Printf**, you need to add the new line symbol yourself, which you do by adding **\n** at the end of the string. Let's get started:

1. Create a new folder and add a **main.go** file to it.

2. In **main.go**, add the **main** package name to the top of the file:

    ```
    package main
    ```

3. Import the packages we'll need:

    ```
    import (
        "fmt"
        "time"
    )
    ```

4. Create the **main()** function:

    ```
    func main() {
    ```

5. Declare and print an integer:

    ```
    var count int
    fmt.Printf("Count   : %#v \n", count)
    ```

6. Declare and print a **float**:

    ```
    var discount float64
    fmt.Printf("Discount : %#v \n", discount)
    ```

7. Declare and print a Boolean:

    ```
    var debug bool
    fmt.Printf("Debug   : %#v \n", debug)
    ```

8. Declare and print a **string**:

    ```
    var message string
    fmt.Printf("Message   : %#v \n", message)
    ```

9. Declare and print a collection of strings:

    ```
    var emails []string
    fmt.Printf("Emails    : %#v \n", emails)
    ```

10. Declare and print a struct (a type composed of other types; we will cover this in a later chapter):

    ```
    var startTime time.Time
    fmt.Printf("Start   : %#v \n", startTime)
    ```

11. Close the **main()** function:

```
}
```

12. Save the file. Then, in the new folder, run the following:

```
go run .
```

The following is the output:

```
~/src/Th…op/Ch…01/Exercise01.12   go run .
Count    : 0
Discount : 0
Debug    : false
Message  : ""
Emails   : []string(nil)
Start    : time.Time{wall:0x0, ext:0, loc:(*time.Location)(nil)}
```

Figure 1.18: Output displaying zero values

In this exercise, we defined a variety of variable types without an initial value. Then, we printed them out using **fmt.Printf** to expose more detail about the values. Knowing what the zero values are and how Go controls them allows you to avoid bugs and write concise code.

Next, we'll look are what pointers are and how they can enable you to write efficient software.

Value versus Pointer

With values such as **int**, **bool**, and **string**, when you pass them to a function, Go makes a copy of the value, and it's the copy that's used in the function. This copying means that a change that's made to the value in the function doesn't affect the value that you used when calling the function.

Passing values by copying tends to end up with code that has fewer bugs. With this method of passing values, Go can use its simple memory management system called the stack. The downside is that copying uses up more and more memory as values get passed from function to function. In real-world code, functions tend to be small, and values get passed to lots of functions, so copying by value can sometimes end up using much more memory than is needed.

There is an alternative to copying that uses less memory. Instead of passing a value, we create something called a pointer and then pass that to functions. A pointer is not a value itself, and you can't do anything useful with a pointer other than getting a value using it. You can think of a pointer as directions to a value you want, and to get to the value, you must follow the directions. If you use a pointer, Go won't make a copy of the value when passing a pointer to a function.

When creating a pointer to a value, Go can't manage the value's memory using the stack. This is because the stack relies on simple scope logic to know when it can reclaim the memory that's used by a value, and having a pointer to a variable means these rules don't work. Instead, Go puts the value on the heap. The heap allows the value to exist until no part of your software has a pointer to it anymore. Go reclaims these values in what it calls its garbage collection process. This garbage collection happens periodically in the background, and you don't need to worry about it.

Having a pointer to a value means that a value is put on the heap, but that's not the only reason that happens. Working out whether a value needs to be put on the heap is called escape analysis. There are times when a value with no pointers is put on the heap, and it's not always clear why.

You have no direct control over whether a value is put on the stack or the heap. Memory management is not part of Go's language specification. Memory management is considered an internal implementation detail. This means it could be changed at any time, and that what we've spoken about are only general guidelines and not fixed rules and could change at a later date.

While the benefits of using a pointer over a value that gets passed to lots of functions are clear for memory usage, it's not so clear for CPU usage. When a value gets copied, Go needs CPU cycles to get that memory and then release it later. Using a pointer avoids this CPU usage when passing it to a function. On the other hand, having a value on the heap means that it then needs to be managed by the complex garbage collection process. This process can become a CPU bottleneck in certain situations, for example, if there are lots of values on the heap. When this happens, the garbage collector has to do lots of checking, which uses up CPU cycles. There is no correct answer here, and the best approach is the classic performance optimization one. First, don't prematurely optimize. When you do have a performance problem, measure before you make a change, and then measure after you've made a change.

Beyond performance, you can use pointers to change your code's design. Sometimes, using pointers allows a cleaner interface and simplifies your code. For example, if you need to know whether a value is present or not, a non-pointer value always has at least its zero value, which could be valid in your logic. You can use a pointer to allow for an `is not set` state as well as holding a value. This is because pointers, as well as holding the address to a value, can also be `nil`, which means there is no value. In Go, `nil` is a special type that represents something not having a value.

The ability for a pointer to be nil also means that it's possible to get the value of a pointer when it doesn't have a value associated with it, which means you'll get a runtime error. To prevent runtime errors, you can compare a pointer to nil before trying to get its value. This looks like **<pointer> != nil**. You can compare pointers with other pointers of the same type, but they only result in true if you are comparing a pointer to itself. No comparison of the associated values gets made.

As a beginner in the language, I suggest avoiding pointers until they become necessary, either because you have a performance problem or because having a pointer makes your code cleaner.

Getting a Pointer

To get a pointer, you have a few options. You can declare a variable as being a pointer type using a **var** statement. You can do this by adding an * at the front of most types. This notation looks like **var <name> *<type>**. The initial value of a variable that uses this method is **nil**. You can use the built-in **new** function for this. This function is intended to be used to get some memory for a type and return a pointer to that address. The notation looks like **<name> := new(<type>)**. The **new** function can be used with **var** too. You can also get a pointer from an existing variable using **&**. This looks like **<var1> := &<var2>**.

Exercise 1.13: Getting a Pointer

In this exercise, we'll use each of the methods we can use to get a pointer variable. Then, we'll print them to the console using **fmt.Printf** to see what their type and value is. Let's get started:

1. Create a new folder and add a **main.go** file to it.

2. In **main.go**, add the **main** package name to the top of the file:

```
package main
```

3. Import the packages we'll need:

```
import (
    "fmt"
    "time"
)
```

4. Create the **main()** function:

```
func main() {
```

5. Declare a pointer using a **var** statement:

```
var count1 *int
```

6. Create a variable using **new**:

```
count2 := new(int)
```

7. You can't take the address of a literal number. Create a temporary variable to hold a number:

```
countTemp := 5
```

8. Using **&**, create a pointer from the existing variable:

```
count3 := &countTemp
```

9. It's possible to create a pointer from some types without a temporary variable. Here, we're using our trusty **time** struct:

```
t := &time.Time{}
```

10. Print each out using **fmt.Printf**:

```
fmt.Printf("count1: %#v\n", count1)
fmt.Printf("count2: %#v\n", count2)
fmt.Printf("count3: %#v\n", count3)
fmt.Printf("time   : %#v\n", t)
```

11. Close the **main()** function:

```
}
```

12. Save the file. Then, in the new folder, run the following:

```
go run .
```

The following is the output:

```
~/src/Th...op/Ch...01/Exercise01.13    go run .
count1: (*int)(nil)
count2: (*int)(0xc0000140c8)
count3: (*int)(0xc0000140f0)
time   : &time.Time{wall:0x0, ext:0, loc:(*time.Location)(nil)}
```

Figure 1.19: Output after creating a pointer

In this exercise, we looked at three different ways of creating a pointer. Each one is useful, depending on what your code needs. With the **var** statement, the pointer has a value of nil, while the others already have a value address associated with them. For the **time** variable, we can see the value, but we can tell it's a pointer because its output starts with an **&**.

Next, we'll see how we can get a value from a pointer.

Getting a Value from a Pointer

In the previous exercise, when we printed out the pointer variables for the **int** pointers to the console, we either got nil or saw a memory address. To get to the value a pointer is associated with, you dereference the value using ***** in front of the variable name. This looks like **fmt.Println(*<val>)**.

Dereferencing a zero or **nil** pointer is a common bug in Go software as the compiler can't warn you about it, and it happens when the app is running. Therefore, it's always best practice to check that a pointer is not **nil** before dereferencing it unless you are certain it's not **nil**.

You don't always need to dereference; for example, when a property or function is on a struct. Don't worry too much about when you shouldn't be dereferencing as Go gives you clear errors regarding when you can and can't dereference a value.

Exercise 1.14: Getting a Value from a Pointer

In this exercise, we'll update our previous exercise to dereference the values from the pointers. We'll also add **nil** checks to prevent us from getting any errors. Let's get started:

1. Create a new folder and add a **main.go** file to it.

2. In **main.go**, add the **main** package name to the top of the file:

    ```
    package main
    ```

3. Import the packages we'll need:

    ```
    import (
        "fmt"
        "time"
    )
    ```

4. Create the **main()** function:

    ```
    func main() {
    ```

5. Our pointers are declared in the same way as they were previously:

```
var count1 *int
count2 := new(int)
countTemp := 5
count3 := &countTemp
t := &time.Time{}
```

6. For count 1, 2, and 3, we need to add a **nil** check and add * in front of the variable name:

```
if count1 != nil {
fmt.Printf("count1: %#v\n", *count1)
}
if count2 != nil {
fmt.Printf("count2: %#v\n", *count2)
}
if count3 != nil {
fmt.Printf("count3: %#v\n", *count3)
}
```

7. We'll also add a **nil** check for our **time** variable:

```
if t != nil {
```

8. We'll dereference the variable using *, just like we did with the **count** variables:

```
fmt.Printf("time  : %#v\n", *t)
```

9. Here, we're calling a function on our **time** variable. This time, we don't need to dereference it:

```
fmt.Printf("time  : %#v\n", t.String())
```

10. Close the **nil** check:

```
}
```

11. Close the **main()** function:

```
}
```

12. Save the file. Then, in the new folder, run the following:

```
go run .
```

The following is the output:

```
 📂   ~/src/Th…op/Ch…01/Exercise01.14    go run .
count2: 0
count3: 5
time   : time.Time{wall:0x0, ext:0, loc:(*time.Location)(nil)}
time   : "0001-01-01 00:00:00 +0000 UTC"
```

Figure 1.20: Output displaying the values that were obtained using pointers

In this exercise, we used dereferencing to get the values from our pointers. We also used nil checks to prevent dereferencing errors. From the output of this exercise, we can see that **count1** was a nil value and that we'd have gotten an error if we tried to dereference. **count2** was created using **new**, and its value is a zero value for its type. **count3** also had a value that matches the value of the variable we got the pointer from. With our **time** variable, we were able to dereference the whole struct, which is why our output doesn't start with an **&**.

Next, we'll look at how using a pointer allows us to change the design of our code.

Function Design with Pointers

We'll cover functions in more detail in a later chapter, but you know enough from what we've done so far to see how using a pointer can change how you use a function. A function must be coded to accept pointers, and it's not something that you can choose whether to do or not. If you have a pointer variable or have passed a pointer of a variable to a function, any changes that are made to the value of the variable in the function also affect the value of the variable outside of the function.

Exercise 1.15: Function Design with Pointers

In this exercise, we'll create two functions: one that accepts a number by value, adds 5 to it, and then prints the number to the console; and another function that accepts a number as a pointer, adds 5 to it, and then prints the number out. We'll also print the number out after calling each function to assess what effect it has on the variable that was passed to the function. Let's get started:

1. Create a new folder and add a **main.go** file to it.

2. In **main.go**, add the **main** package name to the top of the file:

```
package main
```

3. Import the packages we'll need:

```
import "fmt"
```

4. Create a function that takes an **int** as an argument:

```
func add5Value(count int) {
```

5. Add **5** to the passed number:

```
count += 5
```

6. Print the updated number to the console:

```
fmt.Println("add5Value    :", count)
```

7. Close the function:

```
}
```

8. Create another function that takes an **int** pointer:

```
func add5Point(count *int) {
```

9. Dereference the value and add **5** to it:

```
*count += 5
```

10. Print out the updated value of **count** and dereference it:

```
fmt.Println("add5Point    :", *count)
```

11. Close the function:

```
}
```

12. Create the **main()** function:

```
func main() {
```

13. Declare an **int** variable:

```
var count int
```

14. Call the first function with the variable:

```
add5Value(count)
```

15. Print the current value of the variable:

```
fmt.Println("add5Value post:", count)
```

16. Call the second function. This time, you'll need to use **&** to pass a pointer to the variable:

```
add5Point(&count)
```

17. Print the current value of the variable:

```
fmt.Println("add5Point post:", count)
```

18. Close the **main()** function:

```
}
```

19. Save the file. Then, in the new folder, run the following:

```
go run .
```

The following is the output:

```
 ~/src/Th…op/Ch…01/Exercise01.15    go run .
add5Value      : 5
add5Value post: 0
add5Point      : 5
add5Point post: 5
```

Figure 1.21: Output displaying the current value of the variable

In this exercise, we showed you how passing values by a pointer can affect the value variables that are passed to them. We saw that, when passing by value, the changes you make to the value in a function do not affect the value of the variable that's passed to the function, while passing a pointer to a value does change the value of the variable passed to the function.

You can use this fact to overcome awkward design problems and sometimes simplify the design of your code. Passing values by a pointer has traditionally been shown to be more error-prone, so use this design sparingly. It's also common to use pointers in functions to create more efficient code, which Go's standard library does a lot.

Activity 1.02: Pointer Value Swap

In this activity, your job is to finish some code a co-worker started. Here, we have some unfinished code for you to complete. Your task is to fill in the missing code, where the comments are to swap the values of **a** and **b**. The **swap** function only accepts pointers and doesn't return anything:

```
package main
import "fmt"
func main() {
    a, b := 5, 10
    // call swap here
```

```
  fmt.Println(a == 10, b == 5)
}
func swap(a *int, b *int) {
  // swap the values here
}
```

1. Call the **swap** function, ensuring you are passing a pointer.

2. In the **swap** function, assign the values to the other pointer, ensuring you dereference the values.

    The following is the expected output:

    ```
    true true
    ```

    > **Note**
    >
    > The solution for this activity can be found on page 685.

Next, we'll look at how we can create variables with a fixed value.

Constants

Constants are like variables, but you can't change their initial value. These are useful for situations where the value of a constant doesn't need to or shouldn't change when your code is running. You could make the argument that you could hardcode those values into the code and it would have a similar effect. Experience has shown us that while these values don't need to change at runtime, they may need to change later. If that happens, it can be an arduous and error-prone task to track down and fix all the hardcoded values. Using a constant is a tiny amount of work now that can save you a great deal of effort later.

Constant declarations are similar to **var** statements. With a constant, the initial value is required. Types are optional and inferred if left out. The initial value can be a literal or a simple statement and can use the values of other constants. Like **var**, you can declare multiple constants in one statement. Here are the notations:

```
constant <name> <type> = <value>
constant (
  <name1> <type1> = <value1>
  <name2> <type2> = <value3>

  ...

  <nameN> <typeN> = <valueN>
)
```

Exercise 1.16: Constants

In this exercise, we have a performance problem. Our database server is too slow. We are going to create a custom memory cache. We'll use Go's **map** collection type, which will act as the cache. There is a global limit on the number of items that can be in the cache. We'll use one **map** to help keep track of the number of items in the cache. We have two types of data we need to cache: books and CDs. Both use the ID, so we need a way to separate the two types of items in the shared cache. We need a way to set and get items from the cache.

We're going to set the maximum number of items in the cache. We'll also use constants to add a prefix to differentiate between books and CDs. Let's get started:

1. Create a new folder and add a **main.go** file to it.

2. In **main.go**, add the **main** package name to the top of the file:

```
package main
```

3. Import the packages we'll need:

```
import "fmt"
```

4. Create a constant that's our global limit size:

```
const GlobalLimit = 100
```

5. Create a **MaxCacheSize** that is 10 times the global limit size:

```
const MaxCacheSize int = 10 * GlobalLimit
```

6. Create our cache prefixes:

```
const (
    CacheKeyBook = "book_"
    CacheKeyCD   = "cd_"
)
```

7. Declare a **map** that has a **string** for a key and a **string** for its values as our cache:

```
var cache map[string]string
```

8. Create a function to get items from the cache:

```
func cacheGet(key string) string {
    return cache[key]
}
```

9. Create a function that sets items in the cache:

```
func cacheSet(key, val string) {
```

10. In this function, check out the **MaxCacheSize** constant to stop the cache going over that size:

```
if len(cache)+1 >= MaxCacheSize {
    return
}
cache[key] = val
}
```

11. Create a function to get a book from the cache:

```
func GetBook(isbn string) string {
```

12. Use the book cache prefix to create a unique key:

```
    return cacheGet(CacheKeyBook + isbn)
}
```

13. Create a function to add a book to the cache:

```
func SetBook(isbn string, name string) {
```

14. Use the book cache prefix to create a unique key:

```
    cacheSet(CacheKeyBook+isbn, name)
}
```

15. Create a function to get CD data from the cache:

```
func GetCD(sku string) string {
```

16. Use the **CD** cache prefix to create a unique key:

```
    return cacheGet(CacheKeyCD + sku)
}
```

17. Create a function to add CDs to the shared cache:

```
func SetCD(sku string, title string) {
```

18. Use the **CD** cache prefix constant to build a unique key for the shared cache:

```
    cacheSet(CacheKeyCD+sku, title)
}
```

19. Create the **main()** function:

```
func main() {
```

20. Initialize our cache by creating a **map**:

```
cache = make(map[string]string)
```

21. Add a book to the cache:

```
SetBook("1234-5678", "Get Ready To Go")
```

22. Add a **CD** to the cache:

```
SetCD("1234-5678", "Get Ready To Go Audio Book")
```

23. Get and print that **Book** from the cache:

```
fmt.Println("Book :", GetBook("1234-5678"))
```

24. Get and print that **CD** from the cache:

```
fmt.Println("CD   :", GetCD("1234-5678"))
```

25. Close the **main()** function:

```
}
```

26. Save the file. Then, in the new folder, run the following:

```
go run .
```

The following is the output:

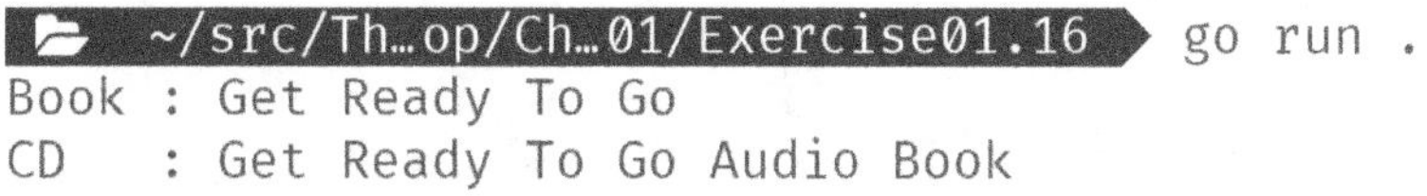

```
          ~/src/Th…op/Ch…01/Exercise01.16    go run .
Book : Get Ready To Go
CD   : Get Ready To Go Audio Book
```

Figure 1.22: Output displaying the Book and CD caches

In this exercise, we used constants to define values that don't need to change while the code is running. We declared then using a variety of notation options, some with the typeset and some without. We declared a single constant and multiple constants in a single statement.

Next, we'll look at a variation of constants for values that are more closely related.

Enums

Enums are a way of defining a fixed list of values that are all related. Go doesn't have a built-in type for enums, but it does provide tools such as **iota** to let you define your own using constants, which we'll explore now.

For example, in the following code, we have the days of the week defined as constants. This code is a good candidate for Go's **iota** feature:

```
...
const (
    Sunday    = 0
    Monday    = 1
    Tuesday   = 2
    Wednesday = 3
    Thursday  = 4
    Friday    = 5
    Saturday  = 6
)
...
```

With **iota**, Go helps us manage lists just like this. Using **iota**, the following code is equal to the preceding code:

```
...
const (
    Sunday = iota
    Monday
    Tuesday
    Wednesday
    Thursday
    Friday
    Saturday
)
...
```

Now, we have **iota** assigning the numbers for us. Using **iota** makes enums easier to create and maintain, especially if you need to add a new value to the middle of the code later.

Next, we'll take a detailed look at Go's variable scoping rules and how they affect how you write code.

Scope

All the variables in Go live in a scope. The top-level scope is the package scope. A scope can have child scopes within it. There are a few ways a child scope gets defined; the easiest way to think about this is that when you see {, you are starting a new child scope, and that child scope ends when you get to a matching }. The parent-child relationship is defined when the code compiles, not when the code runs. When accessing a variable, Go looks at the scope the code was defined in. If it can't find a variable with that name, it looks in the parent scope, then the grandparent scope, all the way until it gets to the package scope. It stops looking once it finds a variable with a matching name or raises an error if it can't find a match.

To put it another way, when your code uses a variable, Go needs to work out where that variable was defined. It starts its search in the scope of the code using the variable it's currently running in. If a variable definition using that name is in that scope, then it stops looking and uses the variable definition to complete its work. If it can't find a variable definition, then it starts walking up the stack of scopes, stopping as soon as it finds a variable with that name. This searching is all done based on a variable name. If a variable with that name is found but is of the wrong type, Go raises an error.

In this example, we have four different scopes, but we define the **level** variable once. This fact means that no matter where you use **level**, the same variable is used:

```
package main
import "fmt"
var level = "pkg"
func main() {
  fmt.Println("Main start  :", level)
  if true {
    fmt.Println("Block start :", level)
    funcA()
  }
}
func funcA() {
  fmt.Println("funcA start :", level)
}
```

The following is the output displaying variables using level:

```
Main start  : pkg
Block start : pkg
funcA start : pkg
```

In this example, we've shadowed the **level** variable. This new **level** variable is not related to the **level** variable in the package scope. When we print **level** in the block, the Go runtime stops looking for variables called **level** as soon as it finds the one defined in **main**. This logic results in a different value getting printed out once that new variable shadows the package variable. You can also see that it's a different variable because it's a different type, and a variable can't have its type changed in Go:

```go
package main
import "fmt"
var level = "pkg"
func main() {
  fmt.Println("Main start  :", level)
  // Create a shadow variable
  level := 42
  if true {
    fmt.Println("Block start :", level)
    funcA()
  }
  fmt.Println("Main end    :", level)
}
func funcA() {
  fmt.Println("funcA start :", level)
}
```

The following is the output:

```
Main start  : pkg
Block start : 42
funcA start : pkg
Main end    : 42
```

Go's static scope resolution comes into play when we call **funcA**. That's why, when **funcA** runs, it still sees the package scope **level** variable. The scope resolution doesn't pay attention to where **funcA** gets called.

You can't access variables defined in a child scope:

```
package main
import "fmt"
func main() {
  {
    level := "Nest 1"
    fmt.Println("Block end   :", level)
  }
  // Error: undefined: level
  //fmt.Println("Main end   :", level)
}
```

The following is the output:

```
📂  ~/src/Th…op/Ch…01/Example01.11    go run .
# github.com/PacktWorkshops/The-Go-Workshop/Chapter01/Example01.11
./main.go:11:31: undefined: level
```

Figure 1.23: Output displaying an error

Activity 1.03: Message Bug

The following code doesn't work. The person who wrote it can't fix it, and they've asked you to help them. Can you get it to work?

```
package main
import "fmt"
func main() {
  count := 5
  if count > 5 {
    message := "Greater than 5"
  } else {
    message := "Not greater than 5"
  }
  fmt.Println(message)
}
```

1. Run the code and see what the output is.

2. The problem is with the **message**; make a change to the code.

3. Rerun the code and see what difference it makes.

4. Repeat this process until you see the expected output.

    The following is the expected output:

```
Not greater than 5
```

> **Note**
>
> The solution for this activity can be found on page 685.

In this activity, we saw that where you define your variables has a big impact on the code. Always think about the scope you need your variables to be in when defining them.

In the next activity, we are going to look at a similar problem that is a bit trickier.

Activity 1.04: Bad Count Bug

Your friend is back, and they have another bug in their code. This code should print **true**, but it's printing **false**. Can you help them fix the bug?

```go
package main
import "fmt"
func main() {
    count := 0
    if count < 5 {
        count := 10
        count++
    }
    fmt.Println(count == 11)
}
```

1. Run the code and see what the output is.

2. The problem is with **count**; make a change to the code.

3. Rerun the code and see what difference it makes.

4. Repeat this process until you see the expected output.

    The following is the expected output:

    ```
    True
    ```

> **Note**
>
> The solution for this activity can be found on page 686.

Summary

In this chapter, we got into the nitty-gritty of variables, including how variables are declared, and all the different notations you can use to declare them. This variety of notation gives you a nice compact notation to use for 90% of your work, while still giving you the power to be very specific when you need to the other 10% of the time. We looked at how to change and update the value of variables after you've declared them. Again, Go gives you some great shorthand to help in the most common use cases to make your life easier. All your data ends up in some form of variable. Data is what makes code dynamic and responsive. Without data, your code could only ever do exactly one thing; data unleashes the true power of software.

Now that your application has data, it needs to make choices based on that data. That's where variable comparison comes in. This helps us see whether something is true or false, bigger or smaller, and to make choices based on the results of those comparisons.

We explored how Go decided to implement their variable system by looking at zero values, pointers, and scope logic. Now, we know that these are the details that can be the difference between delivering bug-free efficient software and not doing so.

We also took a look at how we can declare immutable variables by using constants and how **iota** can help manage lists or related constants to work, such as enums.

In the next chapter, we'll start to put our variables to work by defining logic and looping over collections of variables.

Logic and Loops

Overview

In this chapter, we'll use branching logic and loops to demonstrate how logic can be controlled and selectively run. With these tools, you'll have control of what you do and don't want to run based on the values of variables.

By the end of this chapter, you will be able to implement branching logic using `if`, `else`, and `else if`; use `switch` statements to simplify complex branching logic; create looping logic using a `for` loop; loop over complex data collections using `range`; and use `continue` and `break` to take control of the flow of loops.

Introduction

In the previous chapter, we looked at variables and values and how we can temporarily store data in a variable and make changes to that data. We're now going to look at how we can use that data to run logic, or not, selectively. This logic allows you to control how data flows through your software. You can react to and perform different operations based on the values in your variables.

The logic could be for validating your user's inputs. If we were writing code to manage a bank account, and the user asked to withdraw some money, we could check that they asked for a valid amount of money. We would check that they had enough money in their account. If the validation was successful, we would use logic to update their balance, transfer the money, and show a success message. If the validation failed, we'd show a message explaining what went wrong.

If your software is a virtual world, then logic is the physical law of that world. Like the physical laws of our world, those laws must be followed and can't be broken. If you create a law with a flaw in it, then your virtual world won't run smoothly and could even explode.

Another form of logic is a loop; using loops allows you to execute the same logic multiple times. A common way to use loops is to iterate over a collection of data. For our imaginary banking software, we would use a loop to step over a user's transactions to display them to the user on request.

Loops and logic allow the software to have complex behavior that responds to changing and dynamic data.

if Statements

An **if** statement is the most basic form of logic in Go. An **if** statement either will or won't run a block of logic based on a Boolean expression. The notation looks like this: **if <boolean expression> { <code block> }**.

The Boolean expression can be a simple code that results in a Boolean value. The code block can be any logic that you could also put in a function. The code block runs when the Boolean expression is true. You can only use **if** statements in the function scope.

Exercise 2.01: A Simple if Statement

In this exercise, we'll use an **if** statement to control whether logic will or won't run. We'll define an **int** value to check it's hardcoded, but in a real-world application, this could be user input. We'll then check whether the value is an odd or even number using % operator, also known as a modulus expression on the variable. The modulus gives you the amount remaining after division. We'll use the modulus to get the remainder after dividing by 2. If we get a remainder of 0, we know the number is even. If the remainder is 1, we know the number is odd. The modulus results in an **int**, so we use == to get a Boolean value:

1. Create a new folder and add a **main.go** file.

2. In **main.go**, add the package and imports:

```
package main
import "fmt"
```

3. Create the **main** function:

```
func main() {
```

4. Define an **int** variable with an initial value. We are setting it to 5 here, which is an odd number but we could also set it to 6, which is an even number:

```
input := 5
```

5. Create an **if** statement that uses a modulus expression; then, check whether the result is equal to 0:

```
if input%2 == 0 {
```

6. When the Boolean expression results in **true**, that means the number is even. We then print that it's even to the console using the format package:

```
fmt.Println(input, "is even")
```

7. Close the code block:

```
}
```

8. Now do the same for odd numbers:

```
if input%2 == 1 {
    fmt.Println(input, "is odd")
}
```

9. Close **main**:

```
}
```

10. Save the file, and, in the new folder, **run** the following code snippet:

```
go run main.go
```

The following is the expected output:

```
5 is odd
```

In this exercise, we used logic to run code selectively. Using logic to control what code runs, let's you create flows through your code. This allows you to have code that reacts to its data. These flows allow you to be able to reason about what the code is doing with your data, making it easier to understand and maintain.

Try changing the value of the input to 6 to see how the even block gets executed instead of the odd block.

In the next topic, we'll explore how we can improve this code and make it more efficient.

if else Statements

In the previous exercise, we did two evaluations. One evaluation was to check whether the number was even and the other was to see whether it was odd. As we know, a number can only ever be odd or even. With this knowledge, we can use deduction to know that if a number is not even, then it must be odd.

Using deductive logic like this is common in programming in order to make programs more efficient by not having to do unnecessary work.

We can represent this kind of logic using an **if else** statement. The notation looks like this: **if <boolean expression> { <code block> } else { <code block> }**. The **if else** statement builds on the **if** statement and gives us a second block. The second block only runs if the first block doesn't run; both blocks can't run.

Exercise 2.02: Using an if else Statement

In this exercise, we'll update our previous exercise to use an **if else** statement:

1. Create a new folder and add a **main.go** file.

2. In **main.go**, add **package** and **import**:

```
package main
import "fmt"
```

3. Create the **main** function:

```
func main() {
```

4. Define an **int** variable with an initial value, and we'll give it a different value this time:

```
input := 4
```

5. Create an **if** statement that uses a modulus expression, and then check whether the result is equal to 0:

```
if input%2 == 0 {
    fmt.Println(input, "is even")
```

6. This time, we are not closing the code block but starting a new **else** code block:

```
} else {
    fmt.Println(input, "is odd")
}
```

7. Close **main**:

```
}
```

8. Save the file, and, in the new folder, **run** the following code snippet:

```
go run main.go
```

The following is the expected output:

```
4 is even
```

In this exercise, we were able to simplify our previous code by using an **if else** statement. As well as making the code more efficient, it also makes the code easier to understand and maintain.

In the next topic, we'll demonstrate how we can add as many code blocks as you want while still only letting one execute.

else if Statements

The **if else** solves the problem of running code for only one or two possible logical outcomes. With that covered, what if our preceding exercise's code was intended to only work for non-negative numbers? We need something that can evaluate more than one Boolean expression but only execute one of the code blocks, that is, the code block for negative numbers, even numbers, or odd numbers.

In that case, we can't use an **if else** statement on its own; however, we could cover it with another extension to **if** statements. In this extension, you can give the **else** statement its own Boolean expression. This is how the notation looks: **if <boolean expression> { <code block> } else if <boolean expression> { <code block> }**. You can also combine it with a final **else** statement at the end, which would look like this: **if <boolean expression> { <code block> } else if <boolean expression> { <code block> } else { <code block> }**. After the initial **if** statement, you can have as many **else if** statements as you need. Go evaluates the Boolean expressions from the top of the statements and works its way through each Boolean expression until one results in **true** or finds an **else**. If there is no **else** and none of the Boolean expressions results in true, then no block is executed and Go moves on. When Go gets a Boolean true result, it executes the code block for that statement only and it then stops evaluating any Boolean expressions of the **if** statement.

Exercise 2.03: Using an else if Statement

In this exercise, we'll update our previous exercise. We're going to add a check for negative numbers. This check must run before the even and odd checks, as only one of the code blocks can run:

1. Create a new folder and add a **main.go** file.

2. In **main.go**, add **package** and **import**:

    ```
    package main
    import "fmt"
    ```

3. Create the **main** function:

    ```
    func main() {
    ```

4. Define an **int** variable with an initial value, and we'll give it a negative value:

    ```
    input := -10
    ```

5. Our first Boolean expression is to check for negative numbers. If we find a negative number, we'll print a message saying that they are not allowed:

    ```
    if input < 0 {
        fmt.Println("input can't be a negative number")
    ```

6. We need to move our even check to an **else if** statement:

```
} else if input%2 == 0 {
    fmt.Println(input, "is even")
```

7. The **else** statement stays the same, and we then close **main**:

```
} else {
    fmt.Println(input, "is odd")
}
}
```

8. Save the file, and, in the new folder, **run** the following code snippet:

```
go run main.go
```

The following is the expected output:

```
input can't be a negative number
```

In this exercise, we added even more complex logic to our **if** statement. We added an **else if** statement to it, which allowed complex evaluation. This addition took what is usually a simple fork in the road that gives you many roads to go down but still with the restriction of only going down one of them.

In the next topic, we'll use a subtle but powerful feature of **if** statements that lets you keep your code nice and tidy.

The Initial if Statement

It's common to need to call a function but not care too much about the returned value. Often, you'll want to check that it executed correctly and then discard the returned value. For example, sending an email, writing to a file, or inserting data into a database; most of the time, if these types of operations execute successfully, you don't need to worry about the variables they return. Unfortunately, the variables don't go anywhere as they are still in scope.

To stop these unwanted variables from hanging around, we can use what we know about scope rules to get rid of them. The best way to check for errors is to use "initial" statements on **if** statements. The notation looks like this: **if <initial statement>; <boolean expression> { <code block> }**. The initial statement is in the same section as the Boolean expression, with **;** to divide them.

Go only allows what it calls simple statements in the initial statement section, including:

- Assignment and short variable assignments:

    ```
    E.g.: i := 0
    ```

- Expressions such as math or logic expressions:

    ```
    E.g.: i = (j * 10) == 40
    ```

- Sending statements for working with channels, which we'll cover later.

- Increment and decrement expressions:

    ```
    E.g.: i++
    ```

A common mistake is trying to define a variable using **var**. That's not allowed; you can use the short assignment in its place.

Exercise 2.04: Implementing the Initial if Statements

In this exercise, we're going to continue to build on our previous exercises. We're going to add even more rules about what numbers can be checked as to whether they are odd or even. With so many rules, putting them all in a single Boolean expression is hard to understand. We'll move all the validation logic to a function that returns an **error**. This is a built-in Go type used for errors. It the value of the error is **nil**, then everything is okay. If not, you have an error, and you need to deal with it. We'll call the function in our initial statement and then check for errors:

1. Create a new folder and add a **main.go** file.

2. In **main.go**, add **package** and **import**:

    ```
    package main
    import (
       "errors"
       "fmt"
    )
    ```

3. Create a function to do the validation. This function takes a single integer and returns **error**:

    ```
    func validate(input int) error {
    ```

4. We define some rules, and if any are true, we return a new **error** using the **New** function in the **errors** package:

    ```
    if input < 0 {
       return errors.New("input can't be a negative number")
    } else if input > 100 {
    ```

```
        return errors.New("input can't be over 100")
    } else if input%7 == 0 {
        return errors.New("input can't be divisible by 7")
```

5. If the input passes all the checks, return **nil**:

```
    } else {
        return nil
    }
}
```

6. Create our **main** function:

```
func main() {
```

7. Define a variable with a value of **21**:

```
    input := 21
```

8. Call the function using the initial statement; use the short variable assignment to capture the returned error. In the Boolean expression, check that the error is not equal to **nil** using **!=**:

```
    if err := validate(input); err != nil {
        fmt.Println(err)
    }
```

9. The rest is the same as before:

```
    else if input%2 == 0 {
        fmt.Println(input, "is even")
    } else {
        fmt.Println(input, "is odd")
    }
}
```

10. Save the file, and, in the new folder, **run** the following code snippet:

```
go run main.go
```

The following is the expected output which displays an error statement:

```
input can't be divisible by 7
```

In this exercise, we used an initial statement to define and initialize a variable. That variable can be used in the Boolean expression and the related code block. Once the **if** statement completes, the variable goes out of scope and is reclaimed by Go's memory management system.

Activity 2.01: Implementing FizzBuzz

When interviewing for a programming job, you'll be asked to do some coding exercises. These questions have you writing something from scratch and will have several rules to follow. To give you an idea of what that looks like, we'll run you through a classic one, "FizzBuzz."

The rules are as follows:

- Write a program that prints out the numbers from 1 to 100.
- If the number is a multiple of 3, print "Fizz."
- If the number is a multiple of 5, print "Buzz."
- If the number is a multiple of 3 and 5, print "FizzBuzz."

Here are some tips:

- You can convert a number to a string using **strconv.Itoa()**.
- The first number to evaluate must be 1 and the last number to evaluate must be 100.

These steps will help you to complete the activity:

1. Create a loop that does 100 iterations.

   > **Hint**
   >
   > You'll learn about loops in detail later on in the chapter (in a section titled *Loops*). If you're not sure how to create a loop, use the following block of code as a hint:
   >
   > ```
   > for i := 1; i <= 100; i++{
   >
   > <code>
   >
   > }
   > ```
   >
   > The preceding code should create a **for** loop that starts at **1** and loops until **i** gets to **100**.

2. Have a variable that keeps count of the number of loops so far.
3. In the loop, use that count and check whether it's divisible by 3 or 5 using %.
4. Think carefully about how you'll deal with the "FizzBuzz" case.

The following screenshot shows the expected output:

```
 ▷    ~/src/Th…op/Ch…02/Activity02.01 ▶   go run .
1
2
Fizz
4
Buzz
Fizz
7
8
Fizz
Buzz
11
Fizz
13
14
FizzBuzz
16
17
Fizz
19
Buzz
Fizz
22
23
Fizz
Buzz
26
Fizz
28
29
FizzBuzz
31
```

Figure 2.01: The FizzBuzz output

Note

The solution for this activity can be found on page 686.

In the next topic, we'll see how we can tame **if else** statements that start to get too big.

Expression switch Statements

While it's possible to add as many **else if** statements to an **if** as you want, at some point, it'll get hard to read.

When this happens, you can use Go's logic alternative: **switch**. For situations where you would need a big **if** statement, **switch** can be a more compact alternative.

The notation for **switch** is shown in the following code snippet:

```
switch <initial statement>; <expresion> {
case <expresion>:
  <statements>
case <expresion>, <expresion>:
  <statements>
default:
  <statements>
}
```

The "initial" statement works the same in **switch** as it does in the preceding **if** statements. The expression is not the same because the **if** is a Boolean expression. You can have more than just a Boolean in this expression. The cases are where you check to see whether the statements get executed. Statements are like code blocks in **if** statements, but with no need for the curly brackets here.

Both the initial statement and expression are optional. To have just the expression, it would look like this: **switch <expresion> {**.... To have only the initial statement, you would write **switch <initial statment>; {**.... You can leave them both off, and you'll end up with **switch {**.... When the expression is missing, it's as if you put the value of **true** there.

There are two main ways of using case expressions. They can be used just like **if** statements or Boolean expressions where you use logic to control whether the statements get executed. The alternative is to put a literal value there. In this case, the value is compared to the value in the **switch** expression. If they match, then the statements run. You can have as many case expressions as you want by separating them with a **,**. The case expressions get checked from the top case and then from left to right if a case has multiple expressions.

When a case matches, only its statements are run, which is different from many other languages. To get the fallthrough behavior found in those languages, a **fallthrough** statement must be added to the end of each case where you want that behavior. If you call **fallthrough** before the end of the case, it will fall through at that moment and move on to the next case.

An optional **default** case can be added anywhere in the **switch** statement, but it's best practice to add it to the end. The **default** case works just like using an **else** statement in an **if** statement.

This form of switch statement is called an "expression **switch**" statement. There is also another form of **switch** statement, called a "type **switch**" statement, which we'll look at in a later chapter.

Exercise 2.05: Using a switch Statement

In this exercise, we need to create a program that prints a particular message based on the day someone was born. We are using the **time** package for the set of days of the week constants. We'll use a **switch** statement to make a more compact logic structure:

1. Load the **main** package:

```
package main
```

2. Import the **fmt** and **time** packages:

```
import (
    "fmt"
    "time"
)
```

3. Define the **main** function:

```
func main() {
```

4. Define a variable that is the day of the week someone was born. Use the constants from the **time** package to do it. We'll set it to Monday, but it could be any day:

```
dayBorn := time.Monday
```

5. Create a **switch** statement that uses the variable as it's expression:

```
switch dayBorn {
```

6. Each **case** will try to match its expression value against the switch expression value:

```
case time.Monday:
fmt.Println("Monday's child is fair of face")
case time.Tuesday:
fmt.Println("Tuesday's child is full of grace")
case time.Wednesday:
fmt.Println("Wednesday's child is full of woe")
case time.Thursday:
fmt.Println("Thursday's child has far to go")
case time.Friday:
```

```
fmt.Println("Friday's child is loving and giving")
case time.Saturday:
fmt.Println("Saturday's child works hard for a living")
case time.Sunday:
fmt.Println("Sunday's child is bonny and blithe")
```

7. We'll use the **default** case here as a form of validation:

```
default:
fmt.Println("Error, day born not valid")
}
```

8. Close the **main** function:

```
}
```

9. Save the file, and, in the new folder, **run** the following code snippet:

```
go run main.go
```

The following is the expected output:

```
Monday's child is fair of face
```

In this exercise, we used **switch** to create a compact logic structure that matches lots of different possible values to give a specific message to our users. It's quite common to see **switch** statements used with a constant as we did here, using the day of the week constants from the **time** package.

Next, we'll use the **case** feature that let's us match multiple values.

Exercise 2.06: switch Statements and Multiple case Values

In this exercise, we're going to print out a message that tells us whether the day someone was born was a weekday or the weekend. We only need two cases as each case can support checking multiple values:

1. Load the **main** package:

```
package main
```

2. Import the **fmt** and **time** packages:

```
import (
    "fmt"
    "time"
)
```

3. Define the **main** function:

```
func main() {
```

4. Define our **dayBorn** variable using one of the **time** package's constants:

```
dayBorn := time.Sunday
```

5. **switch** starts the same by using the variable as the expression:

```
switch dayBorn {
```

6. This time, for **case**, we have weekday constants. Go checks each one against the **switch** expression, starting from the left, and sweeps through each one by one. Once Go gets a match, it stops evaluating and runs the statements for that case only:

```
case time.Monday, time.Tuesday, time.Wednesday, time.Thursday, time.Friday:
    fmt.Println("Born on a weekday")
```

7. Then, it does the same for weekend days:

```
case time.Saturday, time.Sunday:
    fmt.Println("Born on the weekend")
```

8. We use **default** for validation again and close out the **switch** statement:

```
default:
    fmt.Println("Error, day born not valid")
}
```

9. Close the **main** function:

```
}
```

10. Save the file, and, in the new folder, **run** the following code snippet:

```
go run main.go
```

The following is the expected output:

```
Born on the weekend
```

In this exercise, we used cases with multiple values. This allowed a very compact logic structure that could evaluate 7 days of the week with validation checking in a few lines of code. It makes the intention of the logic clear, which, in turn, makes it easier to change and maintain.

Next, we'll look at using more complex logic in **case** expressions.

Sometimes, you'll see code that doesn't evaluate anything in the **switch** statement but does checks in the **case** expression.

Exercise 2.07: Expressionless switch Statements

It's not always possible to be able to match values using the value of the **switch** expression. Sometimes, you'll need to match on multiple variables. Sometimes, you'll need to match on something more complicated than an equality check. For example, you may need to check whether a number is in a specific range. In these cases, **switch** is still helpful in building compact logic statements, as **case** allows the same range of expressions that you have in **if** Boolean expressions.

In this exercise, let's build a simple **switch** expression that checks whether a day is a weekend to show what can be done in **case**:

1. Load the **main** package:

   ```
   package main
   ```

2. Import the **fmt** and **time** packages:

   ```
   import (
       "fmt"
       "time"
   )
   ```

3. Define the **main** function:

   ```
   func main() {
   ```

4. Our **switch** expression is using the initial statement to define our variable. The expression is left empty as we'll not be using it:

   ```
   switch dayBorn := time.Sunday; {
   ```

5. **case** is using some complex logic to check whether the day is at the weekend:

   ```
   case dayBorn == time.Sunday || dayBorn == time.Saturday:
       fmt.Println("Born on the weekend")
   ```

6. Add a **default** statement and close the **switch** expression:

   ```
   default:
       fmt.Println("Born some other day")
   }
   ```

7. Close the **main** function:

   ```
   }
   ```

8. Save the file, and, in the new folder, **run** the following code snippet:

   ```
   go run main.go
   ```

The following screenshot shows the expected output:

```
Born on the weekend
```

In this exercise, we learned that you can use complex logic in the **case** expression when a simple **switch** statement match is not enough. This still offers a more compact and easier way to manage a logic statement than **if**, if you have more than a couple of cases.

Next, we'll leave logic structures behind and start to look at ways in which we can run the same statements multiple times to make processing data easier.

Loops

In real-world applications, you're often going to need to run the same logic repeatedly. It's common to have to deal with multiple inputs and give multiple outputs. Loops are the simplest way of repeating your logic.

Go only has one looping statement, **for**, but it's a flexible one. There are two distinct forms: the first is used a lot for ordered collections such as arrays and slices, which we'll cover more later. The sort of loop used for ordered collections looks as follows:

```
for <initial statement>; <condition>; <post statement> {
    <statements>
}
```

The **initial** statement is just like the one found in **if** and **switch** statements. **initial** statement runs before everything else and allows the same simple statements that we defined before. The condition is checked before each loop to see whether the statements should be run or whether the loop should stop. Like **initial** statement, **condition** also allows simple statements. The **post** statement is run after the statements are run at the end of each loop and allow you to run simple statements. The **post** statement is mostly used for incrementing things such as loop counters, which get evaluated on the next loop by **condition**. The statements are any Go code you want to run as part of the loop.

The **initial**, **condition**, and **post** statements are all optional, and it's possible to write a **for** loop like this:

```
for {
    <statements>
}
```

This form would result in a loop that would run forever, also known as an infinite loop, unless the **break** statement is used to stop the loop manually. In addition to **break**, there is also a **continue** statement that can be used to skip the remainder of an individual run of a loop but doesn't stop the whole loop.

Another form the **for** loop can take is when reading from a source of data that returns a Boolean when there is more data to read. Examples of this include when reading from databases, files, command-line inputs, and network sockets. This form looks like this:

```
for <condition> {
    <statements>
}
```

This form is just a simplified version of the form used to read from an ordered list but without the logic needed to control the loop yourself, as the source you're using is built to work easily in **for** loops.

The other form that the **for** loop takes is when looping over unordered data collections such as maps. We'll cover what maps are in more detail in a later chapter. When looping over these, you'll use the **range** statement in your loop. With maps, the form looks like this:

```
for <key>, <value> := range <map> {
    <statements>
}
```

Exercise 2.08: Using the for i Loop

In this exercise, we'll use the three parts of the **for** loop to create a variable and use a variable in the loop. We'll be able to see how the variable changes after each iteration of the loop by printing out its value to the console:

1. Define **package** as **main** and add imports:

    ```
    package main
    import "fmt"
    ```

2. Create the **main** function:

    ```
    func main() {
    ```

3. Define a **for** loop that defines the **i** variable with an initial value of **0** in the **initial** statement section. In the clause, check that **i** is less than **5**. In for the post statement, increment **i** by 1:

    ```
    for i := 0; i < 5; i++ {
    ```

4. In the body of the loop, print out the value of **i**:

    ```
    fmt.Println(i)
    ```

5. Close the loop:

    ```
    }
    ```

6. Close **main**:

```
}
```

7. Save the file, and, in the new folder, **run** the following code snippet:

```
go run main.go
```

The following is the expected output:

```
0
1
2
3
4
```

In this exercise, we used a variable that only exists in the **for** loop. We set up the variable, checked its value, modified it, and output it. Using a loop like this is very common when working with ordered, numerically indexed collections such as arrays and slices. In this instance, we hardcoded the value for when to stop looping; however, when looking over arrays and slices, that value would be determined dynamically from the size of the collection.

Next, we'll use a **for i** loop to work with a slice.

Exercise 2.09: Looping Over Arrays and Slices

In this exercise, we'll loop over a collection of strings. We'll be using a slice, but the loop logic will also be the same set of arrays. We'll define the collection; we'll then create a loop that uses the collection to control when to stop looping and a variable to keep track of where we are in the collection.

The way the index of arrays and slices works means that there are never any gaps in the number, and the first number is always 0. The built-in function, **len**, is used to get the length of any collection. We'll use it as part of the condition to check when we've reached the end of the collection:

1. Create a new folder and add a **main.go** file.

2. In **main.go**, add **package** and **import**:

```
package main
import "fmt"
```

3. Create the **main** function:

```
func main() {
```

4. Define a variable which is a slice of "strings" and initialize it with data:

```
names := []string{"Jim", "Jane", "Joe", "June"}
```

We will cover **collection** and **string** in more detail in the next chapter.

5. The **initial** and **post** statements for the loop are the same as before; the difference is in the **condition**, where we use **len** to check whether we are at the end of the collection:

```
for i := 0; i < len(names); i++ {
```

6. The rest is the same as before:

```
        fmt.Println(names[i])
    }
}
```

7. Save the file, and, in the new folder, **run** the following code snippet:

```
go run main.go
```

The following is the expected output:

```
Jim
Jane
Joe
June
```

The range Loop

The **array** and **slice** types always have the number of an index, and that number always starts at **0**. The **for i** loop we've seen so far is the most common choice you'll see in real-world code for these types.

The other collection type, **map**, doesn't give the same guarantee. That means you need to use **range**. You'll use **range** instead of the **condition** of a **for** loop, and, on each loop, **range** yields both a key and a value of an element in the collection, then, moves on to the next element.

With a **range** loop, you don't need to define a condition to stop the loop as **range** takes care of that for us.

> **Note**
>
> **Callout map Order:** The order of items is randomized to stop developers relying on the order of the elements in a map, which means you can use it as a form of pseudo data randomization if needed.

Exercise 2.10: Looping Over a Map

In this exercise, we're going to create a **map** that has a string for its key and a string for the values. We'll cover **map** types in more detail in a later chapter, so don't worry if you don't quite get what **map** types are yet. We'll then use **range** in the **for** loop to iterate over the map. We'll then write out the key and value data to the console:

1. Create a new folder and add a **main.go** file.

2. In **main.go**, add the **package** and **import**:

```
package main
import "fmt"
```

3. Create the **main** function:

```
func main() {
```

4. Define a **map** with a **string** key and a **string** value of strings variable and initialize it with the data:

```
config := map[string]string{
"debug":    "1",
"logLevel": "warn",
"version":  "1.2.1",
}
```

5. Use **range** to get the **key** and **value** for an array element and assign them to variables:

```
for key, value := range config {
```

6. Print out the **key** and **value** variables:

```
fmt.Println(key, "=", value)
```

7. Close the loop and **main**:

```
    }
}
```

8. Save the file, and, in the new folder, **run** the following code snippet:

```
go run main.go
```

The following is the expected output displaying a map that has a string for its key and a string for the values:

```
debug = 1
logLevel = warn
version = 1.2.1
```

In this exercise, we used **range** in a **for** loop to allow us to read out all the data from a **map** collection. Even though we used an integer for the **map** variable's key, **map** types don't give guarantees like arrays and slices do about starting at zero and having no gaps. **range** creates an integer variable which is the **key**, and the **value** is referenced by the **key**. **range** also controls when to stop the loop.

If you don't need the **key** or the **value** variable, you can use _ as the variable name to tell the compiler you don't want it.

Activity 2.02: Looping Over Map Data Using range

Suppose you have been provided with the data in the following table. You have to find the word with the maximum count and print the word and its count using the following data:

Word	Count
Gonna	3
You	3
Give	2
Never	1
Up	4

Figure 2.02: Word and count data to perform the activity

Note

The preceding words are from the song *Never Gonna Give You Up*, sung by *Rick Astley*.

The steps to solve the activity are as follows.

1. Put the words into a map like this:

```
words := map[string]int{
"Gonna": 3,
"You": 3,
"Give": 2,
"Never": 1,
"Up":   4,
}
```

2. Create a loop and use **range** to capture the word and the count.

3. Keep track of the word with the highest count using a variable for what the highest count is and its associated word.

4. Print the variables out.

   The following is the expected output displaying the most popular word with its count value:

```
Most popular word: Up
With a count of  : 4
```

> **Note**
>
> The solution for this activity can be found on page 688.

Next, we'll look at how we can take manual control of the loop by skipping iterations or stopping the loop.

break and continue

There are going to be times when you need to skip a single loop or stop the loop from running altogether. It's possible to do this with variables and **if** statements, but there is an easier way.

The **continue** keyword stops the execution of the current loop and starts a new loop. The **post** loop logic runs, and the loop **condition** gets evaluated.

The **break** keyword also stops the execution of the current loop and it stops any new loops from running.

Use **continue** when you want to skip a single item in a collection; for instance, perhaps it's okay if one of the items in a collection is invalid, but the rest may be okay to process. Use **break** when you need to stop processing when there are any errors in the data and there's no value in processing the rest of the collection.

Here, we have an example that generates a random number between **0** and **8**. The loop skips on a number divisible by **3** and stops on a number divisible by **2**. It also prints out the **i** variable for each loop to help us see that **continue** and **break** are stopping the execution of the rest of the loop.

Exercise 2.11: Using break and continue to Control Loops

In this exercise, we'll use **continue** and **break** in a loop to show you how you can take control of it. We're going to create a loop that keeps going forever. This means we have to stop it with **break** manually. We'll also randomly skip loops with **continue**. We'll do this skipping by generating a random number, and if that number is divisible by 3, we'll skip the rest of the loop:

1. Create a new folder and add a **main.go** file.

2. In **main.go**, add **package** and **import**:

```go
package main
import (
  "fmt"
  "math/rand"
)
```

3. Create the **main** function:

```go
func main() {
```

4. Create an empty **for** loop. This will loop forever if you don't stop it:

```go
for {
```

5. Use **Intn** from the **rand** package to pick a random number between 0 and 8:

```go
r := rand.Intn(8)
```

6. If the random number is divisible by 3, print **"Skip"** and skip the rest of the loop using **continue**:

```go
if r%3 == 0 {
    fmt.Println("Skip")
    continue
```

7. If the random number is divisible by 2, then print **"Stop"** and stop the loop using **break**:

```go
} else if r%2 == 0 {
    fmt.Println("Stop")
    break
}
```

8. If the number is neither of those things, then print the number:

```
fmt.Println(r)
```

9. Close the loop and **main**:

```
    }
}
```

10. Save the file, and, in the new folder, **run** the following code snippet:

```
go run main.go
```

The following is the expected output displaying random numbers, **Skip**, and **Stop**:

```
1
7
7
Skip
1
Skip
1
Stop
```

In this exercise, we created a **for** loop that would loop forever, and we then used **continue** and **break** to override normal loop behavior to take control of it ourselves. The ability to do this can allow us to reduce the number of nested **if** statements and variables needed to prevent logic from running when it shouldn't. Using **break** and **continue** help to clean up your code and make it easier to work on.

If you use an empty **for** loop like this, the loop continues forever, and you must use **break** to prevent an infinite loop. An infinite loop is a loop in your code that never stops. Once you get an infinite loop, you'll need a way to kill your application; how you do that will depend on your operating system. If you are running your app in a terminal, closing the terminal normally does the trick. Don't panic – it happens to us all – your system may slow down, but it won't do it any harm.

Next, we'll work on some activities to test out all your new knowledge about logic and loops.

Activity 2.03: Bubble Sort

In this activity, we'll sort a given slice of numbers by swapping the values. This technique of sorting is known as the **bubble sort** technique. Go has built-in sorting algorithms in the **sort** package but I don't want you to use them; we want you to use the logic and loops you've just learned.

Steps:

1. Define a slice with unsorted numbers in it.

2. Print this slice to the console.

3. Sort the values using swapping.

4. Once done, print the now sorted numbers to the console.

Tips:

- You can do an in-place swap in Go using:

  ```
  nums[i], nums[i-1] = nums[i-1], nums[i]
  ```

- You can create a new slice using:

  ```
  var nums2 []int
  ```

- You can add to the end of a slice using:

  ```
  nums2 = append(nums2, 1)
  ```

  The following is the expected output:

  ```
  Before: [5, 8, 2, 4, 0, 1, 3, 7, 9, 6]
  After : [0, 1, 2, 3, 4, 5, 6, 7, 8, 9]
  ```

> **Note**
>
> The solution for this activity can be found on page 690.

Summary

In this chapter, we discussed logic and loops. These are the foundational building blocks to build complex software. They allow you to have data flow through your code. They let you deal with collections of data by letting you execute the same logic on every element of the data.

Being able to define the rules and laws of your code are the starting points of codifying the real world in software. If you are creating banking software and the bank has rules about what you can and can't do with money, then you can also define those rules in your code.

Logic and loops are the essential tools that you'll use to build all your software.

In the next chapter, we'll look at Go's type system and the core types it has available.

3

Core Types

Overview

This chapter aims to show you how to use Go's basic core types to design your software's data. We'll work through each type to show what they are useful for and how to use them in your software. Understanding these core types provides you with the foundation required to learn how to create complex data designs.

By the end of this chapter, you will be able to create variables of different types for Go programs and assign values to variables of different types. You will learn to identify and pick a suitable type for any programming situation. You will also write a program to measure password complexity and implement empty value types.

Introduction

In the previous chapter, we learned how to use `if`, `if-else`, `switch`, `continue`, and `break` in Go.

Go is a strongly typed language, and all data is assigned a type. That type is fixed and can't be changed. What you can and can't do with your data is constrained by the types you assign. Understanding exactly what defines every one of Go's core types is critical to success with the Go language.

In later chapters, we'll talk about Go's more complex types, but those types are built on the core types defined in this chapter.

Go's core types are well-thought-out and easy to understand once you understand the details. Having to understand the details means Go's type system is not always intuitive. For example, Go's most common number type, `int`, may be either 32 bits or 64 bits in size depending on the computer used to compile the code.

Types are needed to make data easier for humans to work with. Computers only think about data in binary. Binary is hard for people to work with. By adding a layer of abstraction to binary data and labeling it as a number or some text, humans have an easier time reasoning about it. Reducing the cognitive load allows people to build more complex software because they're not overwhelmed by managing the details of the binary data.

Programming languages need to define what a number is or what a text is for. A programming language defines what you can call a number, and it defines what operations you can use on a number. For example, can a whole number such as 10 and a floating-point number such as 3.14 both be stored as the same type? While it seems obvious that you can multiply numbers, can you multiply text? As we progress through this chapter, we'll clearly define what the rules are for each type and what operations you can use with each of them.

The way data is stored is also a large part of what defines a **type**. To allow for the building of efficient software, Go places limits on how large some of its types can be. For example, the largest amount of storage for a number in Go's core types is 64 bits of memory. This allows for any number up to 18,446,744,073,709,551,615. Understanding these type limitations is critical in building bug-free code.

The things that define a type are:

- The kind of data that you can store in it

- What operations you can use with it

- What those operations do to it

- How much memory it can use

This chapter gives you the knowledge and confidence to use Go's types system correctly in your code.

True and False

True and false logic is represented using the Boolean type, **bool**. Use this type when you need an on/off switch in your code. The value of a **bool** can only ever be **true** or **false**. The zero value of a **bool** is **false**.

When using a comparison operator such as == or >, the result of that comparison is a **bool** value.

In this code example, we use comparison operators on two numbers. You'll see that the result is a **bool**:

```go
package main
import "fmt"
func main() {
   fmt.Println(10 > 5)
   fmt.Println(10 == 5)
}
```

Running the preceding code shows the following output:

```
true
false
```

Exercise 3.01: Program to Measure Password Complexity

An online portal creates user accounts for its users and accepts passwords that are only 8-15 characters long. In this exercise, we write a program for the portal to display whether the password entered meets the character requirements. The character requirements are as follows:

- Have a lowercase letter
- Have an uppercase letter
- Have a number
- Have a symbol
- Be 8 or more characters long

To do this exercise, we're going to use a few new features. Don't worry if you don't quite understand what they are doing; we'll cover them in detail in the next chapter. Consider this a sneak peek. We'll explain what everything is as we go, but your main focus should be on the Boolean logic:

1. Create a new folder and add a **main.go** file.

2. In **main.go**, add the main package name to the top of the file:

    ```
    package main
    ```

3. Now add the imports we'll use in this file:

    ```
    import (
      "fmt"
      "unicode"
    )
    ```

4. Create a function that takes a string argument and returns a **bool**:

    ```
    func passwordChecker(pw string) bool {
    ```

5. Convert the password string into **rune**, which is a type that is safe for multi-byte (UTF-8) characters:

    ```
    pwR := []rune(pw)
    ```

    We'll talk more about rune later in this chapter.

6. Count the number of multi-byte characters using **len**. This code results in a **bool** result that can be used in the **if** statement:

    ```
    if len(pwR) < 8 {
    return false
    }
    if len(pwR) > 15 {
    return false
    }
    ```

7. Define some **bool** variables. We'll check these at the end:

    ```
    hasUpper  := false
    hasLower  := false
    hasNumber := false
    hasSymbol := false
    ```

8. Loop over the multi-byte characters one at a time:

    ```
    for _, v := range pwR {
    ```

9. Using the **unicode** package, check whether this character is uppercase. This function returns a **bool** that we can use directly in the **if** statement:

```
if unicode.IsUpper(v) {
```

10. If it is, we'll set the **hasUpper bool** variable to **true**:

```
    hasUpper = true
}
```

11. Do the same thing for lowercase letters:

```
if unicode.IsLower(v) {
    hasLower = true
}
```

12. Also do it for numbers:

```
if unicode.IsNumber(v) {
    hasNumber = true
}
```

13. For symbols, we'll also accept punctuation. Use the **or** operator, which works with **Booleans**, to result in **true** if either of these functions returns **true**:

```
if unicode.IsPunct(v) || unicode.IsSymbol(v) {
    hasSymbol = true
}
}
```

14. To pass all our checks, all our variables must be **true**. Here, we combine multiple **and** operators to create a one-line statement that checks all four variables:

```
return hasUpper && hasLower && hasNumber && hasSymbol
```

15. Close the function:

```
}
```

16. Create the **main()** function:

```
func main() {
```

17. Call the **passwordChecker()** function with an invalid password. As this returns a **bool**, it can be used directly in an **if** statement:

```
if passwordChecker("") {
fmt.Println("password good")
} else {
```

```
        fmt.Println("password bad")
    }
```

18. Now, call the function with a valid password:

```
    if passwordChecker("This!I5A") {
    fmt.Println("password good")
    } else {
    fmt.Println("password bad")
    }
```

19. Close the **main()** function:

```
    }
```

20. Save the file and in the new folder and then run the following:

```
    go run main.go
```

Running the preceding code shows the following output:

```
password bad
password good
```

In this exercise, we highlighted a variety of ways that **bool** values manifest themselves in the code. **Bool** values are critical to giving your code the ability to make a choice and be dynamic and responsive. Without **bool**, your code would have a hard time doing anything.

Next, we'll take a look at numbers and how Go categorizes them.

Numbers

Go has two distinct number types: integers, also known as whole numbers, and floating-point numbers. A floating-point number allows a number with whole numbers and fractions of a whole number.

1, 54, and 5,436 are examples of whole numbers. 1.5, 52.25, 33.333, and 64,567.00001 are all examples of floating-point numbers.

> **Note**
>
> The default and empty values for all number types is 0.

Next, we'll start our number journey by looking at integers.

Integer

Integer types are classified in two ways, based on the following conditions:

- Whether or not they can store negative numbers
- The smallest and largest numbers they can store

Types that can store negative numbers are called signed integers. Types that can't store negative numbers are called unsigned integers. How big and small a number each type can store is expressed by how many bytes of internal storage they have.

Here is an excerpt from the Go language specification with all the relevant integer types:

uint8	the set of all unsigned 8-bit integers (0 to 255)
uint16	the set of all unsigned 16-bit integers (0 to 65535)
uint32	the set of all unsigned 32-bit integers (0 to 4294967295)
uint64	the set of all unsigned 64-bit integers (0 to 18446744073709551615)
int8	the set of all signed 8-bit integers (-128 to 127)
int16	the set of all signed 16-bit integers (-32768 to 32767)
int32	the set of all signed 32-bit integers (-2147483648 to 2147483647)
int64	the set of all signed 64-bit integers (-9223372036854775808 to 9223372036854775807)
byte	alias for uint8
rune	alias for int32

Figure 3.01: Go language specification with relevant integer types

There are also special integer types as follows:

uint	either 32 or 64 bits
int	same size as uint

Figure 3.02: Special integer types

uint and **int** are either 32 or 64 bits depending on whether you compile your code for a 32-bit system or a 64-bit system. It's rare nowadays to run applications on a 32-bit system, systems so most of the time they are 64 bits.

An **int** on a 64-bit system is not an **int64**. While these two types are identical, they are not the same integer type, and you can't use them together. If Go did allow this, there would be problems when the same code gets compiled for a 32-bit machine, so keeping them separate ensures that the code is reliable.

This incompatibility is not just an **int** thing; you can't use any of the integer types together.

Picking the correct integer type to use when defining a variable is easy: use **int**. When writing code for an application, **int** does the job the majority of the time. Only think about using the other types when an **int** is causing a problem. The sorts of problems you see with **int** tend to be related to memory usage.

For example, let's say you have an app that's running out of memory. The app uses a massive number of integers, but these integers are never negative and won't go over 255. One possible fix is to switch from using **int** to using **uint8**. Doing this cuts its memory usage from 64 bits (8 bytes) per number to 8 bits (1 byte) per number.

We can show this by creating a collection of both kinds of type then asking Go how much heap memory it is using. The output may vary on your computer, but the effect should be similar. This code creates a collection of **int** or **int8**. It then adds 10 million values to the collection. Once that's done, it uses the runtime package to give us a reading of how much heap memory is being used. We convert that reading to MB and then print it out:

```
package main
import (
    "fmt"
    "runtime"
)
func main() {
    var list []int
    //var list []int8
    for i := 0; i < 10000000; i++ {
        list = append(list, 100)
    }
    var m runtime.MemStats
    runtime.ReadMemStats(&m)
    fmt.Printf("TotalAlloc (Heap) = %v MiB\n", m.TotalAlloc/1024/1024)
}
```

Here's the output using **int**:

```
TotalAlloc (Heap) = 403 MiB
```

And here's the output using `int8`:

```
TotalAlloc (Heap) = 54 MiB
```

We saved a good amount of memory here, but we need 10 million variables to make it worthwhile. Hopefully, now you are convinced that it's okay to start with `int` and only worry about performance when it's a problem, not before.

Next, we'll look at floating-point numbers.

Floating Point

Go has two floating-point number types, `float32` and `float64`. The bigger `float64` allows for more precision in the numbers. `float32` has 32 bits of storage and `float64` has 64 bits of storage. Floats split their storage between whole numbers (everything to the left of the decimal point) and decimal numbers (everything to the right of the decimal point). How much space is used for the whole number or the decimal numbers, varies by the number being stored. For example, 9,999.9 would use more storage for the whole numbers while 9.9999 would use more storage for the decimal numbers. With `float64`'s bigger space for storage, it can store more whole numbers and/or more decimal numbers than `float32` can.

Exercise 3.02: Floating-Point Number Accuracy

In this exercise, we're going to compare what happens when we do some divisions on numbers that don't divide equally. We'll be dividing 100 by 3. One way of representing the result is 33 ⅓. Computers, for the most part, can't compute fractions like this. Instead, they use a decimal representation, which is 33.3 recurring, where the 3 after the decimal point repeats forever. If we let the computer do that it uses up all the memory, which is not very helpful.

Luckily for us, we don't need to worry about this happening as the floating-point types have storage limits. The downside is that this leads to a number that doesn't reflect the true result; the result has a certain amount of inaccuracy. Your tolerance for inaccuracy needs and how much storage space you want to give to your floating-point numbers must be balanced out:

1. Create a new folder and add a `main.go` file.

2. In `main.go`, add the main package name to the top of the file:

   ```
   package main
   ```

3. Now add the imports we'll use in this file:

   ```
   import "fmt"
   ```

4. Create the **main()** function:

```
func main() {
```

5. Declare an **int** and initialize it with a value of 100:

```
var a int = 100
```

6. Declare a **float32** and initialize it with a value of 100:

```
var b float32 = 100
```

7. Declare a **float64** and initialize it with a value of 100:

```
var c float64 = 100
```

8. Divide each variable by 3 and print the result to the console:

```
fmt.Println(a / 3)
fmt.Println(b / 3)
fmt.Println(c / 3)
}
```

9. Save the file and in the new folder run the following:

```
go run main.go
```

Running the preceding code shows the following output displaying **int**, **float32**, and **float64** values:

```
33
33.333332
33.333333333333336
```

In this exercise, we can see that the computer is not able to give perfect answers to this sort of division. You can also see that when doing this sort of math on integers, you don't get an error. Go ignores any fractional part of the number, which is usually not what you want. We can also see that the **float64** gives a much more accurate answer than **float32**.

While this limit seems like it would lead to problems with inaccuracy, for real-world business work, it does get the job done well enough the vast majority of the time.

Let's see what happens if we try to get our number back to 100 by multiplying it by 3:

```
package main
import "fmt"
func main() {
    var a int = 100
    var b float32 = 100
```

```
   var c float64 = 100
   fmt.Println((a / 3) * 3)
   fmt.Println((b / 3) * 3)
   fmt.Println((c / 3) * 3)
}
```

Running the preceding code shows the following output:

```
99
100
100
```

In this example, we saw that the accuracy is not as impacted as much as you'd expect. At first glance, floating-point math can seem simple, but it gets complicated quickly. When defining your floating-point variables, typically **float64** should be your first choice unless you need to be more memory efficient.

Next, we'll look at what happens when you go beyond the limits of a number type.

Overflow and Wraparound

When you try to initialize a number with a value that's too big for the type we are using, you get an overflow error. The highest number you can have in an **int8** is 127. In the following code, we'll try to initialize it with 128 and see what happens:

```
package main
import "fmt"
func main() {
   var a int8 = 128
   fmt.Println(a)
}
```

Running the preceding code gives the following output:

```
      ~/src/Th...op/Ch...03/Example03.04    go run main.go
# command-line-arguments
./main.go:6:15: constant 128 overflows int8
```

Figure 3.03: Output after initializing with 128

This error is easy to fix and can't cause any hidden problems. The real problem is when the compiler can't catch it. When this happens, the number will ".wraparound". Wraparound means the number goes from its highest possible value to its smallest possible value. Wraparound can be easy to miss when developing your code and can cause significant problems to your users.

Exercise 3.03: Triggering Number Wraparound

In this exercise, we'll declare two small integer types: **int8** and **uint8**. We'll initialize them near their highest possible value. Then we'll use a loop statement to increment them by 1 per loop then print their value to the console. We'll be able to see exactly when they wraparound.

1. Create a new folder and add a **main.go** file.

2. In **main.go** add the main package name to the top of the file:

```
package main
```

3. Now add the imports we'll use in this file:

```
import "fmt"
```

4. Create the main function:

```
func main() {
```

5. Declare an **int8** variable with an initial value of 125:

```
var a int8 = 125
```

6. Declare an **uint8** variable with an initial value of 253:

```
var b uint8 = 253
```

7. Create a **for i** loop that runs five times:

```
for i := 0; i < 5; i++ {
```

8. Increment the two variables by 1:

```
a++
b++
```

9. Print the variables' values to the console:

```
fmt.Println(i, ")", "int8", a, "uint8", b)
```

10. Close the loop:

```
}
```

11. Close the **main()** function:

```
}
```

12. Save the file, and in the new folder run the following:

```
go run main.go
```

Running the preceding code shows the following output:

```
 📂  ~/src/Th…op/Ch…03/Exercise03.03  ▶  go run main.go
0 ) int8 126 uint8 254
1 ) int8 127 uint8 255
2 ) int8 -128 uint8 0
3 ) int8 -127 uint8 1
4 ) int8 -126 uint8 2
```

Figure 3.04: Output after wraparound

In this exercise, we saw that, for signed integers, you'd end up with a negative number and for unsigned integers, it wraps around to 0. You must always consider the maximum possible number for your variable and be sure to have the appropriate type to support that number.

Next, we'll look at what you can do when you need a number that's bigger than the core types can give you.

Big Numbers

If you need a number higher or lower than **int64** or **uint64** can give, you can use the **math/big** package. This package feels a little awkward to use compared to dealing with integer types, but you'll be able to do everything you can generally do with integers using its API.

Exercise 3.04: Big Numbers

In this exercise, we're going to create a number that's larger than what is possible with Go's core number types. To show that, we'll use an addition operation. We'll also do the same to an **int** to show the difference. Then, we'll print the result to the console:

1. Create a new folder and add a **main.go** file.

2. In **main.go**, add the main package name to the top of the file:

```
package main
```

3. Now add the imports we'll use in this file:

```
import (
  "fmt"
  "math"
  "math/big"
)
```

4. Create the **main()** function:

```
func main() {
```

5. Declare an **int** and initialize with **math.MaxInt64**, which is the highest possible value for an **int64** in Go, which is defined as a constant:

```
intA := math.MaxInt64
```

6. Add 1 to the **int**:

```
intA = intA + 1
```

7. Now we'll create a **big int**. This is a custom type and is not based on Go's **int** type. We'll also initialize it with Go's highest possible number value:

```
bigA := big.NewInt(math.MaxInt64)
```

8. We'll add 1 to our **big int**. You can see that this feels clumsy:

```
bigA.Add(bigA, big.NewInt(1))
```

9. Print out the max **int** size and the values for our Go **int** and our **big int**:

```
fmt.Println("MaxInt64: ", math.MaxInt64)
fmt.Println("Int    :", intA)
fmt.Println("Big Int : ", bigA.String())
```

10. Close the **main()** function:

```
}
```

11. Save the file, and in the new folder run the following:

```
go run main.go
```

Running the preceding code shows the following output:

```
  ~/src/Th…op/Ch…03/Exercise03.04   go run main.go
MaxInt64:  9223372036854775807
Int    : -9223372036854775808
Big Int :  9223372036854775808
```

Figure 3.5: Output displaying large numbers with Go's number types

In this exercise, we saw that while **int** has wrapped around, **big.Int** has added the number correctly.

If you have a situation where you have a number whose value is higher than Go can manage, then the **big** package from the standard library is what you need. Next, we'll look at a special Go number type used to represent raw data.

Byte

The **byte** type in Go is just an alias for **uint8**, which is a number that has 8 bits of storage. In reality, **byte** is a significant type, and you'll see it in lots of places. A bit is a single binary value, a single on/off switch. Grouping bits into groups of 8 was a common standard in early computing and became a near-universal way to encode data. 8 bits have 256 possible combinations of "off" and "on," **uint8** has 256 possible integer values from 0 to 255. All combinations of on and off can are represented with this type.

You'll see **byte** used when reading and writing data to and from a network connection and when reading and writing data to files.

With this, we're all done with numbers. Now, let's look at how Go stores and manages text.

Text

Go has a single type to represent some text, **string**.

When you are writing some text for a **string**, it's called a string literal. There are two kinds of string literals in Go:

- Raw – defined by wrapping text in a pair of `
- Interpreted – defined by surrounding the text in a pair of "

With raw, what ends up in your variable is precisely the text that you see on the screen. With interpreted, Go scans what you've written and then applies transformations based on its own set of rules.

Here's what that looks like:

```
package main

import "fmt"

func main() {
  comment1 := `This is the BEST
thing ever!`
  comment2 := `This is the BEST\nthing ever!`
  comment3 := "This is the BEST\nthing ever!"

  fmt.Print(comment1, "\n\n")
  fmt.Print(comment2, "\n\n")
  fmt.Print(comment3, "\n")
}
```

Running the preceding code gives the following output:

```
📁  ~/src/Th…op/Ch…03/Example03.05    go run main.go
This is the BEST
thing ever!

This is the BEST\nthing ever!

This is the BEST
thing ever!
```

Figure 3.6: Output printing texts

In an interpreted string, **\n** represented a new line. In our raw string, **\n** doesn't do anything. To get a new line in the raw string, we must add an actual new line in our code. The interpreted string must use **\n** to get a new line as having a real new line in an interpreted string is not allowed.

While there are a lot of things you can do with an interpreted string literal, in real-world code, the two you'll see more commonly are **\n** for a new line and occasionally **\t** for a tab.

Interpreted string literals are the most common kind in real-world code, but raw literals have their place. If you wanted to copy and paste some text that contains a lot of new lines, " or \, in it, it's easier to use **raw**.

In the following example, you can see how using raw makes the code more readable:

```go
package main
import "fmt"
func main() {
    comment1 := `In "Windows" the user directory is "C:\Users\"`
    comment2 := "In \"Windows\" the user directory is \"C:\\Users\\\""
    fmt.Println(comment1)
    fmt.Println(comment2)
}
```

Running the preceding code shows the following output:

```
📁   ~/src/Th…op/Ch…03/Example03.06    go run main.go
In "Windows" the user directory is "C:\Users\"
In "Windows" the user directory is "C:\Users\"
```

Figure 3.7: Output for more readable code

One thing you can't have in a raw literal is a `. If you need a literal with a ` in it, you must use an interpreted string literal.

String literals are just ways of getting some text into a **string** type variable. Once you have the value in the variable, there are no differences.

Next, we'll look at how to work safely with multi-byte strings.

Rune

A **rune** is a type with enough storage to store a single UTF-8 multi-byte character. String literals are encoded using UTF-8. UTF-8 is a massively popular and common multi-byte text encoding standard. The **string** type itself is not limited to UTF-8 as Go needs to also support text encoding types other than UTF-8. **string** not being limited to UTF-8 means there is often an extra step you need to take when working with your strings to prevent bugs.

The different encodings use a different number of bytes to encode text. Legacy standards use one byte to encode a single character. UTF-8 uses up to four bytes to encode a single character. When text is in the **string** type, to allow for this variability, Go stores all strings as a **byte** collection. To be able to safely perform operations with text of any kind of encoding, single- or multi-byte, it should be converted from a **byte** collection to a **rune** collection.

> **Note**
>
> If you don't know the encoding of the text, it's usually safe to convert it to UTF-8. Also, UTF-8 is backward-compatible with single-byte encoded text.

Go makes it easy to access the individual bytes of a string, as shown in the following example:

1. First, we define the package, import our needed libraries, and create the **main()** function:

```
package main
import "fmt"
func main() {
```

2. We'll create a string that contains a multi-byte character:

```
username := "Sir_King_Über"
```

3. We are going to use a **for i** loop to print out each byte of our string:

```
for i := 0; i < len(username); i++ {
    fmt.Print(username[i], " ")
}
```

4. Then we will close the **main()** function:

```
}
```

Running the preceding code gives the following output:

~/src/Th…op/Ch…03/Example03.07 go run main.go
83 105 114 95 75 105 110 103 95 195 156 98 101 114

Figure 3.8: Output displaying bytes with respect to input length

The numbers printed out are the byte values of the string. There are only 13 letters in our string. However, it contained a multi-byte character, so we printed out 14 byte values.

Let's convert our bytes back to strings. This conversion uses type conversion, which we'll cover in detail soon:

```
package main
import "fmt"
func main() {
  username := "Sir_King_Über"
  for i := 0; i < len(username); i++ {
    fmt.Print(string(username[i]), " ")
  }
}
```

Running the preceding code gives the following output:

~/src/Th…op/Ch…03/Example03.08 go run main.go
S i r _ K i n g _ Ã   b e r

Figure 3.9: Output displaying bytes converted as strings

The output is as expected until we get to the "Ü." That's because the "Ü" was encoded using more than one byte, and each byte on its own no longer makes sense.

To safely work with interindividual characters of a multi-byte string, you first must convert the strings slice of **byte** types to a slice of **rune** types.

Consider the following example:

```go
package main
import "fmt"
func main() {
  username := "Sir_King_Über"
  runes := []rune(username)
  for i := 0; i < len(runes); i++ {
    fmt.Print(string(runes[i]), " ")
  }
}
```

Running the preceding code gives the following output:

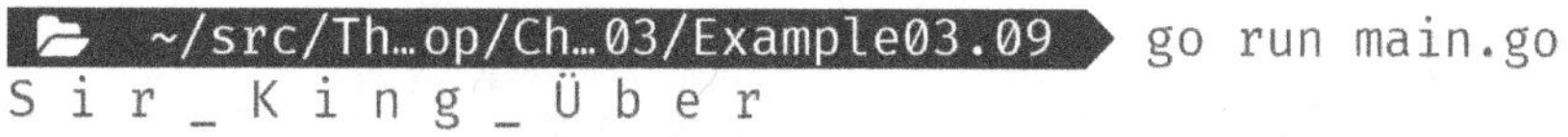

```
 ~/src/Th…op/Ch…03/Example03.09  go run main.go
S i r _ K i n g _ Ü b e r
```

Figure 3.10: Output displaying strings

If we do wish to work with each character in a loop like this, then using a **range** would be a better choice. When using **range**, instead of going one **byte** at a time, it moves along the string one **rune** at a time. The index is the byte offset, and the value is a **rune**.

Exercise 3.05: Safely Looping over a String

In this exercise, we'll declare a string and initialize it with a multi-byte string value. We'll then loop over the string using **range** to give us each character, one at a time. We'll then print out the byte index and the character to the console:

1. Create a new folder and add a **main.go** file.

2. In **main.go**, add the main package name to the top of the file:

```go
package main
```

3. Now add the imports we'll use in this file:

```go
import "fmt"
```

4. Create the **main()** function:

```go
func main() {
```

5. Declare the string with a multi-byte string value:

```
logLevel := "デバッグ"
```

6. Create a **range** loop that loops over the string, then capture the **index** and **rune** in variables:

```
for index, runeVal := range logLevel {
```

7. Print the **index** and **rune** to the console, casting the rune to a string:

```
fmt.Println(index, string(runeVal))
```

8. Close the loop:

```
}
```

9. Close the **main()** function:

```
}
```

10. Save the file and in the new folder run the following:

```
go run main.go
```

Running the preceding code gives the following output:

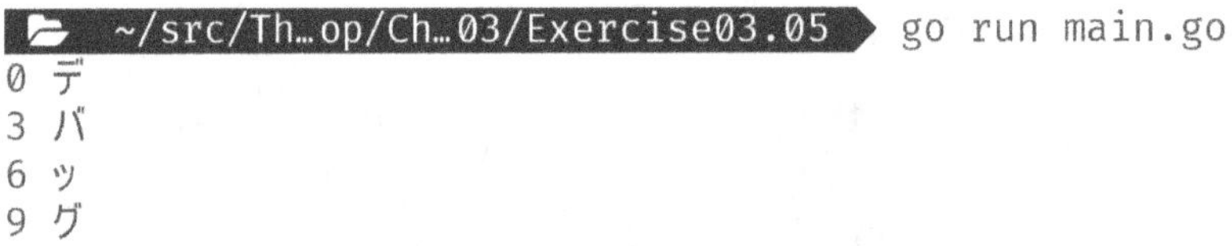

```
  ~/src/Th…op/Ch…03/Exercise03.05    go run main.go
0 デ
3 バ
6 ッ
9 グ
```

Figure 3.11: Output after safely looping over a string

In this exercise, we demonstrated that looping over a string in a multi-byte safe way is baked right into the language. Using this method prevents you from getting invalid string data.

Another common way to find bugs is to check how many characters a string has by using **len** directly on it. Here is an example of some common ways multi-byte strings can get mishandled:

```go
package main
import "fmt"
func main() {
    username := "Sir_King_Über"
    // Length of a string
    fmt.Println("Bytes:", len(username))
    fmt.Println("Runes:", len([]rune(username)))
    // Limit to 10 characters
    fmt.Println(string(username[:10]))
    fmt.Println(string([]rune(username)[:10]))
}
```

Running the preceding code gives the following output:

```
📂  ~/src/Th…op/Ch…03/Example03.10    go run main.go
Bytes: 14
Runes: 13
Sir_King_�
Sir_King_Ü
```

Figure 3.12: Output displaying bugs after using the len function

You can see that when using **len** directly on a string, you get the wrong answer. Checking the length of data input using **len** in this way would end up with invalid data. For example, if we needed the input to be exactly 8 characters long and somebody entered a multi-byte character, using **len** directly on that input would allow them to enter less than 8 characters.

When working with strings, be sure to check the **strings** package first. It's filled with useful tools that may already do what you need.

Next, let's take a close look at Go's special **nil** value.

The nil Value

nil is not a type but a special value in Go. It represents an empty value of no type. When working with pointers, maps, and interfaces (we'll cover these in the next chapter), you need to be sure they are not nil. If you try to interact with a nil value, your code will crash.

If you can't be sure whether a value is nil or not, you can check it like this:

```
package main
import "fmt"
func main() {
   var message *string
   if message == nil {
      fmt.Println("error, unexpected nil value")
      return
   }
   fmt.Println(&message)
}
```

Running the preceding code shows the following output:

```
error, unexpected nil value
```

Activity 3.01: Sales Tax Calculator

In this activity, we create a shopping cart application, where sales tax must be added to calculate the total:

1. Create a calculator that calculates the sales tax for a single item.

2. The calculator must take the items cost and its sales tax rate.

3. Sum the sales tax and print the total amount of sales tax required for the following items:

Item	Cost	Sales Tax Rate
Cake	0.99	7.5%
Milk	2.75	1.5%
Butter	0.87	2%

Figure 3.13:List of items with the sales tax rates

Your output should look like this:

```
Sales Tax Total:   0.1329
```

> **Note**
>
> The solution for this activity can be found on page 691.

Activity 3.02: Loan Calculator

In this activity, we must create a loan calculator for an online financial advisor platform. Our calculator should have the following rules:

1. A good credit score is a score of 450 or above.

2. For a good credit score, your interest rate is 15%.

3. For a less than good score, your interest rate is 20%.

4. For a good credit score, your monthly payment must be no more than 20% of your monthly income.

5. For a less than good credit score, your monthly payment must be no more than 10% of your monthly income.

6. If a credit score, monthly income, loan amount, or loan term is less than 0, return an error.

7. If the term of the loan if not divisible by 12 months, return an error.

8. The interest payment will be a simple calculation of loan amount * interest rate * loan term.

9. After doing these calculations, display the following details to the user:

```
Applicant X
-----------
Credit Score    : X
Income          : X
Loan Amount     : X
Loan Term       : X
Monthly Payment : X
Rate            : X
Total Cost      : X
Approved        : X
```

This is the expected output:

```
 ~/src/Th…op/Ch…03/Activity03.02   go run main.go
Applicant 1
-----------
Credit Score    : 500
Income          : 1000
Loan Amount     : 1000
Loan Term       : 24
Monthly Payment : 47.916666666666664
Rate            : 15
Total Cost      : 150
Approved        : true

Applicant 2
-----------
Credit Score    : 350
Income          : 1000
Loan Amount     : 10000
Loan Term       : 12
Monthly Payment : 1000
Rate            : 20
Total Cost      : 2000
Approved        : false
```

Figure 3.14: Output of loan calculator

> **Note**
>
> The solution for this activity can be found on page 692.

Summary

In this chapter, we took a big step in working with Go's type system. We took the time to define what types are and why they are needed. We then explored each of the core types in Go. We started with the simple **bool** type, and we were able to show how critical it is to everything we do in our code. We then moved on to the number types. Go has lots of types for numbers, reflecting the control that Go likes to give developers when it comes to memory usage and accuracy. After numbers, we looked at how strings work and how they are closely related to the rune type. With the advent of multi-byte characters, it's easy to make a mess of your text data. Go has provided power built-in features to help you get it right. Lastly, we looked at **nil** and how you use it within Go.

The concepts you've learned in this chapter have armed you with the knowledge needed to tackle Go's more complex types, such as collections and structs. We'll be looking at these complex types in the next chapter.

4

Complex Types

Overview

This chapter introduces Go's more complex types. This will build on what we learned in the previous chapter regarding Go's core types. These complex types are indispensable when you build more complex software as they allow you to logically group related data together. This ability to group data makes your code easier to understand, maintain, and fix.

By the end of this chapter, you will be able to use arrays, slices, and maps to group data together. You will learn to create custom types based on the core types. You will also learn to use structs to create structures composed of named fields of any other types and explain the importance of **interface{}**.

Introduction

In the previous chapter, we covered Go's core types. These types are critical to everything you'll do in Go, but it can be challenging to model more complex data. In modern computer software, we want to be able to group data and logic where possible. We also want to be able to make our logic reflect the real-world solutions we're building.

If you were building software for cars, you would ideally want a custom type that embodies a car. This type should be named "car" and it should have properties that can store things about what kind of car it is. The logic that affects the car, such as starting and stopping, should be associated with the car type. If we had to manage more than one car, we need to be able to group all the cars.

In this chapter, we'll learn about the features in Go that allow us to model the data part of this challenge. Then, in the next chapter, we'll solve the behavior part. By using custom types, you can extend Go's core types, and using structs allows you to compose a type made of other types and associate logic with them. Collections let you group data together and allow you to loop over and perform operations on them.

As the complexity of your tasks increase, Go's complex types help you keep your code easy to understand and maintain. Collections such as **arrays**, **slices**, and **maps** allow you to keep related data grouped together. Go's **struct** type allows you to create a single type that's made up of other strings, numbers, and Booleans, giving you the power to build models of complex real-world concepts. Structs also allow you to attach logic to them; this allows you to have the logic that controls your models closely tied together.

When things get complicated with types, we need to know how to use type conversions and assertions to manage type mismatches correctly. We'll also be looking at Go's **interface{}** type. This type is almost magical in that it allows you to overcome Go's struct typing system but in a way that's still type-safe.

Collection Types

If you were dealing with a single email address, you would define a string variable to hold that value for you. Now, think about how you would structure your code if you needed to deal with between 0 and 100 email addresses. You could define a separate variable for each email address, but Go has something else we can use.

When dealing with lots of similar data, we put it in a collection. Go's collection types are array, slice, and map. Go's collection types are strongly typed and are easy to loop over, but they each have unique qualities that mean they are each better suited to different use cases.

Arrays

Go's most basic collection is an array. When you define an array, you must specify what type of data it may contain and how big the array is in the following form: `[<size>]<type>`. For example, `[10]int` is an array of size 10 that contains ints, while `[5] string` is an array of size 5 that contains strings.

The key to making this an array is specifying the size. If your definition didn't have the size, it would seem like it works, but it would not be an array – it'd be a slice. A slice is a different, more flexible, type of collection that we'll look at after arrays. You can set the element values to be any type, including pointers and arrays.

You can initialize arrays with data using the following form: `[<size>]<type>{<value1>,<value2>,…<valueN>}`. For example, `[5]string{1}` would initialize the array with the first value as 1, while `[5]string{9,9,9,9,9}` would fill the array with the value 9 for each element. When initializing with data, you can have Go set the size of the array based on the number of elements you initialize it with. You can take advantage of this by replacing the length number with …. For example, `[...] string{9,9,9,9,9}` would create an array of length 5 because we initialized it with 5 elements. Just like all arrays, the length's set at compile time and is not changeable at runtime.

Exercise 4.01: Defining an Array

In this exercise, we're going to define a simple array of size 10 that takes integers. Then, we'll print out the contents. Let's get started:

1. Create a new folder and add a `main.go` file to it.

2. In `main.go`, add the package and imports:

```
package main
import "fmt"
```

3. Create a function that defines an array and then return it:

```
func defineArray() [10]int {
    var arr [10]int
    return arr
}
```

4. Define `main()`, call the function, and print the result. We'll use `fmt.Printf` with `%#v` to get extra details about the value, including its type:

```
func main() {
    fmt.Printf("%#v\n", defineArray())
}
```

5. Save this. Then, from within the new folder, run the following:

```
go run .
```

Running the preceding code provides us with the following output:

```
[10]int{0, 0, 0, 0, 0, 0, 0, 0, 0, 0}
```

In this exercise, we've defined an array but haven't filled it with any data. Since all arrays have a fixed size, when the array was printed out, it contained 10 values. These values are the empty values for whatever type the array accepts.

Comparing Arrays

The array's length is part of its type definition. If you have two arrays that accept the same type but they're different sizes, they are not compatible and aren't comparable with each other. Arrays of different lengths that are not the same type can can't be compared with each other.

Exercise 4.02: Comparing Arrays

In this exercise, we'll compare arrays. First, we'll define some arrays; some are comparable, while some are not. Then, we'll run the code and fix any problems that come up. Let's get started:

1. Create a new folder and add a `main.go` file to it.

2. In `main.go`, add the package and imports:

```
package main
import "fmt"
```

3. Create a function that defines four arrays:

```
func compArrays() (bool, bool, bool) {
    var arr1 [5]int
    arr2 := [5]int{0}
    arr3 := [...]int{0, 0, 0, 0, 0}
    arr4 := [9]int{0, 0, 0, 0, 9}
```

4. Compare the arrays and return the result of the comparison. This closes off this function:

```
    return arr1 == arr2, arr1 == arr3, arr1 == arr4
}
```

5. Define **main** so that it prints out the results:

```
func main() {
    comp1, comp2, comp3 := compArrays()
    fmt.Println("[5]int == [5]int{0}          :", comp1)
    fmt.Println("[5]int == [...]int{0, 0, 0, 0, 0}:", comp2)
    fmt.Println("[5]int == [9]int{0, 0, 0, 0, 9}  :", comp3)
}
```

6. Save and run the code:

```
go run .
```

Running the preceding code produces the following output:

```
📂    ~/src/Th…op/Ch…04/Exercise04.02 ▸ go run .
# github.com/TrainingByPackt/Get-Ready-To-Go/Chapter04/Exercise04.02
./main.go:10:42: invalid operation: arr1 == arr4 (mismatched types [5]int and [9]int)
```

Figure 4.1: Array type mismatch error

You should see an error. This error is telling you that **arr1**, which is a **[5] int**, and **arr4**, which is a **[9] int**, are not the same type and aren't compatible. Let's fix that.

7. Here, we have the following:

```
arr4 := [9]int{0, 0, 0, 0, 9}
```

We need to replace this with the following:

```
arr4 := [9]int{0, 0, 0, 0, 9}
```

8. We also have the following code:

```
fmt.Println("[5]int == [9]int{0, 0, 0, 0, 9}  :", comp3)
```

We need to replace this with the following:

```
fmt.Println("[5]int == [5]int{0, 0, 0, 0, 9}  :", comp3)
```

9. Save and run the code again using the following command:

```
go run .
```

Running the preceding code produces the following output:

```
📂    ~/src/Th…op/Ch…04/Exercise04.02 ▸ go run .
[5]int == [5]int{0}                : true
[5]int == [...]int{0, 0, 0, 0, 0}: true
[5]int == [5]int{0, 0, 0, 0, 9}  : false
```

Figure 4.2: Output without error

In our exercise, we defined some arrays, and they were all defined in slightly different ways. At first, we had an error because we tried to compare arrays of different lengths, which, in Go, means they are different types. We fixed that and ran the code again. Then, we could see that even though the first three arrays were defined using different methods, they ended up being the same or equal to each other. The last array, now with its type fixed, had different data contained in it, so it's not the same or equal to the other arrays. The other collection types, that is, slice and map, are not comparable in this way. With map and slice, you must loop over the contents of the two collections you're comparing and compare them manually. This ability gives arrays an advantage if comparing data in collections is a hot path in your code.

Initializing Arrays Using Keys

So far, when we've initialized our arrays with data, we've let Go choose the keys for us. Go allows you to pick the key you want for your data if you want using `[<size>]<type>{<key1>:<value1>,…<keyN>:<valueN>}`. Go is flexible and lets you set the keys with gaps and in any order. This ability to set values with a key is helpful if you've defined an array where the numeric keys have a specific meaning and you want to set a value for a specific key but don't need to set any of the other values.

Exercise 4.03: Initializing an Array Using Keys

In this exercise, we'll initialize a few arrays using some keys to set specific values. Then, we'll compare them to each other. After, we'll print out one of the arrays and look at its contents. Let's get started:

1. Create a new folder and add a `main.go` file to it.

2. In `main.go`, add the package and imports:

```
package main
import "fmt"
```

3. Create a function that defines three arrays:

```
func compArrays() (bool, bool, [10]int) {
    var arr1 [10]int
    arr2 := [...]int{9: 0}
    arr3 := [10]int{1, 9: 10, 4: 5}
```

4. Compare the arrays and return the last one so that we can print it out later:

```
    return arr1 == arr2, arr1 == arr3, arr3
}
```

5. Create a **main** function and call **compArrays**. Then, print out the results:

```
func main() {
    comp1, comp2, arr3 := compArrays()
    fmt.Println("[10]int == [...]int{9:0} :", comp1)
    fmt.Println("[10]int == [10]int{1, 9: 10, 4: 5}:", comp2)
    fmt.Println("arr3 :", arr3)
}
```

6. Save the file. Then, in the new folder, run the following:

```
go run .
```

Running the preceding code produces the following output:

```
~/src/Th…op/Ch…04/Exercise04.03   go run .
[10]int == [...]{9:0}              : true
[10]int == [10]int{1, 9: 10, 4: 5}}: false
arr3                               : [1 0 0 0 5 0 0 0 0 10]
```

Figure 4.3: Array initialized using keys

In this exercise, we used keys when initializing the data for an array. For **arr2**, we combined the ... shortcut with setting a key to make the array length directly relate to the key we set. With **arr3**, we mixed it using keys and without using keys, and we also used the keys out of order. Go's flexibility when using keys is strong and makes using arrays in this way pleasant.

Reading from an Array

So far, we've defined an array and initialized it with some data. Now, let's read that data out. It's possible to access a single element of the array using **<array>[<index>]**. For example, this accesses the first element of an array, **arr[0]**. I know 0 is the first element of the array because arrays always use a zero-indexed integer key. The zero index means the first index for an array is always 0 and the last index is always the array's length minus 1.

The order of the items in an array is guaranteed to be stable. Order stability means that an item placed at index 0 is always the first item in the array.

Being able to access specific parts of an array can be helpful in a few ways. It's often necessary to validate the data in an array by checking either the first and/or last elements. Sometimes, the position of the data in an array is important so that you know you can get, for example, a product's name from the third index. This positional significance is common when reading **comma-separated value** (**CSV**) files or other similar delimiter separated value files. CSV is still in common use as it is a popular choice for exporting data from spreadsheet documents.

Exercise 4.04: Reading a Single Item from an Array

In this exercise, we'll define an array and initialize it with some words. Then, we'll read the words out in the form of a message and print it. Let's get started:

1. Create a new folder and add a file named **main.go** to it.

2. In **main.go**, add the package and imports:

```
package main
import "fmt"
```

3. Create a function that defines an array with our words. The order of the words is important:

```
func message() string {
    arr := [...]string{
    "ready",
    "Get",
    "Go",
    "to",
    }
```

4. Now, create a message by joining the words in a specific order and returning it. We're using the **fmt.Sprintln** function here since it allows us to capture the formatted text before it's printed:

```
    return fmt.Sprintln(arr[1], arr[0], arr[3], arr[2])
}
```

5. Create our **main()** function, call the **message** function, and print it to the console:

```
func main() {
    fmt.Print(message())
}
```

6. Save and run the code:

```
go run .
```

Running the preceding code produces the following output:

```
Get ready to Go
```

Writing to an Array

Once an array is defined, you're able to make changes to individual elements using their index using **<array>[<index>]** = **<value>**. This assignment works the same as it does for core type variables.

In real-world code, you often need to modify the data in your collections after it has been defined based on inputs or logic.

Exercise 4.05: Writing to an Array

In this exercise, we'll define an array and initialize it with some words. Then, we'll make some changes to the words. Finally, we'll read the words out to form a message and print it. Let's get started:

1. Create a new folder and add a file named **main.go** to it.

2. In **main.go**, add the package and imports:

```
package main
import "fmt"
```

3. Create a function that defines an array with our words. The order of the words is important:

```
func message() string {
    arr := [4]string{"ready", "Get", "Go", "to"}
```

4. We'll change some of the words in the array by assigning new values using an array index. The order this is done in doesn't matter:

```
arr[1] = "It's"
arr[0] = "time"
```

5. Now, create a message by joining the words in a specific order and return it:

```
    return fmt.Sprintln(arr[1], arr[0], arr[3], arr[2])
}
```

6. Create our **main()** function, call the **message** function, and print it to the console:

```
func main() {
    fmt.Print(message())
}
```

7. Save and run the code:

```
go run .
```

Running the preceding code produces the following output:

```
It's time to Go
```

Looping an Array

The most common way you'll work with arrays is by using them in loops. Due to the way array's indexes works, they are easy to loop over. The index always starts at 0, there are no gaps, and the last element is the array's length, minus 1.

Because of this, it's also common to use a loop where we create a variable to represent the index and increment it manually. This type of loop is often called a **for i** loop since **i** is the name that's given to the index variable.

As you'll remember from the previous chapter, the **for** loop has three possible parts: the logic that can run before the loop, the logic that runs on each loop interaction to check whether the loop should continue, and the logic that runs at the end of each loop iteration. A **for i** loop looks like **i := 0; i < len(arr); i++ {**. What happens is that we define **i** to be zero, which also means **i** only exists in the scope of the loop. Then, **i** is checked on the loop's iteration to ensure it's less than the length of the array. We check that it's less than the length of the array since the length is always 1 more than the last index key. Lastly, we increment **i** by 1 on each loop to let us step over each element in the array, one by one.

When it comes to the length of an array, it can be tempting to hardcode the value of the last index instead of using **len** since you know the length of your array is always the same. Hardcoding length is a bad idea. Hardcoding would make your code harder to maintain. It's common for your data to change and evolve. If you ever need to come back and change the size of an array, having hardcoded array lengths introduces hard-to-find bugs and even runtime panics.

Using loops with arrays allows you to repeat the same logic for every element, that is, validating the data, modifying the data, or outputting the data without having to duplicate the same code for multiple variables.

Exercise 4.06: Looping Over an Array Using a "for i" Loop

In this exercise, we'll define an array and initialize it with some numbers. We'll loop over the numbers and do an operation on each one, putting the result in a message. Then, we'll return the message and print it. Let's get started:

1. Create a new folder and add a file named **main.go** to it.

2. In **main.go**, add the package and imports:

```
package main
import "fmt"
```

3. Create a function. We'll define the array with the data and a m variable before the loop:

```
func message() string {
    m := ""
    arr := [4]int{1,2,3,4}
```

4. Define the start of the loop. This manages the index and the loop:

```
for i := 0; i < len(arr); i++ {
```

5. Then, write the body of the loop, which does an operation on each element of the array and adds it to the message:

```
arr[i] = arr[i] * arr[i]
m += fmt.Sprintf("%v: %v\n", i, arr[i])
```

6. Now, close the loop, return the message, and close the function:

```
    }
    return m
}
```

7. Create our **main** function, call the **message** function, and print it to the console:

```
func main() {
    fmt.Print(message())
}
```

8. Save this code. Then, from the new folder, run the code:

```
go run .
```

Running the preceding code produces the following output after looping over the array using the **for i** loop:

```
0: 1
1: 4
2: 9
3: 16
```

The **for i** loop is very common, so pay close attention to *step* 4, where we defined the loop, and be sure to understand what each of the three parts is doing.

> **Note**
>
> **Using len in a loop**: In other languages, it's not efficient to count the number of elements on each iteration of a loop. In Go, it's okay. The Go runtime tracks the length of the array internally, so it doesn't count the items when you call **len**. This feature is also true for the other collection types, that is, slice and map.

Modifying the Contents of an Array in a Loop

In addition to reading from an array in a loop, you can also change the contents of the array in a loop. Working with the data in each element works like working with variables. You use the same **for i** loops too.

Just like reading data from arrays, being able to change data in collections reduces the amount of code you need to write if each element was a standalone variable.

Exercise 4.07: Modifying the Contents of an Array in a Loop

In this exercise, we're going to define an empty array, fill it with data, and then modify that data. Finally, we'll print the filled and modified array to the console. Let's get started:

1. Create a new folder and add a file named **main.go** to it.

2. In **main.go**, add the package and imports:

```
package main
import "fmt"
```

3. Create a function that fills an array with numbers from 1 to 10:

```
func fillArray(arr [10]int) [10]int {
    for i := 0; i < len(arr); i++ {
    arr[i] = i + 1
    }
    return arr
}
```

4. Create a function that multiples the number from an array by itself and then sets the result back to the array:

```
func opArray(arr [10]int) [10]int {
    for i := 0; i < len(arr); i++ {
      arr[i] = arr[i] * arr[i]
    }
    return arr
}
```

5. In our **main()** function, we need to define our empty array, fill it, modify it, and then print its contents to the console:

```
func main() {
    var arr [10]int
    arr = fillArray(arr)
    arr = opArray(arr)
    fmt.Println(arr)
}
```

6. Save this code. Then, from the new folder, run the code:

```
go run .
```

Running the preceding code produces the following output:

```
[1 4 9 16 25 36 49 64 81 100]
```

Working with data in arrays is simple once you've understood how to use them in a **for i** array. One nice thing about working with arrays over the other collections if their fixed length. With arrays, it's not possible to accidentally change the size of the array and end up in an infinite loop, which is a loop that can't end and results in software that runs forever while using lots of resources.

Activity 4.01: Filling an Array

In this activity, we're going to define an array and fill it using a for-i loop. The following are the steps for this activity:

1. Create a new Go app.

2. Define an array with 10 elements.

3. Use a for-i loop to fill that array with the numbers 1 through 10.

4. Use `fmt.Println` to print the array to the console.

   The expected output is as follows:

   ```
   [1 2 3 4 5 6 7 8 9 10]
   ```

> **Note**
>
> The solution for this activity can be found on page 696.

Slice

Arrays are great, but their rigidity around size can cause issues. If you wanted to create a function that accepted an array and sorted the data in it, it could only work for one size of array. That requires you to create a function for each size of array. This strictness around size makes working with arrays feel like a hassle and unengaging. The flip side of arrays is that they are an efficient way of managing sorted collections of data. Wouldn't it be great if there were a way to get the efficiency of arrays but with more flexibility? Go gives you this in the form of slices.

A slice is a thin layer around arrays that let you have a sorted numeric indexed collection without you having to worry about the size. Underneath the thin layer is still a Go array, but Go manages all the details, such as how big an array to use, for you. You use a slice just like you would an array; it only holds values of one type, you can read and write to each element using `[` and `]`, and they are easy to loop overusing **for i** loops.

The other thing a slice can do is be easily expanded using the built-in **append** function. This function accepts your slice and the values you'd like to add and returns a new slice with everything merged. It's common to start with an empty slice and expand it as needed.

Since a slice is a thin layer around an array, this means it's not a true type like an array. You need to understand how Go uses the hidden array behind the slice. If you don't, it'll lead to subtle and difficult-to-debug errors.

In real-world code, you should be using slices as your go-to for all sorted collections. You'll be more productive because you won't need to write as much code as you would with an array. Most code you'll see in real-world projects use lots of slices and rarely use arrays. Arrays are only used when the size needs to be exactly a certain length, and even then, slices get used most of the time as they can be passed around the code more easily.

Exercise 4.08: Working with Slices

In this exercise, we'll show you how flexible slices are by reading some data from a slice, passing a slice to a function, looping over a slice, reading values from a slice, and appending values to the end of a slice. Let's get started:

1. Create a new folder and add a file named **main.go** to it.

2. In **main.go**, add the package and imports:

    ```
    package main
    import (
      "fmt"
      "os"
    )
    ```

3. Create a function that takes an **int** argument and returns a string slice:

    ```
    func getPassedArgs(minArgs int) []string {
    ```

4. In the function's body, check if we have the correct number of arguments being passed in through the command line. If not, we exit the program with an error. All the arguments that are passed to Go are placed in **os.Args**, which is a slice of strings:

    ```
    if len(os.Args) < minArgs {
        fmt.Printf("At least %v arguments are needed\n", minArgs)
        os.Exit(1)
    }
    ```

5. The first element of the slice is how the code is called and not an argument, so we'll remove that:

    ```
    var args []string
    for i := 1; i < len(os.Args); i++ {
      args = append(args, os.Args[i])
    }
    ```

6. Then, we'll return the arguments:

    ```
    return args
    }
    ```

7. Now, create a function that loops over a slice and finds the longest string. When two words are of the same length, the first word is returned:

```go
func findLongest(args []string) string {
    var longest string
    for i := 0; i < len(args); i++ {
        if len(args[i]) > len(longest) {
            longest = args[i]
        }
    }
    return longest
}
```

8. In the **main()** function, we call the functions and check for errors:

```go
func main() {
    if longest := findLongest(getPassedArgs(3)); len(longest) > 0 {
        fmt.Println("The longest word passed was:", longest)
    } else {
        fmt.Println("There was an error")
        os.Exit(1)
    }
}
```

9. Save the file. Then, in the folder it's saved in, run the code using the following command:

```
go run . Get ready to Go
```

Running the preceding code produces the following output:

```
The longest word passed was: ready
```

In this exercise, we were able to see how flexible slices are and, at the same time, how they work just like arrays. This way of working with slices is another reason why Go has the feel of a dynamic language.

Activity 4.02: Printing a User's Name Based on User Input

It's now your turn to work with maps. We're going to define a map and create logic to print the data in the map based on the key that's passed to your app. The following are the steps for this activity:

1. Create a new Go app.

2. Define a **map** with the following key-value pairs:

    Key: 305, Value: Sue

    Key: 204, Value: Bob

    Key: 631, Value: Jake

    Key: 073, Value: Tracy

3. Using **os.Args**, read a key that's been passed in and print the corresponding name; for instance, **go run . 073**.

4. Correctly handle when no argument gets passed or if the passed argument doesn't match a value in the **map.**

5. Print a message to the user with the name in the value.

    The expected output is as follows:

    ```
    Hi, Tracy
    ```

> **Note**
>
> The solution for this activity can be found on page 697.

Appending Multiple Items to a Slice

The built-in **append** function can add more than one value to a slice. You can add as many parameters to **append** as you need since the last parameter is variadic. Since it's variadic, this means that you can also use the ... notation to use a slice as the variadic parameter, allowing you to pass a dynamic number of parameters to **append.**

Being able to pass more than one parameter to **append** comes up all the time in real-world code, and having it keeps Go code compact by not requiring multiple calls or loops to add multiple values.

Exercise 4.09: Appending Multiple Items to a Slice

In this exercise, we'll use the variadic parameter of **append** to add multiple values in the form of predefined data to a slice. Then, we'll add a dynamic amount of data based on user input to the same slice. Let's get started:

1. Create a new folder and add a file named **main.go** to it.

2. In **main.go**, add the package and imports:

```
package main
import (
  "fmt"
  "os"
)
```

3. Create a function to safely grab user input:

```
func getPassedArgs() []string {
  var args []string
  for i := 1; i < len(os.Args); i++ {
    args = append(args, os.Args[i])
  }
  return args
}
```

4. Create a function that accepts a slice of strings as a parameter and returns a slice of strings. Then, define a slice of strings variable:

```
func getLocals(extraLocals []string) []string {
  var locales []string
```

5. Add multiple strings to the slice using **append**:

```
locales = append(locales, "en_US", "fr_FR")
```

6. Add more data from the parameter:

```
locales = append(locales, extraLocals...)
```

7. Return the variable and close the function definition:

```
  return locales
}
```

8. In the **main()** function, get the user input, pass it to our function, and then print the result:

```
func main() {
    locales := getLocals(getPassedArgs())
    fmt.Println("Locales to use:", locales)
}
```

9. Save the file. Then, in the folder you created in *step* 1, run the code using the following command:

```
go run . fr_CN en_AU
```

Running the preceding code produces the following output:

```
Locales to use: [en_US fr_FR fr_CN en_AU]
```

In this exercise, we used two methods of adding multiple values to a slice. You would also use this technique if you needed to join two slices together.

While exploding a slice like this to add it to another slice may seem inefficient, the Go runtime can spot when you're doing an explode in an append and optimizes the call in the background to ensure no resources get wasted.

Activity 4.03: Creating a Locale Checker

In this activity, we're going to create a locale validator. A locale is an internationalization and localization concept that is a combination of both a language and a country or region. We'll create a struct that represents a locale. After, we're going to define a list of locales our code supports. Then, we'll read in some locale code from the command line and print out whether our code accepts that locale or not.

Here are the steps for this activity:

1. Create a new Go app.

2. Define a struct with a field for language and a separate field for country or region.

3. Create a collection to hold the local definitions for at least five locales, for instance, "en_US", "en_CN", "fr_CN", "fr_FR", and "ru_RU".

4. Read in the local from the command line, for example, using **os.Args**. Be sure to have error checking and validation working.

5. Load the passed locale string into a new locale struct.

6. Use that struct to check whether the passed struct is supported.

7. Print a message to the console stating whether the locale is supported or not.

The expected output is as follows:

```
 ~/src/Th…op/Ch…04/Activity04.03    go run . en_GB
Locale not supported: en_GB
exit status 1
 ~/src/Th…op/Ch…04/Activity04.03    go run . en_CN
Locale passed is supported
```

Figure 4.4: Expected output

Note

The solution for this activity can be found on page 698.

Creating Slices from Slices and Arrays

By using a similar notation to accessing a single element in an array or slice, you can create new slices derived from the contents of arrays and slices. The most common notation is [<low>:<high>]. This notation tells Go to create a new slice with the same value type as the source slice or array and to populate the new slice with values by starting at the low index and then going up to but not including the high index. Low and high are optional. If you omitted low, then Go defaults to the first element in the source. If you omit high, then it goes all the way to the last value. It's possible to skip both, and if you do, then the new slice has all the values from the source.

When you create new slices this way, Go doesn't copy the values. If the source is an array, then that source array is the hidden array for the new slice. If the source is a slice, then the hidden array for the new slice is the same hidden array the source slice uses.

Exercise 4.10: Creating Slices from a Slice

In this exercise, we'll use the slice range notation to create slices with a variety of initial values. Commonly, in real-world code, you need to work with only a small part of a slice or array. The **range** notation is a quick and straightforward way of getting only the data you need. Let's get started:

1. Create a new folder and add a file named **main.go** to it.

2. In **main.go**, add the package and imports:

```
package main
import "fmt"
```

3. Create a function and define a slice with nine **int** values:

```
func message() string {
    s := []int{1, 2, 3, 4, 5, 6, 7, 8, 9}
```

4. We'll extract the first value, first directly as an int, then as a slice using both low and high, and finally using just high and skipping low. We'll write the values to a message string:

```
m := fmt.Println("First   :", s[0], s[0:1], s[:1])
```

5. Now, we'll get the last element. To get the int, we'll use the length and subtract 1 from the index. We use that same logic when setting the low for the range notation. For high, we can use the length of the slice. Finally, we can see we can skip high and get the same result:

```
m += fmt.Println("Last   :", s[len(s)-1], s[len(s)-1:len(s)], s[len(s)-1:])
```

6. Now, let's get the first five values and add them to the message:

```
m += fmt.Println("First 5 :", s[:5])
```

7. Next, we'll get the last four values and add them to the message as well:

```
m += fmt.Println("Last 4   :", s[5:])
```

8. Finally, we'll extract five values from the middle of the slice and get them in the message too:

```
m += fmt.Println("Middle 5:", s[2:7])
```

9. Then, we'll return the message and close the function:

```
    return m
}
```

10. In **main**, we'll print the message out:

```
func main() {
    fmt.Print(message())
}
```

11. Save the file. Then, in the folder you created in *step 1*, run the code using the following command:

```
go run .
```

Running the preceding code produces the following output:

```
 ~/src/Th…op/Ch…04/Exercise04.10  go run .
First    : 1 [1] [1]
Last     : 9 [9] [9]
First 5 : [1 2 3 4 5]
Last 4   : [6 7 8 9]
Middle 5: [3 4 5 6 7]
```

Figure 4.5: Output after creating slices from a slice

In this exercise, we tried out a few ways to create slices from another slice. You can also use these same techniques on an array as the source. We saw that both the start and stop indexes are optional. If you don't have a start index, it'll start at the beginning of the source slice or array. If you don't have the stop index, then it'll stop at the end of the array. If you skip both the start and stop indexes, it'll make a copy of the slice or array. This trick is useful for turning an array into a slice but not helpful for copying slices because the two slices share the same hidden array.

Understanding Slice Internals

Slices are great and should be your go-to when you need an ordered list, but if you don't know how they work under the hood, they cause hard-to-spot bugs.

An array is a value type that's similar to a string or an **int**. Value types can be copied and compared to themselves. These value types, once copied, are not connected to their source values. Slices don't work like value types; they work more like pointers, but they are also not pointers.

The key to staying safe with a slice is to understand that there is a hidden array that stores the values and that making changes to the slice may or may not require that hidden array to be replaced with a bigger one. The fact that the management of the hidden array happens in the background is what makes it hard to reason well about what's going on with your slices.

Slices have three hidden properties: length, a pointer to the hidden array, and where in the hidden array its starting point is. When you append to a slice, one or all of these properties get updated. Which properties get updated depends on whether the hidden array is full or not.

The size of the hidden array and the size of the slice are not always the same. The size of the slice is its length, which we can find out by using the **len** built-in function. The size of the hidden array is the capacity of the slice. There is also a built-in function that tells you the capacity of a slice, that is, **cap**. When you add a new value to a slice using **append**, one of two things happens: if the slice has extra capacity, that is, the hidden array is not full yet, it adds the value to the hidden array and then updates the slices length property. If the hidden array is full, Go creates a new, larger, array. Go then copies all the values from the old array into the new array and adds the new value too. Then, Go updates the slice from pointing to the old array to the new array and updates the length of the slice and possibly its starting point.

The starting point only comes into play if the slice is a subset of values from an array or a slice not starting at the first element, for example, in our example where we got the last five elements of a slice. The rest of the time, it'll be the first element in the hidden array.

It's possible to control the size of the hidden array when you define a slice. Go's built-in **make** function allows you to set the length and capacity of a slice when creating it. The syntax looks like **make(<sliceType>, <length>, <capacity>)**. When creating a slice using **make**, the capacity is optional, but length is required.

Exercise 4.11: Using make to Control the Capacity of a Slice

In this exercise, using the **make** function, we'll create some slices and display their length and capacity. Let's get started:

1. Create a new folder and add a file named **main.go** to it.

2. In **main.go**, add the package and imports:

```
package main
import "fmt"
```

3. Create a function that returns three **int** slices:

```
func genSlices() ([]int, []int, []int) {
```

4. Define a slice using the **var** notation:

```
var s1 []int
```

5. Define a slice using make and set only the length:

```
s2 := make([]int, 10)
```

6. Define a slice that uses both the length and capacity of the slices:

```
s3 := make([]int, 10, 50)
```

Return the three slices and close the function definition:

```
    return s1, s2, s3
}
```

7. In the **main()** function, call the function we created and capture the returned values. For each slice, print its length and capacity to the console:

```
func main() {
    s1, s2, s3 := genSlices()
    fmt.Printf("s1: len = %v cap = %v\n", len(s1), cap(s1))
    fmt.Printf("s2: len = %v cap = %v\n", len(s2), cap(s2))
    fmt.Printf("s3: len = %v cap = %v\n", len(s3), cap(s3))
}
```

8. Save the file. Then, in the folder you created in *step 1*, run the code using the following command:

```
go run .
```

Running the preceding code produces the following output:

```
 ~/src/Th...op/Ch...04/Exercise04.11   go run .
s1: len = 0 cap - 0
s2: len = 10 cap = 10
s3: len = 10 cap = 50
```

Figure 4.6: Output displaying slices

In this exercise, we used **make**, **len**, and **cap** to control and display the length and capacity of a slice when defining one.

If you know how big a slice is, you'll typically need for an operation for setting the capacity, which can be a performance boost as Go has to do less work managing the hidden array.

Background Behavior of Slices

Due to the complexity of what a slice is and how it works, you can't compare slices to one another. If you try, Go gives you an error. You can compare a slice to nil, but that's it.

A slice is not a value, and it's not a pointer, so what is it? A slice is a special construct in Go. A slice doesn't store its own values directly. In the background, it's using an array that you can't access directly. What a slice does store is a pointer to that hidden array, its own starting point in that array, how long the slice is, and what the capacity of the slice is. These values provide slices with a window for the hidden array. The window can be the whole hidden array or just a smaller portion of it. The pointer to the hidden array can be shared by more than one slice. This pointer sharing can result in multiple slices that can share the same hidden array, even though not all the slides contain the same data. This means that one of the slices can have more of the data than the other slices.

When a slice needs to grow beyond its hidden array, it creates a new bigger array and copies the contents from the old array to the new one and points the slice at the new array. This array swap is why our preceding slices became disconnected. At first, they were pointing to the same hidden array, but when we grow the first slice, the array it's pointing to changes. This change means that changes to the grown slice no longer affect the other slices since they are still pointing to the old, smaller, array.

If you need to make a copy of a slice and need to be sure they are not connected, you have a few choices. You can use **append** to copy the contents of the source slice into another array or use the built-in **copy** function. When using **copy**, Go won't change the size of the destination slice, so be sure it has enough room for all the elements you want to copy.

Exercise 4.12: Controlling Internal Slice Behavior

In this exercise, we're going to explore five different ways to copy data from slice to slice and how that has an impact on a slice's internal behavior. Let's get started:

1. Create a new folder and add a file named **main.go** to it.

2. In **main.go**, add the package and imports:

```
package main
import "fmt"
```

3. Create a function that returns three ints:

```
func linked() (int, int, int) {
```

4. Define an int slice, initialized with some data:

```
s1 := []int{1, 2, 3, 4, 5}
```

5. Then, we'll make a simple variable copy of that slice:

```
s2 := s1
```

6. Create a new slice by copying all the values from the first slice as part of a slice range operation:

```
s3 := s1[:]
```

7. Change some data in the first slice. Later, we'll see how this affects the second and third slice:

```
s1[3] = 99
```

8. Return the same index for each slice and close the function definition:

```
    return s1[3], s2[3], s3[3]
}
```

9. Create a function that will return two ints:

```
func noLink() (int, int) {
```

10. Define a slice with some data and do a simple copy again:

```
s1 := []int{1, 2, 3, 4, 5}
s2 := s1
```

11. This time, we'll append to the first slice before we do anything else. This operation changes the length and capacity of the slice:

```
s1 = append(s1, 6)
```

12. Then, we'll change the first slice, return the same indexes from the two slices, and close the function:

```
    s1[3] = 99
    return s1[3], s2[3]
}
```

13. In our next function, we'll be returning two ints:

```
func capLinked() (int, int) {
```

14. We'll define our first slice using make this time. When doing this, we'll be setting a capacity that's larger than its length:

```
s1 := make([]int, 5, 10)
```

15. Let's fill the first array with the same data as before:

```
s1[0], s1[1], s1[2], s1[3], s1[4] = 1, 2, 3, 4, 5
```

16. Now, we'll create a new slice by copying the first slice, like we did previously:

```
s2 := s1
```

17. We'll append a new value to the first slice, which changes its length but not its capacity:

```
s1 = append(s1, 6)
```

18. Then, we'll change the first slice, return the same indexes from the two slices, and close the function:

```
s1[3] = 99
return s1[3], s2[3]
}
```

19. In this function, we'll use make again to set a capacity, but we'll use **append** to add elements that will go beyond that capacity:

```
func capNoLink() (int, int) {
  s1 := make([]int, 5, 10)
  s1[0], s1[1], s1[2], s1[3], s1[4] = 1, 2, 3, 4, 5
  s2 := s1
  s1 = append(s1, []int{10: 11}...)
  s1[3] = 99
  return s1[3], s2[3]
}
```

20. In the next function, we'll use **copy** to copy the elements from the first slice to the second slice. Copy returns how many elements were copied from one slice to another, so we'll return that too:

```
func copyNoLink() (int, int, int) {
  s1 := []int{1, 2, 3, 4, 5}
  s2 := make([]int, len(s1))
  copied := copy(s2, s1)
  s1[3] = 99
  return s1[3], s2[3], copied
}
```

21. In the final function, we'll use **append** to copy the value into the second slice. Using **append** in this way results in the values being copied into a new hidden array:

```
func appendNoLink() (int, int) {
    s1 := []int{1, 2, 3, 4, 5}
    s2 := append([]int{}, s1...)
    s1[3] = 99
    return s1[3], s2[3]
}
```

22. In **main**, we'll print out all the data we returned and print it to the console:

```
func main() {
    l1, l2, l3 := linked()
    fmt.Println("Linked     :", l1, l2, l3)
    nl1, nl2 := noLink()
    fmt.Println("No Link    :", nl1, nl2)
    cl1, cl2 := capLinked()
    fmt.Println("Cap Link   :", cl1, cl2)
    cnl1, cnl2 := capNoLink()
    fmt.Println("Cap No Link :", cnl1, cnl2)
    copy1, copy2, copied := copyNoLink()
    fmt.Print("Copy No Link: ", copy1, copy2)
    fmt.Printf(" (Number of elements copied %v)\n", copied)
    a1, a2 := appendNoLink()
    fmt.Println("Append No Link:", a1, a2)
}
```

23. Save the file. Then, in the folder you created in *step 1*, run the code using the following command:

```
go run .
```

Running the preceding code produces the following output:

```
 ~/src/Th…op/Ch…04/Exercise04.12  go run .
Linked      : 99 99 99
No Link     : 99 4
Cap Link    : 99 99
Cap No Link : 99 4
Copy No Link : 99 4 (Number of elements copied 5)
Append No Link: 99 4
```

Figure 4.7: Output displaying data

In this exercise, we stepped through five different scenarios where we made copies of slice data. In the `Linked` scenario, we made a simple copy of the first slice and then a range copy of it. While the slices themselves are distinct and are no longer the same slices, in reality, it doesn't make a difference to the data they hold. Each of the slices pointed to the same hidden array, so when we made a change to the first slice, it affected all of the slices.

In the `No Link` scenario, the setup was the same for the first and second slice, but before we made a change to the first slice, we appended a value to it. When we appended this value to it, in the background, Go needed to create a new array to hold the now large number of values. Since we were appending to the first slice, its pointer was to look at the new, bigger slice. The second slice doesn't get its pointer updates. That's why, when the first slice had its value change, the second slice wasn't affected. The second slice isn't pointing to the same hidden array anymore, meaning they are not linked.

For the `Cap Link` scenario, the first slice was defined using make and with an oversized capacity. This extra capacity meant that when the first slice had a value appended to it, there was already extra room in the hidden array. This extra capacity means there's no need to replace the hidden array. The effect was that when we updated the value on the first slice, it and the second slice were still pointing to the same hidden array, meaning the change affects both.

In the `Cap No Link` scenario, the setup was the same as the previous scenario, but when we appended values, we appended more values than there was available capacity. Even though there was extra capacity, there was not enough, and the hidden array in the first slice got replaced. The result was that the link between the two slices broke.

In `Copy No Link`, we used the built-in `copy` function to copy the value for us. While this does copy the values into a new hidden array, copy won't change the length of the slice. This fact means that the destination slice must be the correct length before you do the copy. You don't see copy much in real-world code; this could be because it's easy to misuse it.

Lastly, with `Append No Link`, we use `append` to do something similar to `copy` but without having to worry about the length. This method is the most commonly seen in real-world code when you need to ensure you get a copy of the values that are not linked to the source. This is easy to understand since append gets used a lot and it's a one-line solution. There is one slightly more efficient solution that avoids the extra memory allocation of the empty slice in the first argument of append. You can reuse the first slice by creating a 0-capacity range copy of it. This alternative looks as follows:

```
s1 := []int{1, 2, 3, 4, 5}
s2 := append(s1[:0:0], s1...)
```

Can you see something new here? This uses the seldom-used slice range notation of `<slice>[<low>:<high>:<capacity>]`. With the current Go compiler, this is the most memory-efficient way to copy a slice.

Map Fundamentals

While arrays and slices are similar and can sometimes be interchangeable, Go's other collection type, map, is quite different and is not interchangeable with array and slice. Go's map type serves a different purpose.

Go's map is a hashmap in computer science terms. The main difference between a map and the other collections types relates to its key. In an array or slice, the key is a placeholder, and it has no meaning of its own. It's only there to act as a counter and has no direct relationship with the value.

With a map, the key is data – data that has a real relationship with the value. For example, you could have a collection of user account records in a map. The key would be the users' employee ID. An employee ID is real data and not just an arbitrary placeholder. If someone were to give you their employee ID, you'd be able to look up their account records without needing to loop over the data to find it. With a map, you can set, get, and delete data quickly.

You can access the individual elements of a map in the same way as you do with a slice or array: using [and]. Maps can have any type that is directly comparable as a key, such as an int or a string. You can't compare slices, so they can't be keys. A map's value can be of any type, including pointers, slices, and maps.

You shouldn't use a map as an ordered list. Even if you were to use an int for a map's keys, maps are not guaranteed to always start at index 0, and they are not guaranteed to not have any gaps in the keys. This feature could be an advantage, even if you did want int keys. If you had sparsely populated data, that is, values with gaps between keys, in a slice or array, it would contain lots of zero data. In a map, it would only contain the data you set.

To define a map, you use the following notation: `map[<key_type>]<value_type>`. You can use **make** to create maps, but the arguments for **make** are different when using **make** to create a map. Go can't create keys for a map, so it's not possible to create a map of an arbitrary length like you can with a slice. You can suggest a capacity for the compiler to use for your map. Suggesting the capacity for a map is optional, and map can't be used with **cap** to check what its capacity is.

Maps are like slices in that they are not a value and not a pointer. A map is a special construct in Go. You'll need to take the same care when copying the variable or the values. Since you can't control or check the capacity of a map, they are even more challenging when you want to know what's going to happen when you add elements.

Since Go does not help you manage your keys with maps, this means you must specify keys when initializing a map with data. It's the same notation as the other collections, that is, **map[<key_type>]<value_type>{<key1>: <value>, … <keyN>:, <valueN>}**.

Once defined, you can set values without needing to worry about the length of the map like you do with arrays and slices. Setting a value is just like the other collections, that is, **<map>[<key>] = <value>**. Something that you do need to do before setting the value of a map is to make sure you've initialized it first. If you try to set a value of an uninitialized map, it causes a runtime panic. To avoid this, it's good practice to avoid defining a map using **var**. If you initialize the map with data or use **make** to create your maps, you won't have this problem.

Exercise 4.13: Creating, Reading, and Writing a Map

In this exercise, we're going to define a map with some data and then add a new element to it. Finally, we'll print the map to the console. Let's get started:

1. Create a new folder and add a file named **main.go** to it.

2. In **main.go**, add the package and imports:

```
package main
import "fmt"
```

3. Create a function that returns a **map** with string keys and string values:

```
func getUsers() map[string]string {
```

4. Define a **map** with string keys and string values and then initialize it with some elements:

```
users := map[string]string{
    "305": "Sue",
    "204": "Bob",
    "631": "Jake",
}
```

5. Next, we'll add a new element to the **map**:

```
users["073"] = "Tracy"
```

6. Return the **map** and close the function:

    ```
        return users
    }
    ```

7. In the **main** function, print the **map** to the console:

    ```
    func main() {
        fmt.Println("Users:", getUsers())
    }
    ```

8. Save the file. Then, in the folder you created in *step* 1, run the code using the following command:

    ```
    go run .
    ```

    Running the preceding code produces the following output:

    ```
    Users: map[073:Tracy 204:Bob 305:Sue 631:Jake]
    ```

In this exercise, we created a map, initialized it with data, and then added a new element. This exercise shows that working with maps is similar to working with arrays and slices. When you should use a map comes down to the kinds of data you'll store in it and if your access pattern needs access to individual items rather than a list of items.

Reading from Maps

You won't always know whether a key exists in a map before needing to use it to get a value. When you're getting a value for a key that doesn't exist in a map, Go returns the zero value for the map's value type. Having logic that works with zero values is a valid way to program in Go, but that's not always possible. If you can't use zero value logic, maps can return an extra return value when you need it. The notation looks like **<value>, <exists_value> := <map>[<key>]**. Here, **exists** is a Boolean value that is true if a key exists in the map; otherwise, it's false. When looping over a map, you should use the **range** keyword. When looping over a map, never rely on the order of the items in it. Go doesn't guarantee the order of items in a map. To make sure no one replies on the order of the elements, Go purposely randomizes the order of them when you range over a map. If you did need to loop over the elements of your map in a specific order, you'd need to use an array or slice to assist you with that.

Exercise 4.14: Reading from a Map

In this exercise, we're going to read from a map using direct access and a loop. We'll also check to see if a key exists in the map. Let's get started:

1. Create a new folder and add a file named **main.go** to it.

2. In **main.go**, add the package and imports:

```
package main

import (
    "fmt"
    "os"
)
```

3. Create a function that returns a **map** with a string key and a string value:

```
func getUsers() map[string]string {
```

4. Define a **map** and initialize it with data. Then, return the **map** and close the function:

```
    return map[string]string{
        "305": "Sue",
        "204": "Bob",
        "631": "Jake",
        "073": "Tracy",
    }
}
```

5. In this function, we'll accept a string as input. The function will also return a string and a Boolean:

```
func getUser(id string) (string, bool) {
```

6. Get a copy of the **users** map from our earlier function:

```
users := getUsers()
```

7. Get a value from the **users** maps using the passed in ID as the key. Capture both the value and the **exists** value:

```
user, exists := users[id]
```

8. Return both values and close the function:

```
    return user, exists
}
```

9. Create the **main** function:

```
func main() {
```

10. Check that at least one argument gets passed in. If not, exit:

```
    if len(os.Args) < 2 {
      fmt.Println("User ID not passed")
      os.Exit(1)
    }
```

11. Capture the passed argument and call the get user function:

```
    userID := os.Args[1]
    name, exists := getUser(userID)
```

12. If the key is not found, print a message, and then print all the users using a **range** loop. After that, exit:

```
    if !exists {
      fmt.Printf("Passed user ID (%v) not found.\nUsers:\n", userID)
      for key, value := range getUsers() {
        fmt.Println("  ID:", key, "Name:", value)
      }
      os.Exit(1)
    }
```

13. If everything is okay, print the name we found:

```
    fmt.Println("Name:", name)
}
```

14. Save the file. Then, in the folder you created in *step* 1, run the code using the following command:

```
go run . 123
```

15. Then, run the following command:

```
go run . 305
```

Running the preceding code produces the following output:

```
📁  ~/src/Th…op/Ch…04/Exercise04.14    go run . 123
Passed user ID (123) not found.
Users:
    ID: 305 Name: Sue
    ID: 204 Name: Bob
    ID: 631 Name: Jake
    ID: 073 Name: Tracy
exit status 1
📁  ~/src/Th…op/Ch…04/Exercise04.14    go run . 305
Name: Sue
```

Figure 4.8: Output displaying all the users and the name that was found

In this exercise, we learned how we can check to see if a key exists in a map. It may look a little strange coming from other languages that require you check for the existence of a key before getting the value, not after. This way of doing things does mean there is much less chance of runtime errors. If a zero value is not possible in your domain logic, then you can use that fact to check if a key exists.

We used a **range** loop to print all the users in our map nicely. Your output is probably in a different order to the output shown in the preceding screenshot, which is due to Go randomizing the order of the elements in a map when you use **range**.

Activity 4.04: Slicing the Week

In this activity, we're going to create a slice and initialize it with some data. Then, we're going to modify that slice using what we've learned about sub-slices. The following are the steps for this activity:

1. Create a new Go app.

2. Create a slice and initialize it with the all the days of the week, starting on Monday and ending on Sunday.

3. Change the slice using slice ranges and append it so that the week now starts on Sunday and ends on Saturday.

4. Print the slice to the console.

The expected output is as follows:

```
[Sunday Monday Tuesday Wednesday Thursday Friday Saturday]
```

> **Note**
>
> The solution for this activity can be found on page 700.

Deleting Elements from a Map

If you need to remove an element from a map, you'll need to do something different than you would with an array or slice. In an array, you can't remove elements since the length's fixed; the best you can do is zero out the value. With a slice, you can zero out, but it's also possible to use a combination of a slice range and append to cut out one or more elements. With a map, you could zero the value out, but the element still exists, so it causes problems if you're checking whether a key exists in your logic. You can't use slice ranges on a map to cut elements out either.

To remove an element, we need to use the built-in **delete** function. The function signature for **delete**, when used with maps, is **delete(<map>, <key>)**. The **delete** function doesn't return anything and if a key doesn't exist, nothing happens.

Exercise 4.15: Deleting an Element from a Map

In this exercise, we'll define a map and then delete an element from it using user input. Then, we'll print the now possibly smaller map to the console. Let's get started:

1. Create a new folder and add a file named **main.go** to it.

2. In **main.go**, add the package and imports:

```
package main
import (
    "fmt"
    "os"
)
```

3. We're going to define our **users** map in the package scope:

```
var users = map[string]string{
    "305": "Sue",
    "204": "Bob",
    "631": "Jake",
    "073": "Tracy",
}
```

4. Create a function that deletes from the **users** map using a passed in string as the key:

```
func deleteUser(id string){
    delete(users, id)
}
```

5. In **main**, we'll grab the passed in **userID** and print the **users** map to the console:

```
func main() {
    if len(os.Args) < 2 {
        fmt.Println("User ID not passed")
        os.Exit(1)
    }
    userID := os.Args[1]
    deleteUser(userID)
    fmt.Println("Users:", users)
}
```

6. Save the file. Then, in the folder you created in *step 1*, run the code using the following command:

```
go run . 305
```

Running the preceding code produces the following output:

```
Users: map[073:Tracy 204:Bob 631:Jake]
```

In this exercise, we used the built-in **delete** function to totally remove an element from a map. This requirement is unique for maps; you can't use **delete** on arrays or slices.

Activity 4.05: Removing an Element from a Slice

Go doesn't have anything built in to remove elements from a slice, but it's possible with the techniques you've learned. In this activity, we're going to set up a slice with some data and with one element to remove. Then, you need to work out how to do this. There are many ways to get this done, but can you work out the most compact way?

Here are the steps for this activity:

1. Create a new Go app.

2. Create a slice with the following elements in the following order:

   Good

   Good

   Bad

   Good

   Good

3. Write the code to remove the "Bad" element from the slice.

4. Print the result to the console.

   The following is the expected output:

   ```
   [Good Good Good Good]
   ```

> **Note**
>
> The solution for this activity can be found on page 701.

Simple Custom Types

You can create custom types using Go's simple types as a starting point. The notation is **type <name> <type>**. If we were to create an ID type based on a string, this would look like **type id string**. The custom type acts the same as the type you based it on, including getting the same zero value and having the same abilities to compare with other values of the same type. A custom type is not compatible with its base type, but you can convert your custom type back into the type it's based on to allow for interaction.

Exercise 4.16: Creating a Simple Custom Type

In this exercise, we'll define a map and then delete an element from it using user input. Then, we'll print the now possibly smaller map to the console. Let's get started:

1. Create a new folder and add a file named **main.go** to it.

2. In **main.go**, add the package and imports:

```
package main
import "fmt"
```

3. Define a custom type called **id** based on the string type:

```
type id string
```

4. Create a function that returns three ids:

```
func getIDs() (id, id, id) {
```

5. For **id1**, we'll initialize it and leave at its zero value:

```
var id1 id
```

6. For **id2**, we'll initialize it using a string literal:

```
var id2 id = "1234-5678"
```

7. Finally, for **id3**, we'll initialize it to zero and then set a value separately:

```
var id3 id
id3 = "1234-5678"
```

8. Now, return the ids and close the function:

```
    return id1, id2, id3
}
```

9. In **main**, call our function and do some comparisons:

```
func main() {
    id1, id2, id3 := getIDs()
    fmt.Println("id1 == id2   :", id1 == id2)
    fmt.Println("id2 == id3   :", id2 == id3)
```

10. For this preceding comparison, we'll convert the id back into a string:

```
    fmt.Println("id2 == \"1234-5678\":", string(id2) == "1234-5678")
}
```

11. Save the file. Then, in the folder you created in *step 1*, run the code using the following command:

```
go run .
```

Running the preceding code produces the following output:

```
 ~/src/Th…op/Ch…04/Exercise04.16   go run .
id1 == id2        : false
id2 == id3        : true
id2 == "1234-5678": true
```

Figure 4.9: Output after comparison

In this exercise, we created a custom type, set data on it, and then compared it with values of the same type and with its base type.

Simple custom types are a foundation part of modeling the data problems you'll see in the real world. Having types designed to reflect the data you need to work with closely helps keep your code easy to understand and maintain.

Structs

Collections are perfect for grouping values of the same type and purpose together. There is another way of grouping data together in Go for a different purpose. Often, a simple string, number, or Boolean doesn't fully capture the essence of the data you'll have.

For example, for our user map, a user was represented by their unique ID and their first name. That is rarely going to be enough details to be able to work with user records. The data you could capture about a person is almost infinite, such as their given, middle, and family names. Their preferred prefix and suffix, their date of birth, their height, weight, or where they work can also be captured. It would be possible to store this data in multiple maps, all with the same key, but that is hard to work with and maintain.

The ideal thing to do is collect all these different bits of data into a single data structure that you can design and control. That's what Go's struct type is: it's a custom type that you can name and specify the field properties and their types.

The notation for structs looks as follows:

```
type <name> struct {
   <fieldName1> <type>
   <fieldName2> <type>
   ...
   <fieldNameN> <type>
}
```

Field names must be unique within a struct. You can use any type for a field, including pointers, collections, and other structs.

You can access a field on a struct using the following notation: **<structValue>.<fieldName>**. To set a value, you use this notation: **<structValue>.<fieldName> = <value>**. To read a value you use the following notation: **value = <structValue>.<fieldName>**.

Structs are the closest thing that Go has to what are called classes in other languages, but structs have purposely been kept stripped down by Go's designers. A key difference is that structs don't have any form of inheritance. The designers of Go feel that inheritance causes more problems than it solves in real-world code.

Once you've defined your custom struct type, you can use it to create a value. You have several ways to create values from struct types. Let's take a look at them now.

Exercise 4.17: Creating Struct Types and Values

In this exercise, we're going to define a user struct. We'll define some fields of different types. Then, we'll create some struct values using a few different methods. Let's get started:

1. Create a new folder and add a file named **main.go** to it.

2. In **main.go**, add the package and imports:

```
package main
import "fmt"
```

3. The first thing we'll do is define our struct type. You generally do this in the package scope. We need to give it a name that's unique at the package-level scope:

```
type user struct {
```

4. We'll add some fields of different types and then close the struct definition:

```
    name    string
    age     int
    balance float64
    member  bool
}
```

5. We'll create a function that returns a slice of our newly defined struct type:

```
func getUsers() []user {
```

6. Our first user is initialized using this key-value notation. This notation is the most common form to use when initializing structs:

```
u1 := user{
name:    "Tracy",
age:     51,
balance: 98.43,
member:  true,
}
```

7. When using the key-value notation, the order of the fields doesn't matter and any you leave out will get a zero value for their type:

```
u2 := user{
age:  19,
name: "Nick",
}
```

8. It's possible to initialize a struct with values only. If you do this, all the fields must be present, and their order must match how you defined them in the struct:

```
u3 := user{
"Bob",
25,
0,
false,
}
```

9. This **var** notation will create a struct where all the fields have zero values:

```
var u4 user
```

10. Now, we can set values on the fields using . and the field name:

```
u4.name = "Sue"
u4.age = 31
u4.member = true
u4.balance = 17.09
```

11. Now, we will return the values wrapped in a slice and close the function:

```
    return []user{u1, u2, u3, u4}
}
```

12. In **main**, we'll get the slice of **users**, loop over it, and print it to the console:

```
func main() {
  users := getUsers()
  for i := 0; i < len(users); i++ {
  fmt.Printf("%v: %#v\n", i, users[i])
  }
}
```

13. Save the file. Then, in the folder you created in *step 1*, run the code using the following command:

```
go run .
```

Running the preceding code produces the following output:

```
📂  ~/src/Th…op/Ch…04/Exercise04.17   go run .
0: main.user{name:"Tracy", age:51, balance:98.43, member:true}
1: main.user{name:"Nick", age:19, balance:0, member:false}
2: main.user{name:"Bob", age:25, balance:0, member:false}
3: main.user{name:"Sue", age:31, balance:17.09, member:true}
```

Figure 4.10: Output as per the new struct

In this exercise, you defined a custom struct type that contained multiple fields, each of a different type. Then, we created values from that struct using a few different methods. Each of these methods is valid and is useful in different contexts.

We defined the struct at the package scope, and while it's not typical, you can define struct types in the function scope too. If you do define a struct type in a function, it'll only be valid for use in that function. When defining a type at the package level, it's available for use throughout the package.

It's also possible to define and initialize a struct at the same time. If you do this, you can't reuse the type, but it's still a useful technique. The notation looks as follows:

```
type <name> struct {
  <fieldName1> <type>
  <fieldName2> <type>

  ...

  <fieldNameN> <type>
}{
  <value1>,
  <value2>,

  ...

  <valueN>,
}
```

You can also initialize using the key-value notation, but initializing with only the values is the most common when this is done.

Comparing Structs to Each Other

If all of a struct's fields are comparable types, then the struct as a whole is also comparable. So, if your struct is made up of strings and ints, then you can compare whole structs to one another. If your struct has a slice in it, then you can't. Go is strongly typed, so you can only compare values of the same type, but with structs, there is a little bit of flexibility. If the struct was defined anonymously and it has the same structure as a named struct, then Go allows the comparison.

Exercise 4.18: Comparing Structs to Each Other

In this exercise, we'll define a comparable struct and create a value with it. We'll also define and create values with anonymous structs that have the same structure as our named struct. Finally, we'll compare them and print the results to the console. Let's get started:

1. Create a new folder and add a file named **main.go** to it:

2. In **main.go**, add the package and imports:

```
package main
import "fmt"
```

3. Let's define a simple, comparable struct:

```
type point struct {
    x int
    y int
}
```

4. Now, we'll create a function that returns two Booleans:

```
func compare() (bool, bool) {
```

5. Create our first anonymous struct:

```
point1 := struct {
    x int
    y int
}{
    10,
    10,
}
```

6. With the second anonymous struct, we're initializing it to zero and then changing the value after initialization:

```
point2 := struct {
    x int
    y int
}{}
point2.x = 10
point2.y = 5
```

7. The final struct to create uses the named struct type we created previously:

```
point3 := point{10, 10}
```

8. Compare them. Then, return and close the function:

```
    return point1 == point2, point1 == point3
}
```

9. In main, we'll call our function and print the results:

```
func main() {
    a, b := compare()
    fmt.Println("point1 == point2:", a)
    fmt.Println("point1 == point3:", b)
}
```

10. Save the file. Then, in the folder you created in *step 1*, run the code using the following command:

```
go run .
```

Running the preceding code produces the following output:

```
~/src/Th…op/Ch…04/Exercise04.18   go run .
point1 == point2: false
point1 == point3: true
```

Figure 4.11: Output comparing structs

In this exercise, we saw that we can work with anonymous struct values in the same way as named struct types, including comparing them. With named types, you can only compare structs of the same type. When you compare types in Go, Go compares all the fields to check for a match. Go is allowing a comparison of these anonymous structs to be made because the field names and types match. Go is a little flexible with comparing structs like this.

Struct Composition Using Embedding

While inheritance is not possible with Go structs, the designers of Go did include an exciting alternative. The alternative is to embed types in struct types. Using embedding, you can add fields to a struct from other structs. This composition feature has the effect of letting you add to a struct using other structs as components. Embedding is different than having a field that is a struct type. When you embed, the fields from the embedded struct get promoted. Once promoted, a field acts as if it's defined on the target struct.

To embed a struct, you add it like you would a field, but you don't specify a name. To do this, you add a struct type name to another struct without giving it a field name, which looks like this:

```
type <name> struct {
    <Type>
}
```

Though not common, you can embed any other type into structs. There is nothing to promote, so to access the embedded type, you access it using the type's name, for example, `<structValue>.<type>`. This way of accessing the embedded types by their type name is also true for structs. This means there is two valid ways to work with an embedded struct's fields: `<structValue>.<fieldName>` or `<structValue>.<type>.<fieldName>`. This ability to access the type by its name also means that the type's names must be unique between the embedded types and the root field names. When embedding pointer types, the type's name is the type without the pointer notation, so the name `*<type>` becomes `<type>`. The field is still a pointer, and only the name is different.

When it comes to promotion, if you were to have any overlap with your struct's field names, Go allows you to embed, but the promotion of the overlapping field doesn't happen. You can still access the field by going through the type name path.

You can't use promotion when initializing structs with embedded types. To initialize the data, you must use the embedded types name.

Exercise 4.19: Struct Embedding and Initialization

In this exercise, we'll define some structs and custom types. We'll embed those types into a struct. Let's get started:

1. Create a new folder and add a file named `main.go` to it.

2. In `main.go`, add the package and imports:

    ```
    package main
    import "fmt"
    ```

3. Create a custom string type called name:

    ```
    type name string
    ```

4. Create a struct called location with two int fields, that is, **x** and **y**:

    ```
    type location struct {
        x int
        y int
    }
    ```

5. Create a size struct with two int fields, that is, **width** and **height**:

```
type size struct {
    width  int
    height int
}
```

6. Create a struct named **dot**. This embeds each of the preceding structs in it:

```
type dot struct {
    name
    location
    size
}
```

7. Create a function that returns a slice of dots:

```
func getDots() []dot {
```

8. Our first **dot** uses the **var** notation. This will result in all the fields having a zero value:

```
var dot1 dot
```

9. With **dot2**, we're also initializing with zero values:

```
dot2 := dot{}
```

10. To set the name, we use the type's name as if it were a field:

```
dot2.name = "A"
```

11. For size and location, we'll use the promoted fields to set their value:

```
dot2.x = 5
dot2.y = 6
dot2.width = 10
dot2.height = 20
```

12. When initializing embedded types, you can't use promotion. For name, the result is the same but for location and size, you need to put more work into this:

```
dot3 := dot{
name: "B",
location: location{
    x: 13,
    y: 27,
},
size: size{
```

```
      width:  5,
      height: 7,
    },
  }
```

13. For **dot4**, we'll use the type names to set data:

```
dot4 := dot{}
dot4.name = "C"
dot4.location.x = 101
dot4.location.y = 209
dot4.size.width = 87
dot4.size.height = 43
```

14. Return all the dots in a slice and then close the function:

```
  return []dot{dot1, dot2, dot3, dot4}
}
```

15. In **main**, call the function. Then, loop over the slice and print it to the console:

```
func main() {
  dots := getDots()
  for i := 0; i < len(dots); i++ {
    fmt.Printf("dot%v: %#v\n", i+1, dots[i])
  }
}
```

16. Save the file. Then, in the folder you created in *step* 1, run the code using the following command:

```
go run .
```

Running the preceding code produces the following output:

```
📂 ~/src/Th…op/Ch…04/Exercise04.19 ▶ go run .
dot1: main.dot{name:"", location:main.location{x:0, y:0}, size:main.size{width:0, height:0}}
dot2: main.dot{name:"A", location:main.location{x:5, y:6}, size:main.size{width:10, height:20}}
dot3: main.dot{name:"B", location:main.location{x:13, y:27}, size:main.size{width:5, height:7}}
dot4: main.dot{name:"C", location:main.location{x:101, y:209}, size:main.size{width:87, height:43}}
```

Figure 4.12: Output after struct embedding and initialization

In this exercise, we were able to define a complex struct by embedding other types into it. Embedding allows you to reuse common structures by reducing the duplicated code but still giving your struct a flat API.

We won't see much embedding in real-world Go code. It does come up, but the complexity and exception mean that Go developers prefer to have the other structs as named fields.

Type Conversions

There are times when your types won't match up, and with Go's strict type system, if types are not the same, they can't interact with one another. In these cases, you have two options. If the two types are compatible, you can do type conversion – that is, you can create a new value by changing one type to another. The notation to do this is `<value>.(<type>)`. When working with strings, we used this notation to cast a string to a slice of runes or bytes and back again. This works because a string is a special type that stores the string's data as a slice of bytes.

The string type conversion is losses, but that's not true of all type conversions. When working with numeric type conversion, the numbers can change from their original value. If you convert from a large `int` type, for example, `int64`, into a smaller `int` type, for example, `int8`, it causes the number to overflow. If you were to convert from an unsigned int, for example, uint64, into a signed int, for example, `int64`, this overflow happens because unsigned ints can store a higher number than a signed `int`. This overflowing is the same when converting an `int` into a `float` since the `float` splits its storage space between whole numbers and decimals. When converting from a `float` to an `int`, the decimal part is truncated.

It's still perfectly reasonable to do these types of lossy conversions, and they happen all the time in real-world code. If you know that the data you're dealing with doesn't cross these thresholds, then there's no need to worry.

Go does its best to guess at the types that need conversion. This is called implicit type conversion. For example, `math.MaxInt8` is an `int`, and if you try to assign it to a number other than an `int`, Go does an implicit type conversion for you.

Exercise 4.20: Numeric Type Conversion

In this exercise, we'll do some numeric type conversion and intentionally cause some data issues. Let's get started:

1. Create a new folder and add a file named `main.go` to it.

2. In `main.go`, add the package and imports:

```
package main
import (
    "fmt"
    "math"
)
```

3. Create a function that returns a string:

```
func convert() string{
```

4. Define some variables to do our work. Go is doing an implicit conversion of the int **math.MaxInt8** into an **int8**:

```
var i8 int8 = math.MaxInt8
i := 128
f64 := 3.14
```

5. Here, we'll convert from a smaller **int** type into a larger **int** type. This is always a safe operation:

```
m := fmt.Sprintf("int8  = %v  > in64  = %v\n", i8, int64(i8))
```

6. Now, we'll convert from an **int** that's 1 above **int8**'s maximum size. This will cause an overflow to **int8**'s minimum size:

```
m += fmt.Sprintf("int   = %v  > in8   = %v\n", i, int8(i))
```

7. Next, we'll convert out **int8** into a **float64**. This doesn't cause an overflow and the data is unchanged:

```
m += fmt.Sprintf("int8  = %v  > float32 = %v\n", i8, float64(i8))
```

8. Here, we'll convert a float into an **int**. All the decimal data is lost but the whole number is kept as is:

```
m += fmt.Sprintf("float64 = %v > int   = %v\n", f64, int(f64))
```

9. Return the message and then close the function:

```
    return m
}
```

10. In the **main()** function, call the function and print it to the console:

```
func main() {
    fmt.Print(convert())
}
```

11. Save the file. Then, in the folder you created in *step 1*, run the code using the following command:

```
go run .
```

Running the preceding code produces the following output:

```
 ~/src/Th…op/Ch…04/Exercise04.20   go run .
int8    = 127  > in64     = 127
int     = 128  > in8      = -128
int8    = 127  > float32 = 127
float64 = 3.14 > int      = 3
```

Figure 4.13: Output after conversion

Type Assertions and interface{}

We've used **fmt.Print** and its siblings a great deal for writing our code, but how does a function such as **fmt.Print** take any type of value when Go is a strongly typed language? Let's take a look at the actual Go standard library code for **fmt.Print**:

```
// Print formats using the default formats for its operands and writes to standard
output.
// Spaces are added between operands when neither is a string.
// It returns the number of bytes written and any write error encountered.
func Print(a ...interface{}) (n int, err error) {
   return Fprint(os.Stdout, a...)
}
```

I hope you can see that looking at Go's source code is not scary – it's a great way to see how you should do things and I recommend looking at it whenever you are curious about how they do something.

By looking at this code, we can see that **fmt.Print** has a variadic of the **interface{}** type. We'll cover interfaces in more detail later, but for now, what you need to know is that an interface in Go describes what functions a type must have to conform to that interface. Interfaces in Go don't describe fields and don't describe a type's core value, such as being a string or a number. In Go, any type can have functions, including strings and numbers. What **interface{}** is describing is a type with no functions. What use is a value with no function, no fields, and no core value? None, but it's still a value, and it can still be passed around. This interface is not setting the type of the value but controlling what values it will allow for a variable with that interface. What types in Go conform to **interface{}**? All of them! Any of Go's types or any custom type you create conform to **interface{}**, and this is how **fmt.Print** can accept any type. You can also use **interface{}** in your code to achieve the same result.

Once you have your variable that conforms to **interface{}**, what can you do with it? Even if the underlying value of your **interface{}** variable has functions, fields, or a core value, you can't use them because Go is enforcing the interface's contract, which is why this is still all type safe.

To unlock the capabilities of the value masked by **interface{}**, we need to use type assertion. The notation for type assertion is **<value>.(<type>)**. Type assertion results in a value of the type that was requested and optionally a bool regarding whether it was successful or not. This looks like **<value> := <value>.(<type>)** or **<value>, <ok> := <value>.(type)**. If you leave the Boolean value out and type assertion fails, Go raises a panic.

Go doesn't remove anything from a value when you place it in an **interface{}** variable. What happens is the Go compiler prevents you from using it because it's not able to perform its type-safety checks at compile time. Using type assertion is your instruction to Go that you want to unlock the value. When you do type assertion, Go performs the type-safety checks it would have done at compile time at runtime, and those checks may fail. It's then your responsibility to deal with the type-safety checks failing. Type assertions is a feature that causes runtime errors and panics, which means you must be extra careful around them.

Exercise 4.21: Type Assertion

In this exercise, we will perform some type assertions and ensure that all the safety checks are in place when we do so. Let's get started:

1. Create a new folder and add a file named **main.go** to it.

2. In **main.go**, add the package and imports:

```
package main
import (
  "errors"
  "fmt"
)
```

3. Create a function that accepts an **interface{}** and returns a string and an error:

```
func doubler(v interface{}) (string, error) {
```

4. First, we'll check to see if our argument is an int, and if it is, we'll multiply it by **2** and return it:

```
if i, ok := v.(int); ok {
    return fmt.Sprint(i * 2), nil
}
```

5. Here, we'll check if it's a string and if it is, we'll concatenate it to itself and return it:

```
if s, ok := v.(string); ok {
    return s + s, nil
}
```

6. If we don't get any matches, return an error. Then, close the function:

```
    return "", errors.New("unsupported type passed")
}
```

7. In **main**, call **doubler** with a variety of data and print the results to the console:

```
func main() {
    res, _ := doubler(5)
    fmt.Println("5    :", res)
    res, _ = doubler("yum")
    fmt.Println("yum :", res)
    _, err := doubler(true)
    fmt.Println("true:", err)
}
```

8. Save the file. Then, in the folder you created in *step 1*, run the code using the following command:

```
go run .
```

Running the preceding code produces the following output:

```
 ~/src/Th…op/Ch…04/Exercise04.21   go run .
5    : 10
yum : yumyum
true: unsupported type passed
```

Figure 4.14: Output showing matches

The combination of **interface{}** and type assertions allows you to overcome Go's strict type controls, in turn allowing you to create functions that can work with any type of variable. The challenge is that you lose the protection that Go gives you at compile time for type safety. It's still possible to be safe, but the responsibility is yours now – do it wrong, and you'll get a nasty runtime error.

Type Switch

If we wanted to expand our **doubler** function to include all **int** types, we'd end up with a lot of duplicated logic. Go has an excellent way of dealing with more complex type assertions situations, known as the type switch. Here's what it looks like:

```
switch <value> := <value>.(type) {
case <type>:
  <statement>
case <type>, <type>:
  <statement>
default:
  <statement>
}
```

The type switch only runs your logic if it matches the type you're looking for, and it sets the value to that type. You can match on more than one type in a case, but Go can't change the type of the value for you, so you'll still need to do type assertion. One of the things that makes this a type switch and not an expression switch is the **<value>.(type)** notation. You can only use that as part of a type switch. Something else that's unique to type switches is that you can't use the **fallthrough** statement.

Exercise 4.22: Type Switch

In this exercise, we'll update our **doubler** function to use a type switch and expand its abilities to deal with more types. Let's get started:

1. Create a new folder and add a file named **main.go** to it.

2. In **main.go**, add the package and imports:

```
package main

import (
  "errors"
  "fmt"
)
```

3. Create our function, which takes a single **inferface{}** argument and returns a string and an error:

```
func doubler(v interface{}) (string, error) {
```

4. Create a type switch using our argument:

```
switch t := v.(type) {
```

5. For **string** and **bool**, since we're only matching on one type, we don't need to do any extra safety checks and can work with the value directly:

```
case string:
return t + t, nil
case bool:
if t {
    return "truetrue", nil
}
return "falsefalse", nil
```

6. For the floats, we're matching on more than one type. This means we need to do type assertion to be able to work with the value:

```
case float32, float64:
if f, ok := t.(float64); ok {
    return fmt.Sprint(f * 2), nil
}
```

7. If this type assertion were to fail, we'd get a panic, but we can rely on the logic that only **float32** can work directly with the result of type assertion:

```
return fmt.Sprint(t.(float32) * 2), nil
```

8. Match all of the **int** and **uint** types. We've been able to remove lots of code here by not needing to do the type-safety checks ourselves:

```
case int:
return fmt.Sprint(t * 2), nil
case int8:
return fmt.Sprint(t * 2), nil
case int16:
return fmt.Sprint(t * 2), nil
case int32:
return fmt.Sprint(t * 2), nil
case int64:
return fmt.Sprint(t * 2), nil
case uint:
return fmt.Sprint(t * 2), nil
case uint8:
return fmt.Sprint(t * 2), nil
case uint16:
```

```
    return fmt.Sprint(t * 2), nil
case uint32:
    return fmt.Sprint(t * 2), nil
case uint64:
    return fmt.Sprint(t * 2), nil
```

9. We'll use the default to return an error. Then, we'll close the switch statement and function:

```
    default:
        return "", errors.New("unsupported type passed")
    }
}
```

10. In the **main()** function, call our function with even more data and print the results to the console:

```
func main() {
    res, _ := doubler(-5)
    fmt.Println("-5  :", res)
    res, _ = doubler(5)
    fmt.Println("5   :", res)
    res, _ = doubler("yum")
    fmt.Println("yum :", res)
    res, _ = doubler(true)
    fmt.Println("true:", res)
    res, _ = doubler(float32(3.14))
    fmt.Println("3.14:", res)
}
```

11. Save the file. Then, in the folder you created in *step 1*, run the code using the following command:

```
go run .
```

Running the preceding code produces the following output:

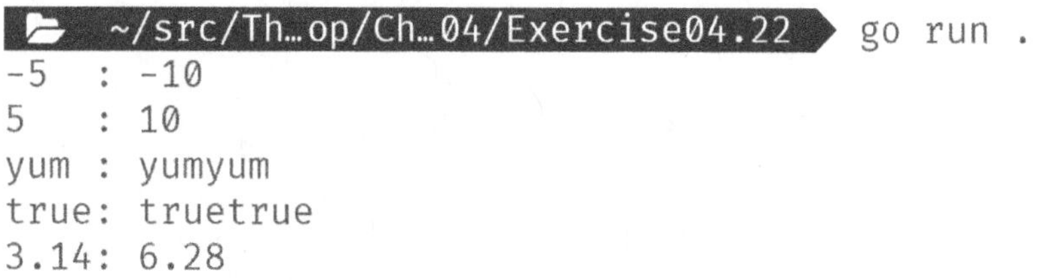

```
  ~/src/Th…op/Ch…04/Exercise04.22   go run .
-5   : -10
5    : 10
yum  : yumyum
true : truetrue
3.14 : 6.28
```

Figure 4.15: Output after calling functions

In this exercise, we used a type switch to build a complex type assertion scenario. Using the type switch still gives us full control of the type assertions but also lets us simplify the type-safety logic when we don't need that level of control.

Activity 4.06: Type Checker

In this activity, you're going to write some logic that has a slice or different types of data. These data types are as follows:

- An int
- A float
- A string
- A bool
- A struct

Create a function that accepts a value of any type. The function returns a string with the name of the type:

- For int, int32, and int64, it returns **int**.
- For all floats, it returns **float**.
- For a string, it returns **string**.
- For a bool, it returns **bool**.
- For anything else, it returns **unknown**.
- Loop all the data by passing each one to your function.
- Then, print the data and its type name to the console.

The expected output is as follows:

```
 ~/src/Th…op/Ch…04/Activity04.06   go run .
1 is int
3.14 is float
hello is string
true is bool
{} is unknown
```

Figure 4.16: Expected output

> **Note**
>
> The solution for this activity can be found on page 702.

Summary

In this chapter, we got into the advanced uses of variables and types in Go. Real-world code gets complicated quickly because the real world is complicated. Being able to model the data accurately and keep that data logically organized in your code helps reduce the complexity of your code to a minimum.

You now know how to group similar data, either in a fixed-length ordered list using an array, in a dynamic length ordered list using a slice, or in a key-value hash using a map.

We learned to go beyond Go's core types and start to create custom types based either directly on the core types or by creating a struct, which is a collection of other types held in a single type and value.

There are times when you'll have type mismatches, so Go gives us the ability to convert compatible types so that they can interact in a type-safe way.

Go also lets us break free of its type safety rules and gives us full control. By using type assertions, we can accept any type using the magic of `interface{}` and then get those types back.

In the next chapter, we'll explore how to group our logic into reusable components and attach them to our custom types to make our code more straightforward and easier to maintain.

5

Functions

Overview

This chapter will describe the various parts of a function in detail, such as defining the function, function identifiers, parameter lists, return types, and the function body. We will also look at some best practices when designing our functions, such as a function performing a single task, how to reduce code, making your function small, and ensuring that functions are reusable.

By the end of this chapter, you will be able to describe a function and the different parts that make up a function and evaluate the scope of variables with functions. You will learn to create and call a function; utilize variadic and anonymous functions and create closures for various constructs. You will also learn to use functions as parameters and return values; and use **defer** statements with functions.

Introduction

Functions are a core part of many languages and Go is no exception. A function is a section of code that has been declared to perform a task. Go functions can have zero or more inputs and outputs. One feature that sets Go apart from other programming languages is the multiple return values; most programming languages are limited to one return value.

In the following section, we will see some features of Go functions that differ from other languages, such as returning multiple types. We will also see that Go has support for first-class functions. This means that Go has the ability to assign a variable to a function, pass a function as an argument, and have a function as a return type for a function. We will show how functions can be used to break up complex parts into smaller parts.

Functions in Go are considered first-class citizens and higher-order functions. First-class citizens are the functions that are assigned to a variable. Higher-order functions are functions that can take a function as an argument. The rich features of Go functions empower them to be used in various segments in the following ways:

- Functions to be passed as an argument to another function

- Return a function as a value from a function

- Functions as a type

- Closures

- Anonymous functions

- Functions assigned to a variable

We will be looking at each of these features that are supported in Go.

Functions

Functions are a critical part of Go and we should understand their place. Let's examine some of the reasons for using functions:

- **Breaking up a complex task**: Functions are used to perform a task, but if that task is complicated, it should then be broken down into smaller tasks. Functions can be used for small tasks to solve a bigger problem. Smaller tasks are more manageable, and using a function to solve specific tasks will make the entire code base easier to maintain.

- **Reducing code**: A good indication that you should use a function is when you see similar code repeating throughout your program. When you have duplicate code, it increases the difficulty of maintenance. If you have one change to make, you will have multiple instances where your code needs to change.

- **Reusability**: Once you have defined your function, you can use it repeatedly. It can also be used by other programmers. This sharing of functions will also reduce lines of code and save time by allowing you to not have to reinvent the wheel. There are a couple of guidelines we should follow when we design functions:

- **Single responsibility**: A function should perform one task. For example, a single function should not calculate the distance between two points and estimate the time to travel between those two points. There should be a function for each of those tasks. This allows for better testing of that function and easier maintenance. It is difficult to narrow a function to perform a single task, so do not get discouraged if you do not get it right the first time. Even seasoned programmers struggle with assigning a single responsibility to a function.

- **Small in size**: Functions should not span over hundreds of lines of code. This is an indication that the code needs some refactoring. When we have large functions, it's more likely that the single responsibility principle will be violated. A good rule of thumb is trying to limit the function size to approximately 25 lines of code; however, that's not a hard-and-fast rule. The benefit of keeping the code concise is that it reduces the complexity of debugging a large function. It also makes writing unit tests with better code coverage easier.

Parts of a function

We will now be looking at the different components involved in defining a function. The following is the typical layout of a function:

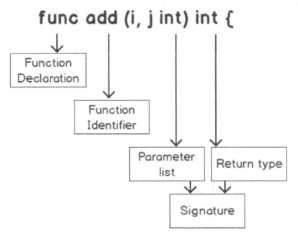

Figure 5.1: Different parts of a function

The different parts of a function are described here:

- **func**: In Go, the function declaration starts with the `func` keyword.

- **Identifier**: This is also referred to as the function name. It is idiomatic in Go to use camelCase for the function name. camelCase is the practice of having the first letter of the function name in lowercase and the first letter of each word following in upper case. Examples of function names that follow this convention include `calculateTax`, `totalSum`, and `fetchId`.

  The identifier should be something descriptive that makes the code easy to read and makes the purpose of the function easy to understand. The identifier is not required. You can have a function with no name; this is known as an anonymous function. Anonymous functions will be discussed in detail in a later part of the chapter.

  > **Note**
  >
  > When the first letter of the function name is in lowercase, then the function is not exportable outside of a package. This means they are private and cannot be called from outside the package. They can only be called within the package.
  >
  > Keep this in mind when you use camelCase naming convention. If you want your function to be exportable, the first letter of the function name must be capitalized.

- **Parameter list**: Parameters are input values to a function. A parameter is data that is required by the function to help solve the task of the function. Parameters are defined as follows: name, type. An example parameter list could be (`name string`, `age int`). Parameters are local variables to the function.

  Parameters are optional for a function. It is possible to not have any parameters for a function. A function can have zero or more parameters.

  When two or more parameters have the same type, you can use what is called shorthand parameter notation. This removes specifying the same type for each parameter. For instance, if your parameters are (`firstName string`, `lastName string`), they can be shortened to (`firstName`, `lastName string`). This reduces the verbosity of the parameter inputs and increases the readability of the function parameter list.

- **Return types**: Return types are a list of data types, such as Boolean, string, map, or another function that can be returned.

  In the context of declaring a function, we refer to these types as return types. However, in the context of calling a function, they are called return values.

  Return types are the output of the function. Often, they are the result of the arguments provided to the function. They are optional. Most programming languages return a single type; in Go, you can return multiple types.

- **Function body**: The function body is the coding statements between curly braces, `{}`.

  The statements in the function are what determine what the function does. The function code is the code that is being used to perform the task that the function was created to accomplish.

  If there were return types defined, then a `return` statement is required in the function body. The `return` statement causes the function to immediately stop and return the value types listed after the `return` statement. The types in the return type list and in the `return` statement must match.

  In the function body, there can be multiple `return` statements.

- **Function signature**: Though not listed in the preceding code snippet, a function signature is a term that references the input parameters combined with the return types. Both of those units make up a function signature.

  Often, when you define the function signature when it is being used by others, you want to strive to not make changes to it as this can adversely impact your code and the code of others.

We will be diving deep into each of the parts of a function as we progress through the chapter. These parts of a function will become easier to understand through the following discussion, so don't worry if you do not quite understand all the parts yet. It will become clearer as we go through the chapter.

fizzBuzz

Now that we have looked at the different parts of the function, let's see how these parts work with various examples. Let's start with a classical programming game called fizzBuzz. The rules of fizzBuzz are straightforward. The fizzBuzz function prints out various messages based on some math results. The rules perform one of the actions based on the number given:

- If the number is divisible by 3, print Fizz.

- If the number is divisible by 5, print Buzz.

- If the number is divisible by 15, print FizzBuzz.

- Else, print the number.

The following is the code snippet to achieve this output:

```
func fizzBuzz() {
    for i := 1; i <= 30; i++ {
        if i%15 == 0 {
            fmt.Println("FizzBuzz")
        } else if i%3 == 0 {
            fmt.Println("Fizz")
        } else if i%5 == 0 {
            fmt.Println("Buzz")
        } else {
            fmt.Println(i)
        }
    }
}
```

Let's look at the code in sections now:

```
func fizzBuzz() {
```

- **func**, as you may recall, is the keyword to declare a function. This informs Go that the following piece of code is going to be a function.

- **fizzBuzz** is the name of our function. It is idiomatic in Go to use a camelCase name.

- **()**, the parenthesis following the name of our function, is empty: our current implementation of the **FizzBuzz** game does not require any input parameters.

- The space between the parameter list, **()**, and the opening brace would be the return type. Our current implementation does not require a return type.

- Regarding **{**, unlike other programming languages that you may know, Go requires that the opening curly brace is on the same line as the function declaration. If the opening brace is not on the same line as the function signature when you attempt to run the program, you will get an error.

```
for i := 1; i <= 30; i++ {
```

The preceding line is a **for** loop that increments the **i** variable from **1** to **30**:

```
if i%15 == 0 {
```

- **%** is a modulus operator; it gives the remainder of the two integers being divided. Using our function, if **i** is **15**, then **15%15** will return zero. We use the modulus operator to determine whether **i** is evenly divisible by **3**, **5**, or **15**.

> **Note**
>
> As we become more familiar with Go concepts and language syntax, the explanation of the code will exclude items that we would otherwise be going over multiple times.

We have now defined our function. It has a specific task we want it to perform, but it doesn't do any good if we do not execute the function. So, how do we execute a function? We must call our function. When we call a function, we are telling our program to execute the function. We will be calling our function inside the **main()** function.

Functions can call other functions. When this occurs, control is given to the function that was called. After the called function has returned data or reached the ending curly brace, **}**, control is given back to the caller. Let's see an example to understand this better:

```
func main() {
   fmt.Println("Main is in control")
   fizzBuzz()
   fmt.Println("Back to main")
}
```

- **}fmt.Println("Main is in control")**: This **print** statement is for demonstration purposes. It shows that we are in the **main()** function.

- **fizzBuzz()**: We are now calling the function inside the **main()** function. Even though there are no parameters for our function the parentheses are still required, control of the program is given to the **fizzBuzz()** function. After the **fizzBuzz()** function completes, control is then given back to the **main()** function.

- **fmt.Println("Back to main")**: The **print** statement is for demonstration purposes to show that control has been given back to the **main()** function.

The output will be as follows:

```
Main is in control
1
2
Fizz
4
Buzz
Fizz
7
8
Fizz
Buzz
11
Fizz
13
14
FizzBuzz
16
17
Fizz
19
Buzz
Fizz
22
23
Fizz
Buzz
26
Fizz
28
29
FizzBuzz
Back to main
```

Figure 5.2: Output for fizzBuzz

> **Note**
>
> The parentheses following the **fizzBuzz** function are still required even though there are no input parameters. If they are omitted, the Go compiler will generate an error that states **fizzBuzz** evaluated but not used. This is a common error.

The output will be as follows:

```
prog.go:9:2: undefined: fizzBuzz
```

Figure 5.3: Output for fizzBuzz without parentheses

Exercise 5.01: Creating a Function to Print Salesperson Expectation Ratings from the Number of Items Sold

In this exercise, we will be creating a function that will not have any parameters or return types. The function will iterate over a map and print the name and number of items sold in the map. It will also print a statement based on how the salesperson performed based on their sales. The following steps will help you with the solution:

1. Use the IDE of your choice.

2. Create a new file and save it as **main.go.**

3. Enter the following code in **main.go**. The first function that **main** will call on **itemsSold()**; it does not have any parameters and has no return values:

```
package main
import (
    "fmt"
)
func main() {
    itemsSold()
}
```

4. In the **itemsSold()** function, initialize a map that will have a key-value pair of **string**, **int**. The map will hold a **name(string)** and the number of **items(int)** sold. The name is the key for the map. We assign various names to number of items sold:

```
func itemsSold() {
    items := make(map[string]int)
    items["John"] = 41
    items["Celina"] = 109
    items["Micah"] = 24
```

5. We iterate over the **items** map and assign **k** to the **key(name)** and **v** to the **value(items)**:

```
for k, v := range items{
```

6. We print out the **Name** and the number of sold **items**:

```
fmt.Printf("%s sold %d items and ", k, v)
```

7. Depending on the value of **v(items)**, we will determine the statement we print:

```
if v < 40 {
   fmt.Println("is below expectations.")
} else if v > 40 && v <= 100 {
   fmt.Println("meets expectations.")
} else if v > 100 {
   fmt.Println("exceeded expectations.")
}
}
}
```

8. Open your terminal and navigate to the code's directory.

9. Run **go build** and then run the executable.

   The expected output is as follows:

```
John sold 41 items and meets expectations.
Celina sold 109 items and exceeded expectations.
Micah sold 24 items and is below expectations.
```

In this exercise, we saw some of the fundamental parts of a function. We demonstrated how to declare a function using the **func** keyword, followed by how to give our function an identifier or name such as itemsSold() We then proceed to add code to the function body. In the next topics, we will expand on these core parts of the function and learn how to pass data into a function using parameters.

> **Note**
>
> It is best to type the code into an IDE. The benefit is that if you type something incorrectly, you will see the error message and can perform some debugging to solve the problem.

Parameters

Parameters define what arguments can be passed to our function. Functions can have zero or more parameters. Even though Go allows us to define multiple parameters, we should take care not to have a huge parameter list; that would make the code harder to read. It also may be an indication that the function is doing more than one specific task. If that is the case, we should refactor the function. Take, for example, the following code snippet:

```
func calculateSalary(lastName string, firstName string, age int, state string, country
string, hoursWorked int, hourlyRate, isEmployee bool) {
// code
}
```

The preceding code is an example of a function whose parameter list is bloated. The parameter list should pertain only to the single responsibility of the function. We should only define the parameters that are needed to solve the specific problem that the function is built for.

Parameters are the input types that our function will use to perform its task. Function parameters are local to the function, meaning they are only available to that function. They are not available outside of the context of the function. Also, the order of the parameters must match the parameter types in the correct sequence.

Correct:

```
func main() {
   greeting("Cayden", 45)
}
func greeting(name string, age int) {
   fmt.Printf("%s is %d",name, age)
}
```

The output when the correct parameter matches would be as follows:

```
Cayden is 45
```

Incorrect:

```
func main() {
   greeting(45,"Cayden")
   }
func greeting(name string, age int) {
   fmt.Printf("%s is %d",name, age)
}
```

The output looks as follows:

```
prog.go:5:11: cannot use 45 (type int) as type string in argument to greeting
prog.go:5:14: cannot use "Cayden" (type string) as type int in argument to greeting

Go build failed.
```

Figure 5.4: Output for incorrect parameter matching

In the incorrect version of the code, we are calling the **greeting()** function with the **age** argument of type **integer** when the parameter is of type **string**. The sequence of your arguments must match the sequence of the parameter input list.

Additionally, users would want to have more control over the data the code iterates over. Going back to the **fizzBuzz** example, the current implementation only does **1** to **100**. Users may need to work on different number ranges and hence we need a way to decide the ending range of the loop. We can change our **fizzBuzz** function to accept an input parameter. This would meet the needs of our user:

```go
func main() {
  fizzBuzz(10)
}
func fizzBuzz(end int) {
  for i := 1; i <= end; i++ {
    if i%15 == 0 {
      fmt.Println("FizzBuzz")
    } else if i%3 == 0 {
      fmt.Println("Fizz")
    } else if i%5 == 0 {
      fmt.Println("Buzz")
    } else {
      fmt.Println(i)
    }
  }
}
```

The preceding code snippet can be explained as follows:

- For **fizzBuzz(10)** in the **main()** function, we pass **10** as an argument to our **fizzBuzz** function.

- For **fizzBuzz(end int)**, **topEnd** is the name of our parameter and it is of type **int**.

- Our function now will only iterate up to the value of our end parameter; in this example, it will iterate to **10**.

The Difference between an Argument and a Parameter

This is a good time to discuss the difference between an argument and a parameter. When you are defining your function, using our example, **fizzBuzz(end int)** is called a parameter. When you call a function, such as **fizzBuzz(10)**, 10 is called the argument. Also, the argument and parameter names do not need to match.

Functions in Go also can have more than one parameter defined. We need to add another parameter to our **fizzBuzz** function to accommodate this enhancement:

```go
func main() {
    s:= 10
    e:= 20
fizzBuzz(s,e)
}
func fizzBuzz(start int, end int) {
    for i := start; i <= end; i++ {
    // code omitted for brevity
    }
}
```

The preceding code snippet can be explained as follows:

- Regarding **fizzBuzz(s,e)**, we are now passing two arguments to the **fizzBuzz** function. When there are multiple arguments, they must be separated by a comma.

- Regarding **func fizzBuzz(start int, end int)**, when multiple parameters are defined in a function, they are separated by commas, following the convention of name type, name type, name type, and so on.

Our **fizzBuzz** parameters are more verbose than what is necessary. When we have multiple input parameters of the same type, you can separate the input name by a comma followed by the type. This is referred to as shorthand parameter notation. See the following example of using shorthand parameter notation:

```go
func main() {
    s,e := 10,20
    fizzBuzz(s,e)
}
func fizzBuzz(start,end int) {
    // code…
}
```

The preceding code snippet can be explained as follows:

- There is no change to the caller when using shorthand parameter notation.

- Regarding **fizzBuzz(start,end int)**, **start** and **end** are of type **int**. Nothing needs to change in the body of the function to accommodate the shorthand parameter notation.

Exercise 5.02: Mapping Index Values to Column Headers

The function that we are going to create will be taking a slice of column headers from a CSV file. It will print out a map of an index value of the headers we are interested in:

1. Open the IDE of your choice.

2. Create a new file and save it **main.go**.

3. Enter the following code in **main.go**:

```
package main
import (
  "fmt"
  "strings"
)
func main() {
  hdr :=[]string{"empid","employee","address","hours worked","hourly rate",
    "manager"}
  csvHdrCol(hdr)
  hdr2 :=[]string{"employee","empid","hours worked","address",
    "manager","hourly rate"}
  csvHdrCol(hdr2)
}
func csvHdrCol   (header []string) {
        csvHeadersToColumnIndex:= make(map[int]string)
```

First, we assign a variable to a key-value pair of **int** and **string**. **key(int)** will be the index of our **header(string)** column. The index will map to a column header.

4. We range over the **header** to process each string that is in the slice:

```
for i, v := range header {
```

5. For each string, remove any trailing spaces in front of and after the string. In general, we should always make the assumption that our data may have some erroneous characters:

```
v = strings.TrimSpace(v)
```

6. In our **switch** statement, we lower all the casing for exact matches. As you may recall, Go is a case-sensitive language. We need to ensure that the casing is the same for matching purposes. When our code finds the header, it sets the index value for the header in the map:

```
switch strings.ToLower(v) {
case "employee":
        csvHeadersToColumnIndex[i] = v
case "hours worked":
        csvHeadersToColumnIndex[i] = v
case "hourly rate":
        csvHeadersToColumnIndex[i] = v
    }
  }
```

7. Typically, we would not print out the results. We should return the **csvHeadersToColumnIndex**, but since we have not gone over how to return a value, we will print it for now:

```
fmt.Println(csvHeadersToColumnIndex)
  }
```

8. Open your terminal and navigate to the code's directory.

9. Run **go build** and run the executable.

   The expected output is as follows:

```
Map[1:employee 3:hours worked 4: hourly rate]
Map[0:employee 2:hours worked 5: hourly rate]
```

In this exercise, we saw how to accept data into a function, by defining a parameter for our function. The callers of our function were able to pass arguments to the function. We will continue to discover various abilities that functions in Go can provide. We have seen how to get data into our function. In the next section, we will see how to get data out of our function.

Function Variable Scope

When designing functions, we need to consider the variable scope. The scope of a variable determines where the variable is accessible or visible to the different parts of the application. Variables declared inside the function are considered local variables. This means that they are only accessible to the code within the body of the function. You cannot access variables from outside of the function. The calling function does not have access to variables inside the called function. The input parameter's scope is the same as the local variable's scope to the function.

Variables declared in the calling function are scoped to that function. This means that the variables are local to the function and those variables are not accessible outside of the function. Our function cannot reach into the calling function's variables. To get access to those variables, they must be passed into our function as input parameters:

```go
func main() {
  m:= "Uncle Bob"
  greeting()
}
func greeting() {
  fmt.Printf("Greeting %s", m)
}
```

```
prog.go:10:28: undefined: m

Go build failed.
```

Figure 5.5: Error output for the m variable being undefined

The previous code snippet will result in an error in **func greeting()** that states that **m** is undefined. That is because the **m** variable is declared inside **main()**. The **greeting()** function does not have access to the **m** variable. For it to have access to, the **m** variable must be passed to the **greeting()** function as an input parameter:

```go
func main() {
  m:= "Uncle Bob"
  greeting(m)
  fmt.Printf("Hi from main: %s", s)
}
func greeting(name string) {
  fmt.Printf("Greeting %o",name)
  s:= "Slacker"
  fmt.Printf("Greeting %s",s)
}
```

```
prog.go:7:33: undefined: s

Go build failed.
```

Figure 5.6: Error output for the s variable being undefined

The previous code snippet will result in an error in **func main()**. The error will state that **s** is undefined. This is because the **s** variable is declared in the **greeting()** function. The **main()** function does not have access to the **s** variable. The **s** variable is only visible to code inside the function body of **greeting()**.

These are just some considerations that we need to keep in mind when we are declaring and accessing variables. It is important to understand the scope of the variables inside a function in relation to the variables declared outside of a function. It can cause some confusion when you are trying to access variables but you are not scoped to the context that you are trying to access. The examples in this chapter should help you in understanding the scope of variables.

Return Values

So far, the functions that we have created do not have any return values. Functions typically accept inputs, perform some action on those inputs, and then return the results of those inputs. Most programming languages return only one value. Go allows you to return multiple values from a function. This is one of the features of Go functions that distinguishes it from other programming languages.

Exercise 5.03: Creating a fizzBuzz Function with Return Values

We are going to make some enhancements to our **fizzBuzz** function. We are going to change it so that it accepts only an integer. We will leave the onus on the caller to perform the looping if they desire to do so. Also, we are going to have two returns. The first will be the number provided and the corresponding text of empty string, **fizz**, **buzz**, or **fizzbuzz**. The following steps will help you with the solution.

1. Open the IDE of your choice.

2. Create a new file and save it at **$GOPATH\functions\fizzBuzzreturn\main.go**.

3. In the **main()** function, assign variables to the return values of our function. The **n**, **s** variables correspond respectively to the values being returned from our function, **int**, **string**:

```go
func main() {
  for i := 1; i <= 15; i++ {
    n, s := fizzBuzz(i)
    fmt.Printf("Results:  %d %s\n", n, s)
  }
}
```

4. The **fizzBuzz** function now returns two values; the first being an **int**, followed by a string.

```
func fizzBuzz(i int) (int, string) {
  switch {
```

5. Simplify the **if{}else{}** statements by replacing them with a **switch** statement. As you are writing code, you should look for ways to simplify things and make the code more readable. **case i%15 ==0** is equivalent to our previous **if i%15 == 0** statements. Instead of our previous **fmt. Println()** statements, replace them with **return**. The **return** statement will immediately stop the execution of the function and return the results to the caller:

```
case i%15 == 0:
  return i, "FizzBuzz"
case i%3 == 0:
  return i, "Fizz"
case i%5 == 0:
  return i, "Buzz"
}
return i, ""
}
```

The expected output is as follows:

```
Results:  1
Results:  2
Results:  3 Fizz
Results:  4
Results:  5 Buzz
Results:  6 Fizz
Results:  7
Results:  8
Results:  9 Fizz
Results:  10 Buzz
Results:  11
Results:  12 Fizz
Results:  13
Results:  14
Results:  15 FizzBuzz

Program exited.
```

Figure 5.7: Output for the fizzBuzz function with return values

In this exercise, we saw how we can return multiple values from a function. We were able to assign variables to the multiple return values from the function. We also noticed that the assigned variables to the function match the order of the return values. In the following section, we will learn that in the body of the function, we can perform naked returns, where we do not need to specify the variable being returned in our return statement.

Activity 5.01: Calculating the Working Hours of Employees

In this activity, we shall be creating a function that will calculate the working hours of employees for a week, which shall be used to calculate the payable salary amount. The developer struct has a field called Individual that is of type Employee. The developer struct keeps track of the HourlyRate that they charge and how many hours they work each day. The following steps shall help you to reach the solution:

1. Create an Employee type that has the following fields: Id as int, FirstName as string, and LastName as string.

2. Create a developer type that has the following fields: Individual Employee, HourlyRate int, and WorkWeek [7]int.

3. Create an enum for the seven days of the week. This will be of type Weekday int with a constant declaration for each day of the week.

4. Create a pointer receiver method called LogHours for Developer that will take the WeekDay type and int type as input. Assign the hours worked that day to the Developer workweek slice.

5. Create a method that is a pointer receiver called HoursWorked(). This method will return the total hours that have been worked.

6. In the main() function, initialize and create a variable of the Developer type.

7. In the LogHours method, call the method for two days (such as Monday and Tuesday).

8. Print the hours for the two days of the previous step.

9. Next, print the results of the **HoursWorked** method.

The following is the expected output:

```
Hours worked on Monday:   8
Hours worked on Tuesday:   10
Hours worked this week:   18
```

> **Note**
>
> The solution for this activity can be found on page 704.

The aim of this activity is to demonstrate the ability to break problems down into manageable tasks to be implemented by functions, such that each of our functions has a single responsibility. **LogHours** is responsible for assigning the hours worked for each day. **HoursWorked** uses the values that were assigned in **LogHours** to display the hours worked each day. We have used return types from our functions to display the data. This exercise demonstrates utilizing functions correctly to provide a solution to a problem.

Naked Returns

> **Note**
>
> Functions that have return values must have a **return** statement as the last statement in the function. If you omit the return statement, the Go compiler will give you the following error: "missing return at the end of function."
>
> Typically, when a function returns two types, the second type is of type **error**. We have not gone over errors yet so in these examples, we are not demonstrating them. It is good to know that it is idiomatic in Go for the second return type to be of type **error**.

Go also allows the ability to ignore a variable being returned. For example, say we are not interested in the **int** value that is being returned from our **fizzBuzz** function. In Go, we can use what is called a blank identifier; it provides a way to ignore values in an assignment:

```
_, err := file.Read(bytes)
```

For example, when reading a file, we might not be concerned about the number of bytes read. So, in that case, we can ignore the value being returned by using the blank identifier, "_". When there is extra data being returned from a function that does not provide any information that is needed by our program, such as the reading of a file, it is a good candidate for ignoring the return.

> **Note**
>
> As you will discover later, many functions return an error as the second return value. You should not ignore return values from functions that are errors. Ignoring an error returned by a function could result in unexpected behavior. Error return values should be handled appropriately.

```
func main() {
    for i := 1; i <= 15; i++ {
        _, s := fizzBuzz(i)
        fmt.Printf("Results: %s\n",s)
    }
}
```

In the preceding example, we are using the blank identifier, _, to ignore the **int** value being returned:

```
    _, s := fizzBuzz(i)
```

You must always have a placeholder for the values being returned when assigning values from a function. When performing an assignment, the placeholders must match the number of return values from the function. _ and **s** are the placeholders for the return values of **int** and **string**.

Go also has a feature that allows you to name your returns. If you use this feature, it can make your code more readable as well as self-documenting. If you name your return variables, they are under the same constraints as the local variables, as discussed in the previous topic. By naming your returns, you are creating local variables in the function. You can then assign values to those return variables, just as you do with input parameters:

```
func greeting() (name string, age int){
    name = "John"
    age = 21
    return name, age
}
```

In the preceding code, (`name string, age int`) are named returns. They are now local variables to the function.

Since **name** and **age** are local variables that were declared in the return list of the function, you can now assign values to them. They can be treated as local variables. In the **return** statement, specify the return values. If you do not specify the variable name in the return, it is called a **naked return**:

```
func greeting() (name string, age int){
    name = "John"
    age = 21
    return
}
```

Consider the preceding code block. This code is the same as before with the exception that the return does not name the variables to return. The **return** statement will return the variables that are named in the return list.

One of the disadvantages of naked returns is that it can cause confusion when reading code. To avoid confusion and the possibility of other issues, it is recommended that you avoid using the naked returns feature. It can make it difficult to follow the variable that is to be returned. There can also be issues with shadowing when using naked returns:

```
func message() (message string, err error) {
    message = "hi"
    if message == "hi"{
        err := fmt.Errorf("say bye\n")
        return
    }
    return
}
```

The preceding code will result in the following error:

```
prog.go:15:7: err is shadowed during return
```

Figure 5.8: Output for shadowing with naked returns

That is because the **err** variable is named in the **return** and is initialized in an **if** statement. Recall that variables that are initialized within curly braces, such as **for** loops, **if** statements, and **switch** statements, are scoped to that context, meaning that they are only visible and accessible within those curly braces.

Exercise 5.04: Mapping a CSV Index to a Column Header with Return Values

In *Exercise 5.02*, *Mapping Index Values to Column Headers*, we only printed the results of the index to the column header. In this exercise, we are going to return the map as the result. The map being returned is the index-to-column header mapping. The following steps will help you with the solution:

1. Open the IDE of your choice.

2. Open the file from the previous exercise: **$GOPATH\functions\indxToColHdr\main.go**.

3. Enter the following code in **main.go**:

```
package main
import (
  "fmt"
  "strings"
)
```

4. Next, in the **main()** function, define the headers for the columns. First, we assign a variable to a key-value pair of **int** and **string**. **key(int)** will be the index of our **header(string)** column. The index will map to a column header:

```
func main() {
    hdr := []string{"empid", "employee", "address", "hours worked", "hourly
      rate", "manager"}
    result := csvHdrCol(hdr)
    fmt.Println("Result:")
    fmt.Println(result)
    fmt.Println()
    hdr2 := []string{"employee", "empid", "hours worked", "address",
      "manager", "hourly rate"}
    result2 := csvHdrCol(hdr2)
    fmt.Println("Result2:")
    fmt.Println(result2)
    fmt.Println()
}
func csvHdrCol(hdr []string) map[int]string {
    csvIdxToCol := make(map[int]string)
```

5. We range over the **header** to process each string that is in the slice:

```
for i, v := range hdr {
```

6. For each string, we remove any trailing spaces in front of and after the string. In general, we should always make the assumption that our data may have some erroneous characters:

```
v = strings.TrimSpace(v)
```

7. In our **switch** statement, we lower all the casing for exact matches. As you may recall, Go is a case-sensitive language. We need to ensure the casing is the same for matching purposes. When our code finds the header, it sets the index value for the header in the map:

```
switch strings.ToLower(v) {
    case "employee":
      csvIdxToCol[i] = v
    case "hours worked":
      csvIdxToCol[i] = v
    case "hourly rate":
      csvIdxToCol[i] = v
    }
  }
    return csvIdxToCol
}
```

8. Open up a terminal and navigate to the code's directory.

9. Run **go build** and run the executable.

    The expected output for return values is as follows:

```
Result1:
Map[1:employee 3:hours worked 4: hourly rate]
Result2:
Map[0:employee 2:hours worked 5: hourly rate]
```

In this exercise, we saw a real-world example of mapping a CSV index to column headers. We used a function to solve this complex problem. We were able to have the function have a single return value of type **map**. In the next section, we are going to see how functions can accept a variable number of argument values within a single argument.

Variadic Function

A variadic function is a function that accepts a variable number of argument values. It is good to use a variadic function when the number of arguments of a specified type is unknown.

```
func f(parameterName …Type)
```

The preceding function is an example of what a variadic function looks like. The three dots (...) in front of the type is called a **pack operator**. The pack operator is what makes it a variadic function. It tells Go to store all the arguments of `Type` into `parameterName`. The variadic variable can accept zero or more variables as the argument:

```go
func main() {
    nums(99,100)
    nums(200)
    nums()
}
func nums(i ...int) {
    fmt.Println(i)
}
```

The `nums` function is a variadic function that accepts a type of `int`. As stated before, you can pass zero or more arguments of the type. If there is more than one value, you separate them with a comma, as in `nums(99,100)`. If there is only one argument to pass, you only pass that argument, as in `nums(200)`. If there isn't an argument to pass, you can leave it empty, as in `nums()`.

Variadic functions can have other parameters. However, if your function requires multiple parameters, the variadic parameter must be the last parameter in the function. Also, there can only be one variadic variable per function. The following function is incorrect and will result in an error at compile time.

Incorrect function:

```go
package main
import "fmt"
func main() {
    nums(99, 100,"James")
}
func nums(i ...int,str person) {
    fmt.Println(str)
    fmt.Println(i)
}
```

```
./prog.go:8:11: syntax error: cannot use ... with non-final parameter i
```

Figure 5.9: Variadic syntax error output

Correct function:

```
package main
import "fmt"
func main() {
   nums("James",99, 100)
}
func nums(str string, i ...int) {
   fmt.Println(str)
   fmt.Println(i)
}
```

The output would look as follows:

```
James
[99 100]
```

You may have guessed by now that the actual type of **Type** inside the function is a slice. The function takes the arguments being passed in and converts them to the new slice being specified. For example, if the variadic type is **int**, then once you are inside the function, Go converts that variadic **int** to a slice of integers:

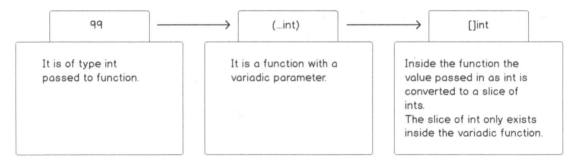

Figure 5.10: Conversion of a variadic int into a slice of integers

```
package main
import "fmt"
func main() {
   nums(99, 100)
}
func nums(i ...int) {
   fmt.Println(i)
   fmt.Printf("%T\n", i)
   fmt.Printf("Len: %d\n", len(i))
   fmt.Printf("Cap: %d\n", cap(i))
}
```

The variadic function's output is as follows:

```
[99 100]
[] int
Len: 2
Cap: 2
```

The **nums()** function is showing that the variadic type of **i** is a slice of integers. Once in the function, **i** will be a slice of integers. The variadic type has length and capacity, which is to be expected for a slice. In the next code snippet, we will try to pass a slice of integers to a variadic function, **nums()**:

```
package main
import "fmt"
func main() {
  i := []int{5,10,15}
  nums(i)
}
func nums(i ...int) {
  fmt.Println(i)
}
```

```
./prog.go:7:6: cannot use i (type []int) as type int in argument to nums
```

Figure 5.11: Variadic function error

Why didn't this code snippet work? We just proved that the variadic variable inside the function is of type **slice**. The reason is that the function is expecting a list of arguments of type **int** to be converted to a slice. Variadic functions work by converting the arguments passed to a slice of the type being specified. However, Go has a mechanism for passing a slice to a variadic function. We need to use the unpack operator; it is three dots (…). When you call a variadic function and you want to pass a slice as an argument to a variadic parameter, you need to place the three dots before the variable:

```
func main() {
  i := []int{5,10,15}
  nums(i…)
}
func nums(i ...int) {
  fmt.Println(i)
}
```

The difference between this version of the function and the previous is the calling code to the function, **nums**. The three dots are put after the **i** variable is a slice of integers. This allows a slice to be passed to the variadic function.

Exercise 5.05: Summing Numbers

In this exercise, we are going to sum up a variable number of arguments. We will pass the arguments as a list of arguments and as a slice. The return value will be an **int**, the sum of the values we passed to the function. The following steps will help you with the solution:

1. Open the IDE of your choice.

2. Create a new file and save it at **$GOPATH\functions\variadic\main.go**.

3. Enter the following code in **main.go**:

```
package main
import (
    "fmt"
)
func main() {
    i := []int{5, 10, 15}
    fmt.Println(sum(5, 4))
    fmt.Println(sum(i...))
}
```

4. The **sum** function accepts a variadic argument of type **int**. Since it gets converted to a slice, we can range over the values and return the sum of all the values that get passed:

```
func sum(nums ...int) int {
    total := 0
    for _, num := range nums {
        total += num
    }
    return total
}
```

5. Open up a terminal and navigate to the code's directory.

6. Run **go build** and run the executable.

   The expected output for summing numbers is as follows:

```
9
30
```

In this exercise, we saw that by using a variadic parameter, we can accept an unknown number of arguments. Our function allows us to sum up any number of integers. We can see that variadic parameters can be utilized to solve specific problems where the number of values of the same type being passed as an argument is unknown. In the next section, we are going to look at how to create a function without a name and assign a function to a variable.

Anonymous Functions

So far, we have been using named functions. As you may recall, named functions are functions that have an identifier or a function name. Anonymous functions can be declared within another function.

Anonymous functions, also referred to as function literals, are functions that do not have a function name, hence the name "anonymous functions." An anonymous function is declared in a similar way to how a named function is declared. The only difference with the declaration is that the name for the function is omitted. Anonymous functions can do basically whatever a normal function in Go does, including accepting arguments and returning values.

In this section, we will be introducing the fundamentals of anonymous functions and some of their basic uses. Later, you will also see how anonymous functions can be fully utilized. Anonymous functions are used for and in conjunction with the following:

- Closure implementations
- defer statements
- Defining a code block to be used with a Goroutine
- Defining a function for one-time use
- Passing a function to another function

    The following is a basic declaration for an anonymous function:

```
func main() {
  func() {
    fmt.Println("Greeting")
  }()
}
```

- Notice that we are declaring a function inside another function. As with named functions, you must start with the **func** keyword to declare a function.

- Following the **func** keyword would normally be the name of the function, but with anonymous functions, there is no function name. Instead, there are empty parentheses.

- The empty parentheses following the **func** keyword is where the function's parameters would be defined for the function.

- Next is the open curly brace, {, which starts the function body.

- The function body is only a one-liner; it will print "**Greeting**".

- The closing curly brace, }, denotes the end of the function.

- The last set of parentheses are called the execution parentheses. These parentheses invoke the anonymous function. The function will execute immediately. Later, we will see how to execute an anonymous function at a later location within the function.

  You can also pass arguments to an anonymous function. To be able to pass arguments to an anonymous function, they must be supplied in the execution parentheses:

```go
func main() {
    message := "Greeting"
    func(str string) {
        fmt.Println(str)
    }(message)
}
```

- **func (str string)**: The anonymous function being declared has an input parameter of type **string**.

- **} (message)**: The argument message being passed to the execution parentheses.

We have currently been executing anonymous functions at the moment they are declared, but there are other ways to execute anonymous functions. You can also save the anonymous function to a variable. This leads to a different set of opportunities that we will look at in this chapter:

```go
func main() {
    f := func() {
        fmt.Println("Executing an anonymous function using a variable")
    }
    fmt.Println("Line after anonymous function")
    f()
}
```

- We are assigning the **f** variable to our anonymous function.

- **f** is now of type **func()**.

- **f** now can be used to invoke the anonymous function, in a fashion similar to that for a named function. You must include the **()** after the **f** variable to execute the function.

Exercise 5.06: Creating an Anonymous Function to Calculate the Square Root of a Number

Anonymous functions are great for small snippets of code that you want to execute within a function. Here, we are going to create an anonymous function that is going to have an argument passed to it. It will then calculate the square root. The following steps will help you with the solution:

1. Use the IDE of your choice.

2. Create a new file and save it at **$GOPATH\functions\anonymousfnc\main.go**.

3. Enter the following code in **main.go**. We are assigning our **x** variable to our anonymous function. Our anonymous function takes a parameter, (**i int**). It also returns a value of **int**:

```
package main
import (
  "fmt"
)
func main() {
   j := 9
   x := func(i int)int {
     return i * i
   }
```

4. Notice that the last curly brace does not have the **()** to execute the function. We call our anonymous function using **x(j)**:

```
fmt.Printf("The square of %d is %d\n", j, x(j))
   }
```

5. Open up a terminal and navigate to the code's directory.

6. Run **go build** and run the executable.

   The expected output is as follows:

```
The square of 9 is 81
```

In this exercise, we saw how to assign a variable to a function and later call that function by using the variable that was assigned to it. We saw that when we need a small function that might not be reusable in our program, we can create an anonymous function and assign it to a variable. In the next section, we are going to expand the use of anonymous functions into closures.

Closures

We have introduced anonymous function syntax using some basic examples. Now that we have a fundamental understanding of how anonymous functions work, we will look at how we can use this powerful concept. Closures are a form of anonymous functions. Regular functions cannot reference variables outside of themselves; however, an anonymous function can reference variables external to their definition. A closure can use variables declared at the same level as the anonymous function's declared. These variables do not need to be passed as parameters. The anonymous function has access to these variables when it is called:

```go
func main() {
    i := 0
    incrementor := func() int {
        i +=1
        return i
    }
    fmt.Println(incrementor())
    fmt.Println(incrementor())
    i +=10
    fmt.Println(incrementor())
}
```

Code synopsis:

1. We initialize a variable in the **main()** function called **i** and set it to **0**.

2. We assign **incrementor** to our anonymous function.

3. The anonymous function increments **i** and returns it. Notice that our function does not have any input parameters.

4. We then print the results of **incrementor** twice and get **1** and **2**.

5. Notice that outside our function we increment **i** by **10**. This is a problem. We want **i** to be isolated and for it not to change, as this is not the desired behavior. When we print the results of **incrementor** again, it will be **13**. We want it to be **3**. We will correct this in our next example.

One problem with the previous example that we notice is that any code in the main function has access to **i**. As we saw in the example, **i** can be accessed and changed outside of our function. This is not the desired behavior; we want the incrementor to be the only one to change that value. In other words, we want **i** to be protected from other functions changing it. The only function that should be changing it is our anonymous function when we call it:

```go
func main() {
    increment := incrementor()
    fmt.Println(increment())
    fmt.Println(increment())
}
func incrementor() func() int {
    i :=0
    return func() int {
        i += 1
        return i
    }
}
```

Code synopsis:

1. We declared a function called **incrementor()**. This function has a return type of **func() int**.

2. **i := 0**: We initialize our variable at the level of the **incrementor()** function; this is similar to what we did in the previous example, except it was at the **main()** function level and anyone at that level had access to **i**. Only the **incrementor()** function has access to the **i** variable with this implementation.

3. We are returning our anonymous function, **func() int**, which increments the **i** variable.

4. In the **main()** function, **increment:=incrementor()** assigns a variable to the **func() int** that gets returned. It is important to note that **incrementor()** only gets executed once here. In our **main()** function, it is no longer being referenced or executed.

5. **Increment()** is of type **func() int**. Each call to **increment()** runs the anonymous function code. It is referencing the **i** variable, even after **incrementor()** has executed.

Exercise 5.07: Creating a Closure Function to Decrement a Counter

In this exercise, we are going to create a closure that decrements from a given starting value. We are combining what we have learned about passing an argument to an anonymous function and using that knowledge with a closure. The following steps will help you with the solution:

1. Open the IDE of your choice.

2. Create a new file and save it at **$GOPATH\closureFnc\variadic\main.go**.

3. Enter the following code in **main.go**:

```
func main() {
import "fmt"
   counter := 4
```

4. We will look at the **decrement** function first. It takes an argument of type **int** and has a return value of **func()int**. In previous examples, the variable was declared inside the function but before the anonymous function. In this exercise, we have it as an input parameter:

```
x:= decrement(counter)
   fmt.Println(x())
   fmt.Println(x())
   fmt.Println(x())
   fmt.Println(x())
}
```

5. We decrement **i** by one inside the anonymous function:

```
func decrement(i int) func() int {
```

6. In the **main()** function, we initialize a variable counter to be used as our starting integer to be decremented:

```
return func() int {
```

7. **x:= decrement(counter)** : x is assigned to **func() int**. Each call to **x()** runs the anonymous function:

```
      i --
      return i
   }
}
```

8. Open up a terminal and navigate to the code's directory.

9. Run **go build** and run the executable.

The expected output for the **decrement** counter is as follows:

```
3
2
1
0
```

In this exercise, we saw that closures have access to variables that are external to them. This allowed our anonymous function to make changes to the variable that a normal function would not be able to make. In the next section, we are going to look at how functions can be passed as arguments to another function.

Function Types

As we have seen so far, Go has rich feature support for functions. In Go, functions are types too, just like **int**, **string**, and **bool** are types. This means we can pass functions as arguments to other functions, functions can be returned from a function, and functions can be assigned to variables. We can even define our own function types. A function's type signature defines the types of its input parameters and return values. For a function to be of the type of another function, it must have the exact signature of the type function that is declared. Let's examine a few function types:

```
type message func()
```

The preceding code snippet creates a new function type called message. It has no input parameters and does not have any return types.

Let's examine another one:

```
type calc func(int, int) string
```

The preceding code snippet creates a new function type called calc. It accepts two arguments of type int and its return value is of type string.

Now that we have a fundamental understanding of function types, we can write some code to demonstrate their uses:

```
package main
import (
    "fmt"
)
type calc func(int, int) string
func main() {
    calculator(add, 5, 6)
}
```

```
func add(i, j int) string {
    result := i + j
    return fmt.Sprintf("Added %d + %d = %d", i, j, result)
}
func calculator(f calc, i, j int) {
    fmt.Println(f(i, j))
}
```

Let's look at the code by the line:

```
type calc func(int, int) string
```

type calc declares **calc** to be of type **func**, determining that it takes two integers as arguments and returns a string:

```
func add(i, j int) string {
    result := i + j
    return fmt.Sprintf("Added %d + %d = %d", i, j, result)
}
```

func add(i,j int) string has the same signature as type **calc**. It takes two integers as arguments and returns a string stating "Adding **i + j = result**". Functions can be passed to other functions just like any other type in Go:

```
func calculator(f calc, i, j int) {
    fmt.Println(f(i, j))
}
```

func calculator(f calc, i, j int) accepts type **calc** as input. The **calc** type, as you may remember, is a function type that has input parameters of **int** and a return type of **string**. Anything that matches that signature can be passed to the function. The **func calculator** function returns the result of the function of type **calc**.

In the **main** function, we call **calculator(add,5,6)**. We are passing it the **add** function. **add** satisfies the signature of type **calc func**.

Figure 5.12 summarizes each of the preceding functions and how they relate to each other. The figure shows how **func add** is of type **func calc**, which then allows it to be passed as an argument to **func calculator**:

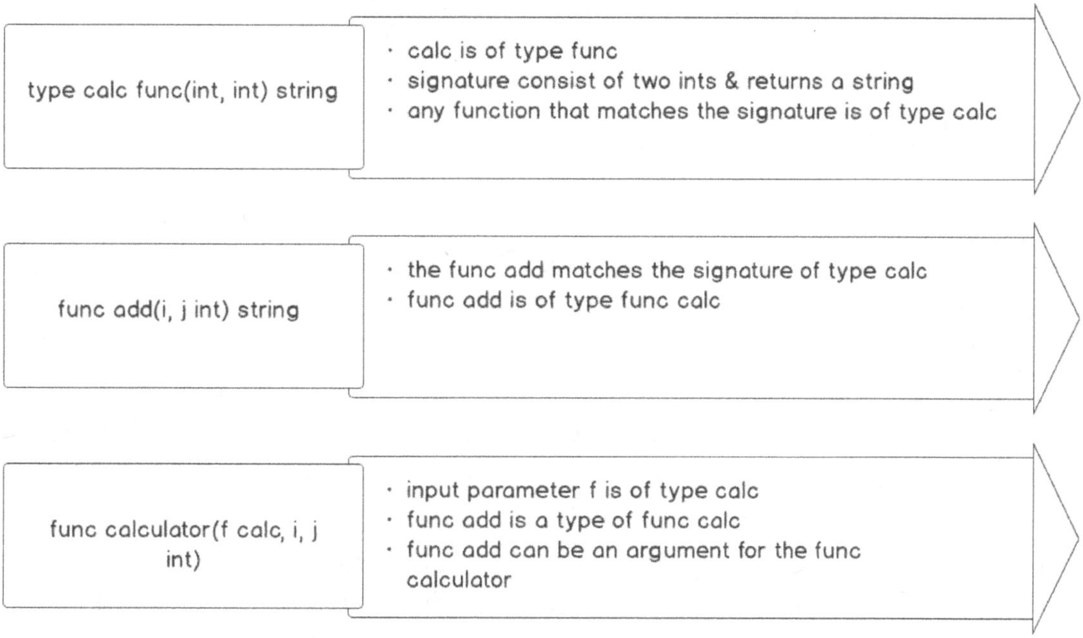

Figure 5.12: Function types and uses

We have just seen how to create a function type and pass it as an argument to a function. It is not that far of a stretch to pass a function as a parameter to another function. We will change our previous example slightly to reflect passing a function as a parameter:

```
func main() {
  calculator(add,5,6)
  calculator(subtract,10,5)
}
func calculator(f func(int,int)int, i, j int) {
  fmt.Println(f(i, j))
}
func add(i, j int) int {
  return i + j
}
func subtract(i, j int) int {
  return i - j
}
```

- We modify the **add** function signature to return an **int** instead of a string.

- We added a second function called **subtract**. Note that its function signature is the same as that of the **add** function. The **subtract** function simply returns the result of subtracting two numbers:

```
func calculator(f func(int,int)int, i, j int) {
   fmt.Println(f(i, j))
}
```

- **calculator(f func(int,int)int,i,j int)**: The **calculator** function now has an input parameter of type **func** The input parameter, **f**, is a function that accepts two integers and returns an **int**. Any function that satisfies the signature can be passed to the function.

- In the **main()** function, **calculator** is called twice: once with the **add** function and some integer values being passed and once with the **subtract** function being passed as an argument with some integer values.

The ability to pass functions as a type is a very powerful feature that can pass different functions to other functions as long as their signatures match the passed-to function's input parameter. It is quite simple when you think about it. An integer type for a function can be any value as long as it is an integer. The same goes for passing functions: a function can be any value as long as it is the correct type.

A function can also be returned from another function. We saw this when using anonymous functions combined with closures. Here, we will take a brief look since we have already seen this syntax in a previous section:

```
package main
import "fmt"
func main() {
   v:= square(9)
   fmt.Println(v())
   fmt.Printf("Type of v:   %T",v)
}
func square(x int) func() int {
   f := func() int {
      return x * x
   }
   return f
}
```

Returning a function looks as follows:

```
81
Type of v: func() int
```

- **square(x int) func() int**: The **square** function accepts an **int** as an argument and returns a function type that returns an **int**:

```
func square(x int) func() int {
  f := func() int {
    return x * x
  }
  return f
}
```

- In the **square** body, we assign a variable, **f**, to an anonymous function that returns the square value of the input parameter, **x**.

- The **return** statement for the **square** function returns an anonymous function that is of type **func() int**.

- **v** is assigned to the return of the **square** function. As you may recall, the return value is of type **func() int**.

- **v** has been assigned type **func ()int**; however, it has not been invoked. We will invoke it inside the **print** statement.

- **fmt.Printf("Type of v: %T",v)**: This statement just prints out the type for **v**, which is **func()int**.

Exercise 5.08: Creating Various Functions to Calculate Salary

We are going to be creating several functions. We need the ability to calculate the salary of a developer and a manager. We want this solution to be extensible for the future possibilities of other salaries to be calculated. We will be creating functions to calculate the developer and manager salary. Then we will create another function that will take the previously mentioned function as input parameter. The following steps will help you with the solution:

1. Use the IDE of your choice.

2. Create a new file and save it at **$GOPATH\function\funcAsParam\main.go**.

3. Enter the following code in **main.go**:

```
package main
import "fmt"
func main() {
    devSalary := salary(50,2080, developerSalary)
    bossSalary := salary(150000,25000,managerSalary)
    fmt.Printf("Boss salary: %d\n",bossSalary)
    fmt.Printf("Developer salary: %d\n",devSalary)
}
```

4. The **salary** function accepts a function that accepts two integers as arguments and returns an int. So, any function that matches that signature can be passed as an argument to the **salary** function:

```
func salary(x,y int, f func(int,int)int)int{
```

5. In the body of the **salary()** function, **pay** is assigned the value that gets returned from the **f** function. It passes **x** and **y** parameters as parameters to the **f** parameter:

```
    pay := f(x,y)
    return pay
}
```

6. Notice that the **managerSalary** and **developerSalary** signatures are identical and they match the function **f** for **salary**. This means that both **managerSalary** and **developerSalary** can be passed as **func(int,int) int**:

```
func managerSalary(baseSalary,bonus int) int {
    return baseSalary + bonus
}
```

7. **devSalary** and **bossSalary** get assigned to the results of the **salary** function. Since **developerSalary** and **managerSalary** satisfy the signature of **func(int,int) int**, they each can be passed in as arguments:

```
func developerSalary(hourlyRate,hoursWorked int) int {
    return hourlyRate * hoursWorked
}
```

8. Open a terminal and navigate to the code's directory.

9. Run **go build** and run the executable.

The expected output is as follows:

```
Boss salary: 175000
Developer salary: 104000
```

In this exercise, we saw how a function type can be a parameter for another function. This allows a function to be an argument to another function. This exercise showed how our code can be simplified by having one **salary** function. If, in the future, we need to calculate the salary for a tester position, we would only need to create a function that matches the function type for **salary** and pass it as an argument. The flexibility that this gives is that we do not have to change our **salary** function's implementation. In the next section, we are going to see how we can change the execution flow of a function, specifically after the function returns.

defer

The defer statement defers the execution of a function until the surrounding function returns. Let's try to explain this a bit better. Inside a function, you have a **defer** in front of a function that you are calling. That function will execute essentially right before the function you are currently inside completes. Still confused? Perhaps an example will make this concept a little clearer:

```
package main
import "fmt"
func main() {
  defer done()
  fmt.Println("Main:  Start")
  fmt.Println("Main:  End")
}
func done() {
  fmt.Println("Now I am done")
}
```

The output for the **defer** example is as follows:

```
Main: Start
Main: End
Now I am done
```

Inside the **main()** function, we have a deferred function, **defer done()**. Notice that the **done()** function has no new or special syntax. It just has a simple print to **stdout**.

Next, we have two print statements. The results are interesting. The two **print** statements in the **main()** function print first. Even though the deferred function was first in **main()**, it printed last. Isn't that interesting? Its ordering in the **main()** function did not dictate its order of execution.

The deferred functions are commonly used for performing "clean-up" activities. That would include the release of resources, the closing of files, the closing database connections, and the removal of configuration\temp files created by a program. The **defer** functions are also used to recover from a panic; this is discussed in a later chapter.

Using the **defer** statement is not limited to just named functions. In fact, you can utilize the defer statement with anonymous functions. Taking our previous code snippet, let's turn it into deferred call with an anonymous function:

```
package main
import "fmt"
func main() {
   defer func(){
      fmt.Println("Now I am done")
   }()
   fmt.Println("Main:  Start")
   fmt.Println("Main:  End")
}
```

- There is not much that has changed from the previous code. We took the code that was in the **done** function and created a deferred anonymous function.

- The **defer** statement is placed before the **func()** keyword. Our function has no function name. As you may recall, a function without a name is an anonymous function.

- The results are the same as those from the previous example. The readability, to a certain extent, is easier than having the deferred function declared as a named function, as in the previous example.

It is also possible and common to have multiple **defer** statements in a function. However, they may not execute in the order that you expect. When using **defer** statements in front of functions, the execution follows the order of **First In Last Out (FILO)**. Think of it as how you would stack plates. The first plate to start the stack will have a second plate placed on it, the second plate will have a third plate placed on it, and so on. The first plate to get taken off the stack is the last plate that was placed on the stack. The first plate that was placed to start the stack will be the last plate to come off the stack. Let's look at an example that declares multiple anonymous functions with the **defer** statement placed in front of them:

```
package main
import "fmt"
func main() {
   defer func() {
```

```
      fmt.Println("I was declared first.")
    }()
    defer func() {
      fmt.Println("I was declared second.")
    }()
    defer func() {
      fmt.Println("I was declared third.")
    }()
    f1 := func() {
      fmt.Println("Main:   Start")
    }
    f2 := func() {
      fmt.Println("Main:   End")
    }
    f1()
    f2()
}
```

The multiple **defer** output looks as follows:

```
Main: Start
Main: End
I was declared third.
I was declared second.
I was declared first.
```

- The first three anonymous functions are having their execution deferred.

- We declare **f1** and **f2** of type **func()**. These two functions are anonymous functions.

- As you can see, our **f1()** and **f2()** executed as expected, but the order of the multiple **defer** statements executed in the reverse order of how they were declared in the code. The first **defer** was the last to execute and the last **defer** was the first to execute.

Careful consideration must be given when using **defer** statements. A situation that you should consider is when you use **defer** statements in conjunction with variables. When a variable is passed to a deferred function, the variable's value at that time is what will be used in the deferred function. If that variable is changed after the deferred function, it will not be reflected when the deferred function runs:

```
func main() {
    age := 25
    name := "John"
    defer personAge(name, age)
```

```
    age *= 2
    fmt.Printf("Age double %d.\n",age)
}
func personAge(name string,i int) {
    fmt.Printf("%s is %d.\n", name,i)
}
```

The output would be as follows:

```
Age double 50.
John is 25.
```

- **age:= 25**: We initialize the **age** variable to **25** before the **defer** function.

- **name:= "John"**: We initialize the **name** variable to **"John"** before the **defer** function.

- **defer personAge(name,age)**: We state that the function is going to be deferred.

- **age*=2**: We double the age after the deferred function. We then print the current value of **age** doubled.

- **personAge(name string, i int)**: This is the function that is deferred; it only prints out the person and age.

- The results show the value of **age** (**25**) after it has been doubled in the **main** function.

- When the execution of the program reaches the line that has **defer personAge(name,age)**, the value of **age** is **25**. Before the **main()** function completes, the deferred function runs and the value of **age** is still **25**. Variables used in the deferred function are the values before it was deferred, regardless of what happens after it.

Activity 5.02: Calculating Payable Amount for Employees Based on Working Hours

This activity is based on the previous activity. We will keep the same functionality but we will be adding three additional features. In this version of the application, we would like to give the employee the ability to track their hours throughout the day without having logged them yet. This will allow the employees to keep better track of their hours before they log them at the end of the day. We are also enhancing the application to calculate the employee's pay. The application will calculate their pay for any overtime they worked. The application will also print out details of how many hours were worked each day:

1. Create a function called **nonLoggedHours() func(int) int**. Each time this function is called, it will calculate the hours of the employee that have not been logged. You will be using a closure inside the function.

2. Create a method called **PayDay()(int,bool)**. This method will calculate the weekly pay. It needs to take into consideration overtime pay. The method will pay twice the hourly rate for hours greater than 40. The function will return **int** as the weekly pay and **bool** for if the pay is overtime pay. The Boolean will be true if the employee worked more than **40** hours and false if they worked less than **40** hours.

3. Create a method called **PayDetails()**. This method will print each day and the hours worked that day by the employee. It will print the total hours for the week, the pay for the week, and if the pay contains overtime pay.

4. Inside of the **main** function, initialize a variable of type **Developer**. Assign a variable to **nonLoggedHours**. Print the variable assigned to **nonLoggedHours** with values of **2**, **3**, and **5**.

5. Also, in the **main()** function, log the hours for the following days: Monday 8, Tuesday 10, Wednesday 10, Thursday 10, Friday 6, and Saturday 8.

6. Then run the **PayDetails()** method.

   The following is the expected output:

```
Tracking hours worked thus far today:  2
Tracking hours worked thus far today:  5
Tracking hours worked thus far today:  10

Sunday hours:  0
Monday hours:  8
Tuesday hours:  10
Wednesday hours:  10
Thursday hours:  10
Friday hours:  6
Saturday hours:  8

Hours worked this week:  52
Pay for the week: $ 544
Is this overtime pay:  true
```

Figure 5.13: Output for payable amount activity

Note

The solution for this activity can be found on page 706.

The aim of this activity is to go a step further than *Activity 5.01, Calculating the Working Hours of Employees*, by using some more advanced programming with Go's functions. In this activity, we will continue to use functions as we did previously; however, we will be returning multiple values and returning a function from a function. We also demonstrate the use of closures for calculating hours not logged by an employee.

Summary

We have studied why and how functions are an essential part of the Go programming language. We also discussed various features of functions in Go that make Go stand apart from other programming languages. Go has features that allow us to solve a lot of real-world problems. Functions in Go serve many purposes, including enhancing the usage and readability of code. We learned how to create and call functions. We studied the various types of functions used in Go and discussed scenarios where each of the function types can be used. We also expounded the concept of closures. Closures are essentially a type of anonymous function that can use variables declared at the same level as that at which the anonymous function was declared. We also discussed various parameters and return types and studied `defer`.

In the next chapter, we shall be exploring errors and error types and learning how to build custom errors, thus building a recovery mechanism to handle errors in Go.

6

Errors

Overview

In this chapter, we will be looking at various code snippets from the Go standard packages to get an understanding of Go's idiomatic way of performing error handling. We will also look at how to create custom error types in Go and see examples in the standard library.

By the end of this chapter, you will be able to distinguish between the different types of errors and compare error handling and exception handling. You will also be able to create error values and use `panic()` to handle errors and recover after a panic.

Introduction

In the previous chapter, we learned about creating functions. We also discovered that functions can be passed as parameters and returned from a function. In this chapter, we will work with errors and learn how to return those from functions.

Developers are not perfect and, by extension, neither is the code that they produce. All software at some point in time has had errors. Handling errors is critical when you are developing software. These errors can have a negative impact of varying degrees on its users. The impact on the users of your software can be more far-reaching than you realize.

For instance, let's consider the Northeast Blackout of 2003. On August 14, there was a blackout for about 50 million people in the United States and Canada that lasted for 14 days. This was due to a race condition bug in the alarm system in a control room. Technically, a race condition bug is when two separate threads try to access the same memory location for a write operation. This race condition can cause a program to crash. In this instance, it resulted in over 250 power plants going offline. One way to handle a race condition is to ensure proper synchronization between the various threads and allow memory locations to be accessed for write operations by only one thread at a time. It is important that we, as developers, ensure proper handling of errors. If we do not handle errors properly, this can have a negative impact on the users of our application and their way of life, as seen by the power outage incident we described.

In this chapter, we will be looking at what an error is, what an error looks like in Go, and, more specifically, how to handle errors the Go way. Let's get started!

What Are Errors?

An error is something that causes your program to produce unintended results. Those unintended results could range from the application crashing, incorrect data calculation (such as a bank transaction not being processed correctly), or not providing any results. These unintended results are referred to as software bugs. Any software would contain errors during its lifetime due to numerous scenarios that programmers do not anticipate. The following are possible outcomes when errors occur:

- The erroneous code could cause the program to crash without warning.

- The output of the program was not the intended result.

- An error message is displayed.

There are three types of errors that you might encounter:

- Syntax errors
- Runtime errors
- Semantic errors

Syntax Errors

Syntax errors result from improper use of the programming language. This often occurs due to mistyping the code. Most modern IDEs will have some visual way of bringing syntax errors to the attention of the programmer; for example, refer to *Figure 6.1*. In most modern IDEs, syntax errors can be caught at an early stage. They may occur more frequently when you are learning a new programming language. A few occurrences of syntax errors could be due to the following:

- Incorrect use of syntax for a loop
- Misplacing or omitting curly braces, parentheses, or brackets
- Misspelled function names or package names
- Passing the wrong type of argument to a function

Here is an example of a syntax error:

```
package main
import (
    "fmt"
)
func main() {
    fmt.println("Enter your city:")
}
```

The output appears as follows:

```
fmt.println("Enter your city:")

cannot refer to unexported name fmt.println
undefined: fmt.println
```

Go is case sensitive, so, **println** should be **Println**.

Runtime Errors

These errors occur when the code is asked to perform a task that it cannot do. Unlike syntax errors, these are typically only found during the execution of the code.

The following are common examples of runtime errors:

- Opening a connection to a database that does not exist

- Performing a loop that is bigger than the number of elements in the slice or array you are iterating over

- Opening a file that does not exist

- Performing a mathematical operation, such as dividing a number by zero

Exercise 6.01: Runtime Errors While Adding Numbers

In this exercise, we are going to write a simple program that sums up a slice of numbers. This program will demonstrate an example of a runtime error and will crash when it is executed.

1. Inside **$GOPATH**, create a directory called *Exercise6.01*.

2. Create a file called **main.go** inside the directory created in *step 1*.

3. This program will be in **package main**. Import the **fmt** package:

```
package main
import "fmt"
```

4. Inside the **main** function, we will have a slice of integers that will have four elements:

```
func main() {
   nums := []int{2, 4, 6, 8}
```

5. We will have a variable, **total**, to be used for the calculation of summing all the integer variables in the slice. Use a **for** loop to sum the variables:

```
total := 0
for i := 0; i <= 10; i++ {
   total += nums[i]
}
```

6. Next, we print the results of the total:

```
fmt.Println("Total: ", total)
}
```

We have introduced an example of a runtime error to the program; so, we will not get the following output:

```
Total: 20
```

7. At the command line, navigate to the directory created in *step 1*.

8. At the command line, type the following:

```
go build
```

The **go build** command will compile your program and create an executable named after the directory you created in *step 1*.

9. Type the name of the file created in *step 8* and hit *Enter* to run the executable:

```
panic: runtime error: index out of range [4] with length 4

goroutine 1 [running]:
main.main()
        /tmp/sandbox265689164/prog.go:9 +0x120
```

Figure 6.1: Output after executing

As you can see, the program crashed. The **index out of range** panic is a common error to new Go developers and veterans alike.

In this example, the error, a panic (we will discuss what a panic is later in the chapter) in this program, is the result of iterating in the **for** loop by a greater number, in our case 10, than the actual number of elements in the slice, in our case 4. One possible solution would be to use a **for** loop with a range:

```
package main
import "fmt"
func main() {
  nums := []int{2, 4, 6, 8}
  total := 0
  for i := range nums {
    total += nums[i]
  }
  fmt.Println("Total: ", total)
}
```

In this exercise, we saw how we can avoid runtime errors by paying attention to minute details.

Semantic Errors

Syntax errors are the easiest to debug, followed by runtime errors, while logic errors are the hardest. Semantic errors are sometimes very hard to spot at first. For example, in 1998, when the Mars Climate Orbiter was launched, its purpose was to study the climate of Mars, but due to a logic error in the system, the Mars Climate Orbiter, valued at $235 million, was destroyed. After some analysis, it was discovered that the calculations of units on the ground controller system were done in imperial units and the software on the Orbiter was done in metric units. This is a logic error that caused the navigation system to incorrectly calculate its maneuvers in space. As you can see, these are defects in the way the code is processing elements of your program. Reasons for semantic errors to occur could be because of:

- Incorrect computations
- Accessing incorrect resources (files, databases, servers, variables, and so on)
- Incorrect setting of variables for negation (not equal versus equal)

Exercise 6.02: Logic Error with Walking Distance

We are writing an application that will determine whether we should walk to our destination or take a car. If our destination is greater than or equal to 2 km, we are going to take a car. If it is less than 2 km, then we will walk to our destination. We are going to demonstrate a semantic error with this program.

The expected output of this exercise is as follows:

```
Take the car
```

1. Create a directory called *Exercise6.02* inside your **$GOPATH**.

2. Save a file called **main.go** inside the directory created in *step 1*. This program will be inside **package main**.

3. Import the **fmt** package:

```
package main
import "fmt"
```

4. Inside of the **main** function, display a message to take the car when **km** is greater than 2, and when **km** is less than 2, to send a message for walking:

```
func main() {
  km := 2
  if  km > 2 {
    fmt.Println("Take the car")
  } else {
```

```
        fmt.Println("Going to walk today")
    }
}
```

5. At the command line, navigate to the directory created in *step 1*.

6. At the command line, type the following:

```
go build
```

The **go build** command will compile your program and create an executable named after the directory you created in *step 1*.

7. Type the name of the file created in *step 6* and hit *Enter* to run the executable. You will get the following output:

```
Going to walk today
```

The program runs with no errors, but the message displayed is not what was expected.

As previously stated, the program runs with no errors, but the results are not what we expected. This is because we have a logic error. Our **if** statement is not accounting for the **km** equal to **2**. It is only checking that the distance is greater than **2**. It is a simple fix. Replace the **>** with **>=** and now the program will give the results that we expect.

```
func main() {
    km := 2
    if  km >= 2 {
        fmt.Println("Take the car")
    } else {
        fmt.Println("Going to walk today")
    }
}
```

This simple program made it easy to debug the logic error, but these types of errors in a larger program may not be as easy to spot.

We will mainly be focusing on the runtime errors in this chapter. It is good to understand the various types of errors that you as a programmer could encounter.

Error Handling Using Other Programming Languages

New programmers to Go who have a background in other programming languages will initially find Go's methodology for dealing with errors a bit odd. Go does not handle errors in the same fashion as other languages, such as Java, Python, C#, and Ruby. Those languages perform exception handling.

The following code snippets are some examples of how other languages handle errors by performing exception handling:

```
//java
try {
  // code
}catch (exception e){
  // block of code to handle the error
}
//python
try:
  //code
except:
  //code
else:
  try:
  // code
  except:
  // code
finally:
  //code
```

Typically, exceptions, if not handled, will crash your application. In most cases, exception handling tends to be implicit checking versus Go's explicit checking for errors returned by its functions. In the exception handling paradigm, anything can fail, and you must account for that. Each function can throw an exception, but you do not know what that exception could be.

In the error handling paradigm that Go uses, it is obvious when the programmer did not handle the error, because the function returns the error code, and you can see that they did not check for the error. We will be looking at the specifics of checking for the error code later in the chapter.

Most programming languages follow a similar pattern to the one shown in the previous code snippet. It is usually some sort of **try..catch..finally** block. One point of contention with the **try..catch..finally** block is that the control flow of the program execution gets interrupted and can follow a different path. This can sometimes lead to a number of logic errors and difficulty in the readability of the code. Here is a quick peek at how Go handles errors:

```
val, err:= someFunc() err
if err !=nil{
   return err
}
return nil
```

The preceding code snippet is a very simple syntax for handling the error. We will see this in much greater detail in the following topics. In this topic, we want to introduce you to the simplicity of how Go handles errors compared to the syntax of other languages.

Error Interface Type

What is an error in Go? An error in Go is a value. Here is a quote from Rob Pike, one of the pioneers of Go:

"Values can be programmed, and since errors are values, errors can be programmed. Errors are not like exceptions. There's nothing special about them, whereas an unhandled exception can crash your program."

Since errors are values, they can be passed into a function, returned from a function, and evaluated just like any other value in Go.

An error in Go is anything that implements the error interface. We need to look at some fundamental aspects that make up the error type in Go. To be an error type in Go, it must first satisfy the **type error interface**:

```
//https://golang.org/pkg/builtin/#error
type error interface {
  Error()string
}
```

The wonderful thing about Go is the simplistic design of the language features. This can easily be seen with the error interface. Go's standard library uses the error interface. To satisfy the error interface, only two things are required:

- The method name, **Error()**
- The **Error()** method to return a string

Those are the two requirements. It is important to understand that an error type is an interface type. Any value that is an error can be described as a string. When performing error handling in Go, the functions will return an error value. The Go language uses this throughout the standard library.

Look at the following code snippet for a starting discussion point on errors:

```go
package main
import (
    "fmt"
    "strconv"
)
func main() {
    v := "10"
    if s, err := strconv.Atoi(v); err == nil {
        fmt.Printf("%T, %v\n", s, s)
    }else{
        fmt.Println(err)
    }
    v = "s2"
    s, err := strconv.Atoi(v)
    if err != nil{
        fmt.Println(s, err)
    }
}
```

We will not go into every detail of the function but focus on the error portion of the code. In *Chapter 5, Functions*, we stated that functions can return multiple values. This is a powerful feature that most languages do not have. It is powerful, especially when dealing with error values. The **strconv.Atoi()** function returns an **int** and an error, as seen in the example stated previously. It is a function that is in the Go standard library (https://packt.live/2YvL1BV). For functions that return error values, it should be the last return value.

It is Go idiomatic to evaluate the error value for functions or methods that return an error. It is generally bad practice to not handle an error that is returned from the function. An error when returned and ignored can lead to lots of wasted debugging efforts. It can also cause unforeseen consequences in your program. If the value is not nil, then we have an error and must decide how we want to handle it. Depending on the scenario, we might want to:

- Return the error to the caller
- Log the error and continue execution

- Stop the execution of the program

- Ignore it (this is highly not recommended)

- Panic (only in very rare conditions, we will discuss this further later)

If the value of error is nil, that means there is no error. No further steps are necessary.

Let's look further into the standard package regarding the error type. We will start by looking at each piece of code in the https://packt.live/2rk6r8Z file.

```
type errorString struct {
s string
}
```

The **struct errorString** is in the **errors** package. The struct is used to store the string version of the error. The **errorString** has a single field of **s** that is of the **string** type. The **errorString** and the field are unexportable. This means that we can't access the **errorString** type or its field, **s**, directly. The following code gives an example of trying to access an unexported **errorString** type and its field, **s**:

```
package main
import (
  "errors"
  "fmt"
)
func main() {
  es := errors.errorString{}
  es.s = "slacker"
  fmt.Println(es)
}
```

```
./prog.go:9:8: cannot refer to unexported name errors.errorString
./prog.go:10:4: es.s undefined (cannot refer to unexported field or method s)
```

Figure 6.2: Expected output for unexported field

On the surface, it appears that **errorString** is neither accessible nor useful but we should keep digging. We are still in the standard library:

```
func (e *errorString) Error() string {
    return e.s
}
```

The **errorString** type has a method that implements the error interface. It satisfies requirements, a method called **Error()**, and it returns a string. The error interface has been satisfied. We now have access to the **errorString** field, **s**, through the **Error()** method. This is how an error gets returned within the standard library.

You should now have a basic understanding of what an error is in Go. Now, we should look at how to create our own error types in Go.

Creating Error Values

In the standard library, the package error has a method that we can use to create our own errors:

```
// https://golang.org/src/errors/errors.go
// New returns an error that formats as the given text.
func New(text string) error {
    return &errorString{text}
}
```

It is important to understand that the **New** function takes a string as an argument and converts it to *errors.**errorString** and returns as an error value. The underlying value of the error type that gets returned is of the *errors.**errorSting** type.

We can prove this by running the following code:

```
package main
import (
  "errors"
  "fmt"
)
func main() {
  ErrBadData := errors.New("Some bad data")
  fmt.Printf("ErrBadData type:  %T", ErrBadData)
}
```

Here is an example from Go's standard library, **http**, that uses the **errors** package to create package-level variables:

```
var (
    ErrBodyNotAllowed = errors.New("http: request method or response status
      code does not allow body")
    ErrHijacked = errors.New("http: connection has been hijacked")
    ErrContentLength = errors.New("http: wrote more than the declared Content-
      Length")
    ErrWriteAfterFlush = errors.New("unused")
)
```

When creating your own errors, it is idiomatic in Go to start with the **Err** variable.

Exercise 6.03: Creating an Application to Calculate Pay for the Week

In this exercise, we are going to create a function that calculates pay for the week. This function will accept two arguments, the hours worked during the week and the hourly rate. The function is going to check whether the two parameters meet the criteria for being valid. The function will need to calculate regular pay, which is hours less than or equal to 40, and overtime pay, which is hours greater than 40 for the week.

We will create two error values using **errors.New()**. The one error value will be used when there is an invalid hourly rate. An invalid hourly rate in our app is an hourly rate that is less than 10 or greater than 75. The second error value will be when hours per week are not between 0 and 80.

Use the IDE of your choice. One option would be Visual Studio Code.

1. Create a directory called *Exercise6.03* inside your **$GOPATH**.

2. Save a file called **main.go** inside the directory created in *step 1*. The **main.go** file will be in **package main**.

3. Import the two Go standard libraries, **errors** and **fmt**:

```
package main
import (
  "errors"
  "fmt"
)
```

4. Now we have declared our error variables using **errors.New()**. We use idiomatic Go for the variable name, starting it with **Err** and camel casing. Our error string is in lowercase with no punctuation:

```
var (
  ErrHourlyRate  = errors.New("invalid hourly rate")
  ErrHoursWorked = errors.New("invalid hours worked per week")
)
```

5. Inside the **main** function, we will be calling our **payday()** function three times. We declared our error variables using **errors.New()**:

```
pay, err := payDay(81, 50)
if err != nil {
  fmt.Println(err)
}
```

6. In the **main()** function, check each **err** after the function. If **err** is not nil, this means there is an error, and we will print that error.

    Create the **payDay** function to accept two arguments (**hoursWorked** and **hourlyRate**). The function will return an **int** and an error:

    ```go
    func payDay(hoursWorked, hourlyRate int) (int, error) {
      if hourlyRate < 10 || hourlyRate > 75 {
        return 0, ErrHourlyRate
      }
      if hoursWorked < 0 || hoursWorked > 80 {
        return 0, ErrHoursWorked
      }
      if hoursWorked > 40 {
        hoursOver := hoursWorked - 40
        overTime := hoursOver * 2
        regularPay := hoursWorked * hourlyRate
        return regularPay + overTime, nil
      }
      return hoursWorked * hourlyRate, nil
    }
    ```

7. We will use an **if** statement to check whether the hourly rate is less than 10 or greater than 75. If **hourlyRate** meets those conditions, we will return a **0** and our custom error, **ErrHourlyRate**. If **hourlyRate** does not meet those conditions, then the returned value will be **return hoursWorked * hourlyRate, nil**. We return **nil** for the error because there was no error:

    ```go
    func payDay(hoursWorked, hourlyRate int) (int, error) {
      if hourlyRate < 10 || hourlyRate > 75 {
        return 0, ErrHourlyRate
      }
      return hoursWorked * hourlyRate, nil
    }
    ```

8. In *step* 7, we validated **hourlyRate**. Now we will need to validate **hoursWorked**. We will add another **if** statement to the **payDay()** function that will check whether **hoursWorked** is less than **0** or greater than **80**. If the **hoursWorked** matches that condition, we will return **0** and the error, **ErrHoursWorked**:

    ```go
    func payDay(hoursWorked, hourlyRate int) (int, error) {
      if hourlyRate < 10 || hourlyRate > 75 {
        return 0, ErrHourlyRate
      }
    }
    ```

```go
    if hoursWorked < 0 || hoursWorked > 80 {
        return 0, ErrHoursWorked
    }
    return hoursWorked * hourlyRate, nil
}
```

9. In the previous two steps, we added **if** statements to validate the arguments being passed to the function. In this step, we will add another **if** statement to calculate overtime pay. Overtime pay is hours greater than **40**. The hours over **40** are double the **hourlyRate**. The hours less than or equal to **40** are at the **hourlyRate**:

```go
func payDay(hoursWorked, hourlyRate int) (int, error) {
    if hourlyRate < 10 || hourlyRate > 75 {
        return 0, ErrHourlyRate
    }
    if hoursWorked < 0 || hoursWorked > 80 {
        return 0, ErrHoursWorked
    }
    if hoursWorked > 40 {
        hoursOver := hoursWorked - 40
        overTime := hoursOver * 2
        regularPay := hoursWorked * hourlyRate
        return regularPay + overTime, nil
    }
    return hoursWorked * hourlyRate, nil
}
```

10. In the **main()** function, we will call the **payDay()** function three times with various arguments. We will check the error after each call and print the error message if applicable. If there is no error, then we print the pay for the week:

```go
func main() {
    pay, err := payDay(81, 50)
    if err != nil {
        fmt.Println(err)
    }
    pay, err = payDay(80, 5)
    if err != nil {
        fmt.Println(err)
    }
    pay, err = payDay(80, 50)
    if err != nil {
```

```
        fmt.Println(err)
    }
    fmt.Println(pay)
}
```

11. In the command line, navigate to the directory created in *step 1*.

12. In the command line, type the following:

```
go build
```

The **go build** command will compile your program and create an executable named after the directory you created in *step 1*.

13. Type the name of the file created in *step 12* and hit *Enter* to run the executable.

The expected output is as follows:

```
Invalid hours worked per week
Invalid hourly rate
4080
```

In this exercise, we saw how to create custom error messages that can be used to easily determine why the data was considered invalid. We also showed how to return multiple values from a function and to check for errors from the function. In the next topic, we will look at how to use panic in our applications.

Panic

Several languages use exceptions for handling errors. However, Go does not use exceptions, it uses something called panic. Panic is a built-in function that causes the program to crash. It stops the normal execution of the Goroutine.

In Go, panic is not the norm, unlike other languages where an exception is a norm. A panic signal indicates something abnormal that is occurring within your code. Usually, when panic is initiated by runtime or the developer, it is to protect the integrity of the program.

Errors and panics differ in their purposes and how they are handled by the Go runtime. An error in Go indicates that something unexpected occurred, but it will not adversely impact the integrity of the program. Go expects that the developer will handle the error properly. The function or other programs will not typically crash if you do not handle the error. However, panics differ in this regard. When panic occurs, it will ultimately crash the system unless there are handlers to handle the panic. If there are no handlers for the panic, it will go all the way up the stack and crash the program.

One example that we will look at later in this chapter is where panic occurs due to an index being out of range. This is typical when trying to access the index of a collection that doesn't exist. If Go did not panic in this case, it could have an adverse impact on the integrity of the program, such as other parts of the program trying to store or retrieve data that is not there in the collection.

> **Note**
>
> Review the topic of Goroutines. The `main()` function is a Goroutine. When panic occurs, you will see references to "Goroutine running" in the error message.

Panics can be initiated by the developer and can be caused during the execution of a program by runtime errors. A `panic()` function accepts an empty interface. For now, suffice to say, this means it can accept anything as an argument. However, in most cases, you should pass an error type to the `panic()` function. It is more intuitive to the user of our function to have some details on what caused the panic. Passing an error to the panic function is also idiomatic in Go. We will also see how recovering from a panic that has an error type passed to it gives us some different options when dealing with panic. When panic occurs, it will generally follow these steps:

- The execution is stopped
- Any deferred functions in the panicking function will be called
- Any deferred functions in the stack of the panicking function will be called
- It will continue all the way up the stack until it reaches `main()`
- Statements after the panicking function will not execute
- The program then crashes

Here is how panic works:

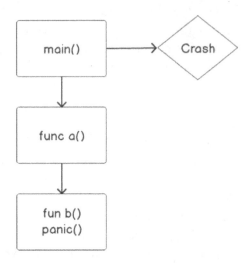

Figure 6.3: The working of panic

The preceding diagram illustrates code in the **main** function that calls function **a()**. Function **a()** then calls function **b()**. Inside of function **b()**, a panic occurs. The **panic()** function is not handled by any of the code upstream (function **a()** or the **main()** function), so the program will crash the **main()** function.

Here is an example of a panic that occurs in Go. Try to determine why this program panics.

```go
package main
import (
    "fmt"
)
func main() {
    nums := []int{1, 2, 3}
    for i := 0; i <= 10; i++ {
        fmt.Println(nums[i])
    }
}
```

An example of panic is as follows:

```
1
2
3
panic: runtime error: index out of range [3] with length 3

goroutine 1 [running]:
main.main()
          /tmp/sandbox076956134/prog.go:10 +0x100
```

Figure 6.4: Panic example

The panic runtime error is a common one that you will encounter while developing. It is an **index out of range** error. Go generated this panic because we are trying to iterate over a slice more times than there are elements. Go felt that this is a reason to panic because it puts the program in an abnormal condition.

Here is a snippet of code that demonstrates the basics of using a panic:

```go
package main
import (
  "errors"
  "fmt"
)
func main() {
  msg := "good-bye"
  message(msg)
  fmt.Println("This line will not get printed")
}
func message(msg string) {
  if msg == "good-bye" {
    panic(errors.New("something went wrong"))
  }
}
```

Code Synopsis:

- The function panics because the argument to the function message is **"good-bye"**.

- The **panic()** function will print the error message. Having a good error message helps with the debugging process.

- Inside the panic, we are using **errors.New()**, which we used in the previous topic to create an error type.

- As you can see, **fmt.Println()** does not get executed in the **main()** function. Since there are no **defer** statements, execution stops immediately.

The expected output for this code snippet is:

```
panic: something went wrong

goroutine 1 [running]:
main.message(...)
        /tmp/sandbox741915746/prog.go:16
main.main()
        /tmp/sandbox741915746/prog.go:10 +0x140
```

Figure 6.5: Panic example output

In the following code snippet, we will see how using **panic** and a **defer** statement functions together.

`main.go`

```
10 func test() {
11   n := func() {
12     fmt.Println("Defer in test")
13   }
14   defer n()
15   msg := "good-bye"
16   message(msg)
17 }
18 func message(msg string) {
19   f := func() {
20     fmt.Println("Defer in message func")
21   }
22   defer f()
23   if msg == "good-bye" {
24     panic(errors.New("something went wrong"))
```

The full code is available at https://packt.live/2qyujFg

The output of the panic example is as follows:

```
Defer in message func
Defer in test
panic: something went wrong

goroutine 1 [running]:
main.message(0x116057, 0x8)
        /tmp/sandbox806116420/prog.go:24 +0x140
main.test()
        /tmp/sandbox806116420/prog.go:16 +0x60
main.main()
        /tmp/sandbox806116420/prog.go:7 +0x20
```

Figure 6.6: Panic example output

Let's understand the code in parts:

- We will start examining the code in the **message()** function since that is where the panic starts. When the panic occurs, it runs the **defer** statement within the panicking function, **message()**.

- The deferred function, **func f()**, runs in the **message()** function.

- Going up the call stack, the next function is the **test()** function, and its deferred function, **n()**, will execute.

- Finally, we get to the **main()** function where the execution is stopped by the panicking function. The print statement in **main()** does not get executed.

> **Note**
>
> You may have seen **os.Exit()** used to stop execution of the program. **os.Exit()** stops execution immediately and returns a status code. No deferred statements are run when **os.Exit()** is performed. **Panic** is preferred over **os.Exit()** in certain cases. Panic will run deferred functions.

Exercise 6.04: Crashing the Program on Errors Using panic

We will be modifying *Exercise 6.03*, *Creating an Application to Calculate Pay for the Week*. Consider the following scenario, where the requirements have changed. We no longer need to return error values from our **payDay()** function. It has been decided that we cannot trust the user of the program to respond properly to the errors. There have been complaints of incorrect paychecks. We believe this is due to the caller of our function ignoring the errors being returned.

The **payDay()** function will only now return the pay amount and no errors. When the arguments provided to the function are invalid, instead of returning an error, the function will panic. This will cause the program to stop immediately and, therefore, not process a paycheck.

Use the IDE of your choice. One option could be Visual Studio Code.

1. Create a new file and save it in **$GOPATH\err\panicEx\main.go**.

2. Enter the following code in **main.go**:

```
package main
import (
  "fmt"
  "errors"
```

```
)
var (
    ErrHourlyRate  = errors.New("invalid hourly rate")
    ErrHoursWorked = errors.New("invalid hours worked per week")
)
```

3. Inside the **main** function, call the **payDay()** function, assign it to only one variable, **pay**, and then print it:

```
func main() {
    pay := payDay(81, 50)
    fmt.Println(pay)
}
```

4. Change the return type of the **payDay()** function to only return **int**:

```
func payDay(hoursWorked, hourlyRate int) int {
```

5. Inside the **payDay()** function, assign a variable, **report**, to an anonymous function. This anonymous function provides details of the arguments provided to the **payDay()** function. Even though we are not returning errors, this will provide some insight as to why the function panics. Since it is a deferred function, it will always execute before the function exits:

```
func payDay(hoursWorked, hourlyRate int) int {
    report := func() {
        fmt.Printf("HoursWorked: %d\nHourldyRate: %d\n", hoursWorked, hourlyRate)
    }
    defer report()
}
```

The business rule for valid **hourlyRate** and **hoursWorked** stays the same as in the previous exercise. Instead of returning an error, we will be using the **panic** function. When the data is invalid, we panic and pass the argument of **ErrHourlyRate** or **ErrHoursWorked**.

The arguments passed to the **panic()** function assist the user of our function in understanding the cause of the panic.

6. When panic occurs in the **payDay()** function, the **defer** function, **report()**, will give the caller some insight into why the panic occurred. The panic will bubble up the stack to the **main()** function and execution will stop immediately:

```
if hourlyRate < 10 || hourlyRate > 75 {
    panic(ErrHourlyRate)
}
if hoursWorked < 0 || hoursWorked > 80 {
```

```
        panic(ErrHoursWorked )
    }
    if hoursWorked > 40 {
        hoursOver := hoursWorked - 40
        overTime := hoursOver * 2
        regularPay := hoursWorked * hourlyRate
        return regularPay + overTime
    }
    return hoursWorked * hourlyRate
```

7. At the command line, navigate to the directory created in *step 1*.

8. At the command line, type the following:

```
go build
```

The **go build** command will compile your program and create an executable named after the directory you created in *step 1*.

9. Type the name of the file created in *step 8* and hit *Enter* to run the executable.

The expected output should be as follows:

```
HoursWorked: 81
HourldyRate: 50
panic: invalid hours worked per week

goroutine 1 [running]:
main.payDay(0x51, 0x32, 0x0, 0x28e8)
        /tmp/sandbox697228173/prog.go:28 +0x1e0
main.main()
        /tmp/sandbox697228173/prog.go:14 +0x40
```

Figure 6.7: Panic exercise output

In this exercise, we learned how to perform **panic** and pass an error to the **panic()** function. This aids the user of the function in gaining a good understanding of the cause of the panic. In the next topic, we will see how to regain control of the program after a panic occurs using **Recover**.

Recover

Go provides us with the ability to regain control after **panic** has occurred. Recover is a function that is used to regain control of a panicking Goroutine.

The signature of the **recover()** function is as follows:

```
func recover() interface{}
```

The **recover()** function accepts no arguments and returns an empty **interface{}**. For now, an empty **interface{}** indicates that any type can be returned. The **recover()** function will return the value sent to the **panic()** function.

The **recover()** function is only useful inside a deferred function. As you may recall, a deferred function gets executed before the encompassing function terminates. Executing a call to the **recover()** function inside a deferred function stops the panicking by restoring normal execution. If the **recover()** function is called outside a deferred function, it will not stop the panicking.

The following diagram shows the steps a program would take when using **panic()**, **recover()**, and a **defer()** function:

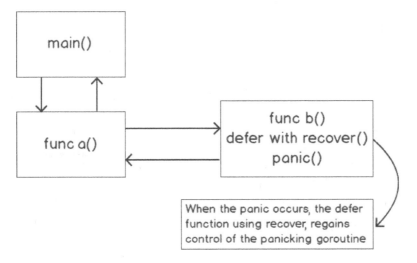

Figure 6.8: Recover function flow

The steps followed in the diagram can be explained as follows:

- The **main()** function calls **func a()**.

- **func a()** calls **func b()**.

- Inside **func b()**, there is a panic.

- The **panic()** function gets handled by a deferred function that is using the **recover()** function.

- The deferred function is the last function to execute inside **func b()**.

- The deferred function calls the **recover()** function.

- The call to **recover()** causes normal flow back to the caller, **func a()**.

- Normal flow continues, and control is finally back with the **main()** function.

The following code snippet mimics the behavior of the preceding diagram:

main.go

```
6  func main() {
7    a()
8    fmt.Println("This line will now get printed from main() function")
9  }
10 func a() {
11   b("good-bye")
12   fmt.Println("Back in function a()")
13 }
14 func b(msg string) {
15   defer func() {
16     if r:= recover(); r!= nil{
17       fmt.Println("error in func b()",r)
18     }
19   }()
```

The full code is available at https://packt.live/2E6j6ig

Code Synopsis

- The **main()** function calls function **a()**. The **a()** function calls function **b()**.

- Function **b()** accepts a string type and assigns it to the **msg** variable. If **msg** evaluates to **true** in the **if** statement, a panic will occur.

- The argument for the panic is a new error created by the **errors.New()** function:

```
if msg == "good-bye" {
    panic(errors.New("something went wrong"))
}
```

Once the panic occurs, the next call will be to the deferred function.

The deferred function uses the **recover()** function. The value of the panic is returned from recover; in this case, the value of **r** is an error type. Then, the function prints out some details:

```
defer func() {
    if r:= recover(); r!= nil{
        fmt.Println("error in func b()",r)
    }
}()
```

- The control flow goes back to function **a()**. Function **a()** prints out some details.

- Then, the control goes back to the **main()** function and it prints out some details and terminates:

```
error in func b() something went wrong
Back in function a()
This line will now get printed from main() function
```

Figure 6.9: Recover example output

Exercise 6.05: Recovering from a Panic

In this exercise, we will enhance our **payDay()** function to recover from a panic. When our **payDay()** function panics, we will inspect the error from that panic. Then, depending on the error, we will print an informative message to the user.

Use the IDE of your choice, one option would be Visual Studio Code.

1. Create a new file and save it in **$GOPATH\err\panicEx\main.go**.

2. Enter the following code in **main.go**:

```go
package main
import (
  "errors"
  "fmt"
)
var (
  ErrHourlyRate  = errors.New("invalid hourly rate")
  ErrHoursWorked = errors.New("invalid hours worked per week")
)
```

3. Call the **payDay()** function with various arguments and then print the return value of the function:

```go
func main() {
    pay := payDay(100, 25)
    fmt.Println(pay)
    pay = payDay(100, 200)
    fmt.Println(pay)
    pay = payDay(60, 25)
    fmt.Println(pay)
}
```

4. Then, add a **defer** function to your **payDay()** function:

```
func payDay(hoursWorked, hourlyRate int) int {
    defer func() {
```

5. We can check for the return value from the **recover()** function, as follows:

```
if r := recover(); r != nil {
        if r == ErrHourlyRate {
```

If **r** is not **nil**, that means a panic occurs and we should perform an action.

6. We can evaluate **r** and see whether it equals our error values, **ErrHourlyRate** or **ErrHoursWorked**:

```
            fmt.Printf("hourly rate: %d\nerr: %v\n\n", hourlyRate, r)
        }
        if r == ErrHoursWorked {
            fmt.Printf("hours worked: %d\nerr: %v\n\n", hoursWorked, r)
        }
    }
```

7. If our **if** statements evaluate to **true**, we print some details about the data and the error values from the **recover()** function. We then print how our pay was calculated:

```
        fmt.Printf("Pay was calculated based on:\nhours worked: %d\nhourly Rate: %d\n",
    hoursWorked, hourlyRate)
    }()
```

8. The rest of the code in the **payDay()** function remains unchanged. To see a description of it, you can refer to *Exercise 6.04, Crashing the Program on Errors Using panic*:

```
if hourlyRate < 10 || hourlyRate > 75 {
    panic(ErrHourlyRate)
}
if hoursWorked < 0 || hoursWorked > 80 {
    panic(ErrHoursWorked)
}
if hoursWorked > 40 {
    hoursOver := hoursWorked - 40
```

```
        overTime := hoursOver * 2
        regularPay := hoursWorked * hourlyRate
        return regularPay + overTime
    }
    return hoursWorked * hourlyRate
}
```

9. At the command line, navigate to the directory created in *step 1*.

10. At the command line, type the following:

```
go build
```

The **go build** command will compile your program and create an executable named after the directory you created in *step 1*.

11. Type the name of the file created in *step 10* and hit *Enter* to run the executable.

The expected output is as follows:

```
                    hours worked: 100
                    err: invalid hours worked per week

                    Pay was calculated based on:
                    hours worked: 100
                    hourly Rate: 25
                    0
                    hourly rate: 200
                    err: invalid hourly rate

                    Pay was calculated based on:
                    hours worked: 100
                    hourly Rate: 200
                    0
                    Pay was calculated based on:
                    hours worked: 60
                    hourly Rate: 25
                    1540
```

Figure 6.10: Recovering from a panic exercise output

In the preceding exercises, we have seen the progression of creating a custom error and returning that error. From this, we have been able to crash programs when needed using **panic**. In the previous exercise, we demonstrated the ability to recover from panics and display error messages based on the error type that was passed to the **panic()** function. In the following topic, we will discuss some basic guidelines when performing error handling in Go.

Guidelines when working with Errors and Panic

Guidelines are just for guidance. They are not set in stone. This means, the majority of the time you should follow the guidelines; however, there could be exceptions. Some of these guidelines have been mentioned previously, but we have consolidated them here for quick reference:

- When declaring our own error type, the variable needs to start with **Err**. It should also follow the camel case naming convention.

```
var ErrExampleNotAllowd= errors.New("error example text")
```

- The **error** string should start with lowercase and not end with punctuation. One of the reasons for this guideline is that the error can be returned and concatenated with other information relevant to the error.

- If a function or method returns an error, it should be evaluated. Errors not evaluated can cause the program to not function as expected.

- When using **panic()**, pass an error type as the argument, instead of an empty value.

- Do not evaluate the string value of an error.

- Use the **panic()** function sparingly.

Activity 6.01: Creating a Custom Error Message for a Banking Application

A bank wants to add some custom errors when checking for last name and valid routing numbers. They have found that the direct deposit procedure allows invalid names and routing numbers to be used. The bank wants a descriptive error message for when these incidents occur. Our job is to create two descriptive custom error messages. Remember to use an idiomatic naming convention for the error variable and a proper structure for the error message.

You need to do the following:

1. Create two error values for **InvalidLastName** and **InvalidRoutingNumber**.

2. Then, print the custom message in the **main()** function to show the bank the error message they will receive when those errors are encountered.

   The expected output is as follows:

```
invalid last name
invalid routing number
```

By the end of this activity, you will be familiar with the steps that are needed to create a custom error message.

> **Note**
>
> The solution to this activity can be found on page 709.

Activity 6.02: Validating a Bank Customer's Direct Deposit Submission

The bank was pleased with the custom error messages that you created in *Activity 6.01, Creating a Custom Error Message for a Banking Application*. They are so pleased that they now want you to implement two methods. These two methods are for validating the last name and the routing number:

1. You will need to create a struct called **directDeposit**.

2. The **directDeposit** struct will have three string fields: **lastName**, **firstName**, and **bankName**. It will also have two **int** fields called **routingNumber** and **accountNumber**.

3. The **directDeposit** struct will have a **validateRoutingNumber** method. The method will return **ErrInvalidRoutingNum** when the routing number is less than 100.

4. The **directDeposit** struct will have a **validateLastName** method. It will return **ErrInvalidLastName** when the **lastName** is an empty string.

5. The **directDeposit** struct will have a method report. It will print out each of the fields' values.

6. In the **main()** function, assign values to the **directDeposit** struct's fields and call each of the **directDeposit** struct's methods.

   The expected output is as follows:

```
invalid routing number
invalid last name
**********************************************************************************
Last Name:
First Name:   Abe
Bank Name:    XYZ Inc
Routing Number:   17
Account Number:   1809
```

Figure 6.11: Validating a bank customer's direct deposit submission

By the end of this activity, you will have learned how to return errors from functions and how to check for errors returned from a function. You will also be able to check for a condition and, based on that condition, return your own custom error.

> **Note**
>
> The solution to this activity can be found on page 710.

Activity 6.03: Panic on Invalid Data Submission

The bank has now decided that they would rather crash the program when an invalid routing number is submitted. The bank feels that the erroneous data validates causing the program to stop processing the direct deposit data. You need to raise panic on an invalid data submission instance. Build this on top of *Activity 6.02*, *Validating a Bank Customer's Direct Deposit Submission*:

1. Change the `validateRoutingNumber` method to not return `ErrInvalidRoutingNum`, but instead perform a panic:

   The expected output is as follows:

   ```
   panic: invalid routing number

   goroutine 1 [running]:
   main.(*directDeposit).validateRoutingNumber(...)
           /tmp/sandbox561135516/prog.go:44
   main.main()
           /tmp/sandbox561135516/prog.go:30 +0x160
   ```

   Figure 6.12: Panic on invalid routing number

By the end of this activity, you will be able to cause a **panic** to occur and see how that impacts the flow of the program.

> **Note**
>
> The solution to this activity can be found on page 713.

Activity 6.04: Preventing a Panic from Crashing the App

After some initial alpha testing, the bank no longer wants the app to crash, Instead, in this activity, we need to recover from the panic that was an added feature in *Activity 6.03, Panic on Invalid Data Submission*, and print the error that caused the panic:

1. Add a **defer** function inside the **validateRoutingNumber** method.

2. Add an **if** statement that checks the error returned from the **recover()** function. If there is an error, then print the error:

    The expected output is as follows:

```
invalid routing number
invalid last name
*************************************************************************
Last Name:
First Name:   Abe
Bank Name:    XYZ Inc
Routing Number:   17
Account Number:   1809
```

Figure 6.13: Recover from panic on an invalid routing number

By the end of this activity, you will cause a panic, but you will be able to prevent it from crashing the application. You will get an understanding of how the **recover()** function, used in conjunction with the **defer** statement, can be used to prevent the application from crashing.

> **Note**
>
> The solution of this activity can be found on page 614.

Summary

In this chapter, we have looked at the different types of errors that you will encounter while programming, such as syntax, runtime, and semantic errors. We focused more on runtime errors. These errors are more difficult to debug.

We examined the difference between various language philosophies when it comes to dealing with errors. We have seen how Go's syntax for errors is simpler to understand compared to the exception handling that various languages are utilizing.

An error in Go is a value. Values can be passed around to functions. Any error can be a value as long as it implements the error interface type. We learned how easily we can create errors. We also learned that we should name our error values starting with `Err` followed by a descriptive camel case name.

Next, we discussed panics and the similarities between a panic and an exception. We also discovered that panics are pretty similar to exceptions; however, if panics are unhandled, they will cause the program to crash. However, Go has a mechanism that will return the control of the program back to normal. We do this by using the `recover()` function. The requirements for recovering from a panic requires the usage of the `recover()` function in a deferred function. We also learned the general guidelines for using `errors`, `panic`, and `recover`.

In the next chapter, we will look at interfaces and their uses, as well as how they differ from how other programming languages implement interfaces. We will see how they can be used to solve various problems that you face as a programmer.

Interfaces

Overview

This chapter aims to demonstrate the implementation of interfaces in Go. It is quite simple compared to other languages because it is done implicitly in Go, whereas other languages require interfaces to be implemented explicitly.

In the beginning, you will be able to define and declare an interface for an application and implement an interface in your applications. This chapter introduces you to use duck typing and polymorphism and accept interfaces and return structs.

By the end of this chapter, you will learn to use type assertion to access our interface's underlying concrete value, and use the type switch statement.

Introduction

In the previous chapter, we discussed error handling in Go. We looked at what an error is in Go. We discovered that an error in Go is anything that implements the error interface. At the time, we did not investigate what an interface was. In this chapter, we are going to look at what an interface is.

For example, your manager requests that you create an API that can accept JSON data. The data contains information about various employees, such as their address and the hours they worked on a project. The data will need to be parsed into an **employee** struct, a relatively simple task. You then create a function called **loadEmployee(s string)**. The function will accept a string that is formatted as JSON, and then parse that string to load the **employee** struct.

Your manager is happy with the work; however, he has another requirement. The clients need the ability to accept a file with the employee data in JSON format. The functionality to be performed is the same underlying task as before. You create another function called **loadEmployeeFromFile(f *os.File)** that reads the data from the file, parses the data, and loads the employee struct.

Your manager has yet another requirement that the employee data should now also come from an HTTP endpoint. You will need to be able to read the data from the HTTP request, so you create another function called **loadEmployeeFromHTTP(r *Request)**.

All three functions that were written have a common behavior that they are performing. They all need to be able to read the data. The underlying type could be different (such as **string**, **os.File**, or **http.Request**) but the behavior, or reading the data, is the same in all cases.

The **func loadEmployee(s string)**, **func loadEmployeeFromFile(f *os.File)**, and **func loadEmployeeFromHTTP(r *Request)** functions can all be replaced using an interface, **func loadEmployee (r io.Reader)**. **io.Reader** is an interface, and we will discuss it in more depth later in the chapter, but for now, it is enough to say it can be used to solve the given problem.

In this chapter, we will see how interfaces can solve such a problem; by defining the behavior that is being performed as an interface type, we can accept any underlying concrete type. Don't worry if that does not make sense right now; it will start to become clearer as we progress in this chapter. We will discuss how interfaces give us the ability to perform duck typing and polymorphism. We will see how accepting interfaces and returning structs will decrease coupling and increase the use of functions in more areas of our programs. We will also examine the empty interface and discuss use cases to fully utilize it, along with type assertion and type switch statements.

Interface

An interface is a set of methods that describe the behavior of the data type. Interfaces define the behavior(s) of the type that must be satisfied to implement that interface. A behavior describes what that type can do. Almost everything exhibits certain behavior. For example, a cat can meow, walk, jump, and purr. All of those are behaviors of a cat. A car can start, stop, turn, and speed up. All of those are behaviors of a car. Similarly, behaviors for types are called methods.

> **Note**
>
> The definition that the https://packt.live/2qOtKrd provides is "Interfaces in Go provide a way to specify the behavior of an object."

There are several ways to describe an interface:

- A collection of method signatures is methods with only the name of the method, its arguments, types and a return type. This is an example of a collection of method signatures for the **Speaker{}** interface:

```
type Speaker interface{
Speak(message string) string
Greet() string
}
```

- Blueprints of the type's methods are needed to satisfy the interface. Using the **Speaker{}** interface, the blueprint (interface) states that to satisfy the **Speaker{}** interface, the type must have a **Speak()** method that accepts a **string** and returns a **string**. It also must have a **Greet()** method that returns a **string**.

- Behaviors are what the interface type must exhibit. For example, the **Reader{}** interface has a **Read** method. Its behavior is the reading of data and the Go standard library's **Reader{}** interface:

```
type Reader interface{
Read(b []byte)(n int, err error)
}
```

- Interfaces can be described as having no implementation details. The **Reader{}** interface only contains the signature of the method but not the method's code. The implementer of the interface has the responsibility of providing the code or implementation details, not the interfaces themselves.

Behaviors of a type can be as follows:

- **Read()**

- **Write()**

- **Save()**

These behaviors are collectively called **methods sets**. A behavior is defined by a set of methods. A method set is a group of method(s). These method sets comprise the method name, any input parameters, and any return types.

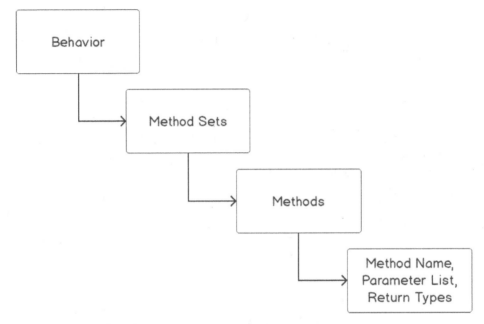

Figure 7.1: Graphic representation of interface elements

When we are talking about behaviors, note that we did not discuss the implementation details. Implementation details are omitted when you define an interface. It is important to understand that no implementation is specified or enforced in the declaration of an interface. Each type that we create that implements an interface can have its own implementation details. An interface that has a method called **Greeting()** can be implemented in different ways by various types. A struct type of person can implement **Greeting()** in a different way than a struct type of animal. Interfaces focus on the behaviors that the type must exhibit. It is not the job of the interface to provide method implementations. That is the job of the type that is implementing the interface. The types, usually a struct, contain the implementation details of the method sets. Now that we have a basic understanding of an interface, in the next topic, we will be looking at how to define an interface.

Defining an Interface

Defining an interface involves the following steps:

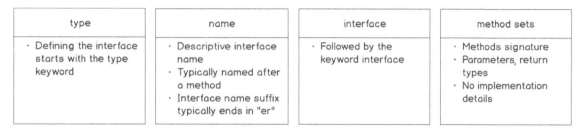

type	name	interface	method sets
· Defining the interface starts with the type keyword	· Descriptive interface name · Typically named after a method · Interface name suffix typically ends in "er"	· Followed by the keyword interface	· Methods signature · Parameters, return types · No implementation details

Figure 7.2: Defining an interface

Here is an example of declaring an interface:

```
type Speaker interface {
    Speak() string
}
```

Let's look at each part of this declaration:

- Start with the **type** keyword, followed by the name, and then the **interface** keyword.

- We are defining an interface type called **Speaker{}**. It is idiomatic in Go to name the interface with an **er** suffix. If it is a one-method interface, it is typical to name the interface after that one method.

- Next, you define the method set. Defining an interface type specifies the method(s) that belong to it. In this interface, we are declaring an interface type that has one method called **Speak()** and it returns a string.

- The method set of the **Speaker{}** interface is **Speak()**.

Here is an interface that is used frequently in Go:

```
// https://golang.org/pkg/io/#Reader
type Reader interface {
    Read(p []byte) (n int, err error)
}
```

Let's look at the parts of this code:

- The interface name is **Reader{}**.

- The method set is **Read()**.

- The signature of the **Read()** method is **(p []byte)(n int, err error)**.

Interfaces can have more than one method as its method set. Let's look at an interface used in the Go package:

```
// https://golang.org/pkg/os/#FileInfo
type FileInfo interface {
        Name() string        // base name of the file
        Size() int64         // length in bytes for regular files; system-dependent for
others
        Mode() FileMode      // file mode bits
        ModTime() time.Time // modification time
        IsDir() bool         // abbreviation for Mode().IsDir()
        Sys() interface{}    // underlying data source (can return nil)
}
```

As you can see, **FileInfo{}** has multiple methods.

In summary, interfaces are types that declare method sets. Similar to other languages that utilize interfaces, they do not implement the method sets. Implementation details are not part of defining an interface. In the next topic, we will be looking at what Go requires for you to be able to implement the interface.

Implementing an Interface

Interfaces in other programming languages implement an interface explicitly. Explicit implementation means that the programming language directly and clearly states that this object is using this interface. For example, this is in Java:

```
class Dog implements Pet
```

The **Dog** class will be implemented by the **Pet** interface. The code segment explicitly states that the **Dog** class will implement **Pet**.

In Go, interfaces are implemented implicitly. This means that a type will implement the interface by having all the methods and their signature of the interface. Here is an example:

```
package main
import (
   "fmt"
)
type Speaker interface {
   Speak() string
}
type cat struct {
}
func main() {
```

```
  c := cat{}
  fmt.Println(c.Speak())
  c.Greeting()
}
func (c cat) Speak() string {
  return "Purr Meow"
}
func (c cat) Greeting() {
  fmt.Println("Meow,Meow!!!!mmmeeeeooooowwww")
}
```

Let's break this code down into parts:

```
type Speaker interface {
  Speak() string
}
```

We are defining a **Speaker{}** interface. It has one method that describes the **Speak()**
behavior. The method returns a string. For a type to implement the **Speaker{}** interface,
it must have the method listed in the interface declaration. Then, we create an empty
struct type called **cat**:

```
type cat struct {
}
func (c cat) Speak() string {
  return "Purr Meow"
}
```

The **cat** type has a **Speak()** method that returns the string. This satisfies the **Speaker{}**
interface. It is now the responsibility of the implementer of **cat** to provide the
implementation details for the cat type's **Speak()** method.

Notice that there was no explicit statement that declares **cat** implements the **Speaker{}**
interface; it does so by just having met the requirements of the interface.

It is also important to notice that the **cat** type has a method called **Greeting()**. The type
can have methods that are not needed to satisfy the **Speaker{}** interface. However, the
cat must have at least the required method sets to be able to satisfy the interface.

The output will be as follows:

```
Purr Meow
Meow,Meow!!!!mmmeeeeooooowwww
```

Advantages of Implementing Interfaces Implicitly

There are some advantages to implementing interfaces implicitly. We have seen that when you create an interface, you have to go to each type and explicitly state that the type implements the interface. In Go, the type that satisfies the interface is said to implement it. There is no `implements` keyword like in other languages; you do not need to say that a type implements the interface. In Go, if it has the method sets and signatures of the interface, it implicitly implements the interface.

When you change the method sets of an interface, in other languages you would have to go to all those types that did not satisfy the interface and remove the explicit declaration for the type. This is not the case in Go, since it is an implicit declaration.

Another advantage is you can write interfaces for types that are in another package. This decouples the definition of an interface from its implementation. We will discuss packages and their scope in *Chapter 8, Packages*.

Let's look at an example of using an interface from a different package in our main package. The `Stringer` interface is an interface that is in the Go language. It is used by several packages through the Go language. One example is the `fmt` package, which is used for formatting when printing values:

```
type Stringer interface {
   String() string
}
```

`Stringer` is an interface that is a type that can describe itself as a string. Interface names typically follow the method name but with the addition of the **er** suffix:

```
package main
import (
   "fmt"
)
type Speaker interface {
   Speak() string
}
type cat struct {
   name string
   age  int
}
func main() {
   c := cat{name: "Oreo", age:9}
   fmt.Println(c.Speak())
```

```
    fmt.Println(c)
}
func (c cat) Speak() string {
    return "Purr Meow"
}
func (c cat) String() string {
    return fmt.Sprintf("%v (%v years old)", c.name, c.age)
}
```

Let's break down this code into parts:

- We have added a **String()** method to our **cat** type. It returns the field data for **name** and **age**.

- When we call the **fmt.Println()** method in **main()** with the argument of **cat**, **fmt.Println()** calls the **String()** method on the **cat** type.

- Our **cat** type now implements two interfaces; the **Speaker{}** interface and the **Stringer{}** interface. It has the methods required to satisfy both of those interfaces:

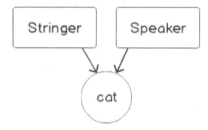

Figure 7.3: Types can implement multiple interfaces

Exercise 7.01: Implementing an Interface

In this exercise, we are going to create a simple program that demonstrates how to implement interfaces implicitly. We will have a **person** struct that will implicitly implement the **Speaker{}** interface. The **person** struct will contain **name**, **age**, and **isMarried** as its fields. The program will call the **Speak()** method of our **person** struct and display a message displaying the **person** struct's **name**. The **person** struct will also satisfy the requirements for the **Stringer{}** interface by having a **String()** method. You may recall previously, in the *Advantages of Implementing Interfaces Implicitly* section, that the **Stringer{}** interface is an interface that is in the Go language. It can be used for formatting when printing values. That is how we are going to use it in this exercise to format the printing of the fields of the **person** struct:

1. Create a new file and save it as **main.go**.

2. We will have **package main** and will be using the **fmt** package in this program:

```
package main
import (
   "fmt"
)
```

3. Create a **Speaker{}** interface with a method called **Speak()** that returns a string:

```
type Speaker interface {
   Speak() string
}
```

We have created a **Speaker{}** interface. Any type that wants to implement our **Speaker{}** interface must have a **Speak()** method that returns a string.

4. Create our **person** struct with **name**, **age**, and **isMarried** as its fields:

```
type person struct {
   name      string
   age       int
   isMarried bool
}
```

Our **person** type contains **name**, **age**, and **isMarried** fields. We will later print the contents of these fields in our **main** function using a **Speak()** method that returns a string. Having a **Speak()** method will satisfy the **Speaker{}** interface.

5. In the **main()** function, we will initialize a person type, print the **Speak()** method, and print the **person** field values:

```
func main() {
   p := person{name: "Cailyn", age: 44, isMarried: false}
   fmt.Println(p.Speak())
   fmt.Println(p)
}
```

6. Create a **String()** method for **person** and return a string value. This will satisfy the **Stringer{}** interface, which will now allow it to be called by the **fmt.Println()** method:

```
func (p person) String() string {
   return fmt.Sprintf("%v (%v years old).\nMarried status: %v ", p.name,
      p.age, p.isMarried)
}
```

7. Create a **Speak()** method for **person** that returns a string. The **person** type has a **Speak()** method that has the same signature as the **Speak()** method of the **Speaker{}** interface. The **person** type satisfies the **Speaker{}** interface by having a **Speak()** method that returns the string. To satisfy interfaces, you must have the same methods and method signatures of the interface:

```
func (p person) Speak() string {
    return "Hi my name is: " + p.name
}
```

8. Open the terminal and navigate to the code's directory.

9. Run **go build**.

10. Correct any errors that are returned and ensure your code matches the code snippet here.

11. Run the executable by typing the executable name in the command line.

   You should get the following output:

```
Hi my name is Cailyn
Cailyn (44 years old).
Married status: false
```

In this exercise, we saw how simple it is to implement interfaces implicitly. In the next topic, we will build on this by having different data types, such as structs, implement the same interface, which can be passed to any function that has the argument of that type of interface. We will go into greater detail of how that is possible in the next topic and see why it is a benefit for a type to appear in various forms.

Duck Typing

We have been basically doing what is called duck typing. Duck typing is a test in computer programming: "*If it looks like a duck, swims like a duck, and quacks like a duck, then it must be a duck.*" If a type matches an interface, then you can use that type wherever that interface is used. Duck typing is matching a type based upon methods, rather than the expected type:

```
type Speaker interface {
    Speak() string
}
```

Anything that matches the **Speak()** method can be a **Speaker{}** interface. When implementing an interface, we are essentially conforming to that interface by having the required method sets:

```go
package main
import (
    "fmt"
)
type Speaker interface {
    Speak() string
}
type cat struct {
}
func main() {
    c := cat{}
    fmt.Println(c.Speak())
}
func (c cat) Speak() string {
    return "Purr Meow"
}
```

cat matches the **Speak()** method of the **Speaker{}** interface, so a **cat** is a **Speaker{}**:

```go
package main
import (
    "fmt"
)
type Speaker interface {
    Speak() string
}
type cat struct {
}
func main() {
    c := cat{}
    chatter(c)
}
func (c cat) Speak() string {
    return "Purr Meow"
}
func chatter(s Speaker) {
    fmt.Println(s.Speak())
}
```

Let's examine this code in parts:

- In the preceding code, we declare a **cat** type and create a method for the **cat** type called **Speak()**. This fulfills the required method sets for the **Speaker{}** interface.

- We create a method called **chatter** that takes the **Speaker{}** interface as an argument.

- In the **main()** function, we are able to pass a **cat** type into the **chatter** function, which can evaluate to the **Speaker{}** interface This satisfies the required method sets for the interface.

Polymorphism

Polymorphism is the ability to appear in various forms. For example, a shape can appear as a square, circle, rectangle, or any other shape:

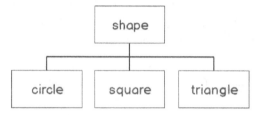

Figure 7.4: Polymorphism example for shape

Go does not do subclassing like other object-oriented languages because Go does not have classes. Subclassing in object-oriented programming is inheriting from one class to another. By doing subclassing, you are inheriting the fields and methods of another class. Go provides a similar behavior through embedding structs and by using polymorphism through interfaces.

One of the advantages of using polymorphism is that it allows the reuse of methods that have been written once and tested. Code is reused by having an API that accepts an interface; if our type satisfies that interface, it can be passed to that API. There is no need to write additional code for each type; we just need to ensure we meet the interface method's set requirements. Obtaining polymorphism through the use of interfaces will increase the reusability of the code. If your API only accepts concrete types such as **int**, **float**, and **bool**, only that concrete type can be passed. However, if your API accepts an interface, then the caller can add the required method sets to satisfy that interface regardless of the underlying type. This reusability is accomplished by allowing your APIs to accept interfaces. Any type that satisfies the interface can be passed to the API. We have seen this type of behavior in a previous example. This is a good time to take a closer look at the **Speaker{}** interface.

As we have seen in previous examples, each concrete type can implement one or more interfaces. Recall that our **Speaker{}** interface can be implemented by a **dog**, **cat**, or **fish** type:

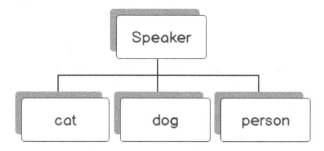

Figure 7.5: The Speaker interface implemented by multiple types

When a function accepts an interface as an input parameter, any concrete type that implements that interface can be passed as an argument. Now, you have achieved polymorphism by being able to pass various concrete types to a method or function that has an interface type as an input parameter.

Let's look at some progressive examples that will enable us to demonstrate how polymorphism is achieved in Go:

```go
package main
import (
    "fmt"
)
type Speaker interface {
    Speak() string
}
type cat struct {
}
func main() {
    c := cat{}
    catSpeak(c)
}
func (c cat) Speak() string {
    return "Purr Meow"
}
func catSpeak(c cat) {
    fmt.Println(c.Speak())
}
```

Let's examine the code in parts:

- **cat** satisfies the **Speaker{}** interface. The **main()** function calls **catSpeak()** and takes a type of **cat**.

- Inside **catSpeak()**, it prints out the results of its **Speak()** method.

We are going to implement some code that takes a concrete type (**cat**, **dog**, **person**) and satisfies the **Speaker{}** interface type. Using the previous coding pattern, it would look like the following code snippet:

```
package main
import (
  "fmt"
)
type Speaker interface {
  Speak() string
}
type cat struct {
}
type dog struct {
}
type person struct {
  name string
}
func main() {
  c := cat{}
  d := dog{}
  p := person{name:"Heather"}
  catSpeak(c)
  dogSpeak(d)
  personSpeak(p)
}
func (c cat) Speak() string {
  return "Purr Meow"
}
func (d dog) Speak() string {
  return "Woof Woof"
}
func (p person) Speak() string {
  return "Hi my name is " + p.name +"."
}
```

```go
func catSpeak(c cat) {
    fmt.Println(c.Speak())
}
func dogSpeak(d dog) {
    fmt.Println(d.Speak())
}
func personSpeak(p person) {
    fmt.Println(p.Speak())
}
```

Let's look at this code in parts:

```go
type cat struct {
}
type dog struct {
}
type person struct {
    name string
}
```

We have three concrete types (**cat**, **dog**, and **person**). The **cat** and **dog** types are empty structs, while the **person** struct has a **name** field:

```go
func (c cat) Speak() string {
    return "Purr Meow"
}
func (d dog) Speak() string {
    return "Woof Woof"
}
func (p person) Speak() string {
    return "Hi my name is " + p.name +" "
}
```

Each of our types implicitly implements the **Speaker{}** interface. Each of the concrete types implements it differently from the others:

```go
func main() {
    c := cat{}
    d := dog{}
    p := person{name:"Heather"}
    catSpeak(c)
    dogSpeak(d)
    personSpeak(p)
}
```

In the **main()** function, we call **catSpeak()**, **dogSpeak()**, and **personSpeak()** to invoke their respective **Speak()** method. The preceding code has a lot of redundant functions that perform similar actions. We can refactor this code to be more simple and easier to read. We will use some of the features you get with implementing interfaces to provide a more concise implementation:

```go
package main
import (
  "fmt"
)
type Speaker interface {
  Speak() string
}
type cat struct {
}
type dog struct {
}
type person struct {
  name string
}
func main() {
  c := cat{}
  d := dog{}
  p := person{name: "Heather"}
  saySomething(c,d,p)
}
func saySomething(say ...Speaker) {
  for _, s := range say {
    fmt.Println(s.Speak())
  }
}
func (c cat) Speak() string {
  return "Purr Meow"
}
func (d dog) Speak() string {
  return "Woof Woof"
}
func (p person) Speak() string {
  return "Hi my name is " + p.name + "."
}
```

Let's look at the code in parts:

```
func saySomething(say ...Speaker)
```

Our **saySomething()** function is using a variadic parameter. If you recall, a variadic parameter can accept zero or more arguments for that type. For more information on variadic functions, review *Chapter 5, Functions*. The parameter type is **Speaker**. An interface can be used as an input parameter:

```
func saySomething(say ...Speaker) {
  for _, s := range say {
    fmt.Println(s.Speak())
  }
}
```

We range over the slice of **Speaker**. For each **Speaker** type, we call the **Speak()** method. In our code, we passed the **cat** and **dog** struct types to the **person** function. The function accepts an argument as an interface of **Speaker{}**. Any of the methods that make up that interface can be invoked. For each of those concrete types, the **Speak()** method is called.

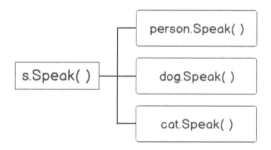

Figure 7.6: Multiple types implementing the Speaker interface

In the **main()** function, we will see the use of polymorphism being demonstrated through the use of interfaces:

```
func main() {
  c := cat{}
  d := dog{}
  p := person{name: "Heather"}
  saySomething(c,d,p)
}
```

We implement each of the concrete types, **cat**, **dog**, and, **person**. The **cat**, **dog**, and, **person** types all satisfy the **Speaker{}** interface. Since they match an interface, you can use that type wherever that interface is used. As you can see, this also includes being able to pass the **cat**, **dog**, and **person** types into a method.

Through the use of interfaces and polymorphism, this code is more concise than the previous code snippets. The example at the beginning of the chapter showed a single concrete type that satisfied the **Speaker{}** interface that invoked the **Speak()** method. We then added a few more concrete types to our running example (**cat**, **dog**, and **person**), each of these separately invoking their own **Speak()** method. We noticed there was a lot of redundant code in that example and started looking for a better way to implement the solution. We discovered that interface types can be parameter input types. Through duck typing and polymorphism, our third and final code snippet was able to have a single function that would call the **Speak()** method on each type that satisfied the **Speaker()** interface.

Exercise 7.02: Calculating the Area of Different Shapes Using Polymorphism

We will be implementing a program that will calculate the area of a triangle, rectangle, and square. The program will use a single function that accepts a **Shape** interface. Any type that satisfies the **Shape** interface can be passed as an argument to the function. This function should then print the area and the name of the shape:

1. Use the IDE of your choice.

2. Create a new file and save it as **main.go**.

3. We will have a package called **main**, and we will be using the **fmt** package in this program:

```
package main
import (
    "fmt"
)
```

4. Create the **Shape{}** interface that has two method sets called **Area() float64** and **Name() string**:

```
type Shape interface {
    Area() float64
    Name() string
}
```

5. Next, we will create **triangle**, **rectangle**, and **square** struct types. These types will each satisfy the **Shape{}** interface. **triangle**, **rectangle**, and **square** have appropriate fields that are needed to calculate the area of the shape:

```
type triangle struct {
    base    float64
    height float64
}
type rectangle struct {
    length float64
    width  float64
}
type square struct {
    side float64
}
```

6. We create the **Area()** and **Name()** methods for the **triangle** struct type. The area of a triangle is **base * height\2**. The **Name()** method returns the name of the shape:

```
func (t triangle) Area() float64 {
    return (t.base * t.height) / 2
}
func (t triangle) Name() string {
    return "triangle"
}
```

7. We create the **Area()** and **Name()** methods for the **rectangle** struct type. The area of a rectangle is **length * width**. The **Name()** method returns the name of the shape:

```
func (r rectangle) Area() float64 {
    return r.length * r.width
}
func (r rectangle) Name() string {
    return "rectangle"
}
```

8. We create the **Area()** and **Name()** methods for the **square** struct type. The area of a square is **side * side**. The **Name()** method returns the name of the shape:

```
func (s square) Area() float64 {
    return s.side * s.side
}
func (s square) Name() string {
    return "square"
}
```

Now, each of our shapes (**triangle**, **rectangle**, and **square**) satisfies the **Shape** interface because they each have an **Area()** and **Name()** method with the appropriate signatures:

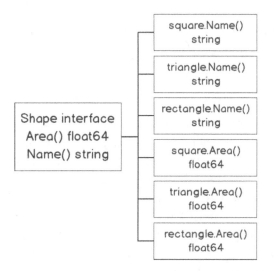

Figure 7.7: square, triangle, rectangle area of the Shape type

9. We will now create a function that accepts the **Shape** interface as a variadic parameter. The function will iterate over the **Shape** type and will execute each of its **Name()** and **Area()** methods:

```
func printShapeDetails(shapes ...Shape) {
    for _, item := range shapes {
        fmt.Printf("The area of %s is: %.2f\n", item.Name(), item.Area())
    }
}
```

10. Inside the **main()** function, set the fields for **triangle**, **rectangle**, and **square**. Pass all three to the **printShapeDetail()** function. All three can be passed because they each satisfy the **Shape** interface:

```
func main() {
    t := triangle{base: 15.5, height: 20.1}
    r := rectangle{length: 20, width: 10}
    s := square{side: 10}
    printShapeDetails(t, r, s)
}
```

11. Build the program by running **go build** at the command line:

```
go build
```

12. Correct any errors that are returned and ensure your code matches the code snippet here.

13. Run the executable by typing the name of the executable and hit *Enter* to run it.

    You should see the following output:

```
The area of triangle is: 155.78
The area of rectangle is: 200.00
The area of square is: 100.00
```

In this exercise, we saw the flexibility and the reusable code that interfaces provide to our programs. Further, we will discuss how accepting interfaces and returning structs for our functions and methods increase code reusability and low coupling by not being dependent on the concrete types. When we use interfaces as input arguments to an API, we are stating that a type needs to satisfy the interface. When using concrete types, we require that the argument for the API must be of that type. For instance, if a function signature is `func greeting(msg string)`, we know that the argument being passed must be a string. Concrete types can be thought of as types that are not abstract (`float64`, `int`, `string`, and so on); however, interfaces could be considered as an abstract type because you are satisfying the method sets of the interface type. The underlying interface type is a concrete type, but the underlying type is not what needs to be passed into the API. The type must meet the requirements of having the method sets the interface type defines.

In the future, if we require another type to be passed, this will mean the code upstream to our API will need to change, or if the caller of our API needs to change its data type, it might request we change our API to accommodate it. If we use interfaces, this is not an issue; the caller of our code needs to satisfy the interface's method sets. The caller can then change the underlying type as long as it complies with the interface requirements.

Accepting Interfaces and Returning Structs

There is a Go proverb that states "*Accept interfaces, return structs.*" It can be restated as accept interfaces and return concrete types. This proverb is talking about accepting interfaces for your APIs (functions, methods, and so on) and the return to be structs or concrete types. This proverb follows Postel's Law, which states "*Be conservative with what you do, be liberal with what you accept.*" We are focusing on the "*be liberal with what you accept.*" By accepting interfaces, you are increasing the flexibility of the API for your function or method. By doing this, you are allowing for the user of the API to meet the requirements of the interface, but not forcing the user to use a concrete type. If our functions or methods only accept concrete types, then we are limiting the users of our functions to a specific implementation. In this chapter, we are going to explore the previously mentioned Go proverb and learn why it is a good design pattern to follow. We will see that as we go over the code example:

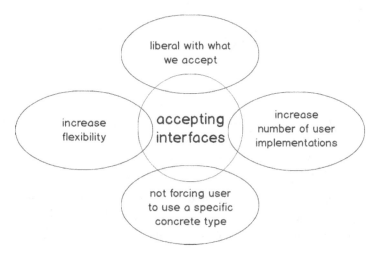

Figure 7.8: Benefits of accepting interfaces

The following example will illustrate the benefits of accepting interfaces versus using concrete types. We will have two functions that perform the same task of decoding JSON, but each has different inputs. One of these functions is superior to the other, and we will go over the reasons why that is the case.

Look at the following example:

main.go

```
1   package main
2   import (
3       "encoding/json"
4       "fmt"
5       "io"
6       "strings"
7   )
8   type Person struct {
9       Name string `json:"name"`
10      Age  int    `json:"age"`
11  }
```

The full code is available at https://packt.live/38teYHn

The expected output is as follows:

```
{Joe 18}
{Jane 21}
```

Let's examine each part of this code. We will discuss some parts of this code in the upcoming chapters. This code decodes some data into a struct. There are two functions being used for that purpose, **loadPerson2()** and **loadPerson()**:

```
func loadPerson2(s string) (Person, error) {
    var p Person
    err := json.NewDecoder(strings.NewReader(s)).Decode(&p)
```

```
    if err != nil {
    return p, err
    }
    return p, nil
}
```

The **loadPerson2()** function accepts an argument that is a concrete **string** and returns a **struct**. The returning of the struct meets half of "*accept interfaces, return structs*". However, it is very limited and not liberal in what it accepts. This limits the user of the function to a narrow implementation. The only thing that can ever be passed is a string. Granted, in some cases that might be acceptable, but in other situations, it could be a problem. For example, if your function or method should only accept a specific data type, then you may not want to accept interfaces:

```
func loadPerson(r io.Reader) (Person, error) {
    var p Person
    err := json.NewDecoder(r).Decode(&p)
    if err != nil {
       return p, err
    }
    return p, err
}
```

In this function, we are accepting the **io.Reader{}** interface. The **io.Reader{}** (https://packt.live/2LRG3Kv) and **io.Writer{}** (https://packt.live/2YIAJhP) interfaces are among the most utilized interfaces in Go packages. **json.NewDecoder** accepts anything that satisfies the **io.Reader{}** interface. The caller code just needs to make sure whatever they pass satisfies the **io.Reader{}** interface:

```
p, err := loadPerson(strings.NewReader(s))
```

strings.NewReader returns a **Reader** type that has a **Read(b []byte) (n int, err error)** method that satisfies the **io.Reader{}** interface. It can be passed to our **loadPerson()** function. You may be thinking that each function still does what it was intended for. You would be correct, but let's say the caller is no longer going to pass a string, or another caller will be passing a file that contains the JSON data:

```
f, err := os.Open("data.json")
if err != nil {
   fmt.Println(err)
}
```

Our **loadPerson2()** function would not work; however, our **loadPerson()** data would work because the return type from **os.Open()** satisfies the **io.Reader{}** interface.

Say, for instance, the data will be coming through an HTTP endpoint. We will be getting the data from ***http.Request**. Again, the **loadPerson2()** function would not be a good choice. We would get the data from **request.Body**, which just so happens to implement the **io.Reader{}** interface.

You may be wondering if interfaces are good for input arguments. If so, why would we not return them too? If you return an interface, it adds unnecessary difficulty to the user. The user will have to look up the interface to then find the method set and the method sets signature:

```
func someFunc() Speaker{} {
// code
}
```

You would need to look at the definition of the **Speaker{}** interface and then spend time looking at the implementation code, all of which is unnecessary for the user of the function. If an interface is needed from the return type of the function, the user of the function can create the interface for that concrete type and use it in their code.

As you start to follow this Go proverb, check to see whether there is an interface in the Go standard packages. This will increase the number of different implementations that your function can provide. Our users of the function can have various implementations using **strings.newReader**, **http.Request.Body**, **os.File**, and many others, just like in our code example, by using the **io.Reader{}** interface from the Go standard packages.

Empty interface{}

An empty interface is an interface that has no method sets and no behaviors. An empty interface specifies no methods:

```
interface{}
```

This is a simple but complex concept to wrap your head around. As you may recall, interfaces are implemented implicitly; there is no **implements** keyword. Since an empty interface specifies no methods, that means that every type in Go implements an empty interface automatically. All types satisfy the empty interface.

In the following code snippet, we will demonstrate how to use the empty interface. We will also see how a function that accepts an empty interface allows any type to be passed to that function:

main.go

```
1   package main
2   import (
3       "fmt"
4   )
5   type Speaker interface {
6       Speak() string
7   }
8   type cat struct {
9       name string
10  }
```

The full code is available at https://packt.live/34dVEdB

The expected output is as follows:

```
({oreo}, main.cat)
({oreo}, main.cat)
(99, int)
(false, bool)
(test, string)
```

Let's evaluate the code in sections:

```
func emptyDetails(s interface{}) {
    fmt.Printf("(%v, %T)\n", i, i)
}
```

The function accepts an empty **interface{}**. Any type can be passed to the function since all types implement the empty **interface{}**. It prints the value and the concrete type. The **%v** verb prints the value and the **%T** verb prints the concrete type:

```
func main() {
    c := cat{name: "oreo"}
    i := 99
    b := false
    str := "test"
    catDetails(c)
    emptyDetails(c)
    emptyDetails(i)
    emptyDetails(b)
    emptyDetails(str)
}
```

We pass a **cat** type, **integer**, **bool**, and **string**. The **emptyDetails()** function will print each of them:

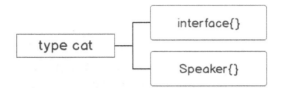

Figure 7.9: The type cat implements an empty interface and the Speaker interface

The **cat** type implements the empty **interface{}** and the **Speaker{}** interface implicitly.

Now that we have a basic understanding of empty interfaces, we will be looking at various use cases for them in the upcoming topics, including the following:

- Type switching
- Type assertion
- Examples of Go packages

Type Assertion and Switches

Type assertion provides access to an interface's concrete type. Remember that **interface{}** can be any value:

```
package main
import (
  "fmt"
)
func main() {
  var str interface{} ="some string"
  var i interface{} = 42
  var b interface{} = true
  fmt.Println(str)
  fmt.Println(i)
  fmt.Println(b)
}
```

The type assertion output would look as follows:

```
some string
42
true
```

In each instance of the variable declaration, each variable is declared as an empty interface, but the concrete value for **str** is a string, for **i** is an integer, and for **b** is a Boolean.

When there is an empty **interface{}** type, sometimes, it is beneficial to know the underlying concrete type. For instance, you may need to perform data manipulation based upon that type. If that type is a string, you would perform data modification and validation different from how you would if it was an integer value. This also comes into play when you are consuming JSON data of an unknown schema. The values in that JSON might be known during the ingesting process. We would need to convert that data to **map[string]interface{}** and perform various data massaging. We have an activity later in this chapter that will show us how to perform such an action. We could perform a type conversion with the **strconv** package:

```
package main
import (
    "fmt"
    "strconv"
)
func main() {
    var str interface{} ="some string"
    var i interface{} = 42
    fmt.Println(strconv.Atoi(i))
}
```

```
prog.go:15:26: cannot use i (type interface {}) as type string in argument to strconv.Atoi: need type assertion
```

Figure 7.10: Error when type assertion is needed

So, it appears we cannot use type conversion because the types are not compatible with type conversion. We will need to use **type** assertion:

```
v := s.(T)
```

The preceding statement says that it asserts that the interface value **s** is of type **T** and assigns the underlying value of **v**:

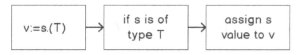

Figure 7.11: Type assertion flow

Consider the following code snippet:

```
package main
import (
  "fmt"
  "strings"
)
func main() {
  var str interface{} ="some string"
  v := str.(string)
  fmt.Println(strings.Title(v))
}
```

Let's examine the preceding code:

- The preceding code asserts that **str** is of the **string** type and assigns it to the variable **v**.

- Since **v** is a **string**, it will print it with title casing.

The result is as follows:

```
Some String
```

It is good when the assertion matches the expected type. So, what will happen if **s** is not of type **T**? Let's take a look:

```
package main
import (
  "fmt"
  "strings"
)
func main() {
  var str interface{} = 49
  v := str.(string)
  fmt.Println(strings.Title(v))
}
```

Let's examine the preceding code:

- **str{}** is an empty interface and the concrete type is of **int**.

- The type assertion is checking whether **str** is of the string type, but in this scenario, it is not, so the code will panic.

- The result is as follows:

```
panic: interface conversion: interface {} is int, not string

goroutine 1 [running]:
main.main()
        /tmp/sandbox011356825/main.go:11 +0x40
```

Figure 7.12: Failed type assertion

Having a panic being thrown is not something that is desirable. However, Go has a way to check whether **str** is a string:

```
package main
import (
  "fmt"
)
func main() {
  var str interface{} = "the book club"
  v, isValid := str.(int)
  fmt.Println(v, isValid)
}
```

Let's examine the preceding code:

- A type assertion returns two values, the underlying value and a Boolean value.

- **isValid** is assigned to a return type of **bool**. If it returns **true**, that indicates that **str** is of the **int** type. It means that the assertion is true. We can use the Boolean that was returned to determine what action we can take on **str**.

- When the assertion fails, it will return **false**. The return value will be the zero value that you are trying to assert to. It also will not panic.

There will be times when you do not know the empty interface concrete type. This is when you will use a type switch. A type switch can perform several types of assertions; it is similar to a regular switch statement. It has a case and default clauses. The difference is that type switch statements evaluate for a type rather than a value.

Here is a basic syntax structure:

```
switch v:= i.(type){
case S:
  // code to act upon the type S
}
```

Let's examine the preceding code:

```
i.(type)
```

The syntax is similar to that of the type assertion, **i.(int)**, except the specified type, **int** in our example, is replaced with the **type** keyword. The type being asserted of type **i** is assigned to **v**; then, it is compared to each of the **case** statements.

```
case S:
```

In the **switch** type, the statements evaluate for types. In regular switching, they evaluate for values. Here, it is evaluated for a type of **S**.

Now that we have a fundamental understanding of the type switch statement, let's look at an example that uses the syntax we have just evaluated:

main.go

```
13 func typeExample(i []interface{}) {
14    for _, x := range i {
15       switch v := x.(type) {
16       case int:
17          fmt.Printf("%v is int\n", v)
18       case string:
19          fmt.Printf("%v is a string\n",v)
20       case bool:
21          fmt.Printf("a bool %v\n", v)
22       default:
23          fmt.Printf("Unknown type %T\n", v)
24       }
25    }
26 }
```

The full code is available at https://packt.live/38xWEwH

Let's now explore the code in pieces:

```
func main() {
   c:=cat{name:"oreo"}
   i := []interface{}{42, "The book club", true,c}
   typeExample(i)
}
```

In the **main()** function, we are initializing a variable, **i**, to a slice of interfaces. In the slice, we have the **int**, **string**, **bool**, and **cat** types:

```
func typeExample(i []interface{})
```

The function accepts a slice of interfaces:

```
   for _, x := range i {
      switch v := x.(type) {
      case int:
         fmt.Printf("%v is int\n", v)
```

```
    case string:
      fmt.Printf("%v is a string\n",v)
    case bool:
      fmt.Printf("a bool %v\n", v)
    default:
      fmt.Printf("Unknown type %T\n", v)
    }
  }
```

The **for** loop ranges over the slice of interfaces. The first value in the slice is 42. The **switch** case asserts that the slice value of 42 is an **int** type. The **case int** statement will evaluate to **true**, and print 42 is int. When the **for** loop iterates over the last value of the **cat** type, the **switch** statement will not find that type in its case evaluations. Since there is no **cat** type being checked for in the **case** statements, the default will execute its print statement. Here are the results of the code being executed:

```
42 is int
The book club is string
a bool true
Unknown type main.cat
```

Exercise 7.03: Analyzing Empty interface{} Data

In this exercise, we are given a map. The map's key is a string and its value is an empty **interface{}**. The map's value contains different types of data stored in the value portion of the map. Our job is to determine each key's value type. We are going to write a program that will analyze the data of **map[string] interface{}**. Understand that the values of the data can be of any type. We need to write logic to catch types we are not looking for. We are going to store that information in a slice of structs that will hold the key name, data, and the type of data:

1. Create a new file called **main.go.**

2. Inside the file, we will have a **main** package and will need to import the **fmt** package:

```
package main
import (
  "fmt"
)
```

3. We will create a **struct** called **record** that will store the key, type of value, and data from **map[string]interface{}**. This struct is used to store the analysis that we are performing on the map. The **key** field is the name as the map key. The **valueType** field is storing the type of data stored as a value in the map. The data field stores the data we are analyzing. It is an empty **interface{}**, since there can be various types of data in the map:

```
type record struct {
    key        string
    valueType string
    data       interface{}
}
```

4. We will create a **person** struct that will be added to our **map[string]interface{}**:

```
type person struct {
    lastName  string
    age        int
    isMarried bool
}
```

5. We will create an **animal** struct that will be added to our **map[string]interface{}**:

```
type animal struct {
    name      string
    category string
}
```

6. Create a **newRecord()** function. The **key** parameter will be our map's key. The function also takes an **interface{}** as an input parameter. **i** will be our map's value for the key that is passed to the function. It will return a **record** type:

```
func newRecord(key string, i interface{}) record {
```

7. Inside the **newRecord()** function, we initialize **record{}** and assign it to the **r** variable. We then assign **r.key** to the key input parameter.

8. The **switch** statement assigns the type of **i** to the **v** variable. The **v** variable type gets evaluated against a series of **case** statements. If a type evaluates to **true** for one of the **case** statements, then the **valueType** record gets assigned to that type, along with the value of **v** to **r.data**, and then returns the **record** type:

```
r := record{}
r.key = key
switch v := i.(type) {
case int:
    r.valueType = "int"
```

```
            r.data = v
            return r
        case bool:
            r.valueType = "bool"
            r.data = v
            return r
        case string:
            r.valueType = "string"
            r.data = v
            return r
        case person:
            r.valueType = "person"
            r.data = v
            return r
```

9. A **default** statement is needed for the **switch** statement. If the type of **v** does not get evaluated to **true** in the **case** statements, then **default** will be executed. The **record.valueType** will be marked as **unknown**:

```
        default:
            r.valueType = "unknown"
            r.data = v
            return r
    }
}
```

10. Inside the **main()** function, we will initialize our map. The map is initialized to a string for the key and an empty interface for the value. We then assign **a** to an **animal** struct literal and **p** to a **person** struct literal. Then, we start adding various key-value pairs to the map:

```
func main() {
    m := make(map[string]interface{})
    a := animal{name: "oreo", category: "cat"}
    p := person{lastName: "Doe", isMarried: false, age: 19}
    m["person"] = p
    m["animal"] = a
    m["age"] = 54
    m["isMarried"] = true
    m["lastName"] = "Smith"
```

11. Next, we initialize a slice of **record**. We iterate over the map and add records to **rs**:

```
rs := []record{}
for k, v := range m {
    r := newRecord(k, v)
    rs = append(rs, r)
}
```

12. Now, print out the record field values. We range over the slice of records and print each record value:

```
for _, v := range rs {
    fmt.Println("Key: ", v.key)
    fmt.Println("Data: ", v.data)
    fmt.Println("Type: ", v.valueType)
    fmt.Println()
}
}
```

The expected output is as follows:

```
Key:   lastName
Data:  Smith
Type:  string

Key:   person
Data:  {Doe 19 false}
Type:  person

Key:   animal
Data:  {oreo cat}
Type:  unknown

Key:   age
Data:  54
Type:  int

Key:   isMarried
Data:  true
Type:  bool
```

Figure 7.13: Output for the exercise

The exercise has demonstrated Go's ability to identify the underlying type of an empty interface. As you can see from the results, our type switch was able to identify each type except for the value for the key of **animal**. It has its type marked as **unknown**. Also, it was even able to identify the **person** struct type, and the data has the field values of the struct.

Activity 7.01: Calculating Pay and Performance Review

In this activity, we are going to calculate the annual pay for a manager and a developer. We will print out the developer's and manager's names and the pay for the year. The developer pay will be based on an hourly rate. The developer type will also keep track of the number of hours they have worked in a year. The developer type will also include their review. The review will need to be a collection of keys of strings. These strings are the category that the developer is being reviewed on, for example, work quality, teamwork, communication, and so on.

The aim of this activity is to use an interface to demonstrate polymorphism by calling a single function called **payDetails()** that accepts an interface. This **payDetails()** function will print the salary information for a developer type and a manager type.

The following steps should help you with the solution:

1. Create an **Employee** type that has **Id**, **FirstName**, and **LastName** fields.

2. Create a **Developer** type that has the following fields: **Individual** of the **Employee** type, **HourlyRate**, **HoursWorkedInYear**, and **Review** of the **map[string]interface{}** type.

3. Create a **Manager** type with the following fields: **Individual** of the **Employee** type, **Salary**, and **CommissionRate**.

4. Create a **Payer** interface that has a **Pay()** method that returns a **string** and **float64**.

5. The **Developer** type should implement the **Payer{}** interface by returning the **Developer** name and returning the developer year pay based on the calculation of **Developer.HourlyRate * Developer.HoursWorkInYear**.

6. The **Manager** type should implement the **Payer{}** interface by returning the **Manager** name and returning the **Manager** year pay based on the calculation of **Manager. Salary + (Manager.Salary * Manager.CommissionRate)**.

7. Add a function called **payDetails(p Payer)** that accepts a **Payer** interface and prints **fullName** and the pay that is returned from the **Pay()** method.

8. We now need to calculate the review rating for a developer. The **Review** is obtained by **map[string]interface{}**. The key of the map is a string; it is what the developer is being rated on, such as work quality, teamwork, skills, and so on.

9. The empty **interface{}** of the map is needed because some managers give the rating as a string and others as a number. Here is the mapping of the **string** to the **integer**:

"Excellent" – 5

"Good" – 4

"Fair" – 3

"Poor" – 2

"Unsatisfactory" – 1

10. We need to calculate the performance review value as a **float** type. It is the sum of the map **interface{}** divided by the length of the map. Take into consideration that the rating can be a string or an integer, so you will need to be able to accept both and convert it to a float.

The expected output is as follows:

```
Eric Davis got a review rating of 2.80
Eric Davis got paid 84000.00 for the year
Mr. Boss got paid 160500.00 for the year
```

> **Note**
>
> The solution for this activity can be found on page 715.

In this activity, we saw the benefits of using an empty interface that allows us to accept any type of data. We then used type assertion and type switch statements to perform certain tasks based on the underlying concrete type of the empty interface.

Summary

This chapter presented some fundamental and advanced topics when using interfaces. We learned that Go's implementation of interfaces has some similarities with other languages; for example, an interface does not contain the implementation details of the behaviors it is representing, and an interface is the blueprint of the methods. The different types that implement the interface can differ in their implementation details. However, Go differs in how you implement an interface compared to other languages. We learned that the implementation is done implicitly and not explicitly, like other languages.

This concludes that Go does not do subclassing, so, for it to implement polymorphism, it uses interfaces. It allows an interface type to appear in different forms, such as a **Shape** interface appearing as a rectangle, square, or circle.

We also discussed a design pattern of accept interfaces and return structs. We demonstrated that this pattern allows for broader uses by other callers. We examined the empty interface and saw how it can be used when you do not know the type being passed or when there could be multiple different types being passed to your API. Even though we did not know the type at runtime, we showed you how to use type assertion and type switching to determine the type. The knowledge and practicing of these various tools will help you build robust and fluid programs.

In the following chapter, we will look at how Go uses packages and how we can use them to further aid in building well-organized and focused code segments.

8

Packages

Overview

This chapter aims to demonstrate the importance of the use of packages in our Go programs. We will discuss how packages can be used to assist our code in being more maintainable, reusable, and modular. In this chapter, you will see how they can be used to bring structure and organization to our code. This will also be seen in our exercises, activities, and some examples from the Go standard library.

By the end of the chapter, you will be able to describe a package and its structure and declare a package. You will learn to evaluate exported and unexported names in a package, create your own package and import your custom package. You will also be able to distinguish between an executable package and non-executable packages, and create an alias of a package.

Introduction

In the previous chapter, we looked at interfaces. We saw how we can use interfaces to describe the behavior of a type. We also discovered that we can pass different types to functions that accept an interface, as long as the type satisfies the interface's method sets. We also saw how we can achieve polymorphism using interfaces.

In this chapter, we will look at how Go organizes its code into packages. We will see how we can hide or expose different Go constructs such as structs, interfaces, functions, and more, using packages. Our programs have been rather small in the number lines of code and in complexity to a certain extent. Most of our programs have been contained in a single code file, often named `main.go`, and inside a single package named `main`. Later in this chapter, we will explore the significance of `package main`, so do not be worried at this juncture if you do not understand it. This will not always be the case when you are working on a development team. Often, your code base can become rather large, with multiple files, multiple libraries, and multiple members of the team. It would be rather restrictive if we could not break our code into smaller, manageable parts. The Go programming language solves the complexity of managing large codebases with the ability to modularize similar concepts into packages. The creators of Go use packages for their own standard libraries to tackle this problem. In this book, you have been working with many Go packages, such as `fmt`, `string`, `os`, `ioutil`, and so on.

Let's look at an example of a package structure from the Go standard library. The Go `strings` package encapsulates string functions that manipulate strings. By keeping the `strings` package focused on only the functions that manipulate strings, we, as Go developers, know that this function should contain all that we need for string manipulation.

The Go package for strings is structured as follows (https://packt.live/35jueEu):

Figure 8.1: The strings package along with the files contained within it

The preceding diagram shows the **strings** package and the files that are in the package. Each file in the **strings** package is named after the functionality it is supporting. The logical organization of the code goes from package to file. We can easily conclude that the **strings** package contains code for manipulating strings. We can then further conclude that the **replace.go** file contains functions for replacing strings. You can already see that the conceptual structure of packages can organize your code into modular chunks. You start with code that is working together to serve a purpose, string manipulation, and it gets stored in a package called **string**. You can then further organize the code into **.go** files and name them according to their purpose. The next step is keeping functions in there that perform a single purpose that reflects the name of the file and the name of the package. We will discuss these conceptual ideas later in the chapter when we discuss structuring code.

It is important to develop software that is maintainable, reusable, and modular. Let's briefly discuss each of these core components of software development.

Maintainable

For code to be maintainable, it must be easy to change, and any changes must have a low risk of having an adverse impact on the program. Maintainable code is easy to modify and extend and is readable. As code progresses through the different stages of the software development life cycle, the cost of changes to the code increases. These changes can be due to bugs, enhancements, or a change in requirements. Costs also increase when code is not easily maintainable. Another reason that code needs to be maintainable is the need to be competitive in the industry. If your code is not easily maintainable, it may be hard to react to a competitor who is releasing a software feature that could be used to outsell your application. These are just some of the reasons for code needing to be maintainable.

Reusable

Reusable code is code that can be used in new software. For example, I have code in my existing application that has a function that returns an address for my mailing application; that function may be used in a new piece of software. That function that returns the address could be used in my new software that returns a customer address for an order the customer has placed.

The advantages of having reusable code are as follows:

- It decreases future project costs by using existing packages.
- It decreases the time it takes to deliver an application, due to not having to reinvent the wheel.
- The quality of the program will increase through increased testing and more usage.
- More time can be spent on other areas of innovation during the development cycle.
- As your packages grow, it becomes easier to lay the foundations for future projects in a timely manner.

Modular

Modular and reusable code is related to a certain extent, in the sense that having modular code makes it more likely that it will be reusable. One of the prominent problems when developing code is the organization of the code. Finding the code that performs a certain function in a large program that is unorganized would be near to impossible, and even finding out whether there is code that performs a certain task would be difficult to ascertain without some code organization. Modularization aids in that area. The idea is that each discrete task that your code performs has its own section of code located in a specific spot.

Go encourages you to develop maintainable, reusable, and modular code by using packages. It was designed to encourage good software practices. We will be diving into how Go utilizes packages to accomplish those tasks:

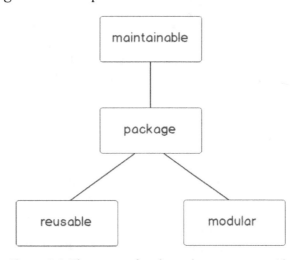

Figure 8.2: The types of code packages can provide

In the next topic, we are going to discuss what a package is and what the components that make up a package are.

What Is a Package?

Go follows the **Don't Repeat Yourself (DRY)** principle. This means that you should not write the same code twice. Refactoring your code into functions is the first step of the DRY principle. What if you had hundreds or even thousands of functions that you used regularly? How would you keep track of all those functions? Some of those functions might even have common characteristics. You could have a group of functions that perform math operations, string manipulations, printing, or file-based operations. You may be thinking of breaking them up into individual files:

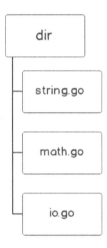

Figure 8.3: Group functions by files

That could alleviate some of the issues. However, what if your string's functionality started to grow further? You would then have a ton of string functions in one file or even multiple files. Every program you build would also have to include all of the code for **string**, **math**, and **io**. You would be copying code to every application that you built. Bugs in one code base would have to be fixed in multiple programs. That kind of code structure is not maintainable, nor does it encourage code reusability. The packages in Go are the next step to organizing your code in a way that makes it easy to reuse the components of your code. The following diagram shows the progression of organizing code from functions to source files to packages:

Figure 8.4: Code progression organization

Go organizes its code for reusability into directories called packages. A package is essentially a directory inside your workspace that contains one or more Go source files, which is used for grouping code that performs a task. It exposes only the necessary parts in order for those using your package to get a job done. The package concept is akin to using directories to organize files on a computer.

Package Structure

It does not matter to Go how many different files are in a package. You should separate code into as many files as makes sense for readability and logic grouping. However, all the files that are in a package must live in the same directory. The source files should contain code that is related, meaning that if the package is for configuration parsing, you should not have code in there for connecting to a database. The basic structure of a package consists of a directory and contains one or more Go files and related code. The following diagram summarizes the core components of a package structure:

Package Structure		
directory	contains one or more files	related code

Figure 8.5: Package structure

One of the commonly used packages in Go is the **strings** package. It contains several Go files that are referred to in the Go documentation as package files. Package files are `.go` source files that are part of the package, for example:

- `builder.go`
- `compare.go`
- `reader.go`
- `replace.go`
- `search.go`
- `strings.go`

Package Naming

Before we discuss how to declare a package, we need to discuss proper Go naming conventions for a package. The name of your package is significant. It represents what your package contains and identifies its purpose. You can think of a package name as self-documentation. Careful consideration needs to go into naming a package. The name of the package should be short and concise. It should not be verbose. Simple nouns are often chosen for a package name. The following would be poor names for a package:

- `stringconversion`
- `synchronizationprimitives`
- `measuringtime`

Better alternatives would be the following:

- `strconv`
- `sync`
- `time`

> **Note**
>
> `strconv`, `sync`, and `time` are actual Go packages found in the standard library.

Also, the styling of a package is something to take into consideration. The following would be poor style choices for a Go package name:

- `StringConversion`
- `synchronization_primitives`
- `measuringTime`

In Go, package names should be all lowercase with no underscores. Don't use camel case or snake case styling. There are multiple packages with pluralized names.

Abbreviations are encouraged, just as long as they are familiar or common in the programming community. The user of the package should easily understand what the package is used for just from its name, for example:

- **strconv** (string conversion)
- **regexp** (regular expression search)
- **sync** (synchronization)
- **os** (operating system)

Avoid package names such as **misc**, **util**, **common**, or **data**. These package names make it harder for the user of your package to understand its purpose. In some cases, there is a deviation from these guidelines, but for the most part, it is something we should strive for:

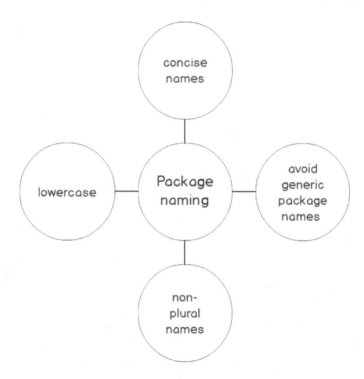

Figure 8.6: Package naming conventions

Package Declarations

Every Go file starts with a package declaration. The package declaration is the name of the package. The first line of executable code must be the package declaration:

```
package <packageName>
```

Recall that the **strings** package from the standard library has the following Go source files:

Each one of those files starts with the package declaration, even though they are all separate files. We will look at an example from the Go standard library. In the Go standard library, there is a package called **strings** (https://packt.live/35jueEu). It is made up of multiple files. We will only be looking at a snippet of code from the files in the package: **builder.go**, **compare.go**, and **replace.go**. We have removed comments and some code just to demonstrate that the package files start with the package name. There will be no output from the code snippet. This is an example of how Go organizes code into multiple files but in the same package:

main.go

```
   // https://golang.org/src/strings/builder.go
1  package strings
2  import (
3     "unicode/utf8"
4     "unsafe"
5  )
6  type Builder struct {
7     addr *Builder // of receiver, to detect copies by value
8     buf  []byte
9  }
10 // https://golang.org/src/strings/compare.go
11 package strings
12 func Compare(a, b string) int {
13    if a == b {
14       return 0
15    }
```

The full code is available at https://packt.live/35sihwF

All the functions, types, and variables that are defined in the Go source file are accessible within that package. Though your package could spread across multiple files, it is all part of the same package. Internally, all code is accessible across the files. Simply stated, code is visible within the package. Notice that not all of the code is visible outside of the package. The preceding snippet is from the official Go libraries. For a further explanation of the code, visit the links in the preceding Go snippets.

Exported and Unexported Code

Go has a very simple way to determine whether code is exported or unexported. Exported means that variables, types, functions, and so on are visible from outside of the package. Unexported means it is only visible from inside the package. If a function, type, variable, and so on starts with an uppercase letter, it is exportable; if it starts with a lowercase letter, it is unexportable. There are no access modifiers to be concerned with in **Go**. If the function name is capitalized, then it is exported, and if it is lowercase, then it is unexported.

> **Note**
>
> It is good practice to only expose code that we want other packages to see. We should hide everything else that is not needed by external packages.

Let's look at the following code snippet:

```
package main
import ("strings"
"fmt"
)
func main() {
  str := "found me"
  if strings.Contains(str, "found") {
    fmt.Println("value found in str")
  }
}
```

This code snippet uses the **strings** package. We are calling a **strings** function called **Contains**. The **stings.Contains** function searchs the **str** variable to see whether it has the value "**found**" within in it. If "**found**" is within the **str** variable, the **strings.Constains** will return **true**; if "**found**" is not within the **str** variable, the **strings.Contains** function will return **false**:

```
strings.Contains(str, "found")
```

To call the function, we prefix it with the package name, then the function name.

This function is exportable, thus is accessible to others outside of the **strings** package. We know it is an exported function because the first letter of the function is capitalized.

When you import a package, you only have access to the exported names.

We can validate whether the function exists in the **strings** package by looking at the **strings.go** file:

```
// https://golang.org/src/strings/strings.go
// Contains reports whether substr is within s.
    func Contains(s, substr string) bool {
    return Index(s, substr) >= 0
    }
```

The next code snippet will attempt to access an unexported function in the **strings** package:

```go
package main
import (
  "fmt"
  "strings"
)
func main() {
  str := "found me"
  slc := strings.explode(str, 3)
  fmt.Println(slc)
}
```

The function is unexported because it starts with a lowercase letter. Only code within the package can access the function; it is not visible outside of the package.

The code is attempting to call an unexported function in the **strings.go** package file:

```
prog.go:10:9: cannot refer to unexported name strings.explode
prog.go:10:9: undefined: strings.explode

Go build failed.
```

Figure 8.7: Program output

The following code snippet is from the Go standard library **strings** package and from the **strings.go** file inside of that package (https://packt.live/2RMxXqh). You can see that the **explode** function is unexportable because the function name starts with a lowercase letter:

main.go

```
1  // https://golang.org/src/strings/strings.go
2  // explode splits s into a slice of UTF-8 strings,
3  // one string per Unicode character up to a maximum of n (n < 0 means no limit).
4  // Invalid UTF-8 sequences become correct encodings of U+FFFD.
```

```
func explode(s string, n int) []string {
5      l := utf8.RuneCountInString(s)
6      if n < 0 || n > l {
7          n = l
8      }
9      a := make([]string, n)
10     for i := 0; i < n-1; i++ {
11         ch, size := utf8.DecodeRuneInString(s)
12         a[i] = s[:size]
13         s = s[size:]
14         if ch == utf8.RuneError {
15             a[i] = string(utf8.RuneError)
```

The full code is available at https://packt.live/2teXDBN.

GOROOT and GOPATH

We have looked at what a package is and its purpose. We have a basic understanding that multiple files can be part of a package construct. We have discussed the idiomatic Go way of naming packages. We have seen all these fundamental concepts being utilized in the Go standard library. We have one more concept to go over before we begin creating our own packages. It is important to understand how the Go compiler looks for the locations of the packages that are used in our applications.

The Go compiler needs a way to know how to find our source files (packages) so that the compiler can build and install them. The compiler utilizes two environmental variables for this job. **$GOROOT** and **$GOPATH** tell the Go compiler where to search for the locations of the Go packages listed by the `import` statement.

$GOROOT is used to tell the Go compiler the location of the Go standard library packages. **$GOROOT** is specific to the Go standard library. It is what Go uses to determine where its standard library packages and tools are located.

$GOPATH is the location for packages we create and third-party packages that we may have imported. At the command line, type the following code:

```
ECHO $GOPATH
```

Inside the **$GOPATH** file structure, there are three directories: **bin**, **pkg**, and **src**. The **bin** directory is the easiest to understand. This is where Go places the binaries or executables when you run the **go install** command. One of the main uses of the **pkg** directory is used by the compiler to store object files for the packages the Go compiler builds. This is to help with speeding up the compiling of programs. The **src** directory is the one we are most interested in understanding as it is the directory where we place our packages. This is the directory where we place files with the `.go` extension.

For example, if we have a package located at **$GOPATH/src/person/address/** and we want to use the address packages, we would need the following `import` statement:

```
import "person/address"
```

Another example would be if we have a package at **$GOPATH/src/company/employee**. If we were interested in using the **employee** package, the **import** statement would be as follows:

```
import "company/employee"
```

Packages that are located in a source code repository would follow a similar pattern. If we wanted to import source code from https://packt.live/2EKp357, the location in the filesystem would be **$GOPATH/src/github.com/PacktWorkshops/The-Go-Workshop/ Chapter08/Exercise8.01**.

The import would be as follows:

```
import "github.com/PacktWorkshops/Get-Ready-To-Go/Chapter08/Exercise8.01"
```

The following is a diagram showing the differences between **$GOROOT** and **$GOPATH**:

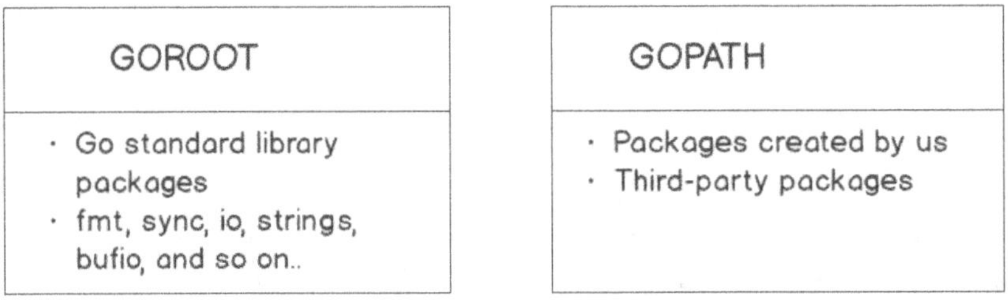

Figure 8.8: GOROOT and GOPATH comparisons

We are going to create a simple package called **msg**. The location of this file is within **$GOPATH $GOPATH/msg/msg.go**:

```
package msg
import "fmt"
//Greeting greets the input parameter
func Greeting(str string) {
    fmt.Printf("Greeting %s\n", str)
}
```

The package is named **msg**.

It has one exported function. The function takes a string and prints **"Greeting"** to the argument passed to the function.

To be able to use Go packages and our custom packages, we must import them. The **import** declaration contains the path location and the name of the package. The name of the package is the last directory that contains the package files. For example, if we have a directory structure in the **$GOPATH** location, **packt/chpkg/test/mpeg**, the package name would be **mpeg**.

The following code snippet is the **main** package file. It is in the following directory structure inside **$GOPATH**:

$GOPATH/demoimport/demoimport.go:

```
package main
import (
  "fmt"
  "msg"
)
func main() {
  fmt.Println("Demo Import App")
  msg.Greeting("George")
}
```

The output will be as follows:

```
Greeting George
```

This basic program imports the **msg** package. Since we have imported the **msg** package, we can then call any exportable function in the package by preferencing it with **"msg.<functionName>"**. We know that our **msg** package has an exportable function called **Greeting**. We call the exportable **Greeting** function from our **msg** package and get the output in the preceding figure.

When creating a package, it can contain multiple files within the same directory. We need to make sure that each of those files in that directory belongs to the same package. If you have a **shape** package and, in that directory, you have two files, but each has a different package declaration, the Go compiler will return an error:

shape.go

```
package shape
```

junk.go

```
package notright
```

If you attempted to perform a build, you would get the following error:

```
can't load package: package github.com/TrainingByPackt/Get-Ready-To-Go/Chapter0
8/Exercise8.01/shape: found packages notright (junk.go) and shape (shape.go) in
```

Figure 8.9: Program output

Package Alias

Go also has the ability to alias package names. There a few reasons that you may want to use alias names:

- The package name may not make it easy to understand its purpose. For the purpose of clarity, it might be better to alias a different name for the package.

- The package name might be too long. In this case, you want the alias to be more concise and less verbose.

- There could be scenarios where the package path is unique but both package names are the same. You would need to then use aliasing to differentiate between the two packages.

The package aliasing syntax is very simple. You place the alias name before the **import** package path:

```
import  f "fmt"
```

Here is a simple example showing how to use package aliasing:

```
package main
import (
   f "fmt"
   //"fmt"
)
func main() {
   f.Println("Hello, Gophers")
}
import (
   f "fmt"
```

We are aliasing the **fmt** package as **f**:

```
   f.Println("Hello, Gophers")
```

In the **main()** function, we are now able to call the **Println()** function using the **f** alias.

Main Package

The main package is a special package. There are two basic types of packages in Go: executable and non-executable. The main package is an executable package in Go. The main package requires there to be a **main()** function in its package. The **main()** function is the entry point for a Go executable. When you perform **go build** on the main package, it will compile the package and create a binary. The binary is created inside of the directory where the main package is located. The name of the binary will be the name of the folder it resides in:

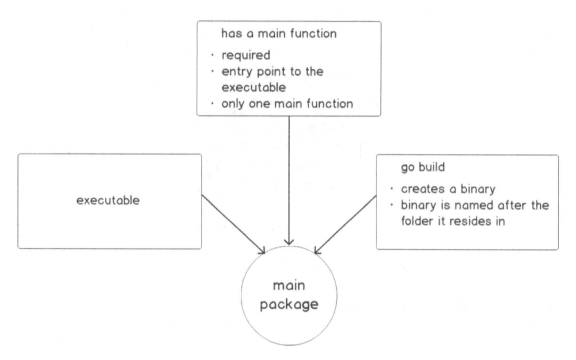

Figure 8.10: Main package functionality

Here's a simple example of the main package code:

```
package main
import (
    "fmt"
)
func main() {
    fmt.Println("Hello Gophers!")
}
```

The expected output is as follows:

```
Hello Gophers !
```

Exercise 8.01: Creating a Package to Calculate Areas of Various Shapes

In *Chapter 7, Interfaces*, we implemented code to calculate areas of different shapes. In this exercise, we will move all the code about shapes into a package called **shape**. We will then update the code in the package shape to be exportable. Then, we will update **main** to import our new **shape** package. However, we want it to still perform the same functionality in the **main()** function of the main package.

Here is the code that we will be converting into packages: https://packt.live/36zt6gv.

You should have a directory structure within your **$GOPATH** and files in those appropriate directories, as displayed in the following screenshot:

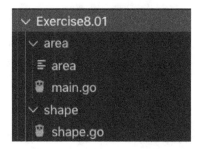

Figure 8.11: Program directory structure

The **shape.go** file should contain the entire code: https://packt.live/2PFsWNx.

We will only be going over the changes that are relevant to making this code a package, and for details on the parts of the code that we have gone over in a previous chapter, please see *Chapter 7, Interfaces*:

1. Create a directory called **Exercise8.01** inside **Chapter08**.

2. Create two more directories called **area** and **shape** inside the **Exercise8.01** directory.

3. Create a file called **main.go** inside the **Exercise8.01/area** directory.

4. Create a file called **shape.go** inside the **Exercise8.01/shape** directory.

5. Open the **Exercise8.01/shape.go** file.

6. Add the following code:

```
package shape
import "fmt"
```

The first line of code in this file tells us this is a non-executable package called **shape**. A non-executable package, when compiled, does not result in binary or executable code. Recall that a `main` package is a package that is executable.

7. Next, we need to make the types exportable. For each **struct** type, we have to capitalize on the type name and its fields to make it exportable. Exportable means that it is visible outside of this package:

```
type Shape interface {
    area() float64
    name() string
}
type Triangle struct {
    Base    float64
    Height float64
}
type Rectangle struct {
    Length float64
    Width   float64
}
type Square struct {
    Side float64
}
```

8. We also have to make the methods non-exportable, by changing the method name to lowercase. There is no need at the moment to make those methods visible outside of the package:

Exercise8.01

```
18 func PrintShapeDetails(shapes ...Shape) {
19   for _, item := range shapes {
20     fmt.Printf("The area of %s is: %.2f\n", item.name(), item.area())
21   }
22 }
23 func (t Triangle) area() float64 {
24   return (t.Base * t.Height) / 2
25 }
26 func (t Triangle) name() string {
27   return "Triangle"
28 }
29 func (r Rectangle) area() float64 {
30   return r.Length * r.Width
31 }
32 func (r Rectangle) name() string {
```

The full code for this step is available at https://packt.live/2rngdHf.

9. The **PrintShapeDetails** function also needs to be capitalized:

```
func PrintShapeDetails(shapes ...Shape) {
  for _, item := range shapes {
    fmt.Printf("The area of %s is: %.2f\n", item.name(), item.area())
  }
}
```

10. Perform a build to ensure that there are no compile errors:

```
go build
```

11. Here is the listing for the **main.go** file. By having a package as **main**, we know that this is executable:

```
package main
```

12. The **import** declaration only has one import. It is the **shape** package. The path location is **$GOPATH** plus the **import** path declaration. We can see the name of the package is **shape** since it is the last directory name in the path declaration. The **$GOPATH** mentioned here may differ from yours:

```
import (
    import "github.com/PacktWorkshops/The-Go-Workshop/Chapter08/Exercise8.01/shape"
)
```

13. In the **main()** function, we are initializing the **shape** package's exportable types:

```
func main() {
    t := shape.Triangle{Base: 15.5, Height: 20.1}
    r := shape.Rectangle{Length: 20, Width: 10}
    s := shape.Square{Side: 10}
```

14. We then call the **shape()** function, **PrintShapeDetails**, to get the area of each shape:

```
    shape.PrintShapeDetails(t, r, s)
}
```

15. At the command line, go to the **\Exercise8.01\area** directory structure.

16. At the command line, type the following:

```
go build
```

17. The **go build** command will compile your program and create an executable named after the **dir** area.

18. Type the executable name and hit *Enter*:

```
./area
```

The expected output is as follows:

```
The area of Triangle is: 155.78
The area of Rectangle is: 200.00
The area of Square is 100.00
```

We now have the functionality that we previously had in the interface chapter's implementation of **shape**. We have the **shape** functionality now encapsulated in the **shape** package. We exposed or made visible only the functions or methods that are needed to maintain the previous implementation. The **main** package has less clutter and imports the **shape** package to provide the functionality that was in the previous implementation.

The init() Function

As we have discussed, every Go program (executable) starts in the **main** package and the entry point is the **main** function. There is another special function that we should be aware of, called **init()**. Each source file can have an **init()** function, but for now, we will look at the **init** function in the context of the **main** package. When you start writing packages, you might need to provide some initialization (the **init()** function) for the package. The **init()** function is used to set up states or values. The **init()** function adds initialization logic for your package. Here are some examples of uses of the **init()** function:

- Setting database objects and connections
- The initialization of package variables
- Creating files
- Loading configuration data
- Verifying or repairing the program state

The **init()** function requires the following pattern to be called:

- Imported packages are initialized first.
- Package-level variables are initialized.
- The package's **init()** function is called.
- **main** is executed.

The following diagram shows the execution order that a typical Go program follows:

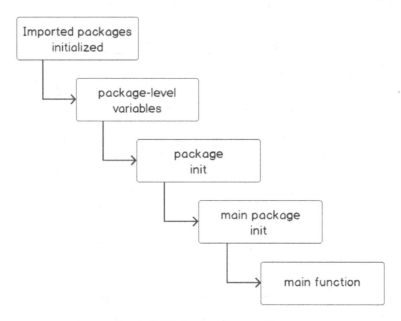

Figure 8.12: Order of execution

Here is a simple example that demonstrates the **package main** order of execution:

```
package main
import (
    "fmt"
)
var name = "Gopher"
func init() {
    fmt.Println("Hello, ",name)
}
func main() {
    fmt.Println("Hello, main function")
}
```

The output of the code is as follows:

```
Hello, Gopher
Hello, main function
```

Let's understand the code in parts:

```
var name = "Gopher"
```

Based on the output of the code, the package level variable declaration got executed first. We know this because the **name** variable is printed in the **init()** function:

```
func init() {
    fmt.Println("Hello, ",name)
}
```

The **init()** function then gets called and prints out **"Hello, Gopher"**:

```
func main() {
    fmt.Println("Hello, main function")
}
```

Finally, the **main()** function is executed:

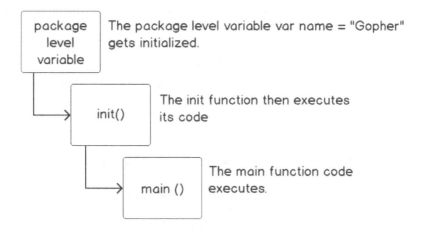

Figure 8.13: Execution flow of the code snippet

The **init()** function cannot have any arguments or return values:

```
package main
import (
    "fmt"
)
var name = "Gopher"
func init(age int) {
    fmt.Println("Hello, ",name)
}
func main() {
    fmt.Println("Hello, main function")
}
```

Running this code snippet will result in the following error:

```
prog.go:8:6: func init must have no arguments and no return values

Go build failed.
```

Figure 8.14: Program output

Exercise 8.02: Loading Budget Categories

Write a program that will load budget categories into a global map, before the **main** function runs. The **main** function should then print out the data on the map:

1. Create a **main.go** file.

2. The code file will belong to **package main** and will need to import the **fmt** package:

```
package main
import "fmt"
```

3. Create a global variable that will contain a map of budget categories with a key of **int** and a value of **string**:

```
var budgetCategories = make(map[int]string)
```

4. We will need to use an **init()** function to load our budget categories before **main** runs:

```
func init() {
    fmt.Println("Initializing our budgetCategories")
    budgetCategories[1] = "Car Insurance"
    budgetCategories[2] = "Mortgage"
    budgetCategories[3] = "Electricity"
    budgetCategories[4] = "Retirement"
    budgetCategories[5] = "Vacation"
    budgetCategories[7] = "Groceries"
    budgetCategories[8] = "Car Payment"
}
```

5. Since our budget categories have been loaded, we can now iterate over the map and print them:

```
func main() {
    for k, v := range budgetCategories {
        fmt.Printf("key: %d, value: %s\n", k, v)
    }
}
```

We will get the following output:

```
Initializing our budgetCategories
key: 5, value: Vacation
key: 7, value: Groceries
key: 8, value: Car Payment
key: 1, value: Car Insurance
key: 2, value: Mortgage
key: 3, value: Electricity
key: 4, value: Retirement
```

The aim here was to demonstrate how the **init()** function can be used to perform data initialization and loading before the **main** function executes. Data that generally needs to be loaded before **main** runs is static data, such as picklist values or some sort of configuration. As demonstrated, after the data gets loaded through the **init** function, it can be used by the **main** function. In the next topic, we will see how multiple **init** functions get executed.

> **Note**
>
> The output may differ in terms of the order displayed; Go maps do not guarantee the order of data.

Executing Multiple init() Functions

There can be more than one **init()** function in a package. This enables you to modularize your initialization for better code maintenance. For example, suppose you need to set up various files and database connections and repair the state of the environment that your program will be executed in. Doing all that in one **init()** function would make it complicated for maintaining and debugging. The order of execution of multiple **init()** functions is the order in which the functions are placed in the code:

```go
package main
import (
  "fmt"
)
var name = "Gopher"
func init() {
  fmt.Println("Hello, ",name)
}
func init(){
```

```
   fmt.Println("Second")
}
func init(){
   fmt.Println("Third")
}
func main() {
   fmt.Println("Hello, main function")
}
```

Let's break the code into parts and evaluate it:

```
var name = "Gopher"
```

Go initializes the **name** variable first, before the **init** function gets executed:

```
func init(){
   fmt.Println("Hello, ",name)
}
```

This prints out first since it is the first **init** in the function:

```
func init(){
   fmt.Println("Second")
}
```

The preceding gets printed out second since it is the second **init** in the function:

```
func init(){
   fmt.Println("Third")
}
```

The preceding gets printed out third since it is the third **init** in the function:

```
func main(){
   fmt.Println("Hello, main function")
}
```

Finally, the **main()** function gets executed.

The results would be as follows:

```
Hello, Gopher
Second
Third
Hello, main function
```

Exercise 8.03: Assigning Payees to Budget Categories

We are going to expand our program from *Exercise 8.02*, *Loading Budget Categories*, to now assign payees to budget categories. This is similar to many budgeting applications that try to match payees to commonly used categories. We will then print the mapping of a payee to a category:

1. Create the **main.go** file.

2. Copy the code from *Exercise 8.02*, *Load Budget Categories*, https://github.com/ PacktWorkshops/The-Go-Workshop/blob/master/Chapter08/Exercise8.02/ main.go into the **main.go** file.

3. Add a **payeeToCategory** map after **budgetCategories**:

```
var budgetCategories = make(map[int]string)
var payeeToCategory = make(map[string]int)
```

4. Add another **init()** function. This **init()** function will be used to populate our new **payeeToCategory** map. We will assign payees to the key value of the categories:

main.go

```
5  func init() {
6      fmt.Println("Initializing our budgetCategories")
7      budgetCategories[1] = "Car Insurance"
8      budgetCategories[2] = "Mortgage"
9      budgetCategories[3] = "Electricity"
10     budgetCategories[4] = "Retirement"
11     budgetCategories[5] = "Vacation"
12     budgetCategories[7] = "Groceries"
13     budgetCategories[8] = "Car Payment"
14 }
```

The full code for this step is available at https://packt.live/2Qdss1E.

5. In the **main()** function, we will print out the payees to categories. We iterate over the **payeeToCategory** map, printing the key **(payee)**. We print the category by passing the value of the **payeeToCategory** map as a key to the **budgetCategories** map:

```
func main() {
    fmt.Println("In main, printing payee to category")
    for k, v := range payeeToCategory {
        fmt.Printf("Payee: %s, Category: %s\n", k, budgetCategories[v])
    }
}
```

Here's the expected output:

```
Initializing our budgetCategories
Assign our Payees to categories
In main, printing payee to category
Payee: First Energy Electric, Category: Electricity
Payee: Ameriprise Financial, Category: Retirement
Payee: Wal Mart, Category: Groceries
Payee: Nationwide, Category: Car Insurance
Payee: Walt Disney World, Category: Vacation
Payee: ALDI, Category: Groceries
Payee: Martins, Category: Groceries
Payee: Chevy Loan, Category: Car Payment
Payee: BBT Loan, Category: Mortgage
```

Figure 8.15: Assign a payee to budget categories

You have now created a program that executes multiple **init()** functions before the execution of the **main** function. Each of the **init()** functions loaded data into our global map variables. We have determined the order of **init** functions executing because of the **print** statements that get displayed. This demonstrates that the **init()** functions print in the order they are present in the code. It is important to be aware of the order of your **init** functions as you may have unforeseen results based on the order of the code execution.

In the upcoming activity, we will be using all these concepts that we have looked at with packages and see how they all work together.

Activity 8.01: Creating a Function to Calculate Payroll and Performance Review

In this activity, we are going to take *Activity 7.01, Calculating Pay and Performance Review*, and modularize it using packages. We will be refactoring the code from https://packt.live/2YNnfS6:

1. Move the types and methods of **Developer**, **Employee**, and **Manager** into their own package. Types, methods, and functions must be properly exported or unexported.

2. Name the package **payroll**.

3. Logically separate the types and their methods into different package files. Recall that good code organization involves separating similar functionality into separate files.

4. Create the `main()` function as an alias to the `payroll` package.

5. Introduce the two `init()` functions in the `main` package. The first `init()` function should simply print a greeting message to `stdout`. The second `init()` should initialize/set up the key-value pairs.

The expected output would be as follows:

```
Welcome to the Employee Pay and Performance Review
++++++++++++++++++++++++++++++++++++++++++++++++++
Initializing variables
Eric Davis got a review rating of 2.80
Eric Davis got paid 84000.00 for the year
Mr. Boss got paid 160500.00 for the year
```

In this activity, we have seen how to use packages to separate our code and then to logically separate the code into individual files. We can see that each of those files make up a package. Each file of the package has internal access to the other files regardless of the fact that they are in separate files. This activity demonstrates how to create a package with multiple files and how those separate files can be used to further organize our code.

> **Note**
>
> The solution for this activity can be found on page 720.

Summary

We looked at the importance of developing software that is maintainable, reusable, and modular. We discovered how Go's packages play an important part in meeting those criteria for developing software. We looked at the overall structure of a package. It is made up of a directory, can contain one or more files, and it has code that is related. A package is essentially a directory inside of your workspace that contains one or more files that are used for grouping code that is to perform a task. It exposes only the necessary parts to those using your package to get a job done. We discussed the importance of naming packages properly. We also learned how to name a package, that is, concisely, in lowercase, descriptively, using non-plural names, and avoiding generic names. Packages can be executable or non-executable. If a package is the main package, then it is an executable package. The main package must have a main function and that is where the entry point is for our package.

We also talked about what is exportable and unexportable code. When we capitalize the name of a function, type, or method, it is visible to others using our package. Lowercasing a function, type, or method makes it not visible to other users from outside our package. When creating a package, we realized that **GOROOT** and **GOPATH** are important to know – they determine where Go looks for a package. We learned that **init** functions can perform the following duties: initializing variables, loading configuration data, setting database connections, or verifying that our program state is ready for execution. The **init()** function has certain rules when it gets executed and on how to utilize it. This chapter will help you to write highly manageable, reusable, and modular code.

In the next chapter, we will be studying basic debugging. We will look at various techniques that help us to locate bugs in our programs. We will also discuss ways to minimize the difficulty of locating bugs and how to increase the chances of locating a bug after making a modification to the codebase.

9

Basic Debugging

Overview

In this chapter, we will look at basic debugging methodologies. We will look at some proactive measures that we can take to reduce the number of bugs that we introduce into our program. Once we understand these measures, we will investigate the ways in which we can locate a bug.

You will be able to acquaint yourself with debugging in Go and implement various ways to format printing. You will evaluate various techniques of basic debugging and find the general location of a bug in the code. By the end of the chapter, you will know to print out variable types and values using Go code and also log the state of an application for debugging purposes.

Introduction

As you develop software programs, there are going to be times that your program behaves in an unintended way. For instance, the program could be throwing an error and might crash. A crash is when our code stops functioning midway and then exits abruptly. Perhaps, the program has given us unexpected results. For example, we request a video streaming service for the movie *Rocky 1*, but instead get *Creed 1*! Or, you deposited a check into your bank account but, instead of being credited, the bank software debited your account. These examples of software programs behaving in an unintended way are called bugs. Sometimes, "bug" and "error" are used interchangeably. In *Chapter 6, Errors*, in the *What Are Errors?* section, we discussed how there are three different types of errors or bugs: syntax errors, runtime errors, and logic errors. We also examined examples and saw the difficulty of discovering the location of each type of error.

The process of determining the cause of unintended behavior is called debugging. There are various causes of bugs that get released into production:

- **Testing is performed at the end of the development**: During the development life cycle, it is tempting to not perform testing incrementally. For instance, we are creating multiple functions for an application, and once we finish all the functions, they then get tested. A possibly better way of testing our code would be to test each function as we complete it. This is known as incrementally testing or delivering code in smaller chunks. This gives us better code stability. This is accomplished by testing a function to ensure it works before continuing to the next function. The function that we just completed could be used by other functions. If we do not test it before we continue, the other functions that use our function could be using a buggy function. Depending on the bug and the change to our function, it could impact other users of our function. Later in the chapter, we will discuss some more benefits of coding and testing incrementally.

- **Application enhancements or changes to requirements**: Our code is often changing between the development phase and when we release it to production. Once in production, we receive feedback from the users; the feedback could be additional requirements or even enhancements to the code. Changing the production-level code in one area could have a negative impact in another area. If the development team uses unit tests, then this would aid in mitigating some of the bugs introduced in a change to the code base. By using unit tests, we could run our unit test before we deliver the code to see whether our change had a negative impact. We will discuss what a unit test is later.

- **Unrealistic development timeframe**: There are times when functionality is requested to be delivered in very tight timeframes. This can lead to taking shortcuts in best practices, shortening the design phase, performing less testing, and receiving unclear requirements. All of those can increase the chance of introducing bugs.

- **Unhanding of errors**: Some developers may choose not to handle errors as they occur. For example, a file that is needed for the application to load configuration data is not found, not handling an error return for an invalid mathematical operation such as dividing by zero, or perhaps a connection to a server could not be established. If your program does not properly handle these and other types of errors, this can cause bugs.

These are just a few causes of bugs. Bugs have a negative impact on our programs. The results of a bug that causes a miscalculation can be life-threatening. In the medical industry, a machine is used to administer a drug called heparin; this drug is a blood thinner, and it is used to prevent blood clots. If the code that determines the calculation of how often and how much heparin can be administered has a bug that causes it to malfunction, the machine could deliver too much or too little of the drug. This could have an adverse effect on the patient. As you can see, it is critical to deliver software that is as bug-free as possible. In this chapter, we are going to look at some ways to minimize the number of bugs that are introduced and ways of isolating the location of the bug.

Methods for Bug-Free Code

We will briefly look at some methods that will help us to minimize the number of bugs that could be introduced into our code. These methods will also aid in giving us confidence as to the portions of the code that introduced the bug:

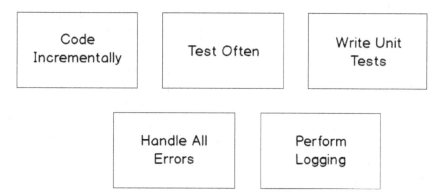

Figure 9.1: Different methods to debug code

Code Incrementally and Test Often

Let's consider the approach of developing incrementally. This means developing the program incrementally and testing it often after adding an incremental piece of code. This pattern will help you to track the bug easily because you are testing every small snippet of code as opposed to one large program.

Writing Unit Tests

When a test is written and code changes occur, the unit test protects the code from potential bugs being introduced. A typical unit test takes a given input and validates that a given result is produced. If the unit test is passing before the code change, but is now failing after the code change, then we can conclude that we introduced some unintended behavior. The unit test needs to pass before we push our code to a production system.

Handling All Errors

This was discussed in *Chapter 6, Errors*. Ignoring errors can lead to potentially unintended results in our program. We need to handle the errors properly to make the debugging process easier.

Performing Logging

Logging is another technique that we can use to determine what is occurring in the program. There are various types of logging; some of the common logging types are debug, info, warn, error, fatal, and trace. We will not go into the details of each type; we will focus instead on performing debug type logging. This type of logging is typically used to determine the state of the program before a bug occurs. Some of the information that is gathered includes the values of the variables, the portion of the code that is being executed (one example would be function name), the values of the arguments being passed, the output of the function or method, and more. In this chapter, we will be performing our own custom debug logging using built-in features of the Go standard library. The built-in log package of Go can provide timestamps. This is useful when trying to understand the timing of various events. When you perform logging, you will need to keep in mind the performance implications. Depending on the application and the load it is under, the logging could be extensive during peak times and may have a negative impact on the performance of the application. In certain circumstances, it could cause it to be unresponsive.

Formatting Using fmt

One of the uses of the **fmt** package is to display data to the console or to the filesystem, such as a text file, that will contain information that could be helpful in debugging the code. We have used the **Println()** function on numerous occasions. Let's take a slightly deeper look at the functionality of **fmt.Println()**. The **fmt.Println()** function places spaces between the variables and then appends a new line at the end of the string. The **fmt.Println()** function prints the default formats of the variables.

Exercise 9.01: Working with fmt.Println

In this exercise, we will print a **hello** statement using **fmt.Println**:

1. Import the **fmt** package:

```
package main
import (
    "fmt"
)
```

2. Declare the **fname** and **lname** variables in a **main()** function, and assign two strings to a variable:

```
func main() {
    fname:= "Edward"
    lname:= "Scissorhands"
```

3. Call the **Println** method from the **fmt** package. It will print **Hello:** and then the value of both variables followed by a space. Then, it will print a \n (newline) to the standard output:

```
    fmt.Println("Hello:",fname,lname)
```

4. The following statement prints **Next Line** plus \n to the standard output:

```
    fmt.Println("Next Line")
}
```

The output is as follows:

```
Hello: Edward Scissorhands
Next Line
```

We have demonstrated the basics of printing out messages. In the next topic, we will look at how we can format the data that we want to print.

Formatting Using fmt.Printf()

The **fmt** package also has numerous ways of formatting the output of our various print statements. We will look next at the **fmt.Printf()**.

The **fmt.Printf()** formats the string according to the verb and prints it to **stdout**. The standard output (**stdout**) is a stream for output. By default, the standard output is pointed to the terminal. The function uses something called format verbs or sometimes called a format specifier. The verbs tell the **fmt** function where to insert the variable. For example, **%s** prints a string; it is a placeholder for a string. These verbs are based upon the C language:

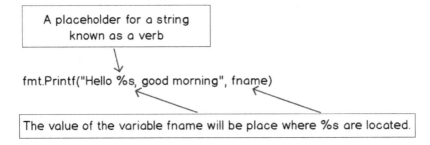

Figure 9.2: Explanation of Printf

Consider the following example:

```
package main
import (
    "fmt"
)
func main() {
    fname:= "Edward"
    fmt.Printf("Hello %s, good morning",fname)
}
```

The **fname** variable is assigned as **Edward**. When the **fmt.Printf()** function runs, the **%s** verb will have the value of **fname**.

The output is as follows:

```
Hello Edward, good morning
```

But what happens when we have more than one variable that we want to print? How can we print more than one variable in the **fmt.Printf()** function? Let's take a look:

```go
package main
import (
    "fmt"
)
func main() {
    fname:= "Edward"
    lname:= "Scissorhands"
    fmt.Printf("Hello Mr. %s %s",fname,lname)
}
```

As you see in the preceding code, we now have **fname** and **lname** assigned to a string. The **fmt.Printf()** function has two verb strings and two variables. The first variable, **fname**, is assigned to the first **%s**. The second variable, **lname**, is assigned to the second **%s**. The variables replace the verbs in the order they are placed in the **fmt.Printf()** function.

The output is as follows:

```
Hello Mr. Edward Scissorhands
```

The **fmt.Printf()** function does not add a new line to the end of the string that it prints. We have to add a newline in the string if we want to return the output with a new line:

```go
package main
import (
    "fmt"
)
func main() {
    fname := "Edward"
    lname := "Scissorhands"
    fmt.Printf("Hello my first name is %s\n", fname)
    fmt.Printf("Hello my last name is %s", lname)
}
```

In Go, you can escape characters using the \. This tells us that a character should not be printed because it has a special meaning. When you use \n, it denotes a newline. We can place a newline anywhere within the string.

The output is as follows:

```
Hello my first name is Edward
Hello my last name is Scissorhands
```

The following would be the result if we did not place the \n in the string:

```
Hello my first name is EdwardHello my last name is Scissorhands
```

The Go language has several printing verbs. We will introduce some of the basic verbs that are frequently used. We will introduce others as they become pertinent to performing basic debugging:

Verb	Meaning
%d	Prints an integer in base-10
%f	Prints a floating point number, default width, default precision
%t	Prints a bool type
%s	Prints a string type
%v	Prints the value in default format
%b	Prints the base two\binary representation
%x	Prints the hex representation

Figure 9.3: Table representing verbs and their meanings

Let's take a look at an example of using verbs for printing out various data types:

```go
package main
import (
    "fmt"
)
func main() {
    fname := "Joe"
    gpa := 3.75
    hasJob := true
    age := 24
    hourlyWage := 45.53
    fmt.Printf("%s has a gpa of %f.\n", fname, gpa)
    fmt.Printf("He has a job equals %t.\n", hasJob)
    fmt.Printf("He is %d earning %v per hour.\n", age, hourlyWage)
}
```

- After initializing the variables of different types, we will use them in our **Printf()** function:

```
fmt.Printf("%s has a gpa of %f.\n", fname, gpa)
```

%s is the placeholder for a string; when the **Printf()** statement runs the value in the **fname** variable, it will replace **%s**. The **%f** is the placeholder for a float; when the **Printf()** statement runs the value in the **gpa** variable, it will replace **%f**.

- Check whether the person has a job as follows:

```
fmt.Printf("He has a job equals %t.\n", hasJob)
```

- **%t** is the placeholder for a **bool**. When the **Printf()** statement runs the value in the **hasJob** variable, it will replace **%t**.

- Print the age of the person and their wage per hour:

```
fmt.Printf("He is %d earning %v per hour.\n", age, hourlyWage)
```

- **%d** is the placeholder for an **int** base-10. When the **Printf** statement runs the value in the **age** variable, it will replace **%d**.

%v is the placeholder for the value in a default format.

The following is the expected output:

```
Joe has a gpa of 3.750000.
He has a job equals true.
He is 24 earning 45.53 per hour.
```

> **Note**
>
> We will demonstrate how to format verbs, such as **gpa**, to make it round to a specific number of decimal places.

Additional Options for Formatting

Verbs can also be formatted by adding additional options to the verb. In our previous example, the **gpa** variable printed out some erroneous zeros. In this topic, we are going to demonstrate how to control the printing of certain verbs. If we want to round to a certain precision when using the %f verb, we can do so by placing a decimal and a number following the % symbol: %.2f. That would specify two decimal places with the second one being rounded. Given the following examples, notice how the **nth** number is rounded to what is specified by the n(number) used in the %.nf verb:

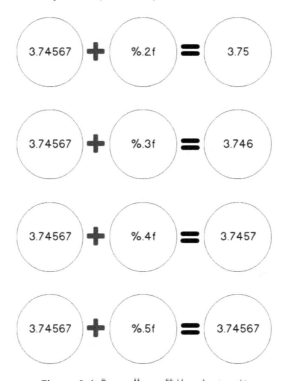

Figure 9.4: Rounding off the decimals

You can also specify the overall width of the number; this includes the decimal point. The width of the number refers to the total characters of the number you are formatting including the decimal point. You can specify the width of the number you are formatting by putting a number before the decimal point. %10.0f states the format will be a total width of 10; this includes the decimal point. It will pad with spaces if the width is less than what is being formatted, and it will be right-aligned.

Let's take a look at an example of formatting various numbers using the width and **%.f** verb together:

```go
package main
import (
    "fmt"
)
func main()
{
  v  := 1234.0
  v1 := 1234.6
  v2 := 1234.67
  v3 := 1234.678
  v4 := 1234.6789
  v5 := 1234.67891
    fmt.Printf("%10.0f\n", v)
    fmt.Printf("%10.1f\n", v1)
    fmt.Printf("%10.2f\n", v2)
    fmt.Printf("%10.3f\n", v3)
    fmt.Printf("%10.4f\n", v4)
    fmt.Printf("%10.5f\n", v5)
}
```

Now, let's understand this code in detail:

- In the **main()** function, we declared variables with different decimal places:

```go
func main() {
    v  := 1234.0
    v1 := 1234.6
    v2 := 1234.67
    v3 := 1234.678
    v4 := 1234.6789
    v5 := 1234.67891
```

- **%10.0f** states that the total width is ten with a precision of zero, using **v** and the verbs total width is 4:

```go
    fmt.Printf("%10.0f\n", v)
```

- **%10.1f** states that the total width is ten with a precision of one, using **v1** and the verbs total width is 6:

```
fmt.Printf("%10.1f\n", v1)
```

- **%10.2f** states that the total width is ten with a precision of two, using **v2** and the verbs total width is 7:

```
fmt.Printf("%10.2f\n", v2)
```

- **%10.3f** states that the total width is ten with a precision of three, using **v3** and the verbs total width is 8:

```
fmt.Printf("%10.3f\n", v3)
```

- **%10.4f** states that the total width is ten with a precision of four, using **v4** and the verbs total width is 9:

```
fmt.Printf("%10.4f\n", v4)
```

- **%10.5f** states that the total width is ten with a precision of five, using **v5** and the verbs total width is 10:

```
fmt.Printf("%10.5f\n", v5)
}
```

The result is as follows:

```
      1234
    1234.6
   1234.67
  1234.678
 1234.6789
1234.67891
```

Figure 9.5: Output after formatting verbs

- To make the results left align your fields, you can use the - flag after the % symbol as follows:

```
fmt.Printf("%-10.0f\n", v)
fmt.Printf("%-10.1f\n", v1)
fmt.Printf("%-10.2f\n", v2)
fmt.Printf("%-10.3f\n", v3)
fmt.Printf("%-10.4f\n", v4)
fmt.Printf("%-10.5f\n", v5)
```

Using the same variables before the results would be as follows:

```
1234
1234.6
1234.67
1234.678
1234.6789
1234.67891
```

Figure 9.6: Output after left aligning the formatted verbs

We have just skimmed the surface of Go's support for using verbs. You should, by now, have a fundamental understanding of how verbs work. We will continue to build on using verbs and the various ways to format **print** in the upcoming topics. This topic laid the groundwork for the techniques that we will be using to do basic debugging.

Exercise 9.02: Printing Decimal, Binary, and Hex Values

In this exercise, we will be printing decimal, binary, and hex values from 1 to 255. The results should be right aligned. The decimal width should be set to three, the binary or base 2 width set to 8, and the hex width set to 2. The aim of this exercise is to properly format the output of our data by using a Go standard library package.

All directories and files created should be within your **$GOPATH**:

1. Create a directory called **Exercise9.02** inside the **Chapter09** directory.

2. Create a file called **main.go** inside the **Chapter09/Exercise9.02/** directory.

3. Using Visual Studio Code, open the **main.go** file.

4. Import the following packages:

```go
package main
import (
    "fmt"
)
```

5. Add the **main()** function:

```go
func main() {
}
```

6. In the **main()** function, use a **for** loop that will loop up to 255 times:

```
func main() {
    for i := 1; i <= 255; i++ {

    }
}
```

7. Next, we want to print the variable three different ways, formatted to the following specifications:

Display **i** as a decimal value with a width of 3 and right aligned.

Display **i** as a base 2 value with a width of 8 and right aligned.

Display **i** as a hex value with a width of 2 and right aligned.

This code should be placed inside of the **for** loop:

```
func main() {
    for i := 1; i <= 255; i++ {
        fmt.Printf("Decimal: %3.d Base Two: %8.b Hex:   %2.x\n", i, i, i)
    }
}
```

8. At the command line, change the directory using the following code:

```
cd Chapter09/Exercise9.02/
```

9. At the command line, type the following:

```
go build
```

10. Type the executable that was created from the **go build** command and hit *Enter*.

Here are the expected results of the program:

```
Decimal:  16 Base Two:   10000 Hex:  10
Decimal:  17 Base Two:   10001 Hex:  11
Decimal:  18 Base Two:   10010 Hex:  12
Decimal:  19 Base Two:   10011 Hex:  13
Decimal:  20 Base Two:   10100 Hex:  14
Decimal:  21 Base Two:   10101 Hex:  15
Decimal:  22 Base Two:   10110 Hex:  16
Decimal:  23 Base Two:   10111 Hex:  17
Decimal:  24 Base Two:   11000 Hex:  18
Decimal:  25 Base Two:   11001 Hex:  19
Decimal:  26 Base Two:   11010 Hex:  1a
Decimal:  27 Base Two:   11011 Hex:  1b
Decimal:  28 Base Two:   11100 Hex:  1c
Decimal:  29 Base Two:   11101 Hex:  1d
Decimal:  30 Base Two:   11110 Hex:  1e
Decimal:  31 Base Two:   11111 Hex:  1f
Decimal:  32 Base Two:  100000 Hex:  20
Decimal:  33 Base Two:  100001 Hex:  21
Decimal:  34 Base Two:  100010 Hex:  22
Decimal:  35 Base Two:  100011 Hex:  23
```

Figure 9.7: Expected output after printing the decimal, binary, and hex values

We have seen how to format our data using the **Printf()** from the Go standard library **fmt** package. We will use this knowledge to perform some basic debugging of printing code markers in our programs. We will learn more about this in the following section.

Basic Debugging

We have been happily coding along. The big moment has arrived; it is time to run our program. We run our program and find the results are not as we expected them to be. In fact, something is grossly wrong. Our inputs and outputs are not matching up. So, how do we figure out what went wrong? Well, having bugs appear in our programs is something that we all face as developers. However, there is some basic debugging that we can perform to aid us in remediating or, at the very least, gathering information about these bugs by:

- **Printing out the code markers in the code**:

  Markers in our code are print statements that help us to identify where we are in the program when the bug occurred:

  ```
  fmt.Println("We are in function calculateGPA")
  ```

- **Printing out the type of the variable**:

  While debugging, it might be useful to know the variable type that we are evaluating:

  ```
  fmt.Printf("fname is of type %T\n", fname)
  ```

- **Printing out the value of the variable**:

  Along with knowing the type of the variable, it is sometimes valuable to know the value that is stored in the variable:

  ```
  fmt.Printf("fname value %#v\n", fname)
  ```

- **Perform debug logging**:

  At times, it might be necessary to print debug statements to a file: maybe there is an error that only occurs in a production environment. Or perhaps we would like to compare the results of data printed in a file for different inputs to our code:

  ```
  log. Printf("fname value %#v\n", fname)
  ```

Here are some basic debugging methods:

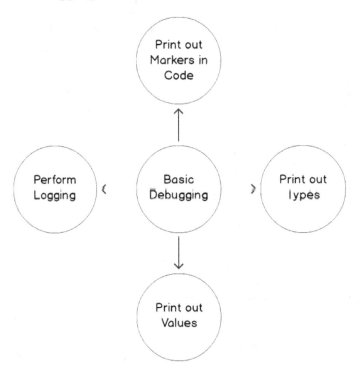

Figure 9.8: Basic debugging methods

One of the first steps in debugging is to identify the general location of where the bug is in the code. Before you can start to analyze any data, we need to know where this bug is occurring. We do this by printing out markers in our code. Markers in our code are typically nothing more than print statements that help us to identify where we are in the program when the bug occurred. They are also used to narrow the scope of the location of the bug. Generally, this process involves placing a print statement with a message that shows us where we are in the code. If our code reaches that point, we can then determine, based on some conditions, whether that area is where the bug is at. If we find that it is not, we potentially remove that print statement and place it in other spots in the code.

Given the following trivial example, here is a bug that returns:

```
Incorrect value
Program exited: status 1.
```

The code is reporting an error, but we do not know where the error is coming from. This code generates a random number and that random number is passed to **func a** and **func b**. Depending on the value of the random number, it will depend on which function the error occurs in. The following code demonstrates the importance of having properly placed **debug** statements to help determine the area of the code that a potential bug is located:

main.go

```
 9  func main() {
10      r := random(1, 20)
11      err := a(r)
12      if err != nil {
13          fmt.Println(err)
14          os.Exit(1)
15      }
16      err = b(r)
17      if err != nil {
18          fmt.Println(err)
19          os.Exit(1)
20      }
21  }
```

The full code is available at https://packt.live/35TQpl0

- We are using the **rand** package to generate a random number.

- **rand.Seed()** is used so that each time you run the program with **rand.Intn**, it lowers the possibility of returning the same number. However, if you use the same seed each time, the random number generator will return the same number the first time you run the code. To minimize the probability of the same number being generated, we need to provide the seed function with a unique number each time. We use **time.Now().UTC.UnixNano()** to help our program get a more random number. It should be noted, though, that if you put this in a loop, the loop could iterate at a speed that **time.Now().UTC.UnixNano()** could generate the same time value. However, for our program, this is not as likely, rather it is just something to consider in future code.

- The **rand.Intn((max-min)+1)+min** is starting to generate a random number between two other numbers. In our program, it is 1 and 20:

```
func a(i int) error {
    if i < 10 {
        fmt.Println("Error is in func a")
        return errors.New("Incorrect value")
    }
    return nil
}
func b(i int) error {
    if i >= 10 {
        fmt.Println("Error is in func b.)
        return errors.New("Incorrect value")
    }
    return nil
}
```

- The preceding two functions evaluate **i** to see whether it falls within a given range. If the value that falls within that range returns an error, but also prints a **debug** statement to let us know where the error occurred.

By strategically placing print statements in our code, we can see which function the error is in.

The output should look something as follows:

```
Error is in func a
Incorrect value

Program exited: status 1.
```

This section covered debugging. We were introduced to using **print** statements for debugging. In the next topic, we will build on our knowledge of printing and look at how to print the variable type.

> **Note**
>
> Due to the randomness of the value of **r**, it can be different, which will impact the results of the program to be either **func a** or **func b**.
>
> Additionally, if you run the preceding program in the Go playground, it will give you the same result every time. This is due to the fact that the playground caches, so it does not adhere to the randomness of the answer.

Printing Go Variable Types

It is often useful to know the type of a variable when debugging. Go provides this functionality through the use of a **%T** verb. Go is case sensitive. A capital **%T** means the type of the variable and a lowercase **%t** means the **bool** type:

```go
package main
import (
    "fmt"
)
type person struct {
    lname string
    age int
    salary float64
}
func main() {
    fname := "Joe"
    grades := []int{100, 87, 67}
    states := map[string]string{"KY": "Kentucky", "WV": "West Virginia", "VA": "Virginia"}
    p:= person{lname:"Lincoln", age:210,salary: 25000.00}
    fmt.Printf("fname is of type %T\n", fname)
    fmt.Printf("grades is of type %T\n", grades)
    fmt.Printf("states is of type %T\n", states)
    fmt.Printf("p is of type %T\n", p)
}
```

Here are the results of the preceding code snippet:

```
fname is of type string
grades is of type []int
states is of type map[string]string
p is of type main.person
```

The **%T** is used in each **print** statement to print the concrete type of the variable. In a previous topic, we printed out values. We can also print out a Go syntax representation of the type using **%#v**. It is useful to be able to print out the Go representation of a variable. The Go representation of a variable is the syntax that can be copied and pasted into the Go code:

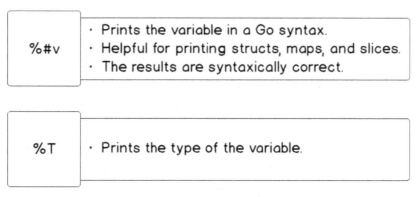

Figure 9.9: Syntax representation of the type using %T and the Go syntax representation, %#v

Exercise 9.03 Printing the Go Representation of a Variable

In this exercise, we will create a simple program that will demonstrate how to print out the Go representation of various variables. We will use various types (such as a string, slice, map, and a struct) and print the Go representations of those types:

1. Create a directory called **Exercise9.03** inside the **Chapter09** directory.

2. Create a file called **main.go** inside the **Chapter09/Exercise9.03/** directory.

3. Using Visual Studio Code, open the **main.go** file.

4. Add the following code to **main.go**:

```
package main
import (
    "fmt"
)
```

5. Next, create a person struct with the same fields listed as follows:

```
type person struct {
    lname string
    age int
    salary float64
}
```

6. Inside the **main** function, assign a value to the **fname** variable:

```
func main() {
    fname := "Joe"
```

7. Create a slice literal and assign to a grades variable:

```
grades := []int{100, 87, 67}
```

8. Create a **map** literal of a key string and a value string, and assign it to a variable of states. This is a map of state abbreviations and their respective names:

```
states := map[string]string{"KY": "Kentucky", "WV": "West Virginia",
    "VA": "Virginia"}
```

9. Create a person literal and assign it to p:

```
p:= person{lname:"Lincoln", age:210,salary: 25000.00}
```

10. Next, we will be printing out the Go representation of each of our variables using **%#v**:

```
fmt.Printf("fname value %#v\n", fname)
fmt.Printf("grades value %#v\n", grades)
fmt.Printf("states value %#v\n", states)
fmt.Printf("p value %#v\n", p)
}
```

11. At the command line, change the directory using the following code:

```
cd Chapter09/Exercise9.03/
```

12. At the command line, type the following:

```
go build
```

13. Type the executable that was created from the **go build** command and hit *Enter*.

You will get the following output:

```
fname value "Joe"
grades value []int{100, 87, 67}
states value map[string]string{"KY":"Kentucky", "VA":"Virginia", "WV":"West Virginia"}
p value main.person{lname:"Lincoln", age:210, salary:25000}
```

Figure 9.10: Go representation of the types

In this exercise, we saw how we can print the Go representation of simple types (the **fname** string) to more complex types such as a **person** struct. This is another tool in our toolbox that we can use for debugging; it allows us to see the data the way Go sees it. In the next topic, we will be looking at another tool to help us debug our code. We will be looking at how we log information that can be used to further aid in debugging.

Logging

Logging can be used to help debug a bug in our program. Operating systems log various information such as access to resources, what an application is doing, the overall health of the system, and much more. It is not doing this because there is an error, rather it is logging to make it easier on the system administrator to determine what is going on with the operating system at various times. It allows for easier debugging when the operating system acts or performs a certain task that was not expected. This is the same attitude we should take when logging our application. We need to think about the information that we gather and how that would help us to debug the application if something is not performing the way we think it should.

We should be performing logging regardless of whether the program needs debugging. Logging is useful for understanding events that happen, the health of the application, any potential issues, and who is accessing our application or data. Logging is an infrastructure to your program that can be utilized when an abnormality occurs in the application. Logging helps us to track abnormalities that we would otherwise miss. In production, our code could be executing in different conditions compared to a development environment, such as an increase in the number of requests to the server.

If we do not have the ability to log this information and how our code performs, we could spend endless hours trying to figure out why our code behaves the way it does in production but not in development. Another example would be that we get some malformed data as a request in production, and our code does not handle the format properly and causes undesired behavior. Without proper logging, it could take an extradentary amount of time to determine that we received data that we were not adequately handling.

The Go standard library provides a package called **log**. It includes basic logging that can be used by our programs. We will look into how the package can be used to log various information.

Consider the following example:

```
package main
import (
    "fmt"
    "log"
)
func main() {
    name := "Thanos"
    log.Println("Demo app")
    log.Printf("%s is here!",name)
    log.Print("Run")
}
```

The log functions, **Println()**, **Printf()**, and **Print()**, perform the same functionality as their **fmt** counterparts with one exception. When the log functions execute, it gives additional details such as the date and time of the execution, as follows:

```
2019/11/10 23:00:00 Demo app
2019/11/10 23:00:00 Thanos is here!
2019/11/10 23:00:00 Run
```

This information can be useful when investigating and reviewing the logs at a later time and for understanding the order of events. We can even get more details to be logged by our logger. The Go log package has a function called **SetFlags** that allows us to be more specific.

> **Note**
>
> Here is a list of the options for logging provided by the Go package that we can set in the function (https://golang.org/src/log/log.go?s=8483:8506#L267):

```go
// These flags define which text to prefix to each log entry generated by the Logger.
// Bits are or'ed together to control what's printed.
// There is no control over the order they appear (the order listed
// here) or the format they present (as described in the comments).
// The prefix is followed by a colon only when Llongfile or Lshortfile
// is specified.
// For example, flags Ldate | Ltime (or LstdFlags) produce,
//       2009/01/23 01:23:23 message
// while flags Ldate | Ltime | Lmicroseconds | Llongfile produce,
//       2009/01/23 01:23:23.123123 /a/b/c/d.go:23: message
const (
        Ldate         = 1 << iota     // the date in the local time zone: 2009/01/23
        Ltime                         // the time in the local time zone: 01:23:23
        Lmicroseconds                 // microsecond resolution: 01:23:23.123123.  assumes Ltime.
        Llongfile                     // full file name and line number: /a/b/c/d.go:23
        Lshortfile                    // final file name element and line number: d.go:23. overrides Llongfile
        LUTC                          // if Ldate or Ltime is set, use UTC rather than the local time zone
        LstdFlags     = Ldate | Ltime // initial values for the standard logger
)
```

Figure 9.11: List of flags in Go

Let's set some of the flags in *Figure 9.11* and observe the difference in behavior that we had before.

Consider the following example:

```go
package main
import (
    "log"
)
func main() {
    log.SetFlags(log.Ldate | log.Lmicroseconds | log.Llongfile)
    name := "Thanos"
    log.Println("Demo app")
    log.Printf("%s is here!", name)
    log.Print("Run")
}
```

Let's break down the code in order to understand it better:

```
log.SetFlags(log.Ldate | log.Lmicroseconds | log.Llongfile)
```

The **log.Ldate** is the date of the local timezone. This is the same information that was logged before.

The **log.Lmicroseconds** will give this is the microseconds of the formatted date. Note that we have not discussed time yet; for further details on time, please refer to *Chapter 10, About Time*.

The **log.LlongFile** will give us the full filename and line number that the log comes from.

The output is as follows:

```
2019/04/30 08:15:57.835521 /go/src/myprojects/scratch/main.go:10: Demo app
2019/04/30 08:15:57.835754 /go/src/myprojects/scratch/main.go:11: Thanos is here!
2019/04/30 08:15:57.835769 /go/src/myprojects/scratch/main.go:12: Run
```

Figure 9.12: Output

Log Fatal Errors

Using the log package, we can also log fatal errors. The **Fatal()**, **Fatalf()**, and **Fatalln()** functions are similar to **Print()**, **Printf()**, and **Println()**. The difference is after the log **Fatal()** functions are followed by an **os.Exit(1)** a system call. The log package also has the following functions: **Panic**, **Panicf**, and **Panicln**. The difference between the **Panic()** functions and the **Fatal** function is that the **Panic** functions are recoverable. When using the **Panic** functions, you can use the **defer()** function, whereas when using the **Fatal** functions, you cannot. As stated earlier, the **Fatal** functions call **os.Exit()**; a **defer** function will not be called when an **os.Exit()** gets called. There may be some instances where you want to abort the program immediately with no possibility of recovery. For example, the application may have gotten to a state where it is best to exit it before data corruption or undesired behavior results. Or you may have developed a command-line utility that is used by others and you need to provide an exit code to the callers of your executable to signal it has completed its tasks.

In the following code example, we will look at how **log.Fataln** is used:

```
package main
import (
    "log"
    "errors"
)
func main() {
```

```
    log.SetFlags(log.Ldate | log.Lmicroseconds | log.Llongfile)
    log.Println("Start of our app")
    err := errors.New("Application Aborted!")
    if err != nil {
        log.Fatalln(err)
    }
    log.Println("End of our app")
}
```

Let's break down the code in order to understand it better:

```
log.Println("Start of our app")
```

The statement prints to **stdout** with the date, time, and line number of the log message:

```
err := errors.New("We crashed!")
```

We create an error to test the logging of the **Fatal()** errors:

```
log.Fatalln(err)
```

We log the error and then it exits the program:

```
log.Println("End of our app")
```

The line did not execute because we logged the error as **fatal** and that causes the program to exit.

Here are the results. Notice that even though it was an error, it still logs the same details about the error as it does the print functionality, and then it exits:

```
2009/11/10 23:00:00.000000 /tmp/sandbox182690719/prog.go:10: Start of our app
2009/11/10 23:00:00.000000 /tmp/sandbox182690719/prog.go:13: Application Aborted!
```

Figure 9.13: Logging a fatal error

Activity 9.01: Building a Program to Validate Social Security Numbers

In this activity, we are going to be validating **Social Security Numbers (SSNs)**. Our program will be accepting SSNs without the dashes. We will want to log the validation process for the SSNs so that we can trace the entire process. We do not want our application to stop if an SSN is invalid; we want it to log the invalid number and continue to the next one:

1. Create a custom error called **ErrInvalidSSNLength** for invalid SSN length.

2. Create a custom error called **ErrInvalidSSNNumbers** for SSNs that have non-numeric digits.

3. Create a custom error called **ErrInvalidSSNPrefix** for an SSN that has three zeros as the prefix.

4. Create a custom error called **ErrInvalidDigitPlace** for SSNs that starts with a 9 it requires 7 or 9 in the fourth place.

5. Create a function that returns an error if the SSN length is not 9.

6. Create a function that checks whether the SSN is a length of 9. The function returns an error that has the SSN that was invalid and the custom error, **ErrInvalidSSNLength**.

7. Create a function that checks whether the SSN contains all numbers. The function returns an error that has the SSN that was invalid and the custom error, **ErrInvalidSSNNumbers**.

8. Create a function that checks whether the SSN does not have a prefix of 000. The function returns an error that has the SSN that was invalid and the custom error, **ErrInvalidSSNPrefix**.

9. Create a function that checks that if the SSN starts with a 9, then it requires a 7 or 9 in the fourth place. The function returns an error that has the SSN that was invalid and the custom error, **ErrInvalidDigitPlace**.

10. In the **main()** function, create a slice of SSN so that your program will validate each of them.

11. For each SSN that you are validating, if errors are returned from your functions that are being used to validate, then log those errors and continue processing the slice.

12. An example slice to validate is as follows:

```
validateSSN := []string{"123-45-6789", "012-8-678", "000-12-0962", "999-33-
    3333", "087-65-4321","123-45-zzzz"}
```

The preceding slice should have the following output:

```
2009/11/10 23:00:00.000000 /tmp/sandbox957632207/prog.go:22: Checking data []string{"123-45-6789", "012-8-678", "000-12-0962", "999-33-3333", "087-65-4321", "123-45-zzzz"}
2009/11/10 23:00:00.000000 /tmp/sandbox957632207/prog.go:24: Validate data "123-45-6789" 1 of 6
2009/11/10 23:00:00.000000 /tmp/sandbox957632207/prog.go:24: Validate data "012-8-678" 2 of 6
2009/11/10 23:00:00.000000 /tmp/sandbox957632207/prog.go:33: the value of 0128678 caused an error: ssn is not nine characters long
2009/11/10 23:00:00.000000 /tmp/sandbox957632207/prog.go:24: Validate data "000-12-0962" 3 of 6
2009/11/10 23:00:00.000000 /tmp/sandbox957632207/prog.go:37: the value of 000120962 caused an error: ssn has three zeros as a prefix
2009/11/10 23:00:00.000000 /tmp/sandbox957632207/prog.go:24: Validate data "999-33-3333" 4 of 6
2009/11/10 23:00:00.000000 /tmp/sandbox957632207/prog.go:41: the value of 999333333 caused an error: ssn starts with a 9 requires 7 or 9 in the fourth place
2009/11/10 23:00:00.000000 /tmp/sandbox957632207/prog.go:24: Validate data "087-65-4321" 5 of 6
2009/11/10 23:00:00.000000 /tmp/sandbox957632207/prog.go:24: Validate data "123-45-zzzz" 6 of 6
2009/11/10 23:00:00.000000 /tmp/sandbox957632207/prog.go:29: the value of 12345zzzz caused an error: ssn has non-numeric digits
```

Figure 9.14: Validating the SSN output

Note

The solution for this activity can be found on page 725.

In this activity, we used the log package to capture information to trace the process of validating an SSN. If we ever need to debug the validation process for our SSN, then we can look at the logging messages and follow the validation failures of the SSN. We also demonstrated how to format the logging messages to contain the information that would be needed for debugging.

Summary

In this chapter, we studied various methodologies for easing the debugging process such as coding incrementally and testing the code often, writing unit tests, handling all errors, and performing logging on the code.

Looking at the `fmt` package, we discovered various ways to output information to help us to find bugs. The `fmt` package offered different print formatting, verbs, and ways to control the output of the verbs by use of various flags.

With the usage of logging from Go's standard library, we were able to see details of how our application is executing. The log package allowed us to see the file path and line number that the log event took place on. The log package came with various print functions that mimic some of the `fmt` print functions, which provided us with various insights into the usage of the verbs we learned in this chapter. We were also able to save the logging information to a file. Each time we call a print function from the log package, it placed the results in the file.

We were able to perform basic debugging by using the standard library that is provided by Go. We looked at the log package and were introduced to the `time` type. We did not go into the details of Go's implementations of time.

In the next chapter, we will be looking at how time is represented in Go. We will be discussing the various functions used with the `time` type. We will also demonstrate how to convert time to various time constructs (such as nanoseconds, microseconds, milliseconds, seconds, minutes, hours, and so on). Then, we will finally learn about the underlying type of time.

10
About Time

Overview

This chapter demonstrates how Go handles variables representing time data, which is a very important aspect of the language.

By the end of this chapter, you will be able to create your own time format, compare and manage time, calculate the duration of time series, and format time according to user requirements.

Introduction

The previous chapter introduced you to basic debugging in Go. The more you develop code in Go, the better you get; however, developing and deploying code may come with corner cases that need to be debugged. The previous chapter showed you how to use the **fmt** package, how to log into files, and how to use the **f** function format.

This chapter is dedicated to teaching you all you need to know about handling variables that represent time data. You will learn how to do it the "Go-way". First, we will start out with basic time creation, timestamps, and more; then, we will learn how to compare and manipulate time, calculate the duration between two dates, and create timestamps. Finally, we will learn how to format the time according to our needs. So, let's not waste any more time and jump right in.

Making Time

Making time means declaring a variable that holds the time formatted in a specific way. Formatting time will be covered at the end of this chapter; so, for now, we will use the default formatting that is provided by Go. In this topic, we will be executing everything in the **main()** function of our script, so the skeleton should look like this:

```
package main
import "fmt"
import "time"
func main(){
   //this is where the code goes.
}
```

Let's look at our skeleton first and learn how to create and manipulate time variables. Our skeleton has the standard **package main** definition that is necessary. We use the **fmt** package to print the output to the console. Since we'll be using the **time** module, we'll need to import that as well.

Whenever we issue **go run <script>.go**, the **main()** function gets called and executes whatever is declared in it.

One of the most common jobs for the **time** module is to measure the duration of the execution for the script. We can do this by capturing the current time in a variable, at the beginning and at the end, so that we can calculate the difference and know how long the specific action took to complete. The very first example is as follows:

```
start := time.Now()
fmt.Println("The script has started at: ",start)
fmt.Println("Saving the world...")
time.Sleep(2 * time.Second)
end := time.Now()
fmt.Println("The script has completed at: ",end)
```

The output from our script should look like this:

```
The script has started at:  2019-09-27 08:19:33.8358274 +0200 CEST m=+0.001998701
Saving the world...
The script has completed at:  2019-09-27 08:19:35.8400169 +0200 CEST m=+2.006161301
```

As you can see, this does not look very fancy; however, by the end of this chapter, you will have learned how to make it more readable.

Consider the following scenario; your employer gives you a task to develop a small Go application that tests a web application based on the day of week. Your employer has the main release of a new web app every Monday at 12:00 AM CEST. With a downtime window from 12:00 AM CEST to 2:00 PM CEST, and the deployment being about 30 minutes, you have 1.5 hours to test the app. This is where Go's time module comes to your rescue. The script performs a **hit-n-run** test on the other days of the week, but, on release day, you are required to perform a **full-blown** functionality test. The first version of the script took the argument to see which test to perform, but the second script version made the decision based on the day and the hour:

Days	Testing strategy
Monday	full-blown
Rest of the week	hit-n-run

Figure 10.1: Testing strategies

Consider the following code:

```
Day := time.Now().Weekday()
Hour := time.Now().Hour()
fmt.Println("Day: ",Day, "Hour: ",Hour)
if Day.String() == "Monday"{
   if Hour >= 1{
     fmt.Println("Performing full blown test!")
   }else{
     fmt.Println("Performing hit-n-run test!")
   }
}else{ fmt.Println("Performing hit-n-run test!")}
```

The current day of the week is captured in the variable called **Day**. The hour of execution is also captured in the variable called **Hour**. When this script is executed, there are two types of output.

The first one is a simple **hit-n-run** output, as follows:

```
Day: Thursday Hour: 14
Performing hit-n-run test!
```

The second one is the **full blown** output, as follows:

```
Day: Thursday Hour: 14
Performing full blown test!
```

In this example, we have seen how the day of execution modifies the behavior of the application.

> **Note**
>
> The actual test was left out intentionally as this is not part of the chapter's topic. However, the output clearly shows which part was responsible for the control of the test.

Another example would be to create the log filenames for scripts in Go. The basic idea is to collect a log per day and have a timestamp concatenated to the name of the log file. The skeleton looks like this:

```
Application_Action_Year_Month_Day
```

In Go, there is an elegant and simple way to do it:

```
import "strconv"
AppName := "HTTPCHECKER"
  Action := "BASIC"
  Date := time.Now()
  LogFileName := AppName + "_" + Action + "_" + strconv.Itoa(Date.Year()) + "_" + Date.
Month().String() + "_" + strconv.Itoa(Date.Day()) + ".log"
  fmt.Println("The name of the logfile is: ",LogFileName)
}
```

The output appears as follows:

```
The name of the logfile is:  HTTPCHECKER_BASIC_2019_September_27.log
```

However, there is a catch. If you want to concatenate strings with **time** types, which are not implicitly convertible, use the **strconv** package, which needs to be imported on top of your script:

```
import "strconv"
```

In turn, this allows you to call the **strconv.Itoa()** function, which converts your **Year** and **Day** values and, finally, lets you concatenate them into a single string.

Now that we have learned how to make time variables, let's learn to compare them.

Exercise 10.1: Creating a Function to Return a timestamp

In this exercise, we will create a function called **whatstheclock**. The goal of this function is to demonstrate how you can create a function that wraps a nice, formatted **time. Now()** function and returns the date in an **ANSIC** format. The **ANSIC** format will be explained in further detail in the *Formatting Time* section:

1. Create a file called **Chapter_10_Exercise_1.go**.

2. Initialize the script with the package and import statements:

    ```
    package main
    import "time"
    import "fmt"
    ```

3. Define the function called **whatstheclock()**:

    ```
    func whatstheclock() string {
      return time.Now().Format(time.ANSIC)
    }
    ```

4. In the **main()** function, define a call to the **whatstheclock()** function and print the result to the console:

```
func main(){
    fmt.Println(whatstheclock())
}
```

5. Save the file and run the code:

```
go run Chapter_10_Exercise_1.go
```

You should see the following output:

```
Thu Oct 17 13:56:03 2019
```

In this exercise, we demonstrated how you can create a small function that returns the current time in an ANSIC format.

> **Note**
>
> Any type of operating system that you work with will provide two types of clocks to measure the time; one is called the "monotonic clock", and the other is called the "wall clock." The wall clock is what you see on a Windows machine in the taskbar; it's subject to change and is usually synchronized with a public or corporate NTP server based on your current location. The **NTP** server stands for **Network Time Protocol** and is used to tell clients the time based on an atomic clock, or from a satellite reference.

Comparing Time

Most of the time, when working with Go on smaller scripts, it is very important for your statistics to know when a script should run, or between what hours and minutes a script should be completed. By statistics, we mean knowing how much time the app saves by executing a specific operation compared to what time cost it would have if we had to perform these manually. This allows us to measure the improvement of the script over time when we develop the functionality further. In this topic, we will look at some live examples demonstrating how you can solve this problem.

Let's take a look at the logic for the first script, which was intended not to run before or after a specified time. This time can arrive either via another automation, or when a trigger file is manually placed there; every day, the script needs to run at different times, specifically, after the specified time as soon as possible.

The time was in the following **2019-09-27T22:08:41+00:00** format:

```
now := time.Now()
only_after, _ := time.Parse(time.RFC3339,"2020-11-01T22:08:41+00:00")
fmt.Println(now, only_after)
fmt.Println(now.After(only_after))
if now.After(only_after){
  fmt.Println("Executing actions!")
}else{
  fmt.Println("Now is not the time yet!!")
}
```

The output of the script when we are not yet at the deadline is as follows:

```
Now is not the time yet!!
```

When we meet the criteria, the output looks like this:

```
Executing actions!
```

Let's examine what is happening here. We create the **now** variable, which is crucial for the execution. We have the **time** string parsed based on RFC3339. RFC3339 specifies the format that should be used for the **date** and **time** strings. This function returns two values: one value is the output if the conversion succeeds, and the other is the error if there is one. We capture the output in the **only_after** variable, and we use a throwaway variable for capturing any output; this is the underscore sign, _. We could use a standard variable such as **only_after_error**, but unless we use that variable later in time, the compiler will throw an error that the variable was declared but never used. This is circumvented by the use of the _ variable. Based on this logic, we could implement the **only_before** argument or variable very simply. The **time** package has two very useful functions: one is called **After()**, and the other is called **Before()**. They allow us to simply compare two **time** variables.

There is a third function in the package called **Equal()**. This function allows you to compare two **time** variables and returns **true** or **false** depending on whether they are equal.

Let's take a look at an example of the **Equal()** function in action:

```
now := time.Now()
   now_too := now
   time.Sleep(2*time.Second)
   later := time.Now()
   if now.Equal(now_too){
     fmt.Println("The two time variables are equal!")
   }else{
     fmt.Println("The two time variables are different!")
   }
   if now.Equal(later){
     fmt.Println("The two time variables are equal!")
   }else{
     fmt.Println("The two time variables are different!")
   }
```

The output looks like this:

```
The two time variables are equal!
The two time variables are different!
```

Let's see what happens here. We have three **time** variables, which are called **now**, **now_too**, and **later**. The **time** module's **Sleep()** function is used to simulate the latency of 2 seconds. This function takes an integer argument and waits for the given time to pass and then continues the execution. The result of this is that the **later** variable holds different time values and allows us to demonstrate the **Equal()** function's purpose, which you can see in the output.

Now, the time has come to check what facilities are provided to calculate the duration or difference between the two **time** variables.

Duration Calculation

The ability to calculate the duration of an execution comes in handy during many aspects of programming. In our everyday life, we can monitor discrepancies and performance bottlenecks that our infrastructure might face. For example, if you have a script that takes only 5 seconds to complete on average and the monitoring execution time shows you a huge bump during certain hours of a day or certain days, it might be wise to investigate. The other aspect is related to web applications. Measuring the duration of request-response in your scripts can give you an insight into how well invested you are in your apps to serve high loads, and it even allows you to expand your capacity on certain days or weeks of the year. For example, if you have an online shop dealing with products, it might be wise to size your capacity according to patterns such as Black Friday or Christmas.

You may do well with a lower capacity during most of the year, but those holidays can result in revenue loss if the infrastructure is not sufficiently well sized. There is very little coding required to add such functionality to your scripts. Let's now take a look at how to do it:

```
Start := time.Now()
fmt.Println("The script started at: ", Start)
sum := 0
for i := 1; i < 10000000000; i++ {
    sum += i
}
End := time.Now()
Duration := End.Sub(Start)
fmt.Println("The script completed at: ", End)
fmt.Println("The task took",Duration.Hours(), "hour(s) to complete!")
fmt.Println("The task took",Duration.Minutes(), "minutes(s) to complete!")
fmt.Println("The task took",Duration.Seconds(), "seconds(s) to complete!")
fmt.Println("The task took",Duration.Nanoseconds(), "nanosecond(s) to complete!")
```

If you execute this script, the result will be something like this, depending on the PC's performance:

```
The script started at:  2019-10-18 09:00:28.1293988 +0200 CEST m=+0.001985801
The script completed at:  2019-10-18 09:00:30.7563703 +0200 CEST m=+2.628957301
The task took 0.0007297143055555556 hour(s) to complete!
The task took 0.043782858333333334 minutes(s) to complete!
The task took 2.6269715 seconds(s) to complete!
The task took 2626971500 nanosecond(s) to complete!
```

Figure 10.2: Measuring the execution time

All that needs to be done is to capture the time when the script starts and ends. Then, we can calculate the duration by subtracting the start time and the end time. After that, we can utilize the **Duration** variable's functions to get the **Hours()**, **Minutes()**, **Seconds()**, and **Nanoseconds()** values of the time it took to complete the task.

There are four resolutions you will be provided with, namely:

- Hours

- Minutes

- Seconds

- Nanoseconds

If you need, for example, days, weeks, or months, then you can calculate it from the resolutions provided.

Back in the day, we had a requirement to measure the duration of transactions, and we had a Service Level Agreement (SLA) that needed to be met. This meant that there were applications that needed to process a request in, let's say, 1,000 ms or 5 s depending on the criticality of the product. The next script will show you how this was implemented. There are 6 different resolutions that you have the option to choose from:

- Hour

- Minute

- Second

- Millisecond

- Microsecond

- Nanosecond

Let's consider the following example:

```
deadline_seconds := time.Duration((600 * 10) * time.Millisecond)
Start := time.Now()
fmt.Println("Deadline for the transaction is  ",deadline_seconds)
fmt.Println("The transaction has started at: ", Start)
sum := 0
for i := 1; i < 25000000000; i++ {
    sum += i
}
End := time.Now()
//Duration := time.Duration((End.Sub(Start)).Seconds() * time.Second)
Duration := End.Sub(Start)
TransactionTime := time.Duration(Duration.Nanoseconds()) * time.Nanosecond
fmt.Println("The transaction has completed at· ", End, Duration)
if TransactionTime <= deadline_seconds{
   fmt.Println("Performance is OK transaction completed in",TransactionTime)
}else{
   fmt.Println("Performance problem, transaction completed
in",TransactionTime,"second(s)!")
 }
```

When we don't meet the deadline, the output is as follows:

```
Deadline for the transaction is 6s
The transaction has started at:  2019-10-18 09:06:54.3287544 +0200 CEST m=+0.001993501
The transaction has completed at:  2019-10-18 09:07:00.8462146 +0200 CEST m=+6.519453701 6.5174602s
Performance problem, transaction completed in 6.5174602s second(s)!
```

Figure 10.3: Transaction deadline not met

When we meet the deadline, it looks like this:

```
Deadline for the transaction is 6s
The transaction has started at:  2019-10-18 09:07:40.9621074 +0200 CEST m=+0.001967701
The transaction has completed at:  2019-10-18 09:07:46.0772246 +0200 CEST m=+5.117084901 5.1151172s
Performance is OK transaction completed in 5.1151172s
```

Figure 10.4: Transaction deadline met

Let's dissect our example. First, we define a deadline for the transaction with the **time. Duration()** variable. In my experience, the **Millisecond** resolution is optimal; however, it does take some time to get used to calculating it. Feel free to use whichever resolution you prefer. We mark the beginning with the **Start** variable, do some calculations, and mark the completion with the **End** variable. The magic happens after this. We would like to calculate the difference between the deadline and the transaction duration, but we cannot do it directly. We need to convert the **Duration** value to **Transaction** time. This is done the same way when we created our deadline. We simply use the **Nanosecond** resolution, which is the lowest resolution we should go to. However, in this case, you can use the resolution you would like. After conversion, we can easily compare and decide whether the transaction is fine or not.

Now, let's see how we can manipulate time.

Managing Time

The Go programming language's **time** package provides two functions that allow you to manipulate time. One of them is called **Sub()**, and the other one is called **Add()**. There have not been many cases, in my experience, where this has been used. Mostly, when calculating the elapsed time of a script's execution, the **Sub()** function is used to tell the difference.

Let's see what the addition looks like:

```
TimeToManipulate := time.Now()
ToBeAdded := time.Duration(10 * time.Second)
fmt.Println("The original time:",TimeToManipulate)
fmt.Println(ToBeAdded," duration later:",TimeToManipulate.Add(ToBeAdded))
```

After execution, the following output welcomes us:

```
The original time: 2019-10-18 08:49:53.1499273 +0200 CEST m=+0.001994601
10s duration later: 2019-10-18 08:50:03.1499273 +0200 CEST m=+10.001994601
```

Let's inspect what happened here. We created a variable to hold our time, which requires some manipulation. The **ToBeAdded** variable represents a duration of 10 seconds, which we would like to add. The **Add()** function of the **time** package expects a variable of the **time.Duration()** type. Then, we simply call the **Add()** function of our date, and the result is visible on the console. The functionality of the **Sub()** function is rather cumbersome, and it is not really intended to remove a specific duration from the time we have. It can be done, but you need many more lines of code to achieve this. What you can do is craft your duration with a negative value. If you swap out the second line to this:

```
ToBeAdded := time.Duration(-10 * time.Minute)
```

It will work just fine and output you this:

```
The original time: 2019-10-18 08:50:36.5950116 +0200 CEST m=+0.001994401
-10m0s duration later: 2019-10-18 08:40:36.5950116 +0200 CEST m=+599.998005599
```

This works as we expected; we have successfully calculated what time it was 10 minutes ago.

Exercise 10.2: Duration of Execution

In this exercise, we will craft a function that allows you to calculate the duration of the execution between two **time.Time** variables and return a string that tells you how long the execution took to complete:

Perform the following steps in order:

1. Create a file called **Chapter_10_Exercise_2.go**.

2. Initialize the script with the following **package** and **import** statements:

```
package main
import "time"
import "fmt"
import "strconv"
```

3. Let's now define our **elapsedTime()** function:

```
func elapsedTime(start time.Time, end time.Time) string {
    Elapsed := end.Sub(start)
    Hours := strconv.Itoa(int(Elapsed.Hours()))
    Minutes := strconv.Itoa(int(Elapsed.Minutes()))
    Seconds := strconv.Itoa(int(Elapsed.Seconds()))
    return "The total execution time elapsed is: " + Hours + " hour(s) and " +
        Minutes + " minute(s) and " + Seconds + " second(s)!"
}
```

4. Now we are ready to define our **main()** function:

```
func main(){
    Start := time.Now()
    time.Sleep(2 * time.Second)
    End := time.Now()
    fmt.Println(elapsedTime(Start,End))
}
```

5. Run the code:

```
go run Chapter_10_Exercise_2.go
```

The following should appear as the output:

```
The total execution time elapsed is: 0 hour(s) and 0 minute(s) and 2
    second(s)!
```

In this exercise, we created a function that shows us how many hours, minutes, and seconds it took to execute the action. This is useful because you can reuse this function in other Go apps.

Now, let's turn our eyes toward the formatting of time.

Formatting Time

So far in this chapter, you may have noticed that the dates are pretty ugly. I mean, take a look at the following lines:

```
The transaction has started at:  2019-09-27 13:50:58.2715452 +0200 CEST
    m=+0.002992801
```

These were intentionally left there to force you to think about whether this is all that Go can do. Is there a way to format down these lines to make them more convenient and easier to read? If so, what are those extra lines?

Here, we will answer those questions. When we talk about time formatting, there are two main concepts we are referring to. The first option is for instances when we would like our time variable to output a desired looking string when we use it in print, and the second option is for when we would like to take a string and parse it to a specific format. Both have their own use cases; we are going to look at them in more detail as I teach you how to use both.

First, we are going to learn about the **Parse()** function. This function has essentially two arguments. The first one is the standard to parse against, and the second one is the string that needs to be parsed. The end of this parse will result in a time variable that can utilize built-in Go functions. Go uses a POSIX-based date format. **Parse()** is very useful when you have an application that is working with time values from different time zones and you would like to convert them, for example, to the same time zone for better understanding and easier comparison:

```
Mon Jan 2 15:04:05 -0700 MST 2006
0      1     2  3  4  5       6
```

This date format is equal to "123456" in POSIX, which can be decoded from the preceding example. There are constants provided in the language to help you deal with parsing different time strings.

There are three main standards against which we can parse the time:

- RFC3339

- UnixDate

- ANSIC

Let's take a look at how **Parse()** works:

```
t1, _ := time.Parse(time.RFC3339,"2019-09-27T22:18:11+00:00")
t2, _ := time.Parse(time.UnixDate,"2019-09-27T22:18:11+00:00")
t3, _ := time.Parse(time.ANSIC,"2019-09-27T22:18:11+00:00")
fmt.Println("RFC3339:",t1)
fmt.Println("UnixDate",t2)
fmt.Println("ANSIC",t3)
```

The output is as follows:

```
RFC3339: 2019-19-27 22:18:11 +0000 +0000
UnixDate 0001-01-01 00:00:00 +0000 UTC
ANSIC 0001-01-01 00:00:00 +0000 UTC
```

What happens behind the scenes is as follows. We have the **t1**, **t2**, and **t3** variables that hold the time, which is parsed against the specified format. The _ variables hold the error results if there are any during the conversion. The output from the **t1** variable is the only one that makes sense; **UnixDate** and the ANSIC are wrong because the wrong string is parsed against the standard. **UnixDate** expects something that they call **epoch**. The epoch is a very unique date; on UNIX systems, it marks the beginning of time, which starts at January 1, 1970. It expects a huge integer, which is the number of seconds elapsed since this date. The format expects something like this as the input: **Mon Sep _27 18:24:05 2019**. Providing such time allows the **Parse()** function to provide the correct output.

Now that we have clarified the **Parse()** function, it's time to look at the **Format()** function.

Go allows you to craft your own **time** variables. Let's learn how we can do that and, afterward, we will format it:

```
date := time.Date(2019, 9, 27, 18, 50, 48, 324359102, time.UTC)
fmt.Println(date)
```

The preceding code demonstrates how you can craft the time for yourself; however, we are going to look at what all those numbers are. The skeleton syntax for that is as follows:

```
func Date(year int, month Month, day, hour, min, sec, nsec int, loc *Location)
    Time
```

Essentially, we need to specify the year, month, day, hour, and so on. We would like to reformat our output based on the input variables; this should appear as follows:

```
2019-09-27 18:50:48.324359102 +0000 UTC
```

Time zones were not important until people started working in big enterprise environments. When you have a global fleet of interconnected devices, it is important to be able to differentiate between time zones. If you want to have an **AddDate()** function, which can be used to add **Year**, **Month**, and **Day** to your current time, then this must enable you to dynamically add to your dates. Let's take a look at an example. Given our previous date, let's add 1 year, 2 months, and 3 days:

```
date := time.Date(2019, 9, 27, 18, 50, 48, 324359102, time.UTC)
next_date := date.AddDate(1, 2, 3)
fmt.Prinln(next_date)
```

You will get the following output upon execution of this program:

```
2020-11-30 18:50:48.324359102 +0000 UTC
```

The `AddDate()` function takes three arguments: the first is `Year`, the second is `Month`, and the third is `Day`. This gives you the opportunity to fine-tune the scripts you have. In order to properly understand how formatting works, you need to know what is under the hood.

One last important aspect of time formatting is to understand how you can utilize the `LoadLocation()` function of the `time` package to convert your local time to the local time of another time zone. Our reference time zone will be the `Los Angeles` time zone. The `Format()` function is used to tell Go how we would like to see our output formatted. The `In()` function is a reference to a specific time zone we want our formatting to be present in.

Let's find out what the time is in Berlin:

```
Current := time.Now()
  Berlin, _ := time.LoadLocation("Europe/Berlin")
  fmt.Println("The local current time is:",Current.Format(time.ANSIC))
  fmt.Println("The time in Berlin is: ",Current.In(Berlin).Format(time.ANSIC))
```

Depending on your day of execution, you should see the following output:

```
The local current time is: Fri Oct 18 08:14:48 2019
The time in Berlin is: Thu Oct 17 23:14:48 2019
```

The key here is that we get our local time in a variable, and then we use the `In()` function of the `time` package to, say, convert that value to a specific time zone's value. It's simple, yet useful.

Exercise 10.03: What Is the Time in Your Zone?

In this exercise, we will create a function that tells the difference between the current time zone and the specified time zone. The function will utilize the `LoadLocation()` function to specify the location based on which a variable will be set to a specific time. The `In()` location will be used to convert a specific time value to a given time zone value. The output format should be in the ANSIC standard.

Perform the following steps in order:

1. Create a file called `Chapter_10_Exercise_3.go`.

2. Initialize the script with the following **package** and **import** statements:

```
package main
import "time"
import "fmt"
```

3. Now is the time to create our function called **timeDiff()**, which will also return the **Current** and the **RemoteTime** variable formatted with ANSIC:

```
func timeDiff(timezone string) (string, string)  {
    Current := time.Now()
    RemoteZone, _ := time.LoadLocation(timezone)
    RemoteTime := Current.In(RemoteZone)
    fmt.Println("The current time is: ",Current.Format(time.ANSIC))
    fmt.Println("The timezone:",timezone,"time is:",RemoteTime)
    return Current.Format(time.ANSIC), RemoteTime.Format(time.ANSIC)
}
```

4. Define the **main()** function:

```
func main(){
    fmt.Println(timeDiff("America/Los_Angeles"))
}
```

5. Run the code:

```
go run Chapter_10_Exercise_3.go
```

The output looks as follows:

```
The current time is: Thu Oct 17 15:37:02 2019
The timezone: America/Los_Angeles time is: 2019-10-17 06:37:02.2440679 -0700
    PDT
Thu Oct 17 15:37:02 2019 Thu Oct 17 06:37:02 2019
```

In this exercise, we saw how easy it is to navigate between different time zones.

Activity 10.01: Formatting a Date According to User Requirements

In this activity, you need to create a small script that takes the current date and outputs it in the following format: "02:49:21 31/01/2019." You need to utilize what you have learned so far regarding the conversion of an integer to a string. This will allow you to concatenate different parts of your **time** variable. Remember that the **date.Month()** function omits the name and not the number of the month.

You have to perform the following steps to get the desired output:

1. Use the **time.Now()** function to capture the current date in a variable.

2. Dissect the captured date to **day**, **month**, **year**, **hour**, **minute**, and **seconds** variables by converting them into strings.

3. Print out the concatenated variables in order.

    Once the script is complete, the output should appear as follows (note that this depends on when you run the code):

    ```
    15:32:30 2019/10/17
    ```

    By the end of this activity, you should have learned how you can craft your custom **time** variables and use **strconv.Itoa()** to convert a number to a string and concatenate the result.

> **Note**
>
> The solution for this activity can be found on page 729.

Activity 10.02: Enforcing a Specific Format of Date and Time

This activity requires you to use the knowledge you have accumulated in this chapter about time. We would like to create a small script that prints out a date with the following format: "02:49:21 31/01/2019."

First, you need to create a **date** variable by utilizing the **time.Date()** function. You then need to recall how we accessed the **Year**, **Month**, and **Day** properties of the variable, and create a concatenation with an appropriate order. Remember that you cannot concatenate string and integer variables. The **strconv()** function is there to help you. You also need to remember that when you omit the **date.Month()** command, it prints the name of the month, but it also needs to be converted into an integer and then back into a string with a number.

You have to perform the following steps to get the desired output:

1. Capture the current date with the **time.Now()** function in a variable.

2. Use the **strconv.Itoa()** function to save the appropriate parts of the captured **date** variable into the following variables: **day**, **month**, **year**, **hour**, **minute**, and **second**.

3. Finally, print these out using the appropriate concatenation.

The expected output should look like this:

```
2:49:21 2019/1/31
```

By the end of this activity, you should have learned how to format the current date to a specific custom format.

> **Note**
>
> The solution for this activity can be found on page 730.

Activity 10.03: Measuring Elapsed Time

This activity requires you to measure the duration of sleep. You should use the `time.Sleep()` function to sleep for 2 seconds, and once the sleep is complete, you need to calculate the difference from the start and end times and show how many seconds it took.

First, you mark the start of the execution, sleep for 2 seconds, and then capture the end of the execution time in a variable. By utilizing the `time.Sub()` function, we can use the `Seconds()` function to output the result. The output will be a bit strange as it will be slightly longer than expected.

You have to perform the following steps to get the desired output:

1. Capture the start time in a variable.

2. Craft a sleep variable that is 2 seconds long.

3. Capture the end time in a variable.

4. Calculate the length by subtracting the start time from the end time.

5. Print out the result.

    Depending on the speed of your PC, you should expect the following output:

    ```
    The execution took exactly 2.0016895 seconds!
    ```

    By the end of this activity, you should have learned how to measure the elapsed time for a specific activity.

> **Note**
>
> The solution for this activity can be found on page 730.

Activity 10.04: Calculating the Future Date and Time

In this activity, we are going to calculate the date that is 6 hours, 6 minutes, and 6 seconds from **Now()**. You will need to capture the current time in a variable. Then, utilize the **Add()** function on the given date to add the previously mentioned length. Please use the **time.ANSIC** format for convenience. There is a catch, however. Because the **Add()** function expects a duration, you need to pick a resolution such as **Second** and craft the duration before you can add it.

You have to perform the following steps to get the desired output:

1. Capture the current time in a variable.

2. Print out this value as a reference in ANSIC format.

3. Calculate the duration with seconds as input.

4. Add the duration to the current time.

5. Print out the future date in ANSIC format.

   Make sure your output looks like this, with the string formatting:

```
The current time: Thu Oct 17 15:16:48 2019
6 hours, 6 minutes and 6 seconds from now the time will be:  Thu Oct 17
  21:22:54 2019
```

   By the end of this activity, you should have learned how you can calculate specific dates in the future by utilizing the **time.Duration()** and **time.Add()** functions.

   Note

   The solution for this activity can be found on page 731.

Activity 10.05: Printing the Local Time in Different Time Zones

This activity requires you to utilize what you learned in the *Formatting Time* section. You need to load an east coast city and a west coast city. Then, print out the current time for each city.

The key here is the **LoadLocation()** function, and you need to use the **ANSIC** format for the output. Remember that the **LoadLocation()** function returns two values!

You have to perform the following steps to get the desired output:

1. Capture the current time in a variable.

2. Create the reference time zone variables for **NYtime** and **LA** using the **time. LoadLocation()** function.

3. Print out, in ANSIC format, the current time in the respective time zones.

   Depending on your day of execution, the following could be your expected output:

   ```
   The local current time is: Thu Oct 17 15:16:13 2019
   The time in New York is: Thu Oct 17 09:16:13 2019
   The time in Los Angeles is: Thu Oct 17 06:16:13 2019
   ```

   By the end of this activity, you should have learned how to convert your time variables to a specific time zone.

   > **Note**
   >
   > The solution for this activity can be found on page 732.

Summary

This chapter introduced you to the **time** package of **go**, which allows you to reuse code that has been invented by other programmers and incorporated into the language. The goal was to teach you how to create, manipulate, and format time variables, and, in general, make you familiar with what you can do with the help of the **time** package. If you would like to further improve or dig deeper into what the package has to offer, you should check out the following link: https://golang.org/pkg/time/.

Timestamps and time manipulation are essential skills for every developer. Whether you have a big or small script put into production, the time module helps you to measure the elapsed time of actions and provide you with the logging of actions that happen during the execution. The most important thing about it, if used correctly, is that it helps you to easily trace back production problems to their roots.

The next chapter will introduce you to encoding and decoding JSON, that is, the JavaScript Object Notation.

11

Encoding and Decoding (JSON)

Overview

This chapter aims to acquaint you with the fundamentals of JavaScript Object Notation (JSON). You will learn how to use Go to parse JSON, and then gain the ability to convert JSON to a struct and back to JSON.

Here, you will learn to describe JSON and unmarshal JSON to a struct. You will also learn to marshal a struct to JSON and set the JSON key name to something different than the struct field name. By the end of the chapter, you will be able to use various JSON tag attributes to control what gets converted to JSON, unmarshal an unknown JSON structure, and use encoding for data transmission.

Introduction

In the previous chapter, we looked at errors in Go and discovered that, in Go, errors are values, which allows us to pass errors around as arguments to functions and methods. We also saw that Go functions can return multiple values, one of which is often an error. We learned that a good practice is to check for the value of an error returned by a function. By not ignoring the error, it prevents unexpected behavior in our program. In Go, we saw that you can create your own custom error types. Finally, we looked at panics and learned how to recover from them.

In this chapter, we will be working with JSON by using only the standard library of Go. Before we start looking at using JSON in Go code, let's have a brief introduction to JSON.

JSON

JSON stands for **JavaScript Object Notation**. It is widely used in many programming languages for transferring and storing data. Often, this is done by transferring data from a web server to a client. JSON is transferred in web applications and is even used to store data in a file for later processing. We will look at various examples of where this is done in this chapter. JSON is minimal; it is not as verbose as XML. It is self-describing; this increases its readability and the ease of writing it. JSON is a text format that is language-independent:

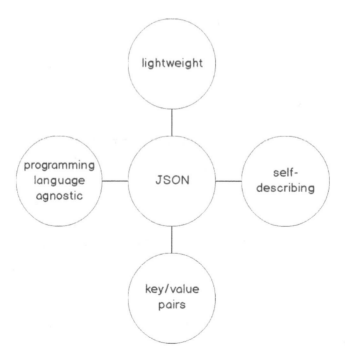

Figure 11.1: Describing JSON

JSON is widely used as a data format for exchanging data between web applications and for various server-to-server communications. A common API that is used in applications is the REST API. JSON is frequently used in applications that utilize the REST API. One of the reasons that JSON is used in the REST API instead of XML is because it is less verbose than XML, more lightweight, and easier to read. Looking at the following JSON and XML, respectively, we can see that JSON is less verbose, easier to read, and more lightweight:

```
{
"firstname":"Captain",
"lastname":"Marvel"
}
<avenger>
<firstname>Captain</firstname>
<lastname>"Marvel"</lastname>
</avenger>
```

Most modern databases also now store JSON as a data type in a field. Static web applications sometimes use JSON for rendering their web pages.

The JSON format is very structured. The primary parts that make up the JSON format consists of a collection of key-value pairs, as shown in the following figure:

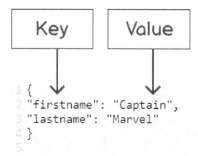

Figure 11.2: JSON key-value pairs

The key is always a string enclosed in quotation marks, whereas the value can encompass a multitude of data types. A key-value pair in JSON is a **key** name followed by a colon, followed by a **value**. If there are additional key-value pairs, they will be separated with a comma.

In *Figure 11.2*, there are two key-value pairs. The **firstname** key and its value of **Captain** is one. The other set is **lastname** and **Marvel**.

JSON can contain arrays. The values are within a set of brackets. In *Figure 11.3*, lines 3 and 4 are the values of the **phonenumbers** key:

```
1 ▾ {
2 ▾     "phonenumbers": [
3           {"type": "business","number": "123-123-1111"},  ⟵────────── value
4           {"type": "home","number": "123-123-2222"}  ⟵───────────
5       ]
6   }
```

Figure 11.3: JSON array

Now that we've seen key-value pairs, let's look at JSON data types. The JSON object supports many different data types; the following diagram shows those data types:

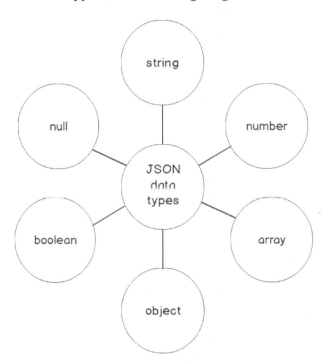

Figure 11.4: JSON data types

Here are a few examples:

- String:

  Example: `{"firstname": "Captain"}`

- Number: This can be a float or an integer:

  Example: `{"age": 32}`

- Array:

  Example: `{"hobbies": ["Go", "Saving Earth", "Shield"]}`

- Boolean: Can only be **true** or **false**:

  Example: `{"ismarried": false}`

- Null:

  Example: `{"middlename": null}`

- Object:

  JSON objects are like structs in Go. The following example shows a Go struct and a JSON object:

```
type person struct {
    firstname string
    middlename string
    lastname string
    age int
    ismarried bool
    hobbies []string
}
{
    "person": {
        "firstname": "Captain",
        "middlename": null,
        "lastname": "Marvel",
        "age": 32,
        "ismarried": false,
        "hobbies": ["Go", "Saving Earth", "Shield"]
    }
}
```

In this section, we provided a brief introduction to JSON. In the following sections, we will look at how Go can decode and encode JSON.

Decoding JSON

When we talk about decoding JSON, what we are stating is that we are taking a JSON data structure and converting it into a Go data structure. Converting the JSON into a Go data structure gives us the benefit of working with the data natively. For example, if the JSON data has a field that is an array in Go, that would get decoded to a slice. We will then be able to treat that slice as we would any other slice, meaning we can iterate over the slice using a **range** clause, we can get the length of the slice, append to the slice, and so on.

If we know what our JSON looks like ahead of time, we can use structs when parsing the JSON. Using Go terms, we need to be able to **unmarshal** the JSON-encoded data and store the results in the struct. To be able to do this, we will need to import the **encoding/json** package. We will be using the JSON **Unmarshal** function. Unmarshaling is the process of parsing JSON to a data structure. Often, you will hear unmarshaling and decoding used interchangeably:

```
func Unmarshal(data []byte, v interface{}) error
```

In the preceding code, the variable data is defined as a slice of bytes. The **v** variable is a pointer to a struct. The **Unmarshal** function takes the slice of bytes of JSON data and stores the results in the value pointed to by **v**.

The argument for **v** must be a pointer and must not be **nil**. If either of those requirements are not met, then an error will be returned as follows:

```
call of Unmarshal passes non-pointer as second argument
```

Figure 11.5: Unmarshal error for a non-pointer passed as an argument

Let's look at the following code as a simple example of unmarshaling data. We will describe each portion of the code in detail to get a better understanding of the program:

```
package main
import (
  "encoding/json"
  "fmt"
)
type greeting struct {
  Message string
}
func main() {
  data := []byte(`
  {
  "message": "Greetings fellow gopher!"
```

```
  }
`)
  var v greeting
  err := json.Unmarshal(data, &v)
  if err != nil {
    fmt.Println(err)
  }
  fmt.Println(v.Message)
}
```

Let's break down the code for better understanding:

```
type greeting struct {
  Message string
}
```

The greeting struct has an exportable field called **Message** of the **string** type:

```
func main() {
  data := []byte(`
  {
  "message": "Greetings fellow gopher!"
  }
`)
```

> **Note**
>
> The ` symbol is a backtick and not a single quote. It is used for string literals.

The **json.Unmarshal** struct requires that the JSON encoded data must be a byte of slices:

```
  var g greeting
```

We are declaring **g** to be of the greeting type:

```
  err := json.Unmarshal(data, &v)
  if err != nil {
    fmt.Println(err)
  }
```

The **Unmarshal()** function takes the slice of bytes of JSON data and stores the results in the value pointed to by **v**.

The **v** variable is pointing to our greeting struct.

It unmarshals the JSON to a greeting instance, as depicted in the following diagram:

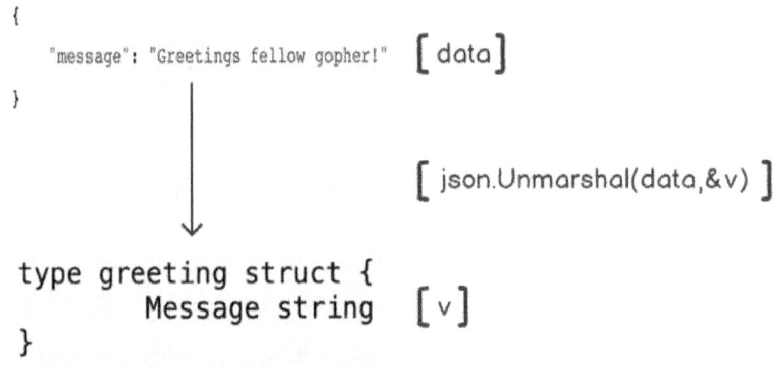

Figure 11.6: Unmarshaling JSON to a Go struct

Now, let's see the output after unmarshaling:

```
fmt.Println(v.Message)
```

It should look as follows:

```
Greetings fellow gopher!
```

In our previous example, the JSON marshaler matched our field name, **Message**, to the JSON key, **message**.

> **Note**
>
> To be able to unmarshal into a struct, the struct field must be exportable. The struct's field name must be capitalized. Only fields that are exportable are visible externally, including the JSON unmarshaler. Only the exported fields will be in the JSON output; other fields are ignored.

Struct Tags

We can use struct tags to provide transformation information on how the struct field is unmarshaled or marshaled. Tags follow the format of `key: "value"`. The tag begins and ends with a backtick (`).

Consider the following example:

```
type person struct {
   LastName string `json:"lname"`
}
```

Using tags gives us more control. We can now name our struct field name anything as long as it is exportable.

The **json** field that will be unmarshaled in this example is **lname**.

Once you use tags for JSON unmarshaling and marshaling, it will not compile if the struct field is not exportable. The Go compiler is smart enough to realize that since there is a JSON tag associated with the struct field, it must be exportable to be used in the JSON marshaling and unmarshaling process. See the following example of the error you will get when **lastname** is lowercase:

```
type person struct {
   lastName string `json:"lname"`
}
```

This is the error message for unexported JSON struct fields:

```
prog.go:13:2: struct field lastName has json tag but is not exported
```

Figure 11.7: Error for unexported JSON struct fields

We have already seen this code before and we know how to unmarshal JSON. However, there is one small change that we will be making, and that is adding a **struct** tag to our code:

```
package main
import (
   "encoding/json"
   "fmt"
)
type greeting struct {
   SomeMessage string `json:"message"`
}
func main() {
   data := []byte(`
   {
   "message": "Greetings fellow gopher!"
   }
```

```
`)
  var g greeting
  err := json.Unmarshal(data, &g)
  if err != nil {
    fmt.Println(err)
  }
  fmt.Println(g.SomeMessage)
}
```

Let's break down the code for better understanding:

```
type greeting struct {
  SomeMessage string `json:"message"`
}
```

We changed our **greeting** struct to use a different exportable field name than what is in JSON.

The `json:"message"` tag states that this exportable field corresponds to the **message** key in the JSON data:

```
err := json.Unmarshal(data, &g)
```

When the data gets unmarshaled, the JSON message value will be placed in the **SomeMessage** struct field.

We will get the following output:

```
Greetings fellow gopher!
```

The Go JSON **unmarshaller** follows a process of determining which struct field to map the JSON data when decoding it:

- An exported field with a tag.
- An exported field name whose case matches the JSON key name.
- An exported field name with a case-insensitive match.
- We could also verify whether the JSON that we are going to unmarshal is valid.

The following is the code to perform the unmarshaling:

```go
package main
import (
  "encoding/json"
  "fmt"
  "os"
)
type greeting struct {
  SomeMessage string `json:"message"`
}
func main() {
  data := []byte(`
  {
  message": "Greetings fellow gopher!"
  }
`)
  if !json.Valid(data) {
    fmt.Printf("JSON is not valid: %s", data)
    os.Exit(1)
  }
  //Code to perform the unmarshal
}
```

The **Valid()** function takes as an argument slice of bytes and will return a Bool that indicates whether the JSON is valid. It will display **True** for valid JSON and **False** for invalid JSON.

This can be useful for checking our JSON before we try to unmarshal it into a struct.

What structs do you think you would need for the following JSON? Let's take a look.

```json
{
"lname": "Smith",
  "fname": "John",
  "address": {
    "street": "Sulphur Springs Rd",
      "city": "Park City",
      "state": "VA",
      "zipcode": 12345
    }
}
```

The preceding JSON has an embedded object called **address**. As you may recall from the introduction of this chapter, objects are one of the types that JSON supports. The Go representation of an object type in JSON is structs. Our **parent** struct would need to have an embedded struct called **address**.

The following code snippet is an example of unmarshaling more than one JSON object into Go structs:

```go
package main
import (
  "encoding/json"
  "fmt"
)
type person struct {
  Lastname  string  `json:"lname"`
  Firstname string  `json:"fname"`
  Address   address `json:"address"`
}
type address struct {
  Street  string `json:"street"`
  City    string `json:"city"`
  State   string `json:"state"`
  ZipCode int    `json:"zipcode"`
}
func main() {
  data := []byte(`
    {
      "lname": "Smith",
      "fname": "John",
      "address": {
        "street": "Sulphur Springs Rd",
        "city": "Park City",
        "state": "VA",
        "zipcode": 12345
      }
    }
  `)
```

```go
    var p person
    err := json.Unmarshal(data, &p)
    if err != nil {
        fmt.Println(err)
    }
    fmt.Printf("%+v",p)
}
```

Let's break the code down for better understanding:

```go
type person struct {
    Lastname   string  `json:"lname"`
    Firstname  string  `json:"fname"`
    Address    address `json:"address"`
}
```

The **person** struct has an embedded struct called **Address**. It is represented in the JSON as an object called **address**. The fields in the **address** struct will have the JSON values unmarshaled to them:

```go
    data := []byte(`
        {
        "lname": "Smith",
        "fname": "John",
        "address": {
            "street": "Sulphur Springs Rd",
            "city": "Park City",
            "state": "VA",
            "zipcode": 12345
        }
    }
    `)
```

The **address** in JSON is an object that will get unmarshaled into our **person struct's** address field:

```
type person struct {
        Lastname  string   `json:"lname"`
        Firstname string   `json:"fname"`
        Address   address  `json:"address"`
}
type address struct {
        Street   string `json:"street"`
        City     string `json:"city"`
        State    string `json:"state"`
        ZipCode  int    `json:"zipcode"`
}


{
"lname": "Smith",
        "fname": "John",
        "address": {
                "street": "Sulphur Springs Rd",
                "city": "Park City",
                "state": "VA",
                "zipcode": 12345
        }
}
```

Figure 11.8: Unmarshaled JSON address to person.address

The **Unmarshal()** function decodes the JSON-encoded **data** into the pointer **p**:

```
var p person
  err := json.Unmarshal(data, &p)
```

The results are as follows:

```
{Lastname:Smith Firstname:John Address:{Street:Sulphur Springs Rd City:Park City State:VA ZipCode:12345}}
```

Figure 11.9: The person struct after decoding JSON

We will be using these concepts that we have learned thus far in the next exercise.

Exercise 11.01: Unmarshaling Student Courses

In this exercise, we will be writing a program that takes a JSON from a web request for college class enrollment. Our program needs to unmarshal the JSON data into a Go struct. The JSON will contain data about a student and the courses that they are taking. After we have unmarshaled the JSON, we will print the struct for verification purposes. The output should be as follows:

```
{123 Smith  John true [{Intro to Golang 101 4} {English Lit 101 3} {World History 101 3}]}
```

Figure 11.10: Printing the student courses struct

All directories and files created need to be created within your **$GOPATH**:

1. Create a directory called **Exercise11.01** within a directory called **Chapter11**.

2. Create a file called **main.go** inside of **Chapter11/Exercise11.01**.

3. Using Visual Studio Code, open the newly created **main.go** file.

4. Add the following package name and import statements:

```go
package main
import (
    "encoding/json"
    "fmt"
)
```

5. We will need to create a **student** struct. The **student** struct will need for all its fields to be exported so that we can unmarshal the JSON data to them. Each struct field will need to have a JSON tag that will be the name of the JSON data fields:

```go
type student struct {
    StudentId      int         `json:"id"`
    LastName       string      `json:"lname"`
    MiddleInitial  string      `json:"minitial"`
    FirstName      string      `json:"fname"`
    IsEnrolled     bool        `json:"enrolled"`
    Courses        []course    `json:"classes"`
}
```

6. We will need to create a **course** struct. The **course** struct will need all its fields to be exported so that we can unmarshal the JSON data to them. Each struct field will need to have a JSON tag that will be the name of the JSON data fields:

```go
type course struct {
    Name    string  `json:"coursename"`
    Number  int     `json:"coursenum"`
    Hours   int     `json:"coursehours"`
}
```

7. Add a **main()** function:

```go
func main() {
    }
```

8. In the **main()** function, add the JSON data that we will be unmarshaling into our structs (**student** and **course**):

```
data := []byte(`
  {
    "id": 123,
    "lname": "Smith",
    "minitial": null,
    "fname": "John",
    "enrolled": true,
    "classes": [{
       "coursename": "Intro to Golang",
       "coursenum": 101,
       "coursehours": 4
    },
   {
       "coursename": "English Lit",
       "coursenum": 101,
       "coursehours": 3
    },
   {
       "coursename": "World History",
       "coursenum": 101,
       "coursehours": 3
    }
  ]
  }
`)
```

0. Declare a variable of the **student** type:

```
var s student
```

10. Next, we will unmarshal the JSON into our **student** struct. We will also handle any errors that get returned from the **json.Unmarshal()** method:

```
err := json.Unmarshal(data, &s)
if err != nil {
  fmt.Println(err)
}
```

11. We will print the **student** struct so that we can see that all the data from the JSON is present:

```
    fmt.Println(s)
}
```

12. Build the program by running **go build** in the command line:

```
go build
```

Correct any errors that are returned and ensure your code matches the code snippet here.

13. Run the executable by typing in the name of the executable and then hit *Enter* to run it.

The output is as follows:

```
{123 Smith  John true [{Intro to Golang 101 4} {English Lit 101 3} {World History 101 3}]}
```

Figure 11.11: Printing the student courses struct

This exercise demonstrated how to unmarshal JSON data into a Go struct successfully.

Encoding JSON

We have studied how to unmarshal JSON into a struct. We will now do the opposite: marshal a struct into JSON. When we talk about encoding JSON, what we mean is we are taking a Go struct and converting it to a JSON data structure. The typical scenario in which this is done is when you have a service that is responding to an HTTP request from a client. The client wants the data in a certain format, and this is frequently JSON. Another situation is that the data is stored in a NoSQL database and it requires JSON as the format, or even a traditional database that has a column with a data type of JSON.

We need to be able to **Marshal** the Go struct into a JSON-encoded structure. To be able to do this, we will need to import the **encoding/json** package. We will be using the **json. Marshal** function:

```
func Marshal(v interface{}) ([]byte, error)
```

The **v** becomes encoded as JSON. Typically, **v** is a **struct**. The **Marshal()** function returns the JSON encoding as a slice of bytes and an error. It is always a good idea to check whether there was an error during the process of encoding **v**. Let's look at a simple example to further explain the marshaling of Go structs to JSON:

```
package main
import (
    "encoding/json"
    "fmt"
)
type greeting struct {
    SomeMessage string
}
func main() {
    var v greeting
    v.SomeMessage = "Marshal me!"
    json, err := json.Marshal(v)
    if err != nil {
        fmt.Println(err)
    }
    fmt.Printf("%s",json)
}
```

Let's break down the code for better understanding:

```
type greeting struct {
    SomeMessage string
}
```

We have a struct with one exportable field. Notice there are no JSON tags. You should be able to guess what the field will be in the JSON data:

```
json, err := json.Marshal(v)
```

The following diagram shows how the **greeting** struct gets marshaled into JSON using the **json.Marshal** method. The v interface argument in the **marshal** method is the **greeting** struct. The **marshal** method will encode the **greeting** field, **SomeMessage**, into JSON. The following diagram shows the process:

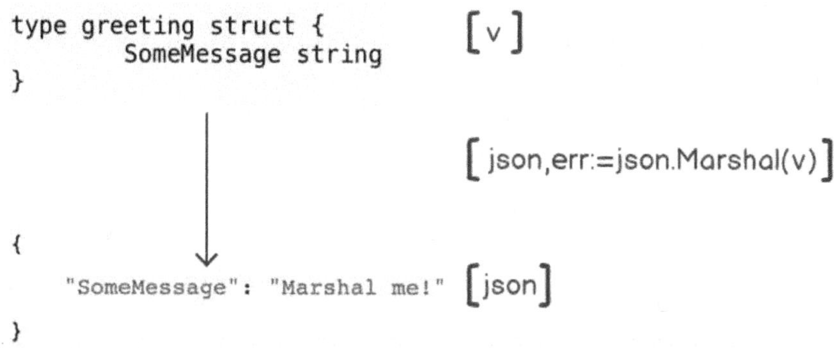

```
type greeting struct {
       SomeMessage string
}
```

$\left[\,v\,\right]$

$\left[\,\text{json,err:=json.Marshal(v)}\,\right]$

```
{
       "SomeMessage": "Marshal me!"
}
```

$\left[\,\text{json}\,\right]$

Figure 11.12: Marshaling a Go struct to JSON

When we call the **Marshal** function, we are passing it a struct. The function will return back an error and the JSON encoding of **g**.

The results of the print statement are as follows:

```
{"SomeMessage":"Marshal me!"}
```

Since we did not provide the JSON tag for the struct greeting, **SomeMessage**, the Go **Marshal** encodes the exportable fields and its values. The Go **Marshal** uses the name of the field, **SomeMessage**, as the name of the **key** field in the JSON data.

The following code produces a result that is not desirable. Examine the following code and notice the result of struct fields that are not set. Pay close attention to the fields that are not being set in the **main()** function.

Consider the following example:

```
package main
import (
  "encoding/json"
  "fmt"
)
type book struct {
    ISBN           string `json:"isbn"`
    Title          string `json:"title"`
    YearPublished int     `json:"yearpub"`
    Author         string `json:"author"`
    CoAuthor       string `json:"coauthor"`
}
func main() {
  var b book
```

```
    b.ISBN = "9933HIST"
    b.Title = "Greatest of all Books"
    b.Author = "John Adams"
    json, err := json.Marshal(b)
    if err != nil {
        fmt.Println(err)
    }
    fmt.Printf("%s", json)
}
```

Marshaling struct data when the field value is not set gives you the following output:

```
{"isbn":"9933HIST","title":"Greatest of all Books","yearpub":0,"author":"John
    Adams","coauthor":""}
```

There are times that we might not want our struct fields to be marshaled to JSON when the fields are not set. Our **CoAuthor** field and **YearPublished** were not set, and thus the JSON values were an empty string and zero, respectively. There is a JSON tag attribute that we can utilize called **omitempty**. It will omit the struct field from the JSON if it is empty:

```
package main
import (
    "encoding/json"
    "fmt"
)
type book struct {
    ISBN          string `json:"isbn"`
    Title         string `json:"title"`
    YearPublished int    `json:"yearpub,omitempty"`
    Author        string `json:"author"`
    CoAuthor      string `json:"coauthor,omitempty"`
}
func main() {
    var b book
    b.ISBN = "9933HIST"
    b.Title = "Greatest of all Books"
    b.Author = "John Adams"
    json, err := json.Marshal(b)
    if err != nil {
        fmt.Println(err)
    }
    fmt.Printf("%s", json)
}
```

Let's break down the code for better understanding:

```
YearPublished int     `json:"yearpub,omitempty"`
CoAuthor       string `json:"coauthor,omitempty"`
```

The two **book** fields' JSON tags use the **omitempty** attribute. If these fields are not set, they will not appear in the JSON. The result is as follows:

```
{"isbn":"9933HIST","title":"Greatest of all Books","author":"John Adams"}
```

When using the JSON tags, you will need to be careful not to have any spaces in the values. Using our previous example, let's change our **YearPublished** JSON tag to this:

```
YearPublished int     `json:"yearpub, omitempty"`
```

Notice the space between the comma and **omitempty**. This would result in the following error if you use **go vet**:

```
prog.go:11:2: struct field tag `json:"yearpub, omitempty"` not compatible with reflect.StructTag.Get: suspicious space in struct tag value
```

Figure 11.13: Go vet error

Another thing to keep in mind is that if you do not properly handle errors, you will get some erroneous results:

```
{"isbn":"9933HIST","title":"Greatest of all Books","yearpub":0,"author":"John
    Adams"}
```

Even though the **json.Marshal(b)** function errored, it still marshaled the struct to JSON. The **yearpub** value was set to zero. That is one of the reasons it is important to handle our errors.

There are other JSON tags that we will look at briefly in the following example:

```
package main
import (
  "encoding/json"
  "fmt"
)
type book struct {
  ISBN          string `json:"isbn"`
  Title         string `json:"title"`
  YearPublished int    `json:",omitempty"`
  Author        string `json:",omitempty"`
  CoAuthor      string `json:"-"`
}
func main() {
  var b book
```

```
  b.ISBN = "9933HIST"
  b.Title = "Greatest of all Books"
  b.Author = "John Adams"
  b.CoAuthor ="Can't see me"
  json, err := json.Marshal(b)
  if err != nil {
    fmt.Println(err)
  }
  fmt.Printf("%s", json)
}
```

Let's break down the code for better understanding:

```
YearPublished int     `json:",omitempty"`
Author        string `json:",omitempty"`
```

- In the above code, `json:",omitempty"` does not have a value for a field. Notice the JSON tag value starts with a comma.

- `json:",omitempty"` will have the field in the JSON if there is a value for the key. If **Author** has a value set, it will appear in the JSON as the **"Author"** :**"somevalue"** key:

```
CoAuthor      string `json:"-"`
```

- The dash is used to ignore the field. The field will not be marshaled to JSON.

The result is as follows:

```
{"isbn":"9933HIST","title":"Greatest of all Books","Author":"John Adams"}
```

The following diagram summarizes the different JSON tag attributes that we have used with our structs when we marshal the struct to JSON:

"keyName,omitempty"	keyName is the name of the key in the JSON.
	If the struct field is not set, the keyName will get omitted from the JSON.
`json:",omitempty"`	The keyName for the JSON will come from the exportable field in the struct.
	If the struct field is not set, the struct field name will get omitted from the JSON.
`json:"-"`	The struct field is ignored and will not appear in the JSON.

Figure 11.14: JSON tag field descriptions

Having the JSON output as a one-liner is not very readable, especially when you start working with larger JSON structures. The Go JSON package provides a way to format the JSON output. The **MarshalIndent()** function provides the same functionality as the **Marshal** function. In addition to encoding JSON, the **MarshalIndent()** function can format the JSON make it easy to read. This is often referred to as "pretty printing." The following code shows an example code for the **MarshalIndent()** function:

```
func MarshalIndent(v interface{}, prefix, indent string) ([]byte, error)
```

We will not be using a prefix in our examples. It just applies a string before our indent string. Each element will begin on a new line:

```
package main
import (
  "encoding/json"
  "fmt"
  "os"
)
type person struct {
  LastName  string  `json:"lname"`
  FirstName string  `json:"fname"`
  Address   address `json:"address"`
}
type address struct {
  Street  string `json:"street"`
  City    string `json:"city"`
  State   string `json:"state"`
  ZipCode int    `json:"zipcode"`
}
func main() {
  p := person{LastName: "Vader", FirstName: "Darth"}
  p.Address.Street = "Galaxy Far Away"
  p.Address.City= "Dark Side"
  p.Address.State= "Tatooine"
  p.Address.ZipCode =12345
  noPrettyPrint, err := json.Marshal(p)
  if err != nil {
    fmt.Println(err)
    os.Exit(1)
  }
  prettyPrint, err := json.MarshalIndent(p, "", "    ")
  if err != nil {
```

```
      fmt.Println(err)
      os.Exit(1)
  }
  fmt.Println(string(noPrettyPrint))
  fmt.Println()
  fmt.Println(string(prettyPrint))
}
```

Let's break down the code for better understanding:

```
type person struct {
   LastName  string  `json:"lname"`
   FirstName string  `json:"fname"`
   Address   address `json:"address"`
}
type address struct {
   Street  string `json:"street"`
   City    string `json:"city"`
   State   string `json:"state"`
   ZipCode int    `json:"zipcode"`
}
```

We have two structs: a **person** struct and an **address** struct. The **address** struct is embedded inside the **person** struct. Both structs have the JSON key names defined in the JSON tags. The **address** struct will be a separate object inside the JSON:

```
p := person{LastName: "Vader", FirstName: "Darth"}
p.Address.Street = "Galaxy Far Away"
p.Address.City= "Dark Side"
p.Address.State= "Tatooine"
p.Address.ZipCode -12345
```

We initialize the **person** struct and set the values for the **person.Address** fields. Every field has a value set, so there will be no empty strings or zero values set in our JSON:

```
noPrettyPrint, err := json.Marshal(p)
if err != nil {
   fmt.Println(err)
   os.Exit(1)
}
```

The **noPrettyPrint** variable is the JSON encoding of **p**.

We, of course, check for any errors returned from the **json.Marshal()** function:

```
prettyPrint, err := json.MarshalIndent(p, "", "    ")
if err != nil {
  fmt.Println(err)
  os.Exit(1)
}
```

The **prettyPrint** variable is the JSON encoding of **p**, by using **json.MarshalIndent()**. We set the prefix argument to an empty string and the indent argument to four spaces.

As with the **json.Marshal()** function, we also check for any errors returned from the **json.MarshalIndent()** function. We can see these various steps using the **json.MarshalIndent()** method depicted in the following diagram:

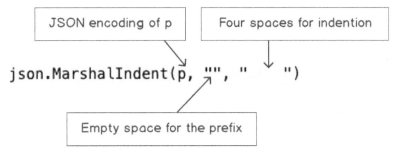

Figure 11.15: The json.MarshalIndent() method

We then print the results of the JSON encoding using the **json.Marshal()** function:

```
fmt.Println(string(noPrettyPrint))
```

As you can see, the readability of the JSON is slightly challenging.

JSON marshaling without **MarshalIndent** looks as follows:

```
{"lname":"Vader","fname":"Darth","address":{"street":"Galaxy Far
  Away","city":"Dark Side","state":"Tatooine","zipcode":12345}}
```

We also print the results of the JSON encoding using the **json.MarshalIndent()** function:

```
fmt.Println(string(prettyPrint))
```

The results are less of a challenge to read using the **json.MarshalIndent()** function. You can clearly read the output more easily than the previous results that were printed:

```
{
    "lname": "Vadar",
    "fname": "Darth",
    "address": {
        "street": "Galaxy Far Away",
        "city": "Dark Side",
        "state": "Tatooine",
        "zipcode": 12345
    }
}
```

Figure 11.16: Using the MarshalIndent JSON result

Exercise 11.02: Marshaling Student Courses

In this exercise, we are going to do the opposite to what we did in *Exercise 11.01, Unmarshaling Student Courses*. We will marshal from a struct into JSON. This is the previous struct:

```
type student struct {
    StudentId      int      `json:"id"`
    LastName       string   `json:"lname"`
    MiddleInitial  string   `json:"minitial"`
    FirstName      string   `json:"fname"`
    IsEnrolled     bool     `json:"enrolled"`
    Courses        []course `json:"classes"`
}
```

We are going to make some changes to the JSON tags.

All directories and files created need to be created within your **$GOPATH:**

1. Create a file called **main.go**.

2. Add the following package name and import statements:

```
package main
import (
    "encoding/json"
    "fmt"
    "os"
)
```

3. Create a **student** struct. All fields will be exportable. The following fields' JSON tags will need the following functionality when they get marshaled:

   MiddleInitial should be omitted if a value is not set; **IsMarried** should not appear in the JSON; and **IsEnrolled** should be the field name and omitted if not set:

```go
type student struct {
    StudentId      int       `json:"id"`
    LastName       string    `json:"lname"`
    MiddleInitial  string    `json:"mname,omitempty"`
    FirstName      string    `json:"fname"`
    IsMarried      bool      `json:"-"`
    IsEnrolled     bool      `json:"enrolled,omitempty"`
    Courses        []course  `json:"classes"`
}
```

4. Create a **course** struct:

```go
type course struct {
    Name    string `json:"coursename"`
    Number  int    `json:"coursenum"`
    Hours   int    `json:"coursehours"`
}
```

5. Create a function called **newStudent()**. This function will return a **student** struct:

```go
func newStudent(studentID int, lastName, middleInitial, firstName string,
    isMarried, isEnrolled bool) student {
    s := student{StudentId: studentID,
        LastName:      lastName,
        MiddleInitial: middleInitial,
        FirstName:     firstName,
        IsMarried:     isMarried,
        IsEnrolled:    isEnrolled,
    }
    return s
}
```

6. Add the **main()** function:

```go
func main() {
}
```

7. In the **main()** function, use the **newStudent()** function to create a **student** struct and assign the result of the function to a variable, **s**:

```
s := newStudent(1, "Williams", "s", "Felicia", false, false)
```

8. Next, marshal **s** to JSON. We want the indenting of the JSON to be four spaces for each field for ease of readability:

```
student1, err := json.MarshalIndent(s, "", "    ")
if err != nil {
  fmt.Println(err)
  os.Exit(1)
}
```

9. Print **student1**:

```
fmt.Println(string(student1))
fmt.Println()
```

10. Create another **student** using the **newStudent()** function:

```
s2 := newStudent(2, "Washington", "", "Bill", true, true)
```

11. We will now add various courses to **s2**:

```
c := course{Name: "World Lit", Number: 101, Hours: 3}
s2.Courses = append(s2.Courses, c)
c = course{Name: "Biology", Number: 201, Hours: 4}
s2.Courses = append(s2.Courses, c)
c = course{Name: "Intro to Go", Number: 101, Hours: 4}
s2.Courses = append(s2.Courses, c)
```

12. Next, marshal **s2** to JSON. We want the indenting of the JSON to be four spaces for each field for ease of readability:

```
student2, err := json.MarshalIndent(s2, "", "    ")
if err != nil {
  fmt.Println(err)
  os.Exit(1)
}
```

13. Print **student2**:

```
fmt.Println(string(student2))
}
```

The result of the **student1** print statement is as follows:

```
{
    "id": 1,
    "lname": "Williams",
    "mname": "S",
    "fname": "Felicia",
    "classes": null
}
```

The result of the **student2** print statement is as follows:

```
{
    "id": 2,
    "lname": "Washington",
    "Fname": "Bill",
    "IsEnrolled": true,
    "classes": [
        {
            "coursename": "World Lit",
            "coursenum": 101,
            "coursehours": 3
        },
        {
            "coursename": "Biology",
            "coursenum": 201,
            "coursehours": 4
        },
        {
            "coursename": "Intro to Go",
            "coursenum": 101,
            "coursehours": 4
        }
    ]
}
```

The aim of this exercise was to demonstrate how to encode JSON. We took a struct and encoded it into JSON. We were able to change the encoding to make it easier to read by indenting the fields. We also saw how to change some of the behavior of how fields are encoded to JSON. We saw that we can omit fields from getting encoded to JSON if the struct field does not have any data. We demonstrated that we can use JSON tags to name the fields in the JSON data differently than the field names in the struct. We also saw how we can even ignore fields in the struct so that they will not appear in the JSON when we marshal it.

So far, we have dealt with knowing the structure of the JSON beforehand and that it is not changing. In the next section, we are going to discuss how to handle situations when you get a JSON structure, but that structure can change and is not stable.

Unknown JSON Structures

When we know the JSON structure beforehand, it allows us the flexibility to design our structs to match the expected JSON. As we have seen, we can unmarshal our JSON values into the destination struct types. Go offers support for encoding (marshaling) and decoding (unmarshaling) to and from struct types.

There are situations in which you may not know the JSON structure. For example, you may be interacting with a third-party tool that posts metrics for a streaming service. This metric is in the format of JSON; however, it is very dynamic and serves various customers. They frequently add new metrics for their various clients. You want to subscribe to this service and report on these various metrics. The problem is that the producer of these metrics changes the JSON data frequently. They change it so often, they do not provide the changes, and not on any prescribed schedule. You need to be able to perform the analysis on new metrics and old ones, and you cannot afford to take your service down to add the new fields from the JSON into your struct. You need the ability to continuously report on their metrics with minimal interruption to the service.

If your JSON is dynamic, it will not work decoding it to a struct. So, what do you do when you do not know the JSON structure or when it changes frequently?

In these cases, we can use `map[string]interface{}`. The keys of the JSON data will be the string key of the map. The `empty interface{}` will be the values of those JSON keys. Every type implements the empty interface:

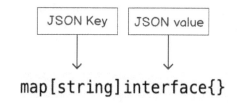

Figure 11.17: Mapping of JSON to a map data type

The **json.Unmarshal** function will decode the unknown JSON structure into the map whose keys are strings and whose values will be empty interfaces. This works out well because JSON keys have to be strings.

Consider the following example:

```
package main
import (
    "encoding/json"
    "fmt"
)
func main() {
    jsonData := []byte(`{"checkNum":123,"amount":200,"category":["gift","clothing"]}`)
    var v interface{}
    json.Unmarshal(jsonData, &v)
    fmt.Println(v)
}
```

Let's break down the code for better understanding:

```
jsonData := []byte(`{"checkNum":123,"amount":200,"category":["gift","clothing"]}`)
```

jsonData represents the JSON that we are given but do not know the structure of:

```
var v interface{}
json.Unmarshal(jsonData, &v)
```

Even though we do not know the JSON structure, we can unmarshal it into an interface.

The **jsonData** gets unmarshaled into v, the empty interface, which will be a map.

The map keys are the strings and the values are empty interfaces. The result of printing out **v** is as follows:

```
map[amount:200 category:[gift clothing] checkNum: 123]
```

The printing of `map[string]interface{}` does not match the order the data is stored. That is because maps are unordered, so their order is not guaranteed.

The Go representation of `v` is as follows:

```
v = map[string]interface{}{
   "amount": 200,
   "category": []interface{}{
      "gift",
      "clothing",
   },
   "checkNum":   123,
}
```

Remember the keys are strings and the values are interfaces. Even when there are slices in the JSON, the values become a slice of `interfaces{}`, represented as `[]interface{}`.

We learned in the *Chapter 7, Interfaces*, that we have the ability to access the concrete types. We can do type assertion to access the underlying concrete type of `map[string]interface{}`. Let's look at another example where we have a variety of data types to work with.

Exercise 11.03: Analyzing College Class JSON

In this exercise, we are going to analyze data from a college administration office and see whether we can replace the current college course grade submission application. The problem is that the old system's JSON data is not well documented. The data types in the JSON are not known, nor is the structure. In some instances, the JSON structure is different. We need to write a program that can analyze an unknown JSON structure and, for each field in the structure, print the data type and the JSON key-value pair.

All directories and files created need to be created within your **$GOPATH**:

1. Create a directory called **Exercise11.03** within a directory called **Chapter11**.

2. Create a file called **main.go** inside of **Chapter11/Exercise11.03**.

3. Using Visual Studio Code, open the newly created **main.go** file.

4. Add the following **package** name and **import** statements:

```
package main
import (
   "encoding/json"
   "fmt"
   "os"
)
```

5. Create a **main()** function and then assign **jsonData** to a **[]byte** that will represent the **JSON** from the college grade submission program:

```go
func main() {
    jsonData := []byte(`
{
    "id": 2,
    "lname": "Washington",
    "fname": "Bill",
    "IsEnrolled": true,
    "grades":[100,76,93,50],
    "class":
        {
            "coursename": "World Lit",
            "coursenum": 101,
            "coursehours": 3
        }
}
`)
```

6. Check whether the **jsonData** is valid **JSON**. If it is not, print an error message and exit the application:

```go
if !json.Valid(jsonData) {
    fmt.Printf("JSON is not valid: %s", jsonData)
    os.Exit(1)
}
```

7. Declare an empty **interface** variable:

```go
var v interface{}
```

8. Unmarshal **jsonData** into an empty interface. Check for any errors. If there is an error, print the error and exit the application:

```go
err := json.Unmarshal(jsonData, &v)
if err != nil {
    fmt.Println(err)
    os.Exit(1)
}
```

9. Perform type switching on each value in the map. Have a case statement for **string**, **float64**, **bool**, **[]interface**, and **default** to capture the unknown type of a value. Each of the **case** statements should print the data type, the key, and the value. Our switch type assertion flow should work as shown in the following diagram:

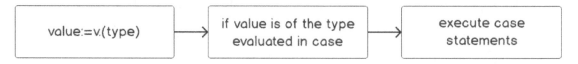

Figure 11.18: Switch type assertion flow

The following is the code for performing type switching on each value in the map:

```
data := v.(map[string]interface{})
for k, v := range data {
  switch value := v.(type) {
  case string:
    fmt.Println("(string):", k, value)
  case float64:
    fmt.Println("(float64):", k, value)
  case bool:
    fmt.Println("(bool):", k, value)
  case []interface{}:
    fmt.Println("(slice):", k)
    for i, j := range value {
      fmt.Println("    ", i, j)
    }
  default:
    fmt.Println( "(unknown):",k, value)
    }
  }
}
```

10. Build the program by running **go build** on the command line:

```
go build
```

11. Correct any errors that are returned and ensure your code matches the code snippet at https://packt.live/2Qr4dNx.

12. Run the executable by typing the name of the executable and then hit *Enter*.

The output from the type **switch** statement should be as follows:

```
(slice): grades
      0 100
      1 76
      2 93
      3 50
(unknown): class map[coursehours:3 coursename:World Lit coursenum:101]
(float64): id 2
(string): lname Washington
(string): fname Bill
(bool): IsEnrolled true
```

Figure 11.19: Output of the college class JSON

> **Note**
>
> The output from the map could differ from the preceding example because iterating over a map with a range loop is not a sure thing from one iteration to the next.

In this exercise, we saw how to parse a JSON structure even if we did not know its content. We learned that by unmarshaling the JSON into an empty interface, we get the structure of **map[string]interface{}**. The key of the map is the field of the JSON and the **interface{}** of the map is the JSON value. We were then able to iterate over the map and perform a switch type statement to get the map value's type and data, and also the key name.

GOB: Go's Own Encoding

Go has its own special data encoding protocol called **gob**. You can only use **gob** when the encoding and decoding are happening in Go. Being limited to Go is only a deal-breaker if you need to communicate with software written in other languages. It's common with software written to be used internally in an organization for both the encoding and decoding software to be written in the same language. As such, it's not a problem in most cases.

If you can use it, gob gives you exceptionally high performance and efficiency. For example, JSON is a string-based protocol that needs to be useable in any programming language. This limits what's possible with JSON and protocols like it. **Gob**, on the other hand, is a binary-based protocol, and gob only needs to work for Go users. This frees gob to become a space- and processing-efficient encoding protocol while still being easy to use.

Gob doesn't require any configuration or setup to use. Also, gob doesn't require the sender and receiver's data model to match exactly. So not only is it efficient and quick, it's also easy to use.

While Go is strict when it comes to types, gob is not. Gob treats all numbers the same be they `int` or `float`. You can use pointers with gob and when encoding, gob will pull the value from the pointer for you. Gob will also happily set values to pointer or value types regardless of whether the value was encoded from a pointer or a value.

Gob can encode complex types such as structs. Gob's flexibility continues because it doesn't require that the properties on the structs match. If there is a matching property on the struct it's decoding to, it'll use it; if not, then it'll discard the value. This fact gives the added benefit that you can add new properties without worrying about it breaking your legacy services.

When using gob for communication between Go web services, it's common practice to use Go's `rpc` package to handle the networking aspects of the communication between the services. The `rpc` package provides a simple way to make calls to other Go web services, and, by default, the `rpc` package uses gob to handle encoding duties. This means you'll get all the benefits of using gob without having to do any extra work.

Using `gob` for `rpc` service-to-service communication will result in lower latency communications. Low latency communications are what allows for modern software architecture designs, such as microservices.

To encode data using the gob protocol in Go directly, you use Go's `gob` package. The package is Go's implementation of the gob protocol. When encoding data using this package, it'll return a `byte` slice. These byte slices are common in code for when dealing with files and networks. This means there are already a great number of helper functions for you to take advantage of.

Gob is not limited to use only in networked solutions. You can also use gob to store data in files. A common use case for writing Go data to files is for making data resilient to server restarts. In modern cloud server deployments, if a server is starting to have problems, it gets killed, and your application is started up again on a new server. If you have any important data that's only in memory, it'll be lost. Prevent this loss by writing that data to a mounted filesystem attached to the server. When the replacement server starts, it attaches to the same filesystem, and on startup, your application recovers the data from the filesystem.

One example of using files for data resilience is in transaction-based workloads. In a transaction-based workload, losing a single transaction can be a big problem. To prevent this from happening, a backup of the transaction is written to disk while your application is processing it. If a restart were to happen, your application would check these backups to ensure everything's in order. Using gob to encode this data would ensure it's written to the filesystem as soon as possible, minimizing the chance of data loss.

Another use case is cold-start cache priming. When using a cache for performance reasons, you need to store it in memory. It's not uncommon for the size of this cache to grow to be gigabytes in size. A server restart means this cache is lost and needs reloading from the database. If a lot of servers get restarted all at once, it causes a cache stampede, which could crash the database. A way to avoid this overload situation is to make a copy of the cache and write it to a mounted filesystem. Then, when your application starts up, it would prime its cache from the files and not the database. Using gob to encode this data would allow much more efficient use of disk space, which, in turn, allows faster reading and more efficient decoding. This also means your server gets back online sooner.

Exercise 11.04: Using gob to Encode Data

In this exercise, we're going to encode and transmit, then decode a transaction using gob. We're going to send a banking transaction from a client to a server using a dummy network. The transaction is a struct that also has an embedded user struct. This shows that complex data can be easily encoded.

To show the flexibility of the **gob** protocol, the client and server structs don't match in several ways. For example, the client's user is a pointer, but the server's user is not. The amounts are of different float types, and the client is a **float64** while the server is a ***float32**. Some of the fields are missing in the server types that are present in the client types.

We'll be using the **bytes** package to store our encoded data. This shows that once encoded, you can use the standard library to work with the gob binary data.

Steps:

1. Define **client** structs.

2. Define **server** structs that differ in a number of ways.

3. Create a byte buffer to act as a dummy network.

4. Create a client value with some dummy data.

5. Encode the client value.

6. Write the encoded data to the dummy network.

7. Create a function that acts as the server.

8. Read the data from the dummy network.

9. Decode the data.

10. Print the decoded data to the console.

Let's get started with the exercise:

1. Create a directory called *Exercise11.04* within a directory called **Chapter11**.

2. Create a file called **main.go** inside of *Chapter11/Exercise11.04*.

3. Using Visual Studio Code, open the newly created **main.go** file.

4. Add the following package name and import statements:

```
package main
import (
   "bytes"
   "encoding/gob"
   "fmt"
   "io"
   "log"
)
```

5. Create a **struct** to be our client-side user model:

```
type UserClient struct {
   ID    string
   Name string
}
```

6. Create a **struct** to be our client-side transaction. **Tx** is a common shorthand for transaction:

```
type TxClient struct {
    ID          string
    User        *UserClient
    AccountFrom string
    AccountTo   string
    Amount      float64
}
```

7. Create a **struct** to be our server-side user model. This model doesn't match the client model because it doesn't have the **Name** property:

```
type UserServer struct {
    ID string
}
```

8. Create a **struct** to be our server-side transaction. Here, the user is not a pointer. The amount is a pointer, however, and the pointer is for a **float32**, not a **float64**:

```
type TxServer struct {
    ID          string
    User        UserServer
    AccountFrom string
    AccountTo   string
    Amount      *float32
}
```

9. Create the **main()** function:

```
func main() {
```

10. Create the dummy network, which is a buffer from the **bytes** package:

```
var net bytes.Buffer
```

11. Create the dummy data using the client-side structs:

```
clientTx := &TxClient{
    ID: "123456789",
    User: &UserClient{
        ID:   "ABCDEF",
        Name: "James",
    },
    AccountFrom: "Bob",
```

```
        AccountTo:    "Jane",
        Amount:       9.99,
    }
```

12. Encode the data. The target for the encoded data is our dummy network:

```
enc := gob.NewEncoder(&net)
```

13. Check for errors and exit if any are found:

```
if err := enc.Encode(clientTx); err != nil {
    log.Fatal("error encoding: ", err)
}
```

14. Send the data to the server:

```
serverTx, err := sendToServer(&net)
```

15. Check for errors and exit if any are found:

```
if err != nil {
    log.Fatal("server error: ", err)
}
```

16. Print the decoded data to the console:

```
fmt.Printf("%#v\n", serverTx)
```

17. Close the **main()** function:

```
}
```

18. Create our **sendToServer** function. This function takes a single **io.Reader** interface and returns a server-side transaction and an **error**:

```
func sendToServer(net io.Reader) (*TxServer, error) {
```

19. Create a variable to be the target for decoding:

```
tx := &TxServer{}
```

20. Create a decoder with the network as the source:

```
dec := gob.NewDecoder(net)
```

21. Decode and capture any errors:

```
err := dec.Decode(tx)
```

22. Return the decoded data and any errors captured:

```
return tx, err
```

23. Close the function:

```
}
```

24. Build the program by running **go build** at the command line:

```
go build
```

25. Run the executable by typing the name of the executable and hitting *Enter*.

The output from the type switch statement should be as follows:

```
~/src/Th…op/Ch…11/Exercise11.04   go run main.go                    ✔
&main.TxServer{ID:"123456789", User:main.UserServer{ID:"ABCDEF"}, AccountFrom:"Bob",
AccountTo:"Jane", Amount:(*float32)(0xc000014588)}
```

Figure 11.20: Gob output

In this exercise, we encoded the data using the client types, **sent** it to the server, and dumped out what the server decoded. In what we get back from the server, we can see it's using different types, that the user has an ID but no name, and that **Amount** is a 32-bit float pointer type.

We can see how easy and flexible gob can be to work with. Gob is also a great choice for performance when you need to communicate between servers, but both servers will need to be written in Go to be able to take advantage of these features.

In the next activity, we're going to test what we've learned so far with JSON.

Activity 11.01: Mimicking a Customer Order Using JSON

In this activity, we are going to mimic a customer order. An online e-commerce portal needs to accept customer orders over its web application. As the customer browses through the site, the customer will add items to their order. This web application will need to be able to take the JSON and add orders to the JSON.

Steps:

1. Create an **address struct** with all the exportable fields (the **Street** string, the **City** string, the **State** string, and the **Zipcode** int).

2. Create an **item struct** with all its exportable fields (the **Name** string, the **Description** string, the **Quantity** int, and the **Price** int). The description field should not show up in the JSON if it has no data.

3. Create an **order struct** with all its exportable fields (the **TotalPrice** int, the **IsPaid** bool, the **Fragile** bool, and **OrderDetail** **[]item**). The **Fragile** field should not show up in the JSON if it has no data.

4. Create a **customer struct** with all its the **UserName** string, the **Password** string, the **Token** string, the **ShipTo** address, and the **PurchaseOrder** order). The **Password** and **Token** fields should never appear in the JSON.

5. The application should check that **jsonData** is valid JSON. The following code snippet is some example JSON to use for a customer order for our application:

```
jsonData := []byte(`
{
    "username" :"blackhat",
    "shipto":
      {
            "street": "Sulphur Springs Rd",
            "city": "Park City",
            "state": "VA",
            "zipcode": 12345
      },
    "order":
      {
        "paid":false,
        "orderdetail" :
          [{
              "itemname":"A Guide to the World of zeros and ones",
              "desc": "book",
              "qty": 3,
              "price": 50
          }]
      }
}
`)
```

6. The application should decode the **jsonData** into the customer struct.

7. Add two additional items to the order include the **TotalPrice** for all the items in the order, whether the order has any fragile items, and whether the items are all paid for in full.

8. Print the customer order so that it is easily readable.

The expected output from the application is as follows:

```
{
    "username": "blackhat",
    "shipto": {
        "street": "Sulphur Springs Rd",
        "city": "Park City",
        "state": "VA",
        "zipcode": 12345
    },
    "order": {
        "total": 475,
        "paid": true,
        "Fragile": true,
        "orderdetail": [
            {
                "itemname": "A Guide to the World of zeros and ones",
                "desc": "book",
                "qty": 3,
                "price": 50
            },
            {
                "itemname": "Final Fantasy The Zodiac Age",
                "desc": "Nintendo Switch Game",
                "qty": 1,
                "price": 50
            },
            {
                "itemname": "Crystal Drinking Glass",
                "qty": 11,
                "price": 25
            }
        ]
    }
}
```

Figure 11.21: Customer order printout

We have seen how to encode and decode complex types such as slices in JSON. We have checked whether the JSON was valid JSON. We also have seen how to control which fields in the struct are displayed, and whether the fields that do not have data were able to omit them from the JSON. When we printed out the JSON, we were able to print it in a format that is easy to read.

> **Note**
>
> The solution for this activity can be found on page 732.

Summary

In this chapter, we studied what JSON is and how we can use Go to store JSON in our structs.

JSON is used by many programming languages including Go. JSON is made up of key-value pairs. These key-value pairs can be any of the following types: string, number, object, array, Boolean, or null.

Go's standard library provides many capabilities that make working with JSON easy. This includes the ability to decode JSON data into structs. It also has the ability to encode structs into JSON.

We have seen that, through the use of JSON tags, we have greater flexibility and control over how the encoding and decoding of JSON occurs. These tags give us the ability to name the JSON key name, ignore fields and not encode them into JSON, and omit fields when they are empty.

The Go standard library gives us the ability to determine how to print in an easy to read format by using the `json.MarshalIndent()` function. We have also seen how to decode JSON structures when we do not know the format of the JSON ahead of time. All of these features and many others demonstrate the powerful functionality that comes in the Go standard library.

In the next chapter, we will be looking at files and systems. The chapter will go over how to interact with the filesystem, including creating and modifying files. You will also learn about file permissions and creating a command-line application that uses various flags and arguments. We will also look at another format for storing data called CSV. All of this and more in the following chapter.

12

Files and Systems

Overview

This chapter aims to give you an understanding of how to interact with the filesystem. This includes creating and modifying files. You will also learn how to check whether the file exists. We will write to the file and save it on disk. We will then create a command-line application that accepts various flags and arguments. We will also be able to catch signals and determine what to do with them before we exit the program.

In this chapter, you will create command-line applications that accept arguments and display help content. By the end of the chapter, you will be able to handle signals that are sent to the application from the operating system (OS), and control the exit from the application when the OS sends a signal to immediately stop the application.

Introduction

In the previous chapter, we looked at how to marshal and unmarshal JSON. We were able to set our struct to the JSON key values and place our struct values into JSON. The Go programming language has great library support for JSON, just like it has good support for the filesystem-type operations (for example, the **open**, **create**, and **modify** files).

In this chapter, we will interact with the filesystem. The levels we are going to be working with the filesystem at are the file, directory, and permission levels. We will tackle everyday issues that developers face when working with the filesystem, including how to write a command-line application that needs to accept arguments from the command line. We will learn how to create a command-line application that will read and write files. Along with discussing what happens when we get a signal interrupt from the OS, we will demonstrate how to perform cleanup actions before our application stops running. We will also handle a scenario of receiving an interrupt to our application and handling how the applications exits. There are times when your application is running, and a signal comes from the OS to shut down the application. In such instances, we may want to log information at the time of the shutdown for debugging purposes; this will help us to understand why the application shut down. We will look at how we can do that in this chapter. However, before we start tackling these issues, let's get a basic understanding of the filesystem.

Filesystem

A filesystem controls how data is named, stored, accessed, and retrieved on a device such as a hard drive, USB, DVD, or another medium. Each filesystem for a specific OS will specify its conventions for naming files, such as the length of the filename, the specific characters that can be used, how long the suffix or file extension can be, and more. There are some file descriptors or metadata about a file that most filesystems contain, such as file size, location, access permissions, date created, date modified, and more:

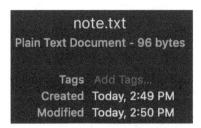

Figure 12.1: Filesystem metadata for a file

Files are generally placed in some sort of hierarchal structure. This structure typically consists of multiple directories and sub-directories. The placement of the files within the directories is a way to organize your data and get access to the file or directory:

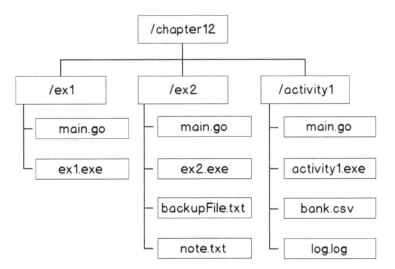

Figure 12.2: Filesystem directory structure

As shown in *Figure 12.2*, the top-level directory is **Chapter12**. This has sub-directories **ex1**, **ex2**, and **activity1**. In this example, those sub-directories organize files according to each of the exercises and activities. The filesystem is also responsible for who or what can access the directories and files. In the next topic, we will be looking at file permissions.

File Permissions

Permissions are an important aspect that you need to understand when dealing with file creation and modifications.

We need to look at various permission types that can be assigned to a file. We also need to look at how those permission types are represented as a symbolic and octal notation.

Go uses the Unix nomenclature for representing permission types. They are represented as symbolic notation or octal notation. The three permission types are *Read*, *Write*, and *Execute*.

Each one has a symbolic and octal notation. The following table explains the permission type and how it is represented:

Read	symbolic: r
	octal: 4
	allows you to open and read a file.
Write	symbolic: w
	octal: 2
	ability to modify the contents of a file.
Execute	symbolic: e
	octal: 1
	ability to execute or run a file if it is a program or script.
no permission	symbolic: -
	octal: 0
	no permission assigned

Figure 12.3: Permissions

For every file, there are three sets of individuals or groups that have their permissions specified:

Owner:

- To an individual, this is a single person such as John Smith or the root user.

Group:

- A group typically consists of multiple individuals or other groups.

Others:

- Those that are not in a group or the owner.
- The following is an example of a file and its permissions on a Unix machine:

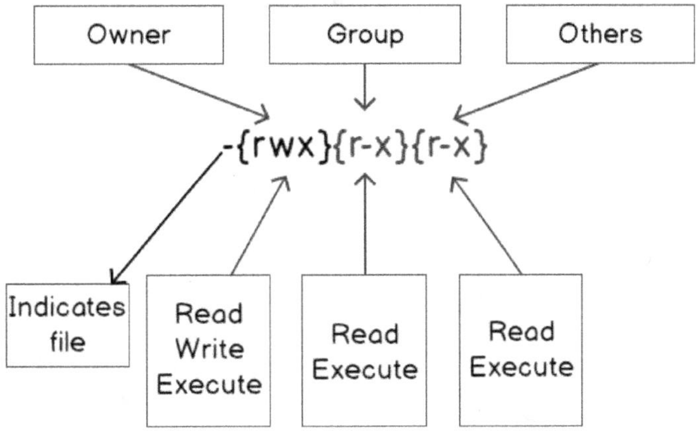

Owner | Group | Others

-{rwx}{r-x}{r-x}

Indicates file

Read Write Execute

Read Execute

Read Execute

Figure 12.4: Permission sets

- The first dash indicates that this is a file; if it was a **d**, that would indicate a directory.

- Octal notation can be used to show multiple permissions types by a single number. For example, if you want to show a permission for **read** and **write** using symbolic notation, it would be **rw-**. If this was to be represented as an octal number, it would be **6**:

Figure 12.5: Permission types

The following table presents the numbers and symbols for the different permission types:

Permission Type	Octal	Symbolic
No Permission	0	---
Execute	1	--x
Write	2	-w-
Execute+Write	3	-wx
Read	4	r--
Read+Execute	5	r-x
Read+Write	6	rw-
Read+Write+Execute	7	Rwx

Figure 12.6: Permission type, octal, and symbolic

The next table is an example of various file permissions for **owner**, **group**, and **others**:

File Permission	Octal	Symbolic
Owner: Read Group: Read Others: Read	0444	-r--r--r--
Owner: Write Group: Write Others: Write	0222	--w--w--w-
Owner: Execute Group: Execute Others: Execute	0111	--x—x—x
Owner: Read Write Execute Group: Read Write Others: Write Execute	0763	-rwxrw-wx
Owner: Read Write Execute Group: Read Write Execute Others: Read Write Execute	0777	-rwxrwxrwx

Figure 12.7: Permissions based on owner, group, and others

Flags and Arguments

Go provides support for creating command-line interface tools. Many times, when we are writing Go programs that are executables, they need to accept various inputs. These inputs could include the location of a file, a value to run the program in the debug state, getting help to run the program, and more. All of this is made possible by a package in the Go standard library called **flag**. It is used to allow the passing of arguments to the program. A flag is an argument that is passed to a Go program. The order of the flags being passed to the Go program using the **flag** package does not matter to Go.

To define your **flag**, you must know the **flag** type you will be accepting. The **flag** package provides many functions for defining flags. Here is a sample list:

```
func Bool(name string, value bool, usage string) *bool
func Duration(name string, value time.Duration, usage string) *time.Duration
func Float64(name string, value float64, usage string) *float64
func Int(name string, value int, usage string) *int
func Int64(name string, value int64, usage string) *int64
```

```
func String(name string, value string, usage string) *string
func Uint(name string, value uint, usage string) *uint
func Uint64(name string, value uint64, usage string) *uint64
```

The parameters of the preceding functions can be explained as follows:

name:

- This parameter is the name of the flag; it is a string type. For example, if you pass **file** as an argument, you would access that flag from the command line by:

```
app.exe -file
```

value:

- This parameter is the default value that the flag is set to.

usage:

- This parameter is used to describe the flag's purpose. It will often show up on the command line when you incorrectly set the value.

- Passing the wrong type for a flag will stop the program and cause an error; the usage will be printed.

return value:

- This is the address of the variable that stores the value of the flag.

Let's take a look at a simple example:

```
package main
import (
    "flag"
    "fmt"
)
func main() {
    v := flag.Int("value", -1, "Needs a value for the flag.")
    flag.Parse()
    fmt.Println(*v)
}
```

The following diagram describes the preceding example when using the flag package.

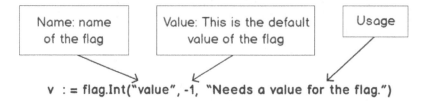

Figure 12.8: flag.Int arguments

We will go over the code in the diagram and the previous code snippet.

- The variable **v** will reference the value for either **-value** or **-value**.

- The initial value of ***v** is the default value of **-1** before calling **flag.Parse()**:

```
flag.Parse()
```

- After defining the flags, you must call **flag.Parse()** to parse the command line into the defined flags.

- Calling **flag.Parse()** places the argument for **-value** into ***v**.

- Once you have called the **flag.Parse() function**, the flags will be available.

- On the command line, execute the following **go build -o exFlag** command and you will get the executable in the directory called **exFlag**:

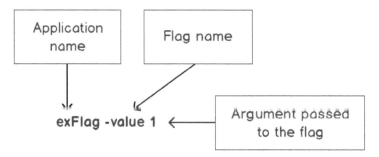

Figure 12.9: Application flag and arguments

Let's look at using flags of various types in the following code snippet:

```go
package main
import (
  "flag"
  "fmt"
)
func main() {
  i := flag.Int("age", -1, "your age")
  n := flag.String("name", "", "your first name")
  b := flag.Bool("married", false, "are you married?")
  flag.Parse()
  fmt.Println("Name: ", *n)
  fmt.Println("Age: ", *i)
  fmt.Println("Married: ", *b)
}
```

Let's analyze the preceding code:

- We define three flags of the **Int**, **String**, and **Bool** type.

- We then call the **flag.Parse()** function to place the arguments for those flags into their respective reference variables.

- Then, we simply print the values.

- Running the executable with no parameters: **./exFlag**

```
Name:
Age:  -1
Married:  false
```

- Running without supplying arguments; the values of the reference pointers are the default values assigned when we defined our flag types: **./exFlag -h**:

```
Usage of ./exFlag:
  -age int
    your age (default -1)
  -married
    are you married?
  -name string
    your first name
```

- Running our application with the **-h** flag prints out the usage statement that we set when we defined our flags:

```
./exFlag -name=John -age 42 -married true results:
```

```
Name:   John
Age:   42
Married:  false
```

There are times when we might want to make a **flag** necessary for the command-line application. Carefully choosing the default value when a flag is required is important. You can check and see whether the value of the flag is the default and whether it is exiting the program:

```go
package main
import (
  "flag"
  "fmt"
  "os"
)
func main() {
  i := flag.Int("age", -1, "your age")
  n := flag.String("name", "", "your first name")
  b := flag.Bool("married", false, "are you married?")
  flag.Parse()
  if *n == "" {
  fmt.Println("Name is required.")
  flag.PrintDefaults()
  os.Exit(1)
  }
  fmt.Println("Name: ", *n)
  fmt.Println("Age: ", *i)
  fmt.Println("Married: ", *b)
  if *n == "" {
  fmt.Println("Name is required.")
  flag.PrintDefaults()
  os.Exit(1)
  }
}
```

Let's review the code in detail:

- The name flag has the default value of an empty string.
- We check to see whether that is the value of ***n**. If it is, we print a message informing the user that **Name** is required.
- We then call **flag.PrintDefaults()**; this prints the usage message to the user.
- The results of calling the application are **/exFlag --age 42 -married true**:

```
Name is required.
  -age int
    your age (default -1)
  -married
    are you married?
  -name string
    your first name
```

Signals

- What is a signal? In our context, a signal is an interrupt that is sent to our program or to a process by the OS. When a signal is delivered to our program, the program will stop what it is doing; either it will handle the signal or, if possible, ignore it. We have seen other Go commands that change the flow of the program; you may be wondering which one to use.

We use **defer** statements in our applications to perform various cleanup activities, such as the following:

- The release of resources
- The closing of files
- The closing of database connections
- Performing the removal of configuration or temporary files

In some use cases, it is imperative that these activities are completed. Using a **defer** function will execute it just before returning to the caller. However, this does not guarantee that it will always run. There are certain scenarios in which the **defer** function won't execute; for example, an OS interrupt to your program:

- **os.Exit(1)**

- *Ctrl* + C

- Other instructions from the OS

- The preceding scenarios indicate where it may warrant using signals. Signals can help us control the exit of our program. Depending on the signal, it could terminate our program. For example, the application is running and encounters an OS interrupt signal after executing **employee.CalculateSalary()**. In this scenario, the **defer** function will not run, thus, **employee.DepositCheck()** does not execute and the employee does not get paid. A signal can change the flow of the program. The following diagram goes over the scenario we discussed previously:

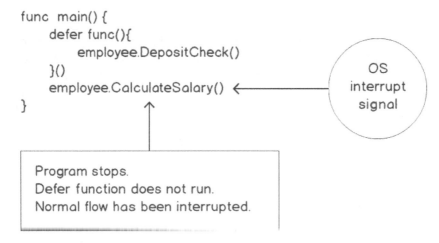

Figure 12.10: Signal changing the flow of the program

- Support for handling signals is built into the Go standard library; it is in the **os/ signal** package. This package will allow us to make our programs more resilient. We want to gracefully shut down when we receive certain signals. The first thing to do when handling signals in Go is to trap or catch the signal that you are interested in. This is done by using the following:

```
func Notify(c chan<- os.Signal, sig ...os.Signal)
```

- The **Notify()** function accepts an **os.Signal** data type on a channel, **c**. The **sig** argument is a variadic variable of **os.Signal**; we specify zero or more **os.Signal** data types that we are interested in.

- The following is an example that handles a **syscall.SIGINT** interrupt, which is akin to **CTRL-C**:

```go
package main
import (
  "fmt"
  "os"
  "os/signal"
  "syscall"
)
func main() {
  sigs := make(chan os.Signal, 1)
  done := make(chan bool)
  signal.Notify(sigs,syscall.SIGINT)
  go func() {
  for {
    s := <-sigs
    switch s {
    case syscall.SIGINT:
    fmt.Println()
    fmt.Println("My process has been interrupted.  Someone might of pressed CTRL-
C")
    fmt.Println("Some clean up is occuring")
    done <- true
    }
  }
  }()
  fmt.Println("Program is blocked until a signal is caught")
  <-done
  fmt.Println("Out of here")
}
```

- Let's look at the preceding code snippet in detail:

```go
    sigs := make(chan os.Signal, 1)
```

- We create a channel of the **os.Signal** type. The **Notify** method works by sending values of the **os.Signal** type to a channel. The **sigs** channel is used to receive these notifications from the **Notify** method:

```go
    done := make(chan bool)
```

- The **done** channel is used to let us know when the program can exit:

```
signal.Notify(sigs,syscall.SIGINT)
```

- The **signal.Notify** method will receive notifications on the **sigs** channel, which is of the **syscall.SIGINT** type:

```
go func() {
for {
  s := <-sigs
  switch s {
  case syscall.SIGINT:
  fmt.Println("My process has been interrupted.  Someone might of pressed
CTRL-C")
  fmt.Println("Some clean up is occurring")
  done <- true
  }
}
```

- We create an anonymous function that is a goroutine. This function currently only has a case statement, which is blocking until it gets a **syscall.SIGINT** type.

- It will print out various messages.

- We send **true** to our **done** channel to indicate that we received the signal. This will stop our channel from blocking:

```
fmt.Println("Program is blocked until a signal is caught")
<-done
fmt.Println("Out of here")
```

- The **<-done** channel will be blocking until our program receives the signal.

- Here are the results:

```
Program is blocked until a signal is caught
^C
My process has been interrupted.  Someone might of pressed CTRL-C
Some clean up is occurring
Out of here
```

Exercise 12.01: Simulating Cleanup

In this exercise, we will be catching two signals: **SIGINT** and **SIGTSTP**. Once those signals have been caught, we will simulate a cleanup of the files. We have not gone over how to remove files yet, so, in this example, we will simply create a delay to demonstrate how we can run a function after a signal is caught. This is the desired output from this exercise:

1. Create a file called **main.go**.

2. Add to the file the package **main** and the following import statements:

```go
package main
import (
    "fmt"
    "os"
    "os/signal"
    "syscall"
    "time"
)
```

3. In the **main()** function, create a channel of the **os.Signal** type. The **sigs** channel is used to receive these notifications from the **Notify** method:

```go
func main() {
    sigs := make(chan os.Signal, 1)
```

4. Next, add a **done** channel. The **done** channel is used to let us know when the program can exit:

```go
    done := make(chan bool)
```

5. We will then add a **signal.Notify** method. The **Notify** method works by sending values of the **os.Signal** type to a channel.

6. Recall that the last parameter of the **signal.Notify** method is a variadic parameter of the **os.Signal** type.

7. The **signal.Notify** method will receive notifications on the channel sigs that are of the **syscall.SIGINT** and **syscall.SIGTSTP** types.

8. Generally speaking, the **syscall.SIGINT** type can occur when you press *Ctrl* + C.

9. Generally speaking, the **syscall.SIGTSTP** type can occur when you press *Ctrl* + Z:

```go
    signal.Notify(sigs, syscall.SIGINT, syscall.SIGTSTP)
```

10. Create an anonymous function as a goroutine:

```
go func() {
```

11. Inside the goroutine, create an infinite loop.

12. Inside the infinite loop, we will receive a value from the **sigs** channel and store it in the **s** variable, **s := <-sigs**:

```
for {
    s := <-sigs
```

13. Create a **switch** statement that evaluates what is received from the channel.

14. We will have two case statements that will check for the **syscall.SIGINT** and **syscall.SIGTSP** types.

15. Each case statement will have a message being printed.

16. We will also call our **cleanup()** function.

17. The last statement in the case statement is sending **true** to the **done** channel to stop the blocking:

```
            switch s {
            case syscall.SIGINT:
              fmt.Println()
              fmt.Println("My process has been interrupted.  Someone might of pressed
    CTRL-C")
              fmt.Println("Some clean up is occuring")
              cleanUp()
              done <- true
            case syscall.SIGTSTP:
              fmt.Println()
              fmt.Println("Someone pressed CTRL-Z")
              fmt.Println("Some clean up is occuring")
              cleanUp()
              done <- true
            }
        }
    }()
    fmt.Println("Program is blocked until a signal is caught(ctrl-z, ctrl-c)")
    <-done
    fmt.Println("Out of here")
}
```

18. Create a simple function to mimic a process performing a cleanup:

```
func cleanUp() {
  fmt.Println("Simulating clean up")
  for i := 0; i <= 10; i++ {
    fmt.Println("Deleting Files.. Not really.", i)
    time.Sleep(1 * time.Second)
  }
}
```

19. You can try running this program and pressing *Ctrl* + Z and *Ctrl* + C to examine the different results of the program. This only works on Linux and macOS:

20. Now run the code:

```
go run main.go
```

The following is the output:

```
Program is blocked until a signal is caught(ctrl-z, ctrl-c)
^Z
Someone pressed CTRL-Z
Some clean up is occuring
Simulating clean up
Deleting Files.. Not really. 0
Deleting Files.. Not really. 1
Deleting Files.. Not really. 2
Deleting Files.. Not really. 3
Deleting Files.. Not really. 4
Deleting Files.. Not really. 5
Deleting Files.. Not really. 6
Deleting Files.. Not really. 7
Deleting Files.. Not really. 8
Deleting Files.. Not really. 9
Deleting Files.. Not really. 10
Out of here
```

Figure 12.11: Simulating cleanup output

In this exercise, we have demonstrated the ability to intercept an interrupt and perform a task before the application closes. We have the ability to control our exit. This is a powerful feature that allows us to perform cleanup actions that include removing files, performing a last-minute log, freeing up memory, and more. In the next topic, we are going to be creating and writing to files. We will be using functions that come from the Go standard package, **os**.

Creating and Writing to Files

The Go language provides support in various ways to create and write to new files. We will examine some of the most common ways in which this is performed.

The **os** package provides a simple way in which to create a file. For those who are familiar with the **touch** command from the Unix world, it is similar to this. Here is the signature of the function:

```
func Create(name string(*File, error)
```

The function will create an empty file just like the **touch** command. It is important to note that if it already exists, then it will truncate the file.

The **Create** function from the **os** package input parameter is the name of the file and the location that you want to create. If successful, it will return a **File** type. It is worth noting that the **File** type satisfies the **io.Write** and **io.Read** interfaces. This is important to know for later in the chapter:

```go
package main
import (
    "fmt"
    "os"
)
func main() {
    f, err := os.Create("test.txt")
    if err != nil {
    panic(err)
    }
    defer f.Close()
}
```

- The preceding code simply creates an empty file:

```go
f, err := os.Create("test.txt")
```

- It creates a file named test.txt.

- If a file by that name already exists, then it will truncate that file.

- Since we did not provide a location for the file, it will create the file in the directory of our executable:

```go
if err != nil {
fmt.Println(err)
}
```

- We then check for errors from the os.Create function. It is a good practice to check for errors immediately, because if an error occurred and we did not check for the error, this would make debugging in our program difficult later.

- We panic if there is an error. It is better to panic and then to exit, because the defer function will not run if you do an os.Exit(1) with a function that has a defer function.

- If an error did occur, then it would be of the *PathError type. For example, say that we gave the os.Create function an incorrect path such as /lol/test.txt. We would get the following error:

```
open /lol/test.txt: no such file or directory
```

Creating an empty file is straightforward, but let's continue with **os.Create** and write to the file we just created. Recall that **os.Create** returns an ***os.File** type. There are two methods of interest that can be used to write to the file:

- **Write**

- **WriteString**:

```
package main
import (
  "os"
)
func main() {
  f, err := os.Create("test.txt")
  if err != nil {
  panic(err)
  }
  defer f.Close()
  f.Write([]byte("Using Write function.\n"))
  f.WriteString("Using Writestring function.\n")
}
```

Let's look at the preceding code in more detail:

```
func (f *File) Write(b []byte) (n int, err error)
```

- The **Write** method accepts a slice of bytes and returns the number of bytes written and an error if there is any. This method also allows the **os.File** type to satisfy the **io.Write** interface:

```
f.Write([]byte("Using Write function.\n"))
```

- We are taking the **"Using Write function.\n"** string and converting it into a slice of bytes.

- Then, we are writing it to our **test.txt** file. The **Write** method accepts **[]byte**:

```
f.WriteString("Using Writestring function.\n")
```

- The **WriteString** method behaves the same as the **Write** method, except that it takes a string as an input parameter versus a **[]byte** data type.

Go provides us with the ability to create and write to a file within a single command. We will be leveraging the **io/ioutil** package in Go to accomplish this task. The **ioutil.WriteFile** method is a very handy method that provides this ability:

```
func WriteFile(filename string, data []byte, perm os.FileMode) error
```

The method writes the data to the file specified in the filename parameter, with the given permissions. It will return an error if one exists. Let's take a look at this in action:

```go
package main
import (
  "fmt"
  "io/ioutil"
)
func main() {
  message := []byte("Look!")
  err := ioutil.WriteFile("test.txt", message, 0644)
  if err != nil {
    fmt.Println(err)
  }
}
```

Let's understand the code in pieces:

```go
err := ioutil.WriteFile("test.txt", message, 0644)
```

- The **WriteFile** method will write the **[]byte** variable message to the **test.txt** file.

- If the **test.txt** file does not exist, it will create the **test.txt** file with the permissions of **0644**. The owner will have read/write permissions. The group and others will have read permissions.

- If the file does exist, it will truncate it.

Both **os.Create** and **ioutil.WriteFile** will truncate the file if it exists. This may not always be the desired behavior. There may be times that we want to check to see whether the file exists before we create the file or before we attempt to read the file. Lucky for us, Go provides a simple mechanism for checking whether a file exists:

> **Note**
>
> The following code snippet requires the **junk.txt** file to not exist. It also requires the **test.txt** file to exist in the same directory as the program's executable.

```go
package main
import (
  "fmt"
  "os"
)
func main() {
  file, err := os.Stat("junk.txt")
  if err != nil {
  if os.IsNotExist((err)) {
    fmt.Println("junk.txt:  File does not exist!")
    fmt.Println(file)
  }
  }
  fmt.Println()
  file, err = os.Stat("test.txt")
  if err != nil {
  if os.IsNotExist((err)) {
    fmt.Println("test.txt:  File does not exist!")
  }
  }
  fmt.Printf("file name: %s\nIsDir: %t\nModTime: %v\nMode: %v\nSize: %d\n", file.Name(),
file.IsDir(), file.ModTime(), file.Mode(), file.Size())
}
```

Let's look at the preceding code snippet in more detail:

```
file, err := os.Stat("junk.txt")
```

- We are calling **os.Stat()** on the **junk.txt** file to check to see whether it exists. The **os.Stat()** method will return a **FileInfo** type if the file exists. If not, **FileInfo** will be **nil** and an error will be returned instead:

```
if err != nil {
if os.IsNotExist((err)) {
  fmt.Println("junk.txt:  File does not exist!")
  fmt.Prinln(file)
}
}
```

- The **os.Stat()** method can return multiple errors. We must inspect the error to determine whether the error is due to the file not being there. The standard library provides **os.IsNotExist(error)**, which can be used to check to see whether the error is the result of the file not existing. Here is the result:

```
IsNotExist returns a boolean indicating whether the error is known to report that
a file or a directory does not exist. It is satisfied by ErrNotExist as well as some
syscall errors.

func os.IsNotExist(err error) bool
```

- The printing of **file(FileInfo)** will be **nil** in this scenario, since **junk.txt** does not exist:

```
file, err = os.Stat("test.txt")
```

- The **test.txt** file does exist in this scenario, so the **err** will be **nil** and the file will contain the **FileInfo** type:

```
fmt.Printf("file name: %s\nIsDir: %t\nModTime: %v\nMode: %v\nSize: %d\n",
  file.Name(), file.IsDir(), file.ModTime(), file.Mode(), file.Size())
}
```

- There are various pieces of information that the **FileInfo** type contains, which can be useful to know.

- The following details on the **FileInfo** interface can be found at https://golang.org/src/os/types.go?s=479:840#L11:

```
// A FileInfo describes a file and is returned by Stat and Lstat.
type FileInfo interface {
Name() string      // base name of the file
Size() int64     // length in bytes for regular files; system-dependent for others
Mode() FileMode   // file mode bits
ModTime() time.Time // modification time
IsDir() bool      // abbreviation for Mode().IsDir()
Sys() interface{}   // underlying data source (can return nil)
}
```

- Here are the results of the executed code:

```
junk.txt:  File does not exist!
<nil>

file name: test.txt
IsDir: false
ModTime: 2019-05-27 11:09:25.106874391 -0400 EDT
Mode: -rw-r--r--
Size: 5
VASML-1587743:ex1 jleaso254$
```

Figure 12.12: os.Stat

Reading the Whole File at Once

In this topic, we will look at two methods that read all the contents of the file. These two functions are good to use when your file size is small. While these two methods are convenient and easy to use, they have one major drawback. That is, if the file size is too large, then it could exhaust the memory on the system. It is important to keep this in mind and understand the limitations of the two methods we will be going over in this topic. Even though these methods are one of the quickest and easiest ways to load data, it is important to understand that they should be limited to small files and not large ones.

The first method we will examine for reading a file is the following:

```
func ReadFile(filename string) ([]byte, error)
```

The **ReadFile** function reads the contents of the file and returns it as a slice of bytes along with any reported errors. We will look at the error return when the **ReadFile** method is used:

- A successful call returns **err == nil**.

- In some of the other read methods for files, EOF is treated as an error. This is not the case for functions that read the entire file into memory:

```
package main
import (
  "fmt"
  "io/ioutil"
)
func main() {
  content, err := ioutil.ReadFile("test.txt")
  if err != nil {
  fmt.Println(err)
  }
  fmt.Println("File contents: ")
  fmt.Println(string(content))
}
```

- For this code snippet, I have a **test.txt** file that is located in the same location as my executable. It contains the following content:

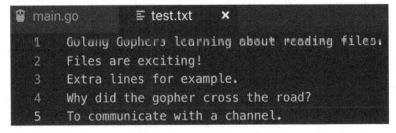

Figure 12.13: Example text file

```
content, err := ioutil.ReadFile("test.txt")
```

- The contents of **text.txt** get assigned as a slice of bytes into the variable content. If there are any errors, they will be stored in the **err** variable:

```
fmt.Println("File contents: ")
fmt.Println(string(content))
```

- Since this is a slice of bytes, it must be converted into a string format for ease of readability. Here are the results of the print statements:

```
File contents:
Golang Gophers learning about reading files.
Files are exciting!
Extra lines for example.
Why did the gopher cross the road?
To communicate with a channel.
```

Figure 12.14: Example output

The next function we will look at that reads the entire content into memory is the following:

```
func ReadAll(r io.Reader) ([]byte, error)
```

Unlike the **ReadFile** method, **ReadAll** takes **io.Reader** as an argument. That is the only real difference in the behavior of **ReadFile** and **ReadAll**:

```go
package main
import (
  "fmt"
  "io/ioutil"
  "os"
  "strings"
)
func main() {
  f, err := os.Open("test.txt")
  if err != nil {
  fmt.Println(err)
  os.Exit(1)
  }
  content, err := ioutil.ReadAll(f)
  if err != nil {
  fmt.Println(err)
  os.Exit(1)
  }
  fmt.Println("File contents: ")
  fmt.Println(string(content))
  r := strings.NewReader("No file here.")
  c, err := ioutil.ReadAll(r)
  if err != nil {
```

```
    fmt.Println(err)
    os.Exit(1)
    }
    fmt.Println()
    fmt.Println("Contents of strings.NewReader: ")
    fmt.Println(string(c))
}
```

Let's understand the code in pieces:

```
f, err := os.Open("test.txt")
```

- The **ioutil.ReadAll** method requires **io.Reader** as an argument. The **os.Open** method returns an ***os.File** type, which satisfies the **io.Reader** interface:

```
    content, err := ioutil.ReadAll(f)
    if err != nil {
    fmt.Println(err)
    os.Exit(1)
    }
```

- The content stores the **[]byte** data from the result of the **ioutil.ReadAll(f)** method. If there are any errors, they will be stored in the **err** variable:

```
    fmt.Println("File contents: ")
    fmt.Println(string(content))
```

- Since this is a slice of bytes, it must be converted to a string format for ease of readability. The results of the print statements are as follows:

```
File contents:
Golang Gophers learning about reading files.
Files are exciting!
Extra lines for example.
Why did the gopher cross the road?
To communicate with a channel.
```

Figure 12.15: Example output

```
    r := strings.NewReader("No file here.")
```

- Since the **ioutil.ReadAll** method accepts an interface, this gives us more flexibility. If you recall *Chapter 7*, *Interfaces*, when using interfaces, it allows for more flexibility and uses.

- We are using **strings.NewReader**, which takes a string and returns a **Reader** type that implements the **io.Reader** interface. This allows us to use the **ioutil.ReadAll()** method without having a file. By doing this, we can perform various tests on the data when we have not yet been given the file:

```
c, err := ioutil.ReadAll(r)
```

- We can use the **ioutil.Readall** method in the same fashion with the results of **strings.Reader()** as we did with **os.Open()**:

```
fmt.Println()
fmt.Println("Contents of strings.NewReader: ")
fmt.Println(string(c))
```

- Following are the results of the print statement:

```
Contents of strings.NewReader:
No file here.
```

Figure 12.16: The strings.NewReader content

We have seen various ways to write to files, create files, and to read from files. However, we have yet to see how to append data to a file. There are times when you would want to append a file with additional information. The **os.OpenFile()** method provides this ability. Most of the time, you will use **Create** or **Open** for your open or create processes; however, when you want to append data to a file, you will need to use **OpenFile**. The signature of the method is as follows:

```
func OpenFile(name string, flag int, perm FileMode) (*File, error)
```

The one parameter that is unique is the **flag** parameter. This is used to determine what actions to allow when opening the file; it is not to be confused with the **FileMode** type, which is what permission types get to assign to the file itself.

Here is a list of flags that can be used to open a file (http://golang.org/src/pkg/os/file. go):

```
// Flags to OpenFile wrapping those of the underlying system. Not all
// flags may be implemented on a given system.
const (
// Exactly one of O_RDONLY, O_WRONLY, or O_RDWR must be specified.
  O_RDONLY int = syscall.O_RDONLY // open the file read-only.
  O_WRONLY int = syscall.O_WRONLY // open the file write-only.
  O_RDWR   int = syscall.O_RDWR   // open the file read-write.
  // The remaining values may be or'ed in to control behavior.
  O_APPEND int = syscall.O_APPEND // append data to the file when writing.
  O_CREATE int = syscall.O_CREAT  // create a new file if none exists.
```

```
  O_EXCL   int = syscall.O_EXCL   // used with O_CREATE, file must not exist.
  O_SYNC   int = syscall.O_SYNC   // open for synchronous I/O.
  O_TRUNC  int = syscall.O_TRUNC  // truncate regular writable file when opened.
)
```

These flags can be used in various combinations when opening a file. Let's take a look at some various examples using the flags:

```go
package main
import (
  "os"
)
func main() {
  f, err := os.OpenFile("junk101.txt", os.O_CREATE, 0644)
  if err != nil {
  panic(err)
  }
  defer f.Close()
}
```

Let's look at **os.OpenFile** in the previous example:

```go
f, err := os.OpenFile("junk101.txt", os.O_CREATE, 0644)
```

- Using **os.OpenFile** with the **os.O_CREATE** file mode will create the **junk101.txt** file if it does not exist, and then open it.

Let's look at an example using different file modes for **os.OpenFile**:

```go
package main
import (
  "os"
)
func main() {
  f, err := os.OpenFile("junk101.txt", os.O_CREATE|os.O_WRONLY, 0644)
  if err != nil {
  panic(err)
  }
  defer f.Close()
  if _, err := f.Write([]byte("adding stuff\n")); err != nil {
  panic(err)
  }
}
```

Let's look at the preceding code in more detail.

```
f, err := os.OpenFile("junk101.txt", os.O_CREATE| os.O_WRONLY, 0644)
```

- Using **os.OpenFile** with the **os.O_CREATE** flag will create the **junk101.txt** file if it does not exist and then open it. If it does exist, it will just open the file. It will also allow the reading and writing of the file while it is open because of the **os.O_WRONLY** flag:

```
if _, err := f.Write([]byte("adding stuff\n")); err != nil {
panic(err)
}
```

- Since we used the **os.O_WRONLY** flag, we can write to the file while it is open.

Let's look at an example of how to append data to a file:

```
package main
import (
  "os"
)
func main() {
  f, err := os.OpenFile("junk.txt", os.O_APPEND|os.O_CREATE|os.O_WRONLY, 0644)
  if err != nil {
    panic(err)
  }
  defer f.Close()
  if _, err := f.Write([]byte("adding stuff\n")); err != nil {
    panic(err)
}}
f, err := os.OpenFile("junk101.txt", os.O_APPEND | os.O_CREATE| os.O_WRONLY,
  0644)
```

- Using **os.OpenFile** with the **os.O_CREATE** flag will create the **junk101.txt** file if it does not exist and then open it. If it does exist, it will just open the file:

- It will also allow the reading and writing of the file while it is open because of the **os.O_WRONLY** flag.

- **os.O_APPEND** will allow you to append data to the bottom of the file:

```
if _, err := f.Write([]byte("adding stuff\n")); err != nil {
panic(err)
}
```

- Since we used the **os.O_WRONLY** flag, we can write to the file while it is open.

The data will be appended to the bottom of the file and not override the existing data since we included the **os.O_APPEND** flag. The following define some common permission flag combinations that can be used for **os.OpenFile**:

os.O_CREATE

- If the file does not exist, it will create the file when attempting to open it.

os.O_CREATE | os.O_WRONLY

- When opening a file, you can now write to it.
- Any data that is in the file will be overwritten.

os.O_CREATE | os.O_WRONLY | os.O_APPEND

- When writing to the file, it will not overwrite the data but rather append the data to the end of the file.

Exercise 12.02: Backing Up Files

Oftentimes, when working with files, we need to back up a file before making changes to it. This is for instances where we might make mistakes or want the original file for auditing purposes. In this exercise, we will take an existing file called **note.txt** and back it up to **backupFile.txt**. We will then open **note.txt** and add some additional notes to the end of the file. Our directory will contain the following files:

Figure 12.17: Backing up files to the directory

1. We must first create the **note.txt** file in the same directory as our executable. This file can be blank or contain some sample data such as this:

```
Notes:
1. Get better at coding.
```

Figure 12.18: Example of the notes.txt file content

2. Create a Go file called **main.go**.

3. This program will be part of the **main** package.

4. Include the imports, as seen in the following code:

```
package main
import (
    "errors"
    "fmt"
    "io/ioutil"
    "os"
    "strconv"
)
```

5. Create a custom error that will be used for when the working file (**note.txt**) is not found:

```
var (
    ErrWorkingFileNotFound = errors.New("The working file is not found.")
)
```

6. Create a function that will be performing the backup. This function is responsible for taking the working file and storing its content into the **backup** file. This function accepts two arguments. The **working** parameter is the file path of the file that you currently are working on:

```
func createBackup(working, backup string) error {
}
```

7. Inside this function, we will need to check to see whether the working file exists. It must first exist before we can read its contents and store them in our backup file.

8. We are able to check to see whether the error is one where the file does not exist by using **os.IsNotExist(err)**.

9. If the file does not exist, we will return with our custom error: **ErrWorkingFileNotFound**:

```
// check to see if our working file exists,
// before backing it up
_, err := os.Stat(working)
if err != nil {
if os.IsNotExist(err) {
    return ErrWorkingFileNotFound
}
return err
}
```

10. Next, we need to open the working file and store the **os.File** return by the function to the **workFile** variable:

```
workFile, err := os.Open(working)
  if err != nil {
  return err
  }
```

11. We need to read the contents of the **workFile**. We will be using the **ioutil.ReadAll** method to get all the contents of the **workFile**. The **workFile** is of the **os.File** type, which satisfies the **io.Reader** interface; this allows us to pass it to **ioutil.ReadFile**.

12. Check to see whether there is an error:

```
content, err := ioutil.ReadAll(workFile)
if err != nil {
return err
}
```

13. The **content** variable contains the data of the **workFile** represented as a slice of bytes. That data needs to be written to the backup file. We will implement the code that will write the data of the **content** variable to the backup file.

14. The content stores the **[]byte** data that gets returned from the function. This is the entire content of the file stored in the variable.

15. We can use the **ioutil.Writefile** method. If the backup file does not exist, it will create the file. If the backup file does exist, it will overwrite the file with the content variable data:

```
err = ioutil.WriteFile(backup, content, 0644)
if err != nil {
fmt.Println(err)
}
```

16. We need to return **nil**, indicating that, at this juncture, we have not encountered any errors:

```
return nil
}
```

17. Create a function that will append data to our working file.

18. Name the function **addNotes**; this will accept the location of our working file and a string argument that will be appended to the working file. The function will need to return an error:

```
func addNotes(workingFile, notes string) error {
   //…
   return nil
}
```

19. Inside the **addNotes** function, add a line that will append a new line to each note's string. This will place each note on a separate line:

```
func addNotes(workingFile, notes string) error {
   notes += "\n"
   //…
   return nil
}
```

20. Next, we will open the working file and allow for appending to the file. The **os.OpenFile()** function will create the file if it does not exist. Check for any errors:

```
func addNotes(workingFile, notes string) error {
   notes += "\n"
   f, err := os.OpenFile(workingFile, os.O_APPEND|os.O_CREATE|os.O_WRONLY, 0644)
   if err != nil {
   return err
   }
   // …
   return nil
}
```

21. After opening a file and checking for an error, we should make sure that it closes when the function exits by using the defer function, **f.Close()**:

```
func addNotes(workingFile, notes string) error {
   notes += "\n"
   f, err := os.OpenFile(workingFile, os.O_APPEND|os.O_CREATE|os.O_WRONLY, 0644)
   if err != nil {
   return err
   }
   defer f.Close()
   //…
   return nil
}
```

22. The final step of the function is to write the contents of the note to the **workingFile** variable. We can use the **Write** method to accomplish this:

```go
func addNotes(workingFile, notes string) error {
    notes += "\n"
    f, err := os.OpenFile(workingFile, os.O_APPEND|os.O_CREATE|os.O_WRONLY, 0644)
    if err != nil {
    return err
    }
    defer f.Close()
    if _, err := f.Write([]byte(notes)); err != nil {
    return err
    }
    return nil
}
```

23. In the **main()** function, we will initialize three variables; the **backupFile** variable contains the name of the file for backing up our **workingFile** variable, while the **data** variable is what we will be writing to our **workingFile** variable:

```go
func main() {
    backupFile := "backupFile.txt"
    workingFile := "note.txt"
    data := "note"
```

24. Call our **createBackup()** function to back up our **workingFile**. Check for errors after calling the function:

```go
    err := createBackup(workingFile, backupFile)
    if err != nil {
    fmt.Println(err)
    os.Exit(1)
    }
```

25. Create a **for** loop that will iterate **10** times.

26. Each iteration we set our **note** variable to the **data** variable plus the **i** variable of our loop.

27. Since our **note** variable is a string and our **i** variable is an **int**, we will need to convert **i** to a string using the **strconv.Itoa(i)** method.

28. Call our **addNotes()** function and pass the **workingFile** and our **note** variables.

29. Check for any errors returned from the function:

```
for i := 1; i <= 10; i++ {
note := data + " " + strconv.Itoa(i)
err := addNotes(workingFile, note)
if err != nil {
  fmt.Println(err)
  os.Exit(1)
}
}
}
```

30. Run the program:

```
go run main.go
```

31. Evaluate the changes to the files after running the program.

Following are the results after running the program:

```
Notes:
1. Get better at coding.
note 1
note 2
note 3
note 4
note 5
note 6
note 7
note 8
note 9
note 10
```

Figure 12.19: The results of backing up the files

CSV

One of the most common ways a file is structured is as a comma-separated value. This is a clear text file that contains data, which is basically represented as rows and columns. Frequently, these files are used to exchange data. A CSV file has a simple structure. Each piece of data is separated by a comma and then a new line for another record. An example of a CSV file would be as follows:

```
firstName, lastName, age
Celina, Jones, 18
Cailyn, Henderson, 13
Cayden, Smith, 42
```

- You will, at some point in your life, come across CSV files as they are very common. The Go programming language has a standard library that is used for handling CSV files: **encoding/csv**:

```go
package main
import (
  "encoding/csv"
  "fmt"
  "io"
  "log"
  "strings"
)
func main() {
  in := `firstName, lastName, age
Celina, Jones, 18
Cailyn, Henderson, 13
Cayden, Smith, 42
`

  r := csv.NewReader(strings.NewReader(in))
  for {
  record, err := r.Read()
  if err == io.EOF {
    break
  }
  if err != nil {
    log.Fatal(err)
  }
  fmt.Println(record)
  }
}
```

The following creates a **reader** type and returns it:

```go
r := csv.NewReader(strings.NewReader(in))
```

The **NewReader** method takes an argument of **io.Reader** and returns a type of **Reader** that is used to read the CSV data:

```go
for {
  record, err := r.Read()
  if err == io.EOF {
    break
  }
```

Here, we are reading in each record one at a time in an infinite loop. After each record we read, we check first to see whether it is the end of the file (**io.EOF**); if so, we break out of the loop. The **r.Read()** function reads one record; it is a slice of strings from the **r** variable. It returns that record as a **[]string** type.

Here is the result of printing the record:

```
[firstName  lastName   age]
[Celina   Jones   18]
[Cailyn   Henderson    13 ]
[Cayden   Smith   42]
```

Figure 12.20: CSV example output

Do you think there might be a way to access each individual value? Currently, we have only looked at printing out of each row. There are instances, however, where we might want to access just the age or the first name. The next example will show us just how to do that:

```go
package main
import (
  "encoding/csv"
  "fmt"
  "io"
  "log"
  "strings"
)
func main() {
  in := `firstName, lastName, age
Celina, Jones, 18
Cailyn, Henderson, 13
Cayden, Smith, 42
`

  r := csv.NewReader(strings.NewReader(in))
  header := true
  for {
  record, err := r.Read()
  if err == io.EOF {
    break
  }
  if err != nil {
    log.Fatal(err)
  }
  if !header {
    for idx, value := range record {
```

```
  switch idx {
    case 0:
      fmt.Println("First Name: ", value)
    case 1:
      fmt.Println("Last Name: ", value)
    case 2:
      fmt.Println("Age: ", value)
    }
    }
  }
  header = false
  }
}
```

We will discuss the new portions of the code in this example:

header := true

We will use the **header** variable as a flag. It will aid us in parsing the headers of the CSV data:

```
for {
```

The infinite loop will stop once the end of the file is reached:

```
record, err := r.Read()
if err == io.EOF {
```

The **r.Read()** function reads a single record and returns a slice of strings that contains the fields of that record:

```
  break
}
// Code omitted for brevity
```

This breaks out of the infinite loop if it is the end of the file.

```
if !header {
```

Next, check to see whether this is the first iteration of the loop. If this is the first iteration of the loop, then the first row would be the headers of the fields; we do not want to parse the headers:

```
for idx, value := range record {
```

Range over the fields in the record:

```
switch idx {
}
```

The **switch** statement is used to perform the specific parsing of each field:

```
        }
    }
    header = false
    }
```

Initially set to **true**, after the first time through the loop, it can be set to **false**. Headers are usually the first row of the file.

The output is as follows:

```
First Name:  Celina
Last Name:   Jones
Age:    18
First Name:  Cailyn
Last Name:   Henderson
Age:    13
First Name:  Cayden
Last Name:   Smith
Age:    42
```

Figure 12.21: Output of parsing CSV fields

Activity 12.01: Parsing Bank Transaction Files

In this activity, we will be ingesting a transaction file from the bank. The file is a CSV file. Our bank also includes budget categories for the transactions in the file. The file is as follows:

```
id,payee,spent,category
1, sheetz, 32.45, fuel
2, martins,225.52,food
3, wells fargo, 1100, mortgage
4, joe the plumber, 275, repairs
5, comcast, 110, tv
6, bp, 40, fuel
7, aldi, 120, food
8, nationwide, 150, car insurance
9, nationwide, 100, life insurance
10, jim electric, 140, utilities
11, propane, 200, utilities
12, county water, 100, utilities
13, county sewer, 105, utilities
14, 401k, 500, retirement
```

The aim of this activity is to create a command-line program that will accept two flags: the location of the CSV bank transaction file and the location of a log file. We will check that the log and bank file location is valid before the application starts parsing the CSV file. The program will parse the CSV file and log any errors it encounters to the log. Upon each restart of the program, it will also delete the previous log file.

Follow these steps to complete the activity:

1. We will need to create budget category types for `fuel`, `food`, `mortgage`, `repairs`, `insurance`, `utilities`, and `retirement`.

2. Create a custom error for when a budget category is not found.

3. Create a struct type transaction that has `ID`, `payee`, `spent`, and `category` fields (the type is what we created in the first step).

4. Create a function that will accept the category from the bank transaction file. This function will map the transaction categories to our categories. Mappings include `fuel` and `gas` maps to `autoFuel`, `food` maps to `food`, `mortgage` maps to `mortgage`, `repairs` map to `repairs`, `car insurance` and `life insurance` maps to `insurance`, `utilities` maps to `utilities`, and everything else will return the custom error that we created in the previous step. The function will return our `budgetCategory` type and an error.

5. Create a `writeErrorToLog(msg string, err error, data string, logfile string) error`. function. This will take the `msg`, `err`, and `data` strings and write them to the log file.

6. Create a function with the following signature: `parseBankFile(bankTransactions io.Reader, logFile string) []transaction`. This function will iterate over the `bankTransaction` file.
   As it is looping, use a `switch` statement and examine the index of the record.

   Each `case` statement assigns the value of the index to the respective value of the `transaction` struct.
   When the case statement index matches the category of the CSV file, we need to call our `convertToBudgeCategory()`. This will map the bank transaction to our budget category.

7. In the `main()` function, we need two `c` flags for the transaction file and `l` for the location of the log file.

8. The bank transaction file and log file are required, so you must ensure they are present before continuing.

9. You will then call the **parsBankFile()** function and print the **[]transactions** that gets returned from the function.

The following is the output:

```
1    id,payee,spent,category
2    1, sheetz, 32.45, fuel
3    2, martins,225.52,food
4    3, wells fargo, 1100, mortgage
5    4, joe the plumber, 275, repairs
6    5, comcast, 110, tv
7    6, bp, 40, fuel
8    7, aldi, 120, food
9    8, nationwide, 150, car insurance
10   9, nationwide, 100, life insurance
11   10, jim electric, 140, utilities
12   11, propane, 200, utilities
13   12, county water, 100, utilities
14   13, county sewer, 105, utilities
15   14, 401k, 500, retirement
```

Figure 12.22: Format of the transaction file

Note

The solution to this activity can be found on page 737.

In this activity, we created a command-line application that accepted flags. We also configured our command-line application to require those flags. In this command-line application, we created and modified files. We also parsed a common file format used in system programming, the comma-separated value (CSV) file. We were able to read from the file and store the data in the file in our various struct types. We were able to continue to process the CSV file when we encountered an error. When we encountered an error, we wrote to a log file for later debugging. This command-line application demonstrated real-world activities that are generally done in programming command-line applications (such as accepting flags, requiring flags, parsing a file such as CSV, modifying and creating files, and logging).

Summary

In this chapter, we gained an understanding of how Go views and uses file permissions. We learned that file permissions can be represented as symbolic and octal notations. We discovered that the Go standard library has built-in support for opening, reading, writing, creating, deleting, and appending data to a file. We looked at the **flag** package and how it provides functionality to create command-line applications to accept arguments.

Using the **flag** package, we could also print out **usage** statements that pertained to our command-line application.

Then, we demonstrated how OS signals can impact our Go program; however, by using the Go standard library, we can capture OS signals and, if applicable, control how we want to exit our program.

We also learned that Go has a standard library for working with CSV files. In working with files previously, we saw that we can also work with files that are structured as CSV files. That Go CSV package provides the ability to iterate over the contents of the file. The CSV file can be viewed as rows and columns similar to database tables. In the next chapter, we will look at how to connect to databases and execute SQL statements against a database. This will demonstrate the ability of Go to be used for applications that require a backend for storing data.

13

SQL and Databases

Overview

This chapter's aim is to enable you to connect to SQL databases with the help of the Go programming language.

You will start by learning to connect to databases, creating tables in a database and insert data into and retrieve data from tables. By the end of this chapter, you will be able to update and delete data in specific tables, and also truncate and drop tables.

Introduction

In the previous chapter, you learned how to interact with the system your Go app is running on. You learned the importance of exit codes and how to customize your scripts to take arguments, thus adding flexibility to your applications. You also learned the mastery of handling different signals that your application receives.

In this chapter, you will further master your Go skills by learning how to use SQL and databases in Go. As a developer, it is impossible to get by without a proper understanding of persistent data storage and databases. Our applications process input and produce output, but most of the time, if not in all cases, a database is involved in the process. This database can be in memory (stored in the computer's RAM) or file-based (a single file in a directory), and it can live on local or remote storage. The cloud can provide you with database services; both Azure and AWS can help you with that.

What we aim to do in this chapter is to make you fluent in talking to these databases and understand the basic concepts of what a database is. Finally, you should extend your skillset to make you a better Go developer as you progress through this chapter.

Let's say your boss wants you to create a Go app that can communicate with a database. By "communicate", we mean that any transaction that is **INSERT**, **UPDATE**, **DELETE**, or **CREATE** can and should be handled by the application. This chapter will show you how to do that.

The Database

In order to make this chapter more appealing, let's see how you can have a database solution called **Postgres** on your system and configure it for yourself so you can try out the following examples.

First, we need to grab the installer from https://packt.live/2RMFPYV. Select the one which is appropriate. The installer is very easy to use, and I suggest you accept the defaults:

1. Run the installer:

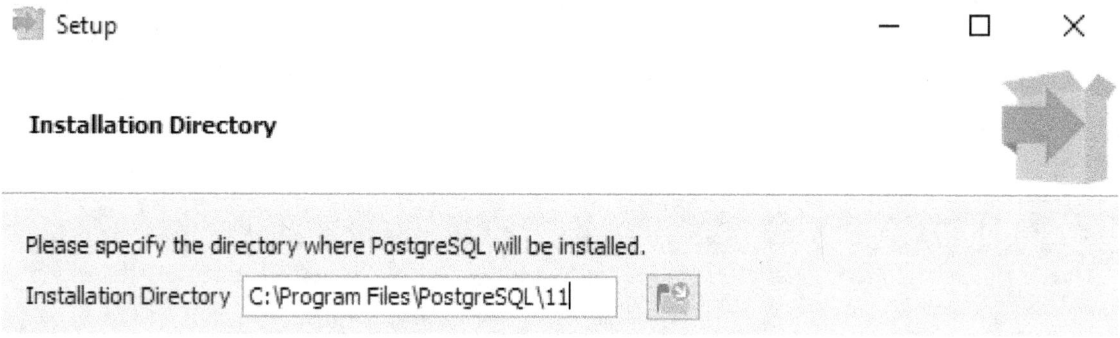

Figure 13.1: Selecting the installation directory

2. Leave the default components:

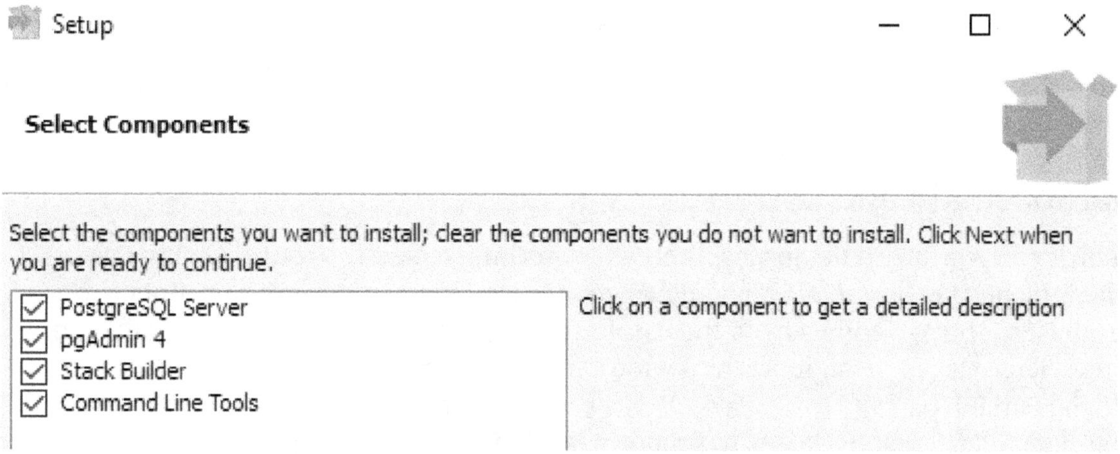

Figure 13.2: Selecting components to install

3. Leave the default data directory:

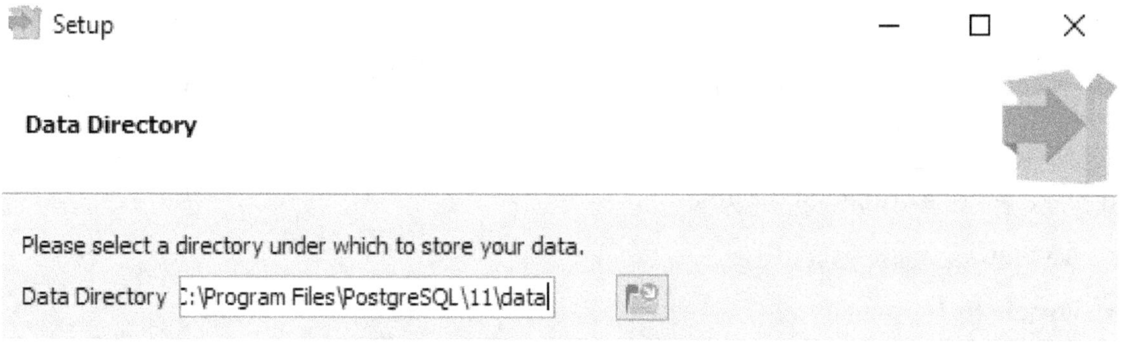

Figure 13.3: Selecting the data directory

It will ask for a password, which you need to remember because this is the master password for your database. **Start!123** is the password for this example. The database is running on the local port 5432. The **pgAdmin** GUI tool will also be installed, and, once the installer completes, you can start **pgAdmin** to connect to the database.

In the browser, the following link can be used to access the admin surface: https://packt.live/2PKWc5w:

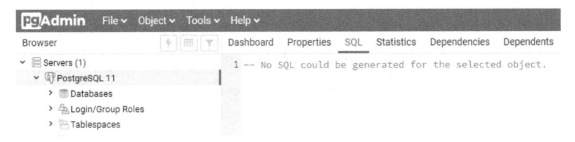

Figure 13.4: The admin interface

Once the installation is complete, we are ready to proceed to the next part and connect to the database via Go.

Database API and Drivers

In order to work with databases, there is something called the "pure" Go approach, which means Go has an API that allows you to use different drivers to connect to databases. The API comes from the **database/sql** package, and the drivers can be of two types. There is native support for a wide variety of drivers, which can be found on the official GitHub page (https://packt.live/2LMzcC4), and there are third-party drivers that need additional packages to function, such as the **SQLlite3** package, which requires you to have **GCC** installed because it is a pure C implementation.

> **Note**
>
> GCC is a compiler system produced by the GNU Project. It takes your source code and translates it to machine code so that your computer can run the application.

Here is a list of a couple of drivers:

- **MySQL** (https://packt.live/38zk9Fw)
- **Oracle** (https://packt.live/34cxwrP)
- **ODBC** (https://packt.live/2EfETV8)
- **Postgres** (https://packt.live/35jKEwL)

The idea behind the API and driver approach is that Go provides a unified interface that allows developers to talk to different types of databases. All you need to do is import the API and the necessary driver and you are able to talk to the database. You don't need to learn driver-specific implementations or how that driver works because the API's sole purpose is to create an abstraction layer that accelerates development.

Let's take an example. Let's say we would like to have a script that queries a database. This database is MySQL. One approach is to take the driver and learn how to code in its language, and then you are good to go. Some time passes by, and you build lots of small scripts that do their job properly. Now the time has come for a management decision that will make you unhappy. They decide that MySQL is not good enough, and they will replace the database with AWS Athena, a cloud-based database. Now, since you wrote your scripts specifically for a certain driver, you will be busy rewriting your scripts in order for them to work properly. The safeguard here is to use a unified API and driver combination. This means writing the scripts against the API and not the driver. The API will translate your wishes for the specific driver. This way, all you need to do is swap out the driver, and the scripts are guaranteed to work. You just saved yourself many hours of scripting and rewriting code, even though the underlying database has been completely replaced.

When we are working with databases in Go, we differentiate these types of databases:

- Relational databases
- NoSQL databases
- Search and analytic databases

Connecting to Databases

Connecting to a database is by far the easiest thing to do; however, we need to keep a few things in mind. In order to connect to any database, we need at least four things to be in place. We need a host to connect to, we need a database to connect to that is running on a port, and we need a username and password. The user needs to have appropriate privileges because we not only want to connect but we would like to perform specific operations, such as query, insert, or remove data, create or delete databases, and manage users and views. Let's imagine that connecting to a database is like walking up to a door as a specific person with a specific key. Whether the door opens or not depends on the key, but what we can do after we have crossed the threshold will depend on the person (which is defined by their privileges).

In most cases, the database server supports multiple databases and the databases hold one or more tables. Imagine that the databases are logical containers that belong together.

Let's take a look at how we can connect to a database in Go. In order to connect, we need to get the appropriate module from GitHub, which needs internet connectivity. We need to issue the following command to get the package needed to interact with the Postgres instance:

```
go get github.com/lib/pq
```

Once this completes, you are ready to start scripting. First, we will initialize our script:

```
package main
import "fmt"
import "database/sql"
import _ "github.com/lib/pq"
```

`import _ <package name>` is a special `import` statement that tells Go to import a package solely for its side effects.

> **Note**
>
> If you would like further information, visit https://packt.live/2PByusw.

Now that we have initialized our script, we can actually connect to our database:

```
db, err := sql.Open("postgres", "user=postgres password=Start!123 host=127.0.0.1
port=5432 dbname=postgres sslmode=disable")
```

This topic is special because the API gives us an `Open()` function, which takes a variety of arguments. There are shorthand ways of doing this, but I would like you to know about all the components that are involved in making the connections, so I will use the longer way. Later, you can decide which one to use. The `Postgres` tells the function to use the Postgres driver to make the connection. The second argument is a so-called connection string, which holds the `user`, `password`, `host`, `port`, `dbname`, and `sslmode` arguments, which will be used to initialize the connection. In this example, we connect to the localhost marked by `127.0.0.1` on the default port 5432, and we don't use `ssl`. For production systems, people tend to change the default port and enforce encrypted traffic via `ssl` toward the database server, and you should always follow the best practices concerning the type of database you're working with. As you can see, the `Open()` function returns two values. One is for the database connection and the other is for the error, if any occurred during initialization. How do we check whether the initialization was success? Well, we can check whether there were any errors by writing the following code:

```
if err != nil {
  panic(err)
}else{
```

```
    fmt.Println("The connection to the DB was successfully initialized!")
}
```

The **panic()** function in Go is used to indicate that something went wrong unexpectedly, and we are not prepared to handle it gracefully, thus stopping the execution. If the connection succeeds, we print out the **The connection to the DB was successfully initialized!** message. When you have a long-running application, it is worth incorporating a way to check whether the database is still reachable, because due to intermittent network errors you could lose the connection and fail to execute whatever you wanted to execute. This can be checked with the following small code snippet:

```
connectivity := db.Ping()
if connectivity != nil{
    panic(err)
}else{
    fmt.Println("Good to go!")
}
```

In this case, we used the **panic()** function to indicate that the connection has been lost. Finally, once our job is done, we need to terminate our connection to the database in order to remove user sessions and free up resources. In big enterprise environments with thousands of users hitting the same database, it's a wise decision to use the database only when necessary, and once the work is done, close the connections. There are two ways to close the connection:

```
db.Close()
defer db.Close()
```

The difference is the scope. **db.Close()** will terminate the connection to the database once the execution arrives at the specific line, while **defer db.Close()** indicates that the database connection should be executed once the function in which it was called goes out of scope. The idiomatic way to do it is with **defer db.Close()**.

Now, in order to further demonstrate this, we will create a table.

> **Note**
>
> The official **Postgres** module of Go can be found at https://packt.live/35jKEwL.

Creating Tables

The act of creating tables aims to make logical containers that persistently hold data that belongs together. Many companies create tables for many reasons, for example, tracking employee attendance, revenue tracking, and statistics. The common goal is to provide a service for applications that make sense of it. How do these database engines control who can access what data? There are basically two approaches. The first one is **Access Control Lists (ACLs)**, which is a simple yet powerful approach. ACL security logic tells us which user has which permissions, such as `CREATE`, `UPDATE`, and `DELETE`. The second approach involves inheritance and roles. This is more robust and is better suited for big enterprises. Before using a database engine, there used to be a precheck to see what the size would be and how many users would use it. There is no point in shooting a sparrow with a shotgun, and there is no shoe size that fits all. It all depends on the situation. `Postgres` uses the second approach, and in this topic, we will see how to create a SQL table and how to create one specifically in `Postgres`.

The general syntax for table creation looks like this:

```
CREATE TABLE table_name (
    column1 datatype constrain,
    column2 datatype constrain,
    column3 datatype constrain,
    ....
);
```

Before we continue, we need to clarify what SQL is. SQL is a standard that stands for **Structured Query Language**. This standard specifies how a specific database engine should respond to specific commands from the user. When we talk via SQL to the `Postgres`, `mysql`, or `mssql` server, they all respond in the same way to a `CREATE TABLE` or `INSERT` command because they are SQL compliant. The idea of the standard is not to specify how the engine works internally but how the interaction with it should happen These database engines usually differ in terms of functionality, speed, and storage approaches; that's where the variety comes from. This is not a full SQL or database engine tutorial. I just wanted to give you a brief explanation so that you understand the commands better. The general command for table creation is `CREATE TABLE`. This command is understood in the context of the database you are connected to. One server can host multiple databases, and connecting to the wrong one can cause headaches when issuing a command that modifies the structure. The command usually takes a column name, which is `column1` in our case, and the type of data in our column, which is `datatype`. Finally, we can set constraints on our columns, which will imbue them with special properties. The supported datatypes for our columns depend on the database engine.

Here are some common datatypes:

- INT
- DOUBLE
- FLOAT
- VARCHAR, which is a string with a specific length

The constraints also depend on the database engine, but some of them are as follows:

- NOT NULL
- PRIMARY KEY
- Named function

The named function is executed every time a new record is inserted or an old one is updated and, based on the evaluation of the transaction, is either allowed or denied.

We are not only able to create a table, but we can also empty the table, remove all of its contents, or remove the table itself from the database. In order to empty a table, we use the following:

```
TRUNCATE TABLE table_name
```

In order to remove the table, we use:

```
DROP TABLE table_name
```

Now create a new table. In **Postgres**, you have a default database you can use; we are not going to create a separate database for the examples.

We would like to initialize our script, which you can find in the examples folder, and it's called **DBInit.go**:

```
package main
import "fmt"
import "database/sql"
import _ "github.com/lib/pq"
```

Now we are ready to define our **main()** function:

DBInit.go

```
5  func main(){
6    db, err := sql.Open("postgres", "user=postgres password=Start!123
       host=127.0.0.1 port=5432 dbname=postgres sslmode=disable")
7    if err != nil {
8      panic(err)
9    }else{
10     fmt.Println("The connection to the DB was successfully
         initialized!")
11   }
12 DBCreate := `
13   CREATE TABLE public.test
14   (
15     id integer,
16     name character varying COLLATE pg_catalog."default"
17   )
18   WITH (
19     OIDS = FALSE
20   )
```

The full code is available at https://packt.live/34Ovy15

Let's dissect what is happening here. We initialize our connection to the database without the default username and password that was previously mentioned, and now we have the **db** variable to interact with the database. Unless there was an error upon execution, the following output will be visible on our console:

```
The connection to the DB was successfully initialized!
The table was successfully created!
```

If we were to rerun the script, the following error would occur:

```
The connection to the DB was successfully initialized!
panic: pq: relation "test" already exists

goroutine 1 [running]:
main.main()
        C:/Users/dszabo/Documents/GitRepos/The-Go-Workshop/Chapter13/Examples/DBInit.go:31 +0x1d3
exit status 2
```

Figure 13.5: Output of failure after consecutive execution

This says that the table already exists. We created a multiline string called **DBCreate** that holds all the table creation information. In this, we have a table called **test**, which has an integer column called **id** and a string column called **name**. The rest of it is **Postgres-**specific configuration. The tablespace defines where our table lives. The **_, err** line with **db.Exec()** is responsible for executing the query.

Since our goal now is to create the table, we only care whether there are any errors; otherwise, we use a throwaway variable to capture the output. If **err** is not **nil**, there was an error, which we saw demonstrated previously. Otherwise, we assume the table was created as expected. Finally, the connection to the database is closed.

Now that we can connect to the database and we have a table, we can insert some data.

Inserting Data

Long ago, when the era of web applications backed by SQL databases started to bloom, there were some gutsy people who invented the SQL injection attack. A type of authentication is done via SQL queries against a database and, for example, after converting the password with mathematical magic into hash functions, all the web app did was execute the query with the username and password coming from the input of the form. Many servers executed something like this:

```
"SELECT password FROM Auth WHERE username=<input from user>"
```

Then, the password gets rehashed; if the two hashes match, the password was good for the user.

The problem with this came from the **<input from user>** part, because if the attacker was smart enough, they could reformulate the query and run additional commands. For example:

```
"SELECT password FROM Auth WHERE username=<input  from user> OR '1'='1'"
```

The problem with this query is that **OR '1' = '1'** always evaluates to **true**, and it does not matter what the username was, all the user's password hash would be returned. This can be further reused to formulate an additional attack. In order to prevent this, Go uses something called the **Prepare()** statement, which provides protection against these attacks.

Go has two types of substitutions. We either use **WHERE col = $1** in the case of queries, or **VALUES($1,$2)** in the case of inserts or updates.

Let's add some values to our tables. We are going to initialize our script in the usual way. The script can be found under the examples folder and is called **DBInsert.go**:

```go
package main
import "fmt"
import "database/sql"
import _ "github.com/lib/pq"
```

In the **main()** function, we connect to the database as usual:

```
func main(){
db, err := sql.Open("postgres", "user=postgres password=Start!123 host=127.0.0.1
port=5432 dbname=postgres sslmode=disable")
if err != nil {
  panic(err)
}else{
  fmt.Println("The connection to the DB was successfully initialized!")
}
insert, err := db.Prepare("INSERT INTO test VALUES ($1, $2)")
if err != nil {
  panic(err)
}
_,err = insert.Exec(2,"second")
if err != nil {
  panic(err)
} else{
  fmt.Println("The value was successfully inserted!")
}
db.Close()
}
```

Upon successful execution, the output is as follows:

```
The connection to the DB was successfully initialized!
The vale was successfully inserted!
```

Let's see what is happening with the insert part. **db.Prepare()** takes a SQL statement and imbues it with protection against SQL injection attacks. The way this works is that it restricts the values of the variable substitutions. In our case, we have two columns, so for the substitution to work we use $1 and $2. You can use any number of substitutions; you only need to make sure they result in a valid SQL statement when evaluated. When the **insert** variable is initialized without errors, it will be responsible for executing the SQL statement. It finds out how many arguments the prepared statement expects, and its sole purpose is to call the statement and perform the operation. **insert. Exec(2,"second")** inserts a new element with **id=2** and **name='second'**. If we were to check what we have in our database, we would see the results.

Now that we have some data in our table, we can query it.

Exercise 13.01: Creating a Table with Numbers

In this exercise, we are going to write a script that is going to create a table called **Numbers**, in which we are going to store numbers. These numbers will be inserted at a later time.

Create two columns, **Number** and **Property**. The **Number** column will hold numbers, and the **Property** column will be either **Odd** or **Even** at the time of creation.

Use the default **Postgres** database for the connection. The numbers should range from 0 to 99.

Perform the following steps in order to complete the exercise:

1. Create a file called **main.go**.

2. Initialize the package with the following lines:

    ```
    package main
    import "fmt"
    import "database/sql"
    import _ "github.com/lib/pq"
    func main(){

    }
    ```

3. Create a **prop string** variable for later use:

    ```
    var prop string
    ```

4. Initialize the database connection:

    ```
    db, err := sql.Open("postgres", "user=postgres password=Start!123 host=127.0.0.1
      port=5432 dbname=postgres sslmode=disable")
    if err != nil {
      panic(err)
    }else{
      fmt.Println("The connection to the DB was successfully initialized!")
    }
    ```

5. Create the multiline string to create the table:

    ```
    TableCreate := `
    CREATE TABLE Number
    (
      Number integer NOT NULL,
      Property text COLLATE pg_catalog."default" NOT NULL
    )
    WITH (
      OIDS = FALSE
    ```

```
    )
    TABLESPACE pg_default;
    ALTER TABLE Number
      OWNER to postgres;
    `
```

6. Create the table:

```
    _,err = db.Exec(TableCreate)
    if err != nil {
      panic(err)
    } else{
      fmt.Println("The table called Number was successfully created!")
    }
```

7. Insert the numbers:

```
    insert, insertErr := db.Prepare("INSERT INTO Number VALUES($1,$2)")
    if insertErr != nil{
      panic(insertErr)
    }
    for i := 0; i < 100; i++ {
      if i % 2 == 0{
          prop = "Even"
      }else{
        prop = "Odd"
      }
      _, err = insert.Exec(i,prop)
      if err != nil{
        panic(err)
      }else{
        fmt.Println("The number:",i,"is:",prop)
      }
    }
    insert.Close()
    fmt.Println("The numbers are ready.")
```

8. Close the database connection:

```
db.Close()
```

When you execute the script, you should see the following output:

```
The connection to the DB was successfully initialized!
The table called Messages was successfully created!
The number: 0 is: Even
The number: 1 is: Odd
The number: 2 is: Even
The number: 3 is: Odd
The number: 4 is: Even
......
The number: 98 is: Even
The number: 99 is: Odd
The numbers are ready.
```

Figure 13.6: Output of the successful property update

> **Note**
>
> Part of the output is omitted from *Figure 13.6* due to its length.

In this exercise, we saw how to create a new table in our database and how to insert new records with the help of a **for** loop and a **Prepare()** statement.

Retrieving Data

SQL injection does not only concern the data being inserted. It also concerns any data that is manipulated in the database. Retrieving data and, most importantly, retrieving it safely is also something we must prioritize and handle with proper caution. When we query data, our results depend on the database we connect to and the table we would like to query. But we must also mention that the security mechanisms implemented by the database engine may also prevent a successful query unless the user has appropriate privileges. We differentiate two types of queries. There are queries that do not take an argument, such as **SELECT * FROM table**, and there are queries that require you to specify filter criteria. Go provides two functions that allow you to query data. One is called the **Query()** function and the other is called the **QueryRow()** function. The availability of these functions depends on the database you are interacting with. As a rule of thumb, you should remember that the **Query()** function is most likely to work. You can also wrap them with the **Prepare()** statement, which will not cover in this topic as it was demonstrated before. Instead, we want to see how these functions work

Let's create a script for **Query()**.

We initialize the script as always. It can be found in the examples and is called **DBQuery. go**:

```go
package main
import "fmt"
import "database/sql"
import _ "github.com/lib/pq"
```

Our **main()** function will be a little bit different because we would like to introduce the **Scan()** function:

```go
func main(){
var id int
var name string
db, err := sql.Open("postgres", "user=postgres password=Start!123 host=127.0.0.1
   port=5432 dbname=postgres sslmode=disable")
if err != nil {
  panic(err)
}else{
  fmt.Println("The connection to the DB was successfully initialized!")
}
rows, err := db.Query("SELECT * FROM test")
if err != nil {
  panic(err)
}
for rows.Next() {
  err := rows.Scan(&id, &name)
  if err != nil {
     panic(err)
  }
  fmt.Println(id, name)
}
err = rows.Err()
if err != nil {
  panic(err)
}
rows.Close()
db.Close()
}
```

The output should look like this:

```
The connection to the DB was successfully initialized!
2 second
```

As we have previously inserted this data to our database, feel free to add some more data based on the previous example. We have defined the **id** and **name** variables, which will help our **Scan()** function. We connect to the database and create our **db** variable. After that, we fill our **rows** variable with the result of the **Query()** function, which will basically hold all the elements from the table. Here comes the tricky part. We use **for rows.Next()** to iterate over the resulting rows. But that is not enough; we would like to assign the results of the query to the corresponding variable, which is returned by **rows. Scan(&id, &name)**. This allows us to refer to the current row's ID and **NAME**, which makes it easier to do whatever we would like to do with the value. Finally, the **rows** and the database connections are gracefully closed.

Let's query a single row with **Prepare()**.

The initialization looks the same as before.

DBPrepare.go

```
1  package main
2  import "fmt"
3  import "database/sql"
4  import _ "github.com/lib/pq"
```

The full code is available at https://packt.live/376LxJo

The main difference is at the beginning of the **main()** function:

```
func main(){
var name string
var id int
id = 2
db, err := sql.Open("postgres", "user=postgres password=Start!123 host=127.0.0.1
  port=5432 dbname=postgres sslmode=disable")
if err != nil {
  panic(err)
}else{
  fmt.Println("The connection to the DB was successfully initialized!")
}
qryrow, err := db.Prepare("SELECT name FROM test WHERE id=$1")
if err != nil{
  panic(err)
}
err = qryrow.QueryRow(id).Scan(&name)
if err != nil {
```

```
    panic(err)
}
fmt.Println("The name column value is",name,"of the row with id=",id)
qryrow.Close()
db.Close()
}
```

The output, if you did everything correctly, should look something like this:

```
The connection to the DB was successfully initialized!
The name column value is second of the row with id= 2
```

Let's inspect our **main** function closely. We defined two variables: the **name** variable will be used when we process the query result, and the **id** variable serves as a flexible input for the query we execute. The usual connection initialization toward our database happens as before. Then comes the **SQL Injection** proof part. We prepare a query that is dynamic in the sense that it accepts a parameter that will be the ID we are looking for. Then, **qryrow** is used to execute the **QueryRow()** function, which in turn takes the **id** variable we specified previously and returns the result in the **name** variable. Then we output the string with an explanation that the value of the column is based on the **id** variable that was specified. At the end, the **qryrow** and **db** resources are closed.

Now that we know how to retrieve data from the database, we need to see how to update existing data in our database.

Updating Existing Data

When you are updating a row or multiple rows with Go, you are in trouble. The **sql** package does not provide any function called **Update()**; however, there is the **Exec()** function, which serves as a universal executor for your queries. You can execute **SELECT**, **UPDATE**, **DELETE**, or whatever you need to execute with this function. This topic will show you how you can do it safely.

We would like to start our script in the usual way. It can be found in the examples folder and is called **DBUpdate.go**:

```
package main
import "fmt"
import "database/sql"
import _ "github.com/lib/pq"
```

Then the magic comes. The idea is to update the **name** column's value for a specific **id** variable that we give as an argument. So, the **main()** function looks like this:

```
func main(){
db, err := sql.Open("postgres", "user=postgres password=Start!123 host=127.0.0.1
port=5432 dbname=postgres sslmode=disable")
if err != nil {
  panic(err)
}else{
  fmt.Println("The connection to the DB was successfully initialized!")
}
UpdateStatement :=`
UPDATE test
SET name = $1
WHERE id = $2
`

UpdateResult, UpdateResultErr := db.Exec(UpdateStatement,"well",2)
if UpdateResultErr != nil {
  panic(UpdateResultErr)
}
UpdatedRecords, UpdatedRecordsErr := UpdateResult.RowsAffected()
if UpdatedRecordsErr != nil {
  panic(UpdatedRecordsErr)
}
fmt.Println("Number of records updated:",UpdatedRecords)
db.Close()
}
```

If everything went well, we see the following output:

```
The connection to the DB was successfully initialized!
Number of records updated: 1
```

Note that you can and should experiment with different inputs and see how the script reacts to different problems/errors.

Let's dissect what is happening here. We initialize our database connection as we did before. We create the `UpdateStatement` variable, which is a multiline string, and it is crafted so that it can be fed to the `Exec()` function, which takes arguments. We want to update the name of the column that has the specified ID. This function either runs the specified statement on its own or can be used to pass arguments that are substituted in the appropriate place. This would be perfectly fine and would do the job for us, but we would like to make sure that the `UPDATE` command actually updates at least one record. To this end, we could use `RowsAffected()`. It will return the number of rows that were updated, and any errors that were faced along the way. Finally, we print to the console how many rows were updated and close the connection.

The time has come to delete data from our database.

Deleting Data

The deletion of data can happen for multiple reasons: we don't need the data anymore, we are migrating to another database, or we are replacing the current solution. We are in luck because the current Go facilities provide a very nice way to do it. The analogy is the same as for the `UPDATE` statement of our records. We formulate a `DELETE` statement and execute it; we can technically modify the action of our `UPDATE` script to delete from the database.

For the sake of simplicity, we only modify the relevant lines.

Our `DELETE` statement will replace the `UPDATE` statement like this:

DBDelete.go

```
12 DeleteStatement :=`
13 DELETE FROM test
14 WHERE id = $1
15 `
```

The full code is available at https://packt.live/371GoCv

We update the line with the `Exec()` statement:

```
DeleteResult, DeleteResultErr := db.Exec(DeleteStatement,2)
if DeleteResultErr != nil {
   panic(DeleteResultErr)
}
```

Also, we update the line with the calculation of updated records:

```
DeletedRecords, DeletedRecordsErr := DeleteResult.RowsAffected()
if DeletedRecordsErr != nil {
  panic(DeletedRecordsErr)
}
fmt.Println("Number of records deleted:",DeletedRecords)
```

Our result of the execution should look like this:

```
The connection to the DB was successfully initialized!
Number of records deleted: 1
```

Basically, that's it. With a little modification, we have a script that can either update or delete records with verification.

Now, let's see how we can create a table that holds prime numbers.

Exercise 13.02: Holding Prime Numbers in a Database

In this exercise, we build on *Exercise 13.01*, *Creating a Table with Numbers*. We would like to create a script that will do the following: first, it will tell us how many prime numbers are in our table and give them to us in order of appearance. We would like to see the sum of prime numbers in the output. Then we would like to remove every even number from the table and see how many were removed. We would like to add the sum of prime numbers to the remaining odd numbers and update the table with the records, changing the property if necessary. Use the **math/big** package for the primality test.

Follow these steps:

1. Create a script called **main.go**.

2. Initialize our script to perform the specific actions:

    ```
    package main
    import "fmt"
    import "database/sql"
    import _ "github.com/lib/pq"
    import "math/big"
    func main(){
    }
    ```

3. Define four variables for later use:

```
var number int64
var prop string
var primeSum int64
var newNumber int64
```

4. Initialize the database connection:

```
db, err := sql.Open("postgres", "user=postgres password=Start!123 host=127.0.0.1
    port=5432 dbname=postgres sslmode=disable")
if err != nil {
    panic(err)
}else{
    fmt.Println("The connection to the DB was successfully initialized!")
}
```

5. Get a list of all the prime numbers:

```
AllTheNumbers := "SELECT * FROM Number"
Numbers, err := db.Prepare(AllTheNumbers)
if err != nil {
    panic(err)
}
primeSum = 0
result, err := Numbers.Query()
fmt.Println("The list of prime numbers:")
for result.Next(){
    err = result.Scan(&number, &prop)
    if err != nil{
    panic(err)
    ]
    if big.NewInt(number).ProbablyPrime(0) {
        primeSum += number
        fmt.Print(" ",number)
    }
  }
Numbers.Close()
```

6. Print the sum of the prime numbers:

```
fmt.Println("\nThe total sum of prime numbers in this range is:",primeSum)
```

7. Remove the even numbers:

```
Remove := "DELETE FROM Number WHERE Property=$1"
removeResult, err := db.Exec(Remove,"Even")
if err != nil {
  panic(err)
}
ModifiedRecords, err := removeResult.RowsAffected()
fmt.Println("The number of rows removed:",ModifiedRecords)
fmt.Println("Updating numbers...")
```

8. Update the remaining records with **primeSum** and print a closing sentence:

```
Update := "UPDATE Number SET Number=$1 WHERE Number=$2 AND Property=$3"
AllTheNumbers = "SELECT * FROM Number"
Numbers, err = db.Prepare(AllTheNumbers)
if err != nil {
  panic(err)
}
result, err = Numbers.Query()
for result.Next(){
    err = result.Scan(&number, &prop)
    if err != nil{
    panic(err)
    }
    newNumber = number + primeSum
    _, err = db.Exec(Update,newNumber,number,prop)
    if err != nil {
      panic(err)
    }
  }
Numbers.Close()
fmt.Println("The execution is now complete...")
```

9. Close the database connection:

```
db.Close()
```

Once the script is executed, the following output should be visible:

```
The connection to the DB was successfully initialized!
The list of prime numbers:
 2 3 5 7 11 13 17 19 23 29 31 37 41 43 47 53 59 61 67 71 73 79 83 89 97
The total sum of prime numbers in this range is: 1060
The number of rows removed: 50
Updating numbers...
The execution is now complete...
```

Figure 13.7: Output of the calculations

In this exercise, we saw how to utilize a built-in Go function to find prime numbers. We also manipulated the table by removing numbers, and then we performed update actions.

> **Note**
>
> Closing the database is important because once our job is done, we do want to release unused resources.

Truncating and Deleting Table

What we would like to achieve in this topic is to empty a table completely and get rid of it. In order to empty the table, we could simply formulate **DELETE** statements that match every record in our table and thus remove every single record from our table. However, there is a more elegant way. We can use the **TRUNCATE TABLE** SQL statement. The result of this statement is a literally empty table. We can use the **Exec()** function from our **sql** package. You already know how to initialize the package with imports. You also know how to connect to the database. This time, we only focus on the statements.

The following statement will achieve a full **TRUNCATE**:

```
EmptyTable, EmptyTableErr := db.Exec("TRUNCATE TABLE test")
if EmptyTableErr != nil {
  panic(EmptyTableErr)
}
```

The result of this is an empty table called **test**.

In order to get rid of the table completely, we should modify our statement as follows.

```
DropTable, DropTableErr := db.Exec("DROP TABLE test")
if DropTableErr != nil {
  panic(DropTableErr)
}
```

If we inspect our database engine, we will not find any trace of the table called **test**. This eradicated the whole table from the very face of the database.

That topic was all about interacting with databases via the Go programming language. Now you have a decent understanding about how to get started.

> **Note**
>
> For further information and extra details, you should check out the official documentation of the SQL API, https://packt.live/2Pi5oj5.

Activity 13.01: Holding User Data in a Table

In this activity, we are going to create a table that is going to hold user information such as **ID**, **Name**, and **Email**. We build on the knowledge you gathered in the *Creating Tables* and *Inserting Data* sections.

Follow these steps to complete this activity:

1. Create a small script that will create a table called **Users**. This table must have three columns: **ID**, **Name**, and **Email**.

2. Add the details of two users with their data into the table. They should have unique names, IDs, and email addresses.

3. Then you need to update the email of the first user to user@packt.com and remove the second user. Make sure that none of the fields are **NULL**, and the ID is the primary key, so it needs to be unique.

4. When you are inserting, updating, and deleting from the table, please use the **Prepare()** function to protect against SQL injection attacks.

5. You should use a struct to store the user information you would like to insert, and when you are inserting, iterate over the struct with a **for** loop.

6. Once the **insert**, **update**, and **delete** calls are complete, make sure you use **Close()** when appropriate and finally close the connection to the database.

Upon successful completion, you should see the following output:

```
The connection to the DB was successfully initialized!
Good to go!
The table called Users was successfully created!
The user with name: Szabo Daniel and email: daniel@packt.com was successfully added!
The user with name: Szabo Florian and email: florian@packt.com was successfully added!
The user's email address was succesfully updated!
The second user was succeesfully removed!
```

Figure 13.8: Possible output

> **Note**
>
> The solution to this activity can be found on page 745.

By the end of this activity, you should have learned how to create a new table called **users** and how to insert data into this table.

Activity 13.02: Finding Messages of Specific Users

In this activity, we will build on *Activity 13.01: Holding User Data in a Table.*

We need to create a new table called **Messages**. This table will have two columns, both of which should have a 280-character limit: one is **UserID** and the other is **Message**.

When your table is ready, you should add some messages with user IDs. Make sure you add **UserID**, which is not present in the **users** table.

Once you have added the data, write a query that returns all the messages a specified user has sent. Use the **Prepare()** function to protect against SQL injection.

If the specified user cannot be found, print **The query returned nothing, no such user: <username>**. You should take the username as input from the keyboard.

Perform these steps in order to complete the activity:

1. Define a **struct** that holds the **userID** and the messages.

2. Messages should be inserted with a **for** loop that iterates over the previously defined **struct**.

3. When the user input is received, make sure you use the **Prepare()** statement to craft your query.

If everything went well, this should be the output, depending on how you fill your database with usernames and messages:

```
The connection to the DB was sucessfully initialized!
Good to go!
The table called Messages was successfully created!
The UserID: 1 with message: Hi Florian, when are you coming home? was successfully added!
The UserID: 1 with message: Can you send some cash? was successfully added!
The UserID: 2 with message: Hi can you bring some bread and milk? was successfully added!
The UserID: 7 with message: Well... was successfully added!
Give me the user's name: Szabo Daniel
Looking for all the messages of user with name: Szabo Daniel ##
The user: Szabo Daniel with email: user@packt.com has sent the following message: Hi Florian, when are you coming home?
The user: Szabo Daniel with email: user@packt.com has sent the following message: Can you send some cash?
```

Figure 13.9: Expected output

> **Note**
>
> The solution to this activity can be found on page 748.

If you want, you can tweak the script to not try and recreate the DB on consecutive runs.

By the end of this activity, you should have learned how to create a new table called **Messages**, then take input from the user and search for related users and messages based on the input.

Summary

This chapter made you efficient in interacting with SQL databases. You learned how to create, delete, and manipulate database tables. You have also become aware of all the different types of databases Go is suited to interact with. As this chapter was made with the **PostgreSQL** engine in mind, you should familiarize yourself with its Go module too. With this knowledge, you will now be able to take your own steps in the realm of database programming with the Go language and be self-sufficient in the sense that you know where to look for solutions to problems and for extra knowledge. The most common use case for this knowledge is when you must build automated reporting apps that pull data from a database and report it as an email. The other use case is when you have an automated app for pushing data to the database server that processes a CSV file or an XML file. This really depends on the situation you are in.

In the next chapter, you will learn how to interact with web interfaces via HTTP clients, which is one of the most interesting topics in Go.

14

Using the Go HTTP Client

Overview

This chapter will equip you to use the Go HTTP client to talk to other systems over the internet.

You will start by learning to use the HTTP client to get data from a web server and to send data to a web server. By the end of the chapter, you will be able to upload a file to a web server and experiment with a custom Go HTTP client to interact with web servers.

Introduction

In the previous chapter, you looked at SQL and databases. You learned how to execute queries, how to create tables, how to insert data into tables and fetch data, how to update data, and how to delete data within a table.

In this chapter, you will learn about the Go HTTP client and how to use it. An HTTP client is something that is used to get data from or send data to a web server. Probably the most well-known example of an HTTP client is a web browser (such as Firefox). When you enter a web address into a web browser, it will have an HTTP client built in that sends a request to the server for data. The server will gather the data and send it back to the HTTP client, which will then display the web page in the browser. Similarly, when you fill out a form in a web browser, for example, when you log in to a website, the browser will use its HTTP client to send that form data to the server and then take appropriate action depending on the response.

This chapter looks at how you can use the Go HTTP client to request data from a web server and send data to a server. You will examine the different ways you can use the HTTP client to interact with a web server and the various use cases for those interactions. The web browser example will be useful in explaining the different interactions. As part of this chapter, you will create your own Go programs that make use of the Go HTTP client to send and receive data from a web server.

The Go HTTP Client and Its Uses

The Go HTTP client is part of the Go standard library, specifically the **net/http** library. There are two main ways to use it. The first is to use the default HTTP client that is included in the **net/http** library. It's simple to use and allows you to get up and running quickly. The second way is to create your own HTTP client based on the default HTTP client. This allows you to customize the requests and various other things. It takes longer to configure, but it gives you much more freedom and control over the requests you send.

When using an HTTP client, you can send different types of requests. While there are many types of requests, we will discuss the two main ones, the GET request and the POST request. For instance, if you wanted to retrieve data from a server, you would send a GET request. When you enter a web address in your web browser, it will send a GET request to the server at that address and then display the data it returns. If you wanted to send data to the server, you would send a POST request. If you wanted to log into a website, you would POST your login details to the server.

In this chapter, there are a few exercises to teach you about the Go HTTP client. They will teach you how to request data from a server in various formats using GET requests. They will also teach you how to POST form data to a web server, similar to how a web browser would send a POST request when you log in to a website. These exercises will also show you how to upload a file to a web server and how to use a customized HTTP client to have more control over the requests you send.

Sending a Request to a Server

When you want to retrieve data from a web server, you send a GET request to the server. When sending a request, the URL will contain the information on the resource you want data from. The URL can be broken down into a few key parts. These include the protocol, the hostname, the URI, and the query parameters. The format of it looks like this:

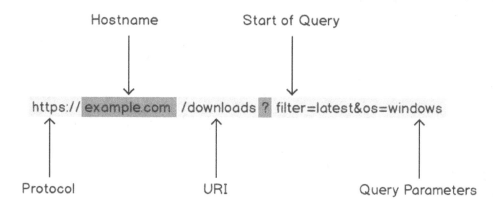

Figure 14.1: URL format breakdown

In this example:

- The **Protocol** tells the client how to connect to the server. The two most common protocols are HTTP and HTTPS. In this example, we have used **https**.

- The **Hostname** is the address of the server we want to connect to. In this example, it is **example.com**.

- The **URI** is the **Uniform Resource Identifier** (**URI**), and this tells the server the path to the resource we want. In this example, it is **/downloads**.

- The **Query Parameters** tell the server of any additional information it needs. In this example, we have two parameters. These are **filter=latest** and **os=windows**. You will notice they are separated from the URI by **?**. This is so the server can parse them from the request. We join any additional parameters to the end of the URI with the **&** symbol, as seen with the **os** parameter.

Exercise 14.01: Sending a Get Request to a Web Server Using the Go HTTP Client

In this exercise, you will be getting data from a web server and printing out that data. You will send a GET request to https://www.google.com and display the data the web server returns:

> **Note**
>
> For this topic, you will need to have Go installed and GOPATH set up on your system. You will also need an IDE that you can use to edit .go files.

1. Open your IDE and create a new directory, **Exercise14.01**, on your GOPATH. Within that directory, create a new Go file called **main.go**.

2. As this is a new program, you will want to set the package of the file to the **main()** function. Import the **net/http** library, the **log** library, and the **io/ioutil** library. Type the following code:

```
package main
import (
    "io/ioutil"
    "log"
    "net/http"
)
```

Now that you have the package set up and the imports you need, you can start creating a function to get data from a web server. The function you are going to create will request data from a web server.

3. Create a function that returns a string:

```
func getDataAndReturnResponse() string {
```

4. Within that function, you can then use the default Go HTTP Client to request data from a server. In this exercise, you will request data from https://www.google.com. To request data from the web server, you use the **GET** function in the **http** library, which looks as follows:

```
r, err := http.Get("https://www.google.com")
if err != nil {
    log.Fatal(err)
}
```

5. The data the server sends back is contained within **r.Body**, so you just to read in that data. To read the data within **r.Body**, you can use the **ReadAll** function within the **io/ioutil** library. The two together would look like this:

```
defer r.Body.Close()
data, err := ioutil.ReadAll(r.Body)
if err != nil {
    log.Fatal(err)
}
```

6. After you have received the response from the server and read the data, you just need to return that data as a string, which looks like this:

```
return string(data)
}
```

The function you have now created will now look like this:

```
func getDataAndReturnResponse() string {
    // send the GET request
    r, err := http.Get("https://www.google.com")
    if err != nil {
        log.Fatal(err)
    }
    // get data from the response body
    defer r.Body.Close()
    data, err := ioutil.ReadAll(r.Body)
    if err != nil {
        log.Fatal(err)
    }
    // return the response data
    return string(data)
}
```

7. Create a **main** function. Within the **main** function, call the **getDataAndReturnResponse** function and log the string it returns:

```
func main() {
    data := getDataAndReturnResponse()
    log.Println(data)
}
```

8. To run the program, open your terminal and navigate to the directory that you created the **main.go** file in.

9. Run **go run main.go** to compile and execute the file:

```
go run server.go
```

The program will issue a GET request to https://www.google.com and log the response in your terminal.

While it may look like gibberish, if you were to save that data to a file called **response.html** and open it in your web browser, it would resemble the Google home page. This is what your web browser will do under the hood when you open a web page. It will send a GET request to the server and then display the data it returns. If we do this manually, it will look as follows:

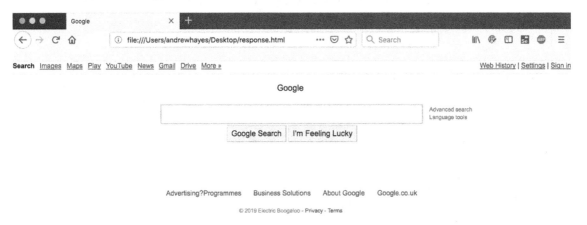

Figure 14.2: Request HTML response when viewed in Firefox

In this exercise, we saw how to send a GET request to a web server and get data back. You created a Go program that sent a request to https://www.google.com and got back the HTML data for the Google home page.

Structured Data

Once you have requested data from a server, the data returned can come in various formats. For example, if you send a request to **packtpub.com**, it will return HTML data for the Packt website. While HTML data is useful for displaying websites, it isn't ideal for sending machine-readable data. A common data type used in web APIs is JSON. JSON provides a good structure for data that is both machine-readable and human-readable. Later, you will learn how to parse JSON and make use of it using Go.

Exercise 14.02: Using the HTTP Client with Structured Data

In this exercise, you will parse structured JSON data in Go. The server will return JSON data and you will use the **json.Unmarshal** function to parse the data and put it into a struct:

1. Create a new directory, **Exercise14.02**, on your GOPATH. Within that directory, create two more directories, **server** and **client**. Then, within the **server** directory, create a file called **server.go** and write the following code:

```go
package main
import (
    "log"
    "net/http"
)
type server struct{}
func (srv server) ServeHTTP(w http.ResponseWriter, r
  *http.Request) {
    msg := "{\"message\": \"hello world\"}"
    w.Write([]byte(msg))
}
func main() {
    log.Fatal(http.ListenAndServe(":8080", server{}))
}
```

This creates a very basic web server that sends back JSON data. We will explain in more detail how this works in the next chapter. For now, we will just use it as an example.

2. Once you have created the server, navigate to the client directory and create a file called **main.go**. Add **package main** and import the packages needed for the file:

```go
package main
import (
    "encoding/json"
    "fmt"
    "io/ioutil"
    "log"
    "net/http"
)
```

3. Then, create a struct with a string parameter that can accept the response from the server. Then, add JSON metadata to it so it can be used to unmarshal the JSON **message** parameter:

```
type messageData struct {
    Message string `json:"message"`
}
```

4. Next, create a function that you can call to get and parse the data from the server. Use the struct you just created as the return value:

```
func getDataAndReturnResponse() messageData {
```

When you run the web server, it will listen on **http://localhost:8080**. So, you need to send a GET request to that URL and then read the response body:

```
r, err := http.Get("http://localhost:8080")
if err != nil {
    log.Fatal(err)
}
defer r.Body.Close()
data, err := ioutil.ReadAll(r.Body)
if err != nil {
    log.Fatal(err)
}
```

5. This time, however, you will parse the response instead of simply returning it. To do that, you create an instance of the struct you created, then pass it along with the response data to **json.Unmarshal**:

```
message := messageData{}
err = json.Unmarshal(data, &message)
if err != nil {
    log.Fatal(err)
}
```

This will populate the **message** variable with the data returned from the server.

6. You then need to return the struct to complete the function:

```
return message
```

7. Finally, call the function you just created from the **main()** function and log the message from the server:

```go
func main() {
    data := getDataAndReturnResponse()
    fmt.Println(data.Message)
}
```

8. To run this, you need to do two steps. The first is navigate to the **server** directory in your terminal and run the following command. This will start the web server:

```
go run server.go
```

9. In a second terminal window, navigate to the **client** directory and run **go run main. go**. This will start the client and connect to the server. It should output the message from the server:

```
client [git::master] > go run main.go
hello world
```

Figure 14.3: Expected output

In this exercise, you sent a GET request to the server and got back structured data in JSON format. You then parsed that JSON data to get the message from it.

Activity 14.01: Requesting Data from a Web Server and Processing the Response

Imagine you are interacting with a web API. You send a GET request for data and get back an array of names. You need to count those names to find out how many of each you have. In this activity, you will do just that. You will send a GET request to the server, get back structured JSON data, parse the data, and count how many of each name you got back in the response:

1. Create a directory called **Activity14.01**.

2. Create two sub-directories, one called **client** and another called **server**.

3. In the **server** directory, create a file called **server.go**.

4. Add the server code in **server.go**.

5. Start the server by calling **go run server.go** in the server directory.

6. In the **client** directory, create a file called **main.go**.

7. In **main.go**, add the necessary imports.

8. Create structs to parse the response data.

9. Create a function called **getDataAndParseResponse** that returns two integers.

10. Send a **GET** request to the server.

11. Parse the response into a struct.

12. Loop through the struct and count the occurrences of the names **Electric** and **Boogaloo.**

13. Return the counts.

14. Print the counts.

The expected output is as follows:

```
solution [git::master *] > go run main.go
Electric Count:  2
Boogaloo Count:  3
```

Figure 14.4: Possible output

> **Note**
>
> The solution for this activity can be found on page 752.

In this activity, we have requested data from a web server and processed the data it returned using the Go HTTP client.

Sending Data to a Server

In addition to requesting data from a server, you will also want to send data to a server. The most common way of doing this is via a POST request. A POST request comes in two main parts: the URL and the body. The body of a POST request is where you put the data you want to send to the server. A common example of this is a login form. When we send a login request, we POST the body to the URL. The web server then checks that the login details within the body are correct and updates our login status. It responds to the request by telling the client whether it succeeded or not. In this chapter, you will learn how to send data to a server using a POST request.

Exercise 14.03: Sending a Post Request to a Web Server Using the Go HTTP Client

In this exercise, you will send a POST request to a web server containing a message. The web server will then respond with the same message so you can confirm that it received it:

1. Create a new directory, **Exercise14.03**, on your GOPATH. Within that directory, create two more directories, **server** and **client**. Then, within the **server** directory, create a file called **server.go** and write the following code:

```go
package main
import (
    "encoding/json"
    "log"
    "net/http"
)
type server struct{}
type messageData struct {
    Message string `json:"message"`
}
func (srv server) ServeHTTP(w http.ResponseWriter, r
  *http.Request) {
    jsonDecoder := json.NewDecoder(r.Body)
    messageData := messageData{}
    err := jsonDecoder.Decode(&messageData)
    if err != nil {
        log.Fatal(err)
    }
    jsonBytes, _ := json.Marshal(messageData)
    log.Println(string(jsonBytes))
    w.Write(jsonBytes)
}
func main() {
    log.Fatal(http.ListenAndServe(":8080", server{}))
}
```

This creates a very basic web server that receives a JSON POST request and returns the message sent to it back to the client.

2. Once you have the server created. Navigate to the client directory and create a file called **main.go**. Add **package main** and the imports needed for the file:

```
package main
import (
    "bytes"
    "encoding/json"
    "fmt"
    "io/ioutil"
    "log"
    "net/http"
)
```

3. Next, you need to create a struct for the data we want to send and receive. This will be the same as the struct used by the server to parse the request:

```
type messageData struct {
    Message string `json:"message"`
}
```

4. You then need to create the function to POST the data to the server. It should accept a **messageData** struct parameter as well as return a **messageData** struct:

```
func postDataAndReturnResponse(msg messageData) messageData {
```

5. To POST the data to the server, you need to marshal the struct into bytes that the client can send to the server. To do this, you can use the **json.Marshal** function:

```
jsonBytes, _ := json.Marshal(msg)
```

6. Now that you have the bytes, you can use the **http.Post** function to send the POST request. Within the request, you just need to tell the function what URL to post to, what kind of data you are sending, and the data you want to send. In this case, the URL is **http://localhost:8080**. The content you are sending is **application/json** and the data is the **jsonBytes** variable you just created. Together, it looks like this:

```
r, err := http.Post("http://localhost:8080", "application/json", bytes.
NewBuffer(jsonBytes))
    if err != nil {
        log.Fatal(err)
    }
```

7. After that, the rest of the function is the same as in the previous exercise. You read the response, parse out the data, and then return the data, which looks like this:

```
defer r.Body.Close()
data, err := ioutil.ReadAll(r.Body)
if err != nil {
```

```
        log.Fatal(err)
    }
    message := messageData{}
    err = json.Unmarshal(data, &message)
    if err != nil {
        log.Fatal(err)
    }
    return message
```

8. Then, you just need to call the **postDataAndReturnResponse** function from your **main** function. This time, however, you need to pass the message you want to send to the function. You just need to create an instance of the **messageData** struct and pass that to the function when you call it, which looks like this:

```
func main() {
    msg := messageData{Message: "Hi Server!"}
    data := postDataAndReturnResponse(msg)
    fmt.Println(data.Message)
}
```

9. To run this exercise, you need to carry out two steps. The first is to navigate to the **server** directory in your terminal and run **go run server.go**. This will start the web server. In a second terminal window, navigate to the **client** directory and run **go run main.go**. This will start the client and connect to the server. It should output the message from the server:

```
client [git::master *] > go run main.go
Hi Server!
```

Figure 14.5: Expected output

In this exercise, you sent a POST request to the server. The server parsed the request and sent the same message back to you. If you change the message sent to the server, you should see the response from the server sending back the new message.

Uploading Files in a Post Request

Another common example of data you might want to POST to a web server is a file from your local computer. This is how websites allow users to upload their photos and so on. As you can imagine, this is a little more complex than sending simple form data. To achieve this, the file needs to be read first, then wrapped in a format that the server can understand. It can then be sent in a POST request to the server in what's called a multipart form. You will learn how to read in a file and upload it to a server using Go.

Exercise 14.04: Uploading a File to a Web Server via a Post Request

In this exercise, you will read in a local file and then upload it to a web server. You can then check that the web server saved the file you uploaded:

1. Create a new directory, **Exercise14.04**, on your GOPATH. Within that directory, create two more directories, **server** and **client**. Then, within the **server** directory, create a file called **server.go** and write the following code:

server.go

```
9  func (srv server) ServeHTTP(w http.ResponseWriter, r
       *http.Request) {
10     uploadedFile, uploadedFileHeader, err :=
         r.FormFile("myFile")
11     if err != nil {
12         log.Fatal(err)
13     }
14     defer uploadedFile.Close()
15     fileContent, err := ioutil.ReadAll(uploadedFile)
16     if err != nil {
17         log.Fatal(err)
18     }
```

The full code for this step is available at https://packt.live/2SkeZHW

This creates a very basic web server that receives a multipart form POST request and saves the file within the form.

2. Once you have created the server, navigate to the client directory and create a file called **main.go**. Add **package main** and the imports needed for the file:

```
package main
import (
    "bytes"
    "fmt"
    "io"
    "io/ioutil"
    "log"
    "mime/multipart"
    "net/http"
    "os"
)
```

3. You then need to create a function to call that you will give a filename to. The function will read in the file, upload it to the server, and return the server's response:

```
func postFileAndReturnResponse(filename string) string {
```

4. You need to create a buffer that you can write the file bytes to, then create a writer to allow bytes to write into it:

```
fileDataBuffer := bytes.Buffer{}
multipartWritter := multipart.NewWriter(&fileDataBuffer)
```

5. Open the file from your local computer using the following command:

```
file, err := os.Open(filename)
if err != nil {
    log.Fatal(err)
}
```

6. Once you have opened the local file, you need to create a **formFile**. This wraps the file data in the right format to upload it to the server:

```
formFile, err := multipartWritter.CreateFormFile("myFile",
    file.Name())
if err != nil {
    log.Fatal(err)
}
```

7. Copy the bytes from the local file into the form file, then close the form file writer so that it knows no more data will be added:

```
_, err = io.Copy(formFile, file)
if err != nil {
    log.Fatal(err)
}
multipartWritter.Close()
```

8. Next, you need to create the POST request you want to send to the server. In the previous exercises, we used shortcut functions such as **http.Post**. However, in this exercise, we need more control over the data being sent. That means we'll need to create an **http.Request**. In this case, you're creating a POST request that you will send to **http://localhost:8080**. As we are uploading a file, the bytes buffer also needs to be included in the request. That looks as follows:

```
req, err := http.NewRequest("POST",
    "http://localhost:8080", &fileDataBuffer)
if err != nil {
    log.Fatal(err)
}
```

9. You then need to set the **Content-Type** request header. This tells the server about the content of the file, so it knows how to handle the upload:

```
req.Header.Set("Content-Type",
    multipartWritter.FormDataContentType())
```

10. Send the request as follows:

```
response, err := http.DefaultClient.Do(req)
if err != nil {
    log.Fatal(err)
}
```

11. After you have sent the request, we can read in the response and return the data within it:

```
defer response.Body.Close()
data, err := ioutil.ReadAll(response.Body)
if err != nil {
    log.Fatal(err)
}
return string(data)
```

12. Finally, you just need to call the **postFileAndReturnResponse** function and tell it what file to upload:

```
func main() {
    data := postFileAndReturnResponse("./test.txt")
    fmt.Println(data)
}
```

13. To run this, you need to carry out two steps. The first is to navigate to the **server** directory in your terminal and run **go run server.go**. This will start the web server:

```
go run server.go
```

14. Next, in the **client** directory, create a file named **test.txt** and put a few lines of text in it.

15. In a second terminal window, navigate to the **client** directory and run **go run main.go**. This will start the client and connect to the server:

```
go run server.go
```

16. The client will then read in **test.txt** and upload it to the server. The client should give the following output:

```
client [git::master *] > go run main.go
./test.txt Uploaded!
```

Figure 14.6: Expected client output

Then, if you navigate to the **server** directory, you should see that the **test.txt** file has now appeared:

```
server [git::master *] > ls
server.go test.txt
```

In this exercise, you sent a file to a web server using the Go HTTP client. You read in a file from disk, formatted it into a POST request, and sent the data to the server.

Custom Request Headers

Sometimes there is more to a request than simply requesting or sending data. This information is stored within the request headers. A very common example of this is authorization headers. When you log into a server, it will respond with an authorization token. In all future requests sent to the server, you would include this token in the request's headers so the server knows you are the one making the requests. You will learn how to add an authorization token to requests later.

Exercise 14.05: Using Custom Headers and Options with the Go HTTP Client

In this exercise, you will create your own HTTP client and set custom options on it. You will also set an authorization token in the request headers, so the server knows it is you requesting the data:

1. Create a new directory, **Exercise14.05**, on your GOPATH. Within that directory, create two more directories, **server** and **client**. Then, within the **server** directory, create a file called **server.go** and write the following code:

```go
package main
import (
    "log"
    "net/http"
    "time"
)
type server struct{}
func (srv server) ServeHTTP(w http.ResponseWriter, r
    *http.Request) {
    auth := r.Header.Get("Authorization")
    if auth != "superSecretToken" {
        w.WriteHeader(http.StatusUnauthorized)
        w.Write([]byte("Authorization token not recognized"))
        return
    }
}
```

```
        time.Sleep(10 * time.Second)
        msg := "hello client!"
        w.Write([]byte(msg))
    }
    func main() {
        log.Fatal(http.ListenAndServe(":8080", server{}))
    }
```

This creates a very basic web server that receives a request, checks the authorization header is correct, waits 10 seconds, then sends back data.

2. Once you have created the server, navigate to the client directory and create a file called **main.go**. Add **package main** and the imports needed for the file:

```
package main
import (
    "fmt"
    "io/ioutil"
    "log"
    "net/http"
    "time"
)
```

3. Then, you need to create a function that will create an HTTP client, set the timeout limitations, and set the authorization header:

```
func getDataWithCustomOptionsAndReturnResponse() string {
```

4. You need to create your own HTTP client and set the timeout to 11 seconds:

```
client := http.Client{Timeout: 11 * time.Second}
```

5. You also need to create a request to send it to the server. You should create a GET request with the URL **http://localhost:8080**. No data will be sent in this request, so the data can be set to nil. You can use the **http.NewRequest** function to do this:

```
req, err := http.NewRequest("POST",
    "http://localhost:8080", nil)
if err != nil {
    log.Fatal(err)
}
```

6. If you look at the server code again, you will notice that it checks for the **Authorization** request header and it expects its value to be **superSecretToken**. So, you need to set the **Authorization** header in your request as well:

```
req.Header.Set("Authorization", "superSecretToken")
```

7. You then get the client you created to do the request:

```
resp, err := client.Do(req)
if err != nil {
    log.Fatal(err)
}
```

8. Then, you need to read in the response from the server and return the data:

```
defer resp.Body.Close()
data, err := ioutil.ReadAll(resp.Body)
if err != nil {
    log.Fatal(err)
}
return string(data)
```

9. Finally, you need to call the function you just created from the **main** function and log the data it returns:

```
func main() {
    data := getDataWithCustomOptionsAndReturnResponse()
    fmt.Println(data)
}
```

10. To run this exercise, you need to carry out two steps. The first is navigate to the **server** directory in your terminal and run **go run server.go**. This will start the web server.

11. In a second terminal window, navigate to the directory you created the **client** in.

12. To execute the client, run the following command:

```
go run main.go
```

This will start the client and connect to the server. The client will send the request to the server and after 10 seconds it should output the following:

```
client [git::master *] > go run main.go
hello client!
```

Figure 14.8: Expected output

> **Note**
>
> Change the timeout settings in the client to be under 10 seconds and see what happens. You can also change or remove the authorization header on the request and see what happens.

In this exercise, you learned how to add custom headers to a request. You learned about the common example of adding an authorization header, which is required by many APIs when you want to interact with them.

Activity 14.02: Sending Data to a Web Server and Checking Whether the Data Was Received Using POST and GET

Imagine you are interacting with a web API and you wish to send data to a web server. You then want to check whether the data was added. In this activity, you will do just that. You will send a POST request to the server, then request the data back using a GET request, parse the data, and print it out.

Follow these steps to get the desired outcome:

1. Create a directory called **Activity14.02**.

2. Create two sub-directories, one called **client** and one called **server**.

3. In the **server** directory, create a file called **server.go**.

4. Add the server code to the **server.go** file.

5. Start the server by calling go run server.go in the server directory.

6. In the **client** directory, create a file called **main.go**.

7. In **main.go**, add the necessary imports.

8. Create structs to host the request data.

9. Create structs to parse the response data.

10. Create an **addNameAndParseResponse** function that posts a name to the server.

11. Create a **getDataAndParseResponse** function that parses the server response.

12. Send a POST request to the server, to add names.

13. Send a GET request to the server.

14. Parse the response into a struct.

15. Loop through the struct and print the names.

This is the expected output:

```
solution [git::go_tools *] > go run main.go
2019/09/19 14:28:52 Electric
2019/09/19 14:28:52 Boogaloo
```

Figure 14.9: Possible output

> **Note**
>
> The solution for this activity can be found on page 754.

In this activity, you saw how to send data to a web server using a POST request and then how to request data from the server to ensure it was updated using a GET request. Interacting with a server in this way is very common when programming professionally.

Summary

HTTP clients are used to interact with web servers. They are used to send different types of requests to a server (for example, GET or POST requests) and then react to the response returned by the server. A web browser is a type of HTTP client that will send a GET request to a web server and display the HTML data it returns. In Go, you created your own HTTP client and did the same thing, sending a GET request to https://www.google.com and then logging the response returned by the server. You also learned about the components of a URL and that you can control what you request from a server by changing the URL.

There is also more to web servers than simply requesting HTML data. You learned that they can return structured data in the form of JSON, which can be parsed and used in your code. Data can also be sent to a server using POST requests, allowing you to send form data to a server. However, the data sent to a server isn't limited to just form data: you can also upload files to a server using a POST request.

There are also ways to customize the requests you send. You learned about the common example of authorization, where you add a token to the header of HTTP requests so that a server can tell who is making that request.

In this chapter, you used some basic web servers in the exercises. However, you didn't learn about the details of what they were doing. In the next chapter, you will learn about web servers in more detail.

15

HTTP Servers

Overview

This chapter introduces you to different ways of creating an HTTP server in order to accept requests from the internet. You will be able to understand how a website can be accessed and how it can respond to a form. You will also learn how to respond to requests from another software program.

You'll be able to create an HTTP server rendering a simple message. You will learn how to create an HTTP server rendering complex data structures which serves local static files. Further you will create an HTTP server rendering dynamic pages and work with different ways of routing. By the end of this chapter you will also learn to create a REST service, accept data through a form, and accept JSON data.

Introduction

In the previous chapter, we saw how to contact a remote server in order to obtain some information, but now we will dig into how the remote server is created, so if you already know how to request information, now you will see how to reply to these requests.

A web server is a program that uses the HTTP protocol, hence, the HTTP server, to accept requests from any HTTP client (web browser, another program, and so on) and respond to them with an appropriate message. When we browse the internet with our browser, it will be an HTTP server that will send an HTML page to our browser and we will be able to see it. In some other cases, a server will not return an HTML page but a different message, appropriate to the client.

Some HTTP servers provide an API that can be consumed by another program. Think of when you want to register with a website, and you are asked if you want to sign up through Facebook or Google. This means that the website you want to register with will consume a Google or Facebook API to get your details. These APIs generally respond with a structured text, which is a text representing a complex data structure. The way these servers expect the requests can be different. Some expect the same type of structured messages they return, while some provide what is called a REST API, which is quite strict with the HTTP methods used and expects inputs in the form of URL parameters or values, like the ones in a web form.

How to Build a Basic Server

The simplest HTTP server that we can create is a Hello World server. This is a server that will return a simple message "Hello World" and will not do anything else. It is not very useful, but it is a starting point to see what Go default packages give us and is the basis for any other more complex server. The aim is to have a server that runs on a specific port on your machine's localhost and accepts any path under it. Accepting any path means that when you test the server with your browser, it will always return the "Hello World" message and a status code of 200. Of course, we could return any other message, but, for historical reasons, the simplest project you learn when you study programming is always some sort of software returning the message "Hello World". In this case, we will see how this can be done and then visualized in a normal browser, before perhaps being put on the internet and shared with billions of users, although users may, in practice, prefer a more useful server. Let's say this is the most basic HTTP server you can create.

HTTP Handler

In order to react to an HTTP request, we need to write something that, we usually say, handles the request; hence, we call this something a handler. In Go, we have several ways to do that, and one is to implement the handler interface of the http package. This interface has one method that is pretty self-explanatory, and this is as follows:

```
ServeHTTP(w http.ResponseWriter, r *http.Request)
```

So, whenever we need to create a handler for HTTP requests, we can create a struct including this method and we can use it to handle an HTTP request. For example:

```
type MyHandler struct {}
func(h MyHandler) ServeHTTP(w http.ResponseWriter, r *http.Request) {}
```

This is a valid HTTP handler and you can use it this way:

```
http.ListenAndServe(":8080", MyHandler{})
```

Here, **ListenAndServe()** is a function that will use our handler to serve the requests; any struct implementing the handler interface will be fine. However, we need to let our server do something.

As you can see, the **ServeHTTP** method accepts a **ResponseWriter** and a **Request** object. You can actually use them in order to capture parameters from the request and write messages to the response. The simplest thing, for example, is to let our server return a message:

```
func(h MyHandler) ServeHTTP(w http.ResponseWriter, r *http.Request) {
   w.Write([]byte("HI"))
}
```

The **ListenAndServe** method might return an error. If this happens, we most likely would like the execution of our program to halt, so one common practice is to wrap this function call with a fatal log:

```
log.Fatal(http.ListenAndServe(":8080", MyHandler{}))
```

This will halt the execution and print the error message returned by the **ListenAndServe** function.

Exercise 15.01: Creating a Hello World Server

Let's start building a simple Hello World HTTP server on the basis of what you've learned in the previous block.

The first thing to do is to create a folder called **hello-world-server**. You can do this via the command line or you can create it with your favorite editor. Inside the folder, create a file called **main.go**. We will not use any external library here:

1. Add the package name:

```
package main
```

   This tells the compiler that this file is an entry point for a program that can be executed.

2. Import the necessary packages:

```
import (
    "log"
    "net/http"
)
```

3. Now, create a **handler**, the struct that will handle the requests:

```
type hello struct{}
func(h hello) ServeHTTP(w http.ResponseWriter, r *http.Request) {
    msg := "<h1>Hello World</h1>"
    w.Write([]byte(msg))
}
```

4. Now that we have our handler, create the **main()** function, which will start the server and produce a web page with our message:

```
func main() {
    log.Fatal(http.ListenAndServe(":8080", hello{}))
}
```

   The entire file should look like this:

```
package main
import (
    "log"
    "net/http"
)
type hello struct{}
func(h hello) ServeHTTP(w http.ResponseWriter, r *http.Request) {
```

```
        msg := "<h1>Hello World</h1"
        w.Write([]byte(msg))
    }
    func main() {
        log.Fatal(http.ListenAndServe(":8080", hello{}))
    }
```

5. If you now go to your Terminal, inside your **hello-world-server** folder, and type in the following command:

```
hello-world-server go run .
```

You should just see nothing; the program has started.

6. If you now open your browser at the following address:

```
http://localhost:8080
```

You should see a page with a big message:

Figure 15.01: Hello world server

If you now try to change path and go to */page1*, you will again see the following message:

Figure 15.02: Hello world server sub-pages

Congratulations! This is your first HTTP server.

In this exercise, we have created a basic hello world server, which returns the message "Hello World" in response to any request on any sub-address.

Simple Routing

The server built just now in the previous exercise does not do much. It just responds with a message and we cannot ask anything else. Before we can make our server more dynamic, let's imagine we want to create an online book and we want to be able to select a chapter just changing the URL. At the moment, if we browse the following pages:

```
http://localhost:8080
http://localhost:8080/hello
http://localhost:8080/chapter1
```

We always see the same message, but we now want to associate different messages with these different paths on our server. We will do this by introducing some simple routing to our server.

A path is what you see after the **8080** in the URL; it can be one number, a word, a set of numbers or character groups separated by a "/". In order to do this, we will use another function of the net/http package, which is:

```
HandleFunc(pattern string, handler func(ResponseWriter, *Request))
```

Here, the pattern is the path we want to be served by the **handler** function. Note how the **handler** function signature has the exact same parameters as the **ServeHTTP** method, which you added to the **hello** struct in the previous exercise.

As an example, the server built in *Exercise 15.01* is not very useful, but we can transform it into something much more useful with the addition of pages other than the **hello world** one, and, in order to do so, we need to do some basic routing. The aim here is to write a book, and the book must have a welcome page with the title, and a first chapter. The book title is **hello world**, so we can keep what we did before. The first chapter will have a heading stating **Chapter 1**. The book is a work in progress, so it does not matter that the content is still poor; what we require is the ability to select the chapter, and we will then add the content later.

Exercise 15.02: Routing Our Server

We are now going to modify the code in *Exercise 15.01* to support different paths. If you haven't gone through the previous exercise, do it now so that you'll have a basic framework for this exercise:

1. Create a new folder and a **main.go** file and add the code from the previous exercise to the definition of the **main** function:

```
package main
import (
    "log"
```

```
    "net/http"
)
type hello struct{}
func(h hello) ServeHTTP(w http.ResponseWriter, r *http.Request) {
    msg := "<h1>Hello World</h1"
    w.Write([]byte(msg))
}
```

2. Create the **main()** function:

```
func main() {
```

3. Then, use **handle** to route "**/chapter1**" through a **handlefunc()** function:

```
    http.HandleFunc("/chapter1", func(w http.ResponseWriter, r *http.Request) {
    msg := "Chapter 1"
    w.Write([]byte(msg))
})
```

This means that we associate the path, **/chapter1**, with a function that returns a specific message.

4. Finally, set the server to listen to a port and to run the following command:

```
    log.Fatal(http.ListenAndServe(":8080", hello{}))
}
```

5. Now, save your file and run the server again with:

```
hello-world-server go run main.go
```

6. Then, go to your browser and load the following URLs:

http://localhost:8080

http://localhost:8080/chapter1

The output for the home page is shown in the following screenshot:

Figure 15.03: Multi-page server – home page

And the output for page 1 is shown in the following screenshot:

Hello World

Figure 15.04: Multi-page server – chapter 1

Note that they both still display the same message. This happens because we are setting our **hello** as the handler for our server, and this overrides our specific path. We can modify our code to look like this:

```
func main() {
    http.HandleFunc("/chapter1", func(w http.ResponseWriter, r *http.Request) {
    msg := "<h1>Chapter 1</h1>"
    w.Write([]byte(msg))
    })
    http.Handle("/", hello{})
    log.Fatal(http.ListenAndServe(":8080", nil))
}
```

What happened here is that you removed the **hello** handler from being the main handler for our server and you associated this handler with the main **/** path:

```
http.Handle("/", hello{})
```

Then, you associated a **handler** function with the specific **/chapter1** path:

```
http.HandleFunc("/chapter1", func(w http.ResponseWriter, r *http.Request) {
    msg := "Chapter 1"
    w.Write([]byte(msg))
})
```

Now, if you stop and then run our server again, you will see that the **/chapter1** path now returns the new message:

Chapter 1

Figure 15.05: Multi-page server repeated – chapter 1

In the meantime, all the other paths return the old **Hello World** message.

Figure 15.06: Multi-page server – base page

Figure 15.07: The page that is not set returns the default setting

Handler versus Handler Function

As you may have noticed, we used two different functions before, **http.Handle** and **http.HandleFunc** , both of which have a path as their first parameter, but which differ in terms of the second parameter. These two functions both ensure that a specific path is handled by a function. **http.Handle**, however, expects **http.Handler** to handle the path, while **http.HandleFunc** expects a function to do the same.

As we've seen before, **http.Handler** is any struct having a method with this signature:

```
ServeHTTP(w http.ResponseWriter, r *http.Request)
```

So, in both cases, there will always be a function with **http.ResponseWriter** and ***http. Request** as parameters that will handle the path. As to when one or the other might be chosen may just be a matter of personal preference in many cases, but it might be important, when creating a complex project, for example, to choose the right method. Doing so will ensure that the structure of the project is optimal. Different routes may appear better organized if handled by handlers belonging to different packages, or might have to perform very few actions, as in our previous case; and a simple function might prove to be the ideal choice.

In general, for simple projects where you have a handful of simple pages, you may opt for **HandleFunc**. For example, let's say you want to have static pages and there is no complex behavior in each page. In this case, it would be an overkill to use an empty struct just for returning a static text. The handler is more appropriate whenever you need to set some parameters, or if you want to keep track of something. As a general rule, let's say that if you have a counter, a **Handler** is the best choice because you can initialize a **struct** with a count of 0 and then increment it, but we will see this in *Activity 15.01*.

Activity 15.01: Adding a Page Counter to an HTML Page

Imagine that you own a website with, say, three pages, where you are writing your book. You earn money depending on how many visits your website receives. In order to understand how popular your website is, and how much money you are earning, you need to keep track of the visits.

In this activity, you will build an HTTP server with three pages, containing some content, and display, in each page, how many visits that page has had so far. You will use the **http.Handler** method, which, in this case, will help you to generalize your counter.

In order to display the dynamic value, you can use the **fmt.Sprintf** function in the **fmt** package, which prints and formats a message to a string. With this function, you can build a string containing characters and numbers. You can find all the information about this method online in the Go documentation.

You will use everything you've learned so far, including how a struct is instantiated, how to set attributes of a struct, pointers, how to increase an integer, and, of course, everything you have learned about HTTP servers hitherto.

Observing the following steps will provide an elegant and effective solution:

1. Create a folder called **page-counter**.

2. Create a file called **main.go**.

3. Add the necessary imports to the **http** and **fmt** packages.

4. Define a struct called **PageWithCounter** with a **counter** as an integer attribute, a **content**, and a **heading** as a text attribute.

5. Add a **ServeHTTP** method to the struct, capable of displaying the content, the heading, and a message with the total number of views.

6. Create your **main** function and, inside, implement the following:

7. Instantiate three handlers of the **PageWithCounter** type, with **Hello World**, **Chapter 1**, and **Chapter 2** headings and some content.

8. Add the three handlers to the routes **/**, **/chapter1**, and **/chapter2**.

9. Run the server on port **8080**.

When you run the server, you should see the following:

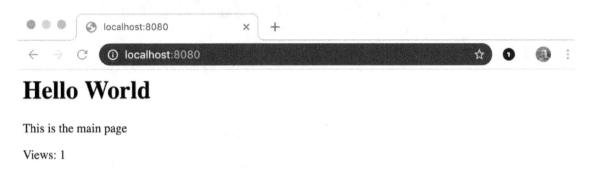

Figure 15.08: Output on the browser when you run the server for the first time

If you refresh the page, you should see the following:

Figure 15.09: Output on the browser when you run the server for the second time

Next, navigate to Chapter 1 by typing **localhost:8080/chapter1** in the address bar. You should be able to see something along the lines of the following:

Figure 15.10: Output on the browser when you visit the chapter1 page for the first time

Similarly, navigate to Chapter 2, and you should be able to see the following increment in terms of the number of views:

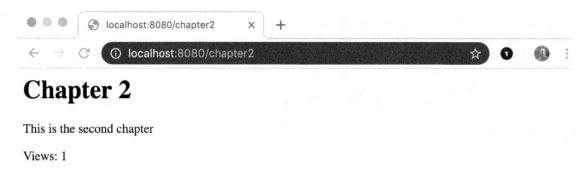

Chapter 2

This is the second chapter

Views: 1

Figure 15.11: Output on the browser when you visit the chapter2 page for the first time

When you revisit Chapter 1, you should see an increase in the number of views as follows:

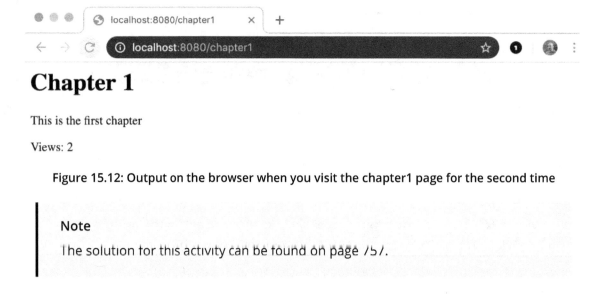

Chapter 1

This is the first chapter

Views: 2

Figure 15.12: Output on the browser when you visit the chapter1 page for the second time

> **Note**
>
> The solution for this activity can be found on page 757.

In this activity, you learned how to create a server that responds to different requests on different pages with a specific static text, along with a counter on each page, with each counter independent from the others.

Returning Complex Structures

What we've seen hitherto is useful when building a website, even though, for this purpose, we still need to see how to better render HTML pages. You might want to use a framework such as **revel** or **gin** for this purpose, although plain Go with a few libraries is more than enough for a production-grade website. You will find, however, that HTTP servers are used not only for building websites, but also for building web services, and especially, nowadays, microservices. Although how to build a web service-based project is beyond the scope of this chapter and book, it is important for you to know how to let your HTTP server serve something that will not be consumed by a human through a browser, but by another program. You may already know what a web service is, but even if you do not, you might have to work on an existing project where you have to modify a web service. There are several ways to present a message to another program, which will be referred to as a client, but, in general, they will all involve some sort of structured texts, which can be parsed easily. The format could be an XML string, but the most common and lightweight format now used is JSON. In the next exercise, we will see how to build a data structure and send it to the client (aq browser or another program) in the form of a JSON string.

Activity 15.02: Serving a Request with a JSON Payload

In this activity, you will create a data structure and you will serve it through an HTTP server. You will make use of what you have already learned about JSON and the encoding/decoding of structs, and you will combine it with what you've learned about HTTP servers. You might have guessed already, but in this exercise, you already have all the knowledge required and you should be able to complete it on your own. Let's now build another book. The title and the chapters are the same, but this time we want to make it accessible to a program that will consume the pages on the server as JSON documents. The document will also include the number of views per chapter, so the code can make use of the one generated in *Activity 15.01*. The steps are as follows:

1. Create a new folder called **book-api**.

2. Create a file called **main.go** in that folder.

3. Add the required imports.

4. Create a struct called **PageWithCounter** representing a book with a title, content, and a counter, with appropriate JSON tags, if necessary.

5. Add a **ServeHTTP** method to the struct, capable of displaying the content, the heading, and a message with the total number of views as a JSON document.

6. Create the **main()** function.

7. Instantiate three handlers of the **PageWithCounter** type, with **Hello World**, **Chapter 1**, and **Chapter 2** headings and some content.

8. Add the three handlers to the routes **/**, **/chapter1**, and **/chapter2**.

9. Run the server on port **8080**.

Running your server, you should see the following for the assigned routes:

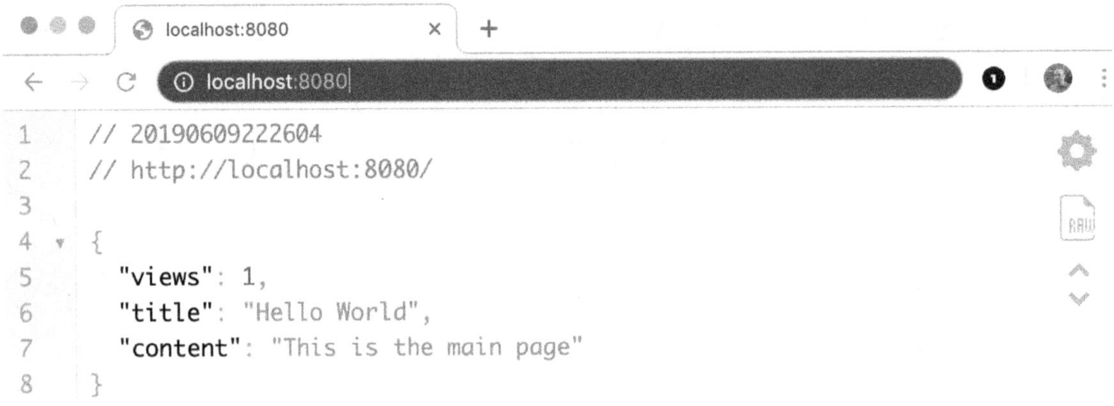

Figure 15.13: Expected output when the handler is /

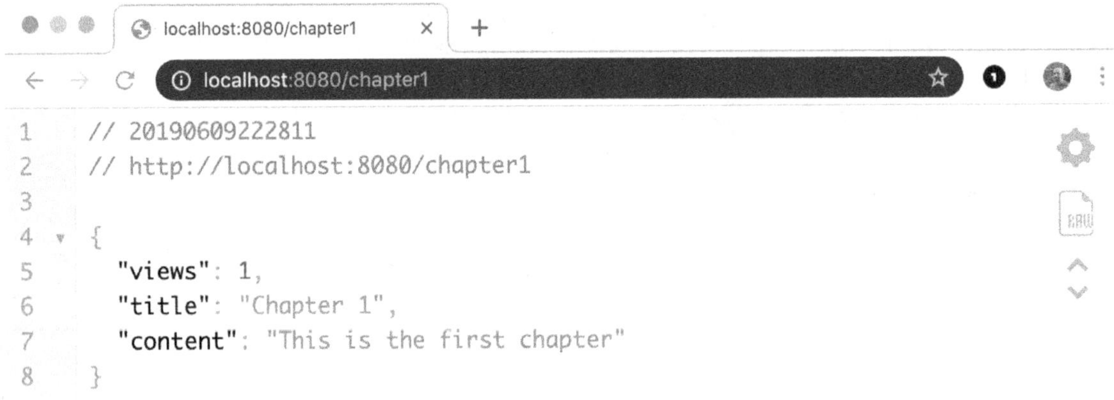

Figure 15.14: Expected output when the handler is /chapter1

```
1   // 20190609222852
2   // http://localhost:8080/chapter2
3
4 ▾ {
5     "views": 1,
6     "title": "Chapter 2",
7     "content": "This is the second chapter"
8   }
```

Figure 15.15: Expected output when the handler is /chapter2

In this activity, you've learned how to return complex structures through an HTTP server. Any kind of complex data structure can be served this way, using a standard format such as JSON.

> **Note**
>
> The solution for this activity can be found on page 761.

Dynamic Content

A server that serves only static content is useful, but there is much more that can be done. An HTTP server can deliver content depending on a more granular request, which is done by passing some parameters to the server. There are many ways to do so, but one simple way is to pass parameters to a **querystring**. If the URL of the server is:

```
http://localhost:8080
```

We can then add something like:

```
http://localhost:8080?name=john
```

Here, the part **?name=john** is called a **querystring** as it is a string representing a query. In this case, this **querystring** sets a variable called **name** with a value of **john**. This way of passing parameters is generally used with **GET** requests, while a **POST** request will generally make use of the body of the request in order to send parameters. This does not mean that a **GET** request does not have a body but is not the standard way to pass parameters to a **GET** request. We will begin by looking at how to accept parameters for a **GET** request, as this request is made by simply opening your browser on a specific address. We will see later how to handle a **POST** request through a form.

In the next exercise, you will be able to return different texts as responses to HTTP requests, where the text depends on what values the user puts in the **querystring** in the address bar.

Exercise 15.03: Personalized Welcome

In this exercise, we will again create an HTTP server that is able to cheer us, but instead of a general "**hello world**" message, we will provide a message depending on our name. The idea is that, by opening the browser on the server's URL and adding a parameter called **name**, the server will welcome us with the message "**hello** ", followed by the value of the **name** parameter. The server is very simple and does not have sub-pages, but contains this dynamic element that constitutes a starting point for more complex situations:

1. Create a new folder called **personalised-welcome** and, inside the folder, create a file called **main.go**. Inside the file, add the package name:

    ```
    package main
    ```

2. Then, add the required imports:

    ```
    import (
        "fmt"
        "log"
        "net/http"
        "strings"
    )
    ```

3. They are all the same imports used in the previous exercises and activities, no there is nothing new. We will not use handlers in this exercise as it is much smaller, but we will make use of the **http.handleFunc** function.

4. Now, add the following code after the imports:

    ```
    func Hello(w http.ResponseWriter, r *http.Request) {
    ```

5. This is the definition of a function that can be used as a handling function for an HTTP path.

6. Now, save the query to a variable using the **Query** method URL from the request:

    ```
    vl := r.URL.Query()
    ```

7. The **Query** method on the **URL** object of the request returns a **map[string][]string** with all the parameters sent through the **querystring** in the URL. We then assign this map to a variable, **vl**.

8. At this point, we need to get the value of a specific parameter called **name**, so we get the value from the **name** parameter:

```
name, ok := v1["name"]
```

9. As you can see, we have an assignment to two variables, but only one value comes from **v1["name"]**. The second variable, **ok**, is a Boolean that tells us whether the "**name**" key exists.

10. If the **name** parameter has not been passed and we want an error message to appear, add it if the variable is not found, in other words, if the **ok** variable is false:

```
if !ok {
    w.WriteHeader(400)
    w.Write([]byte("Missing name"))
    return
}
```

11. The conditional code gets called if the key does not exist in the slice, and it writes a **400** code (bad request) to the header, as well as a message to the response writer stating that the name has not been sent as a parameter. We stop the execution with a **return** statement to prevent further actions.

12. At this point, write the valid message to the response writer:

```
    w.Write([]byte(fmt.Sprintf("Hello %s", strings.Join(name, ","))))
}
```

13. This code formats a string and injects the name into it. The **fmt.Sprintf** function is used to format, while **strings.Join** is used in order to transform the **name** slice into a string. Notice that the **name** variable is set to the value of **v1["name"]**, but **v1** is a **map[string][]string**, which means that it is a map with string keys whose values are slices of strings; hence, **v1["name"]** is a slice of strings and needs to be transformed into a single string. The **strings.Join** function takes all the elements of the slice and builds a single string using "**,**" as a separator. Other characters could also have been used as separators.

14. The last part of the file you have to write is:

```
func main() {
    http.HandleFunc("/", Hello)
    log.Fatal(http.ListenAndServe(":8080", nil))
}
```

15. As always, a **main()** function is created, and then the **Hello** function is associated with the path **"/"** and the server started. Here is the output of three different URLs, two valid ones, and one with a missing parameter:

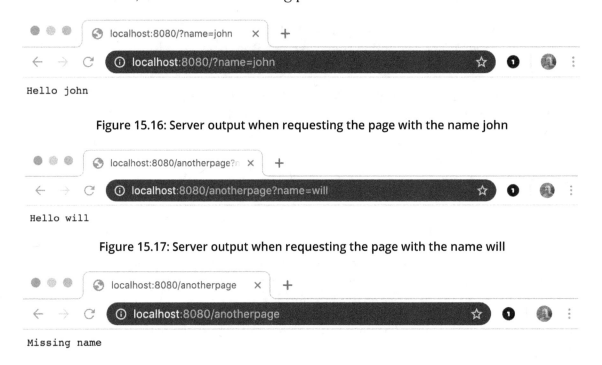

Figure 15.16: Server output when requesting the page with the name john

Figure 15.17: Server output when requesting the page with the name will

Figure 15.18: Server outputting an error message when requesting a page without a name

Templating

Although JSON can be the best choice when complex data structures have to be shared across software programs, this is not the case, in general, when the HTTP server is supposed to be consumed by humans. In the previous exercises and activities, the chosen way to format a text has been the **fmt.Sprintf** function, which is good for formatting texts, but is simply insufficient when a more dynamic and complex text is required. As you will have noticed in the previous exercise, the message returned in case a name was passed as a parameter to the URL observed a specific pattern, and this is where a new concept comes in – the template. A template is a skeleton from which complex entities can be developed. Essentially, a template is like a text with some blanks, and a template engine will take some values and fill the blanks, as you can see in the following diagram:

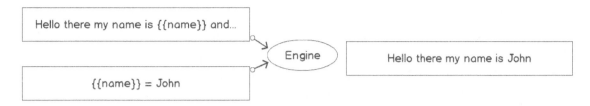

Figure 15.19: Templating example

As you can see, **{{name}}** is a placeholder and, when a value is passed through to the engine, the placeholder is modified with that value.

We see templates everywhere. We have templates for Word documents, where we just fill in what is missing to produce new documents that all differ from one another. A teacher might have some templates for their lessons and will develop different lessons from that same template. Go provides two different templating packages, one for texts and one for HTML. As we are working with HTTP servers and we want to produce a web page, we will use the HTML templating package, but the interface is the same for the text template library. Although the templating packages are good enough for any real-world application, there are also several other external packages that can be used in order to improve performance. One of these is the **hero** template engine, which is much faster than the standard Go templating package.

The Go templating package provides a placeholder language where we can use things such as:

```
{{name}}
```

A simple search and replace block, but more complex situations can be handled via conditionals:

```
{{if age}} Hello {{else}} bye {{end}}
```

Here, if an **age** parameter is not null, the template will have **Hello**; otherwise it has **bye**. Each conditional needs an **{{end}}** placeholder to determine its ending.

Variables in a template, however, do not need to be simple numbers or strings; they can be objects. In this case, if we have a struct with a field called **ID**, we can reference this field in the template this way:

```
{{.ID}}
```

This is very handy, meaning that we can pass a struct to the template instead of many single parameters.

In the next exercise, you will see how to use the basic templating functionalities of Go to create pages with custom messages, like you've done before, but just in a more elegant way.

Exercise 15.04: Templating Our Pages

The aim of this exercise is to build a more structured web page, use a template, and fill it with parameters from the URL's **querystring**. In this scenario, we want to display basic information for a customer and hide some information when the data is missing. A customer has an **id**, **name**, **surname**, and **age** and if any of these items of data are missing, they will not be displayed. Unless the data is the **id**, as in this case, an error message will be displayed:

1. Begin by creating a **server-template** folder with a **main.go** file as usual, and then add the usual package and some imports:

```
package main
import (
    "html/template"
    "log"
    "net/http"
    "strconv"
    "strings"
)
```

2. Here, we use two new imports, **"html/template"** for our templating, and **"strconv"** to convert strings into numbers (this package could also work the other way around, but there are better solutions for formatting text).

3. Now, write the following:

```
var tplStr = `
<html>
  <h1>Customer {{.ID}}
  {{if .ID }}
  <p>Details:</p>
  <ul>
  {{if .Name}}<li>Name: {{.Name}}</li>{{end}}
  {{if .Surname}}<li>Surname: {{.Surname}}</li>{{end}}
  {{if .Age}}<li>Age: {{.Age}}</li>{{end}}
  </ul>
  {{else}}
  <p>Data not available</p>
  {{end}}
</html>
`
```

4. This is a raw string that contains some HTML and templating code, which is wrapped by **{{}}** and which we will analyze now.

5. `{{.ID}}` is essentially a placeholder that tells the template engine that wherever this code is found, it will be substituted by a struct's attribute called `ID`. The Go templating engine works with structs, so essentially, a struct will be passed to the engine and its attributes' values will be used to fill the placeholders. `{{if .ID}}` is a conditional that tells the template that what happens next will depend on the value of `ID`. In this case, if `ID` is not an empty string, the template will display the customer's details, otherwise it will display the message `<p>Data not available</p>`, which is wrapped between the placeholders `{{else}}` and `{{end}}`. As you can see, there are many more conditionals nested inside the first one. At each list item, there is a `<li>` tag, which is wrapped, for example, by `{{if .Name}}` and terminated with `{{end}}`.

6. Now that we have a string template, let's create a struct with the correct attributes. To fill in the template, write the following:

```
type Customer struct {
    ID int
    Name string
    Surname string
    Age int
}
```

This struct is self-explanatory. It contains all the attributes needed by the template.

7. Define the handler function and set a variable to the map of values in the **querystring**:

```
func Hello(w http.ResponseWriter, r *http.Request) {
    vl := r.URL.Query()
```

8. Instantiate a **cust** variable of the **Customer** type:

```
cust := Customer{}
```

9. The variable now has all its attributes set to the default values, and we need to grab the passed values from the URL. In order to do so, write:

```
id, ok := vl["id"]
if ok {
    cust.ID, _ = strconv.Atoi(strings.Join(id, ","))
}
name, ok := vl["name"]
if ok {
    cust.Name = strings.Join(name, ",")
}
surname, ok := vl["surname"]
```

```
    if ok {
        cust.Surname = strings.Join(surname, ",")
    }
    age, ok := vl["age"]
    if ok {
        cust.Age, _ = strconv.Atoi(strings.Join(age, ""))
    }
```

10. As you can see, the parameters are taken as they are from the values map, and if they exist, they are used to set the value of the related **cust** attribute. In order to check whether these parameters exist, we again used the **ok** variable, which is set to a Boolean with a value of **true** in case the map contains the requested key. The last attribute, **Age**, is handled slightly differently:

```
    cust.Age, _ = strconv.Atoi(strings.Join(age, ""))
```

11. This is because **strconv.Atoi** returns an error in case the parameter passed is not really a number. In general, we should handle the errors but, in this case, we just ignore it and we won't display any age-related information if the age provided is not a number.

12. Next, write:

```
    tmpl, _ := template.New("test").Parse(tplStr)
```

13. This creates a template object with the name "**test**" and with the content of the string that you created at the outset. We again ignore the error as we are sure that the template we've written is a valid one. In production, however, all the errors should be dealt with.

14. You can now finish writing the function with:

```
        tmpl.Execute(w, cust)
    }
```

15. Here, the template is actually executed using the **cust** struct and the content is sent directly to **w ResponseWriter** without needing to call the **Write** method manually.

16. What is missing now is the **main** method, which is fairly simple. Write the following:

```
    func main() {
        http.HandleFunc("/", Hello)
        log.Fatal(http.ListenAndServe(":8080", nil))
    }
```

17. Here, simply speaking, the main path is associated with the **Hello** function and the server is then started.

18. The performance of this code is not very high as we create a template in every request. The template could be created in the **main** and then passed to a handler, which could have a **ServeHTTP** method like the **Hello** function you've just written. The code has been kept simple here in order to focus on templating.

19. If you now start the server and visit the following pages, you should see some output similar to the following:

Figure 15.20: Templated response with blank parameters

Now, you can add a query parameter called **id** and put it equal to **1** in the URL visiting this address: **localhost:8080/?id=1**:

Figure 15.21: Templated response with just the ID specified

Then, you can also add a value for the name parameter going to the address **localhost:8080/?id=1&name=John**:

Figure 15.22: Templated response with the ID and name specified

And finally, you can also add an age going to the address
`localhost:8080/?id=1&name=John&age=40`:

Customer 1

Details:

- **Name: john**
- **Age: 40**

Figure 15.23: Templated response with the ID, name, and age specified

Here, each parameter in the **querystring** is displayed, if valid, in the web application.

Static Resources

Everything you've learned so far in this book, up to the last exercise, is sufficient in order to build web applications and dynamic websites; you just need to put all the pieces together. What you've been doing in this chapter is returning messages that are different in nature, but that are all hardcoded as strings. Even dynamic messages have been based on templates hardcoded in the source file of the exercises and activities. Let's now consider something. In the case of the first "**hello world**" server, the message never changed. If we wanted to modify the message and return a "**Hello galaxy**" message, we would have to change the text in the code and then recompile and/or run the server again. What if you wanted to sell your simple "hello" server and give the option to everybody to specify a custom message? Of course, you should give the source code to everybody so that they could recompile and run the server. Although you might want to embrace open source code, this might not be the ideal way to distribute an application, and we need to find a better way to separate the message from the server. A solution to that is to serve static files, which are files loaded by your program as external resources. These files do not change and do not get compiled but are loaded and manipulated by your program. One such example may be templates, as seen before, because they are just text and you can use template files instead of adding the templates as text to your code. Another simple example of static resources are images that you want to include in your web page, or styling files such as CSS. You will see in the following exercises and activities how to do that. You'll be able to serve a specific file or a specific folder, and then you'll see how to serve dynamic files with a static template.

Exercise 15.05: Creating a Hello World Server Using a Static File

In this exercise, you will again create your hello world server but with the use of a static HTML file. What we want is to have a simple server with one handler function that looks for a specific file with a specific name, which will be served as the output for every path. In this case, you will need to create multiple files in your project:

1. Create a folder called **static-file** and, inside it, create a file called **index.html**. Then, insert inside this file the following code for a pretty simple HTML file with a title and an **h1** tag with our welcome message:

```
<!DOCTYPE html>
<html lang="en">
<head>
    <meta charset="UTF-8">
    <title>Welcome</title>
</head>
<body>
    <h1>Hello World</h1>
</body>
</html>
```

2. Now, create a file called **main.go** and start writing the necessary imports:

```
package main
import (
    "log"
    "net/http"
)
```

3. Now, write the **main** function:

```
func main() {
```

4. Now, write the **handler** function:

```
    http.HandleFunc("/", func (w http.ResponseWriter, r *http.Request) {
    http.ServeFile(w, r, "./index.html")
    })
```

5. This is where the magic happens. You can see a normal **http.HandleFunc** called with a **"/"** path as the first parameter, and then a handler function is passed, which contains a single instruction:

```
    http.ServeFile(w, r, "./index.html")
```

6. This essentially sends to **ResponseWriter** the content of the "**index.html**" file.

7. Now, write the last part:

```
    log.Fatal(http.ListenAndServe(":8080", nil))
}
```

8. As is always the case, this starts the server, logs in case of an error, and exits the program.

9. If you now save the file and you run the program with:

```
    go run main.go
```

And then you open your browser on the **localhost:8080** page, you should see the following:

Hello World

Figure 15.24: Hello world with a static template file

10. But now, without stopping your server, just change the HTML file, **index.html**, and modify line **8** where you see:

```
    <h1>Hello World</h1>
```

11. Change the text in the **<h1>** tag:

```
    <h1>Hello Galaxy</h1>
```

12. Save the **index.html** file and, without touching the terminal and without restarting your server, just refresh your browser on the same page, and you should now see the following:

Hello Galaxy

Figure 15.25: Hello world server with the static template file modified

13. So, even if the server is running, it will pick up the new version of the file.

In this exercise, you've seen how to use a static HTML file to serve a web page, and how detaching the static resources from your application makes you able to change your served page without restarting your application.

Getting Some Style

Up to now, you've seen how to serve one static page and you might consider serving a few pages with the same method, maybe creating a handler struct with the name of the file to serve as an attribute. This might be impractical for large numbers of pages, although, in some cases, it is necessary. A web page, however, does not include just HTML code, but also images and styles, and some frontend code. It is not within the scope of this book to teach how to build HTML pages, and even less how to write JavaScript code or CSS style sheets, but you need to know how to serve these documents as we use a small CSS file to build our example. Serving static files and putting templates in different files, or generally using external resources, is a good way to separate concerns on our projects, and makes our projects more manageable and maintainable, so you should try to follow this approach in all your projects.

In order to add a style sheet to your HTML pages, you need to add a tag like this:

```
<link rel="stylesheet" href="file.css">
```

This injects the CSS file into the page as a "stylesheet", but this is reported here just by way of an example, in case you are interested in learning how to write HTML.

You have also seen that we have served files, reading them from the filesystem one by one, but Go provides us with an easy function to do the job for us:

```
http.FileServer(http.Dir("./public"))
```

Essentially, **http.FileServer** creates what the name says: a server serving external files, and it takes them from the directory defined in **http.Dir**. Whatever file we put inside the "**./public**" directory will be automatically accessible, adding in the address bar:

```
http://localhost:8080/public/myfile.css
```

This seems good enough. However, in a real-world scenario, you do not want to expose your folder names and you want to specify a different name for your static resources. This is achieved as follows:

```
http.StripPrefix(
  "/statics/",
  http.FileServer(http.Dir("./public")),
  )
```

You may notice that the **http.FileServer** function is wrapped by an **http.StripPrefix** function that we use in order to associate the requested path with the correct files on the filesystem. Essentially, we want a path of the **/statics** form to be available and to bind it to the content of the **public** folder. The **StripePrefix** function will remove the **"/statics/"** prefix from the request and will pass it to the file server, which will just get the name of the file to serve and will search for it in the **public** folder. It is not necessary, if you do not want to change the name of the path and folder, to use these wrappers, but this solution is general and works everywhere, so you can utilize it in other projects without having to worry.

Exercise 15.06: A Stylish Welcome

The aim of this exercise is to display a welcome page, making use of some external static resources. We will adopt the same approach as in *Exercise 15.05*, but we will add some extra files and code. We will place some stylesheets in a **static** folder, and we will serve them so that they can be used by other pages served by the same server:

1. By way of a first step, create a folder called **stylish-welcome** and, inside this folder, add a file called **index.html** and incorporate the following content:

```
<!DOCTYPE html>
<html lang="en">
<head>
  <meta charset="UTF-8">
  <title>Welcome</title>
  <link rel="stylesheet" href="/statics/body.css">
  <link rel="stylesheet" href="/statics/header.css">
  <link rel="stylesheet" href="/statics/text.css">
</head>
<body>
  <h1>Hello World</h1>
  <p>May I give you a warm welcome</p>
</body>
</html>
```

2. As you can see, there are few differences compared with the previous HTML; we have a paragraph with some more text, wrapped by the **<p>** tag, and, inside the **<head>** tag, we include three links to external resources.

3. Now, create a folder called **public** inside your **stylish-welcome** folder and create three files therein with these names and content:

header.css

```css
h1 {
    color: brown;
}
```

body.css

```css
body {
    background-color: beige;
}
```

text.css

```css
p {
    color: coral;
}
```

4. Now, go back to your main project folder, **stylish-welcome**, and create the **main. go** file. The content at the start corresponds exactly to that in one of the previous exercises:

```go
package main
import (
    "log"
    "net/http"
)
func main() {
    http.HandleFunc("/", func (w http.ResponseWriter, r *http.Request) {
    http.ServeFile(w, r, "./index.html")
    })
```

5. Now, add the following code to handle the static files:

```go
http.Handle(
    "/statics/",
    http.StripPrefix(
    "/statics/",
    http.FileServer(http.Dir("./public")),
    ),
)
```

6. This code adds a handler to the "**/statics/**" path and it does so through an **http. FileServer** function, which returns a static file handler.

7. This function requires a directory to scrape, and we pass one to it as a parameter:

    ```
    http.Dir("./public")
    ```

8. This reads the local "**public**" folder that you created previously.

9. Now, add this final part to the file:

    ```
    log.Fatal(http.ListenAndServe(":8080", nil))
    }
    ```

10. Here again, the server gets created and the **main()** function is closed. If you now run your server, again with:

    ```
    go run main.go
    ```

11. You will now see the following:

Figure 15.26: Styled home page

So somehow, the HTML file is now getting the style from the style sheets you created at the beginning.

12. Let's now examine how the files are injected. If you look back at the **index.html** file, you will see these lines:

    ```
    <link rel="stylesheet" href="/statics/body.css">
    <link rel="stylesheet" href="/statics/header.css">
    <link rel="stylesheet" href="/statics/text.css">
    ```

13. So essentially, we are looking for files under the path **"/statics/"**. Hence, you can go to these addresses and you will see:

Figure 15.27: body CSS file

Figure 15.28: header CSS file

Figure 15.29: text CSS file

14. So, all the style sheets are served. Furthermore, you can even go here:

Figure 15.30: Static folder content visible in the browser

15. And see all the files inside the **public** folder, served under the **/statics/** path. You can see that if you are looking for a simple static files server, Go allows you, with the help of a few lines of code, to create one, and, with a few more lines, you can make it production-ready.

16. If you use Chrome, you can inspect with your mouse by right-clicking, or with any browser if you have a developer tool, and you will see something similar to this:

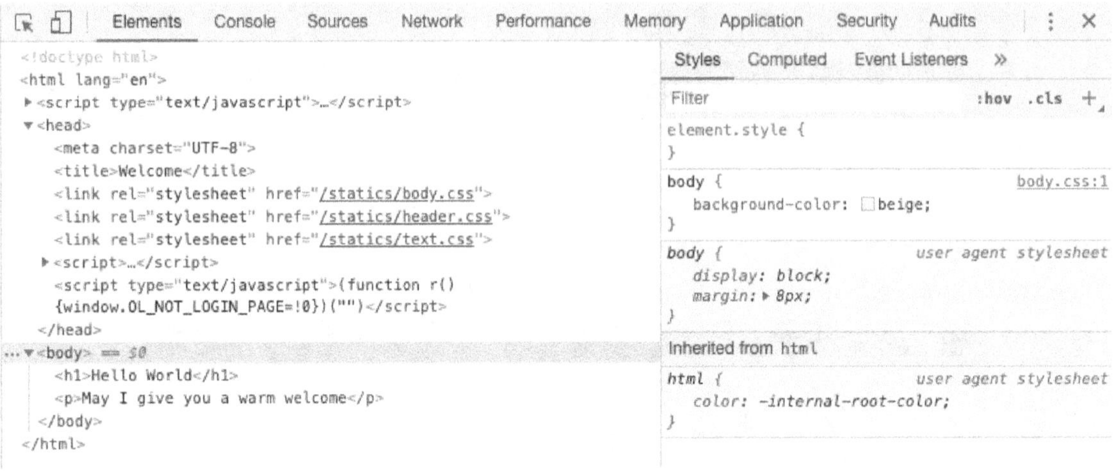

Figure 15.31: Developer tools showing loaded scripts

You can see that the files have been loaded and that the styles are shown as computed from the stylesheet on the right.

Getting Dynamic

Static assets are generally served as they are, but when you want to create a dynamic page, you might want to make use of an external template, which you can use on the fly, so that you can change the template without having to restart your server, or that you can load on startup, which means you will have to restart your server following any change (this is not strictly true, but we need some concepts of concurrent programming in order to make it happen). Loading a file at startup is executed simply for performance reasons. Filesystem operations are always the slowest, and even if Go is a fairly fast language, you might want to take performance into account when you want to serve your pages, especially if you have many requests from multiple clients.

As you will recall from a previous topic, we used the standard Go templates to make dynamic pages. Now, we can use the template as an external resource and put our template code in an HTML file and load it. The template engine can parse it and then fill the blanks with the passed parameters. To do this, we can use the **html/template** function:

```
func ParseFiles(filenames ...string) (*Template, error)
```

This can be called, for example, with:

```
template.ParseFiles("mytemplate.html")
```

In addition, the template is loaded in memory and is ready to be used.

Up to this point, you have been the sole user of your HTTP servers, but in an actual scenario, that is certainly not the case. In the following examples, we will look at performance and will use a resource loaded at startup.

Activity 15.03: External Template

In this activity, you will create a welcome server, like the ones you created before, and you will have to use the template package, as you've done before. In this activity, however, we do not want you to create your template from a hardcoded string but from an HTML file, which will contain all the template placeholders.

You should be able to complete this activity, making use of what you've learned so far in this chapter and in the previous one.

This activity returns a pointer to a **template** and an error from a list of filenames. The error gets returned if any of the files do not exist or if the format of the template is wrong. In any case, do not concern yourself with the possibility of adding multiple files. Stick with one.

Here are the steps to complete the activity:

1. Create a folder for your project.

2. Create a template with a name such as **index.html** and fill it with standard HTML code, with a welcome message and a placeholder for the name. Make sure that if the name is empty, the message inserts the word **visitor** where the name is supposed to be.

3. Create your **main.go** file and add to it the right package and imports.

4. In the **main.go** file, create a **struct** holding a name that can be passed to a template.

5. Create a template from a file using your **index.html** file.

6. Create something that's able to handle the HTTP requests and use the **querystring** to receive parameters and display the data through the template created previously.

7. Set all the paths to the server to use the function or handler created in the previous step and then create the server.

8. Run the server and check the result.

The output will be as follows:

Hello visitor

May I give you a warm welcome

Figure 15.32: Anonymous visitor page

And the visitor page including the name will look something like the following screenshot:

Hello Will

May I give you a warm welcome

Figure 15.33: Visitor page with the name "Will"

> **Note**
>
> The solution for this activity can be found on page 763.

In this activity, you learned how to create a templated HTTP handler as a struct that can be initialized with any external template. You can now create multiple pages, instantiating the same struct with different templates of your choice.

HTTP Methods

Up to this point, you've checked the results of your exercises and activities through your web browser, just visiting an address, your localhost, and getting some results back in the form of a web page. This way of consuming an HTTP server utilizes what is known as the **GET** method. You have seen the methods when you worked with the HTTP clients, which are the only way to use anything other than **GET** or **POST**. Through your web browser, however, you can also use the **POST** method, which is often used in order to send form data. It is possible to send form data through **GET**, but this method pollutes the URL with parameters and has some limitations in terms of the size of the data that can be sent.

There are other methods that are often used, these being **PUT** and **DELETE**, but you need a specific client to utilize them. That is why a set of these four methods is used in order to build what is called a **REST** API. There are other methods, but it is beyond the scope of this book to dig into all the HTTP methods, focusing instead on the ones that are most commonly used. A **REST** API is essentially a set of *paths* and methods that respond to specific requests. An HTTP server exposing a **REST** API is called a **REST server**. In order to understand why different methods are available, you need to understand how are they used. If you need to request some data, you are trying to get this data back, hence, the **GET** method is the most appropriate. If, instead, you want to modify a resource you are already familiar with, you want to put some specific values in a known location, you will use the **PUT** method, which essentially changes the state of the server in a known place. If you need to somehow modify the state of the server, you need to search for the resources to modify. For example, if you do not know their IDs, you will use the **POST** method. This is why you will often find online that the most common explanation for when to use **POST** and **PUT** is that the former is used to add resources, while the latter is used to update resources. Although this is most often true, it is not always the case, as you may also perform updates with the **POST** method.

In the next exercise, you will see how to use the different methods, **GET** and **POST**, to do different things with the same function. Note that in general, you might use more sophisticated external libraries to have more elegant code, but here, we are looking at how to do the basics and show how the standard Go library already offers us much in terms of helping us to do our work.

Exercise 15.07: Completing a Questionnaire

In this exercise, you will build a form and you will send the data to another page. The form will contain questions such as your name, surname, and age, and this data will be sent to another page, which will display them. You will make use of what you've already learned, plus you'll see how to grab **posted** parameters from your **HTTP** request.

1. First of all, create a folder called **questionnaire** and, inside this folder, incorporate a file called **index.html** with the following content:

```html
<!DOCTYPE html>
<html lang="en">
<head>
  <meta charset="UTF-8">
  <title>Welcome</title>
</head>
<body>
  <h1>Details</h1>
  <ul>
  <li>Name: {{.Name}}</li>
  <li>Surname: {{.Surname}}</li>
  <li>Age: {{.Age}}</li>
  </ul>
</body>
</html>
```

2. This is a normal template displaying items of personal information. If any data is missing, we simply display it as empty strings without hiding them.

3. Now, create a file called **form.html** and add the following content:

```html
<!DOCTYPE html>
<html lang="en">
<head>
  <meta charset="UTF-8">
  <title>Form</title>
</head>
<body>
  <form method="post" action="/">
  <ul>
   <li>Name: <input type="text" name="name"></li>
  <li>Surname: <input type="text" name="surname"></li>
  <li>Age: <input type="text" name="age"></li>
  <li><input type="submit" name="send" value="send"></li>
  </ul>
```

```
    </form>
  </body>
</html>
```

4. This is another page inside a form, with three text inputs and a button. The input fields represent the details we want to send. Note that the form has the action set to "/", which means that when clicking the button, the page gets redirected to the main path, but will transport the dataset in the form. The method attribute is set to **post,** which is the HTTP method discussed earlier.

5. You now have to create the actual server in Go. Create a `main.go` file and add the following:

```
package main
import (
    "html/template"
    "log"
    "net/http"
)
```

6. Then, create the struct for the template:

```
type Visitor struct {
    Name string
    Surname string
    Age string
}
```

This holds all the attributes required for the template.

7. Then, execute the following command:

```
type Hello struct {
    tpl *template.Template
}
```

This holds the template, as seen previously.

8. At this point, you need to create the **handler** function for the handler, so add the following:

```
func (h Hello) ServeHTTP(w http.ResponseWriter, r *http.Request) {
    vst := Visitor{}
```

Here, a new empty visitor is created.

9. Check whether the request is a **Post** request, so you need to add:

```
if r.Method == http.MethodPost {
```

This checks the method against a constant provided by the Go **http** package.

10. Parse the form:

```
err := r.ParseForm()
if err != nil {
w.WriteHeader(400)
return
}
```

11. If an error occurs when parsing the form, we return with a **400** code, which is a bad request.

12. If the form gets parsed correctly, we can proceed, so add the following:

```
vst.Name =  r.Form.Get("name")
vst.Surname = r.Form.Get("surname")
vst.Age = r.Form.Get("age")
}
```

Here, all the parameters from the form get assigned to the visitor's attribute. We then close the **if** statement and go to the common part of the handler function.

13. As we have a visitor, empty or not depending on whether the form has been posted and with what values, we can finally return the page, so write:

```
h.tpl.Execute(w, vst)
}
```

14. We need to have a way to create the handler, so, as you've done before, add the following function:

```
func NewHello(tplPath string) (*Hello, error){
    tmpl, err := template.ParseFiles(tplPath)
    if err != nil {
    return nil, err
    }
    return &Hello{tmpl}, nil
}
```

15. At this point, you can write the **main()** function, which creates the handler, assigns it to the main path, and then assigns the static **form.html** file to the **/form** path:

```
func main() {
    hello, err := NewHello("./index.html")
    if err != nil {
    log.Fatal(err)
    }
    http.Handle("/", hello)
    http.HandleFunc("/form", func(writer http.ResponseWriter, request *http.Request)
{
    http.ServeFile(writer, request, "./form.html")
    })
    log.Fatal(http.ListenAndServe(":8080", nil))
}
```

16. Run your server, you will see the following by going to the main page:

Details

- Name:
- Surname:
- Age:

Figure 15.34: Empty details page

17. If you go to the **/form** path, you'll see:

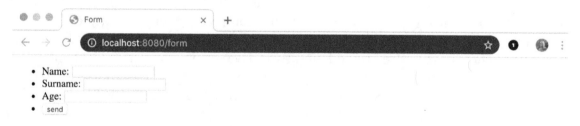

- Name:
- Surname:
- Age:
- send

Figure 15.35: Empty form page

18. And if you fill the data:

Figure 15.36: Filled form page

19. And then press the **send** button, you will be redirected to this page:

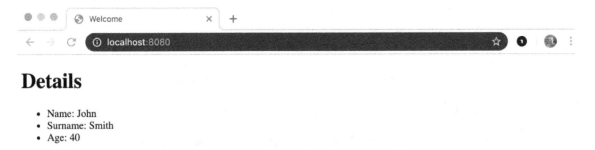

Figure 15.37: Page with details added

This, again, is the main page with the details set via the parameters you put into the form.

JSON loads

Not all HTTP servers are meant to be used by a browser and a human user. Very often, we have different software programs communicating with each other. These programs need to send messages to one another through a commonly accepted format, one of these being JSON. This stands for JavaScript Object Notation, which essentially means that it mimics how objects are created directly in JavaScript (another programming language). It is a simple format, not particularly verbose, and is easy to parse by a piece of software and easy to read for a human. As a user, however, you can use any one of the many tools to send and receive JSON payloads, two of the most common ones being **Insomnia** and **Postman**, which you can easily find online at https://packt.live/2RY13Dt and https://packt.live/2RY13Dt.

They are both free and available for different platforms. You could also use `curl` as a command-line tool, but this becomes more complicated.

Exercise 15.08: Building a Server That Accepts JSON Requests

In this exercise, you will build a server that accepts a JSON message and will respond with another JSON message. You will not be able to use your browser to test it, but you can do it with a client such as **Insomnia** or **Postman**. The example screenshots will be provided using **Insomnia**, so it would be good for you to use the same. The server you will build accepts a message with a name and surname, and returns a message with some personalized greetings:

1. Create a folder called **json-server** and add a file to it called **main.go**. Start adding packages and imports to the file:

```
package main
import (
    "encoding/json"
    "fmt"
    "log"
    "net/http"
)
```

Here, the packages imported are customary for HTTP programming, for logging, for formatting strings, and, of course, for JSON encoding.

2. After this, you need to create models for the incoming and outcoming messages, so write the following:

```
type Request struct {
    Name string
    Surname string
}
type Response struct {
    Greeting string
}
```

These are pretty straightforward structs, including only what we need.

3. Now, add the **main** function:

```
func main() {
```

4. And now set the function to handle the JSON messages:

```
http.HandleFunc("/", func(wr http.ResponseWriter, req *http.Request) {
decoder := json.NewDecoder(req.Body)
```

As you can see, the first thing inside the function is to create a JSON decoder, which will decode the request's body.

5. As a next step, write the following:

```
var data Request
err := decoder.Decode(&data)
if err != nil {
    wr.WriteHeader(400)
    return
}
```

6. Here, we define a data variable of the **Request** type and we decode the body of the HTTP request into it. In case of any error, we return a **400** code for a bad request.

7. Once the data has been decoded correctly, you can now use this data to create the response:

```
rsp := Response{Greeting: fmt.Sprintf("Hello %s %s", data.Name, data.Surname)}
```

8. Here, the name and surname from the request are combined in a personalized greeting message.

9. All that is now left is to send the message back to the requester:

```
bts, err := json.Marshal(rsp)
if err != nil {
wr.WriteHeader(400)
    return
}
wr.Write(bts)
})
```

10. Here, the response is encoded into a JSON string and is sent, writing it as a slice of bytes into the response writer. You can now run the server and open **Insomnia**:

11. Now, create the **main()** function to serve the pages:

```
func main() {
    http.HandleFunc("/", Hello)
    log.Fatal(http.ListenAndServe(":8080", nil))
}
```

Running the preceding code produces the following output:

Figure 15.38: Insomnia response

As you can see, you can make a **post** request with Insomnia and send a JSON string to your server. On the right, you will see the response as a JSON document.

Summary

In this chapter, you've been introduced to the server side of web programming. You've learned how to accept requests from HTTP clients and respond in an appropriate manner. You've learned how to separate the possible requests into different areas of an HTTP server via paths and sub-paths. For this, you used a simple routing mechanism with the standard **Go HTTP** package. You've seen how to return your response in order to suit different consumers: JSON responses for synthetic clients, and HTML pages for human access. You've seen how to use templates in order to format your plain text and HTML messages, using the standard templating package. You've learned how to serve and use static resources, serving them directly through a default file server or through a template object. You've also learned what a **REST** service is, and although we have not built one together, you have all the knowledge necessary to create one, provided you follow the description you've been given. At this stage, you know all the basics for building production-grade HTTP servers, although you might want to use some external libraries to facilitate your hello world example, facilitating better routing by using something such as **gorilla mux** or, generally, the entire **gorilla** package, which is a low-level abstraction on top of the **http** package. You could use **hero** as a template engine to make your page rendering faster. One thing to mention is that you can make pretty much stateless services with what you've learned in this chapter, but you cannot create a production-grade stateful server at the moment as you do not know how to handle concurrent requests. This means that our **views counter** is not suitable for a production server yet, but this will be the subject of another chapter.

In the next chapter, you will see how Go leverages the system of Goroutines to handle multiple work at the same time. This feature is very important, and you can apply it to HTTP servers and other types of projects where you have many concurrent users or whenever you want to do a lot of things at the same time.

16

Concurrent Work

Overview

This chapter introduces you to the Go features that will allow you to perform concurrent work, or, in other words, achieve concurrency. The first feature you will learn is called a Goroutine. You'll learn what a Goroutine is and how you can use it to achieve concurrency. Then, you'll learn how to utilize WaitGroups to synchronize the execution of several Goroutines. You will also learn how to implement synchronized and thread-safe changes to variables shared across different Goroutines using atomic changes. To synchronize more complex changes, you will work with mutexes.

Later in the chapter, you will experiment with the functionalities of channels and use message tracking to track the completion of a task.

Introduction

There is software that's meant to be used by a single user, and most of what you've learned so far in this book allows you to develop such applications. There is other software, however, that is meant to be used by several users at the same time. An example of this is a web server. You created web servers in *Chapter 15, HTTP Servers*. They are designed to serve websites or web applications that are generally used by thousands of users at the same time.

When multiple users are accessing a web server, it sometimes needs to perform a series of actions that are totally independent and whose result is the only thing that matters to the final output. All these situations call for a type of programming in which different tasks can be executed at the same time, independently from each other. Some languages allow parallel computation, where tasks are computed simultaneously. However, in some languages, such as Go, tasks are accomplished by the machine one piece per task; that is, each task, or process, is split into small pieces, and the program will execute a small piece of task at a time, until all the tasks are completed. This is known as concurrent programming.

In concurrent programming, when a task starts, all the other tasks start as well, but instead of completing them one by one, the machine performs a bit of each task at the same time. While Go allows concurrent programming, tasks can also be performed in parallel when the machine has multiple cores. From the perspective of the programmer, however, this distinction is not that important, as the tasks are created with the idea that they will be performed in parallel, and in whatever way the machine will perform them. Let's find out more in this chapter.

Goroutines

Imagine several people have some nails to hammer into a wall. Each person has a different number of nails and a different area of the wall, but there is only one hammer. Each person uses the hammer for one nail, then passes the hammer to the next person, and so on. The person with the fewest nails will finish earlier but they will all share the same hammer; this is how Goroutines work.

Using Goroutines, Go allows multiple tasks to run at the same time (they are also called coroutines). These are routines (read tasks) that can co-run inside the same process but are totally concurrent. Goroutines do not share memory, which is why they are different from threads. However, we will see how easy it is to pass variables across them in your code, and how this might lead to some unexpected behavior.

Writing a Goroutine is nothing special; they are just normal functions. Actually, each function can easily become a Goroutine; all we have to do is to write the word **go** before calling the function.

Let's consider a function called **hello**:

```
func hello() {
    fmt.Println("hello world")
}
```

In order to call our function as a Goroutine, we do the following:

```
go hello()
```

The function will run as a Goroutine. What this means can be understood better through the following code:

```
func main() {
    fmt.Println("Start")
    go hello()
    fmt.Println("End")
```

The code starts by printing **Start**, then it calls the **hello()** function. Then, the execution goes straight to printing **End** without waiting for the **hello()** function to complete. No matter how long it takes to run the **hello()** function, the **main()** function will not care about the **hello()** function as these functions will run independently. In order to better understand how this works, let's do some exercises.

> **Note**
>
> The important thing to remember is that Go is not a parallel language, but concurrent, which means that Goroutines do not work in an independent manner, but each Goroutine is split into smaller parts and each Goroutine runs one of its subparts at a time.

Exercise 16.01: Using Concurrent Routines

Let's imagine we want to make two calculations. First, we sum all the numbers from **1** to **10**, then the numbers from **1** to **100**. In order to save time, we want to make both of these calculations happen independently and see both results at the same time.

1. Create a new folder in your filesystem, and, inside it, create a **main.go** file and write the following:

```
package main
import "fmt"
```

2. Create a function to sum two numbers:

```
func sum(from,to int) int {
    res := 0
    for i:=from;i<=to; i++ {
        res += i
    }
    return res
}
```

This accepts two integers as extremes (the minimum and maximum of an interval) and returns the sum of all the numbers in the range between these two extremes.

3. Create the **main()** function, which sums the numbers **1** and **100**, then print the result:

```
func main() {
    s1 := sum(1,100)
    fmt.Println(s1)
}
```

4. Run the program:

```
go run main.go
```

You will see the following output:

```
5050 55
```

5. Now, let's introduce some concurrency. Modify the **main()** function to look like this:

```
func main() {
    var s1 int
    go func() {
        s1 = sum(1,100)
    }()
    fmt.Println(s1)
}
```

Here, we are running an anonymous function that assigns the value **s1** to the sum as before, but, if we run the code, the result will be **0**. If you try to remove the term **go** before the **func()** part, you will see that the result is **5050**. In this case, the anonymous function will run and start summing the numbers, but then there is a call to **fmt.Println**, which prints the value of **s1**. Here, the program waits for the **sum()** function to end before printing the value of **s1**, hence returning the correct result.

If we call the function and prepend the **go** word, the program prints the current value of **s1** while the function is still computing the sum, which is still **0**, and terminates.

Let's call the **sum** function twice with two different ranges. Modify the **main()** function:

```
func main() {
    var s1,s2 int
    go func() {
        s1 = sum(1,100)
    }()
    s2 = sum(1,10)
    fmt.Println(s1, s2)
}
```

If you run this program, it will print the numbers **0** and **55**. This is because the concurrent function, **go func()**, does not have the time to return the result. The **main()** function is faster as it just has to count to **55** and not **5050**, so the program terminates before the concurrent function is finished.

To solve this problem, we want to find a way to wait for the *concurrent* function to finish. There are some correct ways to do this but, for now, let's do something quite crude but effective, which is to wait for a fixed amount of time. In order to do so, just add this line before the **fmt.Println** command:

```
time.Sleep(time.Second)
```

6. If your IDE does not do it for you, modify the **import** section, just below the **package main** instruction, to look as follows:

```
import (
    "log"
    "time"
)
```

If you run your program now, you should see **5050 55** printed on the screen.

7. In the **main()** function, write code for the log to be printed:

```
log.Println(s1, s2)
```

8. If you run your program now, you will see the same output again, **5050 55**, but prepended by a timestamp representing when you ran the code:

```
2019/10/28 19:23:00 5050 55
```

As you can see, the calculations have happened concurrently, and we have received both the outputs at the same time.

> **Note**
>
> The full code for this exercise is available at: https://packt.live/2Qek69K

WaitGroup

In the previous exercise, we used a not-so-elegant method to ensure that the Goroutine ends by making the main routine wait for a second. The important thing to understand is that even if a program does not explicitly use Goroutines via the **go** call, it still uses one Goroutine, which is the main routine. When we run our program and create a new Goroutine, we are running two Goroutines: the main one and the one we just created. In order to synchronize these two Goroutines, Go gives us a function called `WaitGroup`. You can define a WaitGroup using the following code:

```
wg := sync.WaitGroup{}
```

WaitGroup needs the **sync** package to be imported. A typical code using the WaitGroup will be something like this:

```
package main
import "sync"
func main() {
  wg := &sync.WaitGroup{}
  wg.Add(1)
  ..................
  wg.Wait()
  ...........
  ...........
}
```

Here, we create a pointer to a new WaitGroup, then we mention that we are adding an asynchronous operation that adds 1 to the group using `wg.Add(1)`. This is essentially a counter holding the number of all the concurrent routines that are running. Later, we add the code that will actually run the concurrent call. At the end, we tell the WaitGroup to wait for the Goroutines to end using `wg.Wait()`.

How does the wait group know that the routines are complete? Well, we need to explicitly tell the WaitGroup about it inside the Goroutine with the following:

```
wg.Done()
```

This must be inside the main Goroutine function, which means it needs a reference to the WaitGroup. We will see this in the next exercise.

Exercise 16.02: Experimenting with WaitGroup

Let's say we calculate the addition in *Exercise 16.01, Using Concurrent Routines*, again using a Goroutine that runs concurrently with the main process. However, this time, we want to use a **WaitGroup** to synchronize the results. We have a few changes to make. Essentially, the **sum()** function needs to accept a new parameter for the **WaitGroup**, and there is no need to use the **time** package.

1. Create a new folder and a **main.go** file inside it. The package and import parts of your file will be as follows:

```
package main
import (
    "log"
    "sync"
)
```

Here, we just define the package as the **main** package, and then we import the **log** and **sync** packages. **log** will be used again to print out messages and **sync** will be used for the **WaitGroup**.

2. Next, write the **sum** function:

```
func sum(from,to int, wg *sync.WaitGroup, res *int) {
```

Now, we add a parameter called **wg** with a pointer to the **sync.WaitGroup** along with the result parameter. In the previous exercise, we wrapped the **sum** function with an anonymous function that ran as a Goroutine. Here, we want to avoid that, but we need to somehow get the result of the **sum** function. Hence, we pass an extra parameter as a pointer that will return the correct value.

3. Create a loop to increment the **sum** function:

```
*res = 0
for i:=from;i<=to; i++ {
    *res += i
}
```

Here, we set the value of what is held by the **res** pointer to **0**, then we just use the same loop that we saw earlier, but again associating the **sum** with the value pointed by the **res** parameter.

4. We can now complete this function:

```
wg.Done()
   return
}
```

Here, we tell the **WaitGroup** that this Goroutine is completed and then we return.

5. Now, let's write the **main()** function, which will set up the variables and then run the Goroutine that calculates the **sum**. We will then wait for the Goroutine to finish and display the result:

```
func main() {
    s1 := 0
    wg := &sync.WaitGroup{}
```

Here, the **main()** function is defined, and then a variable called **s1** is set to **0**. Also, a pointer to the WaitGroup is created.

6. Add one to the count of the WaitGroup and then run the Goroutine:

```
    wg.Add(1)
    go sum(1,100, wg, &s1)
```

This code notifies the WaitGroup that there is one Goroutine running and then creates a new Goroutine calculating the **sum**. The **sum()** function will call the.**Done()** method to notify the **WaitGroup** of its completion.

7. We need to wait for the Goroutine to finish. To do so, write the following:

```
    wg.Wait()
    log.Println(s1)
}
```

This also logs the result to the standard output.

8. Run the program:

```
go run main.go
```

You will see the log output for the function using WaitGroups, as follows, with the timestamp:

```
2019/10/28 19:24:51 5050
```

With this exercise, we have explored the functionality of `WaitGroup` by synchronizing Goroutines in our code.

Race Conditions

One important thing to consider is that whenever we run multiple functions concurrently, we have no guarantee in what order each instruction in each function will be performed. In many architectures, this is not a problem. Some functions are not connected in any way with other functions, and whatever a function does in its routine does not affect the actions performed in other routines. This is, however, not always true. The first situation we can think of is when some functions need to share the same parameter. Some functions will just read from this parameter, while others will write to this parameter. As we do not know which operation will run first, there is a high likelihood that one function will override the value updated by another function. Let's see an example that explains this situation:

```
func next(v *int) {
    c := *v
    *v = c+1
}
```

This function takes a pointer to an integer as a parameter. It is a pointer because we want to run several Goroutines with the **next** function and update v. If we run the following code, we would expect that **a** will hold the value 3:

```
a := 0
next(&a)
next(&a)
next(&a)
```

This is perfectly fine. However, what if we run the following code:

```
a := 0
go next(&a)
go next(&a)
go next(&a)
```

In this case, we might see that **a** holds 3, or 2, or 1. Why would this happen? Because when a function executes the following statement, the value of **v** might be 0 for all the functions running in independent Goroutines:

```
c := *v
```

If this happens, then each function will set **v** to **c+1**, which means none of the routines are aware of what the other routines are doing and override any changes made by another routine. This problem is called a *race condition* and happens every time we work with shared resources without taking precautions. Fortunately, we have several ways to prevent this situation and to make sure that the same change is made only once. We will look at these solutions in the next sections, and we will explore the situation we just described in more detail, with a proper solution and race detection.

Atomic Operations

Let's imagine we want to run independent functions again. However, in this case, we want to modify the value held by a variable. We still want to sum the numbers from 1 to 100, but we want to split the work into two concurrent Goroutines. We can sum the numbers from 1 to 50 in one routine and the numbers from 51 to 100 in another routine. At the end, we will need still to receive the value of 5050, but two different routines can add a number at the same time to the same variable. Let's see an example with only 4 numbers where we want to sum 1, 2, 3, and 4, and the result is 10.

Think of it like having a variable called **s:=0** and then making a loop where the value of **s** becomes the following:

```
s=0
s=1
s=3 //(1+2)
s=6
s=10
```

However, we could also have the following loop. In this case, the order in which the numbers are summed is different:

```
S=0
s=1
s=4 //3+1, the previous value of 1
s=6 //2+4 the previous value of 4
s=10
```

Essentially, this is just the commutative property of the sum, but this gives us a hint that we can actually split the sum into two or more concurrent calls. The problem that arises here is that all the functions need to manipulate the same variable, **s**, which can lead to *race conditions* and incorrect final values. A *race condition* happens when two processes change the same variable and one process overrides the changes made by another process without taking into account the previous change. Thankfully, we have a package called *atomic*, which allows us to safely modify variables across Goroutines.

We will take a look at how this package works soon, but, for now, all you need to know is that this package has some functions for executing simple concurrent safe operations on variables. Let's look at an example:

```
func AddInt32(addr *int32, delta int32) (new int32)
```

This code takes a pointer to **int32** and modifies it by adding the value it points at to the value of **delta**. If **addr** holds a value of 2 and **delta** is 4, after calling this function, **addr** will hold 6.

Exercise 16.03: An Atomic Change

In this exercise, we want to calculate the sum of all the numbers between 1 and 100 but with more concurrent Goroutines, let's say 4. So, we have one function summing in the range of 1-25, one in the range of 26-50, then 51-75, and finally 76-100. We will use what we've learned about atomic operations and WaitGroups.

1. Create a new folder and a **main.go** file. Inside it, write the following code:

    ```
    package main
    import (
        "log"
        "sync"
        "sync/atomic"
    )
    ```

    This will import the same packages used for the previous exercises, in addition to the **sync/atomic** package.

2. The next step is to refactor the **sum** function from *Exercise 16.02, Experimenting with WaitGroup*, to use the **atomic** package:

    ```
    func sum(from,to int, wg *sync.WaitGroup, res *int32) {
    ```

    Here, we just changed **res** from **int** to ***int32**. The reason for this is that the **atomic** operations available specifically for arithmetic operations only work on **int32/64** and relative **uint32/64**.

3. At this point, write a loop to add each number to the total:

    ```
    for i:=from;i<=to; i++ {
        atomic.AddInt32(res, int32(i))
    }
    wg.Done()
    return
    }
    ```

As you can see, instead of assigning the value of **res** as **0**, we are now adding **i** to the total value held by **res**. The rest of the code is unchanged.

4. The next step is to write the **main()** function to calculate the **sum** in four different Goroutines:

```
func main() {
    s1 := int32(0)
    wg := &sync.WaitGroup{}
```

Here, we set **s1** to an **int32** type rather than **int** so we can send it as a parameter to the **sum** function. Then we create the pointer to WaitGroup.

5. Now, tell the WaitGroup that we will have four Goroutines running:

```
wg.Add(4)
```

6. Now, run four Goroutines performing the sum over four ranges: 1-25, 26-50, 51-75, and 76-100:

```
go sum(1,25, wg, &s1)
go sum(26,50, wg, &s1)
go sum(51,75, wg, &s1)
go sum(76,100, wg, &s1)
```

7. Now, add the code that waits for the routines to complete and print the result:

```
wg.Wait()
log.Println(s1)
}
```

8. Now, if you run the code with the following:

```
go run main.go
```

You will see something like this:

```
2019/10/28 19:26:04 5050
```

The actual date will be different because it depends on when you run this code.

9. Now, let's test the code. We will use it in order to show you what it means to have a race condition, and why we use this atomic package, and what concurrency safety is. Here is the test code:

```
package main
import (
    "bytes"
    "log"
    "testing"
```

```
    )
    func Test_Main(t *testing.T) {
        for i:=0;i < 10000; i++ {
            var s bytes.Buffer
            log.SetOutput(&s)
            log.SetFlags(0)
            main()
            if s.String() != "5050\n" {
                t.Error(s.String())
            }
        }
    }
```

We will run the same test 10,000 times.

10. Run your test:

```
go test
```

The result of the test on atomic changes is as follows:

```
PASS
Ok      parallelwork/ex3      0.048s
```

11. And now add the **race** flag:

```
go test -race
```

The output when running these tests with the **race** flag is as follows:

```
PASS
Ok      parallelwork/ex3      3.417s
```

Again, everything is fine so far.

12. Let's now remove the **sync/atomic** import and modify the **sum** function where you see this line:

```
atomic.AddInt32(res, int32(i))
```

13. Change it to this:

```
*res = *res + int32(i)
```

14. Now run your program:

```
go run main.go
```

15. The log output for a non-atomic change stays the same when using pointers:

```
2019/10/28 19:30:47 5050
```

16. But if you try running the test multiple times, you may see some different results, even though, in this case, that is quite unlikely. At this point, however, try running the tests with the **-race** flag:

```
go test -race main.go
```

You will see the following output:

```
------------------
WARNING: DATA RACE
Read at 0x00c00008a080 by goroutine 8:
  parallelwork/ex3.sum()
      /Users/deliodanna/goprojects/Get-Ready-To-Go/lesson16/ex3/main.go:11 +0x4a

Previous write at 0x00c00008a080 by goroutine 7:
  parallelwork/ex3.sum()
      /Users/deliodanna/goprojects/Get-Ready-To-Go/lesson16/ex3/main.go:11 +0x5e

Goroutine 8 (running) created at:
  parallelwork/ex3.main()
      /Users/deliodanna/goprojects/Get-Ready-To-Go/lesson16/ex3/main.go:24 +0x12a
  parallelwork/ex3.Test_Main()
      /Users/deliodanna/goprojects/Get-Ready-To-Go/lesson16/ex3/main_test.go:15 +0xe6
  testing.tRunner()
      /usr/local/Cellar/go/1.12.5/libexec/src/testing/testing.go:865 +0x163

Goroutine 7 (finished) created at:
  parallelwork/ex3.main()
      /Users/deliodanna/goprojects/Get-Ready-To-Go/lesson16/ex3/main.go:23 +0xec
  parallelwork/ex3.Test_Main()
      /Users/deliodanna/goprojects/Get-Ready-To-Go/lesson16/ex3/main_test.go:15 +0xe6
  testing.tRunner()
      /usr/local/Cellar/go/1.12.5/libexec/src/testing/testing.go:865 +0x163
------------------
```

Figure 16.1: Race conditions arise when using the pointer here

Note

'GCC' must be installed in order to run this code.

17. Now, let's run the code without the **race** flag:

```
→ ex3 git:(master) × go test
--- FAIL: Test_Main (0.03s)
    main_test.go:18: 5024

    main_test.go:18: 4534

    main_test.go:18: 4100

    main_test.go:18: 4440

    main_test.go:18: 4516

    main_test.go:18: 4878

    main_test.go:18: 4915

    main_test.go:18: 2850

    main_test.go:18: 4903

    main_test.go:18: 4725

    main_test.go:18: 3475

    main_test.go:18: 3741

    main_test.go:18: 4746

    main_test.go:18: 4896

    main_test.go:18: 4978

    main_test.go:18: 4845

    main_test.go:18: 5001

    main_test.go:18: 4935

    main_test.go:18: 4465

    main_test.go:18: 4091

    main_test.go:18: 3655

    main_test.go:18: 4791

    main_test.go:18: 4636

    main_test.go:18: 4978

FAIL
exit status 1
FAIL    parallelwork/ex3        0.038s
```

Figure 16.2: Stack trace with racing conditions

By running the code several times, you can see different results because each routine can change the value of **s1** at any time and in any order, which we cannot know in advance.

In this exercise, you've learned how to use the atomic package to safely modify variables shared by multiple Goroutines. You've learned how direct access to the same variable from different Goroutines can be dangerous and how to use the atomic package to avoid this situation.

> **Note**
>
> The full code for this exercise is available at https://packt.live/35UXbqD.

Invisible Concurrency

We've seen in the previous exercise, the effects of concurrency through race conditions, but we want to see them in practice. It is easy to understand that concurrency problems are difficult to visualize as they do not manifest in the same way every time we run a program. That's why we are focusing on finding ways to synchronize concurrent work. One easy way to visualize it, however, but that is difficult to use in tests, is to print out each concurrent routine and see the order in which these routines are called. In the previous exercise, for example, we could have sent another parameter with a name and printed the name of the function at each iteration in the **for** loop.

If we want to see the effects of concurrency and still be able to test it, we could use the atomic package again, this time with strings so that we can build a string containing a message from each Goroutine. For this scenario, we will use the **sync** package again, but we will not make use of the atomic operations. Instead, we will use a new struct called the **mutex**. Mutex is short for "mutual exclusion" and is essentially a way to stop all the routines, run the code in one, and then carry on with the concurrent code. Let's see how we can use it. First of all, it needs the **sync** package to be imported. Then, we create a mutex like this:

```
mtx := sync.Mutex{}
```

But most of the time we want to pass a mutex across several functions, so we'd better create a pointer to a mutex:

```
mtx := &sync.Mutex{}
```

This ensures we use the same mutex everywhere. It is important to use the same mutex, but the reason why the mutex has to be only one will be clear after analyzing the methods in the Mutex struct; consider the following code:

```
mtx.Lock()
s = s + 5
```

The preceding code snippet will lock the execution of all the routines, except the one that will change the variable. At this point, we will add 5 to the current value of **s**. After this, we release the lock using the following command so that any other routine can modify the value of **s**.

```
mtx.Unlock()
```

From now on, any following code will run concurrently. We will see later some better ways to ensure safety when we modify a variable, but, for now, do not worry about adding much code between the lock/unlock part. The more code there is between these constructs, the less concurrent your code will be. So, you should lock the execution of the program, add only the logic required to ensure safety, and unlock and then carry on with the execution of the rest of the code, which does not touch the shared variables.

One important thing to notice is that the order of asynchronously performed code can change. This is because Goroutines run independently and you cannot know which one runs first. However, each routine runs completely before letting another one run. You should then not rely on Goroutines to order things correctly; you might need to order your results afterward if you need a specific order.

Activity 16.01: Listing Numbers

In this activity, you will need to build a string with all the numbers from 1 to 100. However, instead of using a single loop, you need to split the work across four loops, like in *Exercise 16.03*. Moreover, each loop will add the numbers in its own loop. Here are the steps:

1. Create a folder and a **main.go** file.

2. Create a function that takes a range in its parameters and a string to which you will add all the numbers in its range (also as strings).

3. Wrap each number with the character "**|**", for example, **|4|**, so that the list will have the form **|4||10|**.

4. Create the **main()** function where you will create four Goroutines, each one having a range of 25 numbers.

5. Make sure all the routines modify the same string safely.

6. Make sure the **main()** function will wait for the completion of the routines.

7. Print the final string and run the program.

You should be able to complete this activity using everything you've studied so far in this chapter.

When you run your program, you should see something like this:

```
→ activity1 git:(master) go run .
2019/10/28 19:40:36  |76||51||52||53||54||55||56||57||58||59||60||61||62||63||64||65||66||67||
68||69||70||71||72||73||74||75||1||2||3||4||5||6||7||8||9||10||11||12||13||14||15||16||17||18
||19||20||21||22||23||24||25||77||78||79||80||81||82||83||84||85||86||87||88||89||90||91||92|
|93||94||95||96||97||98||99||100||26||27||28||29||30||31||32||33||34||35||36||37||38||39||40|
|41||42||43||44||45||46||47||48||49||50|
```

Figure 16.3: First output when listing numbers

However, if you run it again multiple times, you will most likely see a different result:

```
→ activity1 git:(master) go run .
2019/10/28 19:42:20  |76||77||78||79||80||81||82||83||84||85||86||87||88||89||90||91||92||93||
94||95||96||97||98||99||100||26||27||28||29||30||31||32||33||34||35||36||37||38||39||40||41||
42||43||44||45||46||47||48||49||50||1||2||3||4||5||6||7||8||9||10||11||12||13||14||15||16||17
||18||19||20||21||22||23||24||25||51||52||53||54||55||56||57||58||59||60||61||62||63||64||65|
|66||67||68||69||70||71||72||73||74||75|
```

Figure 16.4: Second attempt of listing numbers returns with a different order

> **Note**
>
> The solution for this activity can be found on page 766.

Channels

We've seen how to create concurrent code via Goroutines, how to synchronize it with WaitGroup, how to perform atomic operations, and how to temporarily stop the concurrency in order to synchronize access to shared variables. We will now introduce a different concept, the channel, which is typical of Go. A channel is what the name essentially suggests – it's something where messages can be piped, and any routine can send or receive messages through a channel. Similar to a slice, a channel is created the following way:

```
var ch chan int
ch = make(chan int)
```

Of course, it is possible to instantiate the channel directly with the following:

```
ch := make(chan int)
```

Just like with slices, we can also do the following:

```
ch := make(chan int, 10)
```

Here, a channel is created with a buffer of 10 items.

A channel can be of any type, such as **integer**, **Boolean**, **float**, and any **struct** that can be defined, and even slices and pointers, though the last two are generally used less frequently.

Channels can be passed as parameters to functions, and that's how different Goroutines can share content. Let's see how to send a message to a channel:

```
ch <- 2
```

In this case, we send the value of 2 to the **ch** channel, which is a channel of integers. Of course, trying to send something else than an integer to an integer channel will cause an error.

After sending a message, we need to be able to receive a message from a channel. To do that, we can just do the following:

```
<- ch
```

Doing this ensures that the message is received; however, the message is not stored. It might seem useless to lose the message, but we will see that it might actually make sense. Nevertheless, we might want to keep the value received from the channel, and we can do so by storing the value into a new variable:

```
i := <- ch
```

Let's see a simple program that shows us how to use what we've learned so far:

```
package main
import "log"
func main() {
    ch := make(chan int,1)
    ch <- 1
    i:= <- ch
    log.Println(i)
}
```

This program essentially creates a new channel, pipes the integer 1 in, then reads it, and finally prints out the value of **i**, which should be 1. This code is not that useful in practice, but with a small change we can see something interesting. Let's make the channel unbuffered by changing the channel definition to the following:

```
ch := make(chan int)
```

If you run the code, you will get the following output:

```
fatal error: all goroutines are asleep - deadlock!
goroutine 1 [chan send]:
main.main()
    /Users/deliodanna/goprojects/parallelwork/exercise 4/main.go:8 +0x59
Process finished with exit code 2
```

The message may be different depending on the version of Go you are using. Also, some errors like these have been introduced in newer versions. In older versions, though, the compiler was more permissive. In this specific case, the problem is simple: if we do not know how big the channel is, the routines wait indefinitely, and this is called a deadlock. This does not mean we cannot handle unbuffered channels. We will see later how to handle them, as they require more than one routine running. With only one routine, after we send the message, we block the execution and there is no other routine able to receive the message; hence, we have a deadlock.

Before we go further, let's see one more characteristic of the channels, which is that they can be closed. Channels need to be closed when the task they have been created for is finished. In order to close a channel, type in the following:

```
close(ch)
```

Alternatively, you can defer the closing, as shown in the following code snippet:

```
...
defer close(ch)
for i:=0; i< 100; i++ {
    ch <- i
}
return
```

In this case, after the **return** statement, the channel is closed as the closing is deferred to run after the **return** statement.

Exercise 16.04: Exchange Greeting Messages via Channels

In this exercise, we will use a Goroutine to send a greeting message and then we will receive the greeting in the main process. The exercise is very simple and does not need concurrency, but it is a starting point to understand how message passing works.

1. Create a folder. In it, create a **main.go** file with the **main** package:

```
package main
import (
    "log"
)
```

2. Then, create the **greeter()** function:

```
func greet(ch chan string) {
    ch <- "Hello"
}
```

This function just sends a **Hello** message to a channel and ends.

3. Now create the **main()** function where you instantiate a channel and pass it to the **greeter**:

```
func main() {
    ch := make(chan string)
    go greet(ch)
```

Here, only a channel of strings is created and passed as a parameter to the call to a new routine called **greet**.

4. Now print the result and complete the function:

```
log.Println(<-ch)
}
```

Here, we are printing whatever comes from the channel. The following part of the code returns a value, which is passed straight to the **Println** function:

```
<- ch
```

5. Run the program with the following:

```
go run main.go
```

You will see the following output:

```
2019/10/28 19:44:11 Hello
```

Now we can see that the message has been delivered to the **main** function through the channel.

In this exercise, you have seen how to use channels to make different Goroutines communicate with each other and to synchronize their computations.

Exercise 16.05: Two-Way Message Exchange with Channels

What we want now is to send messages from the main routine to the second routine and then get a message back as a response. We will base our code on the previous one and expand it. The main routine will send a **"Hello John"** message, while the second routine will return "**Thanks**" for the message received, stating it in full, and will then add a message: **"Hello David"**.

1. Create a folder. In it, create a **main.go** file with the main package:

```
package main
import (
    "fmt"
    "log"
)
```

With the necessary imports, we will use the **fmt** package to manipulate the strings.

2. Write a **greet()** function to return the expected messages:

```
func greet(ch chan string) {
    msg := <- ch
    ch <- fmt.Sprintf("Thanks for %s", msg)
    ch <- "Hello David"
}
```

The **greet()** function signature has not changed. However, now before sending a message, it will first wait for a message and then reply. After receiving the message, this function sends a message back thanking for the greeting, and then sends its own greeting.

3. Now create the **main()** function and call the **greet()** function as a Goroutine:

```
func main() {
    ch := make(chan string)
    go greet(ch)
```

Here, the main function is created and a string channel is instantiated. Then, the second Goroutine is started. Next, we need to send the first message from the main routine to the second, which is currently waiting.

4. Now, to send the message "**Hello John**" to the channel, write the following code:

```
ch <- "Hello John"
```

5. And finally, add the code that waits for the messages to come back before printing them:

```
    log.Println(<-ch)
    log.Println(<-ch)
}
```

You can see that you need to log twice as you expect two messages to come back. In many cases, you will use a loop to retrieve all the messages, which we will see in the next exercise. For now, try to run your code, and you will see something as follows:

```
2019/10/28 19:44:49 Thanks for Hello John
2019/10/28 19:44:49 Hello David
```

From the output, you can see that both the messages have been received through the channel.

In this exercise, you have learned how a goroutine can both send and receive messages through the same channel and that two goroutines can exchange messages through the same channel in both directions.

Exercise 16.06: Sum Numbers from Everywhere

Imagine you want to add a few numbers but the numbers come from several sources. They might come from a feed or from a database; we just do not know which numbers we are going to add and where they come from. However, we need to add them all in one place. In this exercise, we will have four Goroutines sending numbers in particular ranges, and the main routine, which will calculate their sum.

1. Let's start by creating a new folder and the main file. After you've done that, write the package and imports:

```
package main
import (
    "log"
    "time"
)
```

Here, we also include the **time** package, which we will use to do a small trick that will help us to better visualize the effects of concurrency.

2. Now write the **push** function:

```
func push(from,to int, out chan int) {
    for i:=from;i<=to; i++ {
        out <- i
        time.Sleep(time.Microsecond)
    }
}
```

This sends all the numbers in the **from, to** range to the channel. After each message is sent, the routine sleeps for a microsecond so that another routine will pick up the work.

3. Now write the **main()** function:

```
func main() {
    s1 := 0
    ch := make(chan int, 100)
```

This code creates a variable for the final sum, **s1**, and one for the channel, **ch**, which has a buffer of 100.

4. Now create the four **go** routines:

```
go push(1,25, ch)
go push(26,50,ch)
go push(51,75,ch)
go push(76,100, ch)
```

5. At this point, we need to gather all the numbers to add, so we create a loop of 100 cycles:

```
for c :=0; c< 100; c++ {
```

6. Then read the number from the channel like this:

```
i := <- ch
```

7. We also want to see which number came from which Goroutine:

```
log.Println(i)
```

8. Finally, we calculate the sum and show the result:

```
s1 += i
}
log.Println(s1)
}
```

Here, we have the truncated output once you run the program:

```
2019/07/08 21:42:09 76
2019/07/08 21:42:09 26
2019/07/08 21:42:09 51
2019/07/08 21:42:09 77
2019/07/08 21:42:09 52
.......................................................
2019/07/08 21:42:09 48
2019/07/08 21:42:09 75
2019/07/08 21:42:09 100
2019/07/08 21:42:09 23
2019/07/08 21:42:09 49
2019/07/08 21:42:09 24
2019/07/08 21:42:09 50
2019/07/08 21:42:09 25
2019/07/08 21:42:09 5050
```

Here, based on the results, we can easily guess which number comes from which routine. The last line displays the sum of all numbers. If you run your program multiple times, you will see that the order of the numbers changes as well.

In this exercise, we saw how we can split some computational work across several concurrent routines and then gather all the computation in a single routine. Each routine performs a task. In this case, one sends numbers, while another receives the numbers and performs a sum.

Exercise 16.07: Request to Goroutines

In this exercise, we will solve the same problem mentioned in *Exercise 16.06, Sum Numbers from Everywhere*, but in a different way. Instead of receiving numbers as the routines send them, we will make the main routine ask for the numbers from the other routines. We will play with channel operations and experiment with their blocking nature.

1. Create a folder and a **main.go** file with the main package. Then, add the following import:

```go
package main
import (
    "log"
)
```

2. Then write the signature of the **push** function:

```
func push(from,to int, in chan bool, out chan int) {
```

Here, there are two channels, a Boolean one called **in**, which represents the incoming requests, and **out**, which will be used to send back messages.

3. Now write a loop for sending numbers when a request comes in:

```
    for i:=from;i<=to; i++ {
        <- in
        out <- i
    }
}
```

As you can see, the loop is still for a fixed number of items. Before sending anything, it waits for a request from the **in** channel. When it receives a request, it sends a number.

4. Now create the **main()** function, where you call the **push** function in four different goroutines, each one sending a subset of the numbers 1 to 100:

```
func main() {
    s1 := 0
    out := make(chan int, 100)
    in := make(chan bool,100)
    go push(1,25, in, out)
    go push(26,50,in, out)
    go push(51,75,in, out)
    go push(76,100, in, out)
```

This is pretty similar to the previous exercise, but it creates the extra channel, **in**.

5. Now create a loop to request a number, print it, and add it to the total:

```
    for c :=0; c< 100; c++ {
        in <- true
        i := <- out
        log.Println(i)
        s1 += i
    }
    log.Println(s1)
}
```

In this case, the loop first requests a number, then waits to receive another number. Here, we do not need to sleep for a microsecond because after we receive a number, the next request will go to any active Goroutine. If you run the program, you will again see something similar to what you saw in the previous exercise. Here, we have the truncated output:

```
2019/07/08 22:18:00 76
2019/07/08 22:18:00 1
2019/07/08 22:18:00 77
2019/07/08 22:18:00 26
2019/07/08 22:18:00 51
2019/07/08 22:18:00 2
2019/07/08 22:18:00 78
..............................................
2019/07/08 22:18:00 74
2019/07/08 22:18:00 25
2019/07/08 22:18:00 50
2019/07/08 22:18:00 75
2019/07/08 22:18:00 5050
```

You can see that each number is printed in the order it is received. Then, the sum of all numbers is printed on the screen.

In this exercise, you've learned how you can use channels to request other goroutines to perform some actions. A channel can be used to send some trigger messages and not only to exchange content and values.

The Importance of Concurrency

So far, we've seen how to use concurrency to split the work over several Goroutines, but in all these exercises concurrency was not really needed. In fact, you do not save much time doing what we did, nor do you have any other advantage. Concurrency is important when you need to perform several tasks that are logically independent from each other, and the easiest case to understand is a web server. You saw in *Chapter 15, HTTP Servers*, that several clients will most likely connect to the same server and all these connections will result in the server performing some actions. Also, these actions are all independent; that's where concurrency is important, as you do not want one of your users to have to wait for all the other HTTP requests to be completed before their request gets handled. Another case for concurrency is when you have different data sources to gather data and you can actually gather that data in different routines and combine the result at the end. We will see now some more complex applications for concurrency and learn how to use it for HTTP servers.

Exercise 16.08: Equally Splitting the Work between Routines

In this exercise, we will see how we can perform our sum of numbers in a predefined number of routines for them to gather the result at the end. Essentially, we want to create a function that adds numbers and receives the numbers from a channel. When no more numbers are received by the function, we will send the sum to the main function through the channel.

One thing to note here is that the function performing the sum does not know in advance how many numbers it will receive, which means we cannot have a fixed **from, to** range. So, we have to find another solution. We need to be able to split the work in any number of Goroutines and not be bound by a **from, to** range. Also, we do not want to do the addition in the main function. Instead, we want to create a function that will split the work over several routines.

1. Create a folder and a **main.go** file with the main package and write the following:

```go
package main
import (
    "log"
)
```

2. Now let's write the function to do a partial addition. We will call it **worker()** as we will have a fixed set of routines running this same function, waiting for numbers to arrive:

```go
func worker(in chan int, out chan int) {
sum := 0
    for i := range in {
        sum += i
    }
    out <- sum
}
```

As you can see, we have an **in** channel and an **out** channel of integers. Then, we instantiate the **sum** variable, which will store the sum of all the numbers sent to this worker.

3. At this point, we have a loop that ranges over the channel. This is interesting because we do not use **in** directly as follows:

```go
<- in
```

We, instead, rely only on the range to get the numbers in. In the loop, we just add **i** to the total and, at the end, we send the partial sum back. Even if we do not know how many items are going to be sent to the channel, we can still loop over the range without a problem. We rely on the fact that when no more items are sent, the **in** channel will be closed.

4. Now create the **sum()** function:

```
func sum(workers, from, to int) int {
```

This is the actual **sum** function that has the number of workers and the usual range for the numbers to add.

5. Now write a loop to run the requested number of workers:

```
out := make(chan int, workers)
in := make(chan int,4)
for i:=0;i<workers;i++ {
    go worker(in, out)
}
```

This creates the two **in/out** channels and runs the number of workers set by the **workers** parameter.

6. Then create a loop to send all the numbers to the **in** channel:

```
for i:=from;i<=to; i++ {
    in <- i
}
```

This sends all the numbers to be summed to the channel, which will distribute the numbers across all the routines. If you were to print out the numbers received across with the index of the worker, you could see how the numbers are distributed uniformly across the routines, which does not mean an exact split, but at least it's a fair one.

7. As we sent all the numbers, we now need to receive the partial sums back, but before that we need to notify the function that the numbers to sum are finished, so add the following:

```
close(in)
```

8. And then perform the sum of the partials:

```
sum := 0
for i:=0;i<workers; i++ {
    sum += <-out
}
```

9. Then, finally, close the **out** channel and return the result:

```
close(out)

    return sum
}
```

10. At this point, we need to somehow execute this function. So, let's write a simple main function to do that:

```
func main() {

    res := sum(100,1,100)
    log.Println(res)
}
```

This simply outputs a sum from a function that makes use of concurrency, and then prints out the result.

11. If you run your program, you should see the log output of the sum of numbers split into different routines as follows:

```
2019/10/28 19:49:13 5050
```

As you can see, after splitting the computation across multiple goroutines, the result is synchronized into one single result.

In this exercise, you've learned how to make use of concurrency to split your computation across several concurrent goroutines and then combine all these computations into one single result.

Concurrency Patterns

The way we organize our concurrent work is pretty much the same in every application. We will look at one common pattern that is called a *pipeline*, where we have a source, and then messages are sent from one routine to another until the end of the line, until all the routines in the pipeline have been utilized. Another pattern is the *fan out/ fan in* pattern where, as in the previous exercise, the work is sent to several routines reading from the same channel. All these patterns, however, are generally made of a *source* stage, which is the first stage of the pipeline and the one that gathers, or sources, the data, then some internal steps, and at the end a *sink*, which is the final stage where the results of the process from all the other routines get merged. It is known as a sink because all the data sinks into it.

Activity 16.02: Source Files

In this activity, you will create a program that will read two files at the same time containing some numbers. You will need to pipe those numbers to a function that will split them into even and odd based on their values. It will then send the odd numbers to one routine, even numbers to another. It will then write the addition of all the even and odd numbers to another file.

You will need two files with numbers that you will use as the sources. Then, you will produce one file with the sum of all the odd numbers in one row and then the sum of all the even numbers in the row below. The high-level steps for this activity are as follows:

1. Create two input files. You could use more, but the suggested code will use two.

2. Add some numbers in your input files, one number per line and nothing else. You need an empty line at the end of each file.

3. Create your main program and start with your imports.

4. Create a function to read a file and pipe each line to a channel. Be careful here, though; you may need to add a WaitGroup or something else to avoid any deadlocks.

5. Create a function to receive the numbers and pipe the odd numbers to one channel and the even numbers to another channel.

6. Create a function to sum the numbers and pipe the result to a new channel.

7. Create a merging function to read from the odd and even channels and write to a file called **result.txt**. Each line in this file should contain the word "Odd" or "Even," depending on the value, followed by the sum.

8. Create the main function to run all the Goroutines and handle the WaitGroups, if needed.

If you run your program, you should see nothing in the console, but a file called `result.txt` should have been created. Depending on the numbers in your input files, you will find that the content of the output file is something similar to the following:

```
Odd  9
Even  12
```

> **Note**
>
> The solution for this activity can be found on page 768.

Buffers

You've seen in the previous exercises that there are channels with a defined length and channels with an undetermined length:

```
ch1 := make(chan int)
ch2 := make(chan int, 10)
```

Let's see how we can make use of this.

A buffer is like a container that needs to be filled with some content, so you prepare it when you expect to receive that content. We said that operations on channels are blocking operations, which means the execution of the routine will stop and wait whenever you try to read a message from the channel. Let's try to understand what this means in practice with an example. Let's say we have the following code in a Goroutine:

```
i := <- ch
```

We know that before we can carry on with the execution of the code, we need to receive a message. However, there is something more about this blocking behavior. If the channel does not have a buffer, the Goroutine is blocked as well. It is not possible to write to a channel, nor to receive a channel. We'll get a better idea of this with an example, and we will show how to use unbuffered channels to achieve the same result, so you will get a better understanding of what you've seen in the previous exercises.

Let's have a look at this code:

```
ch := make(chan int, 2)
ch <- 1
ch <- 2
fmt.Println(<-ch)
fmt.Println(<-ch)
```

If you put this code inside a function, you will see that it works perfectly and will display something as follows:

```
1
2
```

But what if you add an extra read? Let's take a look:

```
ch := make(chan int, 2)
ch <- 1
ch <- 2
ch <- 3
fmt.Println(<-ch)
fmt.Println(←ch)
```

In this case, you will see an error:

```
fatal error: all goroutines are asleep - deadlock!
goroutine 1 [chan send]:
main.main()
    /tmp/sandbox223984687/prog.go:9 +0xa0
```

This happens because the routine running this code is blocked after the buffer of size 2 is filled with a data size of 2 coming from the read operations (commonly referred to as reads), which result in the buffer being filled with data, which, in this case, has 2 data and the buffer has a size of 2. We can increase the buffer:

```
ch := make(chan int, 3)
```

And it will work again; we are just not displaying the third number.

Now, let's see what happens if we remove the buffer. Try, and again you will see the previous error. This happens because the buffer is always full and the routine is blocked. An unbuffered channel is equivalent to the following:

```
ch := make(chan int, 0)
```

We've used unbuffered channels without any issues. Let's see an example of how to use them:

```
package main
import "fmt"
func readThem(ch chan int) {
  for {
    fmt.Println(<- ch)
  }
}
func main() {
```

```
    ch := make(chan int)
    go readThem(ch)
    ch <- 1
    ch <- 2
    ch <- 3
}
```

If you run this program, you should see something as follows:

```
1
2
3
```

But there is a chance you could see fewer numbers. If you run this on the Go Playground, you should see this result, but if you run it in your machine, you might see fewer numbers. Try sending more numbers:

```
ch <- 4
ch <- 5
```

At each addition, run your program; you might not see all the numbers. Basically, there are two routines: one is reading messages from an unbuffered channel, and the main routine is sending these messages through the same channel. Due to this, there is no deadlock. This shows that we can make use of unbuffered channels for read and write operations flawlessly by using two routines. We still have, however, an issue with not all numbers showing up, which we can fix in the following way:

```
package main

import "fmt"
import "sync"

func readThem(ch chan int, wg *sync.WaitGroup) {
  for i := range ch {
    fmt.Println(i)
  }
  wg.Done()
}

func main() {
    wg := &sync.WaitGroup{}
    wg.Add(1)
    ch := make(chan int)
    go readThem(ch, wg)
    ch <- 1
```

```
        ch <- 2
        ch <- 3
        ch <- 4
        ch <- 5
        close(ch)
        wg.Wait()
}
```

Here, we iterate over the channel inside the Goroutine, and we stop as soon as the channel gets closed. This is because when the channel gets closed, the range stops iterating. The channel gets closed in the main routine after everything is sent. We make use of a WaitGroup here to know that everything is completed. If we were not closing the channel in the main function, we would be in the main routine, which will terminate before the second routine would print all the numbers. There is another way, however, to wait for the execution of the second routine to be completed, and this is with explicit notification, which we will see in the next exercise. One thing to notice is that even though we close the channel, the messages still all arrive at the receiving routine. This is because the channel is closed only after all the messages are received by the receiver.

Exercise 16.09: Notifying When Computation Has Finished

In this exercise, we want to have one routine to send messages and another one to print them. Moreover, we want to know when the sender has finished sending the messages. The code will be similar to the previous example, with some modifications.

1. Create a new file and import the necessary packages:

```
package main

import "log"
```

2. Then define the function that will first receive the strings and print them later:

```
func readThem(in, out chan string) {
```

3. Then create the loop over the channel until the channel is closed:

```
        for i := range in {
            log.Println(i)
        }
```

4. And finally, send the notification saying that the processing has finished:

```
        out <- "done"
}
```

5. Now, let's build the `main()` function:

```
func main() {
    log.SetFlags(0)
```

Here, we've also set the `log` flags to `0` so we do not see anything other than the strings we send.

6. Now, create the necessary channels and use them to spin up the Goroutine:

```
in, out   := make(chan string), make(chan string)
go readThem(in, out)
```

7. Next, create a set of strings and loop over them, sending each string to the channel:

```
strs := []string{"a","b", "c", "d", "e", "f"}
for _, s := range strs {
    in <- s
}
```

8. After that, close the channel you used to send the messages and wait for the done signal:

```
    close(in)
    <-out
}
```

If you run your program, you will see the log output of code using a **done** channel:

```
a
b
c
d
e
f
```

We see that the main function has received all the messages from the Goroutine and has printed them. The main function terminates only when it has been notified that all the incoming messages have been sent.

In this exercise, you've learned how you can make a Goroutine notify another Goroutine that the work has finished by passing a message through a channel without needing WaitGroup.

Some More Common Practices

In all these examples, we've created channels and passed them through, but functions can also return channels and can also spin up new routines. Here is an example:

```
func doSomething() chan int {
    ch := make(chan int)
    go func() {
        for i := range ch {
            log.Println(i)
        }
    }()
    return ch
}
```

In this case, we can actually have the following in our **main()** function:

```
ch := doSomething()
ch <- 1
ch <- 4
```

We do not need to call the **doSomething** function as a Goroutine because it will actually spin up a new one by itself.

Some functions can also return or accept:

```
<- chan int
```

Or:

```
chan <- int
```

This makes clear what the function does with the channels. In fact, you could try to specify the direction in all the exercises we've done so far and see what happens if you specify an incorrect one.

HTTP Servers

You've seen how to build HTTP servers in *Chapter 15, HTTP Servers*, but you might remember that there was something that's difficult to handle with HTTP servers, and this was the application's state. Essentially, an HTTP server runs as a single program and listens to requests in the main routine. However, when a new HTTP request is made by one of the clients, a new routine is created that handles that specific request. You have not done it manually, nor have you managed the server's channels, but this is how it works internally. You do not actually need to send anything across the different Goroutines because each routine and each request is independent since they have been made by different people.

However, what you must think of is how to not create race conditions when you want to keep a state. Most HTTP servers are stateless, especially if you're building a microservice environment. However, you might want to keep track of things with a counter, or you might actually work with TCP servers or a gaming server or a chat app where you need to keep the state and gather information from all the peers. The techniques you've learned in this chapter allow you to do so. You can use a mutex to make sure a counter is thread-safe, or better, routine-safe, across all the requests. I'd suggest you go back to your code for the HTTP server and ensure safety with mutexes.

Methods as Routines

So far, you've only seen functions used as Goroutines, but methods are simple functions with a receiver; hence, they can be used asynchronously too. This can be useful if you want to share some properties of your struct, such as for your counter in an HTTP server.

With this technique, you can encapsulate the channels you use across several routines belonging to the same instance of a struct without having to pass these channels everywhere.

Here is a simple example of how to do that:

```
type MyStruct struct {}
func (m MyStruct) doIt()

. . . . . .

ms := MyStruct{}
go ms.doIt()
```

But let's see how to apply this in an exercise.

Exercise 16.10: A Structured Work

In this exercise, we will calculate a sum using several workers. A worker is essentially a function, and we will be organizing these workers into a single struct.

1. Create your folder and **main** file. In it, add the required imports and define a **Worker** struct with two channels – **in** and **out**. Ensure that you add a mutex as well:

```
package main
import (
    "fmt"
    "sync"
)
type Worker struct {
```

```
        in, out chan int
        sbw int
        mtx *sync.Mutex
    }
```

2. To create its methods, write the following:

```
func (w *Worker) readThem() {
    w.sbw++
    go func() {
```

Here, we create a method and increment the number of **subworkers**. Sub-workers are basically identical routines that split the work that needs to be done. Note that the function is meant to be used directly and not as a Goroutine, as it itself creates a new Goroutine.

3. Now, build the content of the spawned routine:

```
        partial := 0
        for i := range w.in {
            partial += i
        }
        w.out <- partial
```

4. This is pretty similar to what you've done before; now comes the tricky part:

```
        w.mtx.Lock()
        w.sbw--
        if w.sbw == 0 {
            close(w.out)
        }
        w.mtx.Unlock()
    }()

}
```

Here, we've locked the routine, reduced the counter on the sub-workers safely, and then, in case all the workers have terminated, we've closed the output channel. Then we've unlocked the execution to allow the program to carry on.

5. At this point, we need to make a function that's able to return the sum:

```
func (w *Worker) gatherResult() int {
    total := 0
    wg := &sync.WaitGroup{}
    wg.Add(1)
    go func() {
```

6. Here, we create a total, then a Waitgroup, and we add 1 to it as we will spawn only one routine whose content is as follows:

```
for  i:= range w.out{
        total += i
    }
    wg.Done()
}()
```

As you can see, we have looped until the out channel is closed by one of the sub-workers.

7. At this point, we can wait for the routine to finish and return the result:

```
    wg.Wait()
    return total
}
```

8. The main code just sets up the variables for the worker and its sub-workers:

```
func main() {

    mtx := &sync.Mutex{}
    in := make(chan int, 100)
    wrNum := 10
    out := make(chan int)
    wrk := Worker{in: in, out:out, mtx:mtx}
```

9. Now create a loop where you call the **readThem()** method **wrNum** times. This will create some sub-workers:

```
for i:=1; i<=wrNum; i++ {
    wrk.readThem()
}
```

10. Now send the numbers to be summed to the channel:

```
for i:=1;i<=100; i++ {
    in <- i
}
```

11. Close the channel to notify that all the numbers have been sent:

```
close(in)
```

12. Then wait for the result and print it out:

```
        res := wrk.gatherResult()
        fmt.Println(res)
    }
```

13. If you run the program, you will see the log output of a sum made using structs to organize our work:

```
    5050
```

In this exercise, you've learned how to use a method of a struct to create a new Goroutine. The method can just be called like any function, but the result will be a new anonymous goroutine being created.

Go Context Package

We've seen how to run concurrent code and run it until it has finished, waiting for the completion of some processing through WaitGroup or channel reads. You might have seen in some Go code, especially code related to HTTP calls, some parameters from the **context** package, and you might have wondered what it is and why it is used. All the code we've written here is running in our machines and does not pass through the internet, so we hardly have any delay due to latency; however, in situations involving HTTP calls, we might encounter servers that do not respond and get stuck. In such cases, how do we stop our call if the server does not respond after a while? How do we stop the execution of a routine that runs independently when an event occurs? Well, we have several ways, but a standard one is to use contexts, and we will see now how they work. A context is a variable that is passed through a series of calls and might hold some values or may be empty. It is a container, but it is not used in order to send values across functions; you can use normal integers, strings, and so on for this purpose. A **context** is passed through in order to get back control of what is happening:

```
func doIt(c context.Context , a int, b string) {
  fmt.Println(b)
  doThat(c, a*2)
}
func doThat(c context.Context , a int) {
  fmt.Println(a)
  doMore(c)
}
```

As you can see, there are several calls, and **c** is passed through but we do not do anything with it. However, it can contain data, and it contains functions that we can use in order to stop the execution of the current routine. We will see how it works in the next exercise.

Exercise 16.11: Managing Routines with Context

In this exercise, we will start a Goroutine with an infinite loop counting from zero until we decide to stop it. We will make use of the context to notify the routine to stop and a sleeping function to make sure we know how many iterations we do.

1. Create your folder and a **main.go** file, then write the following:

```
package main
import (
    "context"
    "log"
    "time"
)
```

For the usual imports, we have **logs** and **time**, which we've already seen, plus the **context** package.

2. Let's write a function that counts every 100 milliseconds from 0:

```
func countNumbers(c context.Context, r chan int) {
    v := 0
    for {
```

Here, **v** is the value we count from zero. The **c** variable is the context, while the **r** variable is the channel returning the result. Then, we start defining the loop.

3. Now, we start an infinite loop, but inside it we will have **select**:

```
        select {
    case <-c.Done():
        r <- v
        break
```

In this **select** group, we have a case where we check whether the context is **done**, and if it is, we just break the loop and return the value we have counted so far.

4. If the context is not **done**, we need to keep counting:

```
        default:
        time.Sleep(time.Millisecond * 100)
        v++
    }
    }
}
```

Here, we sleep for 100 milliseconds and then we increment the value by 1.

5. The next step is to write a **main()** function that makes use of this counter:

```
func main() {
    r := make(chan int)
    c := context.TODO()
```

We create an integer channel to pass to the counter and a **context**.

6. We need to be able to cancel the context, so we extend this simple context with a cancellable context:

```
    cl, stop := context.WithCancel(c)
    go countNumbers(cl, r)
```

Here, we also finally call the counting routine.

7. At this point, we need a way to break the loop, so we will use the **stop()** function returned by **context.WithCancel**, but we will do that inside another Goroutine. This will stop the context after 300 milliseconds:

```
    go func() {
        time.Sleep(time.Millisecond*100*3)
        stop()
    }()
```

8. And at this point, we just need to wait for the message with the count to be received and log it:

```
    v := <- r
    log.Println(v)
}
```

After 300 milliseconds have passed, the counter will return 3 since, due to context manipulation, the routine stopped at the third iteration:

```
2019/10/28 20:00:58 3
```

Here, we can see that even though the loop is infinite, the execution stops after three iterations.

In this exercise, you've learned how you can use the context to stop the execution of a routine. This is very useful in many cases, such as when performing long tasks that you want to stop after a maximum amount of time.

One thing to mention is that, in this exercise, we did something that in some situations could lead to problems. What we did was create a channel in one Goroutine, but close it in another one. This is not wrong; in some cases, it might be useful, but try to avoid it as it could lead to problems when somebody looks at the code, or when you look at the code after several months, because it is difficult to track where a channel is closed across several functions.

Summary

In this chapter, you've learned how to create production-ready concurrent code, how to handle race conditions, and how to make sure that your code is concurrent-safe. You've learned how to use channels to make your goroutines communicate with each other and how to stop their executions using the context.

You've worked on several techniques to handle concurrent computation. In many real-life scenarios, you might just use functions and methods that handle concurrency for you, especially if you're doing web programming, but there are cases where you have to handle the work coming from some different sources by yourself. You need to match requests with your response through different channels. You might need to gather different data into one single routine from different ones. With what you've learned here, you'll be able to do all that. You'll be able to ensure you do not lose data by waiting for all the Goroutines to finish. You'll be able to modify the same variable from different routines, making sure you do not override a value if it is not what you want. You've also learned how to avoid deadlocks and how to use channels in order to share information. One of the Go mottos is "share by communicating, do not communicate by sharing." This means that the preferred way to share values is to send them via a channel and not rely on mutexes if not strictly necessary. You now know how to do all that.

In the next chapter, you will learn to make your code more professional. Essentially, you will learn what you are expected to do as a professional in a real working environment, which is testing and checking your code, making sure, essentially, that your code works and is valid.

17

Using Go Tools

Overview

This chapter will teach you how to make use of the Go toolkit to improve and build your code. It will also help you build and improve your code using Go tools and create binaries using **go build**. It will show you how to clean up library imports using **goimports**, detect suspicious constructs with **go vet**, and identify race conditions in your code using the Go race detector.

By the end of this chapter, you will be able to run code with **go run**, format code with **gofmt**, automatically generate documentation using **go doc**, and download third-party packages using **go get**.

Introduction

In the previous chapter, you've learned how to produce concurrent code. Although Go makes the task of creating concurrent code much easier compared to other languages, concurrent code is intrinsically complex. This is when learning to use tools to write better code that will simplify the complexity comes handy.

In this chapter, you will learn about Go tools. Go comes with several tools to help you write better code. For example, in the previous chapters, you came across **go build**, which you used to build your code into an executable. You will also have come across **go test**, which you used to test your code. There are also a few more tools that help in different ways. For example, the **goimports** tool will check if you have all the import statements required for your code to work and if not, it will add them. It can also check if any of your import statements are no longer needed and remove them. While this seems like a very simple thing, it means you no longer need to worry about the imports and can instead focus on the code you are writing. Alternatively, you can use the Go race detector to find race conditions hidden in your code. This is an extremely valuable tool when you start writing concurrent code.

The tools provided with the Go language are one of the reasons for its popularity. They provide a standard way to check code for formatting issues, mistakes, and race conditions, which is very useful when you are developing software in a professional setting. The exercises in this chapter provide practical examples of how to use these tools to improve your code.

The go build Tool

The **go build** tool takes Go source code and compiles it so it can be executed. When creating software, you write code in a human-readable programming language. Then, the code needs to be translated into a machine-readable format to execute. This is done by a compiler that compiles the machine instructions from the source code. To do this with Go code, you would use **go build**.

Exercise 17.01: Using the go build Tool

In this exercise, you will learn about the **go build** tool. This will take your Go source code and compile it into a binary. To use it, run the **go build** tool on the command line, as follows:

```
go build -o name_of_the_binary_to_create source_file.go
```

Let's get started:

1. Create a new directory called **Exercise17.01** on your GOPATH. Within that directory, create a new file called **main.go**:

2. Add the following code to the file to create a simple **Hello World** program:

    ```
    package main
    import "fmt"
    func main() {
        fmt.Println("Hello World")
    }
    ```

3. To run the program, you need to open your Terminal and navigate to the directory that you created the **main.go** file in. Then, run the **go build** tool by writing the following:

    ```
    go build -o hello_world main.go
    ```

4. This will create an executable called **hello_world** that you can execute the binary in by running it on the command line:

    ```
    > ./hello_world
    ```

    The output will look as follows:

    ```
    Hello World
    ```

In this exercise, you used the **go build** tool to compile your code into a binary and execute it.

The go run Tool

The **go run** tool is similar to **go build** in that it compiles your Go code. However, the subtle difference is that **go build** will output a binary file that you can execute, whereas the **go run** tool doesn't create a binary file that you need to execute. It compiles the code and runs it in a single step, with no binary file output in the end. This can be useful if you want to quickly check that your code does what you expect it to do without the need to create and run a binary file. This would be commonly used when you're testing your code so that you can run it quickly without needing to create a binary to execute.

Exercise 17.02: Using the go run Tool

In this exercise, you will learn about the **go run** tool. This is used as a shortcut to compile and run your code in a single step, which is useful if you want to quickly check that your code works. To use it, run the **go run** tool on the command line in the following format:

```
go run source_file.go
```

Perform the following steps:

1. Create a new directory called **Exercise17.02** on your **GOPATH**. Within that directory, create a new file called **main.go**.

2. Add the following code to the file to create a simple **Hello Packt** program:

```
package main
import "fmt"
func main() {
   fmt.Println("Hello Packt")
}
```

3. Now, you can run the program using the **go run** tool:

```
go run main.go
```

This will execute the code and run it all in one step, giving you the following output:

```
Hello Packt
```

In this exercise, you used the **go run** tool to compile and run a simple Go program in a single step. This is useful to quickly check whether your code does what you expect.

The gofmt Tool

The **gofmt** tool is used to keep your code neat and consistently styled. When working on a large software project, an important, but often overlooked factor is code style. Having a consistent code style throughout your project is important for readability. When you have to read someone else's code, or even your own code months after writing it, having it in a consistent style makes you focus on the logic without much effort. Having to parse differing styles when reading code is just one more thing to worry about and leads to mistakes. To overcome this issue, Go comes with a tool to automatically format your code in a consistent way called **gofmt**. This means that, across your project, and even across other Go projects that use the **gofmt** tool, the code will be consistent. So, it will fix the formatting of the code by correcting the spacing and indentation, as well as trying to align the sections of your code.

Exercise 17.03: Using the gofmt Tool

In this exercise, you'll learn how to use the **gofmt** tool to format your code. When you run the **gofmt** tool, it will display how it thinks the file should look with the correct formatting, but it won't change the file. If you would like **gofmt** to automatically change the file to the correct format, you can run **gofmt** with the **-w** option, which will update the file and save the changes. Let's get started:

1. Create a new directory called **Exercise17.03** on your GOPATH. Within that directory, create a new Go file called **main.go**.

2. Add the following code to the file to create a badly formatted **Hello Packt** program:

```
package main
     import "fmt"
func
main(){
  firstVar := 1
        secondVar :=    2
  fmt.Println(firstVar)
                 fmt.Println(secondVar)
  fmt.    Println("Hello Packt")
                    }
```

3. Then, in your Terminal, run **gofmt** to see what the file will look like:

```
gofmt main.go
```

This will display how the file should be formatted to make it correct. The following is the expected output:

```
> gofmt main.go
package main

import "fmt"

func main() {
        firstVar := 1
        secondVar := 2

        fmt.Println(firstVar)
        fmt.Println(secondVar)
        fmt.Println("Hello Packt")
}
```

Figure 17.1: Expected output for gofmt

However, this only shows the changes it would make; it doesn't change the file. This is so you can confirm you are happy with the changes it will make.

4. To actually change the file and save those changes, you need to add the **-w** option:

```
gofmt -w main.go
```

This will update the file and save the changes. Then, when you look at the file, it should look like this:

```
package main
import "fmt"
func main() {
    firstVar := 1

    secondVar := 2

    fmt.Println(firstVar)

    fmt.Println(secondVar)

    fmt.Println("Hello Packt")
}
```

You may observe that the badly formatted code has been realigned after using the **gofmt** tool. The spacing and indentation have been fixed, and the new line between **func** and **main()** has been removed.

> **Note**
>
> Many **Integrated Development Environments (IDEs)** come with a built-in way to use **gofmt** on your code when you save. It is worth researching how to do this with your chosen IDE so that the **gofmt** tool will run automatically and fix any spacing or indentation mistakes in your code.

In this exercise, you used the **gofmt** tool to reformat a badly formatted file into a neat state. This can seem pointless and annoying when you first start coding. However, as your skills improve and you start working on larger projects, you will start to appreciate the importance of a neat and consistent code style.

The goimports Tool

Another useful tool that comes with Go is **goimports**, which automatically adds the imports that are needed in your file. A key part of software engineering is not reinventing the wheel and reusing other people's code. In Go, you do this by importing the libraries at the start of your file, in the **import** section. It can, however, be tedious to add these imports each time you need to use them. You can also accidentally leave in unused imports, which can pose a security risk. A better way to do this is to use **goimports** to automatically add the imports for you. It will also remove unused imports and reorder the remaining imports into alphabetical order for better readability.

Exercise 17.04: Using the goimports Tool

In this exercise, you will learn how to use **goimports** to manage the imports in a simple Go program. When you run the **goimports** tool, it will output how it thinks the file should look with the imports fixed. Alternatively, you can run **goimports** with the **-w** option, which automatically updates the imports in the file and saves the changes. Let's get started:

1. Create a new directory called **Exercise17.04** on your GOPATH. Within that directory, create a new file called **main.go**.

2. Add the following code to the file to create a simple **Hello Packt** program with incorrect imports:

```go
package main
import (
    "net/http"
    "fmt"
)
func main() {
    fmt.Println("Hello")
    log.Println("Packt")
}
```

You will notice that the **log** library has not been imported and that the **net/http** import is unused.

3. In your Terminal, run the **goimports** tool against your file to see how the imports change:

```
goimports main.go
```

This will display the changes it would make to the file to correct it. The following is the expected output:

```
> goimports main.go
package main

import (
        "fmt"
        "log"
)

func main() {
        fmt.Println("Hello")
        log.Println("Packt")
}
```

Figure 17.2: Expected output for goimports

This won't have changed the file but shows what the file will be changed to. As you can see, the **net/http** import has been removed and the **log** import has been added.

4. To write these changes to the file, add the **-w** option:

```
goimports -w main.go
```

5. This will update the file and make it look as follows:

```
package main
import (
  "fmt"
  "log"
)
func main() {
  fmt.Println("Hello")
  log.Println("Packt")
}
```

Many IDEs come with a built-in way to turn on **goimports** so that when you save your file, it will automatically correct the imports for you.

In this exercise, you learned how to use the **goimports** tool. You can use this tool to detect incorrect and unused import statements and automatically correct them.

The go vet Tool

The **go vet** tool is used for static analysis of your Go code. While the Go compiler can find and inform you of mistakes you may have made, there are certain things it will miss. For this reason, the **go vet** tool was created. This might sound trivial, but some of these issues could go unnoticed for a long time after the code has been deployed, the most common of which is passing the wrong number of arguments when using the **Prinf** function. It will also check for useless assignments, for example, if you set a variable and then never use that variable. Another particularly useful thing it detects is when a non-pointer interface is passed to an "unmarshal" function. The compiler won't notice this as it is valid; however, the unmarshal function will be unable to write the data to the interface. This can be troublesome to debug but using the **go vet** tool allows you to catch it early and remediate the issue before it becomes a problem.

Exercise 17.05: Using the go vet Tool

In this exercise, you will use the **go vet** tool to find a common mistake that's made when using the **Printf** function. You will use it to detect when the wrong number of arguments are being passed to a **Printf** function. Let's get started:

1. Create a new directory called **Exercise17.05** on your GOPATH. Within that directory, create a new go file called **main.go**:

2. Add the following code to the file to create a simple **Hello Packt** program:

```go
package main
import "fmt"
func main() {
    helloString := "Hello"
    packtString := "Packt"
    jointString := fmt.Sprintf("%s", helloString, packtString)
    fmt.Println(jointString)
}
```

As you can see, the **jointString** variable makes use of **fmt.Sprintf** to join two strings into one. However, the **%s** format string is incorrect and only formats one of the input strings. When you build this code, it will compile into a binary without any errors. However, when you run the program, the output will not be as expected. Luckily, the **go vet** tool was created for this exact reason.

3. Run the **go vet** tool against the file you created:

```
go vet main.go
```

4. This will display any issues it finds in the code:

```
> go vet main.go
# command-line-arguments
./main.go:9:17: Sprintf call needs 1 arg but has 2 args
```

Figure 17.3: Expected output of go vet

As you can see, **go vet** has identified an issue on line 9 of the file. The **Sprintf** call needs **1** argument, but we have given it **2**.

5. Update the `Sprintf` call so that it can handle both arguments we want to send:

```
package main
import "fmt"
func main() {
    helloString := "Hello"
    packtString := "Packt"
    jointString := fmt.Sprintf("%s %s", helloString, packtString)
    fmt.Println(jointString)
}
```

6. Now, you can run **go vet** again and check that there are no more issues:

```
go vet
```

It should return nothing, letting you know the file has no more issues.

7. Now, run the program:

```
go run main.go
```

The output after making corrections is the string we want, as follows:

```
Hello Packt
```

In this exercise, you learned how to use the **go vet** tool to detect issues that the compiler might miss. While this is a very basic example, **go vet** can detect mistakes such as passing a non-pointer to unmarshal functions or detecting unreachable code. It is encouraged to run **go vet** as part of your build process to catch these issues before they make it into your program.

The Go Race Detector

The Go race detector was added to Go to be able to detect race conditions. As we mentioned in *Chapter 16, Concurrent Work*, you can use goroutines to run parts of your code concurrently. However, even experienced programmers might make a mistake that allows different goroutines to access the same resource at the same time. This is called a race condition. A race condition is problematic because one goroutine can edit the resource in the middle of another reading it, meaning the resource could be corrupted. While Go has made concurrency a first-class citizen in the language, the mechanisms for concurrent code do not prevent race conditions. Also, due to the inherent nature of concurrency, a race condition might stay hidden until long after your code has been deployed. This also means they tend to be transient, making them devilishly difficult to debug and fix. This is why the Go race detector was created.

This tool works by using an algorithm that detects asynchronous memory access, but a drawback of this is that it can only do so when the code executes. So, you need to run the code to be able to detect race conditions. Luckily, it has been integrated into the Go toolchain, so we can use it to do this for us.

Exercise 17.06: Using the Go Race Detector

In this exercise, you will create a basic program that contains a race condition. You will use the Go race detector on the program to find the race condition. You will learn how to identify where the problem lies and then learn ways to mitigate the race condition. Let's get started:

1. Create a new directory called **Exercise17.06** on your GOPATH. Within that directory, create a new file called **main.go**.

2. Add the following code to the file to create a simple program with race conditions:

```
package main
import "fmt"
func main() {
    finished := make(chan bool)
    names := []string{"Packt"}
    go func() {
        names = append(names, "Electric")
        names = append(names, "Boogaloo")
        finished <- true
    }()
    for _, name := range names {
        fmt.Println(name)
    }
    <-finished
}
```

As you can see, there is an array called **names** with one item in it. A goroutine then starts appending more names to it. At the same time, the main goroutine is attempting to print out all the items in the array. So, both goroutines are accessing the same resource at the same time, which is a race condition.

3. Run the code with the **race** flag activated:

```
go run --race main.go
```

Running this command will give us the following output:

```
> go run --race main.go
Packt
==================
WARNING: DATA RACE
Write at 0x00c0000d2000 by goroutine 7:
  main.main.func1()
      /Users/andrew.hayes/go/src/github.com/PacktWorkshops/The-Go-Workshop/Chapter18/Exercise18.06/main.go:10 +0xc8

Previous read at 0x00c0000d2000 by main goroutine:
  main.main()
      /Users/andrew.hayes/go/src/github.com/PacktWorkshops/The-Go-Workshop/Chapter18/Exercise18.06/main.go:15 +0x147

Goroutine 7 (running) created at:
  main.main()
      /Users/andrew.hayes/go/src/github.com/PacktWorkshops/The-Go-Workshop/Chapter18/Exercise18.06/main.go:9 +0x139
==================
Found 1 data race(s)
exit status 66
```

Figure 17.4: Expected output when using the Go race detector

4. In the preceding screenshot, you can see a warning, informing you about the race condition. It tells you that the same resource was read and written in the code on lines **main.go:10** and **main.go:15**, which look as follows:

```
names = append(names, "Electric")
```

and

```
for _, name := range names {
```

As you can see, in both cases, it is the **names** array that is being accessed, so that is where the problem lies. The reason this happens is that the program starts to print the **names** before it waits for the **finished** channel.

5. A solution could be to wait for the **finished** channel before printing the items:

```
<-finished
for _, name := range names {
    fmt.Println(name)
}
```

6. This means the items will have all been added to the array before you start to print them out. You can confirm this solution by running the program again with the race flag activated:

```
go run --race main.go
```

7. This should run the program as normal and show no race condition warnings. The expected output after the corrections have been made is as follows:

```
Packt
Electric
Boogaloo
```

The final program with the race condition now fixed would look as follows:

```go
package main
import "fmt"
func main() {
    finished := make(chan bool)
    names := []string{"Packt"}
    go func() {
        names = append(names, "Electric")
        names = append(names, "Boogaloo")
        finished <- true
    }()
    <-finished
    for _, name := range names {
        fmt.Println(name)
    }
}
```

While the program in this exercise was quite simple, as was the solution, you are encouraged to return to *Chapter 16*, *Concurrent Work*, and use the **race** flag in the activities there. This will provide a better working example of how the Go race detector can help you.

> **Note**
>
> The Go race detector is often used by professional software developers to confirm that their solution doesn't contain any hidden race conditions.

The go doc Tool

The **go doc** tool is used to generate documentation for packages and functions in Go. An often-neglected part of many software projects is the documentation. This is because it can be tedious to write and even more tedious to keep up to date. So, Go comes with a tool to automatically generate documentation for package declarations and functions in your code. You simply need to add comments to the start of functions and packages. Then, these will be picked up and combined with the function header.

This can then be shared with others to help them understand how to use your code. To generate the documentation for a package and its function, you can use the **go doc** tool. Documentation like this helps when you are working on a large project and other people need to make use of your code. Often, in a professional setting, different teams will be working on different parts of a program; each team will need to communicate to the other teams about what functions are available in a package and how to call them. To do this, they could use **go doc** to generate the documentation for the code they've written and share it with other teams.

Exercise 17.07: Implementing the go doc Tool

In this exercise, you will learn about the **go doc** tool and how it can be used to generate documentation for your code. Let's get started:

1. Create a new directory called **Exercise17.07** on your GOPATH. Within that directory, create a new file called **main.go**.

2. Add the following code to the **main.go** file you created:

```go
package main
import "fmt"
// Add returns the total of two integers added together
func Add(a, b int) int {
    return a + b
}
// Multiply returns the total of one integers multiplied the other
func Multiply(a, b int) int {
    return a * b
}
func main() {
    fmt.Println(Add(1, 1))
    fmt.Println(Multiply(2, 2))
}
```

This creates a simple program that contains two functions: one called **Add**, which adds two numbers, and one called **Multiply**, which multiplies two numbers.

3. Run the following command to compile and execute the file:

```
go run main.go
```

4. The output will look as follows:

```
2
4
```

5. You will notice that both functions have comments above them that begin with the name of the function. This is a Go convention to let you know that these comments can be used as documentation. What this means is that you can use the **go doc** tool to create documentation for the code. In the same directory as your `main.go` file, run the following:

```
go doc -all
```

6. This will generate documentation for the code and output it, as follows:

```
> go doc -all

FUNCTIONS

func Add(a, b int) int
    Add returns the total of two integers added together

func Multiply(a, b int) int
    Multiply returns the total of one integers multipled the other
```

Figure 17.5: Expected output from go doc

In this exercise. you learned how to use the **go doc** tool to generate documentation on the Go package you created, as well as its functions. You can use this for other packages you have created and share the documentation with others if they would like to make use of your code.

The go get Tool

The **go get** tool allows you to download and use different libraries. While Go comes with a wide range of packages by default, it is dwarfed by the number of third-party packages that are available. These provide extra functionality that you can use in your own code to enhance it. However, for your code to make use of these packages, you need to have them on your computer so that the compiler can include them when compiling your code. To download these packages, you can use the **go get** tool.

Exercise 17.08: Implementing the go get Tool

In this exercise, you will learn how to download a third-party package using **go get**. Let's get started:

1. Create a new directory called **Exercise17.08** on your GOPATH. Within that directory, create a new file called **main.go.**

2. Add the following code to the **main.go** file you created:

```go
package main
import (
  "fmt"
  "log"
  "net/http"
  "github.com/gorilla/mux"
)
func exampleHandler(w http.ResponseWriter, r *http.Request) {
  w.WriteHeader(http.StatusOK)
  fmt.Fprintf(w, "Hello Packt")
}
func main() {
  r := mux.NewRouter()
  r.HandleFunc("/", exampleHandler)
  log.Fatal(http.ListenAndServe(":8888", r))
}
```

3. This is a simple web server that you can start by running the following command:

```
go run main.go
```

4. However, the web server uses a third-party package called "**mux**." In the import section, you will see that it has been imported from "**github.com/gorilla/mux**." However, since we don't have this package stored locally, an error will occur when we try to run the program:

```
> go run main.go
main.go:8:2: cannot find package "github.com/gorilla/mux" in any of:
        /usr/local/Cellar/go/1.13/libexec/src/github.com/gorilla/mux (from $GOROOT)
```

Figure 17.6: Expected error message

5. To get the third-party package, you can use **go get**. This will download it locally so that our Go code can make use of it:

```
go get github.com/gorilla/mux
```

6. Now that you have downloaded the package, you can run the web server again:

```
go run main.go
```

This time, it should run without any errors:

```
> go run main.go
```

Figure 17.7: Expected output when running the web server

7. While the web server is running, you can open **http://localhost:8888** in your web browser and check that it works:

Hello Packt

Figure 17.8: Web server output when viewed in Firefox

In this exercise, you learned how to download third-party packages using the **go get** tool. This allows the use of tools and packages beyond what comes as a standard package in Go.

Activity 17.01: Using gofmt, goimport, go vet, and go get to Correct a File

Imagine you are working on a project with poorly written code. The file contains a badly formatted file, missing imports, and a log message in the wrong place. You want to use the Go tools you've learned about in this chapter to correct the file and find any issues with it. In this activity, you will use **gofmt**, **goimport**, **go vet**, and **go get** to fix the file and find any issues within it. The steps for this activity are as follows:

1. Create a directory called **Activity 17.01**.

2. Create a file called **main.go**.

3. Add the example code to **main.go**.

4. Fix any formatting issues.

5. Fix any missing imports from **main.go**.

6. Check for any issues the compiler may miss by using **go vet**.

7. Ensure the third-party package, **"gorilla/mux"**, has been downloaded to your local computer.

The following is the expected output:

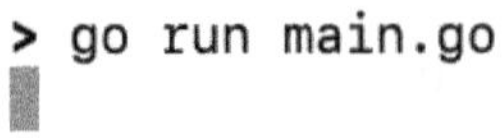

```
> go run main.go
```

Figure 17.9: Expected output when running the code

You can check this worked by going to **http://localhost:8888** in your web browser:

Hello Packt

Figure 17.10: Expected output when accessing the web server through Firefox

> **Note**
>
> The solution for this activity can be found on page 775.

The following is the example code to correct:

```go
package main
import (
  "log"
  "fmt"
  "github.com/gorilla/mux"
)
// ExampleHandler handles the http requests send to this webserver
func
ExampleHandler(w http.ResponseWriter, r *http.Request) {
  w.WriteHeader(http.StatusOK)
fmt.Fprintf(w, "Hello Packt")
  return
  log.Println("completed")
}
func main() {
  r := mux.NewRouter()
  r.HandleFunc("/", ExampleHandler)
  log.Fatal(http.ListenAndServe(":8888", r))
}
```

Summary

Go tools are invaluable to a programmer when they're writing code. In this chapter, you learned about **go build** and how to compile your code into executables. Then, you learned how consistent neat code is important when working on a project and how you can use `gofmt` to automatically neaten up the code for you. This can be further improved with `goimports`, which can remove unnecessary imports for better security and automatically add imports you may have forgotten to add yourself.

After, you looked at **go vet** and how it can be used to help you find any mistakes that the compiler may have missed. You also learned how to use the Go race detector to find race conditions hidden in your code. Then, you learned how to generate documentation for your code, which makes for easier collaboration when working on larger projects. Finally, you looked at downloading third-party packages using the **go get** tool, which allows you to make use of numerous Go packages that are available online to enhance your own code.

In the next chapter, you will learn about security. You will learn how to prevent your code from being exploited and learn how to guard it against common attack vectors.

18

Security

Overview

This chapter aims to equip you with the basic skills to protect your code from attacks and vulnerabilities. You will be able to evaluate the workings of major attack vectors, implement crypto libraries for the encryption and decryption of data and implement communication security by using TLS certificates.

By the end of the chapter, you will be equipped to identify common issues with code that could lead to security loopholes, and refactor code to make it more secure.

Introduction

In the previous chapter, we learned about Go tools such as **fmt**, **vet**, and **race**, which are designed to help you with your code development. Let's now look at how to secure your code by looking at examples of common vulnerabilities. We'll also look at the packages in the standard library that can help you to store your data securely.

Security cannot be an afterthought. It should be part of your code kata, something that you practice every day. Most vulnerabilities in applications stem from the developer not knowing about potential security attacks and from not having a security review of the application before it gets deployed.

If you look at any websites dealing with sensitive data, for example, banking websites, they will have basic security in place, such as the use of a signed SSL certificate. It is always better to design your application with security in mind than to add security layers later, so as to avoid refactoring or redesigning your application. In this chapter, we will cover some major attack vectors and best practices that will guide you in securing your application. The following basic sanity checks in your code will guarantee that you are protected by default from most vulnerabilities and attacks.

Application Security

During the development of your application, you will not be able to anticipate all the possible ways in which it could be compromised. However, you can always try to safeguard the application by following safe coding practices, such as the encryption of data in transit and at rest. It is a well-known fact that if we protect an application from well-known attack vectors such as SQL injection, we will be able to ward off most attacks. We will cover topics such as the use of digital certificates and hashing sensitive data to protect it from attackers.

One of the major attack vectors of a software application is the command or SQL injection, in which malicious user input can change the behavior of a command or query. This can happen with poorly constructed queries in SQL, HTTP URLs, or in OS commands.

Let's look at SQL injection and command injection in detail.

SQL Injection

If you are working on an application that needs to store data, you will most likely be using a database.

SQL injection is a way of injecting malicious code into your database query. Although unintentional, this could have a drastic impact on your application, such as the loss of data or the leaking of sensitive information.

Let's look at some examples to understand what exactly the SQL injection is and how it works.

The following function takes a **userID** parameter and uses it to query the database to return the card number that belongs to the user:

```
func GetCardNumber(db *sql.DB, userID string) (resp string, err error) {
    query := `SELECT CARD_NUMBER FROM USER_DETAILS WHERE USER_ID = ` + userID
    row := db.QueryRow(query)
    switch err = row.Scan(&resp); err {
    case sql.ErrNoRows:
        return resp, fmt.Errorf("no rows returned")
    case nil:
        return resp, err
    default:
        return resp, err
    }
    return
}
```

If the user input is **795001**, the query string will resolve to:

```
query := `SELECT CARD_NUMBER FROM USER_DETAILS WHERE USER_ID = 795001`
```

However, it is possible for a malicious user to construct an input string that will cause the function to retrieve information that does not belong to the user. For example, they could pass in the following input to the function:

```
"" OR '1' == '1'
```

This user input would generate a query that would return the **CARD_NUMBER** of all users:

```
`SELECT CARD_NUMBER FROM USER_DETAILS WHERE USER_ID = "" OR '1' == '1'
```

As you can see, it is very easy to make a mistake when defining a database query.

Along with getting unauthorized access to data, SQL injection can also be used to corrupt or even delete data.

So, what is the idiomatic way of defining a query? We should never construct a query by concatenating user input to form a query string. Instead, use a prepared statement to define a query, in which a placeholder is used to pass the user parameter, as shown in the following example:

```
func GetCardNumberSecure(db *sql.DB, userID string) (resp string, err error){
    stmt, err := db.Prepare(`SELECT CARD_NUMBER FROM USER_DETAILS WHERE USER_ID =
        ?`)
    if err != nil {
```

```
      return resp, err
  }
  defer stmt.Close()
  row := stmt.QueryRow(userID)
  switch err = row.Scan(&resp); err {
  case sql.ErrNoRows:
    return resp, fmt.Errorf("no rows returned")
  case nil:
    return resp, err
  default:
    return resp, err}
  }
  return
}
```

By using placeholders for the user input, we have mitigated potential SQL injection attacks.

Command Injection

Command injection is another possible injection attack vector that you should be aware of. The injection aims to execute OS commands on the application server, which could allow the attacker to get sensitive data, delete files, or even execute malicious scripts on the server. This type of attack can happen when the user input is not sanitized.

We will see how this works by looking at the following example. Consider this function, which takes a string as input and uses it to list files:

```
func listFiles(path string) (string, error) {
  cmd := exec.Command("bash", "-c", "ls"+path)
  var out bytes.Buffer
  cmd.Stdout = &out
  err := cmd.Run()
  if err != nil {
    return "", err
  }
  return out.String(), nil
}
```

There are a few things wrong here:

- The user input is not sanitized.

- The user could pass in any string as a path.

- Along with **path string**, the user could add other commands that could run on the server.

Let's test this by running a unit test on the function. The following test run should prove all the issues previously listed:

```go
package command_injection
import "testing"
func TestListFiles(t *testing.T) {
  out, err := listFiles(" .; cat /etc/hosts")
  if err != nil {
    t.Error(err)
  } else {
    t.Log(out)
  }
}
```

You should get the following output when you run the test using the preceding command:

```
go test -v ./...
```

```
✔ ~/git/The-Go-Workshop/Chapter18/Examples/Example2 [master|✚ 2]
[09:06 $ go test -v - ./...
=== RUN   TestListFiles
--- PASS: TestListFiles (0.01s)
    example_2_test.go:8: example_2.go
        example_2_test.go
        ##
        # Host Database
        #
        # localhost is used to configure the loopback interface
        # when the system is booting.  Do not change this entry.
        ##
        127.0.0.1       localhost
        255.255.255.255 broadcasthost
        ::1             localhost
        fe80::1%lo0     localhost

PASS
ok      github.com/PacktWorkshops/The-Go-Workshop/Chapter18/Examples/Example2
```

Figure 18.1: Expected output

As you can see, instead of passing a valid filename, the user passed a string that made the function return the files in the directory as well as reading the **/etc/hosts** file on the server.

Exercise 18.01: Handling SQL Injection

In this exercise, we will be enabling a function to prevent an SQL injection attack.

> **Note**
>
> In this exercise, we will be using a lightweight database called **Sqlite**, which can run in-memory on your local machine. To use the database, we will need to import a third-party Go library that uses **cgo** under the hood.
>
> https://packt.live/38Bjl3a
>
> If you are on a Windows machine, you will need to have GCC installed and included in your path. You can use the instructions on this website to install GCC for windows: https://packt.live/38Bjl3a.

The following steps will help you with the solution:

1. Create **injection.go** and import the following packages:

```
package exercise1
import (
    "database/sql"
    "fmt"
    "strings"
)
```

2. Define a function, **UpdatePhone()**, that takes a **sql.DB** object and some user information such as an ID and a phone number as a **string**:

```
func UpdatePhone(db *sql.DB, ID string, phone string) error {
    var builder strings.Builder
    builder.WriteString("UPDATE USER_DETAILS SET PHONE=")
    builder.WriteString(phone)
    builder.WriteString(" WHERE USER_ID=")
    builder.WriteString(ID)
    fmt.Printf("Running query: %s\n", builder.String())
    _, err := db.Exec(builder.String())
    if err != nil {
```

```
      return err
   }
   return nil
}
```

The **UpdatePhone()** function inserts a user ID and a phone number into the table by concatenating the data from the input parameters.

The query string in the **UpdatePhone()** function is vulnerable to SQL injection. For example, if an input is passed with the following values:

```
ID: "19853011 OR USER_ID=1007007"
```

This will update the record not only for user ID **"19853011"**, but also for **"1007007"**. This is a simple example. However, there could be worse things that could happen, such as dropping tables in the database.

3. Create another function called **UpdatePhoneSecure()**, which will update the user details securely. Instead of concatenating inputs to form the query, use placeholders for the parameters to pass into the query:

injection.go

```
20 func UpdatePhoneSecure(db *sql.DB, ID string, phone string) error {
21   stmt, err := db.Prepare(`UPDATE USER_DETAILS SET PHONE=? WHERE
     USER_ID=?`)
22   if err != nil {
23     return err
24   }
25   defer stmt.Close()
26   result, err := stmt.Exec(phone, ID)
27   if err != nil {
28     return err
29   }
```

The full code for this step is available at https://packt.live/34QWP31

4. Define a helper function called **initializeDB()** to set up the database and load some test data:

```
func initializeDB(db *sql.DB) error {
    _, err := db.Exec(`CREATE TABLE IF NOT EXISTS USER_DETAILS (USER_ID TEXT,
        PHONE TEXT, ADDRESS TEXT)`)
    if err != nil {

        return err

    }
    stmt, err := db.Prepare(`INSERT INTO USER_DETAILS (USER_ID, PHONE,
        ADDRESS) VALUES (?, ?, ?)`)
    if err != nil {

        return err

    }
```

```go
    for _, user := range testData {
      _, err := stmt.Exec(user.ID, user.CardNumber, user.Address)
      if err != nil {
        return err
      }
    }
    return nil
  }
```

> **Note**
>
> It is good practice to clean up after every test.

5. Define a function called **tearDownDB()** to help you clear the database:

```go
func tearDownDB(db *sql.DB) error {
    _, err := db.Exec("DROP TABLE USER_DETAILS")
    if err != nil {
      return err
    }
    return nil
}
```

6. We will also need a function to help with the setting up of the database connection. Define a function called **getConnection()**, which returns a ***sql.DB** object:

```go
func getConnection() (*sql.DB, error) {
    conn, err := sql.Open("sqlite3", "test.DB")
    if err != nil {
      return nil, fmt.Errorf("could not open db connection %v", err)
    }
    return conn, nil
}
```

7. Define a **TestMain()** function that executes the setup of the test data and then runs the test. This function will also need to call the **tearDownDB()** function to clean up the test data:

```go
func TestMain(m *testing.M) {
    var err error
    db, err = getConnection()
    if err != nil {
      fmt.Println(err)
```

```
      os.Exit(1)
   }
   err = initializeDB(db)
   if err != nil {
      fmt.Println(err)
      os.Exit(1)
   }
   defer tearDownDB(db)
   if m.Run() != 0 {
      fmt.Println("error running tests")
      os.Exit(1)
   }
}
```

8. Finally, define the **TestUpdatePhoneSecure()** function to help you run a test against the **UpdatePhoneSecure()** function:

injection_test.go

```
77 func TestUpdatePhoneSecure(t *testing.T) {
78   var tests = []struct {
79     ID     string
80     Phone  string
81     err    string
82   }{
83     {
84        ID:     "1",
85        Phone: "1234",
86        err:    "",
87     },
```

The full code for this step is available at https://packt.live/34MEJze

9. Run the test using the following command:

```
go test -v ./...
```

You should get the following output:

```
[09:07 $ go test -v ./...
=== RUN   TestUpdatePhoneSecure
--- PASS: TestUpdatePhoneSecure (0.00s)
PASS
ok      github.com/PacktWorkshops/The-Go-Workshop/Chapter18/Exercise18.01
```

Figure 18.2: Expected output

SQL and command injection can occur when user input is not correctly sanitized. Generally, we should avoid passing user input directly into SQL or OS commands.

In this exercise, we have learned how to securely code SQL code to protect an application from SQL injection.

Cross-Site Scripting

Cross-Site Scripting, or XSS, is another major attack type that is frequently listed in the OWASP (**Open Web Application Security Project**) of top ten application vulnerabilities. Similar to SQL injection, this vulnerability is also caused by non-sanitized user input, but in this case, rather than modifying the behavior of a database, it injects scripts into a web page.

Web pages are constructed using html tags. Every html page contains some content bracketed by the html tag, like this:

```
<html>
   Hello World!
</html>
```

One such html tag is the **<script>** tag, which is used to embed executable content – usually, JavaScript code. This tag is used to run client-side code execution on the browser, for example, to generate dynamic content or manipulate data and images.

The code inside the **<script>** tag is not visible on the web page and, as such, it generally goes unnoticed. This feature of the **<script>** tag can be manipulated by attackers to run malicious scripts to steal sensitive data, monitor activity, or perform other unauthorized actions. So, how does the malicious script get injected in the first place? If user data entered through a browser is not sanitized, an attacker can input/inject a malicious script to the web server, which can then be stored on the database.

When a victim visits the page, the script gets loaded onto their browser.

> **Note**
>
> OWASP is an organization that provides useful information to secure your application. They provide rankings for the common application security vulnerabilities such as the OWASP top 10:
>
> https://packt.live/36t6RbU
>
> You can find more information about OWASP here:
>
> https://packt.live/34ioCsZ

Exercise 18.02: Handling XSS Attacks

In this exercise, we will see how an XSS attack can be carried out on a web page, and then we will fix the issue with the code to make it safe from this type of attack:

1. Create a **main.go** file and import the following packages:

```
package main
import (
    "fmt"
    "net/http"
    "text/template"
)
```

2. Define a sample HTML template that can be used to load a web page. For multiline text assignment to a variable, you can use the string enclosed by backticks(`):

```
var content = `<html>
<head>
<title>My Blog</title>
</head>
<body>
    <h1>My Blog Site</h1>
    <h2> Comments </h2>
    {{.Comment}}
    <formaction="/" method="post">
      Add Comment:<input type="text"name="input">
      <input type="submit" value="Submit">
    </form>
</body>
</html>`
```

3. Create a **struct** called **input**, which contains a field called **Comment** as a **string** value. This **struct** will be used to wrap a user comment:

```
type input struct {
    Comment string
}
```

4. Create a **handler()** function to return the response of an HTTP request:

```
func handler(w http.ResponseWriter, r *http.Request) {
    var userInput = &input{
      Comment: r.FormValue("input"),
    }
    t := template.Must(template.New("test").Parse(content))
```

```
    err := t.Execute(w, userInput)
    if err != nil {
      fmt.Println(err)
    }
  }
```

5. Define the **main()** function to run an HTTP server:

```
funcmain() {
    http.HandleFunc("/", handler)
    http.ListenAndServe(":8080", nil)
}
```

6. Run the code:

```
go run main.go
```

7. Open **http://localhost:8080** on the browser. You should be able to see the following page:

Figure 18.3: HTTP server landing page

In a normal scenario, users would input text comments that would get populated on the page. However, if a malicious user wanted to inject an executable script into the page, they could do so by submitting the following input:

```
<script>alert("Hello")</script>
```

This is what you will see:

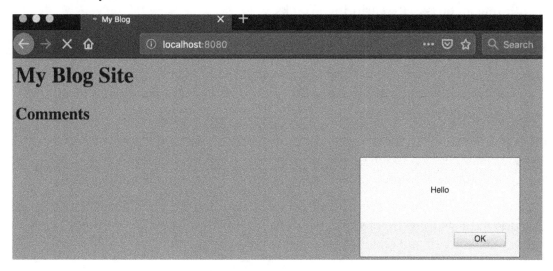

Figure 18.4: XSS execution

8. Let's fix our web application to make it safe from XXS attacks. In this case, the solution is as simple as updating from **text/template** to use the **html/template** package:

```go
package main
import (
  "fmt"
  "net/http"
  "html/template"
)
```

If you run the server again and then submit the same input, your output will be escaped by the **html/template** library and, thus, will not be treated as a script:

Figure 18.5: XSS escaped output

In this exercise, we learned about the proper use of templating in code to protect an application from cross-site scripting attacks.

Cryptography

Go has a very comprehensive crypto library included as part of the standard library, which covers hashing algorithms, PKI certificates, and symmetric and asymmetric encryption algorithms.

While it is convenient to have a collection of different ciphers' encryption and hashing libraries available for us to use, it is important for us to be aware of vulnerabilities in these algorithms, so we can choose the most appropriate algorithm for our use case.

For example, the MD5 and SHA-1 hashing algorithms are not considered safe to use for encrypting data, as they are easily brute-forced. However, they are commonly used by file servers to provide file checksums for error checking.

Hashing Libraries

Hashing is the process of converting plaintext data into an encrypted format by implementing an algorithm to produce the encrypted text. The output of such a process is supposed to be unique and the probability of a hash collision, which is two different inputs producing the same output, is extremely unlikely. Hashing functions are routinely used in databases and in the secure transmission of messages.

We can use the checksum functions to produce a one-way hash. For example, to produce an MD5 checksum, we can use the **Sum()** function, which takes in a **byte** array and returns a **byte** array:

```
Sum(in []byte) []byte
```

For SHA256, the checksum function definition is very similar:

```
Sum256(data []byte) [Size]byte
```

Apart from MD5, the standard library for Go contains implementations for SHA1, SHA256, and SHA512. We will see how to use them in the upcoming exercise.

Exercise 18.03: Using Different Hashing Libraries

In this exercise, we will learn how to use different hashing libraries in Go:

1. Create a **main.go** file and import the following crypto hashing libraries:

```
package main
import (
    "crypto/md5"
    "crypto/sha256"
    "crypto/sha512"
    "fmt"
    "golang.org/x/crypto/blake2b"
    "golang.org/x/crypto/blake2s"
    "golang.org/x/crypto/sha3"
)
```

2. Define a utility function called **getHash()** that takes in an input string to be hashed and the type of hash library to use. Define a **switch** statement that uses the **hashType** input string to decide which type of hashing library to use:

```
func getHash(input string, hashType string) string {
```

3. Inside the **switch** statement, add cases for using MD5, SHA256, SHA512, and SHA3_512. The **switch** cases should return the hash of the input string using the corresponding hashing libraries:

```
switch hashType {
case "MD5":
  return fmt.Sprintf("%x", md5.Sum([]byte(input)))
case "SHA256":
  return fmt.Sprintf("%x", sha256.Sum256([]byte(input)))
case "SHA512":
  return fmt.Sprintf("%x", sha512.Sum512([]byte(input)))
case "SHA3_512":
  return fmt.Sprintf("%x", sha3.Sum512([]byte(input)))
default:
  return fmt.Sprintf("%x", sha256.Sum256([]byte(input)))
}
}
```

4. Add some other hashing libraries that are not available in the standard library:

```go
// from "golang.org/x/crypto/blake2s"
case "BLAKE2s_256":
  return fmt.Sprintf("%x", blake2s.Sum256([]byte(input)))
// from "golang.org/x/crypto/blake2b"
case "BLAKE2b_512":
  return fmt.Sprintf("%x", blake2b.Sum512([]byte(input)))
  }
}
```

> **Note**
>
> Apart from the **blake** libraries mentioned, you can also find packages for MD4 and SHA3 under https://packt.live/2PiwlmH.

5. Define the `main()` function and call the `getHashutility()` function defined previously:

```go
func main() {
  fmt.Println("MD5:", getHash("Hello World!", "MD5"))
  fmt.Println("SHA256:", getHash("Hello World!", "SHA256"))
  fmt.Println("SHA512:", getHash("Hello World!", "SHA512"))
  fmt.Println("SHA3_512:", getHash("Hello World!", "SHA3_512"))
  fmt.Println("BLAKE2s_256:", getHash("Hello World!", "BLAKE2s_256"))
  fmt.Println("BLAKE2b_512:", getHash("Hello World!", "BLAKE2b_512"))
}
```

6. Run the program:

```
go run main.go
```

You should get the following output:

```
gobin:exercise3 Gobin$ go run main.go
MD5: 952d2c56d0485958336747bcdd98590d
SHA256: 334d016f755cd6dc58c53a86e183882f8ec14f52fb05345887c8a5edd42c87b7
SHA512: 3a928aa2cc3bf291a4657d1b51e0e087dfb1dea060c89d20776b8943d24e712ea65778fe608dd
db246be5844
SHA3_512: 5156b8639729070b538a4d57fe78004876376a6503adfe8f48c57da7a959f74162b85f53417
b62d07c4a4240
BLAKE2s_256: 0c55d46f7840a50efa239162ffd9ac7759013bc47d0206c689e45ce110f8df81
BLAKE2b_512: 8af50f029bbce456187b7f9c5da97c12224ecdaed01aa2b27a40bcbc34a7e28c9ea866b6
79d198ca99a93b73
```

Figure 18.6: Expected output

In this exercise, we have learned how to generate ciphertext using different hashing packages available in Go.

> **Note**
>
> In the preceding example, we imported some hashing libraries, such as https://packt.live/2ryy9Ps.
>
> The packages under `golang.org/x/` are still developed as part of the Go project. However, they remain outside of the main installation, so you will have to run **go get** to install them.
>
> You can find a list of these packages here: https://packt.live/2tbThv7.

Encryption

Encryption is the process of converting data into a format in which it cannot be read by an unintended recipient.

When dealing with sensitive data, it is always best practice to encrypt it. The nature of the data will determine the sensitivity. For example, credit card information from your customers can be considered as highly sensitive data, whereas the item being bought could be considered as not very sensitive.

You will probably come across the terms encryption at rest and encryption in transit, referring to how data should be encrypted before being stored (for example, in a database) or transmitted (for example, over a network). We will touch on encryption in transit in a later topic (HTTP/TLS).

In this topic, we will focus on the underlying encryption mechanisms.

Since (good) encryption algorithms are complicated by nature, the general advice is to always use existing encryption algorithms and not invent your own. The strength of an encryption algorithm should lie in the mathematical complexity of the problem, rather than in the secrecy of how the encryption algorithm works. As such, 'safe' encryption algorithms are all public.

Go provides both symmetric and asymmetric encryption libraries. Let's look at the example implementations of both these encryption types.

Symmetric Encryption

With symmetric encryption, the same key is used for encryption and decryption. The Go standard library has implementations of common symmetric encryption algorithms such as AES and DES under **crypto/aes** and **crypto/des**.

The basic steps to encrypt an input byte array using a string key (for example, a password) are as follows:

To create the ciphertext in Go, we can use the **Seal()** function. We also use a **nonce**, which is a single-use random sequence. The **dst** input variable here is a byte array used to store the encrypted data:

```
Seal(dst, nonce, plaintext, additionalData []byte) []byte
```

To decrypt the ciphertext, we need to again use the **crypto/cipher** library to make use of the GCM wrappers:

```
func (g *gcm) Open(dst, nonce, ciphertext, data []byte) ([]byte, error)
```

Exercise 18.04: Symmetric Encryption and Decryption

In this exercise, we are going to make use of the Go crypto libraries for symmetric encryption and learn how to encrypt and decrypt data:

1. Create a **main.go** file and import the following package:

    crypto/cipher: For block cipher implementation.

    crypto/aes: AES is an encryption specification, and **crypto/aes** is the Go implementation.

    crypto/rand: Used for random number generation.

    ```
    package main
    import (
        "crypto/aes"
        "crypto/cipher"
        "crypto/rand"
        "fmt"
    )
    ```

2. Define a function to encrypt data using the **crypto/aes** and **crypto/cipher** libraries. The following function accepts input data in the form of a byte array and a key string, which is typically a secret passphrase. It returns the encrypted data:

    ```
    func encrypt(data []byte, key string) (resp []byte, err error) {
        block, err := aes.NewCipher([]byte(key))
        if err != nil {
    ```

```
      return resp, err
   }
   gcm, err := cipher.NewGCM(block)
   if err != nil {
      return resp, err
   }
   nonce := make([]byte, gcm.NonceSize())
   if _, err := rand.Read(nonce); err != nil {
      return resp, err
   }
   return gcm.Seal(dst, nonce, data, []byte("test")), nil
}
```

The nonce needs to be stored for decryption. There are many ways of doing this. In the preceding implementation, we do this by passing in the nonce in the first input to the **Seal()** function, which is a byte array, **dst**. Since the **Seal()** function appends the encrypted data to the input byte array, the resulting ciphertext will be appended to the nonce and returned as a one-byte array. If you pass in additional data, the value must match when you decrypt the resulting ciphertext.

3. Define a function to decrypt data. It should accept the encrypted data in the form of a byte array and the passphrase as a string. It should return the decrypted data:

```
func decrypt(data []byte, key string) (resp []byte, err error) {
   block, err := aes.NewCipher([]byte(key))
   if err != nil {
      return resp, err
   }
   gcm, err := cipher.NewGCM(block)
   if err != nil {
      return resp, err
   }
   ciphertext := data[gcm.NonceSize():]
   nonce := data[:gcm.NonceSize()]
   resp, err = gcm.Open(nil, nonce, ciphertext, []byte("test"))
   if err != nil {
      return resp, fmt.Errorf("error decrypting data: %v", err)
   }
   return resp, nil
}
```

4. Define the **main()** function to test the **encrypt** and **decrypt** functions:

```go
func main() {
  const key = "mysecurepassword"
  encrypted, err := encrypt([]byte("Hello World!"), key)
  if err != nil {
    fmt.Println(err)
  }
  fmt.Println("Encrypted Text: ", string(encrypted))
  decrypted, err := decrypt(encrypted, key)
  if err != nil {
    fmt.Println(err)
  }
  fmt.Println("Decrypted Text: ", string(decrypted))
}
```

5. Run the program by using the following command:

```
go run main.go
```

You should get the following output.

```
gobin:exercise4 Gobin$ go run main.go
Encrypted Text: d48d0b27b3b1d806d5d464124b3adf12544cbd44f5f3576a0332fdad93527d8a93eb3951ef
Decrypted Text:  Hello World!
```

Figure 18.7: Expected output

In this exercise, we have learned how to perform symmetric encryption and decryption.

Asymmetric Encryption

Asymmetric encryption is also known as public-key cryptography. This encryption mechanism makes use of a pair of keys, a public key and a private key. The public key can be freely distributed to other partners who are willing to exchange data with you. If a partner wants to send encrypted data, they will use your public key to encrypt their data. This encrypted data can be decrypted by you using your private key.

The Go standard library has support for common asymmetric encryption algorithms such as RSA and DSA.

For example, the **rsa.EncryptOAEP()** function is used to encrypt data using the public key:

```
EncryptOAEP(hash hash.Hash,randomio.Reader,pub *PublicKey,msg []byte,label
  []byte)([]byte,error)
```

The **rsa.DecryptOAEP()** function is used to decrypt the ciphertext using the private key:

```
DecryptOAEP(hash hash.Hash, random io.Reader, priv *PrivateKey, ciphertext
   []byte, label []byte) ([]byte, error)
```

The encryption operation takes in **rsa.PublicKey**, and the decryption operation takes **rsa.PrivateKey**. The key pair can be generated using the **rsa.GenerateKey()** function:

```
GenerateKey(random io.Reader, bits int) (*PrivateKey, error)
```

Exercise 18.05: Asymmetric Encryption and Decryption

In this exercise, we will see the encrypt and decrypt operations in action:

1. Create a **main.go** file and import the following packages:

   crypto/rand: The **rand.Reader** from this package will be used to seed the generation of the **rsa.PrivateKey**.

   crypto/rsa: This package is required to generate the private key and for the **encrypt/decrypt** operation.

   crypto/sha256: The symmetric hash function will be used to seed the generation of the **rsa.PrivateKey**.

   ```go
   package main
   import (
     "crypto/rand"
     "crypto/rsa"
     "crypto/sha256"
     "fmt"
     "os"
   )
   ```

2. Define the **main()** function and generate an **rsa** key pair:

   ```go
   func main() {
   privateKey, err := rsa.GenerateKey(rand.Reader, 1024)
     if err != nil {
   fmt.Printf("error generating rsa key: %v", err)
     }
   publicKey := privateKey.PublicKey
   text := []byte("My Secret Text")
   ```

3. Encrypt the data using **publicKey**:

```
    ciphertext, err := rsa.EncryptOAEP(sha256.New(), rand.Reader, &publicKey,
      text, nil)
    if err != nil {
  fmt.Printf("error encrypting data: %v", err)
  os.Exit(1)
  }
  fmt.Println("Encrypted ciphertext: ", string(ciphertext)
```

4. Use **privateKey** to decrypt the ciphertext from *step* 3:

```
  decrypted, err := rsa.DecryptOAEP(sha256.New(), rand.Reader, privateKey,
    ciphertext, nil)
    if err != nil {
  fmt.Printf("error decrypting data: %v", err)
  os.Exit(1)
  }
    fmt.Println("Decrypted text: ", string(decrypted))
}
```

5. Run the program using the following command:

```
  go run main.go
```

You should get the following output:

```
gobin:exercise5 Gobin$ go run main.go
Encrypted cyphertext: 2e8917c088844e14affc13160843d41f2820637021ff1485a34e2e650bf8580727be
f6c808920ab39fb872d7d069497f69d4d0ea579f8abcd2e629fcfeefc8122d672d20b0aaff33b444764ab92b78
0a9235eb61f4dd9542f81abd7f05
Decrypted text:  My Secret Text
```

Figure 18.8: Expected output

We have now learned how to create an RSA public key and use it to encrypt and decrypt data.

Random Generators

The Go standard library provides utility libraries to create random number generators. The implementations are provided in the **crypto/rand** and **math/rand** packages. The **math/rand** library can be used to generate random integers; however, randomness cannot be guaranteed. Therefore, this library should only be used in cases where the number can be generally random and is not security-sensitive.

Otherwise, you should always use **crypto/rand**. As a side note, the **crypto/rand** package relies on OS randomness – for example, on Linux it uses **/dev/urandom**. Therefore, it is generally slower than the math library implementation.

To produce a random integer between 0 and a user-defined number using the **crypto/ rand** library, we can use the following function:

```
funcInt(rand io.Reader, max *big.Int) (n *big.Int, err error)
```

There are many scenarios where we might want to generate a secure random number, for example, when generating unique session IDs. It is important that random numbers used in these scenarios are genuinely random, and do not follow a pattern that can be inferred. For example, if an attacker can infer the next **sessionID** by looking at the last few session IDs, they could potentially gain unauthenticated access to that session.

Let's learn how to generate random numbers using both the **crypto/rand** and **math/rand** libraries.

Exercise 18.06: Random Generators

Random number generation is a common activity when trying to introduce some entropy to encrypt data. In this exercise, we will see how random numbers can be generated using the **math/rand** and **crypto/rand** packages:

1. Create a **main.go** file and import the following packages:

```
package main
import (
   "crypto/rand"
   "fmt"
   "math/big"
   math "math/rand"
)
```

    math "math/rand": We add the **math** namespace to differentiate it from the **crypto/ rand** package.

2. In the **main()** function, create a **for** loop that runs 10 times and prints a random integer between 0 and 1000, generated using the **rand.Int()** function of the **crypto/rand** library:

```
func main() {
   fmt.Println("Crypto random")
   for i := 1; i<=10; i++ {
      data, _:= rand.Int(rand.Reader,big.NewInt(1000))
      fmt.Println(data)
   }
```

3. Create another similar **for** loop using the **math/rand** package:

```
fmt.Println("Math random")
for i := 1; i<=10; i++ {
  fmt.Println(math.Intn(1000))
}
}
```

4. Run the program using the following command:

```
go run main.go
```

You should get the following output:

```
gobin:exercise6 Gobin$ go run main.go
Crypto random
812
155
864
971
216
690
598
909
538
836
Math random
81
887
847
59
81
318
425
540
456
300
```

Figure 18.9: Expected output

While the outputs for the two implementations may appear similar, the underlying mechanism of number generation is important when using random numbers for security purposes.

In this exercise, we have seen how to generate random numbers using the **math/rand** and **crypto/rand** packages.

HTTPS/TLS

When you are developing a web application, it is important to know how to secure your information in transit. This is achieved by using a **Transport Layer Security Protocol**, commonly known as TLS. The standard Go library provides a TLS implementation under the `crypto/tls` package. The TLS protocol ensures:

Identity: Provides both client and server identification using digital certificates.

Integrity: Makes sure that data is not tampered with in transit by calculating a message digest.

Authentication: Both client and server can be required to be authenticated using Public-Key Cryptography.

Confidentiality: The message is encrypted during transit, thus protecting it from any unintended recipient.

In the following topic, we'll see how to use certificates to encrypt traffic between a client and a server.

The first step to encrypting traffic between a client and a server is to generate a digital certificate.

In the next exercise, we will generate a self-signed x509 certificate and a matching RSA private key. This certificate can be used as either a client or server certificate.

> **Note**
>
> You might come across the term CA, which stands for Certificate Authority. The CA is the one who signs certificates and distributes them to users who require a signed certificate.

Exercise 18.07: Generating a Certificate and Private Key

In this exercise, we will learn how to generate a self-signed certificate and a matching private key for the certificate, which can be used in client-server communication:

1. Create a `main.go` file and import the following packages:

```
package main
import (
    "crypto/rand"
    "crypto/rsa"
    "crypto/tls"
    "crypto/x509"
```

```
        "crypto/x509/pkix"
        "encoding/pem"
        "fmt"
        "io/ioutil"
        "math/big"
        "net"
        "net/http"
        "os"
        "time"
    )
```

The crypto packages will be used to generate x509 certificates.

2. To generate the certificate, we first create a template. In the template, we can define criteria for the certificate; for example, the expiry of the certificate is set to a year. The template needs a random seed, which can be generated using the **rand. Int()** function:

main.go

```
28 func generate() (cert []byte, privateKey []byte, err error) {
29    serialNumber, err := rand.Int(rand.Reader, big.NewInt(27))
30    if err != nil {
31      return cert, privateKey, err
32    }
33    notBefore := time.Now()
// Create Certificate template
34    ca := &x509.Certificate{
35      SerialNumber: serialNumber,
36      Subject: pkix.Name{
37        Organization: []string{"example.com"},
38      },
```

The full code for this step is available at https://packt.live/34N7jjT

3. Create **privateKey**, which will be used to sign the certificate:

```
    rsaKey, err := rsa.GenerateKey(rand.Reader, 2048)
    if err != nil {
      return cert, privateKey, err
    }
```

4. Create a self-signed **DER** (binary encrypted) certificate:

```go
DER, err := x509.CreateCertificate(rand.Reader, ca, ca, &rsaKey.PublicKey,
    rsaKey)
if err != nil {
    return cert, privateKey, err
}
```

5. Convert the binary encoded **DER** cert to an ASCII encoded PEM cert. PEM (**Privacy Enhanced Mail**) is a digital certificate format:

```go
b := pem.Block{
    Type:  "CERTIFICATE",
    Bytes: DER,
}
cert = pem.EncodeToMemory(&b)
privateKey = pem.EncodeToMemory(
    &pem.Block{
        Type:  "RSA PRIVATE KEY",
        Bytes: x509.MarshalPKCS1PrivateKey(rsaKey),
    })
return cert, privateKey, nil
}
```

6. Define the **main()** function to call the **generate** function and print the output:

```go
func main() {
    serverCert, serverKey, err := generate()
    if err != nil {
        fmt.Printf("error generating server certificate: %v", err)
        os.Exit(1)
    }
    fmt.Println("Server Certificate:")
    fmt.Printf("%s\n", serverCert)
    fmt.Println("Server Key:")
    fmt.Printf("%s\n", serverKey)
}
```

You should get an output similar to the following:

```
gobin:exercise7 Gobin$ go run main.go
Server Certificate:
-----BEGIN CERTIFICATE-----
MIIC9zCCAd+gAwIBAgIBBzANBgkqhkiG9w0BAQsFADAWMRQwEgYDVQQKEwtleGFt
cGxlLmNvbTAeFw0xOTEwMTcxMTE5NTJaFw0yMDEwMTYxMTE5NTJaMBYxFDASBgNV
BAoTC2V4YW1wbGUuY29tMIIBIjANBgkqhkiG9w0BAQEFAAOCAQ8AMIIBCgKCAQEA
sidxELmEtYVOETkH5DiSbTYh3l0x4W1x9WVzP7t9x6dUUeHOqQoZhzOQBANMJryVV
YryU8PAlcoNhndOk2n3GIahzrBGl8WdrNR1i7AGLCjlq9JTxX/MWRFit+VsJ0Vcl
b2tnuTUqJDkB2+7XmGxYyJV92al7gs2/ghxDJA1Q8qcPQWvKuYvp1pqefPfI1Ptv
VjyEsns5U6SM0z1xoUw2M16b/VEUSgurSiK5REImLBlhoGiJg0GnMetgL2QgL8z9
7O8Rr9dpcKnTsNcyTMJjblizq/fZ9axKa0S5NJz/kl9CCRGMKSnacmWwIXZM22/f
MOBp90aBrxm/dRGCknyI4QIDAQABo1AwTjAOBgNVHQ8BAf8EBAMCBaAwHQYDVR0l
BBYwFAYIKwYBBQUHAwIGCCsGAQUFBwMBMAwGA1UdEwEB/wQCMAAwDwYDVR0RBAgw
BocEfwAAATANBgkqhkiG9w0BAQsFAAOCAQEAVRLN3CKVgjh3EysIlZQmlajtfKxz
ljN6pp8EeyHepS/zyy1OTHKygoNaPM2AaCJJjfXBTl2yviVjfn+yR0XR/hqbgSSe
fisvuq7hEd5yo/0/i01huFm/27/wVBd9wR/Kgbc306AsHX6Bmgm8dlfA8/5/d53W
JbSoBsQoNa53yaJCp+dafzY5u5uJfeBD/XcXJbBHuzR7tOUL19WXyBhoCQTKJM/f
jj4AVMDW9LnzuhulVfFj3gOyASBzUhiZgHghoGa3+z4yTyY0oZdMhvmBbn6J+3XF
lMtjioWWwsdT4GwFY6Hq6eeiq/xGxUE3zk6WNHlbc/kmmjqufAucW4vLGg==
-----END CERTIFICATE-----

Server Key:
-----BEGIN RSA PRIVATE KEY-----
MIIEowIBAAKCAQEAsidxELmEtYVOETkH5DiSbTYh3l0x4W1x9WVzP7t9x6dUUeHO
qQoZhzOQBANMJyVVYryU8PAlcoNhndOk2n3GIahzrBGl8WdrNR1i7AGLCjlq9JTx
X/MWRFit+VsJ0Vclb2tnuTUqJDkB2+7XmGxYyJV92al7gs2/ghxDJA1Q8qcPQWvK
uYvp1pqefPfI1PtvVjyEsns5U6SM0z1xoUw2M16b/VEUSgurSiK5REImLBlhoGiJ
g0GnMetgL2QgL8z97O8Rr9dpcKnTsNcyTMJjblizq/fZ9axKa0S5NJz/kl9CCRGM
KSnacmWwIXZM22/fMOBp90aBrxm/dRGCknyI4QIDAQABAoIBAFk5pcgBkjSzcfjw
PkKQDs4BuY670Dqd7OBBkioORh2TcYic9jr1Ivny2iMYX7CPYydTWakeLTMgF+jK
0hrXuT6sNlqscBbqe+gbMqsOzsstHKMoYYdzoOhUHbXwYYdmBQq7mTRKKzP/FS5I
fdQKF6FGNcSovIIzd8G7U+kffjY4nVuyw015Vi/mNFQWKBEXWTxJot1S3ehOW0t4
PFx68+nxy3L5iqwEl9N7rr7PfFtNZ2tlaNFq4lHjrqnON+fhW/X/aYhQvdglS13u
JxSXIT006ZmsZBjWRPMovHQJly/R3/kSQ0+Uefkb4JP8gLwkIkpv3pKq0kEU3IB7
NOMcPd0CgYEA2LFToXYljYs4gVQ6+WEx8kqvzA3tGerFpBa0XVD/CEfcDAzmYDwc
Sh/ta5o7w9M00qTA4BJdSCD+wNOsXo7aHz/0cEppQyqjDamhbQPPBxlSrDR+VSy/
jXTHj6bS273+mg6a517kXHJK6hsGStJa7dCUHAwvK+32XZ+m3nizZFcCgYEA0nh6
Fe8//XWpKiyQMlDPr7p/zeOBnFLZ17YyvcAQhzFbIhgTridZ7bGsFCu+LwldNbJr
eOAbLgpxZzLfixwtY9kK81LFnl6l6p8Jfkn4gHbTM7FMsIGunhTmuPieJkiAoqbc
GG7lLkcwh02pPgAHGHZcgPAYZXSWC2XfJ0zG+YcCgYBE/rk1KMwuNEzqiOo6KyNf
FT7CRxDedq01YPFO4RJDDbZXs+fKbnlHdMEAyNwMrvwbsc+jyNUguTjEJuG0PeHf
n1pyQo8fjrzaBc/bSSIrDXoQUKqE7jmTjcJYz/JFe0pMvSe/Uax+bvnBbpdjTXUc
UZRHFe4TG7Kc/s9/+IiOAwKBgCK7bPI3tCighRUHm5giC9PlA/g3BgmFBpv5XjBA
BLo6o95heMXxin6WJ16BxXW/ptkYo3GkEfgsEwDDvW4YbUkf5RW4YBI9bkXkjs1/
aXnRohLSvGQYUneV3WlC5d5NcqTkwkdp7XoQl2qMn1Qy7vjTd3pzpKMBdU1WN1gl
7GP7AoGBAKWuotdAWE9SuSgRV37ydL1GqwF2Gae2YwFH3anVZUNCoixypp5lSAxv
i9sIo/R2vsZKzBlvFSpxz/mzKmAxo96rRKUa/V6QAH2/rYKgDyj7bnNtpRzWPOn1
4BLcNojmM6zf/H9mtufbhy8awhy//BMLK4oH4mm/XNlg5JFbdio3
-----END RSA PRIVATE KEY-----
```

Figure 18.10: Expected output

Thus, we have successfully generated a self-signed certificate and a private key for the application. In the output above, the "Server Certificate" is the public certificate, and the "Server Key" is the private key. This can be used to encrypt data between the client and the server. They are particularly useful when there is sensitive data in transit, such as on a banking website.

Exercise 18.08: Running an HTTPS Server

In the following exercise, we'll learn how to use certificates to encrypt traffic between a client and server.

We will learn how to create a public-key certificate. The certificate will be used to encode data between a client and a server:

1. Create a **main.go** file and import the following packages:

    crypto/rand: For random number generation.

    crypto/rsa: Provides a wrapper for RSA certificates.

    crypto/tls: Provides a wrapper for Transport Layer Security (TLS) protocol.

    crypto.x509: Provides a wrapper for X509 digital certificates.

```go
package main
import (
    "crypto/rand"
    "crypto/rsa"
    "crypto/tls"
    "crypto/x509"
    "crypto/x509/pkix"
    "encoding/pem"
    "fmt"
    "io/ioutil"
    "log"
    "math/big"
    "net"
    "net/http"
    "os"
    "time"
)
```

2. Define a function called **runServer()** to run an HTTP server with a TLS configuration. The function should take in the paths of the certificate file, a private key file, and a PEM encoded client certificate. In our TLS configuration, we require both server and client certificates. The server certificate is used by the client to validate the authenticity of the server. The client certificate is verified by the server to validate the client:

main.go

```
117 func runServer(certFile string, key string, clientCert []byte) (err error) {
118   fmt.Println("starting HTTP server")
119   http.HandleFunc("/", hello)
120   server := &http.Server{
121     Addr:    ":443",
122     Handler: nil,
123   }
124   cert, err := tls.LoadX509KeyPair(certFile, key)
125   if err != nil {
126     return err
127   }
```

The full code for this step is available at https://packt.live/39hG58K

3. Define the **hello()** function, which is passed as a handler function when we start the HTTP server. This function will respond with some text whenever the server receives a request:

```
func hello(w http.ResponseWriter, r *http.Request) {
  fmt.Printf("%s: Ping\n", time.Now().Format(time.Stamp))
  fmt.Fprintf(w, "Pong\n")
}
```

4. Now that the server side is done, let's implement the client side:

main.go

```
95  func client(caCert []byte, ClientCerttls.Certificate) (err error) {
96    certPool := x509.NewCertPool()
97    certPool.AppendCertsFromPEM(caCert)
98    client := &http.Client{
99      Transport: &http.Transport{
100       TLSClientConfig: &tls.Config{
101         RootCAs:      certPool,
102         Certificates: []tls.Certificate{ClientCert},
103       },
104     },
105   }
106   resp, err := client.Get("https://127.0.0.1:443")
107   if err != nil {
108     return err
109   }
```

The full code for this step is available at https://packt.live/2PS72Z2

This defines an HTTP client using the TLS implementation. It takes in the certificate of the CA as a parameter to verify the authenticity of the server. In our case, we used a self-signed certificate, so the server certificate will serve the purpose of a CA certificate. The function would also take the client's certificate so that the client can authenticate with the server.

5. Let's now tie these functions and run a client and server handshake.

   First, we generate certificates and keys for both the client and the server. The server is started using a **goroutine** and waits for a request from the client. The client is also started in a **goroutine** and calls the server every 3 seconds:

main.go

```
18 func main() {
19   serverCert, serverKey, err := generate()
20   if err != nil {
21     fmt.Printf("error generating server certificate: %v", err)
22     os.Exit(1)
23   }
24   ioutil.WriteFile("private.key", serverKey, 0600)
25   ioutil.WriteFile("cert.pem", serverCert, 0777)
26   clientCert, clientKey, err := generate()
27   if err != nil {
28     fmt.Printf("error generating client certificate: %v", err)
29     os.Exit(1)
30   }
```

The full code for this step is available at: https://packt.live/2t0IXpW

We can now run the **main()** function. You should see the following output in your console:

```
$ cd../exercise8/
$ go run main.go
starting HTTP server
Oct 17 22:22:28: Ping
Oct 17 22:22:28: Pong
Oct 17 22:22:31: Ping
Oct 17 22:22:31: Pong
```

In this exercise, we demonstrated how a client and server communication could be secured using the TLS protocol. We have learned how to generate digital certificates and used them in the TLS configuration for the client and server.

Password Management

If you are managing user accounts on your website, one common way of verifying user identity is through a combination of usernames and passwords. This authentication mechanism has the risk that, if not properly managed, user credentials can be leaked. This has happened to many of the major websites around the world and remains a surprisingly common security incident.

The main rule of thumb regarding password management is to never store passwords in plaintext (either in memory or in a database). Instead, implement an approved hash algorithm to create a one-way hash of the password so that you can confirm the identity through the hash. However, it is not possible to retrieve the password from the hash. We can see this in action with an example.

The following code shows how to create a one-way hash from a plaintext string. We are using the **bcrypt** package to generate the hash. We then perform a comparison of the password with the hash to verify the match:

```go
package main
import (
  "fmt"
  "golang.org/x/crypto/bcrypt"
)
func main() {
  password := "mysecretpassword"
  encrypted, _ := bcrypt.GenerateFromPassword([]byte(password), 10)
  fmt.Println("Plain Text Password:", password)
  fmt.Println("Hashed Password:    ", string(encrypted))
  err := bcrypt.CompareHashAndPassword([]byte(encrypted), []byte(password))
  if err == nil {
    fmt.Println("Password matched")
  }
}
```

The following is the expected output:

```
gobin:example3 Gobin$ go run main.go
Plain Text Password: mysecretpassword
Hashed Password:     $2a$10$61HFmW/OLppH3GI7138WFur61ICyR9.FtIx26cSOGr5595VX
Password matched
```

Figure 18.11: Expected output

> **Note**
>
> **Elliptic Curve Digital Signature Algorithm** (ECDSA) is a cryptographic algorithm that is used to verify the authenticity of data by providing a mechanism to sign and verify data using a public and private key pair.

Activity 18.01: Authenticating Users on the Application Using Hashed Passwords

You are working on a web application and you need to authenticate users by using hashed passwords.

Create a database with user passwords that are stored as a hash. Define a function to take in a user password as an input and authenticate the user using the stored password in the database. Make sure the SQL query defined to query the database is safe from SQL injection. You can follow these steps to get the desired output.

1. Create a function to load data into the database.

2. Create a function to update a password in the database. Use the **crypto/sha512** library to encrypt the input password before updating the database.

3. Create a function to retrieve the password from the database and confirm whether it matches the hash.

4. In the main function of the program, initialize the database with some test data.

5. Perform the update of the user password using the function defined in *step 2*.

   You should get the following output:

```
gobin:activity1 Gobin$ go run main.go
storing encrypted password:
76243005bcc0bea09d6c0409b6f2e32a8050f31f123b797678e98301ba1822fdfeac10ddfa281b39e9eb5f5a4eddb271b9
retrieving hashed password from db
checking password match
successful password match
```

Figure 18.12: Expected output

Here, we securely store user passwords in a database using a hashing library and then verify a user's identity using a hashed password. You can use this in scenarios where there is sensitive data that needs to be stored.

> **Note**
>
> The solution to this activity can be found on page 777.

Activity 18.02: Creating CA Signed Certificates Using Crypto Libraries

A Certificate Authority(CA) needs to be created to sign certificates. When a new leaf certificate is created, it should be signed using the CA certificate and private key. You will need to define a function to generate ECDSA-encrypted keys using the **crypto/ecdsa** library. The function needs to support the creation of CA certificates as well as leaf certificates. Finally, you will need to verify the newly created leaf certificate.

The aim here is to generate x509 certificates. You can follow these steps to get the desired output:

1. Create a **generateCert()** function to generate an ECDSA certificate and private key using the **crypto/ecdsa** library. It should take in a common name string, a CA certificate, and a CA private key.

   The function should have the following definition:

   ```
   generateCert(cn string, caCert *x509.Certificate, caPrivcrypto.PrivateKey)
       (cert *x509.Certificate, privateKeycrypto.PrivateKey, err error)
   ```

2. Create an ECDSA key using the **ecdsa.GenerateKey()** function.

3. Use the key to generate an x509 certificate.

4. Return the generated certificate and private key.

5. In the **main()** function, generate a CA certificate and private key, as well as a leaf certificate and private key.

6. Verify the leaf certificate generated.

   The output should appear as follows:

   ```
   $ go run main.go
   ca certificate generated successfully
   leaf certificate generated successfully
   leaf certificate successfully verified
   ```

Here, we generate x509 public key certificates. We also saw how using a root certificate to generate a leaf certificate can be handy when you are trying to implement your own PKI server.

> **Note**
>
> The solution to this activity can be found on page 780.

Summary

In this chapter, we have looked at several types of attacks that could be used to compromise an application. We have also covered strategies to mitigate those issues, along with worked examples.

We have presented the use of crypto libraries for the encryption and decryption of data, both at rest and in transit. We have covered hashing libraries, and how they can be used to securely store user credentials. We have also shown how TLS configuration can be used to secure communication between clients and servers. With these tools in mind, you can now start writing secure applications.

In the next chapter, we will be learning about some lesser-known packages in Go, such as reflection and unsafe.

19

Special Features

Overview

In this chapter, we will look at some special features in Go that can be helpful during your application development.

This chapter will first introduce you to use build constraints, to write programs that work on multiple operating systems and architecture and also use command-line options to build Go programs. You will use reflection to inspect objects at runtime. By the end of the chapter you will be able to define build-time behavior for your application and use the **unsafe** package to access runtime memory in Go.

Introduction

In the previous chapter, we learned about vulnerabilities that could affect your application and how to mitigate them. We learned how to secure communication and safely store data.

We will now learn some features in Go that are not obvious and can be hard to find out about. You might come across these features if you are going through the standard library. Knowing about these features will help you to understand what is going on during the execution, as some of these properties are implicitly embedded into the language.

As Go is portable across multiple **operating systems (OSes)** and CPU architectures, Go supports configuring these parameters to build the application. Using these build parameters, you will be able to do things such as cross-compilation, which is very rare in other programming languages.

Concepts such as memory management are hard to master, so the Go runtime manages all memory allocation and deallocation, relieving the coder of the overhead of managing the memory footprint of the application. For rare cases where the coder does need to access memory, Go provides some flexibility by providing a package called **unsafe**, which we will learn about in this chapter.

Build Constraints

Go programs can run on different OSes and different CPU architectures. When you build a Go program, the compilation of your program is done for your current machine's OS and architecture. By using the build constraints, you can set conditions on which a file will be considered for compilation. If you have a function that needs to be overridden for different OSes, you can use build constraints to have multiple definitions of the same function.

You can see lots of examples of this happening in the Go standard library.

The following links are implementations of the same function in darwin and on Linux from the **os** package in the standard library:

- https://packt.live/2RKfydP
- https://packt.live/2PJN957

If you happen to come across a similar requirement, the Go language provides build constraints that can be used to define build conditions.

Build Tags

There are two ways to use build constraints. The first method is to define build tags and the second method is to use filename suffixes.

Build tags should appear before the package clause in your source file. These tags are analyzed at build time and decide whether or not the file is included for the compilation.

Let's take a look at how the tags are evaluated. The following tag means that the source file will only be considered for **build** on Linux machines. So, this file will not be compiled on a Windows machine:

```
// +build linux
```

We can have multiple build constraints defined using build tags:

```
// +build amd64,darwin 386,!gccgo
```

This evaluates to the following:

```
( amd64 AND darwin ) OR (386 AND (NOT gccgo))
```

Note that in the preceding example, we also use negation to avoid certain conditions.

> **Note**
>
> Make sure that there is an empty line between the build constraints and the start of the code, which is the package name.

At build time, Go compares the build tags with the Go environment variables and decides what to do with the tags.

By default, Go will read specific environment variables to set the build and runtime behavior. You can see what these variables are by running the following command:

```
go env
```

```
gobin:activity2 Gobin$ go env
GO111MODULE=""
GOARCH="amd64"
GOBIN=""
GOCACHE="/Users/Gobin/Library/Caches/go-build"
GOENV="/Users/Gobin/Library/Application Support/go/env"
GOEXE=""
GOFLAGS=""
GOHOSTARCH="amd64"
GOHOSTOS="darwin"
GONOPROXY=""
GONOSUMDB=""
GOOS="darwin"
GOPATH="/Users/Gobin/go"
GOPRIVATE=""
GOPROXY="https://proxy.golang.org,direct"
GOROOT="/usr/local/go"
GOSUMDB="sum.golang.org"
GOTMPDIR=""
GOTOOLDIR="/usr/local/go/pkg/tool/darwin_amd64"
GCCGO="gccgo"
AR="ar"
CC="clang"
CXX="clang++"
CGO_ENABLED="1"
GOMOD="/Users/Gobin/git/temp/The-Go-Workshop/go.mod"
CGO_CFLAGS="-g -O2"
CGO_CPPFLAGS=""
CGO_CXXFLAGS="-g -O2"
CGO_FFLAGS="-g -O2"
CGO_LDFLAGS="-g -O2"
PKG_CONFIG="pkg-config"
GOGCCFLAGS="-fPIC -m64 -pthread -fno-caret-diagnostics -Qunused-arguments -fmessage-length=0 -fdebug-prefix
wr/ikdpbaa54vdc4i0zarxv0csr0000gn/T/go-build364854130=/tmp/go-build -gno-record-gcc-switches -fno-common"
```

Figure 19.1: The go env output

The most commonly used variables are **GOOS**, which is the variable for the OS, and **GOARCH**, which is the variable for the CPU architecture. You can cross-compile your application by setting your **GOOS** variable to something other than your current OS. Example values of the **GOOS** variable are Windows, darwin, and Linux.

Let's look at a simple hello world program and use the build tags in action. The following program has a **build** tag that makes the **go build** command ignore the file:

```
// +build ignore
package main
import "fmt"
func main() {
  fmt.Println("Hello World!")
}
```

If you run **go build** in the current directory, you will see the following error output:

```
$ go build
build .: cannot find module for path .
```

If you remove the **build** tag from the file and then run **build** again, it should produce a binary without any errors, as follows:

```
$ go run main.go
Hello World!
```

Let's look at another example of the **build** tag using the **GOOS** variable. We will demonstrate how a combination of **build** tags and environment variables can affect the compilation of your application.

My current operating **GOOS** variable is **darwin**. Replace **darwin** with your own **GOOS** value.

To get your current **GOOS** variable, run the following command:

```
go env GOOS
```

Next:

```
// +build darwin
package main
import "fmt"
func main() {
   fmt.Println("Hello World!")
}
```

If we **build** this file, it should produce an executable binary as follows:

```
$go build -o good
$./goos
Hello World!
```

Now, set your **GOOS** variable to another value other than your own; the build should fail:

```
$GOOS=linux go build -o goos
Build .: cannot find module for path .
```

In this example, we learned how to use **GOOS** values as build constraints.

Filenames

As mentioned earlier, the second method to use build constraints is to use suffixes in the filename to define the constraints.

Using this method, you could define constraints on the OS or CPU architecture or both.

For example, the following files are from the **syscall** package in the standard library. You can see constraints defined on the OS:

```
syscall_linux.go
syscall_windows.go
syscall_darwin.go
```

Another example of using both the OS and CPU architecture can be found in the runtime package:

```
signal_darwin_amd64.go
signal_darwin_arm.go
signal_darwin_386.go
```

To utilize this method, the suffixes have to be of the following form:

```
*_GOOS
*_GOARCH
*_GOOS_GOARCH
```

You can find examples of this naming scheme in the standard library as well:

```
stat_aix.go
source_windows_amd64.go
syscall_linux_386.go
```

Let's look at an example of using filenames to define build constraints. We will define build constraints by CPU architecture. We will use this with the **GOARCH** environment variable to control the build.

We have a file with a suffix of the current **GOARCH**. My current **GOARCH** is **amd64**, so the filename will be **main_amd64.go**. Replace this value for your filename. To get your current **GOARCH**, run the following command:

```
go env GOARCH
```

This will display the following:

```
$go env GOARCH
amd64
```

The filename on my machine will be as follows:

```
main_amd64.go
```

Inside the file, we will define a simple **"Hello World"** program:

```
package main
import "fmt"
func main() {
    fmt.Println("Hello World!")
}
```

The output will be as follows:

```
$ls
main_amd64.go
$go build -o goarch
$./goarch
Hello World!
```

To confirm that the constraint works, we can use another **GOARCH** value to try and check whether the build fails:

```
$ls
main_amd64.go
$GOARCH=386 go build -o goarch
build .: cannot find module for path .
```

In the preceding example, we learned how to use CPU architecture as a build constraint to restrict building files on specific CPU architecture.

Reflection

Reflection is the mechanism of inspecting code at runtime. Reflection is useful when you do not know or cannot guarantee the type of input for a function. In cases such as this, reflection can be used to inspect the type of the object and manipulate values of objects.

The Go **reflect** package gives you features to inspect and manipulate an object at runtime. It can be used not only for basic types such as **int** and **string**, but for inspecting slices, arrays, and structs as well.

Let's create a simple **print()** function to demonstrate how we can use reflection. We define a utility print function called **MyPrint()** that can print different types of objects. This is done by having an interface as an input to the function. Then, inside the function, we make use of the **reflect** package to alter the behavior according to the type of the input. Consider the following code:

```go
package main
import (
  "fmt"
  "reflect"
)
type Animal struct {
  Name string
}
type Object struct {
  Type string
}
type Person struct {
  Name string
}
func MyPrint(input interface{}) {
  t := reflect.TypeOf(input)
  v := reflect.ValueOf(input)
  switch {
  case t.Name() == "Animal":
    fmt.Println("I am a ", v.FieldByName("Name"))
  case t.Name() == "Object":
    fmt.Println("I am a ", v.FieldByName("Type"))
  default:
    fmt.Println("I got an unknown entity")
  }
}
func main() {
  table := Object{Type: "Chair"}
  MyPrint(table)
  tiger := Animal{Name: "Tiger"}
  MyPrint(tiger)
  gobin := Person{Name: "Gobin"}
  MyPrint(gobin)
}
```

Running the preceding program, we get the following output:

```
$go run main.go
I am a Chair
I am a Tiger
I got an unknown entity
```

You can find examples of reflection being used in packages such as **encoding/json** and **fmt**.

Let's look at how to use reflection using some common utility functions in the **reflect** package.

TypeOf and ValueOf

To use reflection, you will need to get familiar with two types defined in the **reflect** package:

```
reflect.Type
reflect.Value
```

Both of these types provide utility functions that give you access to the dynamic runtime information of the object.

These two functions give you a handle on the **Type** and **Value** of the object:

```
func TypeOf( interface{}) Type
func ValueOf( interface{}) Value
```

The following program uses the two functions to print the **Type** and **Value** of the object being passed:

```
func main() {
  var x = 5
  Print(x)
  var y = []string{"test"}
  Print(y)
  var z = map[string]string{"a": "b"}
  Print(z)
}
func Print(a interface{}) {
  fmt.Println("Type: ", reflect.TypeOf(a))
  fmt.Println("Value: ", reflect.ValueOf(a))
}
```

The output of the preceding program should print the **Type** of **x**:

```
$ go run main.go
Type: int
Value 5
Type: []string
Value: [test]
Type: map[string]string
Value: map[a:b]
```

In this example, we observed how two functions are used to print the **Type** and **Value** of the object passed.

> **Note**
>
> It is important to make sure that you use the reflection package carefully. Using the type conversion incorrectly or calling a method on an object that does not support the method will cause the program to panic.

Exercise 19.01: Using Reflection

In this exercise, we will use the reflection package to inspect objects at runtime:

1. Create a file named **main.go**.

2. Import the following packages:

```
package main
import (
    "fmt"
    "math"
    "reflect"
)
```

3. Define a **struct** called **circle** with the **radius** as one of its fields:

```
type circle struct {
    radius float64
}
```

4. Define another **struct** called **rectangle** with **length** and **breadth** as its fields:

```
type rectangle struct {
    length  float64
    breadth float64
}
```

5. Define a function called **area()** that can calculate the area of different shapes. It should take **interface** as its input:

```
func area(input interface{}) float64 {
    inputType := reflect.TypeOf(input)
    if inputType.Name() == "circle" {
        val := reflect.ValueOf(input)
        radius := val.FieldByName("radius")
        return math.Pi * math.Pow(radius.Float(), 2)
    }
    if inputType.Name() == "rectangle" {
        val := reflect.ValueOf(input)
        length := val.FieldByName("length")
        breadth := val.FieldByName("breadth")
        return length.Float() * breadth.Float()
    }
    return 0
}
```

In this function, we use **reflect.TypeOf()** to get a **reflect.Type** object from the input. We then use the **Type.Name()** function to get the name of the **struct**, which, in our case, could be either a circle or a rectangle.

To retrieve the value of the fields in the struct, we first use the **reflect.ValueOf()** function to get a **reflect.Value** object. Then we use **Val.FieldByName()** to get the field value.

6. Define a **main()** function and call the **area()** function:

```
func main() {
    fmt.Printf("area of circle with radius 3 is : %f\n", area(circle{radius:
        3}))
    fmt.Printf("area of rectangle with length 3 and breadth 7 is : %f\n",
        area(rectangle{length: 3, breadth: 7}))
}
```

7. Run the program using the following command:

```
go run main.go
```

You should get the following output when you run the program:

```
$ go run main.go
area of circle with radius 3 is : 28.274334
area of rectangle with length 3 and breadth 7 is : 21.000000
```

In this exercise, we learned how to use reflection to define the different implementations of a function, in this case, by inspecting the input object to determine what object is being passed in.

Activity 19.01: Defining Build Constraints Using Filenames

You have to define a function that behaves differently depending on the OS and CPU architecture. Use build constraints on a filename to achieve this behavior. One file should be set with the OS constraint set to **darwin** and another with the CPU architecture set to **386**.

> **Note**
>
> Substitute **darwin** with your current OS and **386** with another architecture that is not your current machine's architecture.

Perform the following steps:

1. Create a package called **custom**.

2. Create a **print_darwin.go** file and define a function called **Print()** inside the package. It should print the following text: **I am running on a darwin machine**.

3. Create another file in the same package called **print_386.go** and define a function called **Print()** that prints the following text: **Hello I am running on a 386 machine**.

4. Define a **main()** function and import the **custom** package. Call the **Print()** function from the custom package in the **main()** function.

By the end of the activity, you should see the following output:

```
$go run main.go
Hello I am running on a darwin machine.
```

In this activity, we implemented overriding a function using build constraints with filenames. You should be able to see a similar implementation in the Go standard library.

> **Note**
>
> The solution for this activity can be found on page 782.

DeepEqual

The `reflect.DeepEqual()` requires a mention if we are talking about the `reflect` package.

Basic data types in Go can be compared using the `==` or `!=` operator, but slices and maps are not comparable using this method.

The `reflect.DeepEqual()` function can be used in scenarios when the types are incomparable. For example, it can be used for comparing slices and maps. Here is an example that compares maps and slices using `DeepEqual`:

```
package main
import (
  "fmt"
  "reflect"
)
func main() {
  runDeepEqual(nil, nil)
  runDeepEqual(make([]int, 10), make([]int, 10))
  runDeepEqual([3]int{1, 2, 3}, [3]int{1, 2, 3})
  runDeepEqual(map[int]string{1: "one", 2: "two"}, map[int]string{2:
    "two", 1: "one"})
}
func runDeepEqual(a, b interface{}) {
  fmt.Printf("%v DeepEqual %v : %v\n", a, b, reflect.DeepEqual(a, b))
}
```

In the preceding example, we compare different data types using `reflect.DeepEqual()`.

The following are the comparisons done:

- Two nil objects.

- Two empty slices with the same size. The size is important here.

- Two slices with the same data in the same order. Values in a different order will give a different output.

- Two maps with the same data. The order of keys does not matter here as maps are always unordered.

If you run the program, you should get the following output:

```
$go run main.go
<nil> DeepEqual <nil> : true
[0 0 0 0 0 0 0 0 0 0] DeepEqual [0 0 0 0 0 0 0 0 0 0] : true
[1 2 3] DeepEqual [1 2 3] : true
map[1:one 2:two] DeepEqual map[1:one 2:two] : true
```

Figure 19.2: DeepEqual output

Wildcard Pattern

The **go** tool has a number of commands to help you with your code development. For example, the **go list** command helps you list Go files in your current directory, and the **go test** command helps you run test files in your current directory.

Your project may be structured in multiple subdirectories to help organize your code logically. If you wanted to use the **go** tool to run commands over your whole codebase at once, it supports a wildcard pattern that helps you do just that.

To list all the .**go** files in your current directory and its subdirectories, you can use the following relative pattern:

```
go list ./...
```

Similarly, if you wanted to run all the tests in your current directory and subdirectories, the same pattern can be used:

```
go test ./...
```

If you are still using vendor directories, the good thing is that this pattern will ignore the .**/vendor** directories.

Let's try the wildcard patterns on the Go workshop repository.

To list all the .**go** files in the project, you can run the **list** command with the wildcard:

```
go list -f {{.GoFiles}}{{.Dir}} ./...
```

You should get an output similar to the following:

```
[08:53 $ go list -f {{.GoFiles}}{{.Dir}} ./...
[main.go]/Users/Gobin/git/The-Go-Workshop/Chapter19/Activity19.01
[print_darwin.go]/Users/Gobin/git/The-Go-Workshop/Chapter19/Activity19.01/custom
[]/Users/Gobin/git/The-Go-Workshop/Chapter19/Activity19.02
[]/Users/Gobin/git/The-Go-Workshop/Chapter19/Activity19.02/package1
[]/Users/Gobin/git/The-Go-Workshop/Chapter19/Activity19.02/package2
[main.go]/Users/Gobin/git/The-Go-Workshop/Chapter19/Examples/example1
[main.go]/Users/Gobin/git/The-Go-Workshop/Chapter19/Examples/example2
[main_amd64.go]/Users/Gobin/git/The-Go-Workshop/Chapter19/Examples/example3
[main.go]/Users/Gobin/git/The-Go-Workshop/Chapter19/Examples/example4
[main.go]/Users/Gobin/git/The-Go-Workshop/Chapter19/Examples/example5
[main.go]/Users/Gobin/git/The-Go-Workshop/Chapter19/Examples/example6
[]/Users/Gobin/git/The-Go-Workshop/Chapter19/Examples/example7
[main.go]/Users/Gobin/git/The-Go-Workshop/Chapter19/Exercise19.01
[]/Users/Gobin/git/The-Go-Workshop/Chapter19/Exercise19.02
[]/Users/Gobin/git/The-Go-Workshop/Chapter19/Exercise19.04
[]/Users/Gobin/git/The-Go-Workshop/Chapter19/Exercise19.08
```

Figure 19.3: Wildcard pattern

The unsafe Package

Go is a statically typed language, and it has its own runtime that does memory allocation and garbage collection. So, unlike C, all the work related to memory management is taken care of by the runtime. Unless you have some special requirements, you would never have to deal with memory directly in your code. When there is a requirement, though, the **unsafe** package in the standard library gives you features to let you peek into the memory of an object.

As the name suggests, it is normally not considered safe to use this package in your code. Another thing to note is that the **unsafe** package does not come with Go 1 compatibility guidelines, which means that functionalities could stop working in future versions of Go.

The simplest example you can find of using the **unsafe** package can be found in the **math** package:

```
func Float32bits(f float32) uint32
{
    return *(*uint32)(unsafe.Pointer(&f))
}
```

This takes a **float32** as input and returns **uint32**. The **float32** number is converted to an **unsafe.Pointer** object and then dereferenced to convert it to a **uint32**.

The reverse conversion on the preceding function can also be found in the **math** package:

```
func Float32frombits(b uint32) float32 {
    return *(*float32)(unsafe.Pointer(&b))
}
```

Another example of using the **unsafe** package, which you can find in the standard library is when calling C programs from your Go code. This is formally known as **cgo**.

> **Note**
>
> To get **cgo** to work on Windows, you need to have the **gcc** compiler installed on your machine. You can use 'Minimalist GNU for Windows' (https://packt. live/2EbOKuZ).

There are some special functions provided in the pseudo C package that convert Go data types to C data or vice versa, for example:

```
// Converts Go string to C string
func C.CString(string) *C.char
// C data with explicit length to Go []byte
func C.GoBytes(unsafe.Pointer, C.int) []byte
```

You can write your program as normal Go code and call functions written in C, as shown in the following example:

```
package main
//#include <stdio.h>
//#include <stdlib.h>
//static void myprint(char* s) {
//  printf("%s\n", s);
//}
import "C"
import "unsafe"
func main() {
    cs := C.CString("Hello World!")
    C.myprint(cs)
    C.free(unsafe.Pointer(cs))
}
```

You can define functions in C in the following format. To use functions in the standard library, the **import** statement is preceded by a comment, which is treated as the header section of your C code:

```
// #include <stdio.h>
// #include <stdlib.h>
//
// static void myprint(char* s) {
//    printf("%s\n", s);
// }
```

The preceding function prints the input to the console. To be able to use the C code, we need to import the pseudo package called **C**. In the **main** function, we can call the **myprint()** function using the C package.

Running this program should get you the following output:

```
$ go run main.go
Hello World!
```

Exercise 19.02: Using cgo with unsafe

In this exercise, we will learn how to use the **unsafe** package to get hold of the underlying memory of a string:

1. Create a **main.go** file and make the following imports. The C pseudo-package is needed to use the C libraries:

```
package main
// #include <stdlib.h>
import "C"
import (
   "fmt"
   "unsafe"
)
```

2. Define a **main()** function and declare a **C** string:

```
func main() {
   var cString *C.char
```

3. Set the value of the **cString** variable with the text **Hello World!\n**. It is always a good practice to clean up allocated memory when dealing with **C**, so add the **C.free()** function call to perform the cleanup:

```
cString = C.CString("Hello World!\n")
   defer C.free(unsafe.Pointer(cString))
```

4. Declare a variable, **b**, as a byte array to store the output of converting the **CString** into a Go **byte** array:

```
var b []byte
b = C.GoBytes(unsafe.Pointer(cString), C.int(14))
```

The **C.GoBytes()** function converts an **unsafe.Pointer** object into a Go **byte** array.

5. Print the **byte** array to the console:

```
fmt.Print(string(b))

}
```

6. Run the program using the following command:

```
go run main.go
```

You should get the following output:

```
$ go run main.go
Hellow World!
```

In this exercise, we learned how to use **Cgo** and create C objects in Go. We then used the **unsafe** package to convert a **CString** object into an **unsafe.Pointer**, which maps directly to the memory of the **CString**.

Activity 19.02: Using Wildcard with Go Test

You have a project with multiple test files and multiple test cases defined inside them. Create multiple packages and define tests inside them. Using the wildcard pattern, run all test cases in the project with a single command. Make sure that all the unit tests are being run using the command.

Perform the following steps:

1. Create a package called **package1**.

2. Create a file called **run_test.go** and define a unit test called **TestPackage1**.

3. Create a package called **package2**.

4. Create a file called **run_test.go** and define a unit test called **TestPackage2**.

5. Print the results of **TestPackage1** and **TestPackage2** using the wildcard pattern:

```
09:01 $ go test -v ./...
=== RUN    TestPackage1
--- PASS: TestPackage1 (0.00s)
    run_test.go:6: running TestPackage1
PASS
ok      github.com/PacktWorkshops/The-Go-Workshop/Chapter19/Activity19.02/package1    (cached)
=== RUN    TestPackage2
--- PASS: TestPackage2 (0.00s)
    run_test.go:6: running TestPackage2
PASS
ok      github.com/PacktWorkshops/The-Go-Workshop/Chapter19/Activity19.02/package2    (cached)
```

Figure 19.4: Recursive test with wildcard

In this activity, we have learned how to use the wildcard pattern to recursively run tests on all test files inside a project. This will come in handy when you want to automate running tests in your continuous integration pipeline.

> **Note**
>
> The solution to this activity can be found on page 782.

Summary

In this chapter, we learned about the special features in Go that are not so obvious.

We covered the use of build constraints and how they can be used to control the behavior of your application build. Build constraints can be used to perform conditional compilation using the **GOOS** and **GOARCH** variables. They can also be used to ignore a file during compilation. Another common use of **build** tags is to add tags to files that contain integration tests.

We have seen use cases for the **reflect** package and the functions that can be used to access the type and value of objects at runtime. Reflection is a good way to solve scenarios where we can only determine the data type of a variable at runtime.

We also demonstrated how wildcards can be used to perform lists and tests on multiple packages in your project. We also learned the use of the **unsafe** package to access runtime memory in Go. The **unsafe** package is commonly used when using C libraries.

Over the course of the book, we have covered the basics of Go with variables and various type declarations. We have seen the special behavior of interfaces and errors in Go. The book also covered chapters focused on application development. Handling files and JSON data is very common in any application's development, especially web applications. The chapters on databases and HTTP servers delve into how you can manage the communication and storage of data. We also looked at how to easily perform concurrent operations using goroutines. Finally, in the last topic of the book, we covered how to improve your code quality by focusing on testing and securing your application. Last but not least, we explored special features in Go such as build constraints and the use of the **unsafe** package.

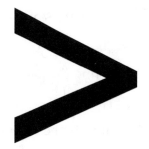

Appendix

Chapter 1: Variables and Operators

Activity 1.01 Defining and Printing

Solution:

1. Define the package name:

```
package main
```

2. Import the required packages:

```
import "fmt"
```

3. Create a **main()** function:

```
func main() {
```

4. Declare and initialize a string variable for the given name:

```
firstName := "Bob"
```

5. Declare and initialize a string variable for the family name:

```
familyName := "Smith"
```

6. Declare and initialize an **int** variable for **age**:

```
age := 34
```

7. Declare and initialize a **bool** variable for **peanutAllergy**:

```
peanutAllergy := false
```

8. Print each variable to the console:

```
fmt.Println(firstName)
fmt.Println(familyName)
fmt.Println(age)
fmt.Println(pean
utAllergy)
```

9. Close the **main()** function:

```
}
```

The following is the expected output:

Figure 1.24: Expected output after assigning the variables

Activity 1.02: Pointer Value Swap

Solution:

1. Let's start the exercise with the following code:

```
package main
import "fmt"
func main() {
    a, b := 5, 10
```

2. You need to get the pointers from **a** and **b** to pass to swap using **&**:

```
    swap(&a, &b)
    fmt.Println(a == 10, b == 5)
}
func swap(a *int, b *int) {
```

3. You need to dereference the values first using *****. You can swap without temporary values by using Go's ability to do multiple assignments. The right-hand side resolves before the left-hand side does:

```
    *a, *b = *b, *a
}
```

The following is the expected output:

```
true true
```

Activity 1.03: Message Bug

Solution:

1. Create **package main** and add the necessary imports:

```
package main
import "fmt"
func main() {
    count := 5
```

2. Define the **message** before the **if** statement:

```
var message string
if count > 5 {
```

3. Define a **message** that would update the **message** in step 2:

```
    message = "Greater than 5"
    } else {
```

4. Define a **message** that would update the message in step 3:

```
message = "Not greater than 5"
    }
    fmt.Println(message)
}
```

The following is the expected output:

```
Not greater than 5
```

Activity 1.04: Bad Count Bug

Solution:

1. Let's start the exercise with the following code:

```
package main
import "fmt"
func main() {
  count := 0
  if count < 5 {
```

2. The assignment here caused the preceding **count** to be shadowed:

```
count = 10
    count++
  }
  fmt.Println(count == 11)
}
```

The following is the expected output:

```
true
```

Chapter 2: Logic and Loops

Activity 2.01: Implementing FizzBuzz

Solution:

1. Define **package** and include **import**:

```
package main
import (
  "fmt"
  "strconv"
)
```

2. Create the **main** function:

```
func main() {
```

3. Create a **for** loop that starts at 1 and loops until **i** gets to 100:

```
for i := 1; i <= 100; i++{
```

4. Initialize a string variable that will hold the output:

```
out := ""
```

5. Using module logic to check for divisibility, **if i** is divisible by 3, then add **"Fizz"** to the **out** string:

```
if i%3 == 0 {
out += "Fizz"
}
```

6. If divisible by 5, add **"Buzz"** to the string:

```
if i%5 == 0 {
out += "Buzz"
}
```

7. If neither, convert the number to a string and then add it to the output string:

```
if out == "" {
out = strconv.Itoa(i)
}
```

8. Print the output variable:

```
fmt.Println(out)
```

9. Close the loop and **main:**

```
}
}
```

10. In the folder you create your code, run:

```
go run main.go
```

The expected output is as follows:

```
 ~/src/Th…op/Ch…02/Activity02.01   go run .
1
2
Fizz
4
Buzz
Fizz
7
8
Fizz
Buzz
11
Fizz
13
14
FizzBuzz
16
17
Fizz
19
Buzz
Fizz
22
23
Fizz
Buzz
26
Fizz
28
29
FizzBuzz
31
```

Figure 2.03: The FizzBuzz output

Activity 2.02: Looping Over Map Data Using range

Solution:

1. Load the **main** package:

```
package main
```

2. Import the **fmt** package:

```
import "fmt"
```

3. Create the **main** function:

```
func main() {
```

4. Initialize the **words** map:

```
words := map[string]int{
    "Gonna": 3,
    "You":   3,
    "Give":  2,
```

```
        "Never": 1,
        "Up":    4,
    }
```

5. Initialize the **topWord** variable to an empty string and the **topCount** variable to 0:

```
topWord := ""
topCount := 0
```

6. Create a **for** loop that uses **range** to get the key and value of each element:

```
for key, value := range words {
```

7. Check whether the current **map** element has a larger count than the top count:

```
if value > topCount {
```

8. If it does, then update the top values with the values from the current element:

```
topCount = value
topWord = key
```

9. Close the **if** statement:

```
    }
```

10. Close the loop:

```
    }
```

11. After the loop is done, you have your result. Print it to the console:

```
    fmt.Println("Most popular word:", topWord)
    fmt.Println("With a count of  :", topCount)
}
```

12. In the folder you created the code, run:

```
go run main.go
```

The following is the expected output displaying the most popular word with its count value:

```
Most popular word: Up
With a count of  : 4
```

Activity 2.03: Bubble Sort

Solution:

1. Define the package and add the imported package:

```
package main
import "fmt"
```

2. Create **main:**

```
func main() {
```

3. Define a slice of integers and initialize it with unsorted numbers:

```
nums := []int{5, 8, 2, 4, 0, 1, 3, 7, 9, 6}
```

4. Print the slice before sorting it:

```
fmt.Println("Before:", nums)
```

5. Create a **for** loop; in the **initial** statement, define a Boolean with the initial value of **true.** In the condition, check that Boolean. Leave the **post** statement empty:

```
for swapped := true; swapped; {
```

6. Set the Boolean variable to **false:**

```
swapped = false
```

7. Create a nested **for i** loop that steps over the whole slice of **int** values. Start the loop from the second element:

```
for i := 1; i < len(nums); i++ {
```

8. Check whether the previous element is bigger than the current element:

```
if nums[i-1] > nums[i] {
```

9. If the previous element is bigger, swap the values of the elements:

```
nums[i], nums[i-1] = nums[i-1], nums[i]
```

10. Set our Boolean to **true** to indicate that we did a swap and we'll need to keep going:

```
swapped = true
```

11. Close the **if** statement and the two loops:

```
        }
    }
}
```

12. Print the now sorted slice and close **main**:

```
    fmt.Println("After :", nums)
}
```

13. In the folder you create the code, run:

```
go run main.go
```

The following is the expected output:

```
Before: [5, 8, 2, 4, 0, 1, 3, 7, 9, 6]
After : [0, 1, 2, 3, 4, 5, 6, 7, 8, 9]
```

Chapter 3: Core Types

Activity 3.01: Sales Tax Calculator

Solution:

1. Create a new folder and add a **main.go** file.

2. In **main.go**, add the **main** package name to the top of the file:

```
package main
```

3. Now add the imports we'll use in this file:

```
import "fmt"
```

4. Create a function that takes two floating-point arguments and returns a floating-point:

```
func salesTax(cost float64, taxRate float64) float64 {
```

5. Multiply the two arguments together and return the result:

```
    return cost * taxRate
```

6. Close the function:

```
}
```

7. Create the **main()** function:

```
func main() {
```

8. Declare a variable to be a floating-point:

```
    taxTotal := .0
```

9. Add **cake** to the **taxTotal**:

```
// Cake
taxTotal += salesTax(.99, .075)
```

10. Add **milk** to the **taxTotal**:

```
// Milk
taxTotal += salesTax(2.75, .015)
```

11. Add **butter** to the **taxTotal**:

```
// Butter
taxTotal += salesTax(.87, .02)
```

12. Print the **taxTotal** to the console:

```
// Total
fmt.Println("Sales Tax Total: ", taxTotal)
```

13. Close the **main()** function:

```
}
```

14. Save the file, and from within the folder you created run the following:

```
go run main.go
```

Running the preceding code shows the following output:

```
Sales Tax Total: 0.1329
```

Activity 3.02: Loan Calculator

Solution:

1. Define the package:

```
package main
```

2. Import the necessary packages:

```
import (
    "errors"
    "fmt"
)
```

3. Define constants for the scores and ratios:

```
const (
    goodScore    = 450
    lowScoreRatio = 10
```

```
        goodScoreRatio = 20
    )
```

4. Pre-define the errors:

```
    var (
        ErrCreditScore = errors.New("invalid credit score")
        ErrIncome      = errors.New("income invalid")
        ErrLoanAmount  = errors.New("loan amount invalid")
        ErrLoanTerm    = errors.New("loan term not a multiple of 12")
    )
```

5. Create a function to check the loan details. This function will accept a **creditScore**, an **income**, a **loanAmount**, and a **loanTerm**, and return an error:

```
    func checkLoan(creditScore int, income float64, loanAmount float64, loanTerm
        float64) error {
```

6. Set a base **interest** rate:

```
    interest := 20.0
```

7. A good **creditScore** gets a better rate:

```
    if creditScore >= goodScore {
        interest = 15.0
    }
```

8. Validate the **creditScore** and return an error if it's bad:

```
    if creditScore < 1 {
        return ErrCreditScore
    }
```

9. Validate the **income** and return an error if it's bad:

```
    if income < 1 {
        return ErrIncome
    }
```

10. Validate the **loanAmount** and return an error if it's bad:

```
    if loanAmount < 1 {
        return ErrLoanAmount
    }
```

11. Validate the **loanTerm** and return an error if it's bad:

```
if loanTerm < 1 || int(loanTerm)%12 != 0 {
    return ErrLoanTerm
}
```

12. Convert the interest rate into something we can use in calculations:

```
rate := interest / 100
```

13. Calculate the payment by multiplying the **loanAmount** by the loan **rate**. Then divide that by the **loanTerm**. Now divide the **loanAmount** by the **loanTerm**.

Finally, add those two amounts together:

```
payment := ((loanAmount * rate) / loanTerm) + (loanAmount / loanTerm)
```

14. Calculate the total cost of the loan by multiplying the payments by the **loanTerm** and then subtracting the **loanAmount**:

```
totalInterest := (payment * loanTerm) - loanAmount
```

15. Declare a variable for **approval**:

```
approved := false
```

16. Add a condition to check that the income is more than the payment:

```
if income > payment {
```

17. Calculate the percentage of their **income** that will be taken up by the payment:

```
ratio := (payment / income) * 100
```

18. If they have a good **creditScore**, allow a higher ratio:

```
if creditScore >= goodScore && ratio < goodScoreRation {
    approved = true
} else if ratio < lowScoreRation {
    approved = false
}
}
```

19. Print out all the details of the application to the console:

```
fmt.Println("Credit Score    :", creditScore)
fmt.Println("Income          :", income)
fmt.Println("Loan Amount     :", loanAmount)
fmt.Println("Loan Term       :", loanTerm)
fmt.Println("Monthly Payment :", payment)
```

```
fmt.Println("Rate          :", interest)
fmt.Println("Total Cost    :", totalInterest)
fmt.Println("Approved       :", approved)
fmt.Println("")
```

20. Return with no error and close the function:

```
    return nil
}
```

21. Create the **main()** function:

```
func main() {
```

22. Create an example that will be approved:

```
// Approved
fmt.Println("Applicant 1")
fmt.Println("-----------")
err := checkLoan(500, 1000, 1000, 24)
```

23. Print out any errors, if found:

```
if err != nil {
   fmt.Println("Error:", err)
   return
}
```

24. Create an example that will be denied:

```
// Denied
fmt.Println("Applicant 2")
fmt.Println("-----------")
err = checkLoan(350, 1000, 10000, 12)
```

25. Print out any errors, if found:

```
if err != nil {
   fmt.Println("Error:", err)
   return
}
```

26. Close the **main()** function:

```
}
```

27. In the folder you wrote the code in, run the following:

```
go run main.go
```

Following is the expected output:

```
📂  ~/src/Th…op/Ch…03/Activity03.02   go run main.go
Applicant 1
-----------
Credit Score    : 500
Income          : 1000
Loan Amount     : 1000
Loan Term       : 24
Monthly Payment : 47.916666666666664
Rate            : 15
Total Cost      : 150
Approved        : true

Applicant 2
-----------
Credit Score    : 350
Income          : 1000
Loan Amount     : 10000
Loan Term       : 12
Monthly Payment : 1000
Rate            : 20
Total Cost      : 2000
Approved        : false
```

Figure 3.15: Output of loan calculator

Chapter 4: Complex Types

Activity 4.01: Filling an Array

Solution:

1. Create a new folder and add a file named **main.go** to it.

2. In **main.go**, add the package and imports:

```
package main
import "fmt"
```

3. Create a function that returns an array:

```
func getArr() [10]int {
```

4. Define an array variable:

```
var arr [10]int
```

5. Use a **for** **i** loop to operate on each element of the array:

```
for i := 0; i < 10; i++ {
```

6. Use **i**, plus a bit of math, to set the correct value:

```
arr[i] = i + 1
}
```

7. Return the array variable and close the function:

```
    return arr
}
```

8. In the **main()** function, call the function and print the returned value to the console:

```
func main() {
  fmt.Println(getArr())
}
```

9. Save the file. Then, in the folder you created in *step* 1, run the code using the following command:

```
go run .
```

Running the preceding code will produce the following output:

```
[1 2 3 4 5 6 7 8 9 10]
```

Activity 4.02: Printing a User's Name Based on User Input

Solution:

1. Create a new folder and add a file named **main.go** to it.

2. In **main.go**, add the package and imports:

```
package main
import (
  "fmt"
  "os"
)
```

3. Define the **map** of user data:

```
var users = map[string]string{
  "305": "Sue",
  "204": "Bob",
  "631": "Jake",
  "073": "Tracy",
}
```

4. Create a function that returns the user's name and whether it exists:

```
func getName(id string) (string, bool) {
    name, exists := users[id]
    return name, exists
}
```

5. In **main()** function, check the passed arguments. Call the function, print if there's an error, and exit if the user doesn't exist. Print a greeting to the user if they do exist:

```
func main() {
    if len(os.Args) < 2 {
        fmt.Println("User ID not passed")
        os.Exit(1)
    }
    name, exists := getName(os.Args[1])
    if !exists {
        fmt.Printf("error: user (%v) not found", os.Args[1])
        os.Exit(1)
    }
    fmt.Println("Hi,", name)
}
```

6. Save the file. Then, in the folder you created in *step* 1, run the code using the following command:

```
go run . 073
```

Running the preceding code produces the following output:

```
Hi, Tracy
```

Activity 4.03: Creating a Locale Checker

Solution:

1. Create a new folder and add a file named **main.go** to it.

2. In **main.go**, add the package and imports:

```
package main
import (
    "fmt"
    "os"
    "strings"
)
```

3. Define a **locale struct** with a **language** and a **territory**, both of which will be strings:

```
type locale struct {
    language string
    territory string
}
```

4. Create a function that returns the test data:

```
func getLocales() map[locale]struct{} {
    supportedLocales := make(map[locale]struct{}, 5)
    supportedLocales[locale{"en", "US"}] = struct{}{}
    supportedLocales[locale{"en", "CN"}] = struct{}{}
    supportedLocales[locale{"fr", "CN"}] = struct{}{}
    supportedLocales[locale{"fr", "FR"}] = struct{}{}
    supportedLocales[locale{"ru", "RU"}] = struct{}{}
    return supportedLocales
}
```

5. Create a function that uses a passed local struct to check the sample data to see if a locale exists:

```
func localeExists(l locale) bool {
    _, exists := getLocales()[l]
    return exists
}
```

6. Create the **main()** function:

```
func main() {
```

7. Check that an argument has been passed:

```
    if len(os.Args) < 2 {
        fmt.Println("No locale passed")
        os.Exit(1)
    }
```

8. Process the passed argument to make sure it's in a valid format:

```
    localeParts := strings.Split(os.Args[1], "_")
    if len(localeParts) != 2 {
        fmt.Printf("Invalid locale passed: %v\n", os.Args[1])
        os.Exit(1)
    }
```

9. Create a local struct value using the passed argument data:

```
passedLocale := locale{
    territory: localeParts[1],
    language:  localeParts[0],
}
```

10. Call the function and print an error message if it doesn't exist; otherwise, print that the locale is supported:

```
if !localeExists(passedLocale) {
    fmt.Printf("Locale not supported: %v\n", os.Args[1])
    os.Exit(1)
}
fmt.Println("Locale passed is supported")
}
```

11. Save the file. Then, in the folder you created in *step 1*, run the code using the following command:

```
go run .
```

Running the preceding code produces the following output:

Figure 4.17: Locale checking result

Activity 4.04: Slicing the Week

Solution:

1. Create a new folder and add a file named **main.go** to it.

2. In **main.go**, add the package and imports:

```
package main
import "fmt"
```

3. Create a function that returns a slice of strings:

```
func getWeek() []string {
```

4. Define a slice and initialize it with the days of the week, starting on Monday:

```
week := []string{"Monday", "Tuesday", "Wednesday", "Thursday", "Friday",
    "Saturday", "Sunday"}
```

5. Create a range that starts at index 6 and goes to the end of the slice. Then, create a slice range that starts at the beginning of the slice and goes up to index 6. Use **append** to add the second range to the first range. Capture the value from append:

```
week = append(week[6:], week[:6]...)
```

6. Return the result and close the function:

```
    return week
}
```

7. In **main**, call the function and print the result to the console:

```
func main() {
    fmt.Println(getWeek())
}
```

8. Save the file. Then, in the folder you created in *step 1*, run the code using the following command:

```
go run .
```

Running the preceding code produces the following output:

```
[Sunday Monday Tuesday Wednesday Thursday Friday Saturday]
```

Activity 4.05: Removing an Element from a Slice

Solution:

1. Create a new folder and add a file named **main.go** to it.

2. In **main.go**, add the package and imports:

```
package main
import "fmt"
```

3. Create a function that returns a slice of strings:

```
func removeBad() []string {
```

4. Define a slice of strings with the **Good** and **Bad** data:

```
sli := []string{"Good", "Good", "Bad", "Good", "Good"}
```

5. Create a slice range from the beginning of the slice up until the **Bad** index. Create another slice range that starts from one index after the **Bad** data and goes until the end of the slice. Append the second slice to the first and capture the result:

```
sli = append(sli[:2], sli[3:]...)
```

6. Return the slice and close the function:

```
    return sli
}
```

7. In **main**, call the function and print the result to the console:

```
func main() {
    fmt.Println(removeBad())
}
```

8. Save the file. Then, in the folder you created in *step 1*, run the code using the following command:

```
go run .
```

The expected output is as follows:

```
[Good Good Good Good]
```

Activity 4.06: Type Checker

Solution:

1. Define the package:

```
package main
```

2. Import the required libraries:

```
import "fmt"
```

3. Create a function that returns a slice of **interface{}** values. This will hold our example values:

```
func getData() []interface{} {
    return []interface{}{
        1,
        3.14,
        "hello",
        true,
        struct{}{},
    }
}
```

4. Create a function that accepts a single **interface{}** value and returns a **string**:

```
func getTypeName(v interface{}) string {
```

5. Use a type **switch**:

```
switch v.(type) {
```

6. Add a **case** for all **int** types:

```
case int, int32, int64:
```

7. Return a string that represents them:

```
return "int"
```

8. Add a **case** for the floats and return a string for them:

```
case float64, float32:
    return "float"
```

9. Add a **case** for the Boolean type and return a string for it:

```
case bool:
    return "bool"
```

10. Then, add a case for strings:

```
case string:
    return "string"
```

11. Add a default case that says you don't know the type:

```
default:
    return "unknown"
```

12. Close the **switch** statement and the function:

```
    }
}
```

13. Create the **main()** function:

```
func main() {
```

14. Get the example data and assign it to a variable:

```
data := getData()
```

15. Use a **for i** loop to step over the example values one by one:

```
for i := 0; i < len(data); i++ {
```

16. Pass each example value to the preceding function and print the result to the console:

```
fmt.Printf("%v is %v\n", data[i], getTypeName(data[i]))
```

17. Close the loop and the function:

```
    }
}
```

18. In the folder you created the code in, run the following command:

```
go run .
```

Running the preceding code will produce the following output:

```
 ~/src/Th…op/Ch…04/Activity04.06  go run .
1 is int
3.14 is float
hello is string
true is bool
{} is unknown
```

Figure 4.18: Output displaying types

Chapter 5: Functions

Activity 5.01: Calculating the Working Hours of Employees

Solution:

All directories and files should be created inside your $GOPATH:

1. Create a directory called Activity5.01.

2. Create a file called main.go inside Activity5.01.

3. Inside Activity5.01/main.go, declare the main package and its imports:

```
package main
import "fmt"
```

4. Create a Developer type. Notice the WorkWeek is an array of 7. This is because the week consists of 7 days and we use an array to ensure the fixed size:

```
type Developer struct {
    Individual Employee
    HourlyRate int
    WorkWeek   [7]int
}
```

5. Create an **Employee** type:

```
type Employee struct {
    Id        int
    FirstName string
    LastName  string
}
```

6. Create a **Weekday** of type **int**:

```
type Weekday int
```

7. Create a constant of type **Weekday**. This is an enumeration of the weekdays:

```
const (
    Sunday Weekday = iota //starts at zero
    Monday
    Tuesday
    Wednesday
    Thursday
    Friday
    Saturday
)
```

8. In the **main()** function, include the following code; initialize **Developer** with the following details:

```
func main() {
    d := Developer{Individual:Employee{Id: 1, FirstName: "Tony", LastName:
    "Stark"}, HourlyRate: 10}
```

9. Next, call the **LogHours** method:

```
    d.LogHours(Monday, 8)
    d.LogHours(Tuesday, 10)
```

10. Print out the workweek and the hours worked for the week:

```
    fmt.Println("Hours worked on Monday:   " ,d.WorkWeek[Monday])
    fmt.Println("Hours worked on Tuesday:  " ,d.WorkWeek[Tuesday])
    fmt.Printf("Hours worked this week:   %d",d.HoursWorked())
}
```

11. Create a **LogHours** method; it is a pointer receiver method. It takes as input a custom type called **Weekday** and an **int**. The method assigns the **WorkWeek** field to the day of the week for hours worked that day. **WorkWeek** is an array with a fixed size of **7**, because there are **7** days in a week:

```
func (d *Developer) LogHours(day Weekday, hours int) {
  d.WorkWeek[day] = hours
}
```

12. Create a **HoursWorked** method that will return an **int**. The **HoursWorked** function ranges over **WorkWeek**, adding the hours for the day to **total**:

```
func (d *Developer) HoursWorked() int {
  total := 0
  for _, v := range d.WorkWeek {
    total += v
  }
  return total
}
```

The following is the expected output:

```
Hours worked on Monday:   8
Hours worked on Tuesday:  10
Hours worked this week:   18
```

Activity 5.02: Calculating Payable Amount for Employees Based on Working Hours

Solution:

1. Create a directory called **Activity5.02**.

2. Create a file called **main.go()** in the directory in step 1.

3. Copy the following code following into **Activity5.02/main.go**. This is the same code from steps 3-7 of Activity5.01, *Calculating the Working Hours of Employees*; see those steps for a description of the code:

main.go

```
3  type Developer struct {
4    Individual Employee
5    HourlyRate int
6    WorkWeek   [7]int
7  }
8  type Employee struct {
9    Id        int
10   FirstName string
11   LastName  string
12 }
13 type Weekday int
14 const (
15   Sunday Weekday = iota //starts at zero
```

The full code for this step is available at https://packt.live/34NsT7T

4. In the **main()** function, place the following code. Assign **x** to the return value of **nonLoggedHours()**. As you may recall, the return value is **func(int)int**. The following three prints pass a value to **x func**. Each time **x func** is called, it adds the value passed to the total:

```
func main() {
    d := Developer{Individual: Employee{Id: 1, FirstName: "Tony", LastName:
        "Stark"}, HourlyRate: 10}
    x := nonLoggedHours()
    fmt.Println("Tracking hours worked thus far today: ", x(2))
    fmt.Println("Tracking hours worked thus far today: ", x(3))
    fmt.Println("Tracking hours worked thus far today: ", x(5))
    fmt.Println()
    d.LogHours(Monday, 8)
    d.LogHours(Tuesday, 10)
    d.LogHours(Wednesday, 10)
    d.LogHours(Thursday, 10)
    d.LogHours(Friday, 6)
    d.LogHours(Saturday, 8)
    d.PayDetails()
}
```

5. The **LogHours** and **HoursWorked** remain unchanged:

```
func (d *Developer) LogHours(day Weekday, hours int) {
    d.WorkWeek[day] = hours
}
func (d *Developer) HoursWorked() int {
    total := 0
```

```
    for _, v := range d.WorkWeek {
        total += v
    }
    return total
}
```

6. Create a method called **PayDay()** that returns an **int** and a **bool**. The method evaluates whether **HoursWorked** is greater than **40**. If it is, then it calculates **hoursOver** as overtime pay. It returns the total pay and **true** if the pay includes overtime:

```
func (d *Developer) PayDay() (int, bool) {
    if d.HoursWorked() > 40 {
        hoursOver := d.HoursWorked() - 40
        overTime := hoursOver * 2 * d.HourlyRate
        regularPay := d.HoursWorked() * d.HourlyRate
        return regularPay + overTime, true
    }
    return d.HoursWorked() * d.HourlyRate, false
}
```

7. Create a function called **nonLoggedHours()**. This is a function that has a return type of **func(int)int**. The function is a closure, it encloses the anonymous function. Each time the function is called, it adds the int that is passed into the running total and returns the total:

```
func nonLoggedHours() func(int) int {
    total := 0
    return func(i int) int {
        total += i
        return total
    }
}
```

8. Create a method called **PayDetails**. Inside the **PayDetails** method, it iterates over **d.WorkWeek**. It assigns the **i** value to the index of the slice and **v** to the value stored in the slice. The **i** switch is the index of the slice; it represents the day of the week. The **case** statement evaluates **i** and based on the value, it prints the day and the hours for that day.

9. The function also prints the hours worked for the week, the pay for the week, and if the pay was overtime pay.

10. The first **print** statement prints out the hours worked.

11. **pay** and **overtime** get assigned the values returned from **d.Payday()**.

12. The following **pay** statements print out the pay, whether it was overtime, and a blank line:

main.go

```
64 func (d *Developer) PayDetails() {
65    for i, v := range d.WorkWeek {
66       switch i {
67       case 0:
68          fmt.Println("Sunday hours: ", v)
69       case 1:
70          fmt.Println("Monday hours: ", v)
71       case 2:
```

The full code for this step is available at https://packt.live/2QeUNEF

The results of this activity being run are as follows:

```
Tracking hours worked thus far today:  2
Tracking hours worked thus far today:  5
Tracking hours worked thus far today:  10

Sunday hours:  0
Monday hours:  8
Tuesday hours:  10
Wednesday hours:  10
Thursday hours:  10
Friday hours:  6
Saturday hours:  8

Hours worked this week:  52
Pay for the week: $ 544
Is this overtime pay:  true
```

Figure 5.14: Output for payable amount activity

Chapter 6: Errors

Activity 6.01: Creating a Custom Error Message for a Banking Application

Solution:

1. Create a directory called *Activity6.01* inside your **$GOPATH**.

2. Save a file inside of the directory created in *step 1* called **main.go**.

3. Define **package main** and import two packages, **errors** and **fmt**:

```
package main
import (
    «errors»
    «fmt»
)
```

4. Next, define our custom error that will return an error that displays **"invalid last name"**:

```
var ErrInvalidLastName = errors.New("invalid last name")
```

5. We need one more custom error that will return an error that displays **"invalid routing number"**:

```
var ErrInvalidRoutingNum = errors.New("invalid routing number")
```

6. In the **main()** function, we will print each of the errors:

```
func main() {
    fmt.Println(ErrInvalidLastName)
    fmt.Println(ErrInvalidRoutingNum)
}
```

7. At the command line, navigate to the directory created in *step 1*.

8. At the command line, type the following:

```
go build
```

The **go build** command will compile your program and create an executable named after the directory you created in *step 1*.

9. Type the name of the file created in *step 8* and hit *Enter* to run the executable.

The expected output is as follows:

```
invalid last name
invalid routing number
```

Activity 6.02: Validating a Bank Customer's Direct Deposit Submission

Solution:

1. Create a directory called *Activity6.02* inside **$GOPATH**.

2. Save a file inside the directory created in *step 1* called **main.go**.

3. Define **package main** and add the following imports for this application:

```
package main
import (
    "errors"
    "fmt"
    "strings"
)
```

4. Define the struct and fields that are mentioned in the activity description:

```
type directDeposit struct {
    lastName      string
    firstName     string
    bankName      string
    routingNumber int
    accountNumber int
}
```

5. Define two errors that will be used by the **directDeposit** method later:

```
var ErrInvalidLastName = errors.New("invalid last name")
var ErrInvalidRoutingNum = errors.New("invalid routing number")
```

6. In the **main()** function, assign a variable of the **directDeposit** type and set its fields:

```
func main() {
    dd := directDeposit{
        lastName:      "   ",
        firstName:     "Abe",
        bankName:      "XYZ Inc",
        routingNumber: 17,
        accountNumber: 1809,
    }
}
```

7. Assign a variable named **err** to the **directDeposit**, **validateRoutingNumber**, and **validateLastName** methods. If an error is returned, print the error:

```
err := dd.validateRoutingNumber()
if err != nil {
    fmt.Println(err)
}
err = dd.validateLastName()
if err != nil {
    fmt.Println(err)
}
```

8. Call the **report()** method to print out the field's values:

```
dd.report()
}
```

9. Create a method that is used to check whether **routingNumber** is less than 100. If that condition is **true**, it will return the custom error, **ErrInvalidRoutingNum**, else it will return **nil**:

```
func (dd *directDeposit) validateRoutingNumber() error {
    if dd.routingNumber < 100 {
        return ErrInvalidRoutingNum
    }
    return nil
}
```

10. Now we are going to add the **validateLastName** method. This method removes all trailing spaces from **lastName** and checks to see whether the **lastName** length equals zero. If the **lastName** length equals zero, the method will return the error, **ErrInvalidLasName**. If **lastName** is not equal to zero, then it will return **nil**:

```
func (dd *directDeposit) validateLastName() error {
    dd.lastName = strings.TrimSpace(dd.lastName)
    if len(dd.lastName) == 0 {
        return ErrInvalidLastName
    }
    return nil
}
```

11. The next **report()** method will print each of the **directDeposit** field's values:

```
func (dd *directDeposit) report() {
    fmt.Println(strings.Repeat("*", 80))
    fmt.Println("Last Name: ", dd.lastName)
    fmt.Println("First Name: ", dd.firstName)
    fmt.Println("Bank Name: ", dd.bankName)
    fmt.Println("Routing Number: ", dd.routingNumber)
    fmt.Println("Account Number: ", dd.accountNumber)
}
```

12. At the command line, navigate to the directory created in *step 1*.

13. At the command line, type the following:

```
go build
```

The **go build** command will compile your program and create an executable named after the directory you created in *step 1*.

14. Type the name of the file created in *step 13* and hit *Enter* to run the executable.

    The expected output is as follows:

```
invalid routing number
invalid last name
*****************************************************************************
Last Name:
First Name:   Abe
Bank Name:    XYZ Inc
Routing Number:   17
Account Number:   1809
```

Figure 6.14: Validating a bank customer's direct deposit submission

Activity 6.03: Panic on Invalid Data Submission

Solution:

1. Navigate to the directory used in *step 1* of *Activity 6.02, Validating a Bank's Customers Direct Deposit Submission*.

2. Change the return **ErrInvalidRoutingNum** to panic with **ErrInvalidRoutingNum** passed to the **panic()** function:

```
func (dd *directDeposit) validateRoutingNumber() {
  if dd.routingNumber < 100 {
    panic(ErrInvalidRoutingNum)
  }
  return nil
}
```

3. At the command line, navigate to the directory used in *step 1*.

4. At the command line, type the following:

```
go build
```

The **go build** command will compile your program and create an executable named after the directory you used in *step 1*.

5. Type the name of the file created in *step 4* and hit *Enter* to run the executable.

The expected output is as follows:

```
panic: invalid routing number

goroutine 1 [running]:
main.(*directDeposit).validateRoutingNumber(...)
        /tmp/sandbox561135516/prog.go:44
main.main()
        /tmp/sandbox561135516/prog.go:30 +0x160
```

Figure 6.15: Panic on invalid routing number

Activity 6.04: Preventing a Panic from Crashing the App

Solution:

1. Navigate to the directory used in *step 1* of *Activity 6.03, Panic on Invalid Data Submission.*

2. Add a **defer** function to the **validateRoutingNumber** method.

3. Inside the **defer** function, check for an error being returned from the **recover()** function.

4. If there is an error, print the error from the **recover()** function.

The only change is adding a deferred function:

```
func (dd *directDeposit) validateRoutingNumber() error {
    defer func() {
        if r:= recover(); r != nil {
            fmt.Println(r)
        }
    }()
    if dd.routingNumber < 100 {
        panic(ErrInvalidRoutingNum)
    }
    return nil
}
```

5. At the command line, navigate to the directory used in *step 1*.

6. At the command line, type the following:

```
go build
```

The **go build** command will compile your program and create an executable named after the directory you used in *step 1*.

7. Type the name of the file created in *step 6* and hit *Enter* to run the executable.

   The expected output is as follows:

```
invalid routing number
invalid last name
********************************************************************************
Last Name:
First Name:  Abe
Bank Name:  XYZ Inc
Routing Number:   17
Account Number:   1809
```

Figure 6.16: Recovering from panic on an invalid routing number

Chapter 7: Interfaces

Activity 7.01: Calculating Pay and Performance Review

Solution:

1. Create a **main.go** file.

2. Inside the **main.go** file, we have a **main** package and we need to import the **errors**, **fmt**, and **os** packages:

```
package main
import (
  "errors"
  "fmt"
  "os"
)
```

3. Create the **Employee** struct as follows:

```
type Employee struct {
  Id         int
  FirstName string
  LastName  string
}
```

4. Create the **Developer** struct. The **Developer** struct has the **Employee** struct embedded into it:

```
type Developer struct {
    Individual        Employee
    HourlyRate        float64
    HoursWorkedInYear float64
    Review            map[string]interface{}
}
```

5. Create the **Manager** struct; it will have the **Employee** struct embedded into it as well:

```
type Manager struct {
    Individual     Employee
    Salary         float64
    CommissionRate float64
}
```

6. The **Pay** interface will be used by both the **Manager** and **Developer** types to calculate their pay:

```
type Payer interface {
    Pay() (string, float64)
}
```

7. Add a **FullName()** method to the **Developer** struct. This is used to concatenate the developer's **FirstName** and **LastName** and return it:

```
func (d Developer) FullName() string {
    fullName := d.Individual.FirstName + " " + d.Individual.LastName
    return fullName
}
```

8. Create the **Pay()** method for the developer that will implement the **Payer** interface.

The **Developer** struct satisfies the **Payer** interface by having a method called **Pay** that returns a string and a float64. The **Developer Pay()** method returns **fullName** of the developer and returns the year's pay by calculating **Developer HourlRate *** **HoursWorkedInYear**:

```
func (d Developer) Pay() (string, float64) {
    fullName := d.FullName()
    return fullName, d.HourlyRate * d.HoursWorkedInYear
}
```

9. Create the **Pay()** method for the **Manager** struct that will implement the **Payer** interface.

10. The **Manager** struct satisfies the **Payer{}** interface by having a method called **Pay()** that returns a string and a **float64**. The **Manager Pay** method returns **fullName** of the **Manager** struct and returns the year's pay by calculating the **Manager** salary plus the **Manager** salary times the manager's **CommissionRate**:

```
func (m Manager) Pay() (string, float64) {
    fullName := m.Individual.FirstName + " " + m.Individual.LastName
    return fullName, m.Salary + (m.Salary * m.CommissionRate)
}
```

11. Create the **payDetails()** function, which accepts a **Payer{}** interface. It will call the **Pay()** method of the type that is passed in; the **Pay()** method is required for the **Payer** interface. Print **fullName** and **yearPay** that gets returned from the **Pay()** method:

```
func payDetails(p Payer) {
    fullName, yearPay := p.Pay()
    fmt.Printf("%s got paid %.2f for the year\n", fullName, yearPay)
}
```

The **payDetails()** function accepts a **Payer{}** interface. It then prints **fullName** and **yearPay**, which get returned from the **Pay()** method.

12. Inside the **main** function, we need to create a **Developer** type and **Manager** type and set their field values:

```
d := Developer{Individual: Employee{Id: 1, FirstName: "Eric", LastName: "Davis"},
HourlyRate: 35, HoursWorkedInYear: 2400, Review: employeeReview}
m := Manager{Individual: Employee{Id: 2, FirstName: "Mr.", LastName: "Boss"},
Salary: 150000, CommissionRate: .07}
```

13. Call **payDetails()** and pass the developer and manager as arguments. Since **Developer** and **Manager** both satisfy the **Payer{}** interface, we can pass them to the **payDetails()** function.

In the **main** function, we initialize **d** as a struct literal of **Developer** and **m** as a struct literal of **Manager**:

```
payDetails(d)
payDetails(m)
```

14. We now need to create the data for the employee review for the developer. We will make a map with a key of string and an interface for the value. As you may recall, different managers can use a numeric value or a string value for the rating to be assigned to the category:

```
employeeReview := make(map[string]interface{})
employeeReview["WorkQuality"] = 5
employeeReview["TeamWork"] = 2
employeeReview["Communication"] = "Poor"
employeeReview["Problem-solving"] = 4
employeeReview["Dependability"] = "Unsatisfactory"
```

15. For the review rating, we need to be able to convert the string rating for the category to an integer version of the category. We will create the **convertReviewToInt()** function to perform this conversion by using a **switch case** statement. The **switch** statement on the string looks at the different string versions of the rating and returns the integer version of the rating. If the string version of the rating is not found, the default clause is executed and returns an error:

```
func convertReviewToInt(str string) (int, error) {
  switch str {
  case "Excellent":
    return 5, nil
  case "Good":
    return 4, nil
  case "Fair":
    return 3, nil
  case "Poor":
    return 2, nil
  case "Unsatisfactory":
    return 1, nil
  default:
    return 0, errors.New("invalid rating: " + str)
  }
}
```

We need to create a function called **OverallReview()** that accepts an interface and returns an integer and an error.

Recall that our review process provides strings and integers for the rating; that is why this function accepts an interface so that we can evaluate either type.

We use the switch type code structure to determine the interface concrete type. The **v** variable gets assigned the concrete type of **i**.

The only valid types for the rating are **int** and a **string**. Anything else is considered invalid and causes the default statement to be executed. The default statement will return an error if the type is not found in the **case** statements.

16. If the type is **int**, it will simply return it as an **int**. If the interface concrete type is a string, the code in the **case string** will execute. It will pass the string to the **convertReviewToInt(v)** function. This function, as explained earlier, will do a lookup of the string version of the rating and return the integer correspondent:

```go
func OverallReview(i interface{}) (int, error) {
  switch v := i.(type) {
  case int:
    return v, nil
  case string:
    rating, err := convertReviewToInt(v)
    if err != nil {
      return 0, err
    }
    return rating, nil
  default:
    return 0, errors.New("unknown type")
  }
}
```

17. Next, create the **ReviewRating()** method to perform the calculation for the developer rating. The **Developer ReviewRating()** method performs the calculation for the **Review**. It loops over the **d.Review** field that is of the **map[string]interface{}** type. It passes each interface value to the **OverallReview(v)** function to get the integer value of the rating. Each loop iteration adds that rating to a total variable. It then calculates the average of the review and prints the results. Here are the results of the performance rating:

```go
func (d Developer) ReviewRating() error {
  total := 0
  for _, v := range d.Review {
    rating, err := OverallReview(v)
    if err != nil {
      return err
    }
```

```
        total += rating
    }
    averageRating := float64(total) / float64(len(d.Review))
    fmt.Printf("%s got a review rating of %.2f\n",d.FullName(),averageRating)
    return nil
}
```

18. In the **main()** function, call **ReviewRating()** and print any errors:

```
err := d.ReviewRating()
    if err != nil {
        fmt.Println(err)
        os.Exit(1)
    }
```

19. Next, call the **payDetails()** function for the **Developer** type and the **Manager** type:

```
        payDetails(d)
        payDetails(m)
    }
```

20. Build the program by running **go build** at the command line:

```
    go build
```

21. Run the program by typing in the name of the executable at the command line.

    The expected output is as follows:

```
Eric Davis got a review rating of 2.80
Eric Davis got paid 84000.00 for the year
Mr. Boss got paid 160500.00 for the year
```

Chapter 8: Packages

Activity 8.01: Creating a Function to Calculate Payroll and Performance Review

Solution:

All directories and files should be created inside of **$GOPATH**:

1. Create a directory called **Activity8.01**.

2. Create a directory called **pay** and **payroll** inside **Activity8.01**.

3. Create a file called **main.go** inside **Chapter08/Activity8.01/pay**.

4. Create the following files: **developer.go**, **employee.go**, and **manager.go** inside **payroll**.

5. The directory structure and files should look similar to the following screenshot:

Figure 8.16: Program directory structure

6. Inside **Chapter08/Activity8.01/payroll/developer.go**, declare the package as **payroll**:

```
package payroll
import (
    "errors"
    "fmt"
)
```

7. The **Developer** type, and the following methods, **Pay()** and **ReviewRating()**, will all be exportable, so the first letter needs to be capitalized. This means that they are visible to other packages outside of **payroll**.

8. From https://packt.live/2YNnfS6, move the code that relates to the developer type and methods to the **Chapter08/Activity8.01/payroll/developer.go** file. It should look like the following code snippet:

developer.go

```
1  package payroll
2  import (
3     "errors"
4     "fmt"
5  )
6  type Developer struct {
7     Individual        Employee
8     HourlyRate        float64
9     HoursWorkedInYear float64
10    Review            map[string]interface{}
11 }
```

The full code for this step is available at https://packt.live/34NTAtn

9. Inside **Chapter08/Activity8.01/payroll/employee.go**, declare the package as **payroll**:

```
package payroll
import "fmt"
```

10. The **Employee** type, **Payer** interface, and its methods will all be exportable, so the first letter needs to be capitalized. This means that they are visible to other packages outside of **payroll**.

11. From https://packt.live/2YNnfS6, move the code that relates to the employee type and methods to **Chapter08/Activity8.01/payroll/employee.go file**. It should look like the following code snippet:

```
package payroll
import "fmt"
type Payer interface {
    Pay() (string, float64)
}
type Employee struct {
    Id        int
    FirstName string
    LastName  string
}
func PayDetails(p Payer) {
    fullName, yearPay := p.Pay()
    fmt.Printf("%s got paid %.2f for the year\n", fullName, yearPay)
}
```

12. Inside **Chapter08/Activity8.01/payroll/manager.go**, declare **package** as **payroll**:

```
package payroll
```

13. In **manager.go**, the **Manager** type and its methods will be exportable. All the types and methods are exportable because the first letter is capitalized. This means that they are visible to other packages outside of **payroll**.

14. From https://packt.live/2YNnfS6, move the code that relates to the employee type and methods to **Chapter08/Activity8.01/payroll/manager.go file**. It should look like the following code snippet:

```
package payroll
type Manager struct {
    Individual     Employee
    Salary         float64
    CommissionRate float64
```

```
    }
    func (m Manager) Pay() (string, float64) {
        fullName := m.Individual.FirstName + " " + m.Individual.LastName
        return fullName, m.Salary + (m.Salary * m.CommissionRate)
    }
```

The **developer.go**, **employee.go**, and **manager.go** files make up the **payroll** package. Even though the **payroll** package is split up between three files: **developer.go**, **employee.go**, and **manager.go**, they are all accessible across files in the **payroll** package. Every file in this directory belongs to the **payroll** package.

15. Next, in the **Chapter08/Activity8.01/pay/main.go** file, by looking at the **package** declaration, we can see this is an executable package. This is because any package that is the main package is an executable. We also know that since this is the main package, it will have a **main()** function:

```
    package main
```

16. We know from the initialization process that the packages will have their variables and **init()** functions initialized first. In the **import** declaration, we are importing our **payroll** package. The **payroll** package is also going to be aliased as **pr**:

```
    import (
        "fmt"
        "os"
        pr "github.com/PacktWorkshops/Get-Ready-To-Go/Chapter08/Activity8.01/payroll"
    )
```

17. The **main** package **employeeReview** variable will be initialized next, after the **import** items:

```
    var employeeReview = make(map[string]interface{})
```

18. Next, create the **init()** function. It will run before the other functions in the **main** package. It will greet users with a message:

```
    func init() {
        fmt.Println("Welcome to the Employee Pay and Performance Review")
        fmt.Println("++++++++++++++++++++++++++++++++++++++++++++++++++++++")
    }
```

19. This is our second **init()** function in the **main** package and it will run next. It initializes the **employeeReview** variables to values that will be used in this package:

```
func init() {
  fmt.Println("Initializing variables")
  employeeReview["WorkQuality"] = 5
  employeeReview["TeamWork"] = 2
  employeeReview["Communication"] = "Poor"
  employeeReview["Problem-solving"] = 4
  employeeReview["Dependability"] = "Unsatisfactory"
}
```

20. We now get to the **main()** function. Every main package has a **main()** function. This is the entry point to our executable:

```
func main() {
```

21. We alias our payroll in the **import** declaration with **pr**. We initialize our exportable **Developer** type through the **payroll** alias of **pr**. Since **Developer** in the **payroll** package is exportable, we will have visibility of it from the **main** package. This is also true for the **Employee** type:

```
  d := pr.Developer{Individual: pr.Employee{Id: 1, FirstName: "Eric", LastName:
"Davis"}, HourlyRate: 35, HoursWorkedInYear: 2400, Review: employeeReview}
```

22. We alias our payroll in the **import** declaration with **pr**. We initialize our exportable **Manager** type through the **payroll** alias of **pr**. Since **Manager** in the **payroll** package is exportable, we have visibility of it from the **main** package. This is also true for the **Employee** type:

```
  m := pr.Manager{Individual: pr.Employee{Id: 2, FirstName: "Mr.", LastName:
"Boss"}, Salary: 150000, CommissionRate: .07}
```

23. The **Developer** method, **ReviewRating()** is also exportable. This allows us to call that method from the **payroll** package:

```
  err := d.ReviewRating()
  if err != nil {
    fmt.Println(err)
    os.Exit(1)
  }
```

24. The **PayDetails** function is exportable, and we can also invoke the function in the **payroll** package. We call it with the alias of **pr**:

```
    pr.PayDetails(d)
    pr.PayDetails(m)
}
```

25. At the command line, go to the **/Exercise8.01/Activity8.01/pay** directory structure.

26. At the command line, type the following:

```
go build
```

27. The **go build** command will compile your program and create an executable named after the **dir** area.

28. Type the executable name and hit *Enter*:

```
./pay
```

The result should be as follows:

```
Welcome to the Employee Pay and Performance Review
+++++++++++++++++++++++++++++++++++++++++++++++++++++
Initializing variables
Eric Davis got a review rating of 2.80
Eric Davis got paid 84000.00 for the year
Mr. Boss got paid 160500.00 for the year
```

Chapter 9: Basic Debugging

Activity 9.01: Building a Program to Validate Social Security Numbers

Solution:

All directories and files created should be within your **$GOPATH**:

1. Create a directory called **Activity9.01** inside the **Chapter09** directory.

2. Create a file called **main.go** inside the **Chapter09/Activity9.01/** directory.

3. Using Visual Studio Code, open the **main.go** file.

4. Add the following code to **main.go**.

Here is the **main** function to build from:

```
package main
import (
    "errors"
    "fmt"
    "log"
    "strconv"
    "strings"
)
```

5. Add the following custom error types. The custom errors that we will be using to log in to our program. These custom errors will be returned by their respective functions. They will appear in the log where applicable:

```
var (
    ErrInvalidSSNLength    = errors.New("ssn is not nine characters long")
    ErrInvalidSSNNumbers   = errors.New("ssn has non-numeric digits")
    ErrInvalidSSNPrefix    = errors.New("ssn has three zeros as a prefix")
    ErrInvalidSSNDigitPlace = errors.New("ssn starts with a 9 requires 7 or
        9 in the fourth place")
)
```

6. Create a function that will check to see whether the SSN length is valid. If the length is not 9, return an error to include the details of which SSN caused the custom error, **ErrInvalidSSNLength**:

```
func validLength(ssn string) error {
    ssn = strings.TrimSpace(ssn)
    if len(ssn) != 9 {
        return fmt.Errorf("the value of %s caused an error: %v\n", ssn,
            ErrInvalidSSNLength)
    }
    return nil
}
```

7. Create a function that will check to see whether all the characters in the SSN are numbers. If the SSN is invalid, return an error to include the details of which SSN caused the custom error, **ErrInvalidSSNNumbers**:

```
func isNumber(ssn string) error {
    _, err := strconv.Atoi(ssn)
    if err != nil {
        return fmt.Errorf("the value of %s caused an error: %v\n", ssn,
            ErrInvalidSSNNumbers)
    }
    return nil
}
```

8. Create a function that will check to see whether the SSN starts with 000. If the SSN is invalid, return an error to include the details of which SSN caused the custom error, **ErrInvalidSSNPrefix**:

```
func isPrefixValid(ssn string) error {
    if strings.HasPrefix(ssn, "000") {
        return fmt.Errorf("the value of %s caused an error: %v\n", ssn,
            ErrInvalidSSNPrefix)
    }
    return nil
}
```

9. Create a function that will check that if the SSN starts with a 9, then the fourth digit of an SSN should be a 7 or a 9. If the SSN is invalid, return an error to include the details of which SSN caused the custom error, **ErrInvalidSSNDigitPlace**:

```
func validDigitPlace(ssn string) error {
    if string(ssn[0]) == "9" && (string(ssn[3]) != "9" && string(ssn[3]) !=
        "7") {
        return fmt.Errorf("the value of %s caused an error: %v\n", ssn,
            ErrInvalidSSNDigitPlace)
    }
    return nil
}
```

10. In the **main()** function, set the flags for our logging:

```
func main() {
    log.SetFlags(log.Ldate | log.Lmicroseconds | log.Llongfile)
```

11. Initialize our **validateSSN** slice to contain various SSN numbers that we will be validating:

```
validateSSN := []string{"123-45-6789", "012-8-678", "000-12-0962", "999-
    33-3333", "087-65-4321","123-45-zzzz"}
```

12. Print the Go representation of the **validateSSN** variable using **%#v**:

```
log.Printf("Checking data %#v",validateSSN)
```

13. Next, create a **for** loop that will iterate over the slice of SSNs using a **range** clause:

```
for idx,ssn := range validateSSN {
```

14. In the **for** loop, for each SSN, we want to print some details about the **ssn**. We want to print the current entry order of the SSN in the slice that we are validating using the **%d** verb. Finally, we need to print the total number of items in the slice using the **%d** verb:

```
log.Printf("Validate data %#v %d of %d ",ssn,idx+1,len(validateSSN))
```

15. Remove any dashes from our SSN:

```
ssn = strings.Replace(ssn, "-", "", -1)
```

16. Call each of the functions we are using for validating the SSN. Log the error that gets returned from the function:

```
Err := isNumber(ssn)
if err != nil {
    log.Print(err)
}
err = validLength(ssn)
if err != nil {
    log.Print(err)
}
err = isPrefixValid(ssn)
if err != nil {
    log.Print(err)
}
err = validDigitPlace(ssn)
if err != nil {
    log.Print(err)
}
}
}
```

17. At the command line, change the directory using the following code:

```
cd Chapter09/Exercise9.02/
```

18. In *Exercise 9.02, Printing Decimal, Binary, and Hex Values*, directory, type the following command:

```
go build
```

Type the executable that was created from the **go build** command and press *Enter*.

The expected output is as follows:

```
2009/11/10 23:00:00.000000 /tmp/sandbox957632207/prog.go:22: Checking data []string{"123-45-6789", "012-8-678", "000-12-0962", "999-33-3333", "087-65-4321", "123-45-zzzz"}
2009/11/10 23:00:00.000000 /tmp/sandbox957632207/prog.go:24: Validate data "123-45-6789" 1 of 6
2009/11/10 23:00:00.000000 /tmp/sandbox957632207/prog.go:24: Validate data "012-8-678" 2 of 6
2009/11/10 23:00:00.000000 /tmp/sandbox957632207/prog.go:33: the value of 0128678 caused an error: ssn is not nine characters long
2009/11/10 23:00:00.000000 /tmp/sandbox957632207/prog.go:24: Validate data "000-12-0962" 3 of 6
2009/11/10 23:00:00.000000 /tmp/sandbox957632207/prog.go:37: the value of 000120962 caused an error: ssn has three zeros as a prefix
2009/11/10 23:00:00.000000 /tmp/sandbox957632207/prog.go:24: Validate data "999-33-3333" 4 of 6
2009/11/10 23:00:00.000000 /tmp/sandbox957632207/prog.go:41: the value of 999333333 caused an error: ssn starts with a 9 requires 7 or 9 in the fourth place
2009/11/10 23:00:00.000000 /tmp/sandbox957632207/prog.go:24: Validate data "087-65-4321" 5 of 6
2009/11/10 23:00:00.000000 /tmp/sandbox957632207/prog.go:24: Validate data "123-45-zzzz" 6 of 6
2009/11/10 23:00:00.000000 /tmp/sandbox957632207/prog.go:29: the value of 12345zzzz caused an error: ssn has non-numeric digits
```

Figure 9.15: Validating the SSN output

Chapter 10: About Time

Activity 10.01: Formatting a Date According to User Requirements

Solution:

1. Create a file called **Chapter_10_Activity_1.go** and initialize it with the following code:

```
package main
import "fmt"
import "time"
import "strconv"
func main(){
```

2. Capture the following values: **date**, **day**, **month**, **year**, **hour**, **minute**, and **second**:

```
date := time.Now()
day := strconv.Itoa(date.Day())
month := strconv.Itoa(int(date.Month()))
year := strconv.Itoa(date.Year())
hour := strconv.Itoa(date.Hour())
minute := strconv.Itoa(date.Minute())
second := strconv.Itoa(date.Second())
```

3. Print the concatenated output:

```
fmt.Println(hour + ":" + minute + ":" + second + " " + year + "/" + month
+ "/" + day)
}
```

The expected output is as follows (note that this depends on when you run the code):

```
15:32:30 2019/10/17
```

Activity 10.02: Enforcing a Specific Format of Date and Time

Solution:

1. Create a file called **Chapter_10_Activity_2.go** and initialize the script as follows:

```
package main
import "fmt"
import "time"
import "strconv"
func main(){
```

2. Capture the following values: **date, day, month, year, hour, minute**, and **second**:

```
date := time.Date(2019, 1, 31, 2, 49, 21, 324359102, time.UTC)
day := strconv.Itoa(date.Day())
month := strconv.Itoa(int(date.Month()))
year := strconv.Itoa(date.Year())
hour := strconv.Itoa(date.Hour())
minute := strconv.Itoa(date.Minute())
second := strconv.Itoa(date.Second())
```

3. Print the concatenated output:

```
fmt.Println(hour + ":" + minute + ":" + second + " " + year + "/" + month +
    "/" + day)
}
```

The expected output is as follows:

```
2:49:21 2019/1/31
```

Activity 10.03: Measuring Elapsed Time

Solution:

1. Create a file called **Chapter_10_Activity_3.go** and initialize it in the following way:

```
package main
import "fmt"
import "time"
func main(){
```

2. Capture the **start** time of execution in a variable, and sleep for 2 seconds:

```
start := time.Now()
time.Sleep(2 * time.Second)
```

3. Capture the end of execution in a variable and calculate the length:

```
end := time.Now()
length := end.Sub(start)
```

4. Print out how long it took to execute **sleep**:

```
fmt.Println("The execution took exactly",length.Seconds(),"seconds!")
}
```

The expected output is as follows:

```
The execution took exactly 2.0016895 seconds!
```

Activity 10.04: Calculating the Future Date and Time

Solution:

1. Create a file called **Chapter_10_Activity_4.go** and initialize it in the following way:

```
package main
import "fmt"
import "time"
func main(){
```

2. Capture and print the **current** time:

```
Current := time.Now()
fmt.Println("The current time is:",Current.Format(time.ANSIC))
```

3. Calculate the specified duration and create a variable called **Future**:

```
SSS := time.Duration(21966 * time.Second)
Future := Current.Add(SSS)
```

4. Print out the time value of **Future** in ANSIC format:

```
fmt.Println("6 hours, 6 minutes and 6 seconds from now the time will be:
  ",Future.Format(time.ANSIC))
}
```

The expected output is as follows:

```
The current time: Thu Oct 17 15:16:48 2019

6 hours, 6 minutes and 6 seconds from now the time will be:  Thu Oct 17
21:22:54 2019
```

Activity 10.05: Printing the Local Time in Different Time Zones

Solution:

1. Create a file called **Chapter_10_Activity_5.go** and initialize it the following way:

```
package main
import "fmt"
import "time"
func main(){
```

2. Capture the following values: **Current**, **NYtime**, and **LA**:

```
Current := time.Now()
    NYtime, _ := time.LoadLocation("America/New_York")
    LA, _ := time.LoadLocation("America/Los_Angeles")
```

3. Print out the values with the following format:

```
fmt.Println("The local current time is:",Current.Format(time.ANSIC))
    fmt.Println("The time in New York is:
    ",Current.In(NYtime).Format(time.ANSIC))
    fmt.Println("The time in Los Angeles is:
    ",Current.In(LA).Format(time.ANSIC))
}
```

The expected output is as follows:

```
The local current time is: Thu Oct 17 15:16:13 2019
The time in New York is: Thu Oct 17 09:16:13 2019
The time in Los Angeles is: Thu Oct 17 06:16:13 2019
```

Chapter 11: Encoding and Decoding (JSON)

Activity 11.01. Mimicking a Customer Order Using JSON

Solution:

All directories and files created need to be created within your **$GOPATH**:

1. Create a directory called **Activity11.01** within a directory called **Chapter11**.

2. Create a file called **main.go** inside **Chapter11/Activity11.01**.

3. Using Visual Studio Code, open the newly created **main.go** file.

4. Add the following package name and import statements:

```
package main
import (
    "encoding/json"
    "fmt"
    "os"
)
```

5. Add the following **customer struct** with the JSON tags set accordingly:

```
type customer struct {
    UserName      string  `json:"username"`
    Password      string  `json:"-"`
    Token         string  `json:"-"`
    ShipTo        address `json:"shipto"`
    PurchaseOrder order   `json:"order"`
}
```

6. Add the following **order struct** with the JSON tags set accordingly:

```
type order struct {
    TotalPrice  int     `json:"total"`
    IsPaid      bool    `json:"paid"`
    Fragile     bool    `json:",omitempty"`
    OrderDetail []item  `json:"orderdetail"`
}
```

7. Add the following **item struct** with the JSON tags set accordingly:

```
type item struct {
    Name        string `json:"itemname"`
    Description string `json:"desc,omitempty"`
    Quantity    int    `json:"qty"`
    Price       int    `json:"price"`
}
```

8. Add the following **address struct** with the JSON tags set accordingly:

```
type address struct {
    Street  string `json:"street"`
    City    string `json:"city"`
    State   string `json:"state"`
    ZipCode int    `json:"zipcode"`
}
```

9. Create a method on the customer type called **Total()**. This method will calculate the **TotalPrice** of the **PurchaseOrder** for the customer type. The calculation is, for each item, **Quantity * price**:

```
func (c *customer) Total() {
  price := 0
  for _, item := range c.PurchaseOrder.OrderDetail {
    price += item.Quantity * item.Price
  }
  c.PurchaseOrder.TotalPrice = price
}
```

10. Add a **main()** function with **jsonData []byte**:

```
func main() {
  jsonData := []byte(`
  {
    "username" :"blackhat",
    "shipto":
      {
        "street": "Sulphur Springs Rd",
        "city": "Park City",
        "state": "VA",
        "zipcode": 12345
      },
    "order":
      {
        "paid":false,
        "orderdetail" :
          [{
            "Itemname":"A Guide to the World of zeros and ones",
            "desc": "book",
            "qty": 3,
            "price": 50
          }]
      }
  }
  `)
```

11. Next, we need to validate that **jsonData** is valid JSON. If it is not, print a message and exit the application:

```
if !json.Valid(jsonData) {
  fmt.Printf("JSON is not valid: %s", jsonData)
```

```
      os.Exit(1)
   }
```

12. Declare a variable of the customer type:

```
   var c customer
```

13. Unmarshal **jsonData** into the customer variable. Check for any errors, and if there is an error, print the error and exit the application:

```
   err := json.Unmarshal(jsonData, &c)
   if err != nil {
     fmt.Println(err)
     os.Exit(1)
   }
```

14. Declare a variable of the **item{}** type and set all the fields:

```
   game := item{}
   game.Name = "Final Fantasy The Zodiac Age"
   game.Description = "Nintendo Switch Game"
   game.Quantity = 1
   game.Price = 50
```

15. Declare another variable of the **item{}** type and set all the fields, except for the **Description** field:

```
   glass := item{}
   glass.Name = "Crystal Drinking Glass"
   glass.Quantity = 11
   glass.Price = 25
```

16. Add the two newly created items to the customer order's **OrderDetail**:

```
   c.PurchaseOrder.OrderDetail = append(c.PurchaseOrder.OrderDetail, game)
   c.PurchaseOrder.OrderDetail = append(c.PurchaseOrder.OrderDetail, glass)
```

17. Now that we have all of our items, we can now calculate the price by calling the **c.Total()** function:

```
   c.Total()
```

18. Set some **PurchaseOrder** fields:

```
   c.PurchaseOrder.IsPaid = true
   c.PurchaseOrder.Fragile = true
```

19. Marshal the customer into JSON. Properly set the indention so that the JSON can be easily read. Check for any errors and if there is an error, print the message, and then exit the application:

```
customerOrder, err := json.MarshalIndent(c, "", "    ")
if err != nil {
   fmt.Println(err)
   os.Exit(1)
}
```

20. Print the JSON:

```
   fmt.Println(string(customerOrder))
}
```

21. Build the program by running **go build** at the command line:

```
go build
```

22. Run the executable by typing in the name of the executable and then hitting *Enter*.

The results are as follows:

```
{
    "username": "blackhat",
    "shipto": {
        "street": "Sulphur Springs Rd",
        "city": "Park City",
        "state": "VA",
        "zipcode": 12345
    },
    "order": {
        "total": 475,
        "paid": true,
        "Fragile": true,
        "orderdetail": [
            {
                "itemname": "A Guide to the World of zeros and ones",
                "desc": "book",
                "qty": 3,
                "price": 50
            },
            {
                "itemname": "Final Fantasy The Zodiac Age",
                "desc": "Nintendo Switch Game",
                "qty": 1,
                "price": 50
            },
            {
                "itemname": "Crystal Drinking Glass",
                "qty": 11,
                "price": 25
            }
        ]
    }
}
```

Figure 11.22: Customer order printout

Chapter 12: Files and Systems

Activity 12.01: Parsing Bank Transaction Files

Solution:

All directories and files created should be inside your **$GOPATH**.

1. Create a **Chapter12/Activity12.01/** directory.

2. Inside **Chapter12/Activity12.01/**, create a **main.go** file.

3. Add the following code to the **main.go** file:

```go
package main
import (
    "encoding/csv"
    "errors"
    "flag"
    "fmt"
    "io"
    "log"
    "os"
    "strconv"
    "strings"
)
```

4. Create budget category types for fuel, food, mortgage, repairs, insurance, utilities, and retirement:

```go
type budgetCategory string
const (
    autoFuel    budgetCategory = "fuel"
    food        budgetCategory = "food"
    mortgage    budgetCategory = "mortgage"
    repairs    budgetCategory = "repairs"
    insurance   budgetCategory = "insurance"
    utilities   budgetCategory = "utilities"
    retirement budgetCategory = "retirement"
)
```

5. Create our custom error type for when the budget category cannot be found:

```go
var (
    ErrInvalidBudgetCategory = errors.New("budget category not found")
)
```

6. Create our **transaction struct** that will hold the data from our bank's transaction file:

```
type transaction struct {
    id       int
    payee    string
    spent    float64
    category budgetCategory
}
```

7. Inside the **main()** function, we need to create two flags. The first flag to create is **bankFile**. The **bankFile** variable is the CSV transaction file. Define our flags for the **bankFile** variable. The flag type is a string. The CLI will have **-c**; this is used to store the location of the CSV **bankFile**. The default value is an empty string, so if the flag does not get set, the value for it will be an empty string. The **bankFile** variable is the address that stores the value of the flag:

```
func main() {
    bankFile := flag.String("c", "", "location of the bank transaction csv file")
    //...
}
```

8. The next flag will be for our **logFile**. This is the file that will be used for logging errors. Define our flags for the log file. The flag type is a string. The CLI will have **-l**; this is used to store the location of the **logFile** variable. The default value is an empty string, so if the flag does not get set, the value for it will be an empty string. The **logFile** variable is the address that stores the value of the flag:

```
logFile := flag.String("l", "", "logging of errors")
```

9. After defining the flags, you must call **flag.Parse()** to parse the command line into the defined flags. Calling **flag.Parse()** places the argument for **-value** into ***bankFile** and ***logFile**. Once you have called **flag.Parse()**, the flags will be available:

```
flag.Parse()
```

10. Our **bankFile** variable is required, so we need to ensure it was provided. When we define our flags, we set the default value to an empty string. If the value of ***bankFile** is an empty string, we know that it was not properly set. If ***bankFile** was not provided, we print a message that the field is required along with the **usage** statement. Then, exit the program:

```
if *bankFile == "" {
fmt.Println("csvFile is required.")
flag.PrintDefaults()
```

```
   os.Exit(1)
}
```

11. If the CSV file was not provided, you should get the following message:

```
csvFile is required.
  -c string
        location of the bank transaction csv file
  -l string
        logging of errors
```

Figure 12.23: The csvFile is required message

12. The **logfile** variable is required and we need to ensure it was provided. Implement the same code you performed in the previous step except for **logfile**:

```
if *logFile == "" {
fmt.Println("logFile is required.")
flag.PrintDefaults()
os.Exit(1)
}
```

13. Implement code to check and see whether the **bankFile** variable exists. We are calling **os.Stat()** on the ***bankFile** file to check to see whether it exists. The **os.Stat()** method will return a **FileInfo** if the file exists. If not, **FileInfo** will be **nil** and an error will be returned instead.

14. The **os.Stat()** method can return multiple errors. We must inspect the error to determine whether the error is due to the file not being there. The standard library provides **os.IsNotExist(error)**, which can be used to check to see whether the error is the result of the file not existing:

```
_, err := os.Stat(*bankFile)
if os.IsNotExist((err)) {
fmt.Println("BankFile does not exist: ", *bankFile)
os.Exit(1)
}
```

15. Likewise, check to see whether the log file exists. If it does, we need to delete it:

```
_, err = os.Stat(*logFile)
if !os.IsNotExist((err)) {
os.Remove(*logFile)
}
```

16. Next, open the **bankFile** variable. Upon opening **bankFile**, the **os.Open** function returns an ***os.File** type that satisfies the **io.Reader** interface, which will allow us to pass it to the next function.

17. As always, check to see whether an error was returned. If so, display the error and exit the program:

```
csvFile, err := os.Open(*bankFile)
if err != nil {
fmt.Println("Error opening file: ", *bankFile)
os.Exit(1)
}
```

18. We will call the **parseBankFile()** function; this is where the bulk of the work occurs. It will transform the CSV file into our transaction struct. We then need to iterate over the slice of transactions and print the data from the transaction:

```
trxs := parseBankFile(csvFile, *logFile)
   fmt.Println()
   for _, trx := range trxs {
   fmt.Printf("%v\n", trx)
}
}
```

19. Create a function called **parseBankFile(bankTransaction io.Reader, logFile string) []transaction**:

```
func parseBankFile(bankTransactions io.Reader, logFile string) []transaction {
/…
}
```

20. Create a reader for the CSV data. The **NewReader** method takes an argument of **io.Reader** and returns a type of **Reader** that is used to read the CSV data.

21. Create a variable of type slice of **transaction**.

22. Create a variable to detect the header of the CSV file:

```
r := csv.NewReader(bankTransactions)
trxs := []transaction{}
header := true
```

23. Implement code that reads each record in one at a time in an infinite loop.

24. After each record we read, we check first to see whether it is the end of the file (**io. EOF**). We need to perform this check to allow us to break out of our infinite loop when it reaches the EOF.

25. The **r.Read()** method reads one record; this is a slice of fields from the **r** variable. It returns that record as **[]string**:

```
for {
  trx := transaction{}
  record, err := r.Read()
  if err == io.EOF {
    break
  }
  if err != nil {
    log.Fatal(err)
  }
}
```

26. We will use the **header** variable as a flag. When header fields are provided, they are typically the first row of the file. We do not need to process the column headers:

```
if !header
```

27. Currently, our first loop iterates over the CSV file, but we also need a loop that iterates over each column in the record. The record is a slice of fields. **idx** is the position of the field in the slice:

```
for idx, value := range record {
```

28. We will use a **switch** statement on the **idx** (index) of the slice to identify the data that is stored at that position:

```
switch idx {
// id
case 0:
// payee
case 1:
// spent
case 2:
// category
}
```

29. Data from the CSV file is in string format; we need to perform various conversions for the fields in the CSV file. The first field is the ID. We need to ensure that there are no trailing spaces in the field.

30. We need to convert the field from a string to an **int**, since our struct is of the integer type for the **id** field:

```
// id
case 0:
value = strings.TrimSpace(value)
trx.id, err = strconv.Atoi(value)
```

31. The second index value is **1**. This column contains the data for the **payee**:

```
// payee
case 1:
    value = strings.TrimSpace(value)
    trx.payee = value
```

The third index value is **2**. This column contains the data for the spent column in the **bankFile** file.

32. **spent** is of the **float** type, so we are converting the **string** type from the **spent** column to a **float** type:

```
// spent
case 2:
    value = strings.TrimSpace(value)
    trx.spent, err = strconv.ParseFloat(value, 64)
    if err != nil {
    log.Fatal(err)
    }
```

The third index value is **3**. This column contains the data for the category provided by the bank.

33. We need to convert the CSV file category column to our **budgetCategory** type.

34. Inside the case statement for the category, we check for any errors returned from the **convertToBudgetCategory** function.

35. If there is an error, we do not want to stop processing the CSV bank file, so we write the error to a log via the **writeErrorToLog** function:

```
// category
    case 3:
    trx.category, err = convertToBudgetCategory(value)
    if err != nil {
      s := strings.Join(record, ", ")
```

```
        writeErrorToLog("error converting csv category column - ", err, s, logFile)
    }
    }
}
```

36. We are at the end of the loop for the fields in the record. We now need to append our transaction to the slice of transactions:

```
trxs = append(trxs, trx)
}
```

37. **header** was **true** at the start of the function; we will set it to **false**, which indicates that in the rest of the CSV file, we will be parsing the data and not the **header** information:

```
    header = false
    }
```

38. We have completed parsing the CSV file. We now need to return the slice of transactions:

```
    return trxs
}
```

39. Create a function named **convertToBudgetCategory(value string)(budgetCategory)**. This function is responsible for mapping the bank categories to our defined categories. If a category is not found, it will return the **ErrInvalidBudgetCategory** error.

40. Use a **switch** statement that evaluates each value. When it matches, return the respective **budgetCategory** type:

```
func convertToBudgetCategory(value string) (budgetCategory, error) {
    value = strings.TrimSpace(strings.ToLower(value))
    switch value {
    case "fuel", "gas":
    return autoFuel, nil
    case "food":
    return food, nil
    case "mortgage":
    return mortgage, nil
    case "repairs":
    return repairs, nil
    case "car insurance", "life insurance":
    return insurance, nil
```

```
    case "utilities":
    return utilities, nil
    default:
    return "", ErrInvalidBudgetCategory
    }
}
```

41. Create a **writeErrorToLog(msg string, err error, data string, logFile string)
    error** function. This function will write a message to the log file.

42. Then, it will need to format the data about the error to include the **msg**, **error**, and
    the **data**:

```
func writeErrorToLog(msg string, err error, data string, logFile string) error {
    msg += "\n" + err.Error() + "\nData: " + data + "\n\n"
    f, err := os.OpenFile(logFile, os.O_APPEND|os.O_CREATE|os.O_WRONLY, 0644)
    if err != nil {
    return err
    }
    defer f.Close()
    if _, err := f.WriteString(msg); err != nil {
    return err
    }
    return nil
}
```

43. Run the program:

```
go run main.go -c bank.csv -l log.log
```

Here is a possible output from the application:

```
{1 sheetz 32.45 fuel}
{2 martins 225.52 food}
{3 wells fargo 1100 mortgage}
{4 joe the plumber 275 repairs}
{5 comcast 110 }
{6 bp 40 fuel}
{7 aldi 120 food}
{8 nationwide 150 insurance}
{9 nationwide 100 insurance}
{10 jim electric 140 utilities}
{11 propane 200 utilities}
{12 county water 100 utilities}
{13 county sewer 105 utilities}
{14 401k 500 }
```

Figure 12.24: Activity output

The possible contents of the **log.log** file are as follows:

```
error converting csv category column -
budget category not found
Data: 5,   comcast,   110,   tv

error converting csv category column -
budget category not found
Data: 14,   401k,   500,   retirement
```

Figure 12.25: The log.log content

Chapter 13: SQL and Databases

Activity 13.1: Holding User Data in a Table

Solution:

1. Initialize your script with the appropriate imports. Let's call it **main.go**. Prepare an empty **main()** function:

```
package main
import "fmt"
import "database/sql"
import _ "github.com/lib/pq"
func main(){
}
```

2. Let's define the **struct** that will hold the users:

```
type Users struct {
    id int
    name string
    email string
}
```

3. Now the time has come to create two users:

```
users := []Users{
    {1,"Szabo Daniel","daniel@packt.com"},
    {2,"Szabo Florian","florian@packt.com"},
}
```

4. Let's open the connection to our **Postgres** server:

```
db, err := sql.Open("postgres", "user=postgres password=Start!123
   host=127.0.0.1 port=5432 dbname=postgres sslmode=disable")
if err != nil {
   panic(err)
}else{
   fmt.Println("The connection to the DB was successfully initialized!")
}
```

5. We should use the `Ping()` function to see whether the connectivity is OK:

```
connectivity := db.Ping()
if connectivity != nil{
   panic(connectivity)
}else{
   fmt.Println("Good to go!")
}
```

6. Now we can create a multiline string for our table:

```
TableCreate := `
CREATE TABLE users
(
   ID integer NOT NULL,
   Name text COLLATE pg_catalog."default" NOT NULL,
   Email text COLLATE pg_catalog."default" NOT NULL,
   CONSTRAINT "Users_pkey" PRIMARY KEY (ID)
)
WITH (
   OIDS = FALSE
)
TABLESPACE pg_default;
ALTER TABLE users
   OWNER to postgres;
`
```

7. Once the string is ready, we should create our table:

```
_,err = db.Exec(TableCreate)
if err != nil {
   panic(err)
} else{
   fmt.Println("The table called Users was successfully created!")
}
```

8. With the **users** struct, we can construct a **for** loop to insert the users:

```
insert, insertErr := db.Prepare("INSERT INTO users VALUES($1,$2,$3)")
if insertErr != nil{
  panic(insertErr)
}
for _, u := range users{
  _, err = insert.Exec(u.id,u.name,u.email)
  if err != nil{
    panic(err)
  }else{
    fmt.Println("The user with name:",u.name,"and email:",u.email,"was
    successfully added!")
  }
}
insert.Close()
```

9. Now with the users in the database, we can update the appropriate field:

```
update, updateErr := db.Prepare("UPDATE users SET Email=$1 WHERE ID=$2")
if updateErr != nil{
  panic(updateErr)
}
_, err = update.Exec("user@packt.com",1)
if err != nil{
  panic(err)
} else{
  fmt.Println("The user's email address was successfully updated!")
}
update.Close()
```

10. The last task is to remove the **user** with **ID=2**:

```
remove, removeErr := db.Prepare("DELETE FROM users WHERE ID=$1")
if removeErr != nil{
  panic(removeErr)
}
_,err = remove.Exec(2)
if err != nil{
  panic(err)
}else{
  fmt.Println("The second user was successfully removed!")
}
remove.Close()
```

11. Since our job is done, we should close the connection to the database:

```
db.Close()
```

Upon successful completion, you should see the following output:

```
The connection to the DB was successfully initialized!
Good to go!
The table called Users was successfully created!
The user with name: Szabo Daniel and email: daniel@packt.com was successfully added!
The user with name: Szabo Florian and email: florian@packt.com was successfully added!
The user's email address was succesfully updated!
The second user was succeesfully removed!
```

Figure 13.10: Possible output

Activity 13.2: Finding Messages of Specific Users

Solution:

1. Initialize your script with the appropriate imports. Let's call it **main.go**. Prepare an empty **main()** function:

```
package main
import "fmt"
import "bufio"
import "os"
import "strings"
import "database/sql"
import _ "github.com/lib/pq"
func main(){
}
```

2. Let's define a **struct** that will hold the messages we want to insert:

```
type Messages struct {
  UserID int
  Message string
}
```

3. We will need four variables that will be used later:

```
var toLookFor string
var message string
var email string
var name string
```

4. Create a **reader** function that will acquire the input from the user when the time comes:

```
reader := bufio.NewReader(os.Stdin)
```

5. Now, create the actual messages:

```
messages := []Messages{
    {1,"Hi Florian, when are you coming home?"},
    {1,"Can you send some cash?"},
    {2,"Hi can you bring some bread and milk?"},
    {7,"Well..."},
}
```

6. Connect to the database:

```
db, err := sql.Open("postgres", "user=postgres password=Start!123
    host=127.0.0.1 port=5432 dbname=postgres sslmode=disable")
if err != nil {
    panic(err)
}else{
    fmt.Println("The connection to the DB was successfully initialized!")
}
```

7. Check the connectivity to the database:

```
connectivity := db.Ping()
if connectivity != nil{
    panic(connectivity)
}else{
    fmt.Println("Good to go!")
}
```

8. If the connection is fine, we can craft our table creation script:

```
TableCreate := `
CREATE TABLE public.messages
(
    UserID integer NOT NULL,
    Message character varying(280) COLLATE pg_catalog."default" NOT NULL
)
WITH (
    OIDS = FALSE
)
```

```
    TABLESPACE pg_default;
    ALTER TABLE public.messages
        OWNER to postgres;
    `
```

9. Create the table to hold the messages:

```
_,err = db.Exec(TableCreate)
if err != nil {
  panic(err)
} else{
  fmt.Println("The table called Messages was successfully created!")
}
```

10. Once the table is ready, insert the messages:

```
insertMessages, insertErr := db.Prepare("INSERT INTO messages
  VALUES($1,$2)")
if insertErr != nil{
  panic(insertErr)
}
for _, u := range messages{
  _, err = insertMessages.Exec(u.UserID,u.Message)
  if err != nil{
    panic(err)
  }else{
    fmt.Println("The UserID:",u.UserID,"with message:",u.Message,"was
    successfully added!")
  }
}
insertMessages.Close()
```

11. Now that you have messages, you can ask for the user's name to look for when filtering the messages:

```
fmt.Print("Give me the user's name: ")
toLookFor, err = reader.ReadString('\n')
toLookFor = strings.TrimRight(toLookFor, "\r\n")
if err != nil{
  panic(err)
} else {
  fmt.Println("Looking for all the messages of user with
  name:",toLookFor,"##")
}
```

12. The following query will give us the desired result:

```
UserMessages := "SELECT users.Name, users.Email, messages.Message FROM
    messages INNER JOIN users ON users.ID=messages.UserID WHERE users.Name
    LIKE $1"
```

13. Now execute the filter query and check how many records were returned:

```
usersMessages, err := db.Prepare(UserMessages)
if err != nil {
    panic(err)
}
result, err := usersMessages.Query(toLookFor)
numberof := 0
for result.Next(){
    numberof++
}
```

14. Based on the number of results, print the appropriate messages:

```
if numberof == 0 {
    fmt.Println("The query returned nothing, no such user:",toLookFor)
}else{
    fmt.Println("There are a total of",numberof,"messages from the
        user:",toLookFor)
    result, err := usersMessages.Query(toLookFor)
    for result.Next(){
        err = result.Scan(&name, &email, &message)
        if err != nil{
        panic(err)
        }
        fmt.Println("The user:",name,"with email:",email,"has sent the following
            message:",message)
    }
}
usersMessages.Close()
```

15. Finally, close the database connection:

```
db.Close()
```

This should be the output, depending on how you fill your database with usernames and messages:

```
The connection to the DB was sucessfully initialized!
Good to go!
The table called Messages was successfully created!
The UserID: 1 with message: Hi Florian, when are you coming home? was successfully added!
The UserID: 1 with message: Can you send some cash? was successfully added!
The UserID: 2 with message: Hi can you bring some bread and milk? was successfully added!
The UserID: 7 with message: Well... was successfully added!
Give me the user's name: Szabo Daniel
Looking for all the messages of user with name: Szabo Daniel ##
The user: Szabo Daniel with email: user@packt.com has sent the following message: Hi Florian, when are you coming home?
The user: Szabo Daniel with email: user@packt.com has sent the following message: Can you send some cash?
```

Figure 13.11: Expected output

Chapter 14: Using the Go HTTP Client

Activity 14.01: Requesting Data from a Web Server and Processing the Response

Solution:

1. Add the necessary imports:

```
package main
import (
    "encoding/json"
    "fmt"
    "io/ioutil"
    "log"
    "net/http"
)
```

Here, **encoding/json** is used to parse the response and marshal it into the structs. **fmt** is used to print out the counts and **io/ioutil** is used to read in the response body. **log** is used if something goes wrong to output the error. **net/http** is what we use to do the GET request.

2. Create structs to parse the data:

```
type Names struct {
    Names []string `json:"names"`
}
```

3. Create a function called **getDataAndParseResponse()** that returns two integers:

```
func getDataAndParseResponse() (int, int) {
```

4. Send a **GET** request to the server:

```
r, err := http.Get("http://localhost:8080")
if err != nil {
    log.Fatal(err)
}
```

5. Parse the response data:

```
defer r.Body.Close()
data, err := ioutil.ReadAll(r.Body)
if err != nil {
    log.Fatal(err)
}
names := Names{}
err = json.Unmarshal(data, &names)
if err != nil {
    log.Fatal(err)
}
```

6. Loop through the names and count the occurrences of each:

```
electricCount := 0
boogalooCount := 0
for _, name := range names.Names {
    if name == "Electric" {
        electricCount++
    } else if name == "Boogaloo" {
        boogalooCount++
    }
}
```

7. Return the counts:

```
return electricCount, boogalooCount
```

8. Print the counts:

```
func main() {
    electricCount, boogalooCount := getDataAndParseResponse()
    fmt.Println("Electric Count: ", electricCount)
    fmt.Println("Boogaloo Count: ", boogalooCount)
}
```

9. Here is the code for the server of this activity:

server.go

```
12 func (srv server) ServeHTTP(w http.ResponseWriter, r
      *http.Request) {
13     names := Names{}
14     // Generate random number of 'Electric' names
15     for i := 0; i < rand.Intn(5)+1; i++ {
16         names.Names = append(names.Names, "Electric")
17     }
18     // Generate random number of 'Boogaloo' names
19     for i := 0; i < rand.Intn(5)+1; i++ {
20         names.Names = append(names.Names, "Boogaloo")
21     }
22     // convert struct to bytes
23     jsonBytes, _ := json.Marshal(names)
24     log.Println(string(jsonBytes))
25     w.Write(jsonBytes)
26 }
```

The full code is available at https://packt.live/2sfnWaR

Add this code to the **server.go** file you created and run it. This will create a server you can connect your client to. Once you have created it, you should be able to run it and see a similar output to this:

```
solution [git::master *] > go run main.go
Electric Count:   2
Boogaloo Count:   3
```

Figure 14.10: Possible output

Activity 14.02: Sending Data to a Web Server and Checking Whether the Data Was Received Using POST and GET

Solution:

1. Add all the required imports:

```
package main
import (
    "bytes"
    "encoding/json"
    "errors"
    "fmt"
    "io/ioutil"
    "log"
    "net/http"
)
```

2. Create the structs needed to send requests and receive responses:

```
var url = "http://localhost:8088"
type Name struct {
    Name string `json:"name"`
}
type Names struct {
    Names []string `json:"names"`
}
type Resp struct {
    OK bool `json:"ok"`
}
```

3. Create the **addNameAndParseResponse** function:

```
func addNameAndParseResponse(nameToAdd string) error {
```

4. Create a **name** struct, **Marshal** it to **json**, and POST it to the URL:

```
name := Name{Name: nameToAdd}
nameBytes, err := json.Marshal(name)
if err != nil {
    return err
}
r, err := http.Post(fmt.Sprintf("%s/addName", url),
    "text/json", bytes.NewReader(nameBytes))
if err != nil {
    return err
}
```

5. Parse the response from the POST request:

```
defer r.Body.Close()
data, err := ioutil.ReadAll(r.Body)
if err != nil {
    return err
}
resp := Resp{}
err = json.Unmarshal(data, &resp)
if err != nil {
    return err
}
```

6. Check that the response returns OK:

```
if !resp.OK {
    return errors.New("response not ok")
}
return nil
```

7. Create the **getDataAndParseResponse** function:

```
func getDataAndParseResponse() []string {
```

8. Send a GET request to the server and read the body:

```
r, err := http.Get(fmt.Sprintf("%s/", url))
if err != nil {
    log.Fatal(err)
}
// get data from the response body
defer r.Body.Close()
data, err := ioutil.ReadAll(r.Body)
if err != nil {
    log.Fatal(err)
}
```

9. Unmarshal the response into the **Names** struct and return the **names** array:

```
names := Names{}
err = json.Unmarshal(data, &names)
if err != nil {
    log.Fatal(err)
}
// return the data
return names.Names
```

10. Create a **main** function to add names, request the names from the server, and print them out:

```
func main() {
    err := addNameAndParseResponse("Electric")
    if err != nil {
        log.Fatal(err)
    }
    err = addNameAndParseResponse("Boogaloo")
    if err != nil {
        log.Fatal(err)
    }
```

```
            names := getDataAndParseResponse()
            for _, name := range names {
                log.Println(name)
            }
        }
    }
```

The server code is as follows:

server.go

```
 1 package main
 2 import (
 3     "encoding/json"
 4     "log"
 5     "net/http"
 6 )
 7 var names []string
 8 type Name struct {
 9     Name string `json:"name"`
10 }
11 type Names struct {
12     Names []string `json:"names"`
13 }
14 type Resp struct {
15     OK bool `json:"ok"`
```

The full code for this step is available at https://packt.live/2Qg5dE8

Start the server and run your client. The client's output should be similar to the following:

```
|solution [git::go_tools *] > go run main.go
2019/09/19 14:28:52 Electric
2019/09/19 14:28:52 Boogaloo
```

Figure 14.11: Possible output

Chapter 15: HTTP Servers

Activity 15.01: Adding a Page Counter to an HTML Page

Solution:

1. First, we import the necessary packages:

```
package main
import (
"fmt"
"log"
"net/http"
)
```

2. Here, **"net/http"** is the usual package for http communication, **"log"** is the package for logging (in this case to the standard output), and **"fmt"** is the package used to format input and output. This can be used to send messages to the standard output, but we use it here just as a message formatter.

3. We define here a type called **PageWithCounter**, which represents our handler, can count visits, and has a heading and some content for the page. The counter will increase every time the page loads:

```
type PageWithCounter struct{
counter int
heading string
content string
}
func(h *PageWithCounter) ServeHTTP(w http.ResponseWriter, r *http.Request)
  {
```

This is the standard handler function for any struct implementing the **http. Handler** interface. Note first the * in the method receiver. In this method, we want to modify a struct's attribute to increment the counter. In order to do so, we need to specify that our method is received by a pointer so that we modify the counter permanently. Without the pointer receiver, we would always see **1** in the page (you can try to modify this and see for yourself).

4. Next, increase the counter, and then we format a string with some HTML tags. The **fmt.Sprintf** function injects the variables on the right in the place where the placeholders, **%s** and **%d**, are located. The first placeholder expects a string, while the second expects a number. After that, we write, as usual, the whole string as a slice of bytes in relation to the response:

```
h.counter++
msg := fmt.Sprintf("<h1>%s</h1>\n<p>%s<p>\n<p>Views: %d</p>", h.heading,
h.content, h.counter)
w.Write([]byte(msg))
}
```

5. Here, we create the **main()** function and we set up three handlers, one with the heading **hello world** and some content, while the other two handlers represent the first two chapters of your book, so are instantiated accordingly. Note that the counter is not explicitly set since any integer will default to **0**, which is where our counter starts:

```
func main() {
  hello := PageWithCounter{heading: "Hello World",content:"This is the main
  page"}
  cha1 := PageWithCounter{heading: "Chapter 1",content:"This is the first
  chapter"}
```

```
    cha2 := PageWithCounter{heading: "Chapter 2",content:"This is the second
    chapter"}
```

6. Add the three handlers to the routes, **/**, **/chapter1**, and **/chapter2**, setting them to use the handlers created previously. Note that we need to pass references with **&** as the **ServeHTTP** method has a pointer receiver:

```
http.Handle("/", &hello)
http.Handle("/chapter1", &cha1)
http.Handle("/chapter2", &cha2)
```

7. Now, complete the code listening to a port:

```
    log.Fatal(http.ListenAndServe(":8080", nil))
}
```

When you run the server, you should see the following:

Figure 15.39: Output on the browser when you run the server for the first time

If you refresh the page, you should see the following:

Figure 15.40: Output on the browser when you run the server for the second time

Next, navigate to **chapter 1** by typing `localhost:8080/chapter1` in the address bar. You should be able to see something along the lines of the following:

Figure 15.41: Output on the browser when you visit the chapter1 page for the first time

Similarly, navigate to *chapter 2*, and you should be able to see the following increment in terms of the number of views:

Figure 15.42: Output on the browser when you visit the chapter2 page for the first time

When you revisit *chapter 1*, you should see an increase in the number of views as follows:

Figure 15.43: Output on the browser when you visit the chapter1 page for the second time

Activity 15.02: Serving a Request with a JSON Payload

Solution:

Although your browser may show the JSON document differently, the full solution to this activity is as follows:

1. We create the package and add the necessary imports, where **"encoding/json"** is the one used for formatting our document as a JSON string:

```
package main
import (
    "encoding/json"
    "log"
    "net/http"
)
```

2. We create the **PageWithCounter** struct, which looks exactly like the one in **Activity 1**. However, some JSON tags need to be added. These tags ensure that when converting the struct into a JSON string, the attributes assume a specific name. **Content** will become **content**, but **Heading** will become **title** and **Counter** will become **views**. Note that all the attributes are now capitalized. As you already know, capitalizing the attributes makes them exported, meaning that every other package can see, and hence use, them:

```
type PageWithCounter struct{
    Counter int `json:"views"`
    Heading string `json:"title"`
    Content string `json:"content"`
}
```

3. We create the usual handler method to serve the page:

```
func(h *PageWithCounter) ServeHTTP(w http.ResponseWriter, r *http.Request) {
```

4. We increase the counter:

```
h.Counter++
```

5. Now, we marshal the struct itself, **h**, into JSON through the **json.Marshal** method, which returns an array of bytes representing the JSON document and an error. Here is where the exported attributes are important. The marshaling function could not otherwise see the attributes and could not convert them, resulting in a JSON string representing an empty document:

```
bts, err := json.Marshal(h)
```

6. We check for an error and, in case there is one, we write the code **400** to the response header. This means that you would not see the actual page in case of a marshaling error, but an error message:

```
if err!=nil {
w.WriteHeader(400)
return
}
```

7. Finally, if there is no error, we write the JSON-encoded struct to the response writer:

```
w.Write([]byte(bts))
}
```

8. The remainder of the code is almost identical to that in *Activity 15.01*, the only difference being that the **PageWithCounter** structs are instantiated with capitalized attributes, given that they are now all exported:

```
func main() {
    hello :=PageWithCounter{Heading: "Hello World",Content:"This is the main
    page"}
    cha1 := PageWithCounter{Heading: "Chapter 1",Content:"This is the first
    chapter"}
    cha2 := PageWithCounter{Heading: "Chapter 2",Content:"This is the second
    chapter"}
    http.Handle("/", &hello)
    http.Handle("/chapter1", &cha1)
    http.Handle("/chapter2", &cha2)
    log.Fatal(http.ListenAndServe(":8080", nil))
}
```

Running your server, you should see the following for the assigned routes:

Figure 15.44: Expected output when the handler is /

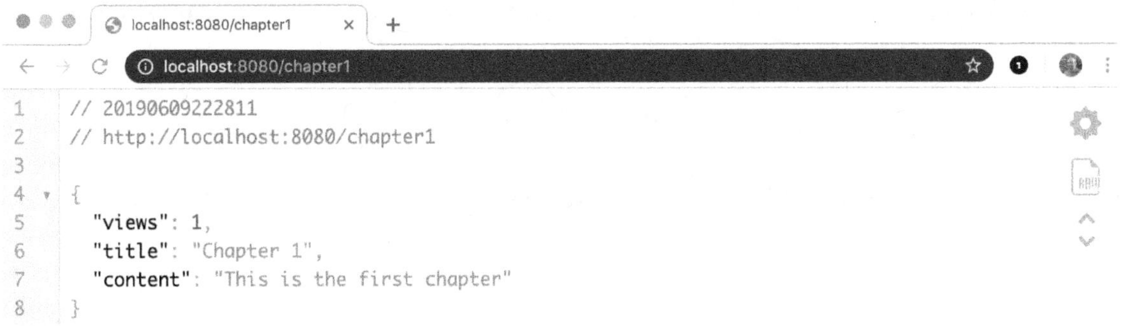

Figure 15.45: Expected output when the handler is /chapter1

Figure 15.46: Expected output when the handler is /chapter2

Activity 15.03: External Template

Solution:

1. Create an HTML file called **index.html**:

```
<!DOCTYPE html>
<html lang="en">
<head>
  <meta charset="UTF-8">
  <title>Welcome</title>
</head>
<body>
```

2. In the body, now add the template tags for the header:

```
<h1>Hello {{if .Name}}{{.Name}}{{else}}visitor{{end}}</h1>
```

You can see that there is an **if** statement that displays the **Name** attribute if it is not empty, otherwise it displays the **visitor** string.

3. Now, complete the HTML file with a welcome message and the closing tags:

```
    <p>May I give you a warm welcome</p>
</body>
</html>
```

4. Now, create a **main.go** file and start adding the package and imports:

```
package main
import (
    "html/template"
    "log"
    "net/http"
    "strings"
)
```

5. Now, create the **Visitor** struct, which is a struct used as a model for our template. It only includes the **Name** field, as this is the only thing we care about. Note that we have been using structs up to this point as they are safer, but you could pass a **map[string]string** to your templates directly and it would work. Structs, however, allow us to perform better sanitization. Write the following:

```
type Visitor struct {
    Name string
}
```

6. Now, create a handler. This is just a struct holding a pointer to a template:

```
type Hello struct {
    tpl *template.Template
}
```

7. This now needs to implement the handler interface:

```
func (h Hello) ServeHTTP(w http.ResponseWriter, r *http.Request) {
```

8. Now, we need to get the requests in the querystring, so write the following:

```
vl := r.URL.Query()
```

9. We now need to create a visitor for this request, so execute the following command:

```
cust := Visitor{}
name, ok := vl["name"]
```

10. If the name exists, then implode the content to have a string in case we have multiple names:

```
    if ok {
    cust.Name = strings.Join(name, ",")
    }
```

11. Now, execute the template to get the full page and pass it to the response writer to serve the file template:

```
    h.tpl.Execute(w, cust)
}
```

12. Now, create a function to instantiate a new page with a specific template file, returning a **Hello** template pointer:

```
    // NewHello returns a new Hello handler
    func NewHello(tplPath string) (*Hello, error){
```

13. Parse the template and assign a variable to it:

```
    tmpl, err := template.ParseFiles(tplPath)
    if err != nil {
    return nil, err
    }
```

14. Return the **Hello** template with the template file set for it:

```
    return &Hello{tmpl}, nil
}
```

15. Create the **main()** function to run:

```
func main() {
```

16. Now, use the **NewHello** function to create a page for the **index.html** template:

```
    hello, err := NewHello("./index.html")
    if err != nil {
    log.Fatal(err)
    }
```

17. Handle the base path with the instantiated template:

```
    http.Handle("/", hello)
```

18. Run the server on your favorite port and exit in the event of an error:

```
    log.Fatal(http.ListenAndServe(":8080", nil))
}
```

The output will be as follows:

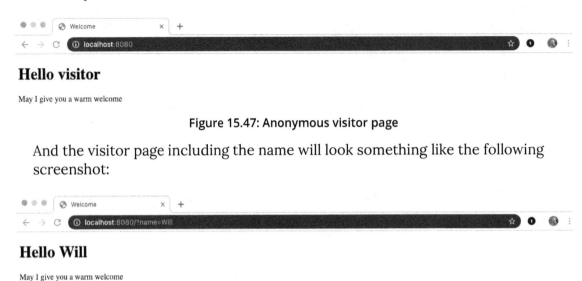

Figure 15.47: Anonymous visitor page

And the visitor page including the name will look something like the following screenshot:

Hello Will

May I give you a warm welcome

Figure 15.48: Visitor page with the name "Will"

Chapter 16: Concurrent Work

Activity 16.01: Listing Numbers

Solution:

1. Create the **main.go** file and import the necessary packages:

```
package main
import (
    "fmt"
    "log"
    "sync"
)
```

2. Define a function called **sum()**, which will use a pointer to a string to hold the result:

```
func sum(from,to int, wg *sync.WaitGroup, res *string, mtx *sync.Mutex) {
    for i:=from;i<=to; i++ {
        mtx.Lock()
        *res = fmt.Sprintf("%s|%d|",*res, i)
        mtx.Unlock()
    }
}
```

```
        wg.Done()
        return
    }
```

3. Create then the **main()** function to perform the sums:

```
func main() {
    s1 := ""
    mtx := &sync.Mutex{}
    wg := &sync.WaitGroup{}
    wg.Add(4)
    go sum(1,25, wg,&s1, mtx)
    go sum(26,50, wg, &s1, mtx)
    go sum(51,75, wg, &s1, mtx)
    go sum(76,100, wg, &s1, mtx)
    wg.Wait()
    log.Println(s1)
}
```

Let's analyze the code in steps:

1. Let's look at the **sum()** function:

```
func sum(from,to int, wg *sync.WaitGroup, res *string, mtx *sync.Mutex) {
    for i:=from;i<=to; i++ {
```

Here, we create a function whose signature contains a range, **from**, **to int**, and then a WaitGroup, a string pointer that is going to be used to modify the value of the shared string, and finally a pointer to a mutex to synchronize the work on the string. After that, we create a loop in the defined range.

2. The next step is:

```
        mtx.Lock()
        *res = fmt.Sprintf("%s|%d|",*res, i)
        mtx.Unlock()
    }
```

Here, we lock the execution and add the current value of **i** as string at the end of the current value of **s**. Then, we unlock the process and end the loop.

3. At this point, we tell the WaitGroup that the routine has finished its computation and that it terminates here:

```
        wg.Done()
        return
    }
```

4. Next, we define the **main()** function:

```
func main() {
    s1 := ""
    mtx := &sync.Mutex{}
    wg := &sync.WaitGroup{}
```

We set a starting string to **""**, then we instantiate a **mutex** and a WaitGroup. The code is then pretty similar to what you've seen in the previous exercises, which is running the four Goroutines and logging the result.

5. When you run your program you should see something like this:

```
→ activity1 git:(master) ✗ go run .
2019/10/28 19:40:36  |76||51||52||53||54||55||56||57||58||59||60||61||62||63||64||65||66||67||
68||69||70||71||72||73||74||75||1||2||3||4||5||6||7||8||9||10||11||12||13||14||15||16||17||18
||19||20||21||22||23||24||25||77||78||79||80||81||82||83||84||85||86||87||88||89||90||91||92|
|93||94||95||96||97||98||99||100||26||27||28||29||30||31||32||33||34||35||36||37||38||39||40|
|41||42||43||44||45||46||47||48||49||50|
```

Figure 16.5: First output when listing numbers

6. However, if you run it again multiple times, you will see that most likely you will have a different result. This is due to concurrency because the order of execution by the machine is uncertain:

```
→ activity1 git:(master) ✗ go run .
2019/10/28 19:42:20  |76||77||78||79||80||81||82||83||84||85||86||87||88||89||90||91||92||93||
94||95||96||97||98||99||100||26||27||28||29||30||31||32||33||34||35||36||37||38||39||40||41||
42||43||44||45||46||47||48||49||50||1||2||3||4||5||6||7||8||9||10||11||12||13||14||15||16||17
||18||19||20||21||22||23||24||25||51||52||53||54||55||56||57||58||59||60||61||62||63||64||65|
|66||67||68||69||70||71||72||73||74||75|
```

Figure 16.6: Second attempt of listing numbers returns with a different order

Activity 16.02: Source Files

Solution:

1. Create the **main** package with the following imports:

```
package main
import (
    "bufio"
    "fmt"
    "os"
    "strconv"
```

```
    "strings"
    "sync"
)
```

2. Create the **source()** function to read numbers from a file and send them to a channel:

```go
func source(filename string, out chan int, wg *sync.WaitGroup)  {
    f, err :=  os.Open(filename)
    if err != nil {
        panic(err)
    }
    rd := bufio.NewReader(f)
    for {
        str, err := rd.ReadString('\n')
        if err != nil {
            if err.Error() == "EOF" {
                wg.Done()
                return
            } else {
                panic(err)
            }
        }
        iStr := strings.ReplaceAll(str, "\n", "")
        i, err := strconv.Atoi(iStr)
        if err != nil {
            panic(err)
        }
        out <- i
    }
}
```

3. Now create the **splitter()** function to receive the numbers and then send them to two different channels, one for **odd** numbers and one for **even** numbers:

```go
func splitter(in, odd, even chan int, wg *sync.WaitGroup)  {
    for i := range in {
        switch i%2 {
        case 0:
            even <- i
        case 1:
            odd <- i
        }
    }
}
```

```
        close(even)
        close(odd)
        wg.Done()
    )
```

4. Now write a function to sum the numbers coming in and send the **sum** to an outbound channel:

```
func sum(in, out chan int, wg *sync.WaitGroup) {
    sum := 0
    for i := range in {
        sum += i
    }
    out <- sum
    wg.Done()
}
```

5. Now create a **merger()** function that will output the **sum** of the even and odd numbers:

```
func merger(even, odd chan int, wg *sync.WaitGroup, resultFile string) {
    rs, err := os.Create(resultFile)
    if err != nil {
        panic(err)
    }
    for i:= 0; i< 2; i++{
        select {
        case i:= <- even:
            rs.Write([]byte(fmt.Sprintf("Even %d\n", i)))
        case i:= <- odd:
            rs.Write([]byte(fmt.Sprintf("Odd %d\n", i)))
        }
    }
    wg.Done()
}
```

6. Now create the **main()** function, where you initialize all the channels and call all the functions you created earlier in order to produce the **sum**:

```
func main() {
    wg := &sync.WaitGroup{}
    wg.Add(2)
    wg2 := &sync.WaitGroup{}
    wg2.Add(4)
    odd := make(chan int)
```

```
      even := make(chan int)
      out := make(chan int)
      sumodd := make(chan int)
      sumeven := make(chan int)
      go source("./input1.dat", out, wg)
      go source("./input2.dat", out, wg)
      go splitter(out, odd, even, wg2)
      go sum(even, sumeven, wg2)
      go sum(odd, sumodd,wg2)
      go merger(sumeven, sumodd, wg2, "./result.txt")
      wg.Wait()
      close(out)
      wg2.Wait()
}
```

Let's analyze the code in a bit more detail.

7. In the **source** function, we have a filename for the input file to open, a channel to pipe messages in, and a WaitGroup to notify the end of the process. This function will run as two Goroutines, one per input file. Inside this function, we read from the file line by line. You should have already learned how to read from files, and there are several optimized ways to do that. Here, we just read line by line with:

```
rd := bufio.NewReader(f)
    for {
        str, err := rd.ReadString('\n')
```

So, we are creating a buffered reader on the file **f** and then looping the **ReadString** function with the newline character **'\n'** as the delimiter. Be mindful that it has to be with single quotes and not **"\n"** because the delimiter is a character and not a string.

8. After that, we handle the errors, and if an end of file error (**EOF**) occurs, we just terminate the function. Note that if we don't do this, the code just panics:

```
if err.Error() == "EOF" {
                wg.Done()
                return
            }
```

9. We also need to strip the line so that we just have the number:

```
iStr := strings.ReplaceAll(str, "\n", "")
        i, err := strconv.Atoi(iStr)
        if err != nil {
            panic(err)
```

```
            }
            out <- i
        }
    }
```

Here, we replace the last part of the string, **"\n"**, with an empty string. After that we convert the text to an integer and if it is not an integer, we panic again. At the end, we just pipe out the number and complete the function.

10. Next step is to create a splitting function:

```
func splitter(in, odd, even chan int, wg *sync.WaitGroup)  {
```

11. This function has a channel to get numbers from the sources and two channels to pipe numbers to; one for the even numbers and one for the odd numbers. A Waitgroup is used again to notify the main routine of completion. The purpose of this function is to split the numbers so we can loop over the channel:

```
    for i := range in {
```

12. Inside the for loop, we can identify the odd and even numbers using **switch**:

```
        switch i%2 {
        case 0:
            even <- i
        case 1:
            odd <- i
        }
    }
```

This code splits the numbers depending on the remainder of division by 2. If the remainder is 0, the number is even and is piped to the even channel, odd otherwise.

13. We close the channels to notify the next process in the line:

```
        close(even)
        close(odd)
        wg.Done()
    }
```

14. We now have the splitter, but we need to sum the messages piped in, and this is done with a function that's similar to what you've seen in the previous exercises:

```
func sum(in, out chan int, wg *sync.WaitGroup) {
    sum := 0
    for i := range in {
        sum += i
    }
```

```
    out <- sum
    wg.Done()
}
```

15. At this point, we need to merge all the results, so we use a merger:

```
func merger(even, odd chan int, wg *sync.WaitGroup, resultFile string) {
```

This function holds the two channels for even and odd numbers, a Waitgroup to handle completion, and a name for the result file.

16. We then begin creating the **results.txt** file:

```
    rs, err := os.Create(resultFile)
    if err != nil {
        panic(err)
    }
```

17. We loop over the two channels for odd and even numbers:

```
    for i:= 0; i< 2; i++{
```

18. And then we write the code to choose the channel based on the type of number:

```
        select {
        case i:= <- even:
            rs.Write([]byte(fmt.Sprintf("Even %d\n", i)))
        case i:= <- odd:
            rs.Write([]byte(fmt.Sprintf("Odd %d\n", i)))
        }


    }
    wg.Done()
}
```

Writing to the file is done using the **Write** method, which in turn needs bytes. That way, we transform the string containing the type of numbers added (**odd**, **even**) and their sum into bytes.

19. We now orchestrate everything in the main function:

```
func main() {
    wg := &sync.WaitGroup{}
    wg.Add(2)
    wg2 := &sync.WaitGroup{}
    wg2.Add(4)
```

20. We used two Waitgroups here; one for the sources and one for the rest of the routines. You will see why soon.

21. Next, we create all the channels we need:

```
odd := make(chan int)
even := make(chan int)
out := make(chan int)
sumodd := make(chan int)
sumeven := make(chan int)
```

out is the channel used by the source functions to pipe the messages to the splitter, **odd** and **even** are the ones where the numbers are piped for being summed, and the last two are the ones holding a single number with the sum.

22. We then start all the routines we need:

```
go source("./input1.dat", out, wg)
go source("./input2.dat", out, wg)
go splitter(out, odd, even, wg2)
go sum(even, sumeven, wg2)
go sum(odd, sumodd,wg2)
go merger(sumeven, sumodd, wg2, "./result.txt")
```

23. We then wait for the routines to finish:

```
wg.Wait()
close(out)
```

Please note that here, we could have used more than two files. You could have even used an arbitrary number of files. Hence, there is no way for the splitter to know how to terminate the execution, so we close the channel after the sources have finished piping numbers in.

24. After that, we have a second Waitgroup for the rest. Essentially, we need to keep all the routines running until the last sum has been added:

```
wg2.Wait()
}
```

25. While the files you can use as input can be different, use the following two files to test the output.

input1.dat

```
1
2
5
```

input2.dat

```
3
4
6
```

Note the newline at the end of each file.

26. Now that you have created the input file, run the following command:

```
go run main.go
```

You should see a file called **results.txt** with the following content.

```
Odd 9
Even 12
```

Chapter 17: Using Go Tools

Activity 17.01: Using gofmt, goimport, go vet, and go get to Correct a File

Solution:

1. Run **gofmt** against the file to check for any formatting issues and see that they make sense:

```
gofmt main.go
```

This should output a much neater-looking file, as follows:

```
> gofmt main.go
package main

import (
        "fmt"
        "github.com/gorilla/mux"
        "log"
)

// ExampleHandler handles the http requests send to this webserver
func ExampleHandler(w http.ResponseWriter, r *http.Request) {
        w.WriteHeader(http.StatusOK)
        fmt.Fprintf(w, "Hello Packt")
        return

        log.Println("completed")
}

func main() {
        r := mux.NewRouter()
        r.HandleFunc("/", ExampleHandler)
        log.Fatal(http.ListenAndServe(":8888", r))
}
```

Figure 17.11: Expected output from gofmt

2. Use the **-w** option on **gofmt** to make the changes to the file and save them:

```
gofmt -w main.go
```

3. Check the imports are correct using **goimports**:

```
goimport main.go
```

4. Use **goimports** to fix the import statements in the file:

```
goimports -w main.go
```

5. The final stage is to use **go vet** to check for any issues the compiler might miss. Run it against **main.go** to check for any issues:

```
go vet main.go
```

6. It will find an issue with unreachable code, as shown in the following output:

```
> go vet main.go
# command-line-arguments
./main.go:17:2: unreachable code
```

Figure 17.12: Expected output from go vet

7. Correct the issue by moving the **log.Println("completed")** line so that it runs before the **return** statement:

```go
func ExampleHandler(w http.ResponseWriter, r *http.Request) {
    w.WriteHeader(http.StatusOK)
    fmt.Fprintf(w, "Hello Packt")
    log.Println("completed")
    return
}
```

8. You should ensure that you have the third-party package downloaded by running **go get**:

```
go get github.com/gorilla/mux
```

9. This will start the web server:

```
> go run main.go
```

Figure 17.13: Expected output when running the code

10. You can check whether it worked by going to **http://localhost:8888** in your web browser:

Hello Packt

Figure 17.14: Expected output when accessing the web server through Firefox

Chapter 18: Security

Activity 18.01: Authenticating Users on the Application Using Hashed Passwords

Solution:

1. Create a **main.go** file and import the following packages:

    crypto/sha512: This package will provide the hashing required to encrypt the password.

    database/sql: The database to store user details will be created using this package.

github.com/mattn/go-sqlite3: This is a third-party library used to create a `sqlite` instance for testing.

```
package main
import (
    "crypto/sha512"
    "database/sql"
    "fmt"
    "os"
    _ "github.com/mattn/go-sqlite3"
)
```

2. Define a function called **getConnection()** to initialize a database connection:

```
func getConnection() (*sql.DB, error) {
    conn, err := sql.Open("sqlite3", "test.DB")
    if err != nil {
        return nil, fmt.Errorf("could not open db connection %v", err)
    }
    return conn, nil
}
```

3. Define helper functions to set up and tear down the database:

main.go

```
13 var testData = []*UserDetails{
14     {
15         Id:       "1",
16         Password: "1234",
17     },
18     {
19         Id:       "2",
20         Password: "5678",
21     },
22 }
23 func initializeDB(db *sql.DB) error {
24     _, err := db.Exec(`CREATE TABLE IF NOT EXISTS USER_DETAILS (USER_ID TEXT,
    PASSWORD TEXT)`)
25     if err != nil {
26         return err
27     }
```

The full code for this step is available at https://packt.live/2sUYVlg

4. Define the **GetPassword()** function to retrieve a user password from the database:

```
func GetPassword(db *sql.DB, userID string) (resp []byte, err error) {
    query := `SELECT PASSWORD FROM USER_DETAILS WHERE USER_ID = ?`
    row := db.QueryRow(query, userID)
    switch err = row.Scan(&resp); err {
    case sql.ErrNoRows:
```

```
        return resp, fmt.Errorf("no rows returned")
      case nil:
        return resp, err
      default:
        return resp, err

      }
    }
```

5. Define a function called **UpdatePassword()** to update the user password in the database with a hashed password:

main.go

```
55 func UpdatePassword(db *sql.DB, Id string, Password string) error {
56   query := `UPDATE USER_DETAILS SET PASSWORD=? WHERE USER_ID=?`
57   cipher := sha512.Sum512([]byte(Password))
58   fmt.Printf("storing encrypted password:\n%x\n", string(cipher[:]))
59   result, err := db.Exec(query, string(cipher[:]), Id)
60   if err != nil {
61     return err
62   }
63   rows, err := result.RowsAffected()
64   if err != nil {
65     return err
66   }
```

The full code for this step is available at https://packt.live/35QwJi8

6. Write the **main()** function. In the **main()** function, you should set up a database connection and initialize the database with some test data. The **UpdatePassword()** function should be called to update the user password to a hashed password. The **GetPassword()** function should be called to verify the hashed password:

main.go

```
87 func main() {
88   db, err := getConnection()
89   if err != nil {
90     fmt.Println(err)
91     os.Exit(1)
92   }
93   err = initializeDB(db)
94   if err != nil {
95     fmt.Println(err)
96     os.Exit(1)
97   }
98   defer tearDownDB(db)
99   err = UpdatePassword(db, "1", "NewPassword")
```

The full code for this step is available at https://packt.live/2PVxWPH

7. Run the program using the following command:

```
go run -v main.go
```

You should get the following output.

```
gobin:activity1 Gobin$ go run main.go
storing encrypted password:
76243005bcc0bea09d6c0409b6f2e32a8050f31f123b797678e98301ba1822fdfeac10ddfa281b39e9eb5f5a4eddb271b9
retrieving hashed password from db
checking password match
successful password match
```

Figure 18.13: Expected output

In this activity, we have implemented a real-world scenario of storing and verifying user passwords with hashing. Should the database details be leaked, the hashed passwords, by themselves, will not be useful to the attacker.

Activity 18.02: Creating CA Signed Certificates Using Crypto Libraries

Solution:

1. Create a **main.go** file and import the following packages:

   The crypto packages here will be used to generate and verify x509 certificates:

```
package main
import (
    "crypto"
    "crypto/ecdsa"
    "crypto/elliptic"
    "crypto/rand"
    "crypto/x509"
    "crypto/x509/pkix"
    "fmt"
    "math/big"
    "os"
    "time"
)
```

2. Create a function called **generateCert()**, which returns an x509 certificate and its private key:

main.go

```
44 func generateCert(cn string, caCert *x509.Certificate, caPriv
      crypto.PrivateKey) (cert *x509.Certificate, privateKey
      crypto.PrivateKey, err error) {
45   serialNumber, err := rand.Int(rand.Reader, big.NewInt(27))
46   if err != nil {
47     return cert, privateKey, err
48   }
49   var isCA bool
50   if caCert == nil {
51     isCA = true
52   }
53   template := &x509.Certificate{
54     SerialNumber:         serialNumber,
```

The full code for this step is available at https://packt.live/39a2R24

3. Create the **main()** function to call the **generateCert()** function. This will generate a root certificate and a leaf certificate from the root certificate. Verify the leaf certificate:

main.go

```
14 func main() {
15   // Generate CA certificates
16   caCert, caPriv, err := generateCert("CA cert", nil, nil)
17   if err != nil {
18     fmt.Printf("error generating server certificate: %v", err)
19     os.Exit(1)
20   } else {
21     fmt.Println("ca certificate generated successfully")
22   }
23   // User CA cert to generate and sign server certificate
24   cert, _, err := generateCert("Test Cert", caCert, caPriv)
```

The full code for this step is available at https://packt.live/398aM04

4. Test the code by running **main.go** using the following command:

```
go run main.go
```

The output should appear as follows:

```
gobin:activity2 Gobin$ go run main.go
ca certificate generated successfully
leaf certificate generated successfully
leaf certificate successfully verified
```

In this activity, we have generated x509 public key certificates. We have also seen how to use a root certificate to generate a leaf certificate. This can be handy when you are trying to implement your own PKI server.

Chapter 19: Special Features

Activity 19.01: Defining Build Constraints Using Filenames

Solution:

1. Create a directory called **custom**.

2. Inside this directory, create a file called **print_darwin.go**.

3. Define a function called **Print()**:

```
package custom
import "fmt"
func Print() {
   fmt.Println("Hello I am running on a darwin machine.")
}
```

4. Create another file inside the **custom** directory called **print_386.go**.

5. Define a function inside this package called **Print()**:

```
import "fmt"
func Print() {
   fmt.Println("Hello I am running on 386 machine.")
}
```

6. Run the program using the following command:

```
go run main.go
```

You should see the following output:

```
$ go run main.go
Hello I am running on a darwin machine.
```

Activity 19.02: Using Wildcard with Go Test

Solution:

1. Create a directory called **package1**:

```
.
├── package1
│   └── run_test.go
```

Figure 19.5: Directory structure

2. Create **run_test.go** in this directory with the following test cases defined:

```
package package1
import "testing"
func TestPackage1(t *testing.T){
    t.Log("running TestPackage1")
}
```

3. In the parent directory, create another directory called **package2**:

```
.
├── package1
│   └── run_test.go
└── package2
    └── run_test.go
```

Figure 19.6: Directory structure

4. Create a file called **run_test.go** in this directory with the following content:

```
package package2
import "testing"
func TestPackage2(t *testing.T){
    t.Log("running TestPackage2")
}
```

5. Run all the test cases using the following command from the parent directory:

```
go test -v ./...
```

You should get the following output:

```
$go test -v ./...
=== RUN   TestPackage1
--- PASS: TestPackage1 (0.00s)
    run_test.go:6: running TestPackage1
PASS
ok      github.com/PacktWorkshops/The-Go-Workshop/Chapter20/Activity20.02/package1
=== RUN   TestPackage2
--- PASS: TestPackage2 (0.00s)
    run_test.go:6: running TestPackage2
PASS
ok      github.com/PacktWorkshops/The-Go-Workshop/Chapter20/Activity20.02/package2
```

Figure 19.7: Recursive test with the wildcard pattern

WHAT NEXT?

Now that you've mastered the fundamentals of Go, continue to build your knowledge and advance your career with one of our other Workshops...

THE SQL WORKSHOP

- Learn how to create normalized databases
- See how to insert data into tables effectively
- Use various techniques to retrieve data from multiple tables
- Build advanced queries using subqueries, joins and views

THE JAVA WORKSHOP

- Write clean and well-commented Java code that's easy to maintain
- Use third-party libraries and software development kits (SDKs)
- Learn how to work with information stored in external databases
- Keep data secure with cryptography and encryption

THE KUBERNETES WORKSHOP

- Learn how to build, deploy and maintain cloud-native applications using Kubernetes
- Create a container image from an image definition manifest
- Construct a Kubernetes-aware continuous integration pipeline for deployments
- Attract traffic to your application using Kubernetes ingress

...or search online for "Packt Workshops" and browse the rest of our range for inspiration.

PLEASE LEAVE A REVIEW

Let us know what you think by leaving a detailed, impartial review on Amazon. We appreciate all feedback – it helps us continue to make great products and help aspiring developers build their skills. Please spare a few minutes to give your thoughts – it makes a big difference to us.

Index

A

agreement: 362
Anonymous function:
169, 170, 172, 197, 198,
199, 200, 201,202, 203,
206, 207, 210, 211, 214,
238, 434, 436, 562, 565,
708argument: 181
array: 111, 114-115,
117, 130, 138
assertion: 161
asymmetric encryption:
638, 641, 644, 645

B

bug: 325-326
bugs: 324
build constraints: 661,
662, 663, 665, 666,
672, 673, 679, 680, 782

C

ca: 649, 655, 658
Certificate Authority:
649, 658
channel: 576-578, 599
checksum: 638
ciphertext: 641-643,
645-646
closure: 200
Command injection:
626, 628, 633
concurrency: 562
Cross-Site Scripting:
634, 638
crypto packages: 650, 780

D

database: 469, 473,
476, 482, 484, 491
databases: 466
date: 366
deadlock: 578
debug: 222-223, 326, 338
debugging: 324, 335, 337,
341, 344, 350, 422
defer: 209
duck: 252, 261, 269

E

ecdsa: 657-658
encoding: 391
enums: 47-48, 53
error: 218, 225, 245,
249, 324, 338
errors: 249, 347
exported: 301-302

F

fatal: 347
filesystem: 421-422
flag: 426-427
format specifier: 328
functions: 197

G

get: 494, 513
goroutines: 560-561,
564, 568, 575, 577

H

handler: 524, 541
hash: 638-639, 656-657
hashing: 626,
638-641, 658

I

identifier: 172
integer: 89
interface: 252-256,
258, 261, 263, 272,
274-275, 286-287

J

json: 498

K

key: 644-646, 649,
653-654, 658

L

level: 362
libraries: 639-640
logging: 320, 344-345
logic: 56, 68, 71, 81, 85
loop: 56, 71, 118

M

map: 138, 140, 144
marshaling: 383
methods: 549
multiline string: 474,
477, 484, 746